THE MATERIALITY OF LANGUAGE

The MATERIALITY of LANGUAGE

GENDER, POLITICS, AND THE UNIVERSITY

David Bleich

Indiana University Press
Bloomington and Indianapolis

This book is a publication of

Indiana University Press
Office of Scholarly Publishing
Herman B Wells Library 350
1320 E. 10th St.
Bloomington, Indiana 47404-3797 USA

iupress.indiana.edu

| Telephone orders | 800-842-6796 |
| Fax orders | 812-855-7931 |

Manufactured in the United States of America

Library of Congress Cataloging-in-Publication Data

Bleich, David.
    The materiality of language : gender, politics, and the university / David Bleich.
        pages cm
    Includes bibliographical references and index.
    ISBN 978-0-253-00771-1 (cloth : alk. paper) — ISBN 978-0-253-00772-8 (pbk. : alk. paper) — ISBN 978-0-253-00773-5 (eb)   1. Language and languages Philosophy.   2. Rhetoric.
3. Academic language.   4. Colloquial language.   5. Language and languages—Political aspects.
6. Language and languages—Sex differences.   I. Title.
    P107.B585 2013
    401—dc23

                                                        2012046669

1 2 3 4 5 18 17 16 15 14 13

Since I find that no one, before myself, has dealt in any way with the theory of eloquence in the vernacular, and since we can plainly see that such eloquence is necessary to everyone—for not only men, but also women and children strive to acquire it, as far as nature allows—I shall try, inspired by the Word that comes from above, to say something useful about the language of people who speak the vulgar tongue, hoping thereby to enlighten somewhat the understanding of those who walk the streets like the blind, ever thinking that what lies ahead is behind them. Yet, in so doing, I shall not bring to so large a cup only the water of my own thinking, but shall add to it more potent ingredients, taken or extracted from elsewhere, so that from these I may concoct the sweetest possible mead.

But since it is required of any theoretical treatment that it not leave its basis implicit, but declare it openly, so that it may be clear with what its argument is concerned, I say, hastening to deal with the question, that I call "vernacular language" that which infants acquire from those around them when they first begin to distinguish sounds: or, to put it more succinctly, I declare that vernacular language is that which we learn without any formal instruction, by imitating our nurses. There also exists another kind of language, at one remove from us, which the Romans called gramatica. . . . *The Greeks and some—but not all—other peoples also have this secondary kind or language. Few, however, achieve complete fluency in it, since knowledge of its rules and theory can only be developed through dedication to a lengthy course of study.*

Of these two kinds of language, the more noble is the vernacular: first, because it was the language originally used by the human race; second, because the whole world employs it, though with different pronunciations and using different words; and third, because it is natural to us, while the other is, in contrast, artificial.

And this more noble kind of language is what I intend to discuss.

—*Dante Alighieri,* De vulgari eloquentia *(1303–1305)*

Yet, having looked through this book [by Matheolus], . . . an extraordinary thought became planted in my mind which made me wonder why on earth it was that so many men, both clerks and others, have said and continue to say and write such awful, damning things about women and their ways. I was at a loss as to how to explain it. It is not just a handful of writers who do this, . . . It is all manner of philosophers, poets, and orators too numerous to mention, who all seem to speak with one voice and are unanimous in their view that female nature is wholly given up to vice.

. . . given that I could scarcely find a moral work by any author which didn't devote some chapter or paragraph to attacking the female sex, I had to accept their unfavorable opinion of women since it was unlikely that so many learned men . . . could possibly have lied on so many different occasions.

—*Christine de Pizan*, Le Livre de la Cité des Dames, *1405*

BRIEF CONTENTS

DETAILED CONTENTS

Part Two: Language in the University

ACKNOWLEDGMENTS

During the writing of this book, my conversations with former students about their teaching and scholarship, and about their classrooms as experienced, have been a continuing stimulation in studying this contested subject of language. I want to thank Mary R. Boland, Lisa De Tora, Jennifer Keating-Miller, Miriam Margala, Chuck Ripley, and Scott Stevens, who were students at the University of Rochester; and Elisabeth Daeumer, Tom Fox, Sally Barr Reagan, Philip Sicks, and Karen Veith at Indiana University. Tom's use of the term "access" gave me the idea to take advantage of its materiality and use it in the same-yet-different sense in this book.

In 1994, Christine Iwanicki, now a faculty member in English at Western Illinois University, finished her dissertation, "The Materiality of Language," at Indiana University; I was her advisor. Chris gives an account of how the topic of language materiality came to her attention. She began thinking of academic discourse as "disembodied"—that is, removed from the daily life of the body: "I first became aware of this phenomenon of disembodiment when I participated as a teaching assistant during the 1987–88 academic year at Indiana University, Bloomington, in a course taught by Prof. David Bleich." Also in her acknowledgments, she writes, "In addition to Professor Bleich, I would like to acknowledge the other members of the L161–162 staff, with whom I worked—and learned from—during that first year: Allison Berg, Jean Kowaleski, Caroline Le Guin, Ellen Weinauer, and Eric Wolfe."[1] That academic year of regular classroom experience, meetings, conversations, and academic socialization a generation ago, is when the present book began to seem possible. So my thanks go to Chris and our literacy collective and to our continuing contact and friendship over the succeeding years.

Chris's dissertation has a spirit and purpose similar to mine in this book. Hers is a different voice covering some of the same sources, and she includes some sources not considered in my book. Chris relates her students' uses of language in each case to the issues raised by the theorists. Readers of her work will see a

---

1. Christine Iwanicki, "The Materiality of Language," Ph.D. diss., Indiana University, 1994, 4.

xiii

circular path from the classroom, to speaking, to reading, to theory, to writing, and back to the languages and conversations found in her classrooms.

I thank Ralph Cohen, Robin Lakoff, Richard Ohmann, Naomi Scheman, and Deborah Tannen for teaching me for the last thirty-five years—even though I was not in their classrooms. A special thanks to John Eakin for his comments on chapter 5. These teachers have modeled the identity of teaching and scholarship.

I wish to thank the dozens of students in my undergraduate "Changing Genres of Erotica" course, my "Family Repression and Rage in Film and Society" course, my "Problems of Western Civilization" course, and my "Orality, Language, and Literacy" course over the last thirteen years. They have given the bases in experience—especially those of how gender politics was developing "out there"—for many of the claims made in this volume about gender, society, and the university. The personal candor of my undergraduate students has been remarkable, as has been their ability to bring out all sides of the many issues that mattered to them.

I am grateful to Matt Bayne, Elizabeth Goodfellow, Julianne Heck, and Dianne Evanochko, all assistants in my courses, for helping to bring undergraduate students to new uses of language. I thank the eight members of my graduate erotica seminar—Catherine Bailey, Carly Chasin, Dave Ewans, Alison Grenert, Acacia O'Connor, Andrew Rhoades, Betsy Woerner, and Jordan Wood—who, I thought, achieved new levels in the uses of language by showing how the combination of courageous talk and writing about social and bodily experience contributes to the building of relaxed, consequential, and humane professional relationships that has begun to change the subjects of language and literature.

Thanks, and brava, to Julianne Heck for finding the dozens of mistranscriptions in the original manuscript and for compiling a dazzling index.

I thank my friends and colleagues Russell Peck, Ken Gross, Sarah Higley, Jeff Tucker, and Stephanie Li, who talked with me, walked with me, ate with me, drank with me, and did not ask how the book was coming along.

At Indiana University Press, my thanks go to Bob Sloan, who helped me get my head around this book and who helped me to teach it to others, and Angela Burton for her focused oversight of the publication process. Thanks to Dawn Ollila for her masterful copyediting and for her total, dedicated manuscript care. I am grateful to the three readers of this manuscript who read it with a heartbeat and a backbone, who were generous in substance and tone, who spotted its problems, and who provided pathways toward a more fluent, thoughtful, fairminded book.

Thanks to Eve Salisbury, who has been a loving companion and partner over the years of writing this book and many years before that. She is a devoted reader and editor, slow to anger, and gentle with insight and alerts for change, and her smile lights up the room.

THE MATERIALITY OF LANGUAGE

Introduction:
The Contested Subject

Language has been our principal means of collective survival, our principal source of interpersonal stability, and the foundation for the growth of all cultures. The use of language is part of every person's daily experience, and has been since birth.

The formal study of language has rarely recognized these facts, partly because the subject is so broad, and partly because there have been political reasons not to ask too many questions about the ubiquity of language use. The university as an institution, in its eight-century history, has been the principal site for the study of language in the West. Although this history is fascinating and instructive, it is also a history of how the subject of language has been avoided, obfuscated, submerged, and repressed during the recorded history of Western societies. In universities, language has been a contested subject matter. Different parts of society, some of them represented in different parts of universities, have had different stakes in which languages are used, how they are used, and, especially, who uses which languages. In spite of the fundamental role of language in all people's lives, most people have not had, and do not now have, access to the full capability of their native languages or other languages they may have learned.

We may view language use as the human way of life, comparable, perhaps, to nest building and calling in birds, dam building for beavers, and the collective cooperation of insects. Researchers have marveled at the swiftness of infantile language acquisition just as they have marveled at the achievements of presumably nonlinguistic creatures. Most of the time, in academic life and in popular culture, people identify such seemingly miraculous behaviors as instinctive or genetic, thus, effectively assigning our understanding of these behaviors to automatic, mechanical, or inevitable factors. These collective behaviors have taken place in elaborate detail in plain sight, and they have been readily available for study.

I undertook this study because I wanted to understand why the issue of language has been the site of so much dispute, so much acrimony, and so much ignoring and repressing of the experiences that all people have. In the course of my reading about the history of the study of language in universities, another fact in plain sight demanded consideration: the sites of dispute, acrimony, and the repression of language have been gender marked. Groups of men, and not groups of men and women, have argued, threatened, fought, and made rules about the uses of language for whole societies. Western societies were governed by these rules, located in the codes of religious and civil law. Many challenged these rules of language use, these widespread forms of coercive censorship, these restrictions on what languages could be used and by whom. But the challengers were themselves ostracized and sometimes executed. These social and political practices of suppression and repression, recorded in history, have not, in general, receded. Some would claim that democratic "free speech" and academic freedom are significant advances toward universal access to language, but I think this is not the case even for most people living in relatively privileged societies. The facts, opinions, and discussions in this study say why: in the academy and in society, extended, serious access to language by the majority of people is still radically limited.

In the middle of the twentieth century, a group of accomplished thinkers noticed the historic limitations of language perpetuated by the recursive prac- tices in formal, professional, and academic language genres. These scholars, with two exceptions, were also men. Members of this group lived and worked in sepa- rate Western societies, and in general, did not work with one another. Ludwig Wittgenstein wrote in German, Mikhail Bakhtin wrote in Russian, Benjamin Whorf wrote in (U.S.) English, John Austin wrote in (British) English, Jacques Derrida wrote in French, Julia Kristeva wrote in French, and Robin Lakoff wrote in (U.S.) English. Each in his and her own way challenged the common West- ern conceptions of language and each presented visions of language that were radically different from what had been previously taken for granted. However, because of the centuries-old tradition of acrimonious dispute about language, the disputes that followed the work of these thinkers looked no different from the previous, usually casuistical, disputes: male scholars blustering in arcane academic language about issues that few ordinary people understood.

There were other influential figures who had similar intuitions about lan- guage: Michel Foucault, Gilles Deleuze and Félix Guattari, and David Silverman and Brian Torode. In the statements of each of these, the applicable sense of "materiality" is based in Marxian perspectives. Each author works strenuously to show how traditional conceptions of language can no longer apply once worldwide economic patterns and social forms are understood to be mutually implicated with language. These works recognize important social and political urgencies brought to the surface by the recognition of the materiality of lan- guage. The single factor missing in each of these works, however, is attention to the class of people—women—who have brought all people into language, and who themselves have been excluded from the public authority over language that has been always held by men.

However, the achievement of all of the foregoing writers may be described as a forceful revocation of binary or dichotomous thinking about language. For example, disputes had repeatedly formed around the dichotomy of thought and language, spirit and matter, words and meaning, *langue* and *parole*, competence and performance, rational and emotional, mind and body, talking and fighting. Each of the foregoing thinkers—in different modes, with different sources, different considerations, different discourse styles, and different vocabularies— aimed to describe a unified conception of language: the materiality of the language we use and see effortlessly. I call this conception of language material because for each thinker, bodily, social, and political factors informed their descriptions of what language is and how it works. Each described language as the embodiment of varieties of social and political relations. Each scholar tried to hold up for reexamination common, easily observable language phenomena, aiming to put an end to speculation about any essence of language beyond the human experience of it. Each tried to assert, and even insist, that the consequential factor of all language experiences—including the uses of artistic and scientific languages—was their palpability, their bodily sources and effects, and above all, their availability for change toward collective interests and benefits.

In spite of the disputes provoked by these figures, I thought they achieved something fundamentally different from several of their precursors who had similar intuitions about language. I wanted to find ways to say how this language dispute was different from the many that preceded it. I found a clue in the work of Julia Kristeva, and so I took the title and the principal issue of this book from the third chapter of her book *Language: The Unknown:* "The Materiality of Language." This idea signaled a key fact about language that has also always been known but was brought to the forefront by *both* the materialist approach and the political emancipation of historically subaltern constituencies: *every* use of language has a political valence. The basis for claiming that something was different about this language dispute has been borne out by the social and political developments that followed later in the twentieth century and that are still growing and transforming today: the active academic initiatives taken by the increasing numbers of women and nonwhite people in the academy, and the increasing volume of work by these groups and their recognized colleagues in *every* academic discipline.

The change in the character of academic practice advocated for and sometimes won by this newly constituted group is comparable in scope and consequence to the proliferation of universities in Europe in the fourteenth century, when the university system became decisively rooted in European culture and Latin became the language of knowledge. Today, a feature of this change is the presence of majority female undergraduate populations feeding into the academic and other professions that were previously male only. Unless this movement of women is physically halted, academic and professional populations will undergo a radical change from their traditionally lopsided male majorities.

Part 2 of this book tries to show the connection between the efforts of this new population and the consequences of the language philosophies articulated by the figures noted above. This task requires a focused discussion of the history of the university, and the reexamination of work in a wide variety of academic disciplines. The changes in thought, language, and academic effort by the materialist perspective on language would remain "academic" if we could not see how language-based forms of academic reporting in the physical sciences, social sciences, and the humanities are affected by this changed sense of language. This book pays specific attention to feminist thinking not simply to include reference to the many women who have contributed to the revision of how we see the languages of understanding. Rather, and especially, academic work has already been shaped by its historic gender markings, and that gender markings—cognizant of the materiality of language to a significant degree in the academy and in society—are changing the nature of academic subject matters themselves. Furthermore, it is not quite enough to notice that interdisciplinary work is becoming more fashionable or more seriously acceptable. It is essential to remind ourselves that the system of disciplines and their corresponding departments have been functioning since the beginning of the university by male-coded rules, mores, and styles of debate and inquiry—all enforced by a tradition of language philosophy developed by and suited to just such a system, as well as to cognate systems of men's organizations. The stakes of this language inquiry are that all aspects of language and knowledge change as the gender socialization of academic work is being revised toward more egalitarian practices and values.

Many have shied away from identifying such change as political. But so-called politics in Western discourse has had a fate similar to that of language, and likely *because* of the practices of limiting our attentions to language. At best, in modern times, politics as a subject matter is circumscribed in academic departments by the disciplinary rules which constrain the exportation of political thinking to other subjects. But the materiality of language refers, in part, to the fact that merely to use language is to participate in social and political relations. Language *matters* because of this participation. As a result, political and language-use issues are features of any subject that presents its understanding in language genres. Because of androcentric domination of societies, the reference of politics, like the reference of language use, is subject to a double standard. The multifarious political and language-use choices available to those who make laws and rules are severely limited for those governed by these laws and rules.

It is certain that a study of this scope will omit key facts or aspects of the collective uses of language that do, after all, require reconsideration. However, I ask readers to focus on how valid the larger picture is to them. In the best outcome, others will add to and change these views and adapt them to the uncountable specific circumstances of their experience. The aim of my presentation is less to persuade others about how correct the description of language as material may be, and more to encourage the academic, pedagogical, social, and political processes of achieving access to language by all people.

Universities, with privileges and time to study everything in our society, have the additional privilege of being able to enlarge the custody of language radically; of being able to listen to everyone's language; of being able to search out hidden constituencies, languages, and interests; of being able to report these again and again in their growing list of conferences and publications. Universities have access to the public and can make themselves accessible to this public. It is a matter of mobilizing the widespread action begun by our love of language, and by the desire to see how the language of all people matters to all other people.

Part One:
The Materiality of Language

CHAPTER ONE

Premises and Backgrounds

I. The Materiality of Language and the Sacralization of Texts

The premise that people exchange language and not meaning governs this study. The materiality of language[1] is a description that follows from this premise.

Uses of language, oral or written, mark the growth and cultivation of language in any society. Different art forms, sciences, and professional interests have distinctive genres of discourse and dialects, which are collective practices—rather than concepts—that are eligible for public assimilation, for testing, and for appropriation toward social adaptation.

Genres in different subject matters are *gestures of language use.* "Gestures" includes reference to the bodily action of speech and writing. This reference contrasts with the common use of the term "language," which usually implies that thought or ideas are prior, more fundamental, and more essential than words. The Platonic tradition, which the common use of the term "language" reflects, is sometimes identified as "realism." According to this tradition, words are transient and mortal. Ideas (meanings), however, are the essence of language and are eternal; they are passed through generations and survive individual human mortality. Emerging from this tradition is the almost universal assumption that language is not bodily because its essence is "meaning"—ideas and thought, which reside in and emerge from an incorporeal zone of existence.

To stipulate the materiality of language is to move away from the Platonic tradition. In classical and medieval times, nominalists questioned the Platonic premise and opposed the tradition that was derived from it.[2] They did not

---

1. The word "material" is used in several senses in different subject matters and contexts of discussion. In this study "materiality" is only somewhat related to the "materialism" of Marxist economics or to the "materialism" that describes people who love acquiring more things. Julia Kristeva gave the title "The Materiality of Language" to chapter 3 of *Language: The Unknown: An Initiation into Linguistics,* trans. Anne M. Menke, (New York: Columbia UP, 1989), 18–42. I added other considerations to her description throughout this study.

2. This is discussed in section 4 of this chapter.

9

attribute to language use its function as a conduit of intangible meaning. They treated the uses of language as self-evident within their immediate contexts and experiences. Seeing language in this way enabled them to use "faith" as a belief in something not in evidence. Yet Church authorities who had custody of language uses and of their study opposed nominalism and maintained, instead, that there was indeed evidence for religious beliefs. If one held a language philosophy that accepted that there was no evidence for faith either within language or outside of it, religious authorities and institutions would be discredited and endangered. Nominalism held that language does not give evidence of anything beyond its living functions, nor does it predict future events.

My extended consideration of the materiality of language is founded on a tradition of language philosophy that had been on the record for (at least) two millennia but has remained a minority perspective. However, the twentieth century's proliferation of popular literacy and greatly increased access to education has brought about a new collective recognition of the materiality of language. This development is due in part to the reduction of religious authority, to the increased respect for secularism, and to the rapid spread of technology and other material benefits such as medicines. In the twentieth century, materiality was urged and suggested by changes in society that brought tangible benefits to millions of people.

From one standpoint, the recognition by several thinkers of the materiality of language could be seen as part of a growing respect for and dependence on material things more generally. The increasing number of educated people willing to challenge the acceptance of transcendental spirituality and God led inevitably to the recognition that language itself—long held to be special, unique to humans, and immaterial—to be, in the final analysis, material like everything else. This view is plausible enough for me to take seriously, but it is not the principal focus of this book. Rather, this study does not seek any explanation of why, in a brief period during the twentieth century, fewer than a dozen figures paying attention to language and how it is conceived arrived at similar understandings of how it worked and how we might continue to view it. I try only to show that these figures are, finally, similar to one another in basic ways, and although they share no one common feature, their similarity may be described as an understanding that language is more usefully treated as a material entity than as an incorporeal, ineffable, intangible, or spiritual phenomenon. I try to show how the work of this group of thinkers shares the sense of the revolutionary role language would take on if consciously received, taught, used, and understood as a material entity.

I hope to show that because these figures came to similar conclusions at more or less the same point in history, those of us who value learning and teaching should pay attention to them—on the grounds that our searches for knowledge and understanding depend on how language is used, who is using it, and what circumstances of its authority are being established. No one locus of language use is more or less important than any other because there is no subject matter that does not finally depend on the use of language. The *use* of language is fundamental throughout the individual life cycle, and throughout history.

I describe the language practice that follows from the use of Platonic realism as the *sacralization of texts*. During times when only a minuscule fraction of the total population was literate, those who could write had the most access to language. Almost automatically, those who could produce texts were in position to proclaim the authority of these texts, as well as their value, to the total population. All cultures have received an array of sacred texts; today we view them as the oldest and most venerated in our possession, and as having the greatest value to our societies. We continue to refer to various bibles as sacred texts, which means that religious institutions have more authority to read, interpret, and use them than those who are not part of such institutions, or who are not religious themselves.

Emerging from this practical religious tradition has been the view that an author of a text has a special claim on our attention by virtue of having *created* that text. Texts created by authors carry a heightened status resembling that of sacred texts. Until recently the creation and production of texts has remained restricted to the most privileged members of society. During the medieval period, authoritative texts were considered valid only if they were written in the one official language, Latin. Those who knew Latin were church members or were trained in universities that were sponsored by the Church. The combination of literacy and the supremacy of the Latin language in the creation of texts lent any text written in Latin a near-sacred, if not altogether sacred, status. Furthermore, the long history of authoritative Latin writing helped to make it seem that anything written was sacred and that anything carrying a Latin name had greater value than something with a vernacular name. Gradually these perceptions took root, leading to the point where any text, even in modern times, could be sacralized.[3]

In practice, sacralization involves viewing a text as fixed, not changeable by those who have access to it. Alteration of sacred texts may be read as sacrilegious, but alteration of any text is understood to be irresponsible and disrespectful. For most received texts, great pains are taken to ascertain the so-called original authenticity of the text and to establish an authoritative version. There is scholarly discomfort when there are different versions of what is ostensibly the same

---

3. Alan Dundes has suggested forcefully that the different versions of the "same" story in the Western Bible must have been transcriptions of oral stories. Biblical scholars try to reconcile the different versions if they view the whole text as sacralized by its having been written. Alan Dundes, *Holy Writ as Oral Lit* (Lanham, MD: Rowman and Littlefield, 1999).

text. There is a silent standard that there must be a final text given by an author, and that incomplete texts are less than satisfactory. In schools students are cautioned to "stick to the text"—that is, to read it in its presumably one and only authoritative form in order to find out its truest possible meaning. In the mid-twentieth century, the highly regarded essay "Heresy of Paraphrase" implied, perhaps in good humor, that paraphrasing a literary text was cause for alarm.[4]

Scientific texts are sacralized somewhat differently than humanistic ones. They formulate so-called laws of nature, and the figures who set down these laws are considered to have given an authoritative formulation that all texts must reproduce. Any reading of a sacralized text must begin with that text, and rephrasing of its language counts only as an interpretation of its language—an attempt at finding its meaning, and not as an improvement or an experiment or a revision for present purposes. Although oral texts, typically conceived of as folklore, have been subject to such socially and politically governed changes, once a text has been written, it is automatically sacralized.[5] In Western culture, there has been a taboo regarding playing with texts, paraphrasing them, or changing them without reference to a fixed original.

The materiality of language is a ground for desacralizing texts. There is no reason automatically to consider written texts to be more permanent or more authoritative than oral texts. There are often occasions to *declare* the permanence of texts, but if such declarations are admissible, then other declarations revoking earlier declarations are equally admissible. The framers of the U.S. Constitution stated that the Constitution could be changed. But for changes to be enacted, 75 percent of the states had to approve the changes. This rule, however, has not been subject to change, so that the political decision to limit the ability to change the Constitution, made over two centuries ago, has remained in effect and can be viewed as having sacralized the Constitution. If political sentiments change, then that text may be desacralized subject to further social and political variation. Any desacralization is a political language gesture that is inhibited by the premise of the permanence of language, but is encouraged by the assumption of the materiality of language.

The nub of the matter is that official and authoritative texts and language remain sacralized by their dependence on established or hegemonic official mediators. While language changes and grows through an increasingly prominent popular culture as well as through a variety of widely read literary works,

---

4. This key founding essay of the New Criticism is the last chapter of Cleanth Brooks's *The Well-Wrought Urn* (New York: Harcourt Brace Jovanovich, 1947). A common reading of that title holds it to be ironic, which is reasonable. But merely using the word "heresy" connotes that the paraphrase, however useful, violates the text.

5. This is one reason Jacques Derrida referred to all semiotic usages as "writing," as considered in chapter 4.

there are very few zones in which the materiality of language has any effect. For example, in legal contexts, the concept of "intent" remains viable: intent to kill. Assuming the materiality of language viewing such a case rules out consideration of intent. The crime is *described* differently if there is no need to specify what the intent was. In sting and entrapment cases, no crime was committed, but legal argument may claim that there was intent. Even in cases in which one person murdered another, one can describe what happened without saying what a person's intent was. But if the law says that intent is part of the crime, juries are likely to be forced to stipulate an intent, something they are not likely to know with certainty. With different descriptions of crimes, the practices of punishment have a different value and a different function.

In science as well, it is hardly possible to contest sacralized phrases such as "the struggle for existence," a carrier of commonly held values that envisions all forms of life in a competition—the outcome of which is the equally sacralized "survival of the fittest." It is assumed that these terms, like "intent," refer to something that exists. But they are abstractions that refer to indefinite, inferred entities that appear to us differently each time they are identified.[6] More often sacralized abstractions are assumed to be causes of important patterns, as it is sometimes thought that an "aggression instinct" is the cause of male violence or war—or that a "maternal instinct" renders those women who decide not to become mothers as maladaptive or otherwise deficient, unable to meet an imaginary phylogenetic standard.

While important texts and familiar phrases are not to be censored, people to whom they matter are in a position to desacralize them, to change their usage and collective function, to make incremental changes of usage by virtue of their materiality. Under these circumstances, changes are tested by the contexts of use, by the political interests of readers and users of language. Whatever the field or zone of inquiry, the language is material in the sense that new uses always retest the received usage, and consensus and mutual comprehension are in position to fix usage—with the understanding that any such fixing is contingent and provisional, and not necessarily denoting the same thing all the time.

Therefore, if, within the study of language-dependent subject matters, there is a tradition of misunderstanding the roles and actions of language in society, it is important to consider the extent of this misunderstanding. The practical result of the present reconsideration is, on the one hand, to lengthen and strengthen the reach of the study of language, and, on the other hand, to extend this study to other semiotic genres—to find, perhaps in a more general way, what claims the use of language has on the ways social and political relations proceed.

---

6. "Survival of the fittest" has been repeatedly discredited as being tautological: if you survive, you must be fit. Yet the term enjoys a good health as part of the narcissism of the survivors. A fuller consideration of this phrase is found in chapter 10.

It will be evident to most readers that this study tries to make assertions that are true relative to contexts of several political considerations. Hopefully, this study's claims are made in a way that promotes discussion and understanding. This common procedure is a political gesture because believing or not believing claims changes their configurations of influence and authority in any social scene. To view claims as political also means assuming that interpersonal and intergroup relationships precede and urge what counts as knowledge and understanding. I assume that all people are members of groups that interact with other groups, and that individuals in each of their memberships have interests that can not be overlooked or assumed not to exist.

I consider that all people share a common interest in achieving *access to language:* people want to be in a position to learn it thoroughly, cultivate it, and use it to enhance their lives; and they expect that others will participate in mutually respectful exchanges of language. This has rarely been the case; access to language has been extremely hard to achieve for most people for most of history. This principal political assumption is considered in some detail in the next section of this chapter in order to enable a more sustained argument that recognizing the materiality of language increases universal access to it. It is also considered with an eye toward justifying it in chapter 6. Another political assumption is that for most of the history of the study of language, we know almost exclusively the contributions of male scholars and thinkers. I assume that as a result of this constellation of contributors, the understanding of language, as well as public access to it, has been limited. Many of the frustrations of the male scholars discussed in this book are the results of their distance from the understanding that women—who play a principal role in teaching all people how to use language—have as much (or more) to contribute to the study of language use as men do. Because these are political issues readers are invited to test them.

I no longer can think of any alternative to engaging political issues when developing formal scholarly treatments of any subject matter. It is not simply that the claims of the disenfranchised must finally be heard and honored, but that it has become self-evident that members of all cultures depend on one another; however tempting it has been for critics, scholars, and researchers to claim isolation, it is simply not possible any longer: we professional readers and researchers are always part of the issues we are investigating. The use of language has been a continuing concern for centuries and is unlikely to abate. This study addresses those who have languages and interests different from mine as much as it does those in my own contexts; it is simultaneously an epistemological, political, and pragmatic gesture to revise a received tradition in the study and use of language. It is not possible to predict what will develop. Philip Lieberman addresses the future in this way: "The purpose of human life is surely that we must use the gift of speech, language, and thought to act to enhance life and love, to vanquish needless suffering and murderous violence."[7] I share this sense of the adaptive function of language. Vivien Law also shares this sense, though with a more specifically located feeling of urgency. She says that the understanding of language gives us the chance to use a "tool which has just as much force as the Bomb, with one big difference: language can be used for good or for ill. We have the choice."[8]

II. Access to Language

Almost everyone acquires language, but most people have only limited access to it. We reach others when what we say matters to them. As we reach more people and more people reach us, we have more access to language. The materiality of our use of language begins with infantile bodily initiatives and, during the years of growth, the initiatives are translated by others' similarly corporeal responses. The processes of bodily change and socialization are stabilized by our exchange of language gestures in our social relations. Access to language and access to society are not the same, yet they can neither be separated from one another nor circumscribed in isolation from one another.[9] With few exceptions, however, higher social standing goes with greater access to language; greater access to language encourages higher social standing.[10]

---

7. Philip Lieberman, *Eve Spoke: Human Language and Human Evolution* (New York: Norton, 1998), 151.

8. Vivien Law, *The History of Linguistics in Europe from Plato to 1600* (Cambridge: Cambridge UP, 2003), 275. Roger Cohen, reflecting on the language of the new American administration, observes, "The power of language to reconcile is as great as its power to kill." The difference between what Law wrote and what Cohen wrote is that Cohen's choice is between two attitudes about language—a traditional choice; language does not actually have the power to kill because when it does not reconcile, it can alienate rather than kill. Law draws the distinction between any use of language and violence-instead-of -language—war—an untraditional, materialist choice. Roger Cohen, "No Time for Retribution," *New York Times,* 23 April 2009.

9. A tree is different from the ground and from the air, yet it cannot be understood in isolation from them.

10. Catharine MacKinnon argues that U.S. law protects inequality through its treatments of free speech. In our society there is "a substantial lack of recognition that some people get a lot more speech than others. In the absence of these recognitions, the power of those who have speech has become more and more exclusive, coercive, and violent as it has become more and more legally protected. . . . [T]he less speech you have, the more the speech of those who have it keeps you unequal; the more the speech of the dominant is protected, the more dominant they become and the less the subordinated are heard from." Catherine MacKinnon, *Only Words* (Cambridge, MA: Harvard UP, 1993), 72–73. I suggest that over centuries the scholarly, formal understanding of language and how it can be used has helped to create the circumstances described by MacKinnon.

To get a sense of how access feels, think of conversations with doctors or lawyers as they explain our situations to us: Do we understand what they are saying, or just their instructions to us? What are the connections between what they say about our bodies and our social relations and their instructions regarding what to do? Each expert has access to a wide range of language and social experiences that we don't have. More comprehensive access to language, which some acquire by spending years in academic and university communities, involves the slow cultivation of familiarity with the languages and contexts of different subject matters and with people from other cultures. Many have studied languages, but when formal, authoritative attention is given to who has how much access to language in different parts of society, the subject matter of language and its use becomes socially disturbing and politically disruptive.

In 1969, Julia Kristeva wrote, "To work on language, to labour in the *materiality* of that which society regards as a means of contact and understanding, isn't that at one stroke to declare oneself a stranger/foreign [*étranger*] to language?"[11] Those who recognized the materiality of language, who made it their business to study the "means of contact and understanding," became socially estranged—heretics, eccentrics, magicians, witches, poets, pornographers, troublemakers, or whistleblowers; each of these groups at different historical periods has challenged conventional pathways of access to language. Yet it is also true that those who have governed societies have learned how to control access, and through this control make use of the materiality of language as an instrument of governance. Most constituents of the general population, which has only local access to language, are not in position either to recognize its materiality or to make use of it if they did recognize it. Toril Moi places Kristeva's observation in the context of another of Kristeva's remarks: "It was perhaps also necessary to be a *woman* to attempt to take up that exorbitant wager of carrying the rational project to the outer borders of the signifying venture of men."[12] Being at the "outer border" means, in part, being female. Women have been at or beyond the border of the "signifying venture of men," Kristeva writes at a new moment in history, when those who were beyond the border for thousands of years have achieved (to some degree) public voices and access to language. Her work, along with that of others, augurs a rearrangement of the public access to language, so that the study of the materiality of language may lead away from estrangement or repression. It may mean access to language for more people.

---

11. Quoted in *The Kristeva Reader,* ed. Toril Moi (New York: Columbia UP, 1986), 3.
12. Julia Kristeva, *Desire in Language: A Semiotic Approach to Literature and Art,* trans. Thomas Gora, Alice Jardine, and Leon S. Roudiez (New York: Columbia UP, 1980), x.

In Kristeva's chapter on materiality cited earlier,[13] of particular relevance are her emphases on the facts about how language is inherently bodily, gestural, social, and graphic, with the latter terms having a reference similar to Derrida's term "writing" or "*écriture*." Reading her discussion makes it seem that these are "obvious" facts about language, yet they have remained in the background of formal study for most of the history of the study of language: they have been repressed, and often enough, suppressed and censored, because of what Kristeva implied above: the uses of language were appropriated to become the "signifying venture of men."[14]

In Hebrew, the word for "speak" has the same consonant root as the word for "thing": *dbr*[15] or *davar,* so that "to speak" (*m'dahbear*) also means "to enthing," or, in more familiar English, to materialize. In Hebrew sometimes one says *ayn davar* for "you're welcome": the Hebrew means literally "no thing" ("it's nothing" in English) and in English, we may say, "Don't mention it." In English "matter" is both a verb and a noun, as is found in the book title *Race Matters.*[16] Both English and Hebrew recognize that words matter and are matter.

---

13. An extended consideration of Kristeva's formulations appears in chapter 4, section 6.

14. Dennis Baron has studied "how attitudes toward men and women have become attitudes toward language." *Grammar and Gender* (New Haven, CT: Yale UP, 1986), 10. These attitudes derive from the "onerous restrictions placed by men upon women's social experience. . . . Men have . . . tried to limit the range of women's linguistic experience to home and hearth" (1). His exhaustive survey of how languages have dealt with grammatical gendering strongly suggests that the gendering of words themselves *does not automatically reflect* the tradition of misogyny. His study shows more that the *specific uses* of received language, including founding myths such as those in Genesis, give a clear rendition of how women's access to language was limited. The study also suggests that, with a few exceptions, such as the unmarked male pronouns, women and men have contributed comparably toward the development of the received language.

15. Thanks to Ayala Emmett for reminding me that the same root, *dbr,* when read *de'ver* in Hebrew, means "pestilence." Conceivably, this sense can be assimilated to the other two: the *aural proximity* in Hebrew of a word or thing and disease may be referencing the vulnerability of the substantive, as well as its ability to do harm, under any circumstances.

Susan Handelman discusses the materiality indicated by the Hebrew word in a reflection on how the rabbinic tradition, which often recognized the materiality of language through certain interpretive styles, contributed to the poststructuralist approach to literary criticism. Susan Handelman, *The Slayers of Moses: The Emergence of Rabbinic Interpretation in Modern Literary Theory* (Albany: SUNY P, 1982). Some of her themes are discussed in chapter 4. Kenneth Dauber cites the identity of word and thing in Hebrew to present a materialist accent on the rabbinic readings of Genesis in "Beginning at the Beginning in Genesis," *Ordinary Language Criticism: Literary Thinking after Cavell and Wittgenstein,* ed. Kenneth Dauber and Walter Jost (Evanston, IL: Northwestern UP, 2003), 336.

16. Cornel West, *Race Matters* (Boston: Beacon P, 1993).

The two meanings of *davar* and the two senses of "matter" allude to a situation that applies to the use of any language. The history of the diminished attention received by the materiality of language, by its regular functions as social and bodily gestures, is like that of a minority party that remained a minority for more than two millennia.

In the twentieth century, women were admitted to academic inquiry in formal contexts. But before this development, several men wrote with approaches to language that challenged language-use orthodoxies. There were the nominalist Roscelin in the eleventh century, Peter Abelard in the twelfth, William Ockham and John Wyclif in the fourteenth century, Lorenzo Valla in the fifteenth, Michael Servetus in the sixteenth, Christian Thomasius in the seventeenth, and Johann Hamann and David Hume in the eighteenth, to name a few.[17] These men are now on the record, but their works had minor influence on how language was studied, understood, and passed along to succeeding generations.[18] Although respected, their works remain in a status of curiosity because they do not fit into the existing language-use practices, even in today's universities. Historically viewed, however, their works are cognate with those of the more central figures in this study—Kristeva, Wittgenstein, Bakhtin, Austin, Whorf, Derrida, Lakoff, and a group of feminist critics of science and social science who have used, de facto, a materialist sense of language.[19] This subordinate, "minority party" tradition has been repressed in the history of cultural life in the West.[20] The recursive attempts to develop a more truthful approach to the uses and study of language may be brought together and applied in collective contexts such as reading lists, scholarship, and different policies toward research in all fields, as part of an effort to create access to language for all people.

Because of the simultaneous independent attention to the materiality of language—by philosophers at mid-century and by gender-equality researchers in different subject matters more recently—the combination of these views is like a Kuhnian paradigm. But it is not such a paradigm because it has not won a consensus.

---

17. Valla and Hamann enter into discussion in chapters 2 and 4, respectively; the others are treated in chapters 8 and 9.

18. An exception to this pattern may be Christian Thomasius (1655–1728), whose use of the vernacular was a key part of the reform and modernization of German universities in the eighteenth century. Some of his efforts are discussed in chapter 8.

19. Among these are Evelyn Fox Keller in biology and physics; Ruth Bleier, Ruth Hubbard, and Emily Martin in biology; Julie Nelson in economics; and Martha Fineman in law. Their critiques are explored in chapters 10 and 11.

20. Chapters 7, 10, and 11 consider the applicability of the term "repression," as well as several instances of how it works in the writing of academics.

III. Limited Access in Education and Total Mediation in Society

Over the course of their years in school, college, and graduate study, when students gain access to their native language their satisfaction, authority, and understanding is unmistakable. Often there is a bodily, behavioral change in a person who has learned the technique of finding the right words for the occasion—the person who feels that there is a way to find what to say, and who does not have to struggle to make the gestures of speaking and writing matter to others? The speakers' demeanors are active, their voices are up a notch in volume, their willingness to interrupt and be interrupted acquires a new flexibility,[21] and a bond is formed, however provisional, with their speaking and writing colleagues. Speakers such as these have materialized their language by gaining access to it. To feel access to language is an uncommon gift, although many who have this gift would not call it "access to language," much less "feeling its materiality."

Most of us have been educated to think of our language as incorporeal or mental, rather than palpable or substantive. Our use of language is something like our heartbeats and the air we breathe: we don't take account of either of them until there is an emergency. Because all people *use* language, all have an interest in gaining access to it, in feeling its materiality. But not everyone achieves access to language or even access to those who do have access in universities, which, in principle, can now provide this access to all. Yet the university, which many take to be a social and political haven characterized by academic freedom and the search for truth,[22] is now and has always been almost fully dependent on larger, richer, more powerful institutions. At its beginnings and up until the nineteenth century, it was dependent on the Church and on monarchies or nobilities. Democratic states then began to support universities, but modern science got its start as an academic subject outside universities thanks to rich men in the seventeenth and eighteenth centuries, and did not begin to move into universities until the end of the eighteenth century. Today, perhaps in an overwhelming way, universities depend on global corporations, and—as in the seventeenth century—on donations by

---

21. Deborah Tannen, *Conversational Styles: Analyzing Talk among Friends* (Norwood, NJ: Ablex, 1984). Tannen characterizes people who are comfortable with interrupting and being interrupted as "high involvement" speakers. In part, interruption is a cultural trait in many cultures, but not in others. But even in "interrupting" cultures, each speaker has to gauge when it is admissible to let the trait function.

22. *Veritas* appears routinely in university mottos—Harvard: *Veritas;* Yale and Indiana: *Lux et veritas;* Brandeis: Truth, even unto its innermost parts. Of these, only Brandeis's motto is not in Latin.

very rich men.[23] Although this form of dependency does not necessarily lead to denigration and diminishment of study and research, more often than not it has. Today, even with the American undergraduate population being majority female, the university is still exclusive, and its mores, customs, traditions of tenure, publication, and teaching are still geared to men's schedules and needs. The university's approach to the study of language still involves the repression of the materiality of language. Those in a position to teach and grant access to language teach instead the need to deny its materiality—and, through this denial, restrict public access by protecting its various subject matters from inquiries into their uses of language.

Here is a more figurative and dramatic picture of the experience of having no access to language in the modern period. In Franz Kafka's *The Trial,* the protagonist, Josef K., listens to a parable told to him by a priest/jailer (someone who works at once for both church and state) just before he is executed, and just after he has tried to find out why he was arrested and scheduled for trial. This frequently anthologized parable tells of a man who waits his lifetime before a door, next to which there is a "doorkeeper" (the lowest member of the Church hierarchy) who will give him access to the law.[24] Just before he dies, he learns that the unopened door was meant only for him. In this way, the parable sums up what happened to Josef K. in this novel. No reasons are given for these events, and the only thing we actually see is the priest/jailer's narrative, and the execution of Josef K by two men. Kafka was a lawyer who used his university training in his day job working for an insurance company. His night job was writing parables, stories, and novels. The novel describes how no one has access to the law, with the implication that the collusion between church and state has successfully prevented it. But Kafka the writer did acquire access to language, as Evelyn Torton Beck has shown in comparisons of the literary style of earlier and later Kafka. His access was the acquisition of his characteristic Kafkaesque style, which he did not have when he first began to write.[25] With regard to gaining access to language, most people are in the same position as is Josef K. when he stands before the law: there is a door, attended by a doorkeeper (one

23. Some, like Frank Donoghue, who cites the previous, comparable studies of Thorstein Veblen and Upton Sinclair, have suggested a certain uniqueness in corporate exploitation of universities, but their behavior remains in the eight-century tradition of university sponsorship. Frank Donoghue, *The Last Professors: The Corporate University and the Fate of the Humanities* (New York: Fordham UP, 2008). Chapter 8 discusses this tradition in more detail.

24. The connections between (lack of) access to the law and (lack of) access to language are discussed in chapter 4.

25. Evelyn Torton Beck, *Kafka and the Yiddish Theater* (Madison: U of Wisconsin P, 1974). She locates the style change during the year 1912—"The Judgment" being the first story that shows what we now recognize the characteristic Kafkaesque style.

who belongs to the so-called club comprising those who have access to language), and access seems like a simple thing—either it will be opened or one can open it—yet this door just for each person is never opened. The majority of people die, many in wars they had no part in waging, without having overtaken their own language in ways that could have provided access to many more parts of society, or simply to a less painful life.

What have universities and other custodians of language done and what can they do with their custody of language, with their ability to grant access, to open the door? What have they said about the language in which every text, every speech, every advertisement, every film, every claim of knowledge and authority, every public pronouncement by political figures, every marital dispute, and every moment of communication has been immersed? How have schools and universities announced their knowledge, or shared the results of their efforts? What have teachers done with the use, study, and dissemination of language—and knowledge of language? Such questions have been asked before, but because this is a new moment in history, we may be in position to consider a new perspective.

From the end of the twelfth century, universities considered Aristotle to be a central figure—perhaps *the* central figure—in scholarship and inquiry. A time-honored postulate is Aristotle's logical principle of non-contradiction, "either A or not-A," sometimes described as "the law of the excluded middle." In its role as a prescriptive principle, one of its effects was to force choices over an extremely narrow range, a practice universities followed in their regular use of disputation as a means of deciding on scholarly competence. In ordinary experience, however, simultaneous A and not-A, with an included middle, are quite common, as Freud began to consider in his essay "The Antithetical Sense of Primal Words" (1910),[26] as well as through his description of "the unconscious" as a part of our minds that affirms everything: there is no "no" in the unconscious mind.[27] Many things are new and not new at once. Most things have "always already" been there. How can this not be the case? For centuries after the founding of the universities, Aristotle was considered to have had the answers to everything. Those who study language more fully, however, learn that, on the one hand, there is no principle of non-contradiction "out there,"[28] and on the other hand,

---

26. Sigmund Freud, *The Standard Edition of the Complete Psychological Works of Sigmund Freud,* trans. James Strachey and Anna Freud, with Alix Strachey and Alan Tyson (London: Hogarth P, 1957), 11:153–161.

27. As discussed in chapter 7, Freud did have trouble with the simultaneous affirmation of opposites in one's *conscious* mind. His principles of rationality led him to segregate this common ability to its cage in unconsciousness: "[I]n analysis, we never discover a 'no' in the unconscious." "Negation," *Standard Edition,* 19:239.

28. Tzvetan Todorov observes, "A and not-A divide up the universe exhaustively, so that to say of an object that it is characterized either by A or by not-A is to say nothing at all" *Genres in Discourse,* trans. Catherine Porter (Cambridge: Cambridge UP, 1990), 61.

announcing it as a principle helps the announcer and his adherents to control access to language of those who have not studied it.

The prescriptive reading of Aristotle's principle discredits the subjunctive and the interrogative moods, while establishing an honored place for the declarative: so-called propositional truth usually is considered the most authoritative form of knowledge. The principle of non-contradiction implies that non-declarative moods are less capable of formulating knowledge, and less welcome in academic writing.[29] When the principle of logic—with its air of inevitability and self-evident truth—is stipulated, it establishes a double standard for understanding potentially any instance language use. Because logical principles cannot apply to ordinary uses of language, to stipulate such a principle is a ruse. With this standard in effect, those who establish preferences and encourage usages on the basis of a stipulated logical principle are those who have access to language and are using this access to limit access of the majority to the language that is actually held and used in common.

I use the phrase "access to language" also to give a gestural, pragmatistic, behavioral, and socially grounded translation, version, or context of the materiality of language. If language is material, one gains access to it in the same sense that one gains access to a house or a driver's license—by using one's body. A material object is something all can grasp; who can grasp an immaterial one? Humpty Dumpty's declarations describe the pragmatic consequences of these phrases.[30] On the one hand, a word can mean "just what I choose it to mean—neither more nor less": access brings the ability to change the use of words in new ways—and to be heard and understood. On the other hand, the question is which [meaning or person, I assume] is to be master: How much power is given by one's recognition of the materiality of language? The "master" meaning or person is created by those with custody of the language, whereas those who are not masters can also make words mean whatever they choose them to mean (that is, what co-speakers will go along with) but because they are not masters, their meanings and usages will not have enough value to become authoritative: Alice says, "The question is . . . whether you *can* make words mean so many different things." For Alice it is a question; for Humpty it is a principle to which he has *taken* access. Geneva Smitherman cites an unidentified linguist who says, "The proper question is not what do words mean but what do the users of the words mean?"[31] To recognize the

---

29. As is now the case in undergraduate writing programs in United States universities. For example, "Such and such is the case, and here are my reasons," as opposed to "The case could be either this, that, or the other thing, and in some situations this is preferred, in others that is preferred, and in still others, something else might be preferred."

30. Lewis Carroll, *Through the Looking Glass* (London: Penguin, Puffin, 1974), 274.

31. Geneva Smitherman, *Talkin' that Talk: Language, Culture, and Education in African America* (New York: Routledge, 2000), 61. The understanding that users, not words,

materiality of language puts one *in a position to present* language as transparent,[32] because sometimes using it that way meets local needs, as in the instructions for assembling furniture. From the standpoint of usage in general, transparency is only one function of language, and not a superior or privileged one. To understand language as material is to recognize that people—individuals and groups who grasp it—can manipulate uses of language, presuppositions about it, and attitudes toward it to an indefinite extent, but that in principle any speaker who *can* gain access to language gets this capability. Yet those on a high wall who present transparency as a principle for all, and materiality for themselves, are fragile and are given to denying, ignoring, or repressing their vulnerability.

Here is an instance that places the question of access to and materiality of language in a different yet related context: the common condition of total mediation in society. Rosalind Morris describes some of the practical consequences of assuming either transparency or materiality, respectively, to understand specific uses of language.[33] In Thailand, on the way to her planned task of studying the Thai stock exchange, Morris came upon a "nationally renowned" Thai spirit medium, Chuchad, who took a recent public occasion to unveil the secret of his magic. He "repudiated mediumship" by revealing the technology of his tricks, which included cutting off a piece of his tongue, walking up a sword ladder, walking over glass, and the like.[34] His work as a medium (a means to reach the dead) was no longer posed as truthful: he no longer promoted the illusion of its truth. For a long time, he posed as a real medium: people considered him a site through which they would communicate with the dead. His self-repudiation meant that his words were no longer magical (efficacious as a material tool: his speaking the words was no longer taken to have physically conjured the dead); his words became, in his moment of revelation, representational: his words (his language use) *described* (in the transparent mode) the tricks he used to deceive people into believing that he could summon the dead, and announced that his words themselves could not really summon the dead. In his having become secularized, the materiality of his language, relative to the religious worldview, was lost, as it no longer had the power to summon the dead. Morris indicates that Chuchad either had to "disavow truth or seek it elsewhere." He chose the latter:

"mean" is characteristic of African American Vernacular English. This issue is discussed further in chapter 6.

32. "Transparency" describes the alleged unambiguous reference of any language: if language is described as transparent, it is taken as a *vehicle* or *conduit* for an unambiguous meaning.

33. Rosalind C. Morris, "Modernity's Media and the End of Mediumship? On the Aesthetic Economy of Transparency in Thailand," *Public Culture* 12.2 (2000): 457–475.

34. Morris, "Modernity's Media," 472.

he became an Amway distributor. Morris identifies this role with Chuchad's earlier role as a medium: the distributor poses as a community member helping the community and its families, but actually he serves the "occult" owners of this company—two Christian men in Michigan. Both the distributor and the medium are frauds. Here is Morris's point:

> Just as Chuchad remade himself a magician [rather than a spirit medium, whose actions are not considered to be tricks] by professing to display his technique, so the confessional disclosures of new capital and the rhetoric of transparency with which they cloak themselves effect the occulting of a system premised on secrecy. . . . [W]hat else is transparency in the massified world but a mediation so total that it has become invisible?[35]

Chuchad traded in one form of total mediation for another. Places in society most dependent on presenting transparent language to the majority are institutions whose function and status are unquestioned and whose uses of language are "total mediations": clerics, the military, the government; today technology, positive science, and commercially motivated corporations join this list of those whose claims are presumed trustworthy but may not be—and often, as in the case of the tobacco companies, they are deliberate lies. The axiomatic grounding of academic work in a search for truth also depends on the total mediation of language between the voices of academic authority and the public—although this assumption is often questioned privately among scholars and teachers. Morris's essay calls attention to how the presumption of the transparency of language has an occulting effect that renders the formulations of the user ineligible to challenge. By contrast, the obfuscating actions of ordinary language—that is, anyone's language—are perceptible in conversation, for example, as we are frequently aware how a person's narratives and explanations and comments are "in the way" of communication; in that situation the transparency of any single use of language is provisional. In ordinary talk, we act on the provisionality of transparency by reserving the option to interrupt in order to clarify; but the authority of *authoritative* pronouncements is derived from the presumption of their *non-provisional* transparency. They mean just what they choose it to mean, neither more nor less.

Shoshana Felman's speech-act analysis of Moliere's *Don Juan* shows the connection between this same language double standard and the familiar sexual double standard.[36] To "Don Juan's antagonists and victims, language is an instrument for transmitting *truth*, . . . a means of *knowing* reality. Truth is a

---

35. Morris, "Modernity's Media," 475.
36. Shoshana Felman, *The Literary Speech Act: Don Juan with J. L. Austin, or Seduction in Two Languages*, trans. Catherine Porter (Ithaca, NY: Cornell UP, 1983), 27.

relation of perfect congruence between an utterance and its referent, and, in a general way, between language and the reality it represents." The group with this view of language ascribes its authority to God, who "underwrites the authority of language." But for Don Juan "[s]aying . . . is in no case tantamount to knowing, but rather to *doing: acting* on the interlocutor, modifying the situation . . . Language, for Don Juan, is performative and not informative; it is a field of enjoyment, not of knowledge." This is the case for any rake or playboy. The women he meets expect (or perhaps only hope) that his words are true. The playboy knows this, but *uses* (plays with?) the language to do something—secure consent to gain access to a body. He is able to move between referential and performative language—he can alternate his standard of language use. But the women he approaches usually have no access to two (or more) standards of language, or to two or more standards of sexual behavior.[37] Don Juan's words mean what he chooses them to mean. But the women he meets do not have this choice. In religion, in commerce, and in sex, the behavioral double standard works because the language double standard is presupposed by the presumed socially superior status of men.[38]

The observations of Morris and Felman are today's versions of a tradition of understanding—nominalism—that has been studied and repeatedly revived in various periods of history. Feminist thinking, politically oriented as it has been, has become one of the modern versions of nominalism. It has, without ideological announcement, and in pursuit of the political purpose of social equality, used assumptions and tropes of language that have a long history. Nominalism is the ancestor of the materiality of language as well as of any social initiative seeking equal access to language and society for all people.

IV. Nominalism

Nominalism[39] rejected the priority and incorporeality of ideas or forms, which were presumed to exist on a plane "higher" than language and for which words

37. If both sexes had about the same access to language, the category terms "rake" and "slut" would have less weight, and bodily access would be a more negotiable event.

38. Today, popular culture in film and subscriber video often shows series or films in which a variable standard applies to both sexes. Yet it still is not the case today that this balance reflects egalitarian gender relations.

39. The philosopher most modern readers might associate with nominalism was the Oxford theologian William of Ockham (c. 1288–1347), who cautioned thinkers to simplify guesses down to what actually can be discovered. Paul Vincent Spade observes, "Ockham holds that for most natural kind terms in the category of substance, and for some in the category of quality, the concrete and the abstract forms are synonymous. Thus 'dog' and 'caninity' are everywhere intersubstitutable." Paul Vincent Spade, ed., *The Cambridge Companion to Ockham* (Cambridge: Cambridge UP, 1999), 105. However, doubt about the reference of abstractions has always been on the record, as suggested

were an inexact substitute.[40] A decisive turn away from nominalism, which did have some currency in the third and fourth centuries, took place with Augustine, who established Platonic realism as the orthodox ideology of language that has persisted since the Church became consolidated in the fifth century. As Augustine moved toward Christianity, he moved toward the Platonic sense of civilization, in which "what is unchangeable is to be preferred to what is changeable."[41] Because ideas were considered to be less changeable than words, because the "spirit" was considered less changeable than matter, and because God was assumed to be less changeable than Man, Augustine ultimately adopted what has been known as the realist sense of how language is to be used.[42] Carre observes that from Augustine, "more than from any other authority, sprang the pronounced Realism that persisted into modern times."[43] Ultimately the approach to language that characterized university subjects from the beginning— through scholasticism, renaissance humanism, experimental science, and modern times—was the combination of Platonic realism and Aristotelian logic.

The third-century *Isagoge* of Porphyry said, "As to whether genera or species really exist or are purely mental constructs, and if they exist whether they are

---

below. In the West, the problem of abstract reference was kept alive by religious debate; however, as discussed in this book, nominalism has led to the modern arrival of materiality, and it plays a considerable role in discussions about what scientific abstractions are worth keeping. Vivien Law has a clear discussion of nominalism and universals, the presupposed problem readdressed by Chomsky. Vivien Law, *History of Linguistics*, 27, 160–162. See also chapters 2 and 5, this volume. Law describes this problem as "one of most urgently debated issues in the cathedral schools and the fledgeling universities" (160). This was a binary debate won by the realists, recursively, into the present day.

40. Bertrand Russell's explanation of nominalism in *A History of Western Philosophy* (New York: Simon and Schuster, 1945), 435–439, is also helpful. There are several sources that engage the "either-or" style of dispute, between nominalism and realism. Some, such as D. M. Armstrong, who advocates for realism, presents viable ways to think about the problem. However, for him, it is a problem of epistemology more than of language. If the focus remains on language, there is no need to continue to assume a radical binarism, as, in language, there are both particulars and universals, as seen in their specific *uses*. D. M. Armstrong, *Nominalism and Realism: Universals and Scientific Realism*, vol. 1 (Cambridge: Cambridge UP, 1978).

41. From *Confessions*, 7:xvii, quoted in Meyrick H. Carre, *Realists and Nominalists* (London: Oxford UP, 1946), 7.

42. This historical fact seems to be why Wittgenstein introduced his *Philosophical Investigations* (see chapter 3, this volume) with a citation from *Confessions* describing Augustine's sense of how language is acquired. Ludwig Wittgenstein, *Philosophical Investigations*, trans. G. E. M. Anscombe (New York: Macmillan, 1958).

43. Carre, *Realists*, v. Peter King states, "In Augustine's view, (Christian) religion and (Platonist) philosophy were engaged in the same enterprise, namely the quest for knowledge." Peter King, introduction to Augustine, *Against the Academicians; The Teacher* (Cambridge: Hackett, 1995), vi. In this case knowledge refers to knowledge of God— theological and spiritual knowledge.

material or immaterial, and whether they are separate from sense-perceptible things or are contained within them—on all of this I am reserving judgment. It is a profound matter which deserves further investigation."[44] Nominalists challenged the inference of universal reference from a local pattern or series of similar experiences, a challenge also called "the problem of universals."[45] Vivien Law describes the Middle Ages' early interest in this problem as deriving from a frustration that exists today as well: "Everyone who worked with language was obliged to confront its essential arbitrariness, and that . . . was something which medieval scholars found very painful. . . . Now, with the new-found interest in universals, the question could be formulated slightly differently: where should one look in language to find universals?"[46] The perception of the arbitrariness of language has never been successfully revoked. The language philosophy of the mid-twentieth century represents an effort to proceed with an understanding of language through discussion of its different forms of arbitrariness. One may think of nominalists as particularly cautious users of language: they assumed reference and communicative efficacy like everyone else, but considered abstraction and generalization to be provisional and to have no claim on us to accept them beyond immediate contexts of use.[47] Nominalists recognized the referential

---

44. Found in, among other sources, Law, *History of Linguistics, 160.* Law identifies Porphyry as a Neo-Platonist, but this statement is a good example of the doubt stimulated in many by the realist perspective. Also quoted in Hastings Rashdall, *The Universities of Europe in the Middle Ages,* vol. 1: *Salerno, Bologna, Paris,* ed. F. M. Powicke and A. B. Emden (New York: Oxford UP, 1997), 40. Rashdall considers this formulation to be a source of "the central problem of the scholastic philosophy" and judges it to "have played perhaps a more momentous part in the history of thought than any other passage of equal length in all literature outside the canonical Scriptures" (40). The ground for this judgment is the inertia of the debate of what took place in the ritual of the Eucharist when the priest declared the wafer and wine to be the body and blood of Christ.

45. Law, *History of Linguistics,* 160.

46. Law, *History of Linguistics,* 163. Grammar has this appeal, since all languages have grammar. In chapter 2, this issue is considered further, with the aim to continue to understand grammar realistically, pragmatically, and responsibly without tying it to a vain search for language universals.

47. Nominalism as a way to approach the study of language poses a psychological challenge similar to those posed by Copernicus, Darwin, and Freud: accepting the nominalist view highlights the contingency of knowledge; it says the human species is less central, less important than we thought. In this light religious claims about transcendental things are exaggerations based on fantasies of things that are altogether unknown.

Sometimes nominalists are considered to be skeptics. But this term is misleading as it presupposes the normative-knowledge status of orthodox believing: one who believes is considered to be more devoted than one who doubts. As Ockham and other nominalists implied, skepticism of abstraction makes faith a more rational stance. The subject of theology converted verbally (and erroneously) faith in God to knowledge of God, thus making those who claimed only faith and not knowledge seem heretical.

insubstantiality of general categories. If an abstraction had no reference in plain sight, its usage was arbitrary and easily appropriated for politically suspicious purposes. If three people are called intelligent, a nominalist does not infer that there is an entity called "intelligence" that could be said to exist in its own right and is in some way *attached* to the three people.[48] Nominalists also do not infer a category of "intelligent person"; rather, they rely on the empirical (or phenomenological) observation of individual cases. This is a question of language because there is no agreement on the reference of so-called intelligence.[49] Classes of similar entities do not necessarily have any one thing in common; rather, our minds approximate the commonality and call the inferred group a class. There is no entity "mind" that exists independently of our use of the word "mind." Similarly, there is no idea of a person (for example) that exists independently of the uses of the word "person"; there are just persons. We persons have no need to find any necessary or logical common feature among them apart from the ordinary recognition of persons. Also, it is not possible to predict which figures will count as members of that class: one counts membership only backward, or in retrospect. We do not list features and say, "Whoever has these features is a person"; rather, we check each being and then *say* it is (or is not) a person. If we decide it is a person, we may also decide that that person has a mind. In addition, there are millions of persons without there being a necessary common feature of personhood.[50] In this way, hesitation about what knowledge is certain is related to a definite view of what language can and can not achieve. We say language "works"—or it can identify things and it can present experience, or objects experienced by two or more people at once, or even things that two or more people *say* are ideas. The certainty of this knowledge derives from the agreement among speakers that it is taken as certain.

Aristotle's concept of substance and accident was thought to be something of a departure from Plato's view—an incremental turn toward nominalism, but as

---

48. Stephen Jay Gould, *The Mismeasure of Man* (New York: Norton, 1983), chapter 6.

49. Alfred North Whitehead presented this point of view as "the fallacy of misplaced concreteness" in his 1925 work *Science and the Modern World,* His use of the term "fallacy" implied that this was a failure of logic and a local caution: be careful how you abstract. The present discussion considers premature abstraction to be a broad, deep, and thoroughgoing habit of thought that is linked to underlying assumptions about language. In the instances considered in this book, the misplacement of concreteness serves the interests of those who depend on the usage yielded by the misplacement. Alfred North Whitehead, *Science and the Modern World* (New York: Free P, 1967).

50. Although, for example, biological principle gives a test for the existence of species: if two organisms can mate with one another, they are members of the same species. But this, too, is limited, as there are organisms of the same species that cannot mate with each other and produce offspring. The mating itself can only be judged to have happened in retrospect from the resulting offspring. Thus, likelihood and the ability of a context to sustain a guess, rather than certainty, are the principles of generalization.

Aristotle was interpreted by orthodox churchmen in the early medieval period, his work was not permitted non-religious reference. When Aristotle separated substance from accident in any entity, individual cases (for example, intelligent people) could be called accidents, but the substance (intelligence) could be claimed to exist as well: the wafer is accidental, but when the priest speaks the words, its substance becomes the body of Christ. The so-called substance of any entity was still a class term that was established as true by the edict of religious authority, and there was no reduction of Plato's claim—or at least that is how many medieval thinkers read Aristotle and adapted his work to Christianity. Both Plato and Aristotle's sense of a transcendental mind or "prime mover" were made to be consistent with the Christian God as the source of the eternal ideas and abstractions.[51] However, nominalists such as Ockham, who were both theologians and faithful Christians, relied on empirical experience to decide whether a class of items should describe a new item that could fit into that class. This simple caveat caused trouble for centuries in disputes over the whether the Trinity was three entities or one entity, and whether the Eucharist was actually the body of Christ, as the priest said it was. Perhaps most noteworthy is that the nominalist perspective rendered faith more necessary and valuable: believing someone else's declaration of the reality of God is not as good as having faith oneself. The nominalist caveat causes trouble now over scientific categories such as instinct and intelligence, political categories such as freedom and bigotry, and gender categories such as masculine and feminine, for example. It could also be said to apply to the dispute over whether light is a particle or a wave, or whether a material essence of things—fundamental particles—is worth seeking.[52] Although some might wonder why this issue was, and still is, important, many who had nominalist approaches to language were considered heretics by the Church; they were excommunicated and sometimes executed.[53] Nominalism might also describe seventeenth- and eighteenth-century empirical philosophers

51. Marcia Colish, *The Mirror of Language* (Lincoln: U of Nebraska P, 1968), has a full discussion of how Aristotle was integrated into Church thinking.

52. Karen Barad, *Meeting the Universe Halfway* (Durham, NC: Duke UP, 2007); Steven Weinberg, *The First Three Minutes: A Modern View of the Origin of the Universe* (New York: Basic, 1993). The views of both of these figures and the language problems they pose are considered in chapter 10.

53. One of the many reasons the church suspected and persecuted Abelard was that one of his teachers was Roscelin, who answered one of Porphyry's questions: no extramental things correspond to concepts. Marilyn McCord Adams states, "Unpopular in the middle ages, this option [that nothing in reality corresponds to concepts] was taken up by Abelard's teacher Roscelin, whose doctrine that a universal is only a spoken sound (*flatus vocis*) was ridiculed by Anselm and Abelard alike." Marilyn McCord Adams, *William Ockham* (South Bend, IN: U of Notre Dame P, 1987), 1:5. In the seventeenth century, the Jewish community of Amsterdam "excommunicated" (but did not execute) Baruch Spinoza (1632–1677), whose philosophy declared the immanence but not the

such as Locke, Berkeley, and Hume. However, their views are usually characterized as "empirical" and "skeptical" because their formulations were taken to apply more to the processes in nature than to the use of language in describing those processes. Yet the problems raised by the empiricists were just as much about language as about nature: they called a cause a "constant conjunction" rather than a "necessary connection." With regard to causes, one cannot with confidence infer necessity if one does not observe it; necessity was an inference that none could observe.

Finally, nominalism made universities anxious.[54] Rashdall observes that in the medieval period, "the concentration of intellectual interest upon a single topic of ancient philosophy originated the never-ending controversy over the reality of universals. . . . He who has given his answer to it [the question of universals] has implicitly constructed his theory of the universe."[55] The most damaging religious disputes over centuries are traceable to this dispute over the nature of language. Of course, it did not, and does not now, seem that a certain take on language can produce far-flung acrimony, violence, or mutually destructive behavior. But Rashdall's judgment is plausible and reasonable, especially if we become aware of the centuries of casuistry devoted to fantasies and to claims that no one could prove. The church and university combined to defeat nominalism in a variety of ways that are discussed in chapters 8 and 9 of this book. However, this defeat was a loss for many others who were not church members. Realism as an approach to language became established as a foundational feature of cultural androcentrism.

---

transcendence of God. He was read by the community as an atheist and a heretic. Steven Nadler says that this heresy consisted of the denial of the immortality of the soul, and claims that this, too, was a fake accusation; in Judaism there is no doctrinal principle of the soul's immortality. Steven Nadler, *Spinoza's Heresy: Immortality and the Jewish Mind* (New York: Oxford UP, 2001). A final similarity of Spinoza's to those Christians who were accused as heretics is in his style of logic. Stuart Hampshire writes, "It is one of the first principles of his logic, throughout nominalistic, that definitions of the abstract, general terms of ordinary language cannot yield genuine knowledge. . . . He strongly insists (*Ethics Pt.* III. *Prop.* LV. *Note* I) that the joy of one man is essentially different from the joy of another, although the common name is properly applicable to them both." Stuart Hampshire, *Spinoza and Spinozism* (New York: Oxford UP, 2005), 108. One sees in Spinoza an issue similar to that in Abelard: a rationalist philosopher being taught by and drawn to nominalism in the cause of rendering faith more reasonable. Spinoza is also relevant to the issue of how scientists describe natural phenomena.

54. Nominalism made anyone adhering to orthodoxy anxious. Brian Stock details how, before the university period, Anselm made it his task to refute the "heretic" Roscelin, who had trouble affirming that the three "forms" of God were in reality one. Brian Stock, *Implications of Literacy: Written Language and Models of Interpretation in the Eleventh and Twelfth Centuries* (Princeton, NJ: Princeton UP, 1983), 359–360.

55. Rashdall, *Universities of Europe,* 1:39–40.

It is worth noting that nominalism has never in its history been discredited. It has been opposed repeatedly, but none have been able to tag it as a false perspective or a useless way of approaching language. Under the hegemony of the church, the opposition to nominalism has been mainly to slander it as a heresy; arguments against it simply were of no avail. Those who had perhaps a reduced taste for feuding, such as Peter Abelard, found value in both ends of the disputed issues as well as in other activities and concerns. Yet, again and again, some form of linguistic pragmatism has returned, as may be seen in the works of the British empiricists in the seventeenth and eighteenth centuries, and of the pragmatists and language materialists of the late nineteenth and early twentieth centuries. Until perhaps the seventeenth century, universities were the only respectable intellectual and educational forums. Since they were overseen by the Church, the chances of achieving credibility for nominalism were virtually nil.

The materiality of language is a descendent of nominalism, empiricism, and phenomenology, but it develops a different perspective and different emphases. It takes language to be inseparable from the total context of its use. Materiality differs from nominalism and empiricism and from most traditional philosophical categories in its self-conscious recognition of the politics of all uses of language in its purview.[56] It differs in its emphasis on the bodily character of language use, and on the role of gender awareness in establishing these uses. Medieval nominalist debates and the later philosophical debates were just as political, but as even contemporary scholars characterize them, the issues appeared in categories—theological, philosophical, or linguistic—that were considered unrelated to political issues, gender being the most distant possible factor.[57] Although materialist thinking discredits the transparency of total mediation, most university-trained people still treat language as a conduit that conveys meaning—meaning being the abstract essences, taken to exist in people's minds as incorporeal things, of particular usages. The Platonic sense that the real action of language does not take place in people's exchange of gestural words but in the exchange of incorporeal meanings or ideas or thoughts is still a majority view today. Although stereotyping is considered to be a form premature generalization and viewed as gauche, impolite, and sometimes bigoted, today other generalizations today—such as *freedom* and *market economics,*—would be

56. The political character of the materiality of language is discussed in chapter 6 and more briefly in all of the following chapters.

57. Rashdall shows the political character of this dispute in his own narrative. Tracing the doctrine of transubstantiation back to the ninth century, he suggests that the "awakening" from this vain belief was connected to the nominalist challenge by Berengar of Tours. There was next a conservative reaction to this challenge: "Realism bespoke the favour of the theologian by supplying a much-needed philosophical dress for his cherished doctrine." In this way, a political interest posed as philosophical truth, which, in turn, sustained the hegemony of the church. Rashdall, *Universities of Europe,* 1:48–49.

rarely challenged on language-materialist grounds; no one can identify stable referents of these common terms, but most people assume that such referents exist.[58] In the school and university teaching of language use and writing—as well as in how these subjects have been taught since the Enlightenment, there are no grounds to find fault with language as conveying meaning. Ordinary teaching of language would not present it as, for example, the gesture exchange of two (or more) speakers. Universities have helped to insure the inertia of this conception of language as conduit.[59] However, recognizing the materiality of language views its "conveyance" function as *one among many* functions taking place at once. Since all academic subjects present themselves through this variety of uses and gestures, academic experience, knowledge, and effort is in a position to help revoke its separation from ordinary lives; it will be easier for all people to have access to language.

Nevertheless, recognizing the materiality of language sounds merely like potentially good advice unless the issue of language is juxtaposed with the equally long history of the abandonment of language and the resulting resort to violence by men who govern (and who sometimes are also scholarly men). It is likely that men themselves are, in part, driven to abandon language because there is no verbal way out of a dispute about an abstraction. The ideological status of abstractions discourages practical application and encourages rigid commitments because they seem like matters of principle. Recognizing the materiality of language makes it easier to see how traditional language-use mores may be inhibiting a greater collective determination to reduce war, killing, cruelty, rape, and other injuries of the most painful and repellent sort.[60]

---

58. The real pragmatistic referents for Americans of "freedom" and "market economics" is something on the order of speaking like us, traveling like us, and doing business like us. Admitting that these are the referents would seem pathologically narcissistic. Therefore, we say "we all know" what the terms "mean." Keeping the referents vague enables us to ignore our habitual narcissistic exceptionalism.

59. An inertia further promoted by the use of the term "media," which started with Marshall McLuhan, and has now assumed a taken-for-granted position in academic discussions. The point being only that interest in media has further obscured the fact that any communication occurs between living people and living constituencies, and not between different technologies.

60. These issues are discussed in chapter 11.

CHAPTER TWO

Received Standards in the Study of Language

I. Language as a Contested Subject Matter

Languages and their uses have remained in university curricula from the beginning. But the study of language as a subject matter has been repeatedly a site of dispute. As with most subject matters, this one followed received standards that resisted change. In antiquity people wrote Latin grammars, and continued to write them through the university period into the present. In addition to learning Latin to enter university, students took introductory courses in rhetoric, which was studied and analyzed to some extent throughout the Middle Ages, usually as a propaedeutic, and this practice has continued into the present day. In several places during the thirteenth and fourteenth centuries, Greek and Hebrew were added to Latin as languages that must be studied; they were formally installed in the sixteenth century in university curricula. During the humanistic period, vernaculars were gradually introduced in universities, and they became the principal languages of classroom education by the eighteenth century, although scholarship and science was still composed in Latin.[1] In the seventeenth century, language was studied in connection with empirical epistemology, a subject that has remained active into the present. In the eighteenth century, there were several efforts (which continue in the present day) to decide how language originated in the human species. Brockliss reports that "at the end of the eighteenth century the first steps were taken towards teaching the native vernacular."[2] In the nineteenth century, the languages of the non-Western world

---

1. "Few of Europe's intelligentsia may have chosen to converse in [Latin] after the Renaissance, but it definitely remained the *lingua franca* of publication." Laurence Brockliss, "Curricula," *A History of the University in Europe,* vol. 2: *Universities in Early Modern Europe: 1500–1800,* ed. Hilde de Ridder-Symoens, gen ed. Walter Rüegg (Cambridge: Cambridge UP, 1996), 570.
2. Brockliss, "Curricula," 570.

were sought out and brought to the university. This collection helped to form comparative philology. In the twentieth century, developing a useful, credible account of the infantile acquisition of language has become one of the principal tasks of language and psychology.

In spite of there having been a variety of approaches to the study of language, and in spite of there being many hypotheses and theories about the origin, nature, and essence of language, there is no consensus in research, scholarship, or science on how to understand the universality of language on the one hand and its indefinite number of variations on the other.[3] Nor is there understanding about how to place it in the collection of other kinds of understanding of humans, of other species, or of living things generally. Almost any kind of language study could make claims that were provocations to other university subject matters. Underlying this historic pattern (in academic life) are the issues raised in the eleventh and twelfth centuries by the considerations of nominalism and realism (as outlined in chapter 1).

Many have regarded language as a hallmark of human distinctiveness or a sign that God has taken special notice of the human species, which makes us, we say, "more" than other species. It has been always considered useful to study language beyond our common intuitive understanding of it, beyond our practical experience, toward the history and function of languages. A great deal of attention to language has been given by speakers of one language trying to learn others. Yet this sort of study also has not led to understanding on which a consensus of observers would develop.[4] With regard to the study of language, the idea of knowledge commonly associated with the sciences does not seem to apply: studies of language have challenged the processes of "seeking knowledge" to begin with.[5]

---

3. This formulation could also be construed as describing the understanding of language in medieval times: there was a search for universals while the fable of the Tower of Babel was understood as an explanation of language diversity.

4. However, there does seem to be a consensus that the surest way to acquire second and third languages is through immersion: learning "takes" when people live among other speakers of the language.

5. This is one of Wittgenstein's starting points and is discussed in chapter 3. Wittgenstein found that philosophy was challenged by a misunderstanding of language, but chapters 10 through 12 in this book discuss how all subjects are thus challenged. One of the symptoms of the provocation by language problems is that the practice of philosophy has barely done anything differently pursuant to Wittgenstein's critique. As discussed in chapter 10, several commentaries on science involve a radical critique of its language, especially its universalist assumptions. The response to such commentaries has been verbally extreme. Paul Gross and Norman Levitt barely contain their outrage that the vocabulary of science has been called "androcentric" and "Western" and that traditional usages have led to erroneous results. Paul Gross and Norman Levitt, *Higher*

In the university the study of language has often been hampered by a variety of factors, one of which is disciplinary disputes that seem bureaucratic but are ideologically substantive. When experts in language appeared and tried to study the language of experts in different subject matters, disputes arose. An accurate description of the study of language during the full university period (from the twelfth century to the present) would include various compartmentalizations of study encouraged by the university structure, a feature common today, and characterized by what must seem to non-academics as pointless disputes over knowledge jurisdictions. Such disputes are partly the result of the agonistic culture.[6] On the one hand, the establishment of a discipline provides space for thought, study, and teaching; on the other hand, because of the agonistic atmosphere, it creates barriers between disciplines that are then justified with ever increasing energy leading to acrimony. However, most such barriers are not only bureaucratic, they also derive from social and political interests that are indirectly promoted and defended.

For example, while both the *trivium* and the *quadrivium* were retained during the first two centuries of the universities' existence, as Louis John Paetow discusses,[7] the emphasis was on logic and dialectic over grammar and rhetoric in order to develop the scholastic style in theology, the highest in the hierarchy of subjects. The subject of language was defined in order to serve the study of theology. Paetow writes that although the Latin literary classics were studied in the eleventh and early twelfth centuries, "[p]robably a university could never have arisen on a purely humanistic basis."[8] He was referring to the roles of logic and dialectic in theology and law—the "establishment" subjects—as being the necessary ingredients for the university to acquire the support of the church and crown. The study of language was present, but its purpose was to serve the language interests of theology.

To study language is to study something that applies to all people, yet at the same time applies to each individual, each community, and each state—perhaps in continuously varying ways. Consequently, serious formal study of language applies to a series of local and individual uses that, when made to seem unstable or contingent, create social and psychological agitation.

Superstition: The Academic Left and Its Quarrels with Science (Baltimore: Johns Hopkins UP, 1994), 144.

6. Or they are the culture of disputation, of struggle, of opposition, of adversariality, described by Walter Ong (chapter 9, and introduced in chapter 7), and challenged by Janice Moulton (chapter 8).

7. Louis John Paetow, *The Arts Course at Medieval Universities with Special Reference to Grammar and Rhetoric,* University of Illinois: The University Studies, vol. 3, no. 7. (Urbana-Champaign, IL: University Press, 1910).

8. Paetow, *Arts Course,* 14.

II. Lorenzo Valla's Challenges

In the fifteenth century, Lorenzo Valla (1406–1457) was a key figure whose erudition, initiatives, and experience provoked but only indirectly affected the existing approach to the study of language in the university. Valla was a well-known professor of rhetoric and a humanist at the University of Pavia.[9] He has been characterized by modern scholars as being more expert in Greek than most of his contemporaries, and as dedicated, more than other humanists, to advocating the greater importance of rhetoric and ordinary language over scholastic philosophy.[10] Jerrold Siegel[11] writes that Valla wanted to "model philosophical discourse on the language of business or politics . . . [and] align [his] conclusions with all the usual notions of common sense."[12] If philosophers try to "refine common language or criticize common ideas of morality, Valla's answer was ready: 'Let the people respond that the rules of speech and all decisions about it lie with them.'"[13] Valla understood that usage and its slow, historical development were fundamental data—perhaps the only data—eligible to guide the understanding of grammar: he treated texts as the evidence for "ordinary" usages of the past. Gradually, a wide split developed between the way Latin was conceived in the academy and the way the vernacular was used by everyone else. Charles Trinkhaus,[14] quoting Luciano Barozzi's 1891 opinion, characterized Valla as "nearer to modern positivist and statistical methods of proof than to rationalism, and, like the

---

9. "The most eminent Humanist . . . of this period was Lorenzo Valla." Frederick B. Artz, *Renaissance Humanism, 1300–1550* (Kent, OH: Kent State UP, 1966), 27. Anthony Grafton and Lisa Jardine state that "Valla . . . became the most original Roman teacher of his generation." Anthony Grafton and Lisa Jardine, *From Humanism to the Humanities: Education and the Liberal Arts in Fifteenth- and Sixteenth-Century Europe* (Cambridge, MA: Harvard UP, 1986), 66.

10. Scholasticism, extolled by Walter J. Ong, was an enterprise that stipulated unprovable abstractions (assumptions, that is, such as are found in theology) and then developed a dialectic method to discuss them. The strenuous curricular attentions and efforts in the universities were thus focused on things that had no bearing on the experience in life of all people. In spite of Abelard's humane values, his work was instrumental in establishing a curriculum based wholly on assumptions that could never be verified. Walter J. Ong, S.J., *Orality and Literacy: The Technologizing of the Word* (New York: Methuen 1982), 109.

11. Jerrold E. Siegel, *Rhetoric and Philosophy in Renaissance Humanism: The Union of Eloquence and Wisdom, Petrarch to Valla* (Princeton, NJ: Princeton UP, 1968).

12. Siegel, *Rhetoric and Philosophy*, 166.

13. Siegel, *Rhetoric and Philosophy*, 167.

14. Charles Edward Trinkhaus, Jr., trans., "Lorenzo Valla," *The Renaissance Philosophy of Man*, ed. Ernest Cassirer, Paul Oskar Kristeller, and John Herman Randall, Jr. (Chicago: U of Chicago P, 1948), 147–182.

positivist philosophers, Valla was concerned with the problems of human liberty."[15] Similarly, Jerrold Siegel writes,

> Valla denied . . .that [syllogistic logic] could ever aid in the pursuit of knowledge. One could not decide about the truth or falsehood of simple statements by any logical test, but only by means of some independently acquired knowledge. . . . He made it quite clear that he did not believe reason, by itself, could add to this knowledge . . . he did not think that dialectic [i.e., scholastic disputation, the means used to certify masters in the university] was therefore any more rigorous a procedure than rhetoric.[16]

For an academic figure, Valla had an unusual respect for ordinary language, and in that regard his stance has something in common with Wittgenstein and other twentieth-century philosophers such as Austin and Bakhtin (chapter 3).[17] According to Walter Rüegg,[18] Valla studied "spoken discourse"[19] and interpreted authors in terms of "his understanding of language and his situation." He was one of the earliest annotators (1444 CE) of the New Testament.[20] He "analysed the Latin language as a living expression of the changing self-understanding of human beings."[21] He tried to create a logic derived from the grammar of ordinary speech. One may describe his approach as "contextualist," as he viewed language as something living in a variety of social situations.[22]

---

15. Trinkhaus, "Lorenzo Valla," 154.

16. Siegel, *Rhetoric and Philosophy*, 167.

17. "In his discussion of Latin style and in his *Dialectics*, Valla proposed a great simplification of logic which he treated ingeniously in close connection with rhetoric. The work contains a strong denunciation of the medieval Aristotelians, and attacks the philosophers of his own time for their belief in the infallibility of Aristotle." Artz, *Renaissance Humanism*, 28.

18. Walter Rüegg gives a full account of Valla's career in "The Rise of Humanism," *A History of the University in Europe*, vol. 1: *Universities in the Middle Ages*, ed. Hilde de Ridder-Symoens, gen. ed. Walter Rüegg (Cambridge: Cambridge UP, 1992), 456–458.

19. Rüegg, "Rise," 456.

20. This work was used by Erasmus, sixty years later, and is discussed below. Rüegg, "Rise," 457.

21. Rüegg, "Rise," 457.

22. Rather than trying to fit Valla into a philosophical genre, a more germane description of his approach to language might emphasize that his own pragmatism comes from knowing many languages and several versions of the key languages, Latin and Greek. The resemblance of his view to materialist views of language derived from his having understood changes in the uses of language as well as the historical abuses. In addition a key point of resemblance are his several intuitions regarding political functions of language.

Grafton and Jardine trace Valla's distinctive understanding to his having overtaken the philosophy of Cicero and the pragmatics of Quintilian.[23] Cicero, in particular, had grown up with Greek and translated his reading of the Greek sources into Latin. In this process Greek culture, frames of mind, and social attitudes made their way into Cicero's vision of the role of language in the education of future statesmen. To both of these figures, language and rhetoric did not mean the study of how to choose words for public speaking. Rather, the study of language was a preparation for the assumption of ethically oriented (and supposedly manly) leadership,[24] something that entailed knowing how to say the truth in ways that will reach the public: this is the source of Valla's reputation for respecting so-called ordinary language. The two classical Roman figures also viewed the use of language as being a bodily as well as a social function.

Valla used his knowledge of classical sources to lay groundwork in language for comprehensive humanistic understanding. He thought scholasticism, with its emphasis on both logic and abstraction, was an erroneous philosophy: "His aim is to show (as he states in the preface to the third book of the *Elegantiae*) that in existing learning and philosophy 'the major source of error stems from their lack of an adequate understanding of language';[25] the humanist who has systematically studied the 'most regularly used conventions of discourse' will have a clearer route to 'truth' than the specialist in logical formalism."[26] Valla's approach to the study of grammar was to search for instances of what appeared to be grammatical ambiguities (Grafton and Jardine give instances from Latin grammar), and find these usages in classical literary texts.[27] Valla argued that the usages were the resolution of the grammatical ambiguities that appear when the

---

23. Grafton and Jardine cite Valla, *Opera* I 266, as quoted in Camporeale, *Lorenzo Valla*, 127: "Concerning the two authors, here is what I feel: . . . No one can understand Quintilian who has not mastered Cicero completely, nor can anyone follow Cicero rightly unless he complies with Quintilian. Nor has anyone ever been eloquent since Quintilian (nor can he be) unless he has devoted himself entirely to the art regulated by him and to imitation. Whoever has not done this, however great he is, I shall set myself far ahead of him in the art of speaking" (*From Humanism*, 68).

24. Like all university members at this time, Valla did not question the presumption of androcentrism as a principle of social leadership. Grafton and Jardine cite Valla's *Institutio oratorio*, 5.11.10: "Courage is more remarkable in a woman than in a man" (*From Humanism*, 79).

25. Compare this formulation to Wittgenstein's (*Philosophical Investigations*, section 109), also cited in chapter 3: "Philosophy is a battle against the bewitchment of our intelligence by means of language." The similarity to Valla is striking. Just as striking is how neither figure is heard by the academy on this issue. Ludwig Wittgenstein, *Philosophical Investigations*, trans. G. E. M. Anscombe (New York: Macmillan, 1958).

26. Grafton and Jardine, *From Humanism*, 73.

27. This strategy may be found the sociolinguistic work of Deborah Tannen in "Oral and Literate Strategies in Spoken and Written Discourse," *Literacy for Life: The Demand*

usages were considered in isolation. Valla was able to use this technique because he knew the classical dialects and others did not. The result was that he taught a rhetorical pragmatism that opposed the sole dependence on uncontextualized logic and reasoning that described scholastic techniques.

In 1440, Valla's specific erudition and testing procedures showed conclusively that the Church's claim to Constantine's territories was based on a forged document. He inferred from the dialect of the document that the Latin of the Church's "will" was eighth-century, and not fourth-century, Latin.[28] Reynolds and Wilson continue, "It is not surprising that he likewise attacked the authenticity of the spurious correspondence between Seneca and Saint Paul, which had had an undeserved run since the days of Jerome."[29] Valla was similar to Abelard, or Wyclif, or Ockham insofar as his extended familiarity with languages and how they have been used led to results that challenged theological and bureaucratic orthodoxies.

Valla's research technique was part of a professional identity that involved other features at odds with conventions of his academic community. He authored *Concerning Pleasure,* in which he criticized monasticism, continence, and the Papacy. The theme of this work "is that 'what nature has created cannot be other than holy and admirable.' 'Would that man had fifty senses since five can give such pleasure.' 'Street women deserve better of the human race than nuns and virgins.'"[30] This is a glimpse of Valla's sympathy with Epicureanism, of his taste for the physicality of experience, as well as of the equalizing effects of this physicality. He may be said to share this perspective with the eighteenth century philosopher Johann Hamann, whose view of language emerges from similar values and perceptions of how human beings are a part of nature rather than separate and distinct from it. But even if Valla criticized the Papacy, he was still a friend of the pope, a friendship that mattered when he tried to apply rhetoric to the study of the law. Furthermore, as he had been private secretary to the king of Naples,[31] he had established himself as a loyal friend of the politically powerful, an identity that permitted his more comprehensive doctrinal iconoclasm.

---

for Reading and Writing, ed. Richard W. Bailey and Robin Melanie Fosheim (New York: MLA, 1983) 79–96. Tannen considers, as a matter of course, that literary conversations are conventionally the same as real recorded oral conversations: the oral and the literate are evidence for each other's usages.

28. Christopher B. Coleman, trans., *The Treatise of Lorenzo Valla on the Donation of Constantine* (Toronto: U of Toronto P, 1993); L. D. Reynolds and N. G. Wilson, *Scribes and Scholars: A Guide to the Transmission of Greek and Latin Literature* (Oxford: Oxford UP, 1968), 126.

29. Reynolds and Wilson, *Scribes and Scholars,* 126.

30. Artz, *Renaissance Humanism,* 27.

31. Artz, *Renaissance Humanism,* 27. Rüegg calls them "the humanistic King Alfonso of Aragon in Naples," and the "humanistic Pope Nicholas V" ("Rise," 456).

In his account of the growth and effects of early-fifteenth-century Italian humanism, Rüegg reports the following:

> It was already clear in the writings of Valla that the humanists, through their teaching in the *trivium,* could reach out beyond the disciplinary boundaries of the faculty of arts and could thereby come into conflict with the other faculties. As a result of such expansion, Valla had to flee from his professorship in Pavia because of the physical dangers arising from his violent persecution at the hands of the members of the faculty of law; in Rome he was protected from the attacks of the theologians only because he enjoyed the favour of the pope.[32]

Valla was considered intrusive because his subject, rhetoric—when pursued without censorship of its political valences—implicated other subject matters.[33] This amounted to an academic heresy, an overstepping of boundaries that threatens to bring unorthodox change. The strong response of the law faculty meant that they were defending at once the language they use, their dominion over this language, and their dominion over the law.[34] The fact that this was a "violent persecution," however, is not a small matter; Rüegg says "physical dangers" forced Valla to leave his appointment because his study of legal rhetoric was taken as a threatening move. A case such as this suggests just why the study of language is threatening to academic interests more generally. If established language conventions, such as those represented by the formal "Donation" document, can be deauthorized by scholarly attention that none can discredit, the

---

32. Rüegg, "Rise," 457.

33. In 1990, Linda Brodkey secured the strong support of the Department of English at the University of Texas, Austin, to teach a required first-year writing course whose subject matter included civil rights cases at the Supreme Court. The University of Texas overrode this formal decision and canceled the course. Brodkey left the University of Texas. Her account of these events can be found in "The Troubles at Texas," *Writing Permitted in Designated Areas Only* (Minneapolis, U of Minnesota P, 1996), 181–192. The syllabus for this course also appears in the volume as "Writing about Difference: The Syllabus for English 306" (211–227). Although Brodkey's life was not threatened, her livelihood was—and for the same reason that Valla's life was threatened: the legal structure and the university structure both viewed her initiative as seditious.

34. Until recently, the language of the law has not come under formal, professional academic scrutiny. Patricia J. Williams's *The Alchemy of Race and Rights: Diary of a Law Professor* (Cambridge, MA: Harvard UP, 1991), brings out a series of incidents in which both the language and the administrators of the law do not admit that its language stands in the way of justice for African Americans. Since then, the field of critical legal studies has asked such questions more frequently, but thus far such questioning has not changed much in how laws are articulated. As broached in chapter 1 of this book, "intent" remains an established term whose reference judges and juries try to determine in actual cases. Imagine how the law would change if the term "intent" were no longer used in the formulations of the law.

authority of those who accept these conventions is jeopardized, as the law faculty knew. Why academic figures are led to physical violence may be related to the gender identity of the academy, as is discussed further in chapter 11.

Valla's detection of forgeries did not move the church to restore the land to its original owners. Nor did his interest in the language of the law have an effect on the thinking of the law faculty. However, both the document and Valla's experience with the law faculty suggests how, historically, the study of language in universities was limited. Valla[35] was a bona fide member of the Church and the university who achieved his position through the conventional path—university training with Church backing. He was acclaimed for his perspicacity and he had no seditious purpose in his scholarship; he involved himself more deeply than most in the study of Greek and Latin and in the study of rhetoric. Enjoying the level of academic freedom any scholar had at that time, he announced discoveries on the assumption that the Church would welcome the truth as the basis of its governance.[36] Because of the political weight of his discovery, it did not count that his knowledge of different dialects of Latin produced practical effects. Had it been taken as consequential, perhaps the Church might have behaved differently, and the law faculty might have welcomed his collaboration. Knowledge of language may well be recognized as true, but this truth lives in isolation when, in the academy, its political character becomes visible—and, therefore, provocative, threatening, or intimidating.

The processes of the Renaissance were characterized by the discovery of new texts and by the increasing ease of reproducing existing texts. Should a scholar of rhetoric not limit the applications of the subject, texts in an indefinite number of subjects would have been eligible for critical study. Those scholars who best comprehended grammar, logic, and rhetoric—and who had the greatest number of languages at their disposal—were in a strong position to recast the received texts in new lights. In modern times, Valla's views on the importance of language have rarely been permitted the space to develop: universities still behave as if full engagement in the study of language as it affects other subjects, and as it takes into account the languages of all populations, is not in its interest.[37] The prevailing attitude toward language is that it is a tool, a helper, something to enable other things to happen, but not, in any event, a primary

---

35. Like Linda Brodkey.

36. Reynolds and Wilson say that he made a practice of attacking sacred cows and that he had a "vain and aggressive" nature (*Scribes and Scholars,* 126). But this is a misleading formulation: the account of Valla's work in Grafton and Jardine documents a principled vision of how his subject—the use of language—integrates into society that derives from Cicero and Quintilian.

37. Practitioners of such subjects as economics or biology, for example, would not cooperate with rhetoricians or sociolinguists in the critical study of the language uses in their disciplines. In the early sixteenth century, Erasmus, who found Valla's work valuable, did not have the same approach to language.

site that reflects and determines human affairs. Valla, on the basis of scholarly knowledge of classical Rome and of his own intuitions, had treated language as being connected with bodily and social experience. Public fear of this approach, rather than any dispute with the validity of his erudition, met his claims and style with suspicion and antagonism.

III. The Humanistic Study of Language

Valla's approach to language was a minority voice in the humanistic period. Yet that was the period, more than the centuries before and after, when the attention to language in universities was greatest. It was the moment when students of languages became aware of how everyone's social and subjective experiences depended on how language was used and studied. The early modern humanist movement took Cicero's *studium humanitatis*,[38] the combination of speech and its use as a path toward moral consciousness, as the distinctive core of the human species.[39] Language in several senses became an important part of the university curriculum because it led to the direct study or contemplation of the mental and cultural lives of people; "humanities" as a subject[40] was understood to revolve around language, especially literary language. During this period, the humanities, rather than just language, rhetoric, grammar, or other languages, became the universal propaedeutic for those seeking advanced degrees.

In discussing "the rise of humanism," Walter Rüegg describes a change in the sense of how to understand what a moral life was from an orientation around the hope for salvation to an orientation around how to behave in this life through "a dialogue over time and space."[41] It could be that war and disease[42] played a major role in shifting the attention of scholars more directly to human dignity and experience. Rüegg observes that the "psychological insecurity which characterized the epoch of humanism is evidence that traditional institutions could no longer form the person. . . . [P]rofessions which used rational and particularly written means of communication and exchange could find no appropriate models for human self-understanding in their own family traditions."[43] There was a surfeit of bookishness, so to speak, and groups with orally transmitted models of human experience were alienated:

38. Rüegg, "Rise," 443.

39. The term "humanism," however, as we use it now, dates from the early nineteenth century. Rüegg cites Niethammer's 1809 definition as "a curriculum based on liberal education and the teaching of language" that "dominated secondary education" since the fifteenth century in Europe ("Rise," 443).

40. Grafton and Jardine say humanism was converted to "humanities" by the pedagogical focus of Peter Ramus (*From Humanism*, chapter 7).

41. Rüegg, "Rise," 446.

42. The Hundred Years' War and the Black Death.

43. Rüegg, "Rise," 446.

The *studia humanitatis* replaced the missing or alienated family traditions of political and social experiences with the study of literary testimonies of alien humanity. They made the analysis of language into the most important part of the educational formation of a human being. . . . [T]hrough his interaction with textual testimonies of alien *humanitas,* the individual human being gives form in language and forms his own *humanitas.* He educates himself thereby into a morally responsible human being who achieves autonomy through a mastery of language.[44]

The reproduction of texts before the printing press was a major undertaking. Very few people were literate, but even those who could write still had to pay a high price to reproduce a document, let alone a book. The desire to recognize openly human passions and experiences without rendering them also as temptations, as was done by Abelard and others like him, was answered through the attention to oral sources of literature—songs, epic poems, and dramatic performances (which began in English churches at about this time).[45]

The approach to language was transformed by the humanists' interest in literature and in studying carefully how things were written in their original languages. These moments in history saw a reduction of the sense of exclusivity created by the mores of the study of Latin, the so-called language of knowledge. The only choice was the vernacular—heresy in some formal contexts, and which was considered incapable and ineligible of articulating authoritative knowledge. Only those literate in Latin could know. To the extent that the language of oral genres of literature—poetry, songs, plays, and speeches—was also considered eligible to transmit knowledge, the use of language became important to scholars. The term "poetry" came to be the "most inclusive term for the formation of human knowledge by language."[46] Scholars in the thirteenth and fourteenth centuries began language-use practices that became the basis for the humanities of today. At that time in the university, the "centre of gravity of the image of the world and of human beings shifted from the

---

44. Rüegg, "Rise," 446.

45. Winfield Parks and Richmond Croom Beatty observe that by the twelfth century in England, "practically all of the Bible had been dramatized" and staged during Christmas and Easter in churches (2). Because of their popularity—and presentation in the vernacular—Church authorities moved them out of the church buildings. They became increasingly secularized and subject to vernacular interpretation and variation; the guilds staged them by the end of the fourteenth century. The story of how these plays expanded is a good index of how and why the times were ready for a scholarly humanism. Winfield Parks and Richmond Croom Beatty, eds., *The English Drama: An Anthology, 900 to 1642* (New York: Norton, 1935), quotation on 2.

46. Rüegg, "Rise," 447.

nature of things to the nature of human beings, who as social beings, were defined by the use of language."[47]

When new universities were founded in the sixteenth century and afterward, and when new groups of students populated the university, they studied in the Faculty of the Arts, which meant the humanities. The movement on the part of both church and state to establish universities owed a great deal to the widespread study of the humanities, which contributed to the other professional schools in considerable degree, as Rüegg describes. Humanities education today means more or less what it meant six centuries ago: the close study of language genres for the purpose of understanding distinctive features of language and moral choices for people.[48]

One other salient fact should be remembered: in universities, the humanities, even when they enjoyed their greatest respect, were secondary to the professional subjects; the humanities were never as important, as theology, law, and medicine.[49] Today, also under circumstances in which the humanities and the study of languages and language use have standing and wide potential application, they remain secondary to science-, technology-, and business-based subject matters. How language works, what the connections may be among the world's several thousand languages, and how these languages may relate to how people behave and to how history has developed are all secondary questions.[50] Similarly, the use of language by the principal subject matters can be analyzed and

47. Rüegg, "Rise," 448.
48. Grafton and Jardine state that "by 1550 'humanism' as an identifiable movement had become 'the humanities' (and their teaching)" (*From Humanism*, 162).
49. Hilde de Ridder-Symoens states in her chapter "Management and Resources," "According to normal standards in Europe outside Italy, a complete university still consisted of four faculties: a lower one (arts) and three higher ones (theology, law, and medicine)" (*History*, ed. Ridder-Symoens, 2:156). Also, Notker Hammerstein states, "theology, which had formerly been the main faculty, paying the highest salaries to its professors, was demoted. The law faculty replaced it. From the mid-eighteenth century at the latest, the 'philosophical faculty'—as the 'arts men' preferred to be called from the seventeenth century onwards—accepted its role as 'handmaiden' to the new leading science, but not very happily. The philosophical faculty sought equal status and independence; it claimed even to be the truly central faculty" ("Epilogue: The Enlightenment," *History*, ed. Ridder-Symoens, 2:629). Walter Rüegg states that in the nineteenth century, at the Humboldtian University of Berlin, "the philosophical faculty advanced from being the maid to the mistress of the *Universitas litterarum*." Walter Rüegg, "Theology and the Arts," *A History of the University in Europe*, vol. 3: *Universities in the Nineteenth and Early Twentieth Centuries (1800–1945)*, ed. Walter Rüegg (Cambridge: Cambridge UP, 2004), 453. The account given by Rüegg suggests that the rank of subject matters is articulated through the underlying gender values of both the universities and its male historians. Compare Rüegg's usage and observation to the Press and Washburn coinage of the "kept" university (see chapter 8).
50. But they are not out of the picture. Such questions have been posed in the twentieth century by anthropologists who have gathered empirical data. Lévi-Strauss's effort

criticized, but such work carries little weight. Because language is assumed to be transparent, practitioners of those subjects see no need for critical inquiry into their various genres and uses. The Renaissance attitude toward the humanities—namely its fascination with and relevance to all human life—is found in some of the world's major universities. But the teaching and study of languages and the use of language in situations in which the social functions of language are paramount—from interpersonal relations to war-avoidance strategies—are not part of the language curriculum.[51]

The medieval approach to morality and its regulator, the Church, may have been underestimated by Rüegg. Morality, understood to apply exclusively to individuals, was then and remains today an underlying measure of education; morality is apart from education's vocational focus, yet is more fundamental. While language was and is thought by many to be a distinctive feature of the human species, it was not recognized as divisible into genres whose characteristics were associated with the social identity of different peoples, nations, or ethnic groups. Morality having always been Church defined and declared to be universal, language genres could not be associated with varying, or group-relative moral standards. Because morality was monolithic (either good or evil), there was no way to perceive, much less account for, the connection of different language uses and values with different moralities. Even if language had been humanized as a subject, with the vernacular and new literature emerging among students, it was still a subject meant to facilitate contact with God,[52] a

---

in this interest is discussed in chapter 4 in connection with Derrida's critique of it. Work by psychologist Alexander Luria is also discussed. Sociolinguistics has also raised such questions, and while the subject is in the curricula, its scope of influence is narrow.

51. This fact may be documented with what is taking place today under the influence of globalization. Tamar Lewin ["Global Classrooms: Universities Rush to Set up Outposts Abroad," (*New York Times,* 10 February 2008), and "Global Classrooms: In Oil-Rich Mideast, Shades of the Ivy League" (*New York Times,* 11 February 2008)] has reported that American and other western universities are establishing campuses in Abu Dhabi and Doha. The principal subjects, however, are business, medicine, and technology, with no humanities courses except practical English. Domestically, the awareness of new cultures and societies still has not resulted in any new support for the teaching of languages, for graduate programs in languages or the study of language. The secondary status of languages and the language-based humanities is quite the same as it has been for centuries. Those who protest this distribution of academic resources are called complainers.

52. Discussing Melanchthon's humanist influence on early Protestantism, "One must learn those alien languages from which the Latins created their works. The study of original texts reveals the brilliant surface and the intrinsic value of words and their true meaning, which leads to the essence of the matter; when 'we turn our attention to the sources, we can begin to understand Christ.'" Walter Rüegg, "Themes," *History,* ed. Ridder-Symoens, 2:35. Language was studied in the service of God, part of which was training Church leaders and their ability to use the language toward Church purposes. Also, according to Artz, the late-fifteenth-century Italian humanist Marsilio Ficino

subject that could be pursued through the vernacular as much as through Latin, with suitable adjustments. From a Protestant point of view, this was very much the case. Thus, even if language had risen in importance—even if humanism was taken seriously—both language and humanism had to be viewed through the perspectives of Christian individualist morality and the sacred status of Latin, which were the loci of this universal sense. Practically, this meant that individualism was an axiomatic social stance: the single person was understood to be a fundamental unit of the human species, that moral education meant teaching one person at a time, and that each soul ultimately had to face God. There were no groups that faced God together; individual conscience was then, and remains today, the only acknowledged regulator of moral values. If both humanities and the study of language(s) are tied to these assumptions about people and society, they are rigged to remain indefinitely at secondary, service, accessory levels of importance.

The secondary status of language has helped to maintain the stability of the university as an institution.[53] As Lorenzo Valla understood, the close study of language brings established usages into question, especially because the political role of these usages is highlighted. For example, scholars use etymologies to consider a different sense of common words, as Rashdall did with the word "universitas"; Madeleine R. Grumet observed that the term "*paidagogos*" once referred to a slave who brought children to school.[54] These are linguistic events that, because they are not followed up with scholarly attention or curricular exploration, do not produce consequences insofar as historically grounded changes in usage, sense, and meaning do not become integrated into the understanding of

---

coined the term "Platonic love" to refer to "a spiritual relationship between persons who share in the contemplation of God" (*Renaissance Humanism,* 44). The principle of individual morality permitted such resourcefulness in scholars who adapted the widespread interest in secular writings to the religious framework of society.

53. Today, there are departments of *foreign* languages. Instead of expanding in response to globalization, they have been reduced in size, and doctoral programs have been cut altogether. Because of corporate interests, English increasingly has become an official language of international scholarship, science, and even international air travel. Universities are barely able to persevere in expanding the study of world languages and their mutual interaction. Economic globalizers want to adopt "'the invisible theory of translation,' the assumption that languages are neutral media for separable 'content.'" Sandra Bermann and Michael Wood, eds., *Nation, Language, and the Ethics of Translation* (Princeton, NJ: Princeton UP, 2005), 1. This means that even if translation is sought, translators are encouraged to seek equivalence in different languages rather than note the mutual contributions of one to the other.

54. Madeleine R. Grumet, *Bitter Milk: Women and Teaching* (Amherst: U of Massachusetts P, 1988), 29. Grumet discusses the devaluation of teachers, and, especially, of female teachers. Such citations by both Grumet and Rashdall remain curiosities instead of being taken as facts urging changes in collective attitudes and behaviors.

language use. George Orwell's novels and essays give modern examples of how a fixed vocabulary is needed in order for a government, a regime, a tyrant, or a democratic head of state to secure the consent of the majority and to minimize the likelihood of popular opposition or uprisings.[55] Fixed references and stable sets of usages help to persuade people and establish in our minds that things are fixed and stable; expectations that they remain so take root and often become efforts to keep things as they are. A common belief in a fixed set of references makes it harder for authorities and easier for the majority to be held accountable for lying. Many believe that politicians, diplomats, generals, and bureaucrats lie routinely. Nevertheless, to a large extent, these lies don't count and are overlooked because people want to accept a stable story: a stable way of saying how things are in order to preserve how they are. The Lee Harvey Oswald story explaining the Kennedy assassination has remained in circulation as plausible in spite of the problems it poses for believers in even rudimentary truths. If language were studied on a scale matching the scale at which software was created, the hierarchical structure of society would feel it. The university has studied language just little enough to prevent the subject from having a salient and salutary impact on society. The academic study of language has not raised the questions about language that assume that each person's use of it, each group's use of it, each institution's use of it, is in principle equal in cogency to official use of language. The repeated search for a pure language standard,[56] a demand now in evidence in many parts of American society,[57] is a way to reduce the study of language by pretending that language can be fixed and ignored

55. In both *Animal Farm* and *1984*, the totalitarian government decrees language usages that cannot be challenged. These instances, and their counterparts in the real societies in Germany and the Soviet Union, and to some degree in all societies, demonstrate Morris's claim regarding the transparency of "total mediators." Some of this function is performed by the U.S. Constitution, although it escapes this criticism in part because amendments are possible. A phrase such as "the right to bear arms" is one such instance. George Orwell, *Animal Farm* (New York: Harcourt, Brace, 1946); *1984* (New York: New American Library, 1983).

56. Miriam Brody describes how in eighteenth-century Britain, George Campbell advocated for a standard, pure English: "Campbell's canon of correct language suppressed the political freedoms implicit in the heterogeneous utterances of a multitude of native dialects." Miriam Brody, *Manly Writing: Gender, Rhetoric, and the Rise of Composition* (Carbondale: Southern Illinois UP, 1993), 54–55. The justification was the same as it was for medieval Latin: one language can give access to all. But that is not how it worked for Latin or for the King's English; rather, the one language belonged to a privileged group of men, and the advocacy for the standardization of that language is felt by all to be the advocacy for the standardization of a class of people: be like us and you will belong.

57. Dennis Baron, *The English Only Question: An Official Language for Americans?* (New Haven, CT: Yale UP, 1990); see also Victor Villanueva, "Spic in English," *Bootstraps* (Urbana, IL: NCTE, 1994), 34–50.

rather than facing the fact that it grows and has to be continuously studied, revised, enriched, and shared.

In this history of the university, few thought language to be unimportant; usually, intimations of its greater importance were suppressed and repressed. The study of language as a series of social phenomena was contained, confined, and studied in certain ways. Fundamentally, as long as the majority of the population had limited access to language either in rhetoric or in literacy, language as a university subject posed few dangers:[58] members of the university (as an institution) would always cooperate and not take the study of language to levels that might disturb official uses of transparent language. Academics have had a strong interest in keeping the university stable. As Mark Lilla[59] has recently suggested, intellectuals have imagined themselves as sharing the power of their benefactors, and have often[60] taken the concept of the philosopher-king seriously enough to anticipate that role.[61]

---

58. This is one basis for reading the crime of Galileo as being his use of the vernacular in addition to his new cosmology. Russell Jacoby claims the vernacular was more of a trespass than the cosmology; Giorgio de Santillana emphasizes the cosmology as being more offensive. Russell Jacoby, *The Last Intellectuals: American Culture in the Age of Academe* (New York: Basic, 1987), 236. It is likely that both scholars are right, and that the combination of the revolutionary cosmology with his use of the vernacular made the threat he posed more acute: heresy would be spread that much more easily. De Santillana's original 1955 explanation is credible and unprovocative: Galileo wrote "in literary style upon philosophical subjects for the open ruling class, which included prelates, princes, gentlemen, and men of business; and this could not but threaten the caste privileges of the average literati." Georgio De Santillana, *The Crime of Galileo* (Chicago: U of Chicago P, 1976), 18. However, in order for Galileo to teach in the Church-sponsored university, he had actually to represent as true a view of the cosmos he knew to be false.

59. "Socrates suggests that such intellectuals play an important role in driving democracies toward tyranny by whipping the minds of the young into a frenzy, until some of them, perhaps the most brilliant and courageous, take the step from thought to action and try to realize their tyrannical ambitions in politics. Then, gratified to see their own ideas take effect, these intellectuals become the tyrant's servile flatterers, composing 'hymns to tyranny' once he is in power." Mark Lilla, *The Reckless Mind: Intellectuals in Politics* (New York: New York Review of Books, 2001), 211. This description applies to the adepts of the Free Spirit discussed by Norman Cohn, as well as, perhaps, to a variety of academics serving in recent American administrations. Public complaints about ideological rigidity are responses to what Lilla describes. A similar danger applies to "defense intellectuals," discussed in chapter 11.

60. In my *Utopia: The Psychology of a Cultural Fantasy* (Ann Arbor: UMI Research P, 1984), the same issue arises in connection with Plato, Thomas More, and other utopists—literary humanist writers who sympathize with the prospect of learned men ruling society. Freud intimated his acceptance of this ideal in his later writings by accepting the need for elite rule (see chapter 7, this volume).

61. As discussed in connection with Wilhelm von Humboldt, this chapter, section 6.

Humanist educators led by Erasmus and Vives began having their effect fifty years after Valla's death.[62] Their energies helped to move European universities from scholasticism to humanism—and then to so-called reason, to experimental science, and to technology in this century. Yet humanism was not urged on by a "search for truth,"[63] as we now routinely describe the purposes of research and scholarship. Rather its energy came from the surprise of discovering that the understanding of many languages and of many forms and dialects in any one language change people's social values and practices.[64] Humanism had purposes opposite to those of the Inquisition and the witch-hunters, both of which practices continued through the humanist period. Humanists wrote that learning could and should be brought before women as well as men, daughters as well as sons. Such learning would bring Utopia.[65] That, certainly, was a motivation, an ideal, a basis for advocating the study of language, literature, history, and society. Over a period of three centuries (about 1450 to 1750) humanists succeeded in introducing into universities a new interest in ancient languages, in the comparison of texts from different periods, and in vernacular translations of these texts.[66] Unquestionably, access to language and to its study was greatly facilitated by the ability to print a wide variety of texts quickly and cheaply.[67] The study of language during this

---

62. According to Artz, "Erasmus had Valla's work printed in 1505, and he always regarded himself as Valla's follower in his interpretations of the New Testament" (*Renaissance Humanism,* 28).

63. This ideal does not enter the picture until the sixteenth century, when—because of, for example, Copernicus—observation and experiment brought new understanding.

64. The truth sought in the study of language was unlike both the revealed truth and the empirical truth that developed more fully in the seventeenth century. The humanists sought a truth designated by the variety of opinions and styles in the list of valuable books available for study.

65. Yet it is equally true that Thomas More wrote the work of that title because nothing of what he described could or would happen no matter how much respect was given to humanist scholars. He was executed for exercising his independence of the king. These early modern advocacies for women's education do contribute to today's efforts toward a more generous pedagogical tradition.

66. Brockliss describes a shift of emphasis in the early sixteenth century from grammar only to grammar plus style and rhetoric as found in the classical texts of Cicero, Virgil, Livy, Horace, and Ovid. In this account, Tacitus was read more outside the university and taught by itinerant scholars as a stylist. Recall Valla's approach a century earlier: use actual texts as models of the language; this approach became orthodoxy in the sixteenth century and stayed that way for a long time. According to Brockliss, "What emerges from recent research is the uniformity of the taste . . . Pupils seldom had direct access to classical texts: authors were bowdlerized according to the confessional, political and moral principles of the institution" ("Curricula," 571–573).

67. At this time Church interests were distracted both by the growth of Protestantism and the impact of the discovery of the heliocentric solar system. Elizabeth L. Eisenstein writes "that the problem of access to publication outlets was a pivotal issue—one that has been unduly neglected and needs to be given more weight." She cites a letter by

period enjoyed the maximum respect in its history in the West. Neither before
nor after was so much academic energy spent on attention to language. How far
did the humanist attention to language proceed, what did it become, and what
might have inhibited it from following through on its intuition regarding the
fundamental status of language in the lives of individuals and of societies?

Buried in the widespread activity of reviewing and retranslating classical texts
was a renewed sense that scholars had become more deeply in touch with a superior language and a superior culture. Juan Luis Vives, seeing that speech "flows at
once from the rational soul as water from a fountain,"[68] and viewing the diversity
of languages as a punishment for arrogance as described in Genesis, takes Latin
to be the "most perfect of all" languages and imagines it to be "probable" that it
was the "original language in which Adam attached the names to things."[69] Vives
understands the wide diffusion of Latin as a sign of the universality and commonality of knowledge, a bulwark against confusion among peoples of various
cultures. He cites Paul to emphasize the sacred character of this diffusion: "For
faith, as Paul says, [Romans 10:17] is through what is heard, for which language
is the instrument"—a proof of divine involvement in the soul's exercise of its
rationality. The language is superior, in part, by virtue of its connection with
faith, one of the proofs of this superiority being its continued widespread use in
Europe as a common language a millennium after the Roman Empire. But Vives
also allows that this language serves as a necessary means of exclusion: "[I]t is
also useful that there should be some language sacred for the learned, to which
might be consigned those hidden things which are unsuitable to be handled by
everybody, and thus become polluted. Probably another language different from
the common language keeps these matters more separate."[70] Fears of pollution and
corruption creep into the discussion of the quality of Latin, signaling that here in
this scholarly, reflective context, the paranoid collective psychology of the Inquisition appears. While there are, of course, considerable benefits to learning through
two languages each having different roles and functions—a common written one
across cultures alongside specific local languages—these benefits are undermined
if the common written language is considered to be superior and sacred. The
arbitrary circumstance of the majority not having access to the common language

Kepler expressing anxiety that printers were being censored by the Church. Elizabeth
L. Eisenstein, *The Printing Press as an Agent of Change: Communications and Cultural
Transformations in Early-Modern Europe* (Cambridge: Cambridge UP, 1979), 636.

68. Foster Watson, ed. and trans., *Vives, On Education: A Translation of* De tradendis
disciplinis *of Juan Luis Vives* (Cambridge: Cambridge UP, 1913), 90. The work of Juan
Luis Vives was not translated into English until Foster Watson did it in 1913. Some now
credit Vives with having as much or greater influence on humanism as Erasmus.

69. Watson, *Vives,* 92. It may be worth asking this: What leads a scholar to such
guesses? Perhaps a *decision about the reference of the abstraction,* Latin, the best language.

70. Watson, *Vives,* 93.

is declared by the lucky and privileged to be a necessary condition. In this way, the arrangement of languages perpetuates many of the damaging social relations of the pre-humanist periods. At the beginning of the humanist period, the axioms of humanism that recognize the exceptional importance of language as a human trait also treat the multiplicity of languages as a punishment, deficit, or burden.

Neither several prominent humanists' advocacy of the education of women, nor, indeed, their assertion that women are the intellectual equals of men, resulted in a substantial change in the admission of women to schools and universities.[71] Vives maintained, moreover, that subjects like "grammar, logic, histories, the rule of governance of the commonwealth . . . they [women] shall leave it unto men. Eloquence is not convenient nor fit for women."[72] These subjects, concerned with the subtleties of language and the mores of public rule, create more access for women to public life, just as they do for men. But for this reason, to educate women did *not* mean for humanists to integrate them into the all-male social institutions, but to create, rather, a nominally equal but separate policy that some might or could accept, and which did not doubt the presumption of male superiority. Tacitly, "separate" meant "not part of the professional institutions." Those seeking the education of women did not reject the fundamental rule that women must obey their husbands. This social division furthered the practices of education that had no interest in creating social and intellectual access for women. The normative status of the hierarchical family structure in Vives and other apparently sympathetic humanist writers is ordinarily ignored in the academic presentation of humanism. Meanwhile, the writings of humanists show that they are implicated in the authoritarian mores of the scholasticism they are leaving behind in other senses: the presumption of male superiority connects them to the practices of the scholastic tradition.[73]

---

71. J. L. Vives, " The Learning of Women," *Vives and the Renascence Education of Women,* ed. Foster Watson (London: Edward Arnold, 1912), 195–210. Also in the volume is Thomas Elyot's "The Defence of Good Women" (211–239), which is a Platonic dialogue in honor of the recently deceased Queen Catharine of Aragon. To say that a queen is the equal of men, however, has other weights attached to it, and the gender issue may be presented somewhat disingenuously.

72. Vives, "Learning," 205–206.

73. The second chapter of Grafton and Jardine's *From Humanism,* "Women Humanists: Education for What?" discusses exchanges of letters between three accomplished female humanists and male counterparts. All of the exchanges demonstrate the sense in which the presumptions of male superiority are not surmounted, showing that the education of women is only for "decorative" purposes: no professional roles are to be taken up by educated women (*From Humanism,* 57). One exchange in 1491 between Cassandra Fedele and Angelo Politian is especially remarkable. Grafton and Jardine write this: "Politian's enthusiasm culminates in an outburst of personal desire actually to confront this paragon of female virtue—a passion which, remember, precedes his ever having set eyes on her. So vividly has he [Politian] conjured up the warrior-maiden from her literary

This connection must be borne in mind while considering how, relative to the scholastic tradition, the humanists' emphasis on language added up to a set of progressive values. The pursuit of these values through male-coded social gestures resulted in an agonistic strategy of advocacy and defense, and by the eighteenth century left the humanists no longer able to claim leadership roles in universities. The new force—the new "primal horde"[74]—natural philosophy and then science and technology, had, proceeding under the same code, won the day. Experimental science, which required more a system of notation and an established logic (mathematics) than a language, had restored the ideal of transparency for the use of language and continued a tradition of doctrinaire misogyny[75] in an altogether new enterprise that claimed a transcendental authority analogous to that claimed in the Church.

Part of Vives's progressive stance[76] is related to his respect for the vernacular; his love of his own native language, Castilian; his fluency in Flemish and French; and his understanding that the teaching of the superior language itself had to proceed through the vernacular. Woodward says Vives thought "the master ought to be competent in the vernacular of his pupils or he will fail to teach adequately the learned tongues by its means."[77] Vives was well oriented around the pedagogical process, and his respect for his native language led him toward such pupil-centered values in pedagogy. He overtook the languages given to him,

productions that her physical person, like her intact virginity, is vividly present to him in them: 'O how I should like to be transported where I might actually contemplate your most chaste visage, sweet virgin; if I might admire your appearance, your cultivation, your refinement, your bearing; if I might drink in your pronouncements, inspired into you by your Muses, as it were with thirsty ears; so that finally infused with your spirit and inspiration I might become most consummate Poet'" (50) Such instances, of which there are several in this chapter, enact how women's sexual identity simply can not be put aside regardless of their scholarly accomplishments. Moreover, the shameless exaggeration of Fidele's achievement in the tradition of games played toward seduction takes the correspondence fully out of the realm of scholarly issues. There is no thought in such circumstances produced by a balanced professional exchange. Remember Valla's observation that courage is more remarkable in women than in men: a similar explanation applies.

74. Freud's term, discussed in chapter 7, used here to mean "group or gang of authoritative men bringing revolution by replacing the leader."

75. Noble observes that during the humanist period, women had "only temporary entry" to mainstream European culture. David F. Noble, "The Scientific Restoration," *A World without Women: The Christian Clerical Culture of Western Science* (New York: Oxford, 1993), 205. See also Roy Porter, "The Scientific Revolution and Universities," *History,* ed. Ridder-Symoens, 2:531–564.

76. Vives was more progressive than Erasmus, according to William Harrison Woodward, *Studies in Education during the Age of the Renaissance, 1400–1600* (New York: Columbia UP, 1967), 197.

77. Woodward, *Studies,* 197.

and in the process of teaching, he made use of his immersion in these languages. Although he continued to view Latin as the language of authority, he promoted the value of knowing the native language just as well.

Because of the license taken by increasing numbers of scholars to study materials written in the vernacular, the humanist movement—even if most of its constituents were university trained—was external to universities but nevertheless influenced them. Their way in was similar to the entrance of practical scientists (chapter 8, sections 7–8): groups with outside support established their values and juxtaposed them to existing curricular orthodoxies in the universities. Woodward observes that the new values entailed using "classical antiquity as a factor making for progress."[78] However, the "universities, broadly regarded, could find no place for the new interests," and "they seemed incapable of reforming their methods of teaching, or adapting their organisation to changing conditions."[79] In several countries, royal secular influence was applied to dislodge scholastic attitudes toward language study.

Although one of the reasons for the universities' stubbornness is connected to their sense of dominion over doctrine and curriculum, they resisted the expansion of curriculum. The habits of agonism and disputation suggest that change implies replacement—a zero-sum game: if the new is coming, then the old must have been wrong. However, the expansion of curriculum was threatening as much because change tended toward broadened access and new populations, especially those in the mercantile middle class and the aristocratic diplomatic sectors.[80] Broadened access showed the limits of the zero-sum assumption. Knowledge of different, modern, and literary languages meant a series of new genres that simply did not fit traditional pedagogical styles and purposes. It

---

78. Woodward, *Studies*, 229.

79. Woodward, *Studies*, 229.

80. Marie Rosa Di Simone describes the student populations of sixteenth-century universities as coming from all classes. An upsurge in aristocratic students was due to the increase in secular power as a result of the Reformation. Also, grammar schools proliferated and the need for teachers led middle-class and poor students to enroll in universities. Such changes in social needs were steady, yet changes in university curricula took place over centuries rather than over generations. Di Simone describes the development from the sixteenth to eighteenth century: "From being corporate and independent bodies, the universities were transformed into public institutions serving to create a ruling class." Marie Rosa Di Simone, "Students," *History*, ed. Ridder-Symoens, 2:285–325, quotation on 324. Thus, even as universities became more public, authority over the university was shifting from Church to secular aristocracies. In the chapter following Di Simone's, Rainer A. Müller describes the "laicizing trend in the universities," in which the law faculty began to supplant the theology faculty as the most influential group. Rainer A. Müller, "Student Education, Student Life," *History*, ed. Ridder-Symoens, 2:327. Again, the universities did not add new faculties—there was just a shift of influence within the universities.

meant a greater airing of so-called pagan stories and actions, no longer under the strict supervision of doctrinaire authorities. It was not enough that universities would continue to train students in theology and feature this training even into the twenty-first century. But if other subjects and other kinds of students were also in the university, the institution itself was different—secular in several ways—and the governance, more than the training of leaders, would change. Finally, the fact that the foundations of these other subjects, and the interests of the new populations, were languages and literatures that were hitherto not a part of traditional university training, was indeed a provocation to the language and doctrine orthodoxies of the university curricula.

The provocative role of humanism may be traced backward in different ways, but Valla's approach to language scholarship affected the specific language practices advocated by humanists. Woodward observes that "the medievalist had treated grammar as an end in itself: to Erasmus, emphatically, it was but an instrument: to the School-men it was indistinguishable from the laws of thought of which it was an expression; to Valla, and all humanists after him, it was but a summary of classical usage."[81] In this small formulation there is an issue about language that has made its way, in a variety of schools of thought, into contemporary (twentieth- and twenty-first-century) discussions: Just how does one understand the orderliness of language that shows up in grammar? How grammar is studied in relation to other features of language reflects underlying approaches to language. To the scholastics, grammar and logic were locked together; the structural appearance of grammar demonstrated the relation of language and thought. Scholastic curricula were dominated by studies in logic, an item taken from Aristotle that had minimal danger of being considered pagan. Yet thought was understood as being *different* from language, grammar, or even logic. Thought was something real and internal, connected to the eternal through the soul, and ushered and carried out into public contexts by language.

Valla's attention to language and the resulting problems of authority evinced by this attention implied that thought did not matter as much as language itself. Language could be recognized as authentic in historical senses: *this* language belonged to *this* society; when the society changed, the language changed. With Valla, usage became the important factor in the study of all languages—classical, vernacular, and current versions of each. Valla combined his interest in usage with his knowledge of rhetoric. In addition, Valla mastered Greek before it was a university subject; it became so at the beginning of the sixteenth century, when the Reformation movement back to the text made it important to know the language of the first stories of Christ. Valla's challenging roles and actions were real threats because of his erudition in both Latin and Greek.

---

81. Woodward, *Studies*, 120.

Specifically, he knew how the usages in these languages could be shown to have been historically authentic. His knowledge of the languages threatened to change established authoritative uses of these languages. As the humanist movement progressed, it did just that, and so contributed to the most important schism of all, the Reformation.

Perhaps a key event in the documentation of Valla's influence[82] was Erasmus's own edition of *Valla's Annotations on the New Testament* (1505).[83] Erasmus re-affirmed Valla's principle that "sound learning," sooner than "divine inspiration," would best serve to provide authoritative readings of the sacred texts. Joan Simon describes how Erasmus and other humanist educators used this commitment to learning to expand the responsibility to study to all people—to "ordinary men and women,"[84] and not just to theologians. To live "wisely and well" you had to study the works of classical Athens, know your native language, and learn practical skills and crafts. Erasmus and other humanists wanted the language of prayer to be understood by all, and as much attention to be given to educating the young in comprehension of the language as in the singing of hymns.

The British universities resisted these ideals for a long time. They continued to teach grammar and logic and to eschew classical literature.[85] But when Corpus Christi College was founded at Oxford in 1517, there was an explicitly humanist curriculum, including the Latin and Greek poets, dramatists, historians, with the lectures on grammar connected with the study of these authors. Among those recommended for study in this regard was Lorenzo Valla.[86] In further recommending the study of the Church fathers rather than the scholastics of the previous three centuries, the curriculum emphasized reading the two testaments themselves. Valla's interest in the study of language use led to humanist principles that stressed the close connection between texts and language rather than between language and thought. As the humanistic styles and program grew and spread, this emphasis established itself in the university. The importance of learning texts and usage over thought was a value that has lasted into today's universities. But texts and usage have not entered prominently into today's study of language. Compared to scholastic education this was increasingly secular in substance and in sponsorship, as royalty now started to oversee the universities

---

82. On individual scholars rather than on the university curriculum, or on the standards for studying language.

83. Joan Simon, *Education and Society in Tudor England* (Cambridge and New York: Cambridge UP, 1966), 70.

84. Simon, *Education,* 71.

85. Simon makes a point of noting that the Corpus Christi curriculum was the exception. The reaction against the new curriculum "was violent enough to suggest that . . . study of classical poets was a startling innovation" (*Education,* 84).

86. Simon, *Education,* 83.

in more active ways. However, the subjective sites of mental activity (thought, mind, and soul) as things to be represented and accounted for in the study of language have remained a fundamental issue; those who doubted the importance of these sites, such as Valla and language materialists, have remained ancillary in the study of language.

Because of the religious belief in the reality of the spirit of human beings, the recognition of language's importance would not go even as far as Valla's perspective and was limited to what the category "thought" would allow. First, thought (rather than language usages) was what classical texts contained, so only they were studied; second, the ancient languages were still considered superior, and Latin in particular was the sacred language—the main path toward spiritual, divinely sanctioned truths; third, rhetoric, virtually eliminated from the curriculum during the first two centuries of the universities' founding,[87] never acceded again to a position of influence, and remained throughout university history in a propaedeutic role. Fourth, modern vernacular languages, while increasingly used, did not ask for the same highly motivated inquiry that Latin, Greek, and, occasionally, Hebrew demanded—owing to their role in establishing the structures of belief, history, and destiny. Even the study by secular students of classical languages in the university took on the role of character cultivation and status creation. One learned these subjects to *seem* educated, cultivated, polished, or worldly in preparation for political service in international affairs.[88] This took only a few years, in contrast with the professionals who took much longer preparing for church, law, or medicine. The majority of those attending the university went for a relatively short period.[89]

---

87. Paetow, *Arts Course*. This study suggests that, actually, the prosperity of twelfth- and thirteenth-century Italy led to the need for the cultivation of the *ars dictaminis,* which taught university students to write different sorts of documents. Rhetoric as an art of public speaking was not needed. In other universities, especially those in France, grammar became an ever-narrower subject. Rhetoric taught people how to speak when one did not expect an answer. The universities needed to teach disputation, which relied more on how to manipulate logic than on how to reach and persuade others.

88. Walter Rüegg describes how Ciceronian standards of eloquence have always been part of the university. However, the purpose of learning eloquence was to refine and stylize the graduates' uses of language so as to create a presentational image for aristocratic figures. Learning eloquence to be a so-called finished person contrasts significantly with Valla's regular search through different texts for the practical uses of language. Walter Rüegg, "Themes," *History,* ed. Ridder-Symoens, 2:28.

89. Rainer Christof Schwinges, "Student Education, Student Life," *History,* ed. Ridder-Symoens, 1:195–243. In the medieval university the majority of students studied "the arts" (the trivium and quadrivium) and attended for less than two years; most did not earn degrees. This course of study was roughly comparable to a secondary education today (197). According to Willem Frijhoff, the situation was similar from the sixteenth to the eighteenth centuries, although the percentages of matriculants (perhaps a third to half)

Perhaps the matter can be put this way: the three-century humanistic period sought to establish accurate knowledge of the languages and texts of antiquity. Teachers sought to reform the long path of education in a major way that emphasized developing familiarity with two or more languages. But the quest was for knowing the language from a practical standpoint: language as access to texts and as cultivators of the mind and soul. This attitude is not philological, although it introduced questions of comparative grammar and etymology that later philologists pursued. The focus on language was an attempt, perhaps, to win back the experiences of living from the dominion of the Church, to recreate for an increasing fraction of the population the collective experience that comes through literature and consciousness of the language in use. As much as it has been promoted by universities after the humanistic period—in the study of vernacular literatures in universities beginning in the nineteenth century—this goal has remained secondary, and thus supported only in limited ways as items in the curriculum. In this sense, the universities were successful in turning back the challenges of Valla and others who understood the degree to which knowledge of language is perhaps the most influential available to all people.

IV. Language and Knowledge

Mordechai Feingold writes that "the inseparability of language and thought as expounded by Erasmus was a dominant feature of renaissance culture, one that was challenged—though not yet rejected—only in the latter part of the seventeenth century."[90] Feingold's opinion immediately follows his citation from Erasmus's *Aim and Method of Education,* but the latter's formulation does not describe just the "inseparability," but rather, the proximity of language and thought; thought is given priority: "all knowledge falls into one of two divisions: the knowledge of 'truths' and the knowledge of 'words,' and if the former is *first in importance* [my emphasis] the latter is required first in order of time." In the words of one of the most widely recognized humanists, the knowledge of truth is more important than the knowledge of words; or perhaps, the truth of knowledge is more important than the words of knowledge, where truth is understood to refer to the established correspondence of words to people's experience. Both of the latter two formulations place the priority of truth over language, rather than declaring that each matters fundamentally to the other because they are not separable. That the humanists' searches for truth involved knowledge of language more than previous searches is not enough to confirm

---

in law and medicine who got degrees was much higher than the percentages pursuing arts degrees. Willem Frijhoff, "Patterns," *History,* ed. Ridder-Symoens, 2:43–110.

90. Mordechai Feingold, "The Humanities," *The History of the University of Oxford,* ed. Nicholas Tyacke (Oxford: Clarendon P, 1997), 4:242.

Feingold's somewhat misleading formulation. It was fundamental for intellectual life inside and outside the academy that words mattered less than truth. Although many may have been tempted to identify language and truth, few would doubt that words *served* truth; none would say that words and truth served one another as relatively equivalent factors. The priority of truth was inherited from the scholastics,[91] whose formulations of theological truth, presented in the sacred language, rendered the language invisible, or spiritually eternal. In this sense, the humanists upgraded the status of language to something that, because it was in some degree material and available in different genres (different languages and dialects), materially affected how to recognize the truth. But the language itself was still secondary, still a tool to disclose an abstract immaterial entity connected through divine means to the human spirit—the truth.

After Erasmus and the humanists' successes in different universities, the value of truth led away from language in a new way: through mathematics and empirical science. It has been noted that the scientific achievements of the seventeenth century, for many, served the traditional religious cosmology: the order and lawfulness of the universe was evidence and, for some, proof of God's dominion.[92] The scientists themselves affirmed their religious loyalties over and above the variations of their religious visions. The empirical study of the natural world, whose forms and behaviors could be expressed mathematically, represented a new form of learning: investigating and observing natural phenomena, recording the quantitative as well as qualitative findings, comparing them to others' findings, and generalizing the results into "laws" of nature. Copernicus, Bacon, Galileo, Kepler, and Newton—helped by philosophers such as Descartes, Locke, and Leibniz—created the foundation and rationale for modern science. The inclusion of quantitative data in an investigation of nature with qualitative judgments shifted the locus of authority from exclusively verbal formulations to formulations that were authorized by measurements that could be performed, in principle, by anyone. This new procedure for reaching understanding took attention away from language; more than ever before, it seemed that when the language was in the hands of clerics, words were subordinate to the truth, which could now be given mathematically, thus adding the sense of logical certainty to empirical observations. The reliance on mathematical formulations implied that logic and truth were, after all, equivalent—a principle contradicted by Valla. Logic seemed to be required

---

91. And ultimately, perhaps, from Plato. Following Plato, truth was not something that became established in social, political, or other collective ways. It was eternally there, waiting to be found.

92. Perhaps it is also germane to say that empirical inquiries were oriented toward finding more rather than less authority for the biblical views of the cosmos as having been created by God.

to certify natural truth; this requirement closely resembles the rule of logic in the practices of scholastic theology. Figures such as Bacon and Locke did not conceal their distrust of words and language, and each thought knowledge to be much deeper than the language that articulated it. Regardless of how many claimed that logic added no new knowledge (especially if its role as an approximation of reality were acknowledged), the combination of measurement, mathematics, and observation—and their apparent harmony with one another—could not be gainsaid. It became the basis of the Royal Society and of several other scientific associations in Europe in the seventeenth century. The value of words took a significant loss.[93] Truth, long felt to be accessible only through words, as Erasmus had written, could now be understood as being located in something more reliable: observations and mathematical calculation. Almost two centuries after Erasmus and almost a century after Shakespeare, but contemporaneously with Newton, John Locke said as much when he commented on those not careful about how they use the language in the study of natural philosophy:

> I can easily forgive those who have not been at the pains to read the third book of my essay [*An Essay Concerning Human Understanding* (1689)], if they make use of expressions that, when examined, signify nothing at all, in defence of hypotheses, that have long possessed their minds . . . I find none so fit, nor so fair judges, as those whose minds the study of mathematics has opened, and dis-entangled from the cheat of words, which has too great an influence in all the other, which go for sciences: and I think (were it not for the doubtful and fallacious use that is made of those signs) might be made much more sciences than they are.[94]

In noting the fitness of those who studied mathematics as having escaped the "cheat of words," Locke articulates succinctly that by the end of the seventeenth century, scientific knowledge is held in the highest esteem, whereas language, having been shown by mathematical knowledge to be slippery and uncertain, needs the detailed attention he gives it in the third book of his *Essay*. Locke

---

93. In *Hamlet*, a play roughly contemporaneous with Bacon's writings, one sign of Hamlet's self-disgust is his self-observation, "like a whore, [I] unpack my heart with words" (2.2.587). It is not clear why this line is powerful in a context—the public performance of a play—that actually values words maximally, unless one already has in mind the Renaissance suspicion of words as "mere words," in contrast to the "action" that Hamlet is told to take by the ghost. A whore's action is insincere, using only words, and not actions, to unpack his or her heart—and falsely at that.

94. John Locke, *Works*, 8:300–301. Quoted in Hans Aarsleff, *From Locke to Saussure: Essays on the Study of Language and Intellectual History* (Minneapolis: U Minnesota P, 1982), 70.

aims to discipline language, to outline its uses toward the responsible practice of natural philosophy and science.[95]

The last chapters of book 3 present Locke's sense of the "imperfection" of words, their "abuse" and the means of counteracting these problems. Although the results are worth studying, the basis of this discussion is the assumption that the problems caused by multiple uses of the same words (or the same conventions in language), the multiple contexts of use, and the differences between public and private reference—among other things—are features that can be brought under control through a rational discussion such as his, and that the uses of language can be held to a standard of plain talk. But while Locke writes as if the "cheat of words" can be minimized, he also writes as if it cannot be eliminated, that the use of language is inherently susceptible to abuse, and that this is a feature of language and the basis of his distrust of it.[96] Like the medieval scholastics who held Aristotelian logic in the highest esteem, Locke is not expecting simple improvement: rather, he sees perfection in mathematics.

V. Condillac's Search for Origins

Locke's discussion of language is cited by Hans Aarsleff[97] as one of the earliest sources for a theme in language study dating from the seventeenth century (including the advocacy of universal grammar) running through Condillac, Humboldt, and Saussure. This tradition,[98] as well as Chomsky's variation of it, helps to demonstrate how language as transparent reference continued to be the fundamental axiom and ideal in this three-century period.[99] In spite of the differences between those searching for an essence of language in its historical

---

95. This is what Wittgenstein tried to do in the *Tractatus,* and then changed his mind and rejected this ideal.

96. Vivien Law describes how Locke's essay was translated in the eighteenth century and "spread swiftly across Europe, instilling doubt in the hitherto unchallenged universality of the signified by the words we use. That doubt opened the way to the linguistic relativity which plays so large a part in our experience of language today, particularly in cross-cultural encounters." Law, *The History of Linguistics in Europe from Plato to 1600* (Cambridge: Cambridge UP, 2003), 265. But before that view was taken up (chapter 3, section 6, this volume), the French Enlightenment had to consider, still in the tradition of the search for universals, the origin of language.

97. Aarsleff, *From Locke,* 24–31.

98. Hans Aarsleff's and Roger Brown's accounts, respectively, give complementary views of this tradition without serious dispute; they trace it from the high middle ages, through the Port-Royalists, Humboldt, and several others. See Aarsleff, *From Locke;* Roger Brown, *Wilhelm von Humboldt's Conception of Linguistic Relativity* (The Hague: Mouton, 1967).

99. Chomsky's theory, discussed later in this chapter (section 7), holds that the real-life use of language does not require explanation, but the ability to learn transformational

origin and those searching for it in universal grammars, each group assumes that there *is* a discoverable essence to language and differ from one another only in where they look for it.[100] This essence is considered either remote in time or deep in our minds, souls, or inner being—or both. But that there is such a discoverable essence is not doubted. The belief in an abstract, universal essence of language that produces extralinguistic thought is friendly to the protected status of universities as well as to their protectors.[101] If thought is believed to be an impalpable abstract essence, it would follow that the words themselves—the language-in-use—are interchangeable with other words and other languages: it is "the thought that counts."[102] If, on the other hand, the ideology no longer stipulates that the same thought can be carried by different words, and if citizens have access to the (oral and written) language, the usages of faculty members and governments become active political and social gestures rather than inert vessels for ineffable laws, edicts, rights of governments.[103]

The belief in an essence of language is a version of Plato's belief in the permanence of ideals that are then identified differently from one another by particular languages using different sounds and words. It is also a version of Latinists' beliefs in the ability of the sacred language to yield the closest approach to divine, transcendental truth. It is further related to the sense that because

---

rules is the innate source of our knowledge of language. The "deep structure" of language comprises simple referential statements, but his theory has since moved beyond the specification of transformational rules and toward the justification of innateness. Language-learning ability is to be sought in the brain, assuming that an abstract representation of the grammatical rules is possible in principle. To date such representations have not appeared, nor has any discrete bodily locus of language been identified. Further discussion of this issue can be found in notes 155–162 to this chapter.

100. Aarsleff's critique of Chomsky's account of the history of linguistics suggests that beliefs in universal grammar were consistent with the desire to stipulate an origin of language and that their formulations overlapped: Chomsky misrepresents that history, Aarsleff implies, to put into relief a single theme consistent with the universal-grammar or deep-structure view of language. The distinction between Chomsky and Aarsleff is that Chomsky approaches the subject of language as if it were an objective science, and searches for a logic that will confirm this view, whereas Aarsleff treats the study of language as a humanist project, with no stipulation as to what will count as an explanation of language, or even that it is needed.

101. Chapter 8 considers the history of the university as a protected institution.

102. This is a phrase many use. But isn't it the case that when this phrase it applied, it refers to the *gesture* that is being made? So if we hear "Get well soon," we can complain that it is trite, but we are quietly pleased that someone took the trouble to say it. Read in this way, the phrase suggests that the use of the word "thought" derives from the ideology of the primacy of one's immaterial inner being. In everyday life we do credit such conventional usages as gestures, but the academic study of language still assumes an inner mental authority over the words that emerge.

103. This issue is taken up in more detail in chapter 4.

only humans have language, this linguistic capability must emanate from a divinely given soul, from a mind that is constituted differently—spiritually, incorporeally—in humans than in any other species. The belief in an essence of language is part of the historically recursive attempt to identify the uniqueness of language-using people with a living essence, that, thus far, has been understood as being immaterial. In the eighteenth century, the origin of language was stipulated as its essence.[104] "Origin as essence" as an explanatory strategy, in spite of—or perhaps because of—its religious tone, has appeared repeatedly in Western writings and continues to be used today.[105] Because of this belief, Darwin's description of the origin of species was also taken to be the essence of species (for example, "because we are descended from simians, we are *essentially* simians"), a view that amounted to fighting words in some religious orthodoxies. Similarly, Freud's theory of infantile sexuality, his technique of interpreting dreams, and his speculations about the origins of civilization stipulate past origins as explanations of present-day phenomena. Today, the search for the origin of the universe is considered a reasonable, plausible, and viable approach to explaining the universe as we now see it.[106]

Aarsleff's several treatments of the history of the study of language (from before 1600 to after 1900) identify Condillac's theory of the origin of language as the extended speculative formulation most relevant to the ways language is approached and conceived now. Aarsleff traces Condillac's influence in the works of several of his near contemporaries, and suggests that Humboldt's establish-

---

104. A starting point for informing oneself about eighteenth-century originology of language might be *Two Essays On the Origin of Language: Jean-Jacques Rousseau and Johann Gottfried Herder,* trans. John H. Moran and Alexander Code (Chicago: U of Chicago P, 1986). However, efforts to infer the origin of language are found in classical culture, as studied by Deborah Levine Gera, in *Ancient Greek Ideas on Speech, Language, and Civilization* (New York: Oxford UP, 2003). If anything, the classical guesses about language origins do indeed show that there is nothing new under the sun. According to Gera, several texts stipulate that gestures and behavioral tropes, possibly associated with danger or food or fire, were repeated and gradually came to be recognized collectively. This recognition rendered the gestures signs or symbols (159–161). A salient point in the present context would be the premise that the use of language was necessarily collective, based in social experience.

105. Aarsleff, *From Locke,* 24. Yet in Locke there is a clue as to the path away from this belief: he observes that the word for soul "originated" in "sense data": the Hebrew *nishama* for "breath of life" is also understood as "soul." The term "soul" as an English translation of the Hebrew is a figuration, used as an idealization, of a body-bound term. Although the origin of the word "soul" does not affect how the word is understood in individual cases, it is important to notice the historical marker of the materiality of the soul. If a nominalist uses the phrase *flatus vocis* to characterize abstractions such as the soul, religious language realists might hear heresy even if the nominalist were using the Hebrew etymology.

106. The big bang theory is discussed in greater detail in chapter 10.

ment of philology as a formal discipline owes a great deal to Condillac's account of the origin of language. This account, a product of Enlightenment liberalism, consists in his trying to explain the use of language in all of its contexts, including aesthetic and affective contexts. Aarsleff also considers Condillac to emphasize the social character of language, a value that has remained in modern and contemporary investigations of language use. To Aarsleff, Condillac provided a plausible narrative that *could* explain its origin. Although this is a reasonable stance to take by both Condillac and Aarsleff, it is not clear that a search for an origin of language contributes to an understanding of its uses and its various appearances in our lives, or that the search for an essence of language is of any use at all. In fact, Aarsleff's most recent introduction to Condillac[107] relates his work to that of Wittgenstein, who rejected a search for either the origin or the essence of language. Aarsleff implies that Condillac's theory may well be a forerunner of Wittgenstein's, even though he seems certain that Wittgenstein did not read Condillac.[108]

Condillac's account of the origin of language is given for the same reason as that given by Locke for his discussion of language: to establish how knowledge reaches its authoritative state by way of its emergence through language.[109] This is an often-asked modern question, found as much in Chomsky's *Language and Mind* as in Hobbes and Descartes. Students of the acquisition of knowledge have always had the intuition that language was essential to knowledge, but none doubted that knowledge was a thing in itself, language a thing in itself, and the challenge for philosophy was to identify how they were related. Although language was treated as the key to knowledge, it was assumed by all that knowledge, and not language, was the real, important riddle. Language was merely the complex mechanical vessel that conveyed knowledge.

As Roger Brown discusses in his introduction to Humboldt,[110] the riddle goes something like this: People existed before language, and they must have known enough to invent language; yet how could they have known anything without

---

107. Hans Aarsleff, "Introduction," Etienne Bonnot de Condillac, *Essay on the Origin of Human Knowledge*, trans. and ed. Hans Aarsleff (Cambridge: Cambridge UP, 2001), xi–xxxviii.

108. Aarsleff writes, "There is no likelihood that Wittgenstein had looked at Condillac" ("Introduction," Condillac, *Essay*, xxxvii). Condillac's name does not appear in Ray Monk's biography of Wittgenstein. But who can be certain about what he read?

109. Aarsleff, "Introduction," Condillac, *Essay*, xviii.

110. Brown cites Rousseau's version: "[M]an is only man through language; to invent language, he would have to be man already" (*Wilhelm von Humboldt's*, 38). Condillac wrote, "It seems that one would not know how to make use of instituted signs if one was not already capable of sufficient reflection to choose them and attach ideas to them: how then, so goes the objection, is it that the exercise of reflection can only be acquired by the use of signs?" (Aarsleff, "Introduction," Condillac, *Essay*, 42).

language? Thus, language must have preceded knowledge. But if so, how did this invention take place and develop into knowledge that now seems universal and "the same" for speakers of different languages?[111] Condillac's speculation on the origin of language addresses this formulation, trying to provide an account of how language could have developed. However, the key to his effort, as to other prior efforts, is the reliance on a false reading of the account of creation given in Genesis, regardless of its possible figurative status. No mention is made in Genesis of the first people getting, being given, or otherwise *acquiring* language at all, or of language being a separate part of creation. Because of this erroneous reading, the account projected onto Genesis is a fantasy of the existence of people without language in some state of innocence, goodness, and peacefulness—a kind of "ignorance is bliss" state. The philosopher or theorist tries to imagine how humans moved from the presumed innocent and primitive state, to the state we are in now—fallen, yet in possession of a knowledge superior to that of those who lived in the prelapsarian state.[112] Calling the story "the Fall" to begin with is a Christian reading. The story must be read as one of disobedience of God, but not necessarily of sin, original or imitated, and thus of characters not necessarily in need of any redemption. According to Genesis, the soul is breath of life (*nishama*) or a bodily object (*nefesh*) and not language.[113]

Aarsleff has repeatedly reviewed Condillac's account of the origin of language, emerging each time over a period of three decades with a stronger sense of its value to the contemporary study of language. Except for certain key factors,[114] Aarsleff's view contributes to the search for sources of the twentieth century's movement toward a view of language that is not derived from a formal theory such as Chomsky's or Searle's,[115] and that recognizes the impossibility of its study

---

111. That it should appear in riddle form at all is a sign that the issue is not usefully conceived.

112. One can think of this investigative strategy this way: we are going to imagine as fully and carefully as we can how language originated in the human species. Our one constraint is that it has to be consistent with an erroneous reading of the account of creation in Genesis.

113. "We now know that the *nefesh* is connected to 'physical body,' to 'blood,' and to 'breath.' *Nefesh,* in short, is about the tangible aspects of life we can touch or feel. One can hold flesh, touch blood, and feel breath.

"This is why 'soul' is a particularly poor translation of *nefesh*. In English, 'soul' almost always emphasizes the untouchable, ethereal, amorphous aspects of life. The physical *nefesh* is just the opposite." Joel M. Hoffman, "Lost in Mistranslation." *Reform Judaism Online* Fall 2010.

114. These factors will be treated shortly, and again in chapter 5: they involve the lack of perception of the involvement of women and children in the ontogenetic and phylogenetic development of language.

115. See, for example, John Searle, *Speech Acts: An Essay in the Philosophy of Language* (Cambridge: Cambridge UP, 1969). Searle's theory is less of a formal theory and more of

as a subject separate from its contexts of functioning. Aarsleff puts Condillac's theory in the context of the humanistic study of language, and he used Valla's intuition that the study of language must, sooner or later, involve other subject matters that themselves depend on the appropriation and reapplication of the received language (or translating received language to new contexts).

Roger Brown cites three other figures in the early eighteenth century who were, like Condillac, willing to contemplate the role of emotional and aesthetic life in the collective acquisition of language—Giambattista Vico, Thomas Blackwell,[116] and Johann Georg Hamann; Condillac's presentation is the most elaborate.[117] Condillac stipulated that in the early stages of the development of the human species—the Adam and Eve stage—so-called linguistic interaction between people took place through movements, gestures, cries of pleasure and pain, and other voluntary and involuntary vocalizations. Gradually, the habituation of such sounds and gestures regularized and ritualized the vocal sounds (due to their convenience), and related them to the feelings and gestures that accompanied them. This view could be consistent with Vico's emphasis on poetry, song, and dance as pre-linguistic practices.[118] Though there is no reason to single out this affective or aesthetic account as the most compelling, its virtue is that it considers language as part of the total semiotic repertoire of people, or as Langer[119] and Cassirer[120] put it, the total collection of each culture's "symbolic forms." This part of Condillac's account makes it possible to conceive of language as a broad spectrum of activities, each of which (that is, the arts and the sciences) bears some kinship or "family resemblance"[121] to verbal language, and all of which taken together are found as features of all human cultures, all civilizations.

But Condillac, like Locke, was focused on knowledge; he allowed, but tended not to emphasize, this broad spectrum described by Langer, Cassirer, and others in the twentieth century. Because of this preference, he wanted to find a way to account for the apparent separability of ideas from everything else, a view usually

---

a philosophical attitude than Chomsky's, which searches for a formalism that will articulate a universal linguistic "deep structure." Like Chomsky's, this theory has lost its early momentum. J. L. Austin is the originator of speech act theory, and his formulations, which have received contemporary attention, are considered in chapter 4.

116. Brown, *Wilhelm von Humboldt's*, 27–32.

117. Chapter 4 discusses Johann Georg Hamann in connection with this issue.

118. And it is consistent with Kristeva's semiotic considerations discussed in chapter 3. It is also consistent with—but not the same as—the accounts of infantile language acquisition given in chapter 5.

119. Susanne K. Langer gives a full comprehensible account in *Philosophy in a New Key* (New York: New American Library, 1941).

120. Ernst Cassirer, *The Philosophy of Symbolic Forms,* (1923) trans. Ralph Manheim, preface and intro. Charles W. Hendel (New Haven, CT: Yale UP, 1953).

121. Wittgenstein's phrase, elaborated in a wider context in chapter 3, section 3.

attributed to Plato. Through the story of the development of language, Condillac wanted to account for the ways the announcement of knowledge seems to go beyond the particular language to represent a certain orientation toward experience that people who speak any language would have. The explanation of knowledge sought by Locke and Condillac was to be *like* quantitative knowledge in its mobility beyond local circumstances: *philosophical* knowledge that was not bound to one language. This preference also helped establish philosophy as a new academic subject, something that grew out of natural philosophy and which then became science.

Aarsleff says Condillac's main point is that the "connection of ideas" is the explanatory principle of human understanding.[122] This principle, consistent with a materialist sense of language, is a part of materiality as discussed in the present context. The principle holds that although verbal usage was first dependent on present-at-the-time sense or affective experience for it to acquire meaning, gradually the repetition of linguistic usage evoked earlier experiences in new contexts and thus became independently usable—abstract, or removable from specific contexts.[123] The vocalizations were abstracted—that is, *removed*—from their earlier context of use, found to be useful in a new context, and then—by mutual experience—referred to something common among two or more people. At that point, different language uses—different abstractions—were connected— presented as dependent on one another—in ways analogous to, similar to, the ways the language was once dependent on experience.[124] Thus, understanding was the creation, in language, of relationships perceived in experience or relationships as experienced. The process of forming linguistically interdependent relationships created the impression that knowledge was separable from experience and formulatable in propositional form—a sentence with mutually dependent subject and predicate—applicable to new situations and, if users agree on it, rendered into knowledge beyond its contexts of use. This much is suggested by Condillac and served as an explanation of the use of language as it was then

---

122. Aarsleff, "Introduction," Condillac, *Essay,* xi.

123. Throughout his 1746 treatise, Condillac shows different ways in which thinking and imagination take two or more "ideas" previously known, and put them together to make a new idea. This could also describe how sentences work, or how groups of sentences go together, and so on. It is a description of how things are known as well as how language developed phylogenetically. Etienne Bonnot de Condillac, *Essay on the Origin of Human Knowledge,* trans. and ed. Hans Aarsleff (Cambridge: Cambridge UP, 2001).

124. I outline a similar path for Helen Keller's ultimate acquisition of language, after her development was interrupted for about five years when she was eighteen months old. David Bleich, "New Considerations of the Infantile Acquisition of Language and Symbolic Thought," *The Psychoanalytic Review* 63.1 (Spring 1976): 49–71. This history is elaborated and further considered in chapter 5; see chapter 4 for continuing discussion of this *model.*

understood. From our standpoint, however, the independence of the new linguistic formulations from the earlier experience was taken, erroneously, to mean that the new contexts of use did not equally enclose, interact with, or identify with the supposedly independent linguistic formulations. Once an abstraction was agreed upon in one context, its provisionality—and its materiality, its context specificity—was forgotten, as it was assumed to have a meaning. The interest in establishing independent, so-called objective knowledge was the temptation or incentive that led to the treatment of language as transparent: perceiving meaning behind the transparent word. People may well have intuited that knowledge was more easily seen as non-contingent if the language were transparent. But, as people may have wondered, could real knowledge be merely contingent in a rational, Godly universe? In any event, the establishment of the ideals of transparent language and fixed, objective knowledge are tied to one another.

Suppose, unlike Locke and Condillac, one's interest was not in explaining the independence of knowledge or its common availability to speakers of all languages. Suppose that one's idea of knowledge were not that it necessarily lived in laws of nature, but that the latter were conventional formulations that had local application—practical uses, that is. The connections between knowledge and language would, then, no longer be a philosophical problem—and perhaps not a problem at all. Would one then want to know, furthermore, about the origin of language? Would one imagine that language, as an independent entity, originated at all? Wouldn't the question of the origin of language be similar to the question of, if asked, the origin of the human species? And then, would one ask about the origin of the human species in a context separate from the origin of all species, or the origin of life? To ask for the origin of anything that is so distant in time is to invite speculative answers, with little hope of actually discovering them.

Yet Locke's and Condillac's considerations, and the works of those, such as Rousseau and Herder, who followed them, moved the search for the understanding of language out of the purely sacral contexts and into natural philosophy and science. As Aarsleff maintains, this was the beginning of the *study of language* in the sense that *language as a subject matter* became separated from the study and inquiry into the specific languages that had to be learned, mastered, translated, and retextualized into the vernaculars. It is noteworthy how the establishment of this subject required a convergence of effort, discernable in retrospect as an Enlightenment effort, into which the earlier work of Valla first falls, but which fell on deaf ears in his own time. Yet, as these theories emerged, religious mythologies continued to command respect: thinkers were careful, almost without exception, to reconcile their senses of language with religious orthodoxies regarding the history of the cosmos and of the human species. From one standpoint, Aarsleff's enthusiasm for this enlightenment history of the study of language is justified: developments and insights into the nature of language are useful and appealing. But, from another standpoint, there remains a strange inconsequentiality to these new views of language, as their only practical effects were to fix the use of vernacular and to justify the ideal of abstract knowledge—knowledge as, perhaps, having a life of its own—and urging scientists to pursue it wherever it may lead because it is autonomous and intrinsically good.

VI. Many Languages and the Enlightened University

Into this axiomatic belief in abstract knowledge came the work of Wilhelm von Humboldt at the beginning of the nineteenth century. His contributions are wide ranging, and they have been a major factor, since his time, in the language-study techniques in Western universities. Among other things, Humboldt's study of the world's languages have helped to place the study of language on a more realistic ground: scholars could use knowledge of the languages of distant cultures as well as their own to think about how to study language. His work was characterized by multiple beliefs, and, as Roger Brown has said more than once, his views and opinions changed and developed, although there is no reason to think that his later views were truer than his earlier ones; several of the views he held at different periods in his life contribute to the present inquiry. Except for his thinking that Indo-European languages were superior to others,[125] the kind of work he did—the writing of grammars and speculation about the relations of language and thinking—remains a basis for continuing research on language. His work as a minister of education, as one of the founders of the new University of Berlin, as well as of a scholar of languages, embodied the ideal of *Wissenschaft*—knowledge or science or disciplined study—or what Charles E. McClelland[126] identifies as "neo-humanist" endeavor, which held the ideal of knowledge for its own sake. He was one who helped recast the university as the site of both research and teaching that we take it to be today.[127] His interest in language was one of the motivations for his thinking of the university in those terms. His work reflects a diffuse love of language in several of its manifestations, such that scholars seeking a point of view in his work could not find any one dogma or theory in it. Brown's view seems most accurate[128] in the following sense: whether he did it deliberately, Humboldt

125. A point to which I return shortly.

126. Charles E. McClelland, *State, Society, and University in Germany, 1700–1914* (Cambridge: Cambridge UP, 1980).

127. A more detailed discussion of Humboldt's role in the development of the modern university may be found in William Clark, *Academic Charisma and the Origins of the Research University* (Chicago: U of Chicago P, 2006), 435–476.

128. Brown, *Wilhelm von Humboldt's,* 109–120. He says that the outcome of Humboldt's efforts was to present the first important statement of linguistic relativity, discussed further in chapter 4. Brown's view is also consistent with that of Marianne Cowan

directed his studies after his changing interests, trying at every moment to make a synthesis of a subject so large as to defy any one person's attempt.

Humboldt's efforts can be put in terms of the two main perspectives on language that had defined the subject in Europe in the seventeenth and eighteenth centuries, and often beforehand: grammar and the origin of words. One group, such as the Port-Royalists,[129] asked this: Doesn't the existence of grammar in every language, of similar parts of speech in every language, suggest the universality of grammar, of a language capability that can be identified with the essentially human? Others, such as Condillac, asked this: How did words come about to guide us to recognize the knowing human mind? Brown says that Humboldt as he grew older moved from a greater sympathy with the search for universal grammar to an emphasis on disclosing the diversity of human languages and their relativity to nation and culture. Although he did not resolve either question, the scope of his work suggests that both factors are fundamental to the understanding of language, even if they do not remain in the forms of their Renaissance and Enlightenment presentations.

Students of Humboldt seem to agree that his work did more than place the origin question and the universal-grammar question on the research table; Humboldt strove for formulations that would show, first, the connection between language and thought, and then the identity of the two. From a scientific viewpoint, this movement treated language as a more important subject than it had been previously in non-sacral contexts. By characterizing language as an activity rather than a thing or a product,[130] he emphasized its living qualities: language is "the ever-repetitive work of the spirit to make articulated sounds capable of expressing thought." Here is Aarsleff's characterization:

> Only by virtue of language do we gain self-awareness, knowledge, and mastery of reality. It is like a second world in which we know both our own selves and the outward face of things, like a middle ground between

in her introduction to *Humanist without Portfolio* (Detroit: Wayne State UP, 1963) 1–25. Cowan portrays Humboldt as a lover, a husband, a friend, a public figure, and a scholar, whose approach to work was both pragmatic and scholarly. His more doctrinaire views emerged after he had collected his materials, relatively late in life.

129. Seventeenth-century French philosophers searching for language universals. For a comprehensive review of the search for universals, see Robin Lakoff, review of *Grammaire générale et raisonnée*, *Language* 45.2 (June 1969): 343–364. The search for language universals is still taking place, following some of Chomsky's more recent formulations. See Morton H. Christiansen, Chris Collins, and Shimon Edelman, eds., *Language Universals* (New York: Oxford UP, 2009). The intellectual and verbal acrobatics seen in this volume resemble, perhaps, the Ptolemaic acrobatics justifying the earth at the center of the solar system.

130. Brown, *Wilhelm von Humboldt's*, 118; Hans Aarsleff, "Introduction," Wilhelm von Humboldt, *On Language*, trans. Peter Heath (Cambridge: Cambridge UP, 1988), xix.

subjective being and objective existence. This philosophy does not have room for the copy-theory of knowledge; language is not merely designative; it is not representation but expression. Language is a constituent of thought and for that reason it must stand at the center of any viable epistemology.

It is possible to see this view in Romantic terms, as it stresses the role of people's inner being, the experiences of feeling and passion as well as of thought, in the uses of language. It transforms Condillac's interest in reflection to a more intense idea of self-awareness, a feeling that differentiates humans from other species more elaborately than just the attribution of language, which might also be applied loosely to other primates, birds, insects, and marine mammals. Humboldt says that universal grammar is evidence of the relatedness of different peoples, as opposed to evidence of the innateness of language. Aarsleff writes that all of Humboldt's work explores the possible identity of thought and language.[131]

As he investigated languages from distant parts of the world, Humboldt developed a sense of the individuality of different language-cultures, suggesting that each culture had its characteristic "genius"—its special idioms and ways of knowing discernable through understanding the special features of grammar in the lexicon in each language. When Brown was working on Humboldt, the work of Sapir and Whorf[132] was being debated, and he found a basis in Humboldt's study of many languages for the mid-twentieth-century interest in linguistic relativity.[133]

Humboldt was involved in one of the most consequential initiatives in university life in the West, the founding of the University of Berlin in 1810. This event is comparable to the recognition of the University of Bologna in 1155 by Frederick Barbarossa[134] and to the founding of the University of Halle at the end of the seventeenth century.[135] Following Halle, progressive universities were founded at Göttingen in 1734 and Erlangen in 1743, each with some

131. Aarsleff, "Introduction," Humboldt, *On Language,* xviii.
132. Brown, *Wilhelm von Humboldt's,* 10–13. The Sapir-Whorf hypothesis about the relativity of language to culture is treated in chapter 4.
133. There has been renewed interest in the Sapir-Whorf hypothesis, possibly as a result of translation needs related to economic globalization. Madeleine Mathiot, ed., *Ethnolinguistics: Boas, Sapir, and Whorf Revisited* (The Hague: Mouton, 1979); J. J. Gumperz and S. C. Levinson, eds., *Rethinking Linguistic Relativity* (Cambridge: Cambridge UP, 1996); Dedre Gentner and Susan Goldin-Meadow, eds., *Language in Mind: Advances in the Study of Language and Thought* (Cambridge, MA: MIT P, 2003).
134. Discussed in chapter 8.
135. According to McClelland, "The beginning of the first eighteenth-century university reform movement in Germany may be dated from the founding of the University of Halle" (*State,* 34–35). A key figure in the founding of this university in 1694 was Christian Thomasius, a law professor known for his opposition to witch trials and his lecturing in the vernacular. His educational philosophy advocated so-called gentleman's

strong intention to provide a new, rich enlightened background for the nobility (and more practical education for everyone else), and all of which may be understood as precursors to Berlin, whose shape and curriculum most resembles those of today's universities. The founding of these universities also resembles the overtaking of Oxford by Henry VIII in the sixteenth century. Heads of state perceived how valuable the universities were in training high-level bureaucrats,[136] and they essentially imitated the Church in this practice; they had a new curriculum, conservative in different ways, but which also added some of the newer interests. The German initiatives from Halle to Berlin were among the most progressive in Europe.

During Humboldt's younger years, he was active in the politics of public education. He was independently wealthy, already a member of the elite who did not have to find employment. While learned and interested in learning more, much of his time was spent helping the king of Prussia establish the new university at Berlin. His views about language were developing at the end of the eighteenth century, but it was not until two decades into the nineteenth century, when he retired,[137] that he started on his major scholarly work on languages, about sixteen years before he died. Before that, he did the institutional work of creating a wide-ranging university in a city that already had an established Academy of Sciences—a group of learned men engaged in *wissenschaftliche* (scientific, disciplinary, academic, philosophical, intellectually rigorous) activities—and a series of collections, libraries, and other resources needed by a forward-looking university.

McClelland says that the so-called neo-humanist founders of the University of Berlin thought of themselves as philosopher-kings: "the university that emerged from the neo-humanists' plans was an elite institution in more than an intellectual sense."[138] Johann Fichte, one of the founders in addition to Humboldt and Friedrich Schleiermacher, had a "social vision [that] included the rule of the academics (who would have a monopoly in the state) over the rest of the *Volk*—a revolutionary idea implying the supplanting of the old birth elites by a consolidated elite with a common experience of high education. Fichte and even Humboldt intended to produce, if not philosopher-kings, philosopher-

---

subjects such as fencing, riding, languages, and science. The full, interesting career of Thomasius is recounted by Andrew Dickson White, *Seven Great Statesmen in the Warfare of Humanity with Unreason* (New York: Century, 1910), 113–164.

136. Walter Rüegg, "Themes," *History*, ed. Rüegg, 3:6–7. In the beginning of the nineteenth century, the state on the Continent became increasing involved in the university bureaucracy, and often ran it. Members of the university faculty were themselves civil servants who trained others for administrative jobs.

137. Marianne Cowan, in *Humanist*, views this period as his second and last "retirement," referring to his getting out of public life.

138. McClelland, *State*, 119.

bureaucrats to rule Prussia."[139] It is unlikely that scholarship and research in any one subject would have led to this sense of an academic mission. Rather, the combination of independent wealth, indulgence by royalty, and a sense of self-regard might produce such political visions. In medieval France, when members of the university were privileged clerics, they behaved with almost identical values, and generally felt free to challenge the pope.[140] The political placement of the founders of the University of Berlin and their sense, perhaps, of entitlement as well as enlightenment create a context for Humboldt's approaches to the study of language.

Humboldt's shift toward studying the many non-European languages, and his efforts to write grammars for them led him, once the data were assembled, toward the task of distinguishing the languages according to their quality. Because all languages are rooted inside (that is, in the soul, spirit, or mind of) individual members of each culture, each language was assumed to reflect a collective inner capability of that people, a collectively held essential style of thinking that was responsible for the speech-forms found in that language. Abstractions such as "national character" were used to describe the belief in the connection between features of the language and an assumed inner source in

---

139. McClelland, *State*, 120. Schleiermacher's formulation is more idealistic: the "business of a university" is "to awaken the idea of scholarship in noble-minded youths already equipped with knowledge of many kinds, to help them to a mastery of it in the particular field of knowledge to which they wish to devote themselves, so that it becomes second nature for them to view everything from the perspective of scholarship, and to see every individual thing not in isolation, but in its closest scholarly connections, relating it constantly to the unity and entirety of knowledge, so that in all their thought they learn to become aware of the principles of scholarship, and thus themselves acquire the ability to carry out research, to make discoveries, and to present these, gradually working things out in themselves. This is the business of a university." Quoted in Christophe Charle, "Patterns," *History*, ed. Rüegg, 3:48. This ideal is still today's ideal, as well as Freud's ideal, but in today's ideal the corollary of the wish to rule society indicated by McClelland is not acknowledged. A manifestation of this idea is described by William Clark, who uses Max Weber's term "charisma" as a university trope that perpetuated the earlier idealism: "The original charismatic figure [for Weber] was the sorcerer, then later the priest and especially the prophet, the herald of the new cult. Regarding academia, part of academic charisma sprang from this topos—the teacher as spiritual or cultic leader. In the field of politics and economics the original charismatic leader was the warrior, then later the general or king. Part of academic charisma sprang from this topos—the martial, agonistic, polemical cast of academic knowledge as it developed in medieval Europe" (*Academic Charisma and the Origin of the Research University*, Chicago: U of Chicago P, 2006, 14–15).

140. An instance of which is discussed in chapter 8. As considered in modern times by Mark Lilla, in *The Reckless Mind*, intellectuals favored by heads of state tend to think of themselves as eligible to become heads of state. The continuing honor accorded Plato has familiarized the term "philosopher-king" to such an extent that it has become romanticized and, too often, entertained as realistic.

thought of that language. Humboldt's movement toward identifying language and thought quietly placed the emphasis on thought, just as Locke and Condillac did, and quietly stipulated an essential inner self that was responsible for the thought represented by the texts, oral and written, in the language. The principle of the relativity of language to culture as used by Humboldt did not consider just the language and just the culture: it assumed, in addition, a collectively held inner character shared by all users of the language. Thus, the (culturally produced) thought of different peoples were different from one another because the peoples were different. This assumption is the nineteenth-century version of the antique and humanist intuitions regarding how language was the sign of the essentially human or the gift of God. The assumption would not apply if there were no expectation of reaching a subjective essence of each person and the collectivity of people in each nation.[141] Without the aforementioned expectation, we would observe different languages' ways of expressing different experiences without our trying to infer either an individual or a collective inner life: perceptible features would show both individual and collective difference clearly. The traditional and Humboldtian views, as compared to a materialist view, search for an inferred essence of language. I use the term "repression" to describe the action by Locke, Condillac, and Humboldt of noticing and then refusing to accept the unity of language and thought. Pursuant to the received tradition of treating thought and the inner life as prior entities, their ways of describing language and knowledge show their having presupposed the priority of thought.[142]

If we consider the recrudescence of this religious fantasy about the origin of language in this case, and if we remember that the founding of the University of Berlin entailed other fantasies of intellectual superiority on the part of its

---

141. This assumption was held by Edmund Husserl over a century later; it led to frustration when he was unable to enlarge his philosophy of individual subjectivity to collective situations.

142. Brown gives an account of how Leibniz argues for the near identity of language and thought—that language was the *medium* of thought. He then observes: "But despite the apparently close identification made here by Leibniz between language and mental processes, the underlying opinion, which was to be carried on by later enlightened thinkers, was still that language was the creation of human Reason, and although perhaps a necessary outward vehicle for its more complex operations, yet still essentially subordinate to it. Any closer identification of language and thought was dependent on a thoroughgoing attack on the Enlightenment view of the primacy of Reason. Hamann based such an attack on his own idiosyncratic view of language" (*Wilhelm von Humboldt's*, 57–58, quotation on 58). Brown's view suggests that reason played a role similar to that played by God or the Holy Spirit (during the medieval period) as the justification for the ultimate and ineffable, but also divine, authority of one's inner being. Little has to be said about the similarity of status between reason and Platonic ideas. Hamann's work is discussed in chapter 4, which examines the unity of thought and language more fully.

academic participants, these two orientations could have contributed to Humboldt's arrival at the conclusion that the ancestor language for all European languages is objectively superior to other languages. Although Napoléon was no longer ruling in Europe, there were still other monarchs, and the expansion of empire was continuing for several European countries. Conquered nations were considered barbaric and savage. They were termed "not civilized." Reasons had to be found, especially by a public figure such as Humboldt, to show in an apparently *wissenschaftliche* way why the European languages were superior.

The reasons given by Humboldt may matter in some other kind of discussion; they resemble in tone and conviction the reasons that were given a century later to justify the claims of lower intelligence for women and nonwhite people.[143] As Aarsleff recounts, two Americans objected to Humboldt's judgments. It seems he was surprised by them, as he answered their objections with purely speculative reasons about the origin of all languages. The so-called savage nations merely inherited a language that was less "preferable for giving the mind the habit of reasoning and for the development of all intellectual forms of man." Humboldt's judgment resembles that of Walter Ong (discussed in chapter 9), who, in retrospect, presents an account of the influence of learned Latin of the "How could it have been otherwise?" variety: because Western civilization is considered to be most advanced, its history of language use and development must also be more advanced, owing to the role of language as reflecting the essence and origin of being human. Humboldt is a nineteenth-century instance of the long tradition of students of language in the academic West who thought that the languages of our ancestors were superior to other languages. In this way, academics, scholars, and others committed to the scientific study of language participated in the politics of the superiority of one's own, the characteristic collective narcissism of the male groups who worked independently, participated in the cycle of power struggles giving rise new leadership, and took androcentrism to be "the way things are."

This unashamed theme of superiority is found less ambiguously in Humboldt's remarks about women. The style and tone of these remarks follows the tradition of Enlightenment individualism, which is part of the work of other men who believed in the promise of Enlightenment emancipation.[144] First, there is a carefully articulated admiration of women's abilities and social action; then

---

143. Aarsleff does not politically endorse Humboldt's views of the superiority of Sanskrit, although his discussion is consistent with those views. He says, "Humboldt's argument was chiefly the consequence of combining determined insistence on the unforgiving demands of universal grammar with the aesthetic view of the nature of language" ("Introduction," Humboldt, *On Language,* xxxii). I agree with this formulation and that these reasons do apply to Humboldt, but they are rationalizations rather than reasons.

144. For example, the work of historian J. L. Talmon, discussed in chapter 11.

there is the decisive proviso that gives the basis for not admitting women into society as equal members in all social contexts. With regard to language,

> [w]omen generally express themselves more naturally, delicately, and yet more forcefully than men. Their speech is a more faithful mirror of their thoughts and feelings and—even if this has been rarely recognized or said—they preserve especially the richness, strength, and naturalness of language in the midst of a culture which ever robs language of these qualities. . . . Women in their handling of language lessen the disadvantage of the split which culture always produces between the common people and the rest of the nation. Truly more closely bound to nature by their own nature; . . . women refine and beautify the naturalness of language without robbing or violating it.[145]

The effusiveness of this description is immediately suspicious, and reminds us of the repeated exaggeration of both welcome and unwelcome qualities men have found in women. The clichés about women are in evidence: women's "nature" is to be bound to nature; women's language is delicate and close to their thoughts and feelings, closer than the language of men to theirs, whose language is prone to abstractions that render them more "one-sided."[146] Women's beauty is "more notable for the graceful freedom of its materiality rather than the rule of form in well-defined features."[147] Humboldt recognizes materiality in women's beauty and spontaneously in the many languages he studied. Yet he seemed driven toward form in writing the grammars of these languages. In Humboldt's writings on women, the Greek tradition asserts itself in spite of his own tendencies toward identifying the materiality of language.

With regard to women as a class, Humboldt's attachment to tradition remains: "but their [women's] nature also contains a lack or a failing of analytic capacity which draws a strict line of demarcation between ego and world; therefore they will not come as close to the ultimate investigation of truth as man."[148] In addition, "[f]emininity in general must have undergone considerable refinement before scientific or poetic productivity becomes possible. Without it, even the most superior feminine individuals lack sufficient clarity and peace, and even more the strength and even the inclination to separate a whole series

---

145. Cowan, *Humanist,* 344. This quotation (6:204–205) is from the German seven-volume edition of Humboldt's writings and correspondence with Caroline von Humboldt.

146. Cowan, *Humanist,* 345. Humboldt's full discussion of gender is worth studying but probably not necessary to the present context.

147. Cowan, *Humanist,* 348.

148. Cowan, *Humanist,* 349.

of thoughts or feelings from their kind and work on them in isolation."[149] Like Freud a century later, Humboldt has an appreciative admiration for women, but this sympathy acts in both men's work to disable women's membership among the builders of civilization.

If the history of ideas is considered without taking into account this presumption about gender and its justifications, there is also a progressive history in the study of language, especially because an eighteenth-century thought like Hamann's regarding the identity of thought and language[150] continues on the record but is overwhelmed by the work of figures such as Humboldt and his accomplishments in general university education. Who would maintain that the liberalization of universities is less urgent than understanding the dubiousness of the category "thought"? Humboldt's having placed before us such a wide range of languages is a valuable achievement. Because of his work these sources for understanding language use became available to us. But also because of the honor accorded to him, because of his standing and his role as a public figure, and because of his gender, there is an inclination among scholars to overlook the relation of his sense of personal and cultural superiority to the substantive views of language he presents. In the academy the nineteenth-century scientific value of "disinterested knowledge"[151] perpetuates the belief in the separation of human knowledge from the rest of nature, as subsequent scholars of language see Humboldt's views of language only in relation to other views of language, and not in relation to the practices of scholars or of the university as a protected institution.[152]

---

149. Cowan, *Humanist*, 353.

150. Brown, *Wilhelm von Humboldt's*, 57; this is also discussed more fully in chapter 4. Brown (*Wilhelm von Humboldt's*, 60) considers Isaiah Berlin's summary of Hamann's to be authoritative: "[P]hilosophers who think that they are studying concepts or ideas or categories of reality are in fact studying means of human expression—language—which is at once the vehicle of men's view of the universe and of themselves, and part and parcel of that world itself, which is not separable from the ways in which it is experienced or thought about." Isaiah Berlin, *The Age of Enlightenment* (New York: Mentor, 1956), 273. This view anticipates Wittgenstein's, and is considered in connection with Wittgenstein in chapters 3 and 4.

151. Arnold claims for criticism the Enlightenment ideal in the search for any knowledge "disinterestedness," which is achieved by the "free play of the mind on all subjects which it touches." Matthew Arnold, "The Function of Criticism in the Present Time," *Critical Theory since Plato,* ed. Hazard Adams (New York: Harcourt Brace Jovanovich, 1971), 588.

152. This is not true of Aarsleff, who took into account a host of contextual factors in his discussions of Condillac and Humboldt. One of his most valuable external points is his view of the study of language as a project in humanism that includes science and philosophy. Aarsleff also discussed the criticism of Humboldt's racism by American linguists. (Aarsleff, "Introduction," Humboldt, *On Language,* lxiii).

VII. Modern Standards

As the interest in science grew in the nineteenth and twentieth centuries, the authority of science grew in proportion to its reputation for objectivity and disinterestedness, and for its presumed immunity to political, social, psychological, and affective influence. This standard was so authoritative that social scientists searched for ways to emulate the techniques that could claim certainty and mathematical precision. At the same time, Humboldt's accomplishment called for anthropological investigative research to follow it through. Franz Boas and Edward Sapir observed the embeddedness of languages in the cultures of real societies. These enterprises contrasted with the more traditionally academic subjects of language philosophy and comparative philology. Other types of language study took place in literature and history departments. The various interests in language did little to increase the social value of language study because the various lines of inquiry were not coordinated with one another. A large part of this inertia was that in universities disciplines generally did not work with one another; they usually occupied and protected their own fields. The study of language has not been a single shared subject[153] amenable to several approaches as seen by Aarsleff, but was compartmentalized by universities into different subject matters. The departmental structure of the university helped to narrow the definition of fields. But, additionally, the axiomatic epistemological principle of any formal research inside and outside the university was to remove (abstract) the item of interest from its context—isolate it, analyze it, and then try to reconcile the analysis with one's prior sense of the whole. This procedure has been true of sciences—except, and only recently, for a few social sciences. In a sense, the university as designed by Humboldt did not allow any subject to predominate, as theology once did, and as medicine does today. But Schleiermacher's ideal of various subjects relating to one another did not materialize either. The rule of the university has been that subjects that have political, economic, and technological contributions to make to government and industry—and that are supported by such institutions—have the greatest share of resources within the university. The humanist ideals regarding the fundamental role of language in culture, a view that required alertness to the culture as a whole—held in the Renaissance, in the Enlightenment, and in the Romantic periods[154]—became

---

153. As Christine Kenneally states, "We have believed for a long, long time that language is a monolithic thing. But all the evidence reported in this book argues that it is not." Christine Kenneally, *The First Word: The Search for the Origins of Language* (New York: Viking, 2007), 289. This study does show that the various parts in the study of language hang together while showing the practical value of not thinking of language as monolithic.

154. These were humanist ideals, but were not generally accepted or promoted by university curricula.

diffused in the research university as founded by Humboldt, as humanism was treated in universities as a fragmented, decorative, ancillary enterprise. The new authority (on the university "block") was physical, chemical, and, in part, biological science—and each of these enterprises depended on the assumption of language transparency.

The commanding authority of modern science, which began in the eighteenth century,[155] was responsible, in part, for the enormous attention given to Noam Chomsky's linguistics in the twentieth century.[156] For the first time, someone proposed a formal theory of language that was at least potentially articulable in rules and propositions that were derived logically from axioms and other fundamental principles, some of which could be claimed to be observable in experience, as principles of physics seemed to be (as related to, say, gravity or billiard balls).[157] If, as Aarsleff suggests, the work of Saussure was the culmination of the humanistic (and also *wissenschaftliche*) study of language, Chomsky's theory, a subtle but consequential variation of Saussure's tradition of the structural linguistics that was consistent with the principle of the relativity of language to culture, reemphasized the older principle of linguistic universals, which he called "Cartesian Linguistics."[158] Its approach was based on the

155. "So great was the faith in science that man tried to bring every field of knowledge under scientific discipline." Pierre Juliard, *Philosophies of Language in Eighteenth-Century France* (The Hague: Mouton, 1970), 90. This attitude has intensified and is still strengthening today.

156. The fact that Chomsky was a faculty member at MIT contributed to this perception of his linguistics. Chomsky also attracted attention with his strongly negative review of B. F. Skinner's 1957 *Verbal Behavior, Language* 35 (1959): 26–58. Many looked askance at Skinner, as he seemed to want to reduce language to "behavior" (which conjured images of rats in mazes). Skinner's sense of language was not as interesting as Austin's (discussed in chapter 3), given at about the same time, but "behavior" as understood by Skinner is closer to language as gesture than to language as genetically innate.

157. In oral presentations, Chomsky characterized his procedures in transformational linguistics by claiming their similarity to the so-called model science, physics.

158. Aarsleff vigorously rejects Chomsky's use of the term "Cartesian," and offers that the history given in this name is "fundamentally false." He claims that Chomsky has distorted the actual paths of influence by making it seem that there was a clear line of development of the belief in universal grammar from the seventeenth century onward. Aarsleff shows, however, that the people cited by Chomsky as believers in universal grammar actually believed *both* in a possible universal grammar and in an origin-of-language explanation that emphasized the gradual growth of abstraction and interdependency of verbal forms from sensual, emotional experience in social situations. Hans Aarsleff, "The History of Linguistics and Professor Chomsky," *From Locke*, 101–119. Robin Lakoff, in her review of a 1966 publication of a history of the Port-Royal grammarians, also writes that "it is a mistake to consider *Grammaire générale et raisonnée* a work of 'Cartesian linguistics.' Linguistically, its theory is pre-Cartesian; that marriage of proto-transformational linguistics and rationalist philosophy and psychology that

belief that there were common characteristics of all languages, that grammar was the most likely place to look for these characteristics, and that, if found, they could be understood as being attached to the human essence, whether conceived of as the spirit, soul, mind—or now, for the first time, the brain and, perhaps, the genes.[159]

This approach, in Chomsky's hands, made a distinction between the supposedly universal aspects of language (competence) and the accidental "sense data" aspects—the sounds, the vocabulary, the habits and genres of use: the perceptible features of all languages (performance). Why did Chomsky take this path? Why—to explain language, as, more or less, the same phenomenon identified by the post-Valla humanists—did one have to stipulate an inner language, a "natural property of the human mind"?[160] His repeatedly claimed evidence for it is the creativity of language use[161] and the rapidity of the infantile acquisition of grammatical language. The term "creativity" is used often interchangeably with the terms "unbounded" and "stimulus-free" to emphasize how significant it is that it is not possible to predict what a person will say.[162]

---

has been termed Cartesian actually does not come into being . . . until the work of Cordemoy and DuMarsais" (review of *Grammaire*, 363). An equally questionable aspect of Chomsky's project is its relationship to the work of Wittgenstein. Norman Malcolm writes, "One striking feature of Chomsky's views about language is that they have a strong resemblance to the conceptions of the *Tractatus* (published with English translation in 1922); and a second striking feature is that they seem to *totally ignore* the devastating criticism of those conceptions in the *Philosophical Investigations* (published with English translation in 1951)" Norman Malcolm, *Wittgenstein: A Religious Point of View?* (Ithaca, NY: Cornell UP, 1994), 48. There is additional discussion of this issue in chapter 3, considering Malcolm's more general point regarding the lack of uptake of Wittgenstein's sense of language until very recently. Further discussion of Chomsky's work is in chapter 5, section 1.

159. However, when Chomsky started writing in the late 1950s and 1960s, enthusiasm for genetic research had not yet established itself.

160. Noam Chomsky, *Cartesian Linguistics: A Chapter in the History of Rationalist Thought* (New York: Harper and Row, 1966), 14. This phrase is used as a description of how Herder thought of language. Chomsky cites the key figures in the three-century modern history of the study of language to show how frequently scholars sought ways to locate the essence of language in the mind.

161. The most recent version of this creativity is recursion, the ability to embed sentences in other sentences indefinitely (actually, until they become too long to understand). Examples are found in Kenneally, *First Word*, 261. These examples also show that it is not just sentences that can be recursively embedded in an abstract sense, but experiences that are arranged hierarchically and then marked as sentences. Therefore, recursion cannot be indefinite: social relationships and actual memory capacity both limit recursion, and all speakers learn these limits.

162. It should also be clear that no language is free of stimulus. If it were, there would be no point to language at all. Dogs bark and birds chirp because of stimuli.

The characterization of speech as creative due to its unpredictability is doubtful. Ordinary speech acts usually have been understood to be generic or conventional. The dialogue on soap operas, while scripted, suggests that it is possible to write an original hour-long play in which every line is clearly identifiable as cliché. The *appearance* of unpredictability derives from a part of experience that Chomsky had ruled out as being of interest in the scientific study of language: social context. Because each social context is new, it seems as if the language is new. Yet how can there be such a thing as really new language that has been generated? When there is neologism, or an unconventional syntactical variation, everyone focuses on it and asks about it. Poets and novelists do it; this is not the creativity referred to by Chomsky. Rather, combinations of known and repeated uses reappear with new voices, new characters, new times and places, and thus the language seems to have been freshly generated, leading Chomsky to the strange claim that the new language was "creative."

If the usage of language is not predictable, he reasons, it must be "generated"[163] by an inner grammar. Because all languages have a grammatical structure, grammar itself must be specific to the human species and, thus, innate. Consequently, if the ability to construct a grammar is part of the mind, it must be in the brain and in the genes. The latter search is a scientific project, and it might render the study of language a science in the Newtonian sense.[164] So the answer to the question above is that Chomsky took the approach of the universal grammarians because it casts linguistics as a real science without underestimating the complexity of language.

Chomsky's approach is similar to that of the humanists and to other students of language in the past: it considers language in ways that show the how language decisively separates the human species from other species. A cornerstone of the transformational generative theory of language is this conviction that first, humans are radically different from other species, and second, that language is the one clear demonstration that this is so.[165] However, there is

---

163. This is also a strange term: imagine people "generating" language the way power plants generate electrical power. The term also implies that people's use of language is a spontaneous, self-oriented process. This may happen in very marginal cases of mental illness, but usually, people make new sentences on the basis of the socially encouraged repertoire of language habits and uses. Almost all the time, people use the language in social situations, where they *say* things rather than *generate* them. Would it be sensible to say that a dancer or athlete generates gestures?

164. However, because of considerations discussed in chapter 10, it is no longer possible to identify Newtonian thinking with science. Physics has moved into areas that contest the traditional senses of certainty and predictability.

165. It is not clear why a factor such as brain size would not provide an equally decisive piece of evidence regarding the difference between humans and other species. However, one wonders why one needs any evidence at all: to be a member of a species

some ambiguity in the following sense: Is Chomsky's theory an inquiry into the nature of language, or is it an attempt to say why the human species is superior to other species? Or both? If both, Chomsky's effort seems similar to Humboldt's: a thoughtful figure, fascinated and immersed in language, imaginative in his stipulation of explanations, yet committed to the inexplicable[166] principle of articulating the terms of human superiority. Because regardless of what is discovered about the use of language in the human brain or genes, there is no conceivable reason for defining and deciding on the humanness of language. None dispute that all people speak and have a grammar, that children do not need long explanations (or any explanation, for that matter) of the difference between themselves and their pets. Why would one want a scientific theory to prove that human beings are superior?

Suppose this is not what Chomsky is trying to do, as he likely would deny that this purpose motivates his work. The question then arises of why is it important to show why or how language is a property of the mind. Is it true that those, such as Leonard Bloomfield and Charles Hockett,[167] who claimed that language is learned by analogy do not believe that language is a property of the mind? Does it matter whether or not they believed it? Does it have any consequence in the study of language whether we students think of it as originating in the mind, in a grammar, or in a primordial garden? Do we need to prove or disprove the well-known "bow-wow" and "pooh-pooh" theories? The search for the essence of language in a language acquisition device in the mind, for an innate ability to construct grammars, for wired-in chemistry in the genes, in the DNA, is not different in status from the many speculative searches in the seventeenth and eighteenth centuries (and, in our time, several in evolutionary psychology, reviewed in chapter 5) for the prehistoric origin of language.[168] It seems from the many considerations brought to bear by historians of the study of language, such as those discussed by Aarsleff, that the history of the study of language has been constantly, almost inevitably, tied to the fantasy of human superiority,

---

means that you can only reproduce with another member of your species. Why isn't this sense of species enough? Ockham's minimalist approach to such problems is applicable in this case.

166. Except as crass, uncomprehending, we-are-the-center-of-the-universe narcissism.

167. Robin Lakoff reviews the positions of Bloomfield, Hockett, and Jesperson as "pre-transformational treatments of philosophical grammars" that are contested by Chomsky's theory (review of *Grammaire*, 343). In chapters 3 and 5, there is discussion of research that suggests that analogy, which takes place thousands of times during infancy and expands as the child grows, is part of the understanding needed to explain how infants acquire language.

168. Chomsky has dismissed the evolutionary study of language—with some justification—as being "just stories." His own path of study is similarly speculative, even wishful.

of the elite status of the human species. People did not study language because there was a need—or even just an interest—but because it was taken to be the human essence: of the human soul, the human spirit, consciousness, the mind, and—in the modern period—knowledge. At least, these were the kind of justifications given by the scholars.

The disturbing result of this history is that the actual sites at which people spoke and wrote or sang and painted became, in modern academic contexts (starting, perhaps with Humboldt), compartmentalized—separated from the study of language to such a degree that it became very hard to see in any contemporary context how these sites might provide the insight into language[169] that has been, habitually, sought in speculation.[170] The case of Chomsky is particularly frustrating, as, early in his theoretical writing, he put aside "performance" as an inconsequential category[171] and declared instead that the study of "competence"—an abstract, logically defined innate structure of some sort—was the scientific path in linguistics. This study could be carried out with invented language formulations rather than with people's actual usage.[172] Chomsky, and others who believed in this approach, invented what are now frequently cited imaginary sentences[173] in order to establish the existence of grammatical transformations: "Golf plays John"; "John is eager/easy to please," and so on. Invented sentences are tied to the context of their invention. They are discussed as if they are standing alone, uncontextualized. In this way language appears to be capable of examination as if there were no context. Yet this is never the case for any use of language, including those used in discussions of transformational grammar. If you invent a sentence, its context has to be part of how it is taken by readers or hearers: the contexts become part of the sentence.[174] It was obvious that if

---

169. The work of Susanne K. Langer has proceeded in this direction, yet has not been followed up by others.

170. As Kenneally reports, current interest in the origin of language is tied to studies in human evolution. Chapter 5 discusses some of these efforts.

171. Noam Chomsky, *Aspects of the Theory of Syntax* (Cambridge: MIT P, 1965), 3.

172. Ad hoc formulations, such as "colorless green ideas sleep furiously," are given as uncontextualized nonsense language and are used, presumably, only for purposes of demonstration at that moment. However, this actual sentence must have appeared originally in context—the so-called research context of Chomsky's discussion—but has acquired over time a much larger context of use, which enables me to cite it at this moment. Many cite the sentence for amusement or for semi-serious purposes in discussions of language. It has become a piece of literature in a scholarly canon upon which all language users may draw.

173. Is there such a thing as an imaginary sentence? (No, there is not; nor are there fictional sentences. Every sentence inevitably is real.)

174. The sociolinguists Robin Tolmach Lakoff and Deborah Tannen have repeatedly written about language as it appears in a wide variety of real contexts. Both authors discuss things that were actually said and then reflect on what can be learned from their

the contexts of use were considered in the search for grammars, the searches would be fruitless, because the sentences' only context would be that in which they were presented, subject to the uncertainties of real life actions—that is to say, performance. The language samples used by transformational linguists are the performances of the group of men undertaking this project. And if it were accepted that language cannot be removed from contexts of its use for the purposes of studying the language, it would not be possible to maintain the theory of generative grammar.[175]

To date, researchers have not discovered the language acquisition device that Chomsky said must be innate. Nor has there been any other theory of language that resembles the scientific, logical ideals Chomsky held for such a theory— ideals that were rejected by Wittgenstein. In universities, the study of language continues to be divided among different departments, as it was in the nineteenth century, with a great deal of the work taking place in cognitive science studies, sometimes called "brain and cognitive science." The desire to study language as a science is not misguided: rather, science as an ideal with a fixed standard of research obscures the fact that the reference of science has been changing, for Chomsky as well as for those succeeding him. This topic is discussed in chapter 10, but merely to contrast the way "science" is used in English with *Wissenschaft* in German suggests that the two words reflect different social purposes. If a scientific enterprise is understood in its actual relativity to culture and interest, this opens the question not of what science is, but to what things shall it turn its attention. Few doubt the value of seeking new understanding, but what things require more understanding more urgently?

The study and uses of language in the university have been distracted by a belief, with several versions, in the inner essence of human beings. Universities have collaborated in promulgating this belief because it limits the study of

---

materials. Lakoff's several works include *Language and Woman's Place* (New York: Harper, 1975); *Talking Power: The Politics of Language in Our Lives* (New York: Basic, 1990); and *The Language War* (Berkeley: U of California P, 2000). Chapter 6 considers Lakoff's work in detail. Tannen's books include *Conversational Style: Analyzing Talk among Friends* (Norwood, NJ: Ablex, 1984); *You Just Don't Understand: Women and Men in Conversation* (New York: William Morrow, 1990); *The Argument Culture: Moving from Debate to Dialogue* (New York: Random House, 1998). This work is treated in chapter 7. These studies are all consistent with and pursuant to an assumption of the materiality of language. Lakoff was once a student of Chomsky's, but she worked in an entirely different direction, namely, the study of performance and language politics, eschewing the dichotomy altogether. Tannen did the same thing on a somewhat different set of subjects.

175. Some critics have moved on to text linguistics and the study of discourse, but the same caveat applies: if you remove the texts or discourses from the contexts of use, new theories need to be developed for every new context studied: the same language is no longer the same when used in a new context.

language in ways that comply with the hierarchical governance of the university and society. Many academic men who oppose such governance—and Noam Chomsky is one of the best known among them—collaborate with its perpetuation through a language-constrained, dogmatic ideal of scientific truth, thereby ignoring or cordoning off or repressing the materiality of language. Chomsky shares such repression with Humboldt and with Freud (see chapter 7, section 3): championing science as academically educated men advocating for truth, they repress the antisocial features of science that assume the referential use of language is its standard, normal use. The materiality of language has always been in plain sight, and unrecognized. Recognizing it permits uses of language that change science and other academic subject matters so that any speaker can gain full access to language.

CHAPTER THREE

Materiality and Genre

I. Materiality from Nominalism

Materiality is the twentieth-century form of nominalism. Whereas nominalism in the past did not challenge beliefs in spirituality, the materiality of the present exists without reference to spiritual categories.[1] Nominalists had faith in such things as spiritual, incorporeal entities, but they did not argue that their existence could be proven. They did not expect that identifying the mind or the soul implied their destiny, nor did their belief in God lead to claims about ideas being more permanent or higher than words.[2] To traditional realists, however, language has been understood as the key to this sense of an immaterial essence of our lives: "In the beginning was the Word, and the Word was with God, and the Word was God." Ways were found to understand language as spiritually substantive, a category whose constituents had no perceptible substance yet which act as if they had such substance (a paradox); one of these ways has been the continuing Platonic belief in the stability and permanence of ideas.[3] This solution has been appealing because, as the author of Ecclesiastes—

---

1. Walter Stephens writes that people have always doubted the reality of spirits: "If spirit was imaginary, was matter the only reality? . . . This is not a modern or 'postmodern' idea. It was pre-Christian, and Christianity never entirely stamped it out." Walter Stephens, *Demon Lovers: Witchcraft, Sex, and the Crisis of Belief* (Chicago: U of Chicago P, 2002), 356.

2. Stanley Cavell characterizes the philosophical tradition as marked by an "obsessional searching for mind, innerness, understanding that seems suspiciously close to searching for substance." Stanley Cavell, *Philosophical Passages: Wittgenstein, Emerson, Austin, Derrida* (Cambridge, MA: Blackwell, 1995), 148. This judgment does not refer to such facts as the equivalence of matter and energy, the meaning of the convertibility of one into the other. Are matter and energy both substantive, as compared to what nothing is? Lawrence M. Krauss has written that "empty space can have a non-zero energy associated with it, even in the absence of any matter or radiation"—that is, nothing is something. Lawrence M. Krauss, *A Universe from Nothing: Why There Is Something Rather than Nothing* (New York: Free P, 2012), 150. Is this verbal sleight of hand? By a physicist who opposes all theology? See chapter 10.

3. Cavell also says, "The origin and status of this language [of Western philosophy] has been the incessant question of philosophy since, I guess, Plato, until by now it can

sometimes thought to be Solomon, a philosopher-king before Plato—had written, "there is nothing new under the sun."[4] Anyone who has read books from
different historical periods understands that similar ideas appear again and
again in different words and different languages, which suggests that they
could be permanent.

General and abstract knowledge represented in language cannot be considered applicable or even relevant to all people. Language cannot be assumed to
be lawful in the physical-science sense, either within or beyond the contexts of
use.[5] Put another way, language cannot identify what is true beyond its uses by
living people,[6] while these are also often open to doubt. Through the path of
trust between speakers, the materiality of language brings with it the relativity
of truth, regardless of how much physical, nonverbal evidence is adduced in
the service of a particular usage. The words used to identify the truth remain
material to the issue of what is considered true because they are themselves
material.[7] Every usage is a test of trust as well as of truth among speakers.[8] Yet
this relativity does not discredit the traditional sense of truth as a knowledge

---

seem philosophy's only question" (*Philosophical*, 143). Vivien Law says that when the
study of grammar was growing at the beginning of the thirteenth century, the application
of Aristotle's four causes to grammar "placed [it] in a broader context: the development
of our intellectual soul, or mind, and the quest for spiritual fulfillment." Vivien Law, *The
History of Linguistics in Europe from Plato to 1600* (Cambridge: Cambridge UP, 2003),
165. Although Chomsky is not spiritual, his aim resembles this traditional one, insofar
as it honors the concept of mind as a discoverable thing.

4. Solomon, however, unlike the envisioned ideal ruler in Plato, was a poet whose
work "watered the passions." His father, David, was also a poet whose work continues
to water the passions. These figures distinguish, perhaps, the materialist view from
the spiritualist view of Plato, which came to govern Christianity even as Aristotle's
techniques also contributed to Christian doctrine. Furthermore, Solomon's view that
there is "nothing new" bears little resemblance to the affirmative enthusiasm of Plato's
ideal forms: Solomon's observation was more akin to the present-day principle of the
conservation of matter and energy: just a cyclical repetition, which might even become
monotonous and depressing.

5. This formulation likely applies to Locke's concern about the "cheat of words"
discussed in chapter 2, section 3. Locke was among those who sought nonverbal evidence
for what the words denoted, and then considered this evidence superior to words as the
path to true knowledge.

6. Such uses include readings, and readings of readings of past texts by us who have
inherited these texts.

7. Readers could apply this principle to this text, assuming the author and reader
are in conversation; Isn't the language—the words, the uses, the grammatical forms—
germane to what you readers will do with a text?

8. This issue is taken up in chapter 10, which discusses Naomi Scheman's recasting
of objectivity as acts of collective trust.

of how things are or of "what is the case."[9] It is merely that such knowledge is provisional or "local."[10]

The medieval heretics were language skeptics but not theological skeptics. None of these men doubted the divinity of God and Jesus. But in order to articulate a faith, one had also to articulate a secular skepticism. Having faith to begin with means that experience does not make one certain.[11] Church dogma preferred declarations of faith without there being a separate category of secular knowledge that recognizes contradictions. To recognize a contradiction follows from the use of language and not from religious faith.[12] Just to use the language fully and to articulate its implications represented a threat to the church as a social institution. Descartes and Galileo were heretical[13] for recognizing the same division between the secular and religious knowledge.[14] In the interest of self-perpetuation the Church took dominion over the language, which was rep-

---

9. "The world is everything that is the case." Ludwig Wittgenstein, *Tractatus Logico-Philosophicus,* trans. C. K. Ogden (New York: Routledge, 1981), 31. Theodor Adorno wrote, "As long as philosophy is no more than the cult of what 'Is the case,' in Wittgenstein's formula it enters into competition with the sciences to which in delusion it assimilates itself—and loses. If it dissociates itself from the sciences, however, and in refreshed merriment thinks itself free of them, it becomes a powerless reserve, the shadow of shadowy Sunday religion." Quoted in Marjorie Perloff, *Wittgenstein's Ladder: Poetic Language and the Strangeness of the Ordinary* (Chicago: U of Chicago P), 1996, 12. Perloff says, however, that Adorno was mistaken in his reading of Wittgenstein, whose anti-philosophical stance might have something in common with Adorno's perspective. Wittgenstein's second opinion (discussed in this chapter) yields the view that language is neither in competition with science nor can it be dissociated from science.

10. Clifford Geertz's term "local knowledge," referring to how culture circumscribes the meaning and status of what is considered known.

11. This is what William of Ockham did and what led to his being considered heretical: he showed the grounds for secular lacks of knowledge and understanding that made his faith necessary. Today, he is remembered for his "razor," namely the principle that argues that the most responsible philosophical strategy is to think with the fewest possible assumptions. Ockham's challenges to language made him appear heretical to the doctrinaire (see chapter 9).

12. All believers who are also scholars labor at reconciling various contradictions in the sacred texts. But their contradictions likely appear because different oral sources were all included when the text were written. See Alan Dundes, *Holy Writ as Oral Lit* (Lanham, MD: Rowman and Littlefield, 1999). In this case, writing (the conversion of oral language to a different material) obscures, through the lack of popular access to literacy, the materiality of the original oral histories.

13. As suggested in chapter 9, the word "heresy" need not have come to mean "oppositional choice," and many so-called heretics merely had differences but were not oppositional. The Church declared them oppositional and thus potentially seditious.

14. Discussed in chapter 9.

resented in public ideology as a spiritual entity.[15] Because of this history, it took until the point of recession of religious authority in the middle of the twentieth century for a materialist sense of language to emerge from several sources at once from students of language and literature: it became safe to assert outright that nonmaterial entities are imaginary—fantasies given as total mediators. Nevertheless, the materiality of language, if acknowledged to any significant extent, remains an inherent challenge to dogmas and orthodoxies—religious and secular—that have characterized the history of civilizations. It is especially a challenge to the hierarchical rule of society, which needs a formal discourse to specify the ideology that legitimates its action. Proponents of the materiality of language themselves have not often recognized the political valence of this understanding of language. The modern academy, the "kept" institution,[16] has neither pursued nor recognized the value of a materialist sense of language.

II. Genre as a Language Function

Genres and categories are uses of language, gestures of naming patterns that are collectively established and perceived.[17] Their use changes if they are understood to be part of the materiality of language. The reference of genre names becomes fixed if it is in the interest of those who declare and identify them. It could be political sedition or heresy when the reference of a genre is challenged or rejected. Platonic realism, with its vision of permanent ideas, has normalized practices of overfixing received categories. Modern students have become familiar with the rigid, formulaic use of genres through Aristotle, and we have learned to arrange the collection of literary works, for example, by understanding how individual works fit into a taxonomy of genres.[18] Although it simplifies conversations to assume stable genres, it also promulgates a false sense that because the names of

---

15. Plato's argument in favor of censoring poets is the same as the Church's for censoring language through its *Index librorum prohibitorum* (List of prohibited books) and its designations of heresy. Plato's and the Church's censorship preserve the rule of the elite. The Church's policy represents an understanding by heads of state that the universal access to language is a real, perhaps ultimate, danger to elite rule.

16. Eyal Press and Jennifer Washburn. "The Kept University." *Atlantic Monthly* March 2000: 39–54. Discussed further in chapter 8, note 1.

17. As Wittgenstein described in his toolbox metaphor, names for individual items and names for categories both seem to be names. Because their function is so different, however, the fact that both are names becomes a source of confusion.

18. Probably the most influential modern treatment, use, and reflection on genre is Northrop Frye's *Anatomy of Criticism* (1957), which aimed to identify relatively fixed genres in the total collection of Western literature. Frye's own wish to render criticism as authoritative as physical science suggests further his own realist sense of the fixity of genres once they are established. Northrop Frye, *Anatomy of Criticism: Four Essays,* ed. Robert D. Denham (Toronto: U of Toronto P, 2006).

genres remain stable over time, the genres themselves are also stable or unified by a single common feature. The dispute between nominalists and realists is about the extent to which a language gesture can fix generic identities. The formulation that genres are "both necessary and loose"[19] is more radical than it may seem, as it provides a ground for understanding genre to be a principal constituent of a materially conceived sense of language. The loose aspect of genres is not usually contemplated because of the assumption that the immaterial words—the class names, universals—refer to real, material things. People do not view a class noun as having uncertain members and no essential feature to tie them together; the use of the term "genre" is a proposal to understand something as a member of a class, but it is not possible to prove that the class exists in some sense beyond the collective agreement to use the class name in ways that work in specific conversations or texts. Newton's laws stipulate that any body in motion stays in motion; they do not say "sometimes" or "most of the time."[20] People do not say, "Well, it looks like there really is a class, so let's speak as if there really is one." People do say, "Science must be exact." If the class term were taken as a language gesture rather than as a declarative name or other rigid designation, it would not demand an exclusive reference. If you presuppose the materiality of this gesture, it would entail assuming its reference to be relative only to this or other local conversations; the contingent status of the genre name would be assumed. To use a generic designation would presuppose that the designation applies only for now. Because naming and identifying classes usually had sacred status as a result of the status of Latin (or, perhaps, the King's English), and because the words were considered transcendental signifiers, their gestural character was repressed, suppressed, and censored. The use of genres for any purpose tended toward the merely taxonomical.

The twentieth-century language materialists whose work is discussed in this and the following chapters have described language in such a way that its materiality and the language gestures that designate genres are part of a single sense of language that has no spiritual or incorporeal parts. The combination of the genre idea with the materialist perspective has made it easier to view materiality as a

---

19. Ralph Cohen, "The Autobiography of a Critical Problem," Midwest Modern Language Association, Bloomington, IN, 4 November 1984.

20. However, it has become very clear by now, as more people become familiar with medical knowledge, that so-called lawful behavior of medicines and bodily substances such as hormones almost always show variations as they are observed in different people under different circumstances. The contemporary phenomenon of immunity to antibiotics does not predict in any fixed way who will be immune, but instead one waits to see when and how quickly the "lawful" action of antibiotics lose their scientific predictability. If some witches were accused on medical grounds, the predicted action of some cures used by some women was *not always* in effect, and the cures did harm, thus providing a pretext for accusing these women.

Kuhnian paradigm and as a basis for the study of language. Such study focuses on the action of language in a sense similar to the focus given by Isocrates and some of his contemporary Sophist colleagues: the study of language in use.[21]

III. Wittgenstein's Second Opinion

Students of Wittgenstein's work agree that one of Wittgenstein's career efforts was to make philosophy into a new kind of subject: one that describes but does not try to explain. His approach was to focus on the use of language in philosophy and in general. Hannah Fenichel Pitkin writes, "Wittgenstein's early work may be seen as the culmination of an ancient and well-established tradition which conceives of language as reference, as our way of referring to things in the world.[22] That tradition still predominates, and is deeply ingrained in our unexamined assumptions. In his later writings, Wittgenstein develops a powerful and original version of a different view, also with some antecedents in the tradition but much less influential."[23] Norman Malcolm writes that for Wittgenstein, "The aim of philosophical analysis, when considered at the highest level of abstraction, was to reveal the essential nature of *language,* of the sentences (propositions) we utter, of what it is to *say* something."[24] He then wonders why Wittgenstein's having pursued this goal was not more widely recognized: "One might imagine that philosophers would react with relief and joy to Wittgenstein's view that everything necessary for the treatment of philosophical problems 'lies before us,' that 'nothing is hidden.' But, in fact, this is not so. Wittgenstein's writings have not had a great impact on present-day philosophical work. Many

---

21. In this regard Kathleen E. Welch observes that generally, classical rhetoric had the "ability to account for all aspects of written and spoken discourse: producing both kinds of discourse, analyzing them, and manipulating and responding to the cultural and political contexts from which discourse must emerge. In each of these interrelated capacities, an emphasis on function is always present. The functionalism of language, a new awareness of its capacities, appears with the many teachers and schools of rhetoric." Kathleen E. Welch, *The Contemporary Reception of Classical Rhetoric: Appropriations of Ancient Discourse* (Hillsdale, NJ: Erlbaum, 1990), 114–115. Welch contrasts Isocrates to Plato, in that the former did not promote the permanent forms claimed by Plato to govern the use of language.

22. Hannah Fenichel Pitkin, *Wittgenstein and Justice* (Berkeley: U of California P, 1972), 24. It is noteworthy that the title of this early work, *Tractatus Logico-Philosophicus,* is in Latin. This gesture could not be fortuitous, as Wittgenstein's career development shows that he first regarded the sacral Latinate world of philosophy in the traditional way only later to become a principal voice of so-called ordinary language philosophy. The historical roles of Latin in academic subjects are discussed in chapter 9.

23. Pitkin, *Justice,* 24.

24. Norman Malcolm, *Wittgenstein: A Religious Point of View?* (Ithaca, NY: Cornell UP, 1994), 40. Italics in original.

individuals have been influenced—but the major tendency continues to be to formulate theories: theories about the nature of *meaning,* of *thinking,* of *representation,* of *belief* and so on."[25]

Wittgenstein's unorthodox presentational style—a series of loosely connected questions and subjunctive stipulations—seemed not to guide the majority of readers toward the view that a new philosophical gesture was being made; those who intuited something new could not identify it. However, the new item was not all that new. The materiality of language might be called an "old" answer that was rarely used to read Wittgenstein's prolific output. Yet every philosophical issue raised by Wittgenstein turns on language usages associated with nominalism—the use of category names as gestures rather than as rigid designators[26]—and materiality. Each of these uses is like one of the tools in his well-known toolbox.[27] In spite of the fact that the uses are in the box of "language games,"[28] they are radically different from one another; each is contingent on both the changing character of the games themselves and on the dependence of these games on the changing contexts of use.

Among commentators on Wittgenstein over the past several decades, there is some consensus as to how to identify his achievement. A recent one, given by Marie McGinn, is that "the Augustinian impulse to abstract language from its natural setting in our form of life, and think of it as a system of meaningful signs, has been repeatedly shown to produce over-simplification, idealization, spurious explanation, empty concepts and pictures which either make no contact with anything that actually happens, or which simply cannot be applied. . . . [Wittgenstein urged a] reorientation of our thought away from abstractions and generalizations towards a careful attention to what lies before our eyes, in the forms of our concrete practice of using language, . . . [T]he real lesson of Wittgenstein's remarks . . . is something that cannot be expressed in a generalization."[29] Readers of Wittgenstein agree that "natural setting" refers

---

25. Malcolm, *Wittgenstein,* 80.

26. This term is contributed by Saul Kripke, *Naming and Necessity* (Cambridge, MA: Harvard UP: 1980). His *use* of this term is different from the present use; yet the *sense* of the term is the same as his.

27. Ludwig Wittgenstein, *Philosophical Investigations,* trans. G. E. M. Anscombe (New York: Macmillan, 1958), 12.

28. This English term, which has retained a respectable degree of currency in Wittgenstein studies, is itself different from the German term used by Wittgenstein, *Sprachspiel.* As discussed below in this and the next chapter in reference to Derrida's "play of language" (which is closer to the English "game," although it is not rule bound), the German *Spiel* might be viewed as akin to the English "play" (as in drama)—a verbally scripted event usually tied to performance. Austin made this connection by introducing the performativity of language, also discussed below.

29. Marie McGinn, *Wittgenstein and the* Philosophical Investigations (New York: Routledge, 1997), 111. McGinn also writes, "It is only if we have already taken the step

to how conventions of speech and writing appear in every context in which people actually use language. They agree that philosophy has, traditionally, removed some of these usages and considered them (as if) in isolation. Some of the clearest instances of Wittgenstein's critique of the practices of isolation are found in the opening parts of the *Blue Book*,[30] the first organized text showing and using his revised approach to philosophy. Therein he raises the question of substantives by asking why people and philosophers ask for the meaning of words that pose no problems when used in everyday life: length, time, pencil, and banjo. He makes a considerable effort to show how it is not possible to give a fixed meaning for such nouns and why there is no need to do so.[31] On such grounds, McGinn and others[32] sum up Wittgenstein's work by saying that it provides a reorientation in which we study language by observing it in use as opposed to abstracting it from its context. When McGinn says that the real lesson of Wittgenstein's work is that it cannot be expressed as a generalization, she is referring to Wittgenstein's having avoided articulating a formal theory

---

of abstracting language from its use that we will be tempted to ignore the differences in our practice and go in search of the essence of assertions, questions, names, and so on" (60).

30. Ludwig Wittgenstein, *The Blue and Brown Books* (New York: Harper, 1965).

31. Alexander Luria, the Russian psychologist, asked a peasant, "Try to explain to me what a tree is." The peasant answered, "Why should I? Everyone knows what a tree is, they don't need me telling them." Quoted in Michael Cole, ed., *Cognitive Development: Its Cultural and Social Foundations,* trans. Martin Lopez-Morillas and Lynn Solatoroff (Cambridge: Harvard UP, 1976), 86. Daniel L. Everett's recent work on the Piraha language and culture in Brazil shows a similar situation with many more instances than shown by Luria. Speakers do not have words like "left" and "right" that give directions relative to the body; they give directions with reference to the environment: "upriver" and "downriver," "toward the jungle," "away from the jungle." Color words derive from the colors experienced in the jungle. Everett's point is that language uses, vocabulary, and grammar derive from an "immediate experience" orientation, that the specifics of the language is continuous with and embedded in the functioning of the total culture, a situation similar to that of Luria's experimental subjects. (*Language: The Cultural Tool,* (New York: Pantheon, 2012), 265. Luria considered the response of his informants a failure of intelligence. Everett insists, based on his having lived among the Piraha for two decades, that their intelligence is no different in capability from ours. Wittgenstein's body of work justifies the peasant's perspective on the ground that the peasant's language-in-use, his contexts for attending to and speaking about trees, had no need for the abstractions common in our Western, industrial societies. One might even wish to view members of such cultures as nominalists: Describing Everett's findings, John Colapinto writes, "Committed to an existence in which only observable experience is real, the Piraha do not think, or speak, in abstractions—and thus do not use color terms, quantifiers, numbers, or myths." John Colapinto, "The Interpreter," *New Yorker* 16 April 2007: 118–137, quotation on 130.

32. Including Norman Malcolm, Stanley Cavell, Hannah Pitkin, Ray Monk, Naomi Scheman, and A. J. Ayer.

of language, such as he tried to do in the *Tractatus Logico-Philosophicus* (1919; published 1922)—and whose approach to philosophy Wittgenstein renounced when he returned to its study after a ten-year hiatus.[33] Thus two salient points made by Wittgenstein's commentators are that the practice of philosophy—for centuries since Plato—has been misled by the abstraction of language from its contexts of actual use, and that no formal theory of language is either needed or possible.

It could be that his work has not been applied because it did not come in a declarative form. Its teaching has been that the history of Western philosophy is based on a confused sense of language. Plato's theory of abstract forms was accepted as true and then preserved for centuries, even while Aristotle's different approach was folded into formal thinking about language and knowledge. Wittgenstein's often-repeated citation of Augustine at the beginning of the *Brown Book* (1935) and of *Philosophical Investigations* (1953) cites a point (from Augustine's *Confessions*) eight hundred years after Plato, and fifteen hundred years before from Wittgenstein that represents (as McGinn suggests) a key yet distant enough location in the history of Western thought to show the inertia of this problematic view of language and of its acquired authoritative standing.[34]

Thinking of Wittgenstein's work as a principal source for the movement toward the materiality of language reduces the impression of the diffuseness of his total effort because each of his broad and different discussion points addresses what happens when language is in use. Issues that Wittgenstein articulates in the interrogative and subjunctive moods in his writings become eligible for a more affirmative articulation in addition to and not in replacement of those articulations already given. A second point is that the attitude of materiality encourages the association of Wittgenstein's work with that of several of his contemporaries with whom, except for (perhaps) J. L. Austin, he had no contact, and of whom he had little or no knowledge. Third, materiality is a useful means of drawing connections between his achievement and that of more contemporary commentators on language, whose work may provide an answer to Wittgenstein's own frustration at feeling misunderstood even by those who had an interest in

---

33. Norman Malcolm goes through Wittgenstein's second and major phase of writing and, point by point, shows that if "repudiation" is too strong a word to describe Wittgenstein's view of his earlier work, then Wittgenstein's criticism of it can be convincingly documented. Earlier, Stanley Cavell and Hannah Pitkin subscribed to this view of the development of Wittgenstein's philosophy. Norman Malcolm, *Nothing Is Hidden* (Cambridge, MA: Blackwell, 1986).

34. From the standpoint of this discussion, the fact that Augustine was one of the four Church fathers is also relevant, though this fact does not play a role in Wittgenstein's discussion. Augustine is a Church father partly because the Church requires that theory of language.

his work.[35] Finally, Wittgenstein's citation of Augustine's theory of childhood language acquisition as a point of contrast, also guides us, if indirectly, to an issue treated by Wittgenstein that has been taken up by few other philosophers,[36] but has been addressed by the psychologists Lev Vygotsky and Jean Piaget[37] with limited success. In the *Investigations,* the process of infantile and childhood language acquisition (mentioned several times but not extensively treated) is a suggestive strain in Wittgenstein's overall discussion.[38] It has been addressed

---

35. "People imitated his gestures, adopted his expressions, even wrote philosophy in a way that made use of his techniques—all, it seems, without understanding the point of his work." Ray Monk, *Ludwig Wittgenstein: The Duty of Genius* (New York: Penguin, 1991), 499.

36. One who took up this issue is George Herbert Mead, who speculated that children acquire language from having lived in conversational situations. George Herbert Mead, *Mind, Self, and Society from the Standpoint of a Social Behaviorist,* ed. Charles W. Morris (Chicago: U of Chicago P, 1962), 50, 225–226. Cavell writes, "one line of thought, or emphasis, that I began, or first made explicit in an extended form, in 1984, has become increasingly critical for me . . . It concerns the remarkable fact of the presence of the figure of the child in Wittgenstein's thoughts, announced with its opening quotation from Augustine. It is not a figure one expects to find in philosophical texts. . . . [M]y interest in ordinary language philosophy has from the beginning been tied up with the idea of the child as a necessary figure, however obscure and untheorized, for philosophy's stake (or repression of the stake) in the ordinary" (*Philosophical,* 167).

37. At about the same time Wittgenstein was writing the *Blue and Brown Books.* This issue is taken up in detail in chapter 5, as it is the starting point for a view of language consistent with the views given by members of a mixed-gender cohort of researchers.

38. Although there are several different approaches to children's acquisition of language, the prevailing attitude toward the study of language is the so-called wired-in perspective that emphasizes study of the brain on the one hand, and study of the abstract form of grammar on the other. Stanley Cavell considers Wittgenstein's approach to children's acquisition of language an important theme in his work, discussed in *The Claim of Reason: Wittgenstein, Skepticism, Morality, and Tragedy* (New York: Oxford UP, 1979), 171–174. However, none in the field of philosophy have pursued this theme, although psychologists' approaches to it are discussed in chapter 5 (see also notes 31 and 32, above). The empirical strategy of studying language-in-use in children is a minority view, even though several psychologists are taking this path. Although Chomsky dates his approach to Descartes, McGinn suggests that the wired-in view is attributable to Augustine: "Within Augustine's account of how we come to acquire language, there is contained the idea of a completed, or structured, human consciousness inside the child, which exists prior to the child's acquisition of language. According to Augustine, the child acquires language in order to express the thoughts and wishes that are already there inside it" (*Wittgenstein,* 51). It might be fair to say that Chomsky does not care about "thoughts and wishes that are already there inside" people's minds; he cares mainly about the principles of how such material is grammatically structured and formed. Other reasons for the prevalence of the innatist view, which has been expanded by Steven Pinker to other zones of mental activity, are social and political, and are discussed at the beginning of chapter 5.

with greater success by contemporary psychologists[39] who, like Vygotsky and Piaget, can be understood to be following Wittgenstein's advice to "look and see." Nevertheless, there is today still no widely accepted explanatory description (no accepted theory) of the infantile acquisition of language. In modern philosophy that does pay attention to the use of language, reference is seldom made to the relatively long period of time each person spends in the presence of involved parents, family, and other caregivers in the process of acquiring and cultivating language.[40] Among philosophers, Stanley Cavell discussed how language acquisition needed to be included in the general discussion of language.[41] However, as observed by Malcolm, philosophy has not moved in this direction, whereas psychologists have worked, more or less according to the academic style, in disciplinary isolation gathering data on how language develops in individual children with an eye toward generalizing about childhood. A partial explanation of the separation of "look and see" study of language from the language philosophy practiced by Wittgenstein is suggested by the fact that Wittgenstein's main body of work came about as a reaction against his own earlier work: his work became an issue in the discipline of analytic philosophy more than in the wider circles of intellectual and cultural life.

It is striking how, in one individual, there can have taken place such an important change of view.[42] World War I produced many changes in Western societies, and some of these are reflected in works such as Freud's *Beyond the Plea-*

---

39. Lois Bloom, Catherine Snow, Elinor Ochs, Bambi Shieffelin, Michael Tomasello, Elizabeth Bates, and Eve Clark are treated in chapter 5.

40. The trait of overlooking or dismissing the common process of child development was characteristic of those seeking to formulate an origin of language, as discussed in chapter 2.

41. His thoughts first appeared in his 1962 dissertation, "The Claim of Rationality," cited frequently by Hannah Pitkin, and published subsequently in 1979 as *The Claim of Reason.* Cavell, himself an unusual member of the philosophical community, integrated his discussions of Wittgenstein with his several other interests, which include American transcendentalism, Hollywood, and Shakespeare, to name a few. Cavell also integrates the history of his own development in many of his works, trying to tease out different strains of thought, and showing when and how they appeared.

42. Yet it is common among those now considered to have achieved a great deal. There has been debate recently about how Freud changed his view of infantile trauma from "things that happened" to "things that were imagined," and his view that free association was more effective than hypnosis to uncover unconscious mentation. Evelyn Torton Beck's *Kafka and the Yiddish Theater* (Madison: U of Wisconsin P, 1971) described how Kafka changed from a conventional writer to *Kafka* in 1912; in 1916 James Joyce changed from a Hero to a Daedalus. As discussed by Erik Erikson in many attempts to show how childhood mores emerge in people's adult social lives, biographical factors are continuous with cultural and collective factors. When individuals change radically, it is useful to identify how childhood cultural values found the chance to emerge in new cultural and biographical circumstances. This procedure helps to reduce the temptation

sure Principle (1920)—which speculated on the existence of a "death instinct," and in literary works such as T. S. Eliot's "The Waste Land" and James Joyce's *Ulysses,* both published in 1922, the same year of publication as the *Tractatus.* Wittgenstein's positivist treatise, unlike the literary ones whose moods were bleak, was affirmative and confident, and it was the culmination of his work with Bertrand Russell; it was Wittgenstein's best effort at thinking governed by mathematical ideals and the quest for a standard of purity in thought.[43] But just after this work appeared, Wittgenstein withdrew from philosophy and became a primary school teacher for ten years, until 1929.[44] He then returned to philosophy with a series of formulations, questions, and issues that most judge to be a critique of his earlier work, representing a revolutionary change in his understanding of philosophy, language, and the role of explanation in the study of nature. This style of work lasted to the end of his life.

If the later period began about 1929 or 1930, it is close to when G. H. Mead and L. S. Vygotsky[45] (each) formulated a view of the social basis of language; John Dewey, a pragmatist, described a basis for recognizing the social basis of knowledge and education. These figures, although they did not draw boundaries around their own work, were located by the academy in specific disciplines, where, more or less, they stayed. As a result, disciplinary constraints helped to inhibit interaction among those in different countries and different subject matters. Wittgenstein was impatient with academic life and with the failure of others to be more responsive or to see the sense in what he proposed.[46] He continued to produce new formulations, but he remained obscure and his major work was not published until after he died in 1951. In spite of its publication and the continuing currency of his reputation in professional contexts, the effect on intellectual life and on society of his many works was, and still is, small, compared, for example, to the effects of Freud's and Marx's works.

---

to attribute such changes to "genius" or other transcendental factors. The concept of genius has itself been challenged by Christine Battersby, *Gender and Genius: Toward a Feminist Aesthetics* (Bloomington: Indiana UP, 1988); as has the idea of scalar intelligence by Stephen Jay Gould, *The Mismeasure of Man* (New York: Norton, 1981). Some of these challenges are considered in chapter 10.

43. Norman Malcolm's *Nothing Is Hidden* details fifteen features of the *Tractatus* that are revoked and revised in the *Philosophical Investigations* (viii). This study—as well as those by Cavell, Pitkin, McGinn, and others—shows a consensus for recognizing this change in Wittgenstein's work.

44. One of his several non-philosophical enterprises, the others being engineering, architecture, and music. See Monk, *Ludwig Wittgenstein,* on music (13–14), engineering (33–34), and architecture (235–238).

45. Mead, *Mind;* L. S. Vygotsky, *Mind in Society,* ed. Michael Cole, Vera John-Steiner, Sylvia Scribner, and Ellen Souberman (Cambridge, MA: Harvard UP, 1978).

46. Monk, *Ludwig Wittgenstein,* 496–498.

Four key expressions are germane to reading the later Wittgenstein as pursuing the understanding of language as a generically differentiated material entity: the *Sprachspiel* (Anscombe's translation, "language game," is discussed shortly), the form of life, the family resemblance, and the substitution of description for explanation as the fundamental mode of philosophical work.[47] Taken together, these also add up to changes in pedagogical stances and attitudes and form the basis of a fundamentally different conceptual (Kuhnian) paradigm to guide and characterize the study of language. They also amount to a warning against the search for palpable inner or subjective entities that are reflected by language. The category of thought was removed from what was considered separate from language, and even if the word "thought" was used, it was to be understood, according to Wittgenstein, as a language use and not, in some deeper sense, a reference to events in a physically locatable and nonlinguistic mind.[48] If this is so, and if language is then understood as Wittgenstein understood it, it would not be surprising, finally, that the uptake of this view would be slow: it took about two hundred years from the time of Copernicus for geocentrism to become the prevailing view, and in that case, there were measurable parameters providing data. Darwin's work of one hundred fifty years ago still meets with resistance. If the scale of change implied by Wittgenstein's work is taken to be comparable to the scale of change initiated by figures like Copernicus and Darwin, one might well have expected this level of inertia in the uptake of the new idea. Furthermore, the subject matters presented by Copernicus and Darwin both involved revisions in the use of language. But given the history of the study and use of language in universities over the past eight centuries, any strong revision of the identity and function of language would be strongly resisted, just as nominalism was resisted and censored in order to promote the belief in a holy, spiritual, and incorporeal conception of language.

III-1. Sprachspiel[49]

The *Sprachspiel*'s English life as "language game" may be somewhat misleading. In German *Spiel* can mean "play" or "game" but in English, "game" cannot mean "play" in the sense that at the theater, we do not see a game, which we do see in a large stadium that seats tens of thousands of people. Although "game" and

47. Section 124 of *Philosophical Investigations* is often cited in this discussion: "Philosophy may in no way interfere with the actual use of language; it can in the end only describe it. For it cannot give it any foundation either. It leaves everything as it is."

48. The identity of thought and language is another philosophical issue often considered in isolation. This issue is central in the consideration of Whorf's work, below, and in the matter of understanding the diversity of languages, discussed in chapter 4.

49. The convention is to print the word in italics because it is in a so-called foreign language. But suppose I want to say that I am admitting *Sprachspiel* to English and

"play" both imply a ludic atmosphere, the theatrical sense of *Spiel* is partially ludic, partially aesthetic, partially referential, and partially serious. Games, however, require a more punctilious observance of rules. When Wittgenstein likens the *Sprachspiel* to a "form of life" (*Lebensform*),[50] the emphasis is on its living existence: a living person performing an activity (*Taetigkeit*)—acting, doing—in the presence of other living persons. In *On Certainty,* Wittgenstein writes, "[I]t is our *acting* [*Handeln*], which lies at the bottom of the language-game."[51] In this case (in contrast to the case of *Spiel* and game) the German and English words have, more or less, a similar range of usages: acting as behaving, performing, and gesturing—each of which has both theatrical and non-theatrical reference. *Handeln* might be used as a synonym, in German, for *Schauspielen,* a term that looks (sounds and is?) somewhat like *Sprachspielen.*[52] Informal speaking might also be said to have the contingency of child's play, as well as its experimental feel. However, plays and speech also are orderly, if not rigidly so. Their order is like the order of living things: there are some accidental elements, but the whole organism or script follows a pattern and a schedule of development that is similar from instance to instance—as with different species of trees or canines, or as with the combination of individual differences and similarities in human faces as we look from person to person. The term *Sprachspiel* is inclusive; every instance of language use falls into one form of *Sprachspiel* or another. The material dimension of this usage is the reference to life, the reminder that language always appears as an aspect of the behaviors (actions, gestures, conventions) of living people, and never without them.[53] Some might say that the *Sprachspiel*

---

leave it in roman type? May I do that? May I treat Sprachspiel as a new English word that refers to things that "language game" cannot refer to? What then? Countless other words have undergone the same fate: substitute words just don't do what original words do. The originals then enter the other language. Wittgenstein writes, "I shall also call the whole, consisting of language and the actions into which it is woven, the 'language-game.'" (*Philosophical Investigations,* section 7). One can see that language with action is not necessarily a game, but could also be called a language play or a language scene. Many rituals fit this description, and some behaviors that are not formal rituals also fit it, such as family dinner. A list of ordinary activities in section 23 shows even more clearly how the word "game" is not the best description.

50. "Here the term 'language-*game*' is meant to bring into prominence the fact that *speaking* of language is part of an activity, or of a form of life" (*Philosophical Investigations,* section 23). This has a family resemblance (some might call it a metaphorical connection) to the life forms referred to in the "play" *Star Trek,* although this life form is simpler and different from the ones referred to by Wittgenstein.

51. Ludwig Wittgenstein, *On Certainty,* ed. G. E. M. Anscombe and G. H. von Wright, trans. Denis Paul and G. E. M Anscombe (New York: Harper, 1972), section 204.

52. One easily sees the close connection between this vocabulary and Austin's "speech acts," discussed section 4 of this chapter.

53. Cavell cites and discusses one of his early lectures on Wittgenstein and writes, "But another motive for [Wittgenstein's] stressing the primitive is to prepare the idea of

identifies members of the human species; yet other living things such as simians, bees, marine mammals, or birds show behaviors that would also be describable as *Sprachspiele*. If the total behavioral interaction between and among individual members of a species is taken as the context for study, the term could apply to non-humans also. This would change the reference of language, removing it from its place of privilege as a sign of distinct and transcendent human spirituality.[54]

Also in section 23 of *Philosophical Investigations,* Wittgenstein gives a list of examples of what would count as *Sprachspiele.* The list includes such ritualized activities as giving orders, reporting an event, forming a hypothesis, and making up a story, as well as less elaborate but equally ritualized activities such as asking, thanking, cursing, greeting, and praying. The list raises the question of the extent to which any use of language can be described as conventional. Each activity listed by Wittgenstein has a conventional character that changes in different circumstances within each culture and from culture to culture. But regardless of which language is involved, if you use the term *Sprachspiel* it implies a ritual or conventional character to, at least, the occasions of the uses of language. In television soap operas, almost all uses of language can be characterized as conventional, or clichéd (and thus learned by having been heard hundreds of times in a variety of circumstances). Nevertheless, it is clear that given the list of conventions in section 23, there is plenty of room for individual initiative in which words, sentences, moods, and neologisms may enter in and produce what would reasonably be called new language or even a new (if only slightly altered) *Sprachspiel.* And in addition to the conventional usages listed by Wittgenstein, an indefinite number of activities we call conversations can be added, as these *Sprachspiele* will vary according to which people are speaking, as well as according to the wider contexts of their conversational exchanges. Even if the open-ended character of conversations is taken into consideration in such rituals as the teacher-student conference,[55] the speech exchanges still follow

---

our words as [lived,] of our language as containing what Wittgenstein will shortly call, in one of his most familiar turns of thought, 'forms of life'" (*Philosophical*), 158.

54. Any living thing could be said to have a spirit—a belief held by those who assume the immanence as well as the transcendence of God. This belief might also remove the axiom of human transcendental uniqueness.

55. Laurel Johnson Black, *Between Talk and Teaching: Reconsidering the Writing Conference* (Logan: Utah State UP, 1998), presents a wide professional context for these conventional and multifarious conversations. Deborah Tannen's *Conversational Style: Analyzing Talk among Friends* (Norwood, NJ: Ablex, 1984), belongs in this category. She was perhaps preceded by sociolinguists William Labov and Erving Goffman, as well as by many researchers in folklore. Studies have also been done on medical and legal conversations, whose actions are hidden by so-called confidentiality protections. By keeping these related efforts in different departments separate, universities have reduced the possibility of principles such as Wittgenstein's drawing different sorts of research together toward a comprehensive view of how language works.

certain conventions as well as grammatical rules and semantic customs. In this way, the term *Sprachspiel* calls attention to the dramatistic use of all language in regard to its possible conventionality, its art, its ludic potential, and its necessary association with interpersonal and social relations. In fact, only a tiny minority (certain screams or other interjections, perhaps[56]) of the uses of language is not describable in these terms.

III-2. LIFE FORMS[57]

The "life forms" that Wittgenstein suggests as a provisional synonym for *Sprachspiele* may be also described as social forms. But in reading Wittgenstein's commentaries in English, one is only rarely inclined to think of society or of collective practices in particular cultures. His word is actually "life forms" and not social forms, yet how else does one read this term "life forms"? Again, *Lebensformen* in German has a somewhat different connotation than "life forms" has in English: it implies more decisively "living people," as the term *Lebensraum* meaning "life space" implies "space, cultural as much as physical, for people to live." The term also suggests that language use (not language alone) is itself alive, having both the autonomy of living things—a life of its own, so to speak—and their connectedness to the earth and their dependence on the ecosphere at once.[58] As a life form, the language folds into the users, and, although they are not identifiable as an essential source of life, language behaviors are viewable as a part of the collection of movements that give the overall sense that something is living. Understood to be something already alive, language uses can only be stopped and inspected with the same caveats that human lives can be stopped and treated surgically. Elaborate measures are taken in cardiac surgery, for example, to preserve a path back from the heart stoppage to the usual situation of living: the heart beating inside a closed chest. The stopping of language for its inspection in this radical way would be, if the term "life forms" were taken seriously, as invasive as surgery—although, like surgery, it works in many cases. However, the analysis of language is not usually as urgent as surgery, although one could think of situations in which it is: negotiations in which large-scale confrontations (wars, strikes, or riots, for example) need to be avoided. Such situations usually

---

56. In performances of Eve Ensler's *The Vagina Monologues,* there is a review of different sounds of female orgasm. If you have seen the performance more than once, it becomes clear that even the screams and interjections are conventional—sounds held in common by an indefinite number of women. Perhaps it is fair to say that any human sound given in social circumstances is a kind of *Sprachspiel.*

57. "And to imagine a language means to imagine a form of life" (*Philosophical Investigations,* section 19). "Here the term 'language-*game*' is meant to bring into prominence the fact that the *speaking* of language is part of an activity, or of a form of life" (section 23).

58. "Every sign *by itself* seems dead. *What* gives it life?—In use it is *alive.* Is life breathed into it there?—Or is the *use* its life?" (*Philosophical Investigations, section 432*).

do have a way of preserving a path back to pre-crisis conditions: the language is pressed into agreements that save face for all the participants. Now, however, analysts think little of stopping language use for a lengthy examination: a great deal of literary criticism has assumed the right to remove the literary works from their living contexts for analysis, unmindful that this removal places the work in a new living context. Since written texts have been used, readers have promoted the illusion that the texts themselves have stopped the language, thus making them eligible for dissection (as if they were dead). This illusion should be easily discredited by the fact that the analyst is a living person who is socially derived, constituted, and located, and who is expecting to present any analysis back to community and society. However, this fact is also suppressed, and the analysis then achieves the dead status of the text as an object—rather than the living thing it is—as soon as it is taken up by others.[59] This assumption of the dead text—that is, its fluent separability, removability, and its abstractability from living people—is a foundation of the comprehensive sense of literacy that has governed Western civilization. Yet in practice it is illusory and, in many cases, maliciously mendacious.[60]

III-3. FAMILY RESEMBLANCE

Although Wittgenstein did not emphasize this point himself, his movement toward recognizing the living status of language is enough to suggest how deep a change is implied if his formulations are recognized as descriptions of how language works.[61] Thinking of language as living extends the processes of comparison of language experience into the orderliness of how living things behave. It seems plausible, consequently, to think of the term "family resemblance"[62]

---

59. *In Wittgenstein's Ladder,* Marjorie Perloff tries to use Wittgenstein's sense of language to counteract this approach to literature. Cavell's discussion of Derrida's response to Austin reflects that texts might be considered actions comparable to wills: behaviors (language acts) meant to act on survivors and materializing the continuity of relationships (*Philosophical,* 65).

60. I am referring here to the sacralization of texts, discussed in chapters 1 and 7. If they are dead objects, they can belong to or be owned by, first, authors, and then religious institutions. Such ownership of texts is illusory, as long as people can read them and assimilate them. However, this illusion becomes malicious, for example, when different readings are then censored by authoritative figures and institutions, and legitimate uses of these texts are suppressed. Censorship keeps texts at once sacred and dead, alive only for their owners.

61. Wittgenstein seemed to believe that the consequence of his revision of philosophy had mainly to do with philosophy. I cannot say that with certainty. However, the present study aims to emphasize how every specific use of language, every "*Sprachspiel,*" with revisions pursuant to discussions in the next chapters, is affected by his approach to language.

62. "[W]e see a complicated network of similarities [found in different *Spiele*— translated as "games"] overlapping and criss-crossing: sometimes overall similarities,

as emerging from the term "life form." Here, again, the reference is indirect and identifiable as figurative. Yet the thought that different language conventions and usages are related to one another the way family members are related implies a way to understand the now-rejected concept of a common essence that links similar *Sprachspiele* to one another: the family resemblance in people refers to more than appearance. It refers also to relatedness, which likely involves genetic factors that can be identified substantively in laboratories. But in the overwhelming majority of cases in which family relatedness matters, there is no need to consult a laboratory to confirm it. A similar argument emerges from Wittgenstein in his discussions of mental states and private language: one may be able to find physical correlatives for mental states, but there would be no need to look for them, as their life is actually between and among the linguistic exchanges of living people: brain activity is not a factor while the language is in use, except, perhaps, in extreme circumstances when individuals lose control of themselves. And if physical correlatives were found for mental states, could they still be considered *mental* states?[63] Wouldn't the category of mental be put out of play permanently? Or would it just resume its present role as an element of various *Sprachspiele*? In most of the social circumstances we will encounter in our lifetimes, the issue is what to say that will fit into and enhance our speech

---

sometimes similarities of detail [section 67]. I can think of no better expression to characterize these similarities than 'family resemblances'; for the various resemblances between members of a family: build, feature, colour of eyes, gait, temperament, etc. etc. overlap and criss-cross in the same way.—And I shall say: 'games' form a family." (*Philosophical Investigations,* sections 66–67). But consider, again, the difference between that last sentence and "'Spiele' or perhaps 'playings' form a family."

63. Cavell (in a citation from his early lectures) asks in regard to this issue, "When would saying 'There's a mechanism inside' be informative? . . . [T]he mechanism of connection is here not supplying *understanding.*" (*Philosophical,* 150). Wittgenstein writes, "The feeling of confidence. How is this manifested in behaviour? [section 580]. An 'inner process' stands in need of outward criteria." (*Philosophical Investigations,* sections 579–580). This is one of many formulations that show not the absence of mental states, but the uselessness of stipulating them as things that exist and about which more can be discovered. As Freud proceeded with dreams, only the verbal presentation is, so to speak, in play as something that matters. The physiology of dreaming, while not irrelevant, has a different locus of application—health and survival. The report of dreams has a social locus. "When a dream is interpreted we might say that it is fitted into a context in which it ceases to be puzzling. In a sense the dreamer re-dreams his dream in surroundings such that its aspect changes." Ludwig Wittgenstein, *Lectures and Conversations on Aesthetics, Psychology, and Religious Belief,* ed. Cyril Barrett (Berkeley: U of California P, 1967), 45. That is to say, just as Freud practiced, the subsequent social and verbal circumstances remove the puzzle. The dream now looks like something other than it seemed when it was dreamed. And there is no search for the inner mental state. In any event, *there is no way to say that a wish preceded and caused* the dream. That Freud stipulated precedence and causation testifies to his belief in origin as essence.

or language situation at that time.[64] Referring to mental states counts as some of the things people want to say, but being certain that those references are utterly true—as pieces of correspondence creating truth—is not needed.[65]

At the same time, the family resemblances of different individual *Sprachspiele* or of language conventions are the grounds for variations that produce the effect of language creativity.[66] Each variation of language tropes, gestures, and movements that are already familiar may produce new resemblances that are unfamiliar yet have a family resemblance whose continuity with the earlier usage authorizes the new usage and provides a moment of insight, surprise, comprehension, or release. Puns are a common instance of such action, but there are many complex verbal moves that have similar effects and seem to give "insight." The weight of Wittgenstein's discussion of the family resemblances of different *Sprachspiele* is to claim that no further form of the explanation of belonging to the same category is either needed or possible.[67] The considerations of similarity and difference always matter in the judgment of verbal constructions. The provisional reference of terms does not require reification beyond the commonly accepted senses, which change and are clarified during

---

64. Austin, in his "theory of performatives," tried to change the focus of language analysis from the search for truth to "felicity": whether different uses of language work in a social sense (Cavell, *Philosophical,* 50–51). It is just in this area, where several male philosophers have proceeded toward a threshold of understanding without actually crossing it. The missing element is the social alertness that has been systematically suppressed in the Western intellectual tradition. Since this is a major point of this book, it is addressed in the next chapters in a variety of contexts.

65. "Now, what about the language which describes my inner experiences and which only I myself can understand? *How* do I use words to stand for my sensations?—As we ordinarily do? Then are my words for sensations tied up with my natural expressions of sensation? In that case my language is not a 'private' one" (*Philosophical Investigations,* section 256). The point is this: to use the word "language" means that it is never private. Also, there is always a socially perceptible gesture—which could be language—for, for example, pain; and that is how pain is identified by others.

66. This factor plays a decisive role in Chomsky's starting postulates. Chomsky omits the principal factor that gives the impression of creativity: previously learned usages, eligible for arbitrary variation, are applied to situations that may well be unprecedented, and in one sense, are unprecedented. But what is creative about adapting existing language gestures to new situations? What else can any speaker do? The adaptation may or may not be creative.

67. Chapter 4 reflects on Derrida's "Law of Genre" and *Monolingualism of the Other,* both of which suggest that groups and genres entail *participation* of individual members *without belonging:* that is, there is no necessary linkage of an element viewed as a member of the genre or class or items, a point similar to Wittgenstein's view of family resemblances. Jacques Derrida, "The Law of Genre," trans. Avital Ronell, *Critical Inquiry* 7.1 (Autumn 1980): 55–81; *Monolingualism of the Other, or The Prosthesis of Origin,* trans. Patrick Mensah (Stanford, CA: Stanford UP, 1998).

conversational exchanges, readings, and interpretations. If the conversations are not curtailed, interrupted, or overruled by violent behaviors—that is, the abandonment of language use altogether[68]—they may continue indefinitely toward judgments of similarity and difference, and the creativity of use then gains performative status: the new formulations are the agreements—the contracts of various applications—between parties, and the temporary stabilization of relationships in a new situation.

III-4. DESCRIPTION INSTEAD OF EXPLANATION[69]

When new language uses are understood to be gesturing and acting socially, the effects of the differences between description and explanation are clearer: they are different social actions. Explanation is a response to an inquiry, to an organized search for answers, to an attempt to get to the bottom of things, to first causes. Description is part of a language activity of sharing views. It is possible and appropriate to seek explanations as well as descriptions in benign, stable circumstances. Yet the history of formal inquiry (the search for knowledge, or truth for its own sake), which includes the humanities and the sciences, shows that these scholarly efforts seek ultimate answers: the term *explanation,* Wittgenstein's work suggests,[70] carries the connotation of final explanation—the origin of the universe, the reasons for mortality, the suffering of the innocent,[71] and so

---

68. This issue is considered in chapter 11.

69. "And we may not advance any kind of theory. There must not be anything hypothetical in our considerations. We must do away with all *explanation,* and description alone must take its place. . . . [philosophical] problems are solved, not by giving new information, but by arranging what we have always known. Philosophy is a battle against the bewitchment of our intelligence by means of language" (*Philosophical Investigations,* section 109).

70. This principle is particularly germane with regard to understanding how language works: "Philosophy may in no way interfere with the actual use of language; it can in the end only describe it. For it cannot give any foundation either. It leaves everything as it is" (*Philosophical Investigations,* section 124). "Grammar does not tell us how language must be constructed in order to fulfill its purpose, in order to have such-and-such an effect on human beings. It only describes and in no way explains the use of signs" (*Philosophical Investigations,* section 496). Chomsky took this principle in the direction opposite to what appears in this statement: his work identifies grammar as the ground on which to search for an *explanation* of language, especially of the rapid acquisition of language in infancy.

71. Susan Neiman's philosophical study, *Evil in Modern Thought: An Alternative History of Philosophy* (Princeton, NJ: Princeton UP, 2003), studies how, in the West, both natural disasters and social disasters, in each of which innocent people die and are harmed, can be placed in the category "evil." If, however, we do not automatically assume a referent for evil, we are in a better position to distinguish among the different kinds of adversity we normally face. The use of the word "evil" deposits into our discourse a

on. It is commonly held that biologists seek the "secret" of life, and physicists the "fundamental" particles, the beginning and end of the universe. Wittgenstein's critique of explanation casts doubt on the practice of asking such questions; he puts the purpose of such inquiries into question.

Although some have viewed Wittgenstein respectfully as a skeptic like Hume and Berkeley, there may be more affirmative ways to characterize his approach to philosophy.[72] His sense of language is itself affirmative, in that every part of it matters when we ask questions of either experience or language or both. Wittgenstein departs from the tradition of philosophy he first tried to accept because the claims of language became too great. In his own judgment, the living action of language overwhelmed his attempt to bring clarity to the view of language most people consider normal—the correspondence or propositional view that places reference at the foundation of language: "if language functions ideally, it is transparent."[73] As detailed by Malcolm, Wittgenstein rejected this view; he understood that neither he nor anyone else can see through language. Language is there, acting on him and others at once: its own claims had to be recognized; but unlike Heidegger, Wittgenstein did not attribute a constraining function or

genre name that refers to the transcendental presupposition of devils and demons and other imaginary forces that some will blame for the adversity.

72. There are grounds for reducing the use of the term "skeptic" in formal discussions. It implies something on the order of doubting universal truths. It is more fruitful to think of cautious figures, such as Hume, as simply modest and comprehending of what can and cannot be believed. Cavell, citing his previous lecture, writes, "Wittgenstein's answer [to the 'philosophical search for a connection between language and mind'] . . . has something to do with what I understand as skepticism, and what I might call skeptical attempts to defeat skepticism" (*Philosophical*, 152; italics in original). Saul A. Kripke writes, "A sceptical problem is posed, and a sceptical solution to that problem is given. The solution turns on the idea that each person who claims to be following a rule can be checked by others. Others in the community can check whether the putative rule follower is or is not giving particular responses that they endorse, that agree with their own." Saul A. Kripke, *Wittgenstein on Rules and Private Language: An Elementary Exposition* (Cambridge, MA: Harvard UP, 1982), 101. Kripke's answer takes Wittgenstein's work in this more affirmative direction, but he does not use some of the novel features of Wittgenstein's discourse; he advances Wittgenstein's project somewhat, but not as much as the ethnographers and sociolinguists who study living, speaking people: groups and different people in speech situations in various zones in society. These researchers use the principles proposed by Wittgenstein.

73. Or, writes Cavell, "the view of language as the transferring of a something called a meaning from one place to another (communicating) place" (*Philosophical*, 60). Wittgenstein announces this problem in the very first section of *Philosophical Investigations*, where Augustine's description is cited. Wittgenstein then comments, "[T]he individual words in language name objects—sentences are combinations of such names.—In this picture of language we find the roots of the following idea: Every word has a meaning. This meaning is correlated with the word. It is the object for which the word stands" (section 1).

autonomy to the claims of language.[74] His achievement has been to reflect on the references of language while continuing to recognize its living status, its capacity to change its value and function while it is being used. His discourse, still distinctive among formal academic writings in the humanities, enacts a stance of linguistic self-reflection, self-inclusion, self-critique, and analytical effort at once. Wittgenstein developed a unified double perspective which held language use to be *simultaneously referential and gestural.* In order to recognize the claims of this perspective on any effort at understanding, Wittgenstein used his characteristic techniques of presentation, of discussion, and of learning and teaching—which I identify as a materialist sense of language. This description puts Wittgenstein's writing in "a context in which it ceases to be puzzling."

III-5. ORDINARY LANGUAGE: ACCESS IN PLAIN SIGHT

This ordinary language philosopher uses ordinary language most of the time.[75] Indirectly, Wittgenstein establishes the authority of ordinary language by ask-

---

74. "The results of philosophy are the uncovering of one or another piece of plain nonsense and of bumps that the understanding has got by running its head up against the limits of language" (*Philosophical Investigations,* section 119). These "bumps" are the same as "entanglement in our rules" (section 125). The limits are not identifiable, and the rules permit the ascribing of fixed references to received abstractions—Platonic realism that is supported by ordinary grammar. Wittgenstein did not see grammar as a limit, but tried to say how the belief in its supremacy led to confusion.

Some may wish to include Heidegger's "way to language" as a contribution to the materiality of language, but Heidegger does not belong to this group of thinkers, even as some of his formulations seem to be related. Heidegger asked if "the way to language" is "the longest road" as well as "a way lined with obstacles that come from language itself." To study speech using speech involves us in a "web of relations in which we ourselves are included." Heidegger, unlike the materialists considered in this study, treats this circumstance as a limit, an impediment to understanding. He writes, "A web compresses, narrows, and obstructs the straight clear view inside its mesh. At the same time, however, the web . . . is the proper matter of language." He views language as a necessary constraint that obstructs understanding. Furthermore, he says, "Language . . . is the foundation of human being." Built into Heidegger's perspective is a declaration of necessary frustration of understanding of language. This is not the case for the materialists discussed in this book. Martin Heidegger, *On the Way to Language,* trans. Peter D. Hertz (New York: Harper and Row, 1971), 112–113.

75. An interesting feature of ordinary language philosophy is that it may be read as vernacular philosophy. Using the term "vernacular" relates this sort of philosophical language to the contrast between the sacred language and the oppositional recursive efforts in medieval times to use the vernacular to get access to important texts. This issue is considered in chapter 9 in regard to the action of language hegemony. Most of Wittgenstein's writing is non-jargonized prose that is accessible by ordinary speakers of vernaculars. There are regular forays into logic and reflections on logic and mathematics (owing to its logical character) that do not seem like ordinary language. Yet these, such as his long reflection on the use of "plus" in mathematics, also seem available to reflective people, even if they are not experts in logic and mathematics.

ing, supposing, and imagining: using the subjunctive mode, which stipulates a different sort of audience than one expected by someone writing or speaking in the traditional declarative mode. This is one of the major contrasts between the *Tractatus* and his subsequent work. He did not say that he is looking for a new readership; but his use of language suggests such a search. Some philosophers responded with enthusiasm, and others critically, as may be expected. But his use of conversational modes suggests that his work was addressed to others who were similarly inclined—a group that includes philosophers interacting with one another informally. But it might also include those eligible to be educated but now excluded. Moreover, and most likely, his address is to others in his own community suffering from the burden of abstract language.[76] He wrote,

> It is the business of philosophy . . . to make it possible for us to get a clear view of the state of mathematics that troubles us: the state of affairs *before* the contradiction is resolved. . . . The fundamental fact here is that we lay down rules, a technique, for a game [*Spiel*], and that then when we follow the rules, things do not turn out as we had assumed. That we are therefore as it were entangled in our own rules. This entanglement in our rules is what we want to understand. . . . The civil [*bürgerliche*[77]] status of a contradiction, or its status in civil life [*der bürgerlichen Welt*]: there is the philosophical problem.[78]

Wittgenstein's move to "ordinary" language (after *Tractatus*) is partly a new statement of the responsibility of the academic discipline of philosophy. But this is also a new kind of statement and a new kind of philosophy: it is a change in the genre of doing philosophy or in philosophical writing. The German term of interest here is *bürgerliche,* translated as "civil." This term has a family resemblance to the French *bourgeois,* which has made its way into English without translation. In both French and German, the term has the connotation of ordinary in addition to meaning civil or civic. In Wittgenstein's writing, it

---

76. An example of which could be Husserl, with whom Wittgenstein did not appear to have any contact. Monk, writing on Husserl, gives an example (*Ludwig,* 286). According to Monk, Wittgenstein's earlier work showed what seemed to Moritz Schlick and the Vienna Circle of positivists a "pseudo-Kantian strain." He referred to the "synthetic *a priori*" as practiced in phenomenology as making up words with which he "cannot associate a thought." But he also observed that arithmetic equations might count as a "synthetic *a priori*." The equations would *show* what is meant by "synthetic *a priori*" to begin with. These thoughts seem to illustrate the phrase in the passage cited in note 73, above, and in the text below: entanglement in our own rules.

77. Here is another translation difficulty. The French *bourgeois* has a pejorative connotation in English. The German term used is less pejorative, but it should not be taken to mean "urban" or "mercantile."

78. *Philosophical Investigations,* section 125.

is plausible to consider this connotation, as this group of academics (ordinary language philosophers) in Cambridge came to be identified with it. Relating what is ordinary to the civil world renders the heavier term, civilization, more a part of the ordinary world; whereas in Freud, *Kultur*, when translated into the English "civilization," seems to be referring to a glorious complex edifice to be identified with master builders and great minds,[79] something more often than not made possible by war and conquest rather than by the independent efforts of just, constructive, and creative societies.[80] The role of the philosopher in the Athens of Plato, someone appreciated by Wittgenstein,[81] is being reread, interpreted, and changed by Wittgenstein—away, it seems, from philosopher-kings and guardians, and reoriented toward teaching the total public about something each member of the public is connected to in a serious way: gaining access to language. Wittgenstein continues the foregoing discussion:

126. Philosophy simply puts everything before us, and neither explains nor deduces anything.—Since everything lies open to view there is nothing to explain. For what is hidden, for example, is of no interest to us.

One might also give the name "philosophy" to what is possible *before* all new discoveries and inventions.

127. The work of the philosopher consists in assembling reminders for a particular purpose.

128. If one tried to advance *theses* in philosophy, it would never be possible to debate them, because everyone would agree to them.[82]

---

79. But in German it refers more to something like "civilized life," or life that has taken on social and physical organization that includes *cultivation* of people through education.

80. Cavell sees Wittgenstein as being opposed to deconstructionist styles and values, which, Cavell describes, "stretches from a horror of the human, to a disgust with bourgeois life, to a certain condescension toward the popular" Yet, in his discussion of Austin and Derrida, Cavell says that they, and, by implication, Wittgenstein, each are trying to overturn the same tradition in Western philosophy. He does not discuss, finally, why he thinks Derrida opposed Austin. He suggests that Derrida is more part of the Continental style, and took some of his views from Heidegger: "It is with respect to their apparently opposite attitudes toward the ordinary that I have sometimes distinguished the philosophizing of Heidegger and that of Wittgenstein, the former seeking distinction from the ordinary, conceived as 'averageness' the latter practicing transformation into it." (*Philosophical*, 156).

81. According to A. J. Ayer, "A philosopher whom he is known to have read and enjoyed is Plato, though there are no signs in his own work of Platonic ideas. [G. H., a pupil of Wittgenstein's] Von Wright suggests that he may have found Plato's temperament congenial." A. J. Ayer, *Wittgenstein* (London: Weidenfeld and Nicolson, 1985), 14. Plato's ironic interrogatives do bear a family resemblance to Wittgenstein's subjunctive interrogatives.

82. This formulation has the sentiment found in Janice Moulton: the common premises held by philosophers produce fluent agreement. Janice Moulton, "A Paradigm of

129. The aspects of things that are most important for us are hidden because of their simplicity and familiarity. (One is unable to notice something—because it is always before one's eyes.) The real foundations of his enquiry do not strike a man at all. Unless *that* fact has at some time struck him.—And this means: we fail to be struck by what, once seen, is most striking and most powerful.

130. Our clear and simple language-games are not preparatory studies for a future regularization of language—as it were first approximations, ignoring friction and air-resistance. The language-games are rather set up as *objects of comparison* which are meant to throw light on the facts of our language by way not only of similarities, but also of dissimilarities.

The "ordinary" user of language, and everyone else, has "no interest" in what is hidden. But what is "most important for us" is always hidden in plain sight—too obvious to be observed.[83] These formulations represent a different articulation of the stance of formal research in philosophy, humanities, and science. No longer committed to discovering secrets,[84] science and philosophy rearrange entities that are already in plain sight. Wittgenstein implies that in principle, if it is not in plain sight, it is not important to us: this statement means no more and no less than the decision to cope only with what is observable, including what one needs instruments to observe. What this perspective rules out is the stipulation of entities or forces that one finally cannot observe, such as "instinct," "ether," or "mental states." The latter term, through the use of words that identify feelings, appears in ordinary language, which then becomes its locus of reality—rather than, as it is more often taken to be, a locus inside the person. In his discussion of pain,[85] Wittgenstein says that the mutual understanding of pain does not admit of testing (does it really hurt?) but is either understood directly or not based on the use of common gestures and language. The subjective locus of pain, while named, admits of no verification beyond the verbal or gestural. *Sprachspiele* bring these internal states into discussion: "nothing is hidden" means that language is the best proof of pain one can

Philosophy: The Adversary Method," *Discovering Reality: Feminist Perspectives on Epistemology, Metaphysics, Methodology, and Philosophy of Science,* ed. Sandra Harding and Merrill B. Hintikka (Dordrecht: D. Reidel, 1983), 149–164.

83. The title of Norman Malcolm's reading of Wittgenstein is *Nothing Is Hidden.* This phrase may also be read as a new use of the psychoanalytic term *repression:* the repressed is in plain sight but unnoticed, and causes interpersonal or collective discomfort.

84. Chapter 10 considers how some scientists proceed with a more descriptive purpose, renouncing the search for the "secrets" of nature. This issue is treated in Evelyn Fox Keller, *Secrets of Life, Secrets of Death: Essays on Language, Gender, and Science* (New York: Routledge, 1992).

85. *Philosophical Investigations*, section 246.

get.[86] Although it may sound extreme, Wittgenstein suggests that experience cannot be apprehended beyond its linguistic and gestural translations; to stipulate subjective locations is just that: a linguistic materializing of such locations or events, and this (material) language then leads us to continue speaking *as if* a real entity is inside our minds or bodies. The fact that there is almost always some degree of doubt about what is happening inside of us also lets us see the provisionality of the language used to describe internal experience.[87]

Wittgenstein says that philosophical issues are connected to what we decide is "important for us." Philosophy's role is to "assemble reminders" of these important matters. It describes things before arguments (theses) are formulated, and the descriptions presuppose a purpose of mutual agreement. This is a postulate of cooperation[88] that accompanies the inspection and identification of *Sprachspiele*. The commonness of people's participation in language use implies a common, ongoing, regular, daily need for finding consensus, regardless of how temporary.[89] This procedure is also contrary to the "adversary method" of traditional philosophy,[90] which agrees not to debate premises, but only to debate on a common premise. Sticking to a received common premise has made logic and the skill in its manipulation more germane than the free comparison of values and assumptions in philosophical inquiry; it has also inhibited the cooperative exchange of different premises and thereby encouraged repression and territorial disputes. Wittgenstein's formulation describes an ordinary language

86. Another person's observation of an infection or of a fracture is an equivalent sort of confirmation. Still, there are reports of pain whose site or cause cannot be identified by a physician or anyone else.

87. Cavell shows the uselessness of stipulating an internal (to the mind) mechanism in order to explain an observation: "When would saying 'There's a mechanism inside' be informative? . . . 'Try to figure out where a mechanism might be that runs this apparently transparent object' (a toy car, a real clock) is hardly an explanation of its working. In any case, the mechanism of connection is here not supplying *understanding*" (*Philosophical*, 150). This is also an argument against the innatist perspective on the acquisition of language.

88. A postulate used in speech act analyses: Grice's "Cooperative Principle." Paul Grice, *Studies in the Way of Words* (Cambridge, MA: Harvard UP, 1989), 29.

89. Temporary consensus could be understood as a form of felicity in conversation and other speech acts. Or a felicitous speech act is one that has reached temporary consensus (even if it should change in the next utterance).

90. Janice Moulton, "The Adversary Method" (this essay is also discussed in chapter 8, note 86, in connection with the unchanging curriculum in universities). It may be useful to characterize the group of philosophers treated in the present study as operating on *premises different* from those of traditional philosophy. However, it is likely truer to say that this group is *moving toward* different premises, as some old premises (those of Western metaphysics, for example) remain to support some of the philosophical critiques. In both Wittgenstein and Derrida one sees adversarial movements—less so in Bakhtin, Austin, and Whorf.

discussion of premises based on agreed-upon descriptions: the role of philosophy is to create such descriptions for comparison, while leaving everything as it is. The phrase "particular purpose"[91] might also be phrased "particular practical purpose," an issue needing attention. An example would be finding a way to fight an illness, or to prevent it. The reminders are different ways to describe the presentation of the illness, whose different aspects are (potentially) in plain sight, while there is uncertainty as to how much weight each of these aspects is to be given in the research project. The view that we "fail to be struck" by what is "most striking and powerful" refers to the automatic selection of what is remembered, to the reduction of the rest of the observed, and to the related assumption that something unseen must be at work. It *is* unseen, but not because it is hidden. Rather, it does not register because of the *expectations* of secret origins, causes, and explanations that are in a zone presumably deeper than anything perceptible. The assumption of such depth is often automatic, as in the fluent uses of such phrases as "depth psychology," 'deep thinking,' and "deep structure."

In light of the steady pursuit of explanation in contemporary research, Wittgenstein's reducing the standing of explanation seems incommensurate with contemporary preferences. For those to whom it does seem that way, the claim that language use is material might seem too extravagant in a different direction: it might seem to attribute too much to the words of description, or claim too much for their effects. The issue at hand is the failure to recognize how the axiom of language transparency creates confusions in philosophy and science, as well as in public policies based on such confusions. It has led, in addition, to the failure to recognize what the use of language is in position to do: contribute substantively to a variety of activities directed toward the survival of our species. Recognizing the materiality of language helps override the drifts toward violence, and work against the tacit, default dependence on the efficacy of force and other destructive practices.[92] Wittgenstein's stipulation that what we need for new descriptions of phenomena is always in "plain sight" takes on a more political cast in this context,[93] and gives a degree of specificity to the view that perception of the materiality of language is repressed in the psychoanalytic sense: an unpleasant but acknowledged fact is put out of mind—that is, put out of attention or awareness on a collective scale. Wittgenstein's stipulation that the repressed is in plain sight applies to political issues as much as to philosophi-

---

91. Wittgenstein, *Philosophical Investigations,* section 127.

92. The failure of the uses of language to override the movement to violence is discussed in chapter 11.

93. Wittgenstein may not have recognized the political vector of his work. Robin Lakoff, in our own time, made the political actions of language her principal issue (see chapter 6).

cal inquiry, as Rosalind Morris's account (see chapter 1) suggests. Collective repression—meaning in this case a society that does not recognize its perception of materiality—and individual repression have this feature in common: the unseen is only that; it is not hidden.[94] We "fail to be struck" by the materiality of language only because we are not looking.

IV. Austin and Speech Action

The speech act theory introduced by J. L. Austin (and pursued further by John Searle and Paul Grice) carries Wittgenstein's underlying sense of language use to specific classes of use in English.[95] In the *Philosophical Investigations*[96] Wittgenstein writes, "And words can be wrung from us,—like a cry. Words can be *hard* to say: such, for example, as are used to effect a renunciation, or to confess a weakness. (Words are also deeds.)"[97] The parenthetical sentence sums up Austin's work, whose issue was: which words are deeds and how shall the different deed-words (speech acts), understood as material, be described, be placed into plausible categories? What kinds of deeds are performed by the different categories of words? The performative role (*Spiel*)[98] of words is implicit in most of what Wittgenstein wrote, but he says it directly only in the foregoing sentence and a few others. Because Wittgenstein identified as a professional, academic philosopher, he discusses, through attention to language, the traditional issues of truth, explanation, epistemology, and certainty; he addresses, mainly, other philosophers. Yet if his critique of language is applied, philosophy as a discipline leaves its fraternal conventions and traditions and becomes less isolated from other groups with access to language who speak differently on many subjects: changing the uses of language applies to all subjects and all issues.

Austin might qualify as one of those who, as a custodian of language, will practice philosophy ordinarily, and change its narrow address to other philosophers. Although the term "ordinary language" is given partly to oppose the

94. In chapter 10 there is discussion of how several critiques of science and language exposed factors that have been in plain sight but have not been included in scientific deliberations.

95. Cavell discerned a fundamental connection between Wittgenstein and Austin after first hearing Austin's lectures in 1955, a feeling he refers to as a "conversion experience" (*Philosophical*, 43).

96. *Philosophical Investigations*, section 546.

97. A good elucidation of Wittgenstein's approach to language as an activity is found in Pitkin, *Justice*, 36–39, where she relates it to Austin's discussion of performativity. If there are two categories, words and deeds, the "also" is salient and does apply in some cases. It may be clearer to say, "to use words is to do something," a thought suggested in Austin's title.

98. Both senses of the word "perform" apply at once: to do and to act within a scene.

unfamiliar language of formal logic in the regular pursuits of philosophy,[99] Austin's studies addressed what most people would understand to be ordinary language: usages, conventions, rituals, and tropes we use in everyday life.

One may hesitate about uses of language, viewed as behaviors, being called "material." Austin's study of words in their role as deeds counteracts this hesitation by contesting the seventeenth-century view of language as an airy nothing or as spiritual entities as the opposite of deeds, the opposite of experience.[100] Austin says that words (usages) are in the same category as other behaviors, other experiences: we feel and do them. Saying is just a different style or genre of doing and feeling, or doing and causing feeling. In this sense claiming the materiality of language is relative to a different claim about language: if the effects and the feel of language are recognized, there is no need to stipulate a spiritual (immaterial, intangible) identity for the words. More importantly, once the histories of individuals' childhood language acquisition are taken into account, the connection of language to behaviors and social relations is apparent: language use is the site of infants' and children's circle of relationships.[101] Understanding language to be speech acts presupposes the materiality of language.

When Austin's work was first recognized, literary critics Richard Ohmann, Mary Louise Pratt, and Shoshana Felman,[102] like Cavell, considered if speech act theory was a new path for the study of language and literature: they saw in this theory a way to ground literary study as part of the study of language and an integration of disciplines while expanding the scope of both language

---

99. Mary Louise Pratt, *Toward a Speech Act Theory of Literary Discourse* (Bloomington: Indiana UP, 1977), 80. The interest in so-called ordinary language bears some resemblance to the preference for the vernacular in Christian Thomasius (chapter 8) as well as in Galileo and Descartes (chapter 9). Like these ancestors in their own time, however, Austin was a member of the elite in mid-twentieth-century British intellectual life. The American Benjamin Lee Whorf (discussed later in this chapter) may qualify as a more ordinary person. His work in the study of language was a second career, almost an avocation. He, too, however, was in conversation with those who were more unequivocally members of the elite.

100. Hamlet's "native hue of resolution" is "sicklied o'er by the pale cast of thought / And enterprises of great pitch and moment / . . . lose the name of action" (3.1.94–96, 98). Also, Hamlet's use of "the play" (*Spiel*) to catch the conscience of the king is an action helping to carry out the ghost's command.

101. This topic is elaborated in chapter 5.

102. Richard Ohmann, "Speech Acts and the Definition of Literature," *Philosophy and Rhetoric* 4 (1971): 1–19; Ohmann, "Speech, Literature and the Space Between," *New Literary History* 5 (1974): 37–63; Mary Louise Pratt, *Speech Act Theory*; Shoshana Felman, *The Literary Speech Act: Don Juan with J. L. Austin, or Seduction in Two Languages*, trans. Catherine Porter (Ithaca, NY: Cornell UP, 1983); reissued as *The Scandal of the Speaking Body: Don Juan with J. L. Austin, or, Seduction in Two Languages* (Palo Alto, CA: Stanford UP, 2003).

and literary study. They took from this set of considerations the means to take account of what Wittgenstein introduced by understanding the *Sprachspiel* as a total scene of social and language action. Pratt wrote,

> [S]peech act theory provides a way of talking about utterances not only in terms of their surface grammatical properties but also in terms of the context in which they are made, the intentions, attitudes, and expectations of the participants, the relationships existing between participants, and generally, the unspoken rules and conventions that are understood to be in play when an utterance is made and received.[103]

Pratt saw oral and written, literary and nonliterary "utterances" as language use. Key terms for this broader categorization are "context" and "unspoken rules." By focusing on the deed or action aspects of speech, the social and interpersonal contexts of language use come into view, as do the "unspoken rules" such as those that were in effect in Wittgenstein's building scene (starting at section 8) early in the *Philosophical Investigations*. Austin's work is what first made students of language aware of the ubiquity of the *action* of language.[104] Where Wittgenstein identified the scenes of language use, as well as their likeness to dramatic plays, Austin emphasized that the words used within that scene were specific behaviors: this person acting on that person, or on a group of people. Today, Austin's description has only a partial reception. Although it is becoming increasingly clear that words can hurt,[105] few conduct their work (or lives) aware of the tangible effects of language use in our living relationships. Yet this intuition—that language has a greater palpability than we expect across the range of interpersonal experience—has not found its way into our taken-for-granted ways of conducting our lives. The action

103. Pratt, *Speech Act Theory*, 86.

104. Plato and the classical rhetoricians were also aware of the action of poetry and rhetoric, but they did not write about the action of the speech of other citizens in illiterate classes, whose language also could do what that of poets and rhetors did.

105. Judith Butler, *Excitable Speech: A Politics of the Performative* (New York: Routledge, 1997), reflects on the actual damage done by hate speech or name-calling. Catharine MacKinnon, in *Only Words* (Cambridge, MA: Harvard UP, 1992), makes a related point regarding pornography. Kent Greenawalt's *Fighting Words: Individuals, Communities and Liberties of Speech* (Princeton, NJ: Princeton UP, 1995) is relevant and useful. Stanley Fish describes how no speech can be free because of its ever present interpersonal contexts in "There's No Such Thing as Free Speech, and It's a Good Thing, Too," *There's No Such Thing as Free Speech, and It's a Good Thing, Too* (New York: Oxford UP, 1994), 102–119. The global reach of this issue is treated in Mari J. Matsuda et al., eds., *Words That Wound* (Boulder, CO: Westview P, 1993); and in Michael E. Brown and Sumit Ganguly, eds., *Fighting Words: Language Policy and Ethnic Relations in Asia* (Cambridge, MA: MIT P, 2003).

or acting of language as presented by Austin is still just an unused thought in most academic contexts.

Austin's general term for speech acts is "the performative." It is easy to read his 1955 Harvard lectures and not notice that wedding vows, bets, promises, or warnings are more than local rituals. His cute title (*How to Do Things with Words*), although literally accurate, is misleading in its appearance of under-statement and its giving a sense of quaintness to the idea of doing things with words. However, the scope of application of speech act theory since then has been narrow; few have heard the challenge that both of these subjects present. The positivist philosophy of language is, more or less, still in effect.[106]

Although the inertia in academic contexts is due mainly to a political comfort with the positivist hegemony, speech act theorists themselves were not able to move very far beyond what Austin proposed: John Searle seemed to want to scientize the study of language by establishing fixed taxonomies and by using a Chomsky-style notation as well as Chomsky's tautological habit of inventing the sentences, as if without any context, that illustrate the rules or principles he wanted to discuss. Chomsky, Searle, and those who accepted their perspectives presupposed that the study of language must be a formal science.[107] The tech-nique of inventing sentences used by both men, however, departed from, rather than demonstrated, the creative element in Austin's first proposals: the under-standing that contexts were fundamental factors in the use of sentences, and that it was the changes of context that rendered old,—that is, conventional— usages new. Chomsky and Searle worked under the assumption that the lan-guage itself was new and creative; but how can there ever be new language? The earlier figures, Wittgenstein and Austin, did understand that conventional language placed in necessarily new contexts *became* new language viewed from a pragmatic standpoint. Except for the literary critics cited above, scholars who aimed to follow up on Austin's theory paid more attention to how to establish categories than to the continuous action of contexts on the processes of language change.[108] Loyalty to positivism does not describe Austin's formulations, nor is

---

106. Cavell says that when Austin gave his lectures, it was in a "climate in which positivism was pervasive and dominant in the Anglo-American academic world from the mid-1940s through the 1950s and beyond, almost throughout the humanities and the social sciences, a hegemonic presence more complete, I believe, than that of any one of today's [1995] politically or intellectually advanced positions: positivism during this period was virtually unopposed on any intellectually organized scale" (*Philosophical*, 51).

107. John R. Searle *Speech Acts: An Essay in the Philosophy of Language* (New York: Cambridge UP, 1969).

108. Rather, Searle and other researchers paid a great deal of attention to intention, an issue that Wittgenstein did much to revoke in the study of language. See John Searle, *Intentionality: An Essay in the Philosophy of Mind* (New York: Cambridge UP, 1983); and Georgia M. Green, *Pragmatics and Natural Language Understanding* (Hillsdale, NJ:

such loyalty found in most of Wittgenstein's later work, which identified the frustration of philosophy as a confusion about the use of language: philosophy and other language-intensive disciplines continued to assume the Augustinian theory—correspondence of notations (oral and written) with facts.[109] Austin died prematurely and did not develop his thought beyond the Harvard lectures. He was drawn to try to consider as many instances of the use of language he could find and to try to describe them. The result was the description of a series of (illocutionary, perlocutionary) forces that different uses of language exert in conversation. These might be thought of as indirect performatives or as genres of performatives. Although a degree of taxonomy is usually needed if a new general conception of the field is proposed, Austin tried to refine his taxonomy, to which end he studied individual cases more thoroughly and improved their articulation.

Austin's description of the different kinds of (locutionary) speech acts in *How to Do Things with Words* was the culmination of his thinking for over a decade before the lectures. His posthumous collection of essays,[110] which were written before his Harvard lectures, shows several points of similarity with Wittgenstein's approach, suggesting that the kind of questioning of the tradition in

---

Erlbaum, 1989). Intentionalists were unwilling to give up on the Husserlian search for an inner essence of language phenomena, and unwilling to see the speech community as the limit of inquiry on this issue. In the subdiscipline pragmatics, which was started with speech act theory, textbooks such as Jacob L. Mey's perennially reprinted *Pragmatics: An Introduction* (Malden, MA: Blackwell, 1993)—although they are generally aware of the largeness and ungainliness of the contexts of language use—spend most of their time on individual sentences used in relatively narrow, or even imaginary, contexts. This gross distortion of central issues of language use is the result of the structures of knowledge and understanding having been created by the institution of the university and the scientific convention of dividing and studying tiny parts of the subject: disciplinary departments have their territories and prescribed conventions of inquiry; and science separates atomistic units, studies each alone, and then puts all the knowledge together under the assumption that this will compose an accurate big picture. Some pragmatics scholars, such as Robin Lakoff (whose academically courageous claims have helped to define the materiality of language in contemporary times; see chapter 6), are exceptions to this description.

109. Although Pitkin suggests "that in criticizing Augustine, Wittgenstein is really criticizing his own earlier views" (*Wittgenstein's*, 31), Richard Rorty presents an extended refutation of the correspondence theory of truth from a pragmatic standpoint. One of his "heroes" is Wittgenstein. Richard Rorty, *Philosophy and the Mirror of Nature* (Princeton, NJ: Princeton UP, 1979), 382. J. L. Austin is discussed in several contexts. However, Rorty's focus is on knowledge rather than language: the task of philosophy is to put the search for knowledge on pragmatic grounds. Language is a factor, but Rorty does not see language as the key to changing philosophy; rather, philosophy should be changed by adopting a pragmatic stance.

110. J. L. Austin, *Philosophical Papers* (Oxford: Clarendon P, 1961).

philosophy, and of the more influential Western approach to language was on the table. Much as Wittgenstein rejected the atomistic status of propositions in his own earlier work, Austin also began to question the philosophical axiom that propositional formulations are the starting point for the study of language and truth. He observed that when grammatically declarative statements appear in other contexts, they no longer act as statements:

> When is a statement not a statement? When it is a formula in a calculus: when it is a performatory utterance: when it is a value-judgement: when it is a definition: when it is part of a work of fiction—there are many such suggested answers. It is simply not the business of such utterances to "correspond to the facts" (and even genuine statements have other businesses besides that of so corresponding).[111]

Austin's emphasis is on the combination of the grammatical form of the utterance or text and its various contextual placements—including its language genres, such as mathematics or literature. This paragraph demonstrates its point: more often than not, propositional statements are not statements.[112] Differing genres, contexts, and uses—all of which attach to any one particular use—change the genre of the "same" statement and make it into something else, into a different speech genre. Austin says that philosophy has not heard ordinary usage and instead "lumped them [statements] all together under the term of art 'proposition.'"[113] In his essay "How to Talk," Austin observed how fully language may be described as the regular production of different kinds of speech acts and that this multifariousness made their identification especially difficult:[114]

> Names for speech-acts are more numerous, more specialized, more ambiguous and more significant than is ordinarily allowed for: none of them can be safely used in philosophy in a general way (for example, 'statement' or 'description') without more investigation than they have,

---

111. Austin, *Philosophical*, 99.

112. This is also a challenge to the principle of non-contradiction. Many uses of language welcome contradiction and variation. Sentences of the form "Statements are not statements" make sense when read in the context of the essay. This issue is even more prominent in the work of Derrida, discussed in chapter 4. Freud observed this feature of language in his 1910 essay, "The Antithetical Sense of Primal Words," *Collected Papers*, trans. Joan Riviere (New York: Basic, 1959), 4:184–191.

113. Austin, *Philosophical*, 99.

114. And, as a result, this is one of the tasks he set for himself in the Harvard lectures: classifying speech acts. This claim corresponds to Wittgenstein's "language-as-a-toolbox" figure in section 11 of *Philosophical Investigations*.

I think, yet received. Here of course we have been concerned with only a few speech-acts of a single family, but naturally there are other whole families besides.[115]

In this preliminary context, there is another connection to Wittgenstein's formulations: the "whole families" of speech acts. Austin is observing that similar speech acts need a separate notice: they need to be identified and differentiated, much as family members do beyond the family resemblance. Then he identifies different classes of speech acts as different families. This style of discourse is connected to Wittgenstein's by virtue of both viewing language use (the *Sprachspiel* and the speech act) as living: Austin's approach to the uses of language are founded on his treating language as a living thing.[116]

Finally, Austin's earlier work challenged the "correspondence" theory of truth through his neo-nominalist view of class concepts and his rejection of an idea of verbal meaning as something that can be abstracted from verbal usage. In "The Meaning of a Word," he wrote that "a 'class of particular ideas' is every bit as fictitious an entity as a 'concept' or 'abstract idea.'" He criticizes Charles Morris for affirming that "every sign has a designatum, which is not a particular thing but a *kind* of object or *class* of object. Now this is quite as fictitious an entity as any 'Platonic idea': and is precisely due to the same fallacy of looking for 'the meaning (or designatum) of a word.'"[117] The larger picture Austin is drawing emerges from this statement: what were once called meanings are localized in living, contextualized speech acts, and not in words, whereas the concept of meaning as something separate but attached to words is itself no longer useful as a path toward describing how language works. He is not rejecting the use of categories; he used them freely in identifying so-called families of speech acts. Like the nominalists, he rejects only the sense that class identification isolates essential or common features of different members of a class.

Austin, like Wittgenstein, understood language to be alive. Although "materiality of language" was not a phrase either figure used, they recognized it in their understanding that the use of language was gestural. Austin opposed the historic assumptions regarding classes of objects and the thought that words have meanings that are stable independently of the ways they are used in different

---

115. Austin, *Philosophical*, 197.

116. Categories of nonliving things are not usually referred to (in English) as families, although they could be.

117. Austin, *Philosophical*, 29. As a semiotician, Morris's formulations are similar to the French language theorists—who, since Saussure, have maintained the formula to describe language as a relation between the signifier and the signified. Poststructuralism challenged this formula but retained this usage and thus caused confusion: that is one factor the renders Derrida so much more difficult to read than Wittgenstein, whose terminology is drawn from more familiar zones of social interaction.

speech situations. His last work started on the process of thinking about how the families of speech acts could become the genres whose descriptive capability would be useful in studying the indefinite number of speech acts, and of classes of speech acts, in different contexts and different societies.

Austin's work went against the disciplinary momentum and toward the possibility of imagining a leap toward the subject matter and interest of disciplines such as sociology or psychology, two subjects to which Wittgenstein was drawn. Movements toward literature and literary criticism might well have helped speech act theory grow[118] or move it toward the ways, for example, that psychoanalysis grew and developed as it was revised away from its individualistic and androcentric emphases.[119] By contrast, speech act theory and language philosophy remained

---

118. Richard Ohmann, Mary Louise Pratt, and Shoshana Felman (see note 102) were virtually the only ones who tried to move to literature, but the lack of response to their efforts saw all three of them move toward other political interests: gender and economic equality. Reading speech act theory as a form of language materiality helps to highlight the role of language in the promotion of egalitarian politics. Jacob Mey's textbook also engages literature, although his focus is on discussing literature as it presents examples of different cases of speech acts (within the taxonomy), rather than looking at the social action of literary texts—a project undertaken, for example, by Andrea Dworkin's *Woman Hating* (New York: Penguin Books, 1974); Janice A. Radway's *Reading the Romance: Women, Patriarchy, and Popular Literature* (Chapel Hill: U of North Carolina P, 1984); and Toni Morrison's *Playing in the Dark: Whiteness and the Literary Imagination* (New York: Vintage, 1990). Although Mey's examples are of interest, Mey does not explore the wider issue raised by Plato : What about the ability of literature—its so-called lying fiction, stories, plays, and poems—to have material effects and actual roles to play in society? Mey offers a two-page section on language and gender and another three pages on critical pragmatics, which studies political issues. Each of Robin Tolmach Lakoff's books stipulate contexts of attention: see *Language and Woman's Place* (New York: Harper, 1975); *Face Value: The Politics of Beauty* (New York: Routledge, 1984 [with Raquel L. Scherr]), *Talking Power: The Politics of Language In Our Lives* (New York: Basic, 1990); *Father Knows Best: The Use and Abuse of Power in Freud's Case of Dora* (New York: Teachers College P, 1993 [with James C. Coyne]); and *The Language War* (Berkeley: U of California P, 2000). The precedent-setting political emphasis of her linguistic work is discussed in chapter 6. Lakoff describes language action as political action. Her work may be associated with linguistic pragmatics; it fits well into sociolinguistics, linguistic anthropology, and U.S. cultural studies. A few, such as Deborah Tannen, approach the study of language as Robin Lakoff does. Lakoff's work does have kinship with ethnographic and social studies that start, as she does, with specific contexts. Examples of related studies would include Sherry Turkle's *The Second Self: Computers and the Human Spirit* (New York: Simon and Schuster, 1984); Anne Allison's *Nightwork: Sexuality, Pleasure, and Corporate Masculinity in a Tokyo Hostess Club* (Chicago: U of Chicago P, 1994); and Allison Leigh Brown's *Subjects of Deceit: A Phenomenology of Lying* (Albany: SUNY P, 1998).

119. I am referring to different therapy styles that have grown in the twentieth century, such as group therapy as well as different forms of family and couples counseling. These all involve changes in the way language is used in psychotherapy. Speech conven-

academic: a subject that could be summarized in textbooks and taught easily in the rigid mores of academic life.[120] Yet only Austin's work is still viewed with more than local disciplinary interest, and it plays an important role in Judith Butler's *Excitable Speech*. Perhaps it can be said that there is a desire to pursue the understanding of speech acts, but few contexts or situations seem to accommodate this project.

A sophisticated, enriched sense of context is usually part of the descriptions of language uses given by Wittgenstein and Austin. It may be asking too much of academic linguistics to recognize the sites of living people as the optimum place to study the action of language.[121] That would be the consequence of studying language by recognizing its materiality: looking and seeing how it is used and how it acts among people, especially in the many "constative"[122] and "illocutionary"[123] cases that outnumber the ordinary performative. Understanding language as both uses (or gestures or behaviors or actions) and genres of uses shows how collective as well as individual actions emerge from living bodies. Any utterance and its accompanying social arrangements—the interpersonal and collective relationships (living groups, families, communities, neighborhoods, clubs, teams, executive boards, classrooms, or societies)—must be understood to be a material site of language. Austin's new vocabulary, which includes the interesting and

tions also have changed; for example, the term "client" is used now used in addition to the traditional "patient." More importantly, perhaps, the actual discourse styles of therapeutic situations have proliferated. "Talk (psycho)therapy" has adapted to changes in history and society.

120. The Kuhnian textbook effect that is responsible for the formulaic quality of "normal science." Kuhn did not thus characterize it, but this normality may not have been so normal: it was only bureaucratically convenient, as it depended on questionable assumptions—the fixity and lawfulness of knowledge—about what teaching and learning science really are.

121. The subject is studied by some researchers in children's language acquisition, sociolinguistics, linguistic anthropology, and in a variety of education researches, though these are not large-scale enterprises in universities. The main tendency of any discipline that studies living people is to become statistical rather than ethnographic. Both approaches yield pertinent understanding, however.

122. This is Austin's term for the heretofore privileged "propositional" statements that had been taken by positivists to be the "atomistic" or fundamental form. It is noteworthy that early versions of Chomsky's transformational grammar were built on permutations and combinations of sentences in propositional form. For example, the adjectival phrase "the red ball" is a transformation of the proposition "the ball is red." Propositional statements identified what Chomsky termed "deep structure."

123. J. L. Austin, *How to Do Things with Words*, ed. J. O. Urmson (New York: Oxford UP, 1962), 99–107. An illocutionary act is *like* a performative ("I thee wed") but the words themselves can vary; a warning has to be uttered, but there are many kinds of warnings and many ways to warn people of different things or events. An illocutionary act may be thought of as a *speech genre* whose many subgenres include warning, promising, and threatening.

sometimes contested term "force" to describe what may relate to the traditional term "intention," aims to take seriously the "occasion of an utterance."[124] This occasion includes "effects upon the feelings, thoughts, or actions of the audience, or of the speaker, or of other persons: and it may be done with the design, intention, or purpose of producing them."[125] Austin recognizes the dynamics[126] of a speech situation—the stimulation of feelings that are palpable—and understands these feelings to be both in the language and in the context. His moves away from relying on the meanings of the words as explanation and his moves toward taking into account the total situation show that every speech situation has at least some degree of conventionality, something generic that helps to identify it: lovers' conversation, pillow talk, parent-child chats, and so on. Language-use situations are not unique, and are acquired—or learned—through a variety of developmental experiences. Once it is allowed that the contexts themselves are generic, then it is not difficult to accept that the language is conventional or socially structured in some way that is already learned by all the participants. An expectation of genres is then useful as an analytical pathway: the stipulation of a kind already means that it is not new, and that speakers are now in the process of reliving and perhaps changing the genres of speech-action to what will then seem new and, if the term must be used, "creative."[127]

Thinking of genres of speech action renders it less urgent to refine the meaning of the different locutionary levels: Just how speakers are acting on one another relates to the speech and social genres that are in effect. The disputes about whether particular usages are constative, perlocutionary, or illocutionary tend to re-essentialize the categories,[128] removing from them the provisional

---

124. Austin observes, "[F]or some years we have been realizing more and more clearly that the occasion of an utterance matters seriously, and that the words used are to some extent to be 'explained' by the 'context' in which they are designed to be or have actually been spoken in a linguistic interchange. Yet still perhaps we are too prone to give these explanations in terms of 'the meanings of words.' . . . I want to distinguish *force* and meaning in the sense in which meaning is equivalent to sense and reference, just as it has become essential to distinguish sense and reference within meaning" (*How to Do Things with Words*, 100).

125. Austin, *How to Do Things with Words*, 101.

126. I use this term, also used in psychoanalysis, to refer to the pull of feelings and because Austin refers to this pull as a "force."

127. The concept and use of the genre idea has no formal place in transformational linguistics, which concentrates on how individuals are in position to "create" the "new" combination of words and sentences. Language acquisition seems far less miraculous if it is understood that children acquire genres and ways to combine them, as opposed to a "language generating system." Extended discussion of the acquisition process is in chapter 5.

128. Manfred Bierwisch discusses whether the distinction between constative and performative statements is basic. We are asked to consider in isolation the two sentences, "I tell you that the earth is flat" and "The earth is flat." No specific contexts are stipulated

status that makes them useful to begin with. But if a generic identification is anticipated, the effort to understand the speech action will call for thinking about the scene of speech in interpersonal and social terms rather than exclusively about individual intentions and the levels of influence the speakers exercise on one another. Furthermore, each local genre is embedded in larger communal and societal genres, and the language used on the local scale has meaning in the series of larger genres in which it may be found; but, again, this meaning now refers to the context in which language is used.[129]

V. Bakhtin's Speech Genres and National Languages

Bakhtin's essay on speech genres was already published when Austin gave his Harvard lectures as well as when Pratt wrote her study, but it had not yet been translated from the Russian. Written in the early 1950s, it was translated into English in 1986.[130] By entertaining the "general linguistic problem of the utterance,"[131] Bakhtin stipulates a territory that shares a key feature of Austin's performatives: attention to the social circumstances of speech and language. The utterance—which he describes as a departure from the word, sentence, and

---

for this discussion. Yet it is not that subtle a matter to see that in some speech situations the distinction will be more germane than in others; similarly, each sentence can have a use in different contexts: the general issue needs no decision and no decisions can be made on the sole basis of comparing the sentences. Manfred Bierwisch, "Semantic Structure and Illocutionary Force," *Speech Act Theory and Pragmatics*, ed. John R. Searle, Ferenc Kiefer, and Manfred Bierwisch (Boston: D. Reidel, 1980), 10–11.

129. Wittgenstein, in his remarks on dream interpretation cited above, pays no attention to whether this context stipulates a past wish that has been fulfilled. He has identified the principle of speech action in psychoanalysis. Because psychoanalysis has indeed relied on speech action as has been described by Wittgenstein, it has remained a living institution, responsive to the uses of language its participants have contributed to it. Freud implicitly relied on a sense of the materiality of language in his therapeutic practices, but tended toward traditional sense of language in his theoretical writings.

130. M. M. Bakhtin, *Speech Genres and Other Essays*, ed. Caryl Emerson and Michael Holquist, trans. Vern W. McGee (Austin: U Texas P, 1986), 60–102. Since Bakhtin's work became available, it has achieved currency in critical theory—including its use by scholars in rhetoric and composition. It has proved valuable to critics who were responding to political calls for multivocality—for the recognition of the different voices within cultures as well as the different constituents of Western civilization, including especially the non-Western and postcolonial constituents.

131. Bakhtin, *Speech Genres*, 61. The use of the term "utterance," also used by Austin, is a sign of the wider scope of language genres that began to be included in language and literary studies at mid-twentieth century; the term is used instead of "words" or "sentences," so that paragraphs, turns in a conversation, or other units of discourse may be considered generically. It may be viewed as an "oral" counterpart of Derrida's inclusive term "writing."

paragraph as ways into discourse—increasingly resembles Austin's speech acts and Wittgenstein's *Sprachspiele*. However, Bakhtin sees each "concrete utterance" in a context that is described differently from the sense of context found in the other two: "Any concrete utterance is a link in the chain of speech communication of a particular sphere."[132] His emphasis is on the embeddedness and continuity associated with utterances. An utterance ends, he considers, when a new speaker takes the floor.[133] The embeddedness of each utterance resides in the fact that "the topic of the speaker's speech, regardless of what this topic may be, does not become the object of speech for the first time in any given utterance; a given speaker is not the first to speak about it. . . . Various viewpoints, world views, and trends cross, converge, and diverge in it."[134] Counterintuitive though it may seem, even conversations about the weather fit this description as easily as conversations about pregnancies or car accidents. The only new element in such speech is the new scene of speech created by the new speakers speaking at new moments in history. This is the significance of what Bakhtin calls "addressivity."[135] The words and sentences themselves "belong to nobody"[136] but once they are used in concrete utterances (that is, taken up by a specific speaker), they must engage an addressee. Otherwise there is no sense in calling the utterance language. Language as addressed must also appear in genres: "Each speech genre in each area of speech communication has it own typical conception of the addressee, and this defines it as a genre."[137] Bakhtin is using the genre idea—there are always more than a few instances of any usage—to identify the living quality of language, the sense that it is not actual language until it appears in a genre—which, in his description, is a category that is necessarily associated with, and part of, a social situation. This description is similar to those given by Wittgenstein and Austin in that all three writers try to find descriptions of the living quality of language use. Each found a different description, yet they have a family resemblance. These three figures, writing in

---

132. Bakhtin, *Speech Genres*, 91.

133. Bakhtin, *Speech Genres*, 93.

134. Bakhtin, *Speech Genres*, 93. It is interesting that, in a completely different direction from that taken in Ecclesiastes (discussed in chapter 7, section 2), Bakhtin discusses how "there is nothing [linguistically] new under the sun." Yet each writer is referring to understanding as given by texts. In Ecclesiastes, the theme of knowledge is frequently in evidence; the writer sees knowledge as inevitably leading to disappointment: people will all soon find out the same bad news ("Whoever increases knowledge increases pain" [Ecclesiastes 1:18]), so to speak, because it is all there, on the record, in plain sight.

135. Bakhtin, *Speech Genres*, 95.

136. Bakhtin, *Speech Genres*, 95.

137. Bakhtin, *Speech Genres*, 95. Again, "[t]he various typical forms this addressivity assumes and the various concepts of the addressee are constitutive, definite features of various speech genres" (99).

different contexts, societies, and cultures, come to understandings of language use that are similar to one another, and that seem to be advocating for recognition of mutual and collective social circumstances that must be considered part of the subject of language.

Bakhtin remains in the disciplines of linguistics and literary theory, although perhaps in his academic tradition these subjects may be considered to be closer to philosophy than they are in Western Europe. He is aware, moreover, of how his subject matter relates to the traditional subject of rhetoric, but observes that "not much has been added [to rhetoric] in subsequent epochs to classical theory."[138] Furthermore, he writes, the sociolinguistic approaches that have studied merely "everyday speech" were "limited" in their tendency toward the "primitive," the American "behaviorists"[139] being his example. In any case, Bakhtin's long involvement in literary discussions, along with his underlying view that literature reflects the range of speech genres, characterize in a more general way the importance of identifying all language genres.

In her earlier work, and often enough later on, Deborah Tannen has drawn "data"—examples of speech and speech acts—from literary sources, presupposing (and sometimes claiming directly) the continuity between literary and oral speech. Bakhtin is reacting to the Russian Formalists of the 1920s, who, like Roman Ingarden,[140] followed their aesthetic intuition that there was something distinctive about literary language that separated it from other language. They tried to find the differences in uses of language, but they had trouble because the uses of language in literature deliberately resemble those in everyday life. They wanted to say that literature defamiliarizes experience, although it does not do so any more than does any language in new contexts. Bakhtin, and later Tzvetan Todorov,[141] removed the ground for dispute about what the difference was: literature appeared in different genres of language. The genre idea makes it clear that there is both similarity and difference between literary and other language uses, and guides scholarship toward consideration of the general issue of how language is social action and is part of social action. Toril Moi[142] says that Julia Kristeva[143] "follows Bakhtin in insisting on the subversive political

---

138. Bakhtin, *Speech Genres*, 61.

139. He may have been referring to the anthropologists Franz Boas and Edward Sapir, as well as Sapir's collaborator Benjamin Lee Whorf, who did refer to the societies they studied as primitive. Bakhtin also sees Saussure and his structuralist heirs as having this limitation. See Boas, *The Mind of Primitive Man*, rev. ed. (New York: Macmillan, 1938).

140. Roman Ingarden, *The Literary Work of Art*, trans. George G. Grabowicz (Evanston, IL: Northwestern UP, 1973).

141. Tzvetan Todorov, *Genres in Discourse*, trans. Catherine Porter (Cambridge, Cambridge UP, 1990).

142. *The Kristeva Reader*, ed. Toril Moi (New York: Columbia UP, 1986), 35.

143. Discussed further in chapter 4.

effects of such [dialogic senses of] language, and thus also comes to prefigure Kristeva's later analysis of the politics of marginality."[144] Moi is one of a minority in academic life that has made use of the political character of these new views of language.[145]

Through his work on speech genres, Bakhtin contributed to the study of language use something that was not treated by Wittgenstein and Austin: the "problem of the national and the individual in language . . . in the utterance, is the national language embodied in individual form."[146] This consideration enlarges the scale at which language must be studied.[147] Different national languages may also be understood as different speech genres, different language behaviors, *Sprachspiele,* or speech acts. If a national language is viewed as a speech genre, the term "national language" can become also a reference to a national culture.[148] If this wider reference is taken, it discloses issues of sense and usage that attach, for example, to how the term *Sprachspiel* is to be translated. It might be that a reason for Wittgenstein's claim that he is not understood is that *cultural* translation was needed for his language uses in addition to language translation. It could happen (and usually does in situations that require translators[149]) that the similar usages in different languages—"It's nothing"

---

144. Alluded to in chapter 1.

145. Moi's work on Ibsen's plays similarly highlights the plays' political achievements: Ibsen's "wish to write about strong, complex, and free women forced him to break with the idealist [aesthetic] framework." Toril Moi, *Henrik Ibsen and the Birth of Modernism: Art, Theater, Philosophy* (New York: Oxford UP, 2006), 187. That language and literature perform similar functions of social action connected to efforts for bodily emancipation is considered in chapter 12.

146. Bakhtin, *Speech Genres,* 63.

147. John Guillory notes that Bakhtin considered the novel non-canonical because it was such a loose genre. It was a change in genre that reflected the "heteroglossic" changes in society. John Guillory, *Cultural Capital: The Problem of Literary Canon Formation* (Chicago: U Chicago P, 1993), 67. Humboldt is the modern scholar who opened the way to comparative philology, the academic treatment of heteroglossia, in the beginning of the nineteenth century (see chapter 2). The work of Whorf and in general the Sapir-Whorf hypothesis, discussed below, casts comparative philology in ways that call attention to the materiality of language.

148. This is another situation in which the German *Kultur* may be a better word than the English "civilization," which does not as easily include the idea of a national language as does the German term. Some readers may be familiar with Bruno Bettelheim's complaint that Freud's "*das Ich*" and "*das Es*" were translated—in the English translations—into Latin and not English, thus taking on an attribute they do not have in German. Might psychoanalysis be different in English-speaking societies if they used "the I" and "the it" instead of "the ego" and "the id"?

149. Stuart Chase observes how, in the United Nations, the English "I assume" got translated as "I deduce" and "I consider." Although these may have preserved the English speaker's sense, these differences could matter a great deal of the situation were urgent.

(said in response to an apology) and *ayn davar* ("It's nothing," meaning "You're welcome" in Hebrew)—have a different speech action; to put it another way, non-equivalent usages, such as "You're welcome" and *bitte* have similar speech action. (And there are similar usages that have similar functions: "See you later," *au revoir* and *auf Wiedersehen*.).[150]

The wider net cast by Bakhtin's awareness of national languages is another way his work finds the common ground of literature and language. He sees in the "vast majority of literary genres" the use of ordinary speech genres such as "the rejoinder in dialogue, everyday stories, letters, diaries, minutes, and so forth."[151] To these he could have added less-ordinary written genres and philosophy and history.[152] He views literature as analogous to speech situations: there is a "real" speaker or author and a "real"[153] addressee. There is always in speech situations a variety of genres—a condition resulting from the embeddedness of language in society, but also from the embeddedness of one language, one literature, in other languages and literatures and other cultures.

Tzvetan Todorov was perhaps more explicit in his viewing the genre function as applying to the embeddedness of language in society:

> Genres communicate indirectly with the society where they are operative through their institutionalization. This aspect of genre study is the one

---

Stuart Chase, "Foreword," Benjamin Whorf, *Language, Thought, and Reality: Selected Writings of Benjamin Lee Whorf,* ed. John B. Carroll (Cambridge, MA: MIT P, 1997), vii–viii.

150. One of Whorf's examples along these lines is his contrast of the physicist's and the psychologist's uses of the word "space." Another is the contrast between the English "sentiment" and the French *le sentiment.* Benjamin Lee Whorf, *Language, Thought, and Reality: Selected Writings,* ed. John B. Carroll (Cambridge, MA: MIT P, 1997), 246–247. A common problem caused by lack of attention to this issue is the name of the school and university subject "English." It is used as the name of a specific language, but also as the name of the differently specific first language in English-speaking cultures. In school the confusion has been between studying the language and studying the literature. Sometimes the national identity of the term English is ignored, and students think they are studying literature, as if this were the same entity in every language and every culture. Curricula could change significantly if academic departments were named something like "Native Language" or "First Language" rather than "English."

151. Bakhtin, *Speech Genres,* 98.

152. In this discussion, I am overlooking Bakhtin's distinction between primary and secondary genres. This point may be worth considering, but it is not directly germane to his broader sense of how genres work and how important they are to the understanding of the uses of language. His distinction is similar to Walter Ong's distinction between primary and secondary orality—which, I think, is also only of tangential relevance to his main discussion of orality and literacy.

153. Bakhtin, *Speech Genres,* 99.

that most interests the ethnologist and the historian. In fact the former will see in a genre system first of all the categories that differentiate it from that of the neighboring peoples; . . . The same is true for the historian: each epoch has its own system of genres, which stands in some relation to the dominant ideology, and so on. Like any other institution, genres bring to light the constitutive features of the society to which they belong.[154]

The identification of genres of discourse is given as a practice of use to every subject matter that addresses history and society. It is also a guide to studying disciplines themselves. History may be told through its succession of historiographcial genres as well as literary, legal, medical, or popular genres. Similar techniques apply to synchronic studies of society. Observing the arrangement of genres in a sample of history, society, or an academic discipline is an action that orients the understanding of that sample.[155] The constitutive role of genres of discourse and language disabuses us of any expectation of their fixity, urges us to look for patterns of social change, and depends on the assumption of their materiality.

This perspective, which is not a theory in the traditional sense, is no more exact than Wittgenstein's or Austin's; it may be a view that is to be used like the many descriptive formulations given as a collection in *Philosophical Investigations*. Although Bakhtin and Todorov did not present it as such, and although "literary response" criticism of the 1970s and 1980s did not refer to Bakhtin and Todorov, that style of criticism is enriched by their conceptions of language and discourse. The "response" is the process of reading or viewing the literary texts and performances and reconstructing or resymbolizing these texts. Readings are viewed as answers to texts, or translations of them, within the dialogues of text and society and among members of society. Different answers follow different conventions, but respondents answer both texts and one another. In this sense respondents relive the texts and rearticulate them, as the exchange of language marks a living community. This style of reading was only indirectly conscious of the material action of language, if at all. Yet response processes, like psychoanalysis, because of their living status, have remained viable as evolving orientations within literary pedagogy, as suggested by the many textbooks and approaches that cultivate different genres of literary response.

---

154. Tzvetan Todorov, *Genres in Discourse* (New York: Cambridge UP, 1990), 19.

155. As discussed in chapter 12, Andrea Dworkin assembled different literary genres which show how the structure of their society promotes misogyny.

156. To pursue such understanding usually falls into the discipline of linguistic or cultural anthropology or anthropological linguistics. A recent example of such a study is Daniel L. Everett's *Language*, cited in section 3, above. Perhaps it is necessary for us who have grown up in large societies that have multiple global connections to study an isolated

VI. Whorf and Linguistic Relativity

Bakhtin's indirect awareness of the generic behavior of whole languages has not been pursued.[156] However, during the same period in the early twentieth century, some anthropologists and linguists were moving in that direction independently, most notably Franz Boas and Edward Sapir. In part Saussure, a theoretical linguist of a more traditionally scientific bent, was responsible for the relativistic approach to language, which is characteristic of the structural linguistics that followed. Saussure and linguistic structuralism helped to make it possible to entertain ideas of linguistic relativity: if national languages each had their own independent structure, and if these structures were embedded in national cultures, then the thought of each culture had to be understood relative to the language, and the language had to be understood relative to the culture. This meant that the referential function of language could vary from culture to culture as well as within individual cultures. Although Boas and Sapir laid a groundwork in anthropology for linguistic relativity,[157] the efforts of Benjamin Lee Whorf produced the data—the admittedly small range of instances from Native American and Native Mexican cultures that persuaded many to consider the importance of at least the possibility of thinking of each national language as a source of and influence on the total culture that includes nonlinguistic customs, habits, and mores.

Whorf did his work between the late 1920s and 1941, when he died in his early forties. He had gotten encouragement during his graduate studies in anthropology at Yale with Edward Sapir in the early 1930s. Gumperz and

---

culture in order to grasp the idea of a comprehensive continuity between language and culture. If one accepts this sense of total language embeddedness in culture, it may not be surprising to learn that the Pirahas "view all non-Piraha people as 'crooked,' that is bent and not working properly" (Everett, *Language,* 304). They exhibit a chauvinism for their language that we Westerners have, historically, shown for our own. Perhaps the missing language "universal" is cultural: androcentric narcissism.

157. This field has an interesting history, traced recently in several volumes that have reviewed the Sapir-Whorf hypothesis as a result of new studies in sociolinguistics and in childhood language acquisition. These studies suggest (in reverse chronology) a lineage from Whorf to Sapir to Boas to Humboldt to Herder to Hamann (the latter two writing in the eighteenth century). Julia M. Penn, *Linguistic Relativity versus Innate Ideas: The Origins of the Sapir Whorf Hypothesis in German Thought* (The Hague: Mouton, 1972), 54. Scholars have disputed just how important each of these figures has been, but few deny that they are all involved in this line of developing thought over a period of more than two centuries. Chapters 4 and 5 consider some of these sources in connection with a discussion of other contributors to a sense of the materiality of language, and then to the founding of the effort to understand childhood language acquisition more comprehensively. The present discussion depicts Whorf's work folding evenly into the general picture of materiality deriving from Wittgenstein's perspective.

Levenson describe linguistic relativity thus: "[S]emantic structures of different languages might be fundamentally incommensurable, with consequences for the way in which speakers of specific languages might think and act. On this view, language, thought, and culture are deeply interlocked, so that each language might be claimed to have associated with it a distinctive world view."[158]

This perception emerges from the anthropological research that came to Whorf through Sapir. Starting with Humboldt in the early nineteenth century, Western familiarity with occult languages was accompanied by discussions of whether some languages were superior to others. This thought was closely associated with the Western perception that the unfamiliar cultures were primitive, backward, and culturally unsophisticated as compared to Western Christian cultures. The imperial frame of mind touched most scholarly researchers as, on the one hand, there was a sense of enlightenment about other peoples, and on the other hand, there was the persistent sense that their local technologies and unfamiliar social and religious rituals meant that they were behind the West in social evolution, not as developed, slower, and so forth. Such thoughts began to change with Sapir, who referred more to difference than to superiority and inferiority. Whorf carried this perspective further, and became outspoken to the point of identifying language forms in Native American societies that seemed preferable to Western forms. These different senses pointed up the local status of European usages, which Whorf called "Standard Average European" (SAE).[159] The differences were striking enough to promote the belief that a language may itself carry a certain view of the world, that an individual's version of a language may be understood as that person's worldview, and that fundamental perceptions of how things are vary with the languages people speak.

The controversy surrounding this research path is also about the materiality of language, although materiality as discussed here does not enter into the earlier arguments. Perhaps one reason—in addition to professional and national political reasons—that the theory of linguistic relativity was upstaged by cognitive psychology in the positivistic early 1960s[160] is that there was uncertainty about

---

158. John J. Gumperz and Stephen C. Levinson, eds., *Rethinking Linguistic Relativity* (Cambridge: Cambridge UP, 1996), 2. Penny Lee observes that Whorf's version of linguistic relativity recognizes both relativity and universality, as also implied in the work of Wittgenstein, Austin, and Bakhtin. "One of the attractions of the Whorf theory complex is that it allows us the flexibility of relativism along with the comforting (and necessary) affirmation of universality in core dimensions of human experience and thought." Penny Lee, *The Whorf Theory Complex: A Critical Reconstruction* (Philadelphia: John Benjamins, 1996), 223. Globalization has encouraged further review of the principle of language relativity. Guy Deutscher, *Through the Language Glass: Why the World Looks Different in Other Languages* (New York: Metropolitan, 2010).

159. Whorf, *Language*, 138.

160. Gumperz and Levenson, *Rethinking*, 3.

the difference between relativity as it appears in individuals as compared to its appearance in cultures. Individual informants were the source of anthropological generalizations, which, despite being provisional in any case, could not be documented. The only form of clear documentation was the language uses—the tropes, the rituals, the conventions—themselves, and these were the items in question to begin with. To document this view meant only to compare uses in two or more different societies. But how to observe the relativity of language was as much an issue as whether it was there at all.

Two instances given by Whorf suggest how tempting a perspective it had become. Both are in one of his last essays, "The Relation of Habitual Thought and Behavior to Language" (1941).[161] First, Whorf's point is given in an epigraph cited from Sapir: "Human beings . . . are very much at the mercy of the particular language which has become the medium of expression for their society. . . . The fact of the matter is that the 'real world' is to a large extent unconsciously built up on the language habits of the group . . . We see and hear and otherwise experience very largely as we do because the language habits of our community predispose certain choices of interpretation."[162] One of Whorf's instances from Hopi relates to how objects of quantity are described[163]—mass nouns such as water, coffee, flour, wood, cloth, and the like[164]—and another instance reflects on the Hopi use of grammatical tenses. In ordinary conversation in English, he writes, we ask for "a glass of" water or refer to "a piece of" wood. There is a form and content structure ("a formless item plus a form"[165]) in speaking about mass nouns.[166] In Hopi, phrases like "piece of meat," "pool of water," and "dish of cornflour" get only a single term; the context of use fixes the scale at which the item is understood. This may not seem to be a radical difference, except in this respect: if there is a habit (or informal rule) that separates used portions of mass nouns from the abstraction, the abstraction itself then asks for definition.

---

161. An important feature of this title is the use of the word "habitual," a term that refers to living generic usage, consciousness of which almost certainly comes from the experience of anthropologists. Moreover, a habit is likely to have exceptions that document the habitual status. In his 1940 essay "Science and Linguistics," Whorf observes that "if a rule has absolutely no exceptions, it is not recognized as a rule or as anything else" (*Language*, 209). This observation is itself an awareness of how total mediation works: when it is there, we do not see it.

162. Whorf, *Language*, 134.

163. An issue that resembles the nominalist view of how language relates to experience.

164. Whorf, *Language*, 141.

165. Whorf, *Language*, 141.

166. It is true that we sometimes say, "Let's go for a coffee" rather than "Let's go for a cup of coffee," but the former is understood to be an abbreviation of the latter. The *habit* in English is not to fold in the quantity in the particular word, or to distinguish with different *single* words a *cup of milk* from a *glass of milk*. English mostly has different form words that limit the content.

Suppose a definition of water is its chemical formula H_2O, which for speakers of European languages is a reasonable response. Although this does not pose a problem for chemists, for ordinary uses of language there is no reason for this definition to play a role in the use of the term "water." To ask for a definition of an abstraction is, in this case, to ask for a person's knowledge of a different activity—chemical analysis. If chemical language is considered definitive, then it assumes an authoritative and dominant role in language uses. If no definitions of abstract nouns are demanded, but only different ways of referring to them are needed, linguistic authority is more diffuse: there is no essential definition given by a secret language or jargon whose speakers are more authoritative than ordinary speakers. This political issue was lost neither on Whorf nor on those who objected to his theory.

The matter of authority applies more dramatically to the different grammatical renditions of time in SAE and in Hopi. Whorf describes Hopi's two "tenselike forms," earlier and later, as compared to the three tenses in SAE: past, present, and future:[167]

> Languages by the score get along well with two tenselike forms answering to this paramount relation of "later" to "earlier." We can of course construct and contemplate in thought a system of past, present, future, in the objectified configuration of points on a line. This is what our general objectification tendency leads us to do and our tense system confirms.[168]

The practical difference between Hopi (and similar other languages) and SAE is in the latter's habit of nominalizing time. In Hopi, the phenomenology of time is represented thus: we can experience earlier and later—we acknowledge that the present is unstable—but we cannot experience what English speakers call "the past," "the present," and "the future." None of these categories, in experience, is stable; rather, they are abstractions (of experience) that do not record (in the tenses) information about the sequence of memories. One could describe the Hopi language as being more at peace with the constant changes marked by time, and SAE as being more at peace with the *habit* of fixing events within tenses; put this way, one is not better than the other. But Whorf makes an additional point that does imply a certain kind of superiority in Hopi tense usage: reduced objectification of experience. This becomes a political matter because objectivity is also the authoritative basis of epistemology in Western society. The objectification of time (through accurate measurement and sophisticated clocks) is part of the objectification of nature or of different parts of the cosmos; in turn, this habit has removed people from this picture. If nature

---

167. Whorf, *Language,* 143.
168. Whorf, *Language,* 143–144.

is objectified, it has to be so under the assumption that human observers are outside of it. It is assumed that human time is different from cosmic time. By contrast, the comparative sense of time and its correspondence to memory and experience teaches that we are not thus removed but a part of the total system of change in the cosmos. Scientific authority, although it would not disappear, would then be considerably reduced from what it is now if we did not rely so deeply on the habit of objectification that is taught by the SAE languages we use. The implication of Whorf's work is not that objectification is erroneous, but that its scope of use is very broad as compared with its use by languages in other cultures, and perhaps that scope is too broad for our own good.[169] If, in turn, we accept that there is a relation between language and culture (between language and science in this case), we are in a better position to adopt features of other cultures, owing to linguistic relativity's revocation of the question of linguistic superiority.[170] However, just such political considerations have kept linguistic relativity a minority position, and in the same ways that *Sprachspiele*, speech acts, and heteroglossia (the principle of mixed genres, further discussed in chapter 4) have been repressed and kept in a minority status.

VII. Academic Resistance to Materiality

Whorf approaches language with as strong a sense of its force or its effects or its palpability in the growth of culture as do Wittgenstein, Austin, and Bakhtin. Bakhtin was the least controversial of these four figures, but each developed ways of thinking about language that, as Stuart Chase says of Whorf, challenge a twenty-five-hundred-year-old view of language that "a line of thought expressed in any language could be translated without loss of meaning into any other language"[171] and asserted, rather, that "a change in language can transform our appreciation of the Cosmos."[172] It is necessary to take the view of these figures

---

169. Naomi Scheman's discussion of objectivity (commented upon in chapter 10) specifies how the exaggeration of objectivity has a paranoid cast—a disease so common and ubiquitous that it seems normal and ordinary.

170. Although I claim this to be true of linguistic relativity, one cannot make this claim about Whorf, as he writes, "Does the Hopi language show here a higher plane of thinking, a more rational analysis of situations than our vaunted English? Of course it does. In this field and in various others, English compared to Hopi is like a bludgeon compared to a rapier" (*Language*, ix). However, the sense of how to understand a local superiority over an essential one has not been aired out. The chance to learn from other languages has been denied, historically, because of various forms of cultural chauvinism created by social psychology—either we are better or they are—when, actually, in cases in which languages mix with one another, each takes from the others and both are enriched.

171. Chase, in Whorf, *Language*, vii.

172. Quoted by Chase, in Whorf, *Language*, vii (but the source is not given).

together. Academic mores have kept them apart, except in the work of very few scholars; certainly there is no consensus about their relationship to one another. Yet at more or less the same time—during the third, fourth, fifth, and sixth decades of the twentieth century—they arrived, from different cultural standpoints, at views of language that challenge a fixed Western approach to language and its use as the foundation for objectivity.

The modern academy has been one of the institutions that have slowed the development of this approach to language. John Lucy's discussion[173] of the slow uptake of linguistic relativity also applies to the materiality of language. He presents four different reasons, each of which emerges from the history of the university discussed in chapters 2, 8, and 9. First, he suggests, academic attention to the issue of linguistic relativity has cast the question in extreme terms: few will accept that language determines thought, although all accept that, to some degree, language influences thought. Thus, no research is needed. This result leads us to ask how this could have happened. Second, study of this issue requires interdisciplinary work: knowledge of linguistics as well as other fields in language, literature, social science, and psychology would be needed to conduct inquiries that yield results. Lucy observes that the interdisciplinarity of the issue "represents a significant obstacle given the present state of research training, which sharply limits the acceptable topics and methods in most social science fields."[174] In other words, the "rule" of disciplines stands in the way of combining disciplinary work to the extent needed by this approach to the study of language use. In part this is a bureaucratic circumstance, but the third obstacle suggests otherwise. Third, research into linguistic relativity (and into materiality) is "intrinsically contrary to some of the central assumptions of the relevant disciplines." He observes that there is an academic hypocrisy at work when there is "widespread lip service" paid to the belief in the human embeddedness in culture, history, and society, but no attempt at serious research that could speak to the matter of language from this standpoint. Linguistic relativity challenges the beliefs in cognitive and behavioral psychology that language, its uses, and its cultural embeddedness must be pursued using positivist, objectivist assumptions—ones rejected by Kristeva, Whorf, Sapir, Bakhtin, Austin, and Wittgenstein. Lucy suggests, further, that the humanist approach implies that there are limits to the kind of understanding available, a point made repeatedly by Wittgenstein, and that the Enlightenment ideal of the free autonomous individual would be cast into doubt.[175] The fourth obstacle mentioned by Lucy

173. John A. Lucy, *Language Diversity and Thought: A Reformulation of the Linguistic Relativity Hypothesis* (New York: Cambridge UP, 1992).

174. Lucy, *Language Diversity*, 4.

175. This point is treated in chapter 4 in connection with the theme of the identity of language and thought articulated by eighteenth-century philosopher Johann Georg

is that the social sciences have not yet found a way to focus both on individual development and on "radically different, socially constituted contextual systems. . . . Even the preliminaries for a comparative psychology of this sort remain undeveloped."[176] The underlying view for studying people is governed almost altogether by individualism: the axiom that the human situation is understood if the individual person is understood. Feminists have challenged this view for decades,[177] but there is still a strong animus in the academy against the study, at the same time, of (1) individuals as participating in different social genres and (2) the growth of the communities, collectivities, and constituencies themselves.

Even though Lucy does not have the academy in mind, his explanations of why linguistic relativity has not been pursued are consistent with political themes already developed in the present discussion. It may be true that Enlightenment individualism—the ideal of the autonomous individual—now stands in the way of this research. Yet the primacy of the individual person (or soul) dates back to Plato, and was emphasized for centuries by the Christian orthodoxy and its theology of individual salvation that governed the Western universities and had dominion over the use of language. The hypothesis of linguistic relativity reevaluates the habits and mores of individual-centered discourse. It urges an altered sense of an individual as one constituted by collective values articulated by commonly held languages. If a ritual such as confession is understood to be local, and connected to particular language communities, it is harder to say, for example, that participating in the *Sprachspiel* of confession represents a unique path to God. The confession as we know it is private—a secret, in fact, between the subject and the confessor. But if there is no private language, no special unique event taking place except in its identity as a local ritual, all matters of faith remain, more or less, in the status of inaccessible mental states referred to in Wittgenstein's discussion. It is reasonable to ask if they exist, but more than this verbal stipulation is not possible.[178] Those philosophers—such as Ockham and Wyclif, Galileo and Descartes—who welcomed faith in God on the basis of their understanding of the provisionality of language, and on the further basis of a rigid separation of language from the transcendental, were

---

Hamann, someone who Herder admired greatly, and who likely affected Humboldt. The critique of individual autonomy as a political ideal is discussed in chapter 11.

176. Lucy, *Language Diversity*, 4.

177. The feminist challenges and their consequences are discussed in chapters 5 and 6, and again in chapters 10, 11, and 12.

178. Derrida made a similar argument about Husserl in Speech and Phenomena, discussed in chapter 4, as part of the mid-twentieth-century's movement toward a consensus about materiality. See also my more detailed discussion of Derrida's critique of Husserl in *The Double Perspective: Language, Literacy, and Social Relations* (New York: Oxford UP, 1988), 40–49.

considered heretical. Orthodoxy demanded correspondence between language and the world as stipulated by the agents of transcendental authority in just the way explained by Augustine at the beginning of *The Confessions*. Orthodoxy requires total mediation.

Custodians of universities have eschewed the materiality of language because they measured the viability of universities according to the interests of their sponsors and protectors. The institution has remained stable largely because of this censorship, which helped to slow the dissemination of language and literacy and which kept language in a community of privilege by resisting the vernacular, by maintaining the superstition that a language can be intrinsically sacred or superior, by limiting access to universities themselves, and by declaring that authoritative knowledge can only appear in one language—by keeping an absolutist sense of language firmly in front of the total population who could do nothing without this language. Although it remained stable, the university as an institution collaborated with institutions and values that have endangered the majority of populations. The resistance to Whorf's, Bakhtin's, Austin's, and Wittgenstein's works emerge from this traditional attitude toward language and knowledge. This attitude is promoted by a view of language that nevertheless is the majority view today. It is characterized by the belief in the separation of language and thought.

CHAPTER FOUR

The Unity of Language and Thought

I. Enlightenment and Other Values

Eighteenth-century Europe sought individual autonomy, independence, and popular freedom. Reason became a standard and an ideal, a path to rational and fair government. Subsequent historians considered this period to be more enlightened than previous ones. In actuality, oligarchic and elitist rule continued in both church and state regardless of movements toward democracy and civil liberty. The enthusiasm for individualism and democracy did not affect the continued hegemony of Platonic realism as the basis of the public uses of language—slogans, rallying cries, and revolutionary zeal. In some cases, Platonic realism aggravated the effects of dogmatists and ideologues during the Enlightenment; political abstractions were as much the announced pretexts for executions and wars as they had been in previous eras. Some social arrangements changed, but the fundamental temptations of power and war in international relations did not change. J. L. Talmon's lifelong effort[1] to understand the Enlightenment and its legacy concluded that totalitarian democracy (communism and fascism) were as much the product of the Enlightenment as was liberal democracy, whose unwillingness to fight permitted the growth of totalitarian states. Talmon described this result as "paradoxical."[2]

In this historical period, as in the others considered so far, there were departures from the intellectual orthodoxies regarding language.[3] One of these, Johann Georg Hamann, had a strong faith in common with the religious iconoclasts of previous times. This is a salient factor because heretics who were also

---

1. J. L. Talmon's three-volume work is discussed in chapter 11.
2. J. L. Talmon, *The Myth of the Nation and Vision of the Revolution: Ideological Polarization in the Twentieth Century* (Piscataway, NJ: Transaction, 2005), 554.
3. There were Porphyry, the nominalist of the third century; Roscelin in the tenth century; John Wyclif and William Ockham in the fourteenth century; Lorenzo Valla in the fifteenth, Sebastian Castellio in the sixteenth; and Christian Thomasius in the seventeenth—as well as, to different degrees, Galileo, Berkeley, and Hume (the latter two tending to discredit language as a foundation of intellectual life).

religious were not recognized for their faith, but were accused because of their claims of their own independence. Church and state used coercive tactics and demonized independent choices. In the eighteenth century, as before, the use of state violence as a standard gesture of governance derived from the underlying traditions of hierarchical power-oriented government. The cycle of the "primal horde" remained as the presumed basis of society.[4]

Hamann was not persecuted, but he remained an eccentric figure. His ludic conception of language and its imagined origins is an ancestor to the twentieth-century continental group of the language materialists, the poststructuralists. And in his time he may have occupied a position similar to Derrida's today: unique, idiosyncratic, imaginative, and respected by other major figures, yet not quite trustworthy and possibly subversive in his message. This take on such figures may also be described as repression (in addition to suppression, denial, or censorship) by the linguistically orthodox: there is something to this Hamann, but we dare not admit it.

II. Hamann, the Magician

Although Johann Georg Hamann was not alone in his critical response to Enlightenment rationalism,[5] his voice had, perhaps, a note of conviction uncommon in academic claims. He came to this position through a religious rebirth, not unlike today's born-again believers: those who were born into collective religious values, then became disoriented, and then returned to such values with a new sense of how to assimilate them. Because of the strong role of religious thinking in his life, his many nicknames, among them "Magus of the North,"[6] lent him a mystical identity, a factor which further removed him from mainstream scholarly consideration.[7] The consensus about Hamann's work is that his

---

4. Freud's use of this figure in his descriptions of religion and civilization is discussed in chapter 7, section 3. Briefly: an oligarchic gang of followers periodically overthrow and replace the leader, sometimes subsequently extolling him in his death.

5. Isaiah Berlin, *Three Critics of the Enlightenment: Vico, Hamann, Herder,* ed. Henry Hardy (Princeton, NJ: Princeton UP, 2000). These were the major figures, but others presented similar critiques.

6. Berlin, *Three,* 310, lists all the soubriquets applied to Hamann, a list which could suggest both eccentricity and uncomprehended distinctiveness. "Magus of the North" is the name used by James C. O'Flaherty for the first chapter his *Johann Georg Hamann* (Boston: Twayne, 1979). It is not surprising that few understood the value of his perspective: Enlightenment "reason" was as overwhelming then as positivism was when Wittgenstein and Austin wrote. And both situations—both movements against the grain—are analogous to, and perhaps actual continuations of, opposition to Church-style hegemony before the eighteenth century.

7. He communicated with principal scholars of his time, such as Kant, and he was the teacher and inspiration for Johann Herder. He also attracted Hegel's attention. Hamann's

overall perspective derives from his reading of what language is, although there is no certain way to account for the actual path of his thinking: the reading of the Bible ("God's word") as the instrument of the divine gift of language to the human species. This particular fantasy is a version of the traditional belief that language is the sign of the transcendental divine in humans—the capability separating us from other species and the world. However, Hamann took it in the opposite direction, and used it as a way of declaring the immanence, in addition to the transcendence, of God. He emphasized the connectedness of people to nature, to the universe, and to one another. In this context, Hamann contributed to the secular philosophical discussions about the origins of language and the identity of language and thought.

In the history of language philosophy as represented by Condillac, Rousseau, and Herder, the question of how to think about the relations of language and thought was confounded by the belief that language must have had an independent origin in the history of the human species.[8] The oldest bases for this belief are the accounts of creation in Genesis and the story of the Tower of Babel. However, individual experience and intuition do not suggest much about the origin of language: it is not a concern as we speak and write. Moreover, in the seventeenth and eighteenth centuries, the intense interest and faith in reason raised the status of abstract thinking to a level greater than it was in some earlier periods in Europe: reason, as distinguished from passion or feeling, was accepted as the path to secular social amelioration and individual refinement.[9]

work was first taken up in the United States in the 1950s by James C. O'Flaherty, whose discussions and editions might have been enough to stimulate interest in philosophical circles; but they did not, probably because of the positivist domination of philosophy alluded to by Cavell, cited in chapter 3. Something to consider is this: When does work recognized as cogent come to join prevailing orthodoxies?

8. As Berlin describes in *Three* (313–314), this issue presented as a conundrum. Which came first, thought or language? Some said symbols must have preceded thought, and that thought would have been impossible without symbols, while others said that one must be able to think before creating symbols. Chomsky's work represents a contemporary effort to solve this problem. Approaches that rejected the search for origins—that is, approaches that rejected the premise of this eighteenth-century debate—could not join it and today such approaches are still marginal.

9. Today, this dualism continues. Academic psychology honors a division between cognitive and emotional realms of mental functioning, strongly privileging the cognitive. Generally, however, conventional ways of speaking counsel us not to act on emotion, as well as to be suspicious of those who speak and write emotionally. Emotion is thought of as interfering with rational deliberation. The assumption is embedded in a variety of laws that indulge so-called crimes of passion more than premeditated crimes, as if one sort of crime were less governed by affect than another. I discuss how cognitive science understands knowledge to be free of emotion, passion, or feeling that such knowledge is, in some sense pure thought. David Bleich, *Know and Tell: A Writing Pedagogy of Disclosure, Genre, and Membership* (Portsmouth, NH: Heinemann, 1998), 178–179.

Because reason and knowledge seemed to be present in all societies, it seemed that they transcended language; that they were, unlike specific languages, universal, and were consequently independent of language. Yet this orientation was not different from Plato's, which, in its (perhaps ironic) suspicion of poets and poetry, seemed to be saying that in order to establish the well-governed society, the separation of ideas from language was essential. Western societies have taken this view to be axiomatic. Those who considered language to be the sole locus of ideas were in the minority.

Hamann was a member of this minority: he trusted poets and poetry with respect to the authority of the language they formulated. His sense of the integration of language with other aspects of experience and civilized life would not recognize a privileged role for reason as a transcendental guide toward understanding the practical functions of society. Although he was not alone in his opposition, his views were not thought to carry weight in discussions of society and philosophy.[10] One would not want to say that Hamann's work was censored, but its relative lack of influence is similar to the peripheral status of nominalism in medieval and early modern thought: other philosophical positions were more acceptable to Church and other authorities.

Scholars have generally agreed that the distinctive feature of Hamann's work that attracted the attention of more famous peers and that provides an anchor for the rest of his thought is his sense of what language is, is its "primacy," as O'Flaherty put it. Here is Berlin's description of this philosophy:

> Hamann's claim was in effect this: the notion that there is a process called thought or reasoning that is an independent activity "within" man, in some part of his brain or mind, which he can choose at will to articulate into a set of symbols that he invents for the purpose (or derives from others, fully formed), but which, alternatively, he can also conduct by means of unverbalised or unsymbolised ideas in some non-empirical medium, free from images, sounds, visual data, is a meaningless illusion—yet that is, of course, what men have often thought to be true, and indeed perhaps, for the most part, still think. Hamann is one of the first thinkers to be quite clear that thought *is* the use of symbols, that non-symbolic thought, that is, thought without either symbols or images—whether visual or auditory,

---

10. Discussing Josef Nadler's assessment of Hamann, O'Flaherty writes, "[Hamann's] language theory is the one positive side of Hamann's work which has had no historically visible effect in the sense in which the language theories of Herder and Humboldt have." James C. O'Flaherty, *Unity and Language: A Study in the Philosophy of Johann Georg Hamann* (Chapel Hill: University of North Carolina Studies in the Germanic Languages and Literatures, 1952), 10. Isaiah Berlin writes, "Hamann remains . . . in the margin of the central movement of ideas, an object of mild astonishment, of some interest to historians of Protestant theology, or, more often, altogether unnoticed" (*Three*, 256).

or perhaps a shadowy combination of the two, or perhaps derived from some other sense, kinaesthetic or olfactory (though this is less likely in man as we know him)—is an unintelligible notion.[11]

The separation of language and thought became more of a problem and less of an assumption as scholarly work was produced increasingly in the vernacular. If Latin is the universally accepted language of knowledge, it is more easily identifiable with thought. But when knowledge is given in not-Latin, one had to determine if it could count as knowledge and not not-knowledge. Hamann returns to the state of mind of the Latin users, but with a difference: the holy texts were the model of *language use* and not the model of language. And within those texts, it was the *genres* that created their authority:

> The Scriptures cannot speak with us as human beings otherwise than in parables, because all our knowledge is sensory, figurative, and because reason makes the images of external things everywhere into signs of more abstract, more intellectual concepts. . . . All mortal creatures are only able to see the truth and the essence of things in parables.[12]

Languages, in this view, work through processes of figuration, a position that Hamann derived from considering how sacred texts kept their authority. This position could not have come through Catholic orthodoxy, and did not obtain in the societies of Greece and Rome, whose slave economies limited access to language. The emphasis on figuration was encouraged by the Protestant principle that people do and shall have direct access to the transcendental through texts. To Hamann, the sacred text is both a speech genre and a text genre: figurative speech and parables in texts. Hamann understood this use of language as being natural in religious and secular senses. As Berlin described it, getting access to language is the same as getting access to thought. In the Hebrew tradition, the situation is similar, although the language is itself often considered holy, as Latin was, and was to be approached through another (vernacular) language. The

---

11. Berlin, *Three,* 315. Julia Penn writes, "Hamann was the first to completely identify thought and language, i.e., the first to advocate the extreme hypothesis of linguistic relativity." Penn describes the "extreme hypothesis" thus: "language and thought are identical" Julia Penn, *Linguistic Relativity versus Innate Ideas* (The Hague: Mouton, 1972), 51, 49. Hamann wrote, "Vernuft ist Sprache, *logos.*" Johann George Hamann, *Schriften,* ed. F. Roth, G. J. Herder, and G. A. Wiener, 8 vols. (Berlin: Bey G. Reimer, 1821–1843), 7:151–152 (quoted in Penn, *Linguistic Relativity,* in which she translates his words thus: "For him reason *is* language; language is reason" [49]). Hamann's and Whorf's understandings of language were similar to one another, relative to other beliefs in rationalism and linguistic realism.

12. Hamann, quoted in O'Flaherty, *Unity,* 12–13.

Hebrew tradition considered the text to be law ("Torah" means, among other things, [God's] law, a guide and standard for conducting one's daily life), and its use was that on the Sabbath, the day of religious observance, the law was to be read orally, one portion at a time over the whole year, while the part of the population that did not study the law (but who could if they wished and could afford to) in the text would at least hear the law read in its entirety: a speech genre, called, perhaps, "the public reading of the law." This hearing, however, is also access to language in the sense that the knowledge provided by the hearing of the law was pointed toward the regulation of people's everyday conduct of life. Given this sense of how the law functioned through the holy text in both oral and written genres, it is not surprising that the Hebrew language would recognize its social role through the term *davar*.[13] Without there being a separate, abstract, rabbinically approved language doctrine about the nature of language, language was understood to be, and used as, a material entity, yet without any danger or opposition to the religious belief in a transcendental custodian of the universe. By coincidence or not, within Christianity Hamann articulated a principle of language that describes fairly well a feature of the historic handling of Hebrew among Jews.[14]

Recall the discussion of Franz Kafka's parable "Before the Law" in chapter 1. Kafka, the secular Czech lawyer who was also familiar with the Jewish use of the law, portrayed in his novel *The Trial* how the secular, state law was perverted by the collusion of church and state.[15] His stories and novels have been often taken

---

13. This fact might also lend support to the Sapir-Whorf hypothesis, to wit: the culturally specific language recognizes Hebrew speakers' tacit sense of the materiality of language. Other languages (such as those Whorf called Standard Average European) function in cultures that have accepted the Church's axiom of the transparency of language. As suggested in chapter 1 about English (and implied about any language), there are places and usages found in rituals and other social conventions that demonstrate the materiality of that language. The eligibility of Latin to hold abstract knowledge undoubtedly derives from the fact that it is not a vernacular for any group of living people. When Latin was a vernacular, it was not sacred. By social action, Latin was sacralized.

14. For Jews, the materiality of the law is also demonstrated by their practices of multiple readings. Sometimes a biblical account is read as a parable, and sometimes as a literal event. Jewish tradition relied on rabbinic interpretation to decide how to approach each textual feature. Possibly, a century earlier, Spinoza also intuited this feature of Hebrew language and culture, and when he announced it, he was ostracized. It is sometimes implied that the presence of the Inquisition inhibited Jews from *endorsing* Spinoza's work, even if they did not see it as undermining Jewish senses of the divine.

15. In the novel, the priest is also the jailer—he works for both church and state, thus clouding the actual sources of authority in the law. During the witch-hunting period in Europe, the Church routinely "outsourced" execution orders to the state, as the Church wanted to be able to claim that it was obeying the sixth commandment. Both religious and secular laws were perverted by such action.

to be parables. Although Kafka, throughout his work, almost never identifies any people or places with things Jewish—his characters and locations are usually completely unidentified culturally—it is possible that this portrayal dramatizes the contrast between the access of Jews to their law, and Kafka's perception of the denial of access of those living under Catholic Church or state rule.[16]

Kafka's gestural style is usually perceived as ordinary language, except with something new and strange about it. Hamann perceived a similar sense of the gestural function of language in the biblical texts. Once language is seen as a gesture—a *speech/text act*—it is a short step to come to the conclusion that, regardless of what thought it is taken to be representing, the language gestures, given among living people, are meaningful in consequence of their having provided *access* to society, to God, to others in the process of granting access to themselves. For Hamann, the language is part of its genres, its genres part of society—genres themselves understood as social gestures—and the whole process of getting access to the sacred text a coherent social process.[17] It was Hamann's return to Lutheranism that led to this insight into language. As Berlin describes, Hamann's having included language in the category of all symbolic action—music, dance, poetry, and so on—anticipates the symbolic-forms philosophy of Ernst Cassirer, Susanne Langer, and Kenneth Burke, as well as the European and American attention to semiotics. The latter subject, although it was the result of thinking like Hamann's, lacks a key element found in Hamann and emphasized by Susanne Langer, but was generally disregarded by the rest of philosophical treatment of language until Wittgenstein, Austin, and Cavell: the use of symbolic forms is governed as much by feeling and passion as by reason and cognition. In consideration of symbolic forms, none of these factors can be excluded, nor can feeling and cognition be separated from one another. If any one item would have led to the marginalization of Hamann, it would be his insistence on acknowledging the presence of feeling and passion in all uses of language.[18] By the time he wrote, the rule of reason had established its claim as the acknowledged means for regulating passions, the feature of our makeup more usually associated, as in Plato's *Republic,* with women.[19]

---

16. This does not imply that Kafka thought Jewish law more reasonable; rather, it was a response to the feeling that laws are not related to justice. In Kafka's life, "law" meant "Catholic law in Prague."

17. Perhaps one may allow that readers make texts their own—internalize them—by reading. But the present discussion puts aside the use of the internal-external distinction in favor of a process of mutualization among readers, texts, and their cultures.

18. Isn't it plausible that women were accused as witches for similarly unacknowledged reasons: investing feeling and passion into their cures and pronouncements? (See chapter 9, sections 3 and 4.)

19. Hamann was not a feminist in any modern sense; he had four children with a servant woman, whom he did not marry, and remained with her until death. In reflecting

In regard to his recognition of emotion and feeling in the regular uses of language, Hamann's work is also to be distinguished from that of Condillac, Rousseau, and Herder, who emphasized the roles of passions and feelings in their accounts of the *origins* of language. Their rationalist stories envision a "primitive" origin of language, a capacity maturing—progressing—over the millennia to the sophistication of Enlightenment rationality. Although the philosophers had no basis for guessing the time periods of human evolution, few doubted that there were pre-linguistic creatures who, collectively, *acquired* language and thought. The human species was thought of, naturally, as independent from the rest of living things, and there was no thought to consider how the totality of life may have developed, or that humans were a species within that much broader category. The Enlightenment and Romantic stories of the human acquisition of language usually involved a strong aesthetic element associated with the emotional marking of oral and verbal sounds, which put the sounds into memory and made them available for iteration, socialization, and permanence. Thus, during "original" times, there were pictures, poetry, and song (according to Condillac) which advanced toward a more deliberate referential and abstract use.

This Enlightenment story is itself strange, even if one accepts, provisionally, that there is such a thing as an origin of language. The pictures, poetry, and song must have been abstractions themselves. The account does not detail how scientific abstraction followed and then improved upon the emotionally motivated figurations: it does not say or show how development rendered reason superior to the passion-motivated primitive art works. There is nothing to say that the use of art-making capabilities and scientific abstraction or abstract reason should not all develop at the same time and pace, and as mutual influences on one another. Rather these kinds of language/thoughts—science and reason— are related to social functions in the later periods of civilization, especially the need to, for example, build cities or pyramids—or to find ways to destroy the cities of others, whereas art and poetry are characteristic of uncivilized humans. Hamann used the biblical creation accounts in a novel way: to perceive that the connectedness implied by the biblical accounts is before us now ("nothing new

---

on the need to renounce the ideal of a pure language, he wrote, "The purity of a language diminishes its riches; a too strict correctness diminishes its strength and manhood" (O'Flaherty, *Unity,* 20). The ideal of language purity was pursued vigorously and with a sense of its masculine superiority by Joseph Campbell and other British teachers in the eighteenth century. Miriam Brody, *Manly Writing* (Carbondale: Southern Illinois UP, 1993). Hamann did not renounce the superiority of men, but like Abelard (and perhaps for similar reasons), he began to see men as being implicated in the passions of social and domestic life, and his vision of what language is participated in this shift away from conventional ideas of manhood.

under the sun"), and perhaps in plain sight. Berlin cites Hamann's formulation, "Language is the first and last organ and criterion of reason."[20] Rationalism moved language away from the life processes through which humans are connected to nature and other living beings:

> The Cartesian notion that there are ideas, clear and distinct, which can be contemplated by a kind of inner eye, a notion common to all the rationalists, and peddled in its empirical form by Locke and his followers—ideas in their pure state, unconnected with words and capable of being translated into any of them indifferently—this is the central fallacy that for him needed eliminating. The facts were otherwise. Language is what we think with, not translate into: the meaning of the notion of "language" is symbol-using. Images [figures] came before words, and images are created by passions.[21]

Viewing language and thought (reason) to be a unified human capability derives from an underlying view of the living world, rather than from a need to solve the conundrum of whether or not language preceded thought. According to this view, it could not have been the case that reason was an independent faculty of superior beings to begin with. The "which came first" conundrum of thought and language was *created* by philosophy, by Plato, and then revised in Renaissance Europe.[22] Hamann's image of the human species (subsequently supported by Boas's observations) considers this a miscarriage of civilization (as opposed to simply a philosophical error) that, if approached philosophically, calls for radical revision of the roles of intellectual lives, not just a revision of thought.

Hamann's perception provides a wider historical context for the pointed critique of philosophy by Wittgenstein, and for the approaches to the study of language given by Austin and Whorf. Hamann's view helps to take their thinking out of the philosophical box, out of the space of academic work, and places it in

---

20. Berlin, *Three*, 316.

21. Berlin, *Three*, 316.

22. Franz Boas suggested that the abstractions on which "abstract thought" depends were created by philosophers: "Terms like 'essence, substance, existence, idea, reality,' many of which are now commonly used, are by origin artificial devices for expressing the results of abstract thought. In this way they would resemble the artificial, unidiomatic abstract terms that may be formed in primitive languages." Franz Boas, *The Mind of Primitive Man,* rev. ed. (New York: Macmillan, 1938), 219. Although Boas's sense of the word "primitive" is no longer used, he observed that different societies created different levels and kinds of abstraction. Abstract thought is not peculiar to Western civilization, but is created in different styles, depending on what a culture needs, tolerates, and welcomes. The conundrum of thought and language was, according to this view, created by Western learned society.

the larger space of society, viewing academic work as needing to belong more to all people. But Hamann's work is noteworthy in another important sense: it is an ancestor of the different style of materiality found in the work of poststructural-ist philosopher Jacques Derrida, whose work is with the *figurative character of all language,* a topic related to but not emphasized by Wittgenstein's reflections. The concepts of figuration cancel the distinction used by eighteenth-century rationalists between primitive and advanced, between savage and civilized, as categories of language.

III. Figuration

It might be said that Derrida tried to live out his philosophy of language. Like Wittgenstein, he spoke differently to his academic colleagues, and spoke enough to make the point that something "*différant*" was up. His speaking was writing, and his writing speaking. His erudition enabled him to take liberties with the use of language that in most instances are forbidden to students and junior academics, but are taken routinely by many of us who participate in ordinary language conversations.[23] He introduced into academic discourse practices which confound this discourse, but which nevertheless can be understood to be genres in the category of *Sprachspiele,* which, in this chapter, could be translated as "the plays of language." Understood in the context of play, Derrida's uses of language are unremarkable; but in academic contexts, they are a provocation just as Wittgenstein's uses were. If one remembers Derrida's sources in Nietzsche and Heidegger—if one entertains the mystical thought that language functions on its own—that language, alive, is constraining human action rather than its being human action—then the "play of language" has one sort of reference: one not different from the traditional one, a conduit carrying "meaning" to other destinations. If, on the other hand, Derrida's play *with* language is understood as an instance of the play of language, we have introduced a factor rarely mentioned by Derrida: the speech action of the living speakers. I say "rarely" because Derrida's discussions do not use the discourses of subjective experience to refer to his own speech action; rather, his discussions refer only to his own texts (such as his signature) as his means of discussing speech acts.

---

23. A close counterpart of Derrida in literary history is James Joyce, whose vision and uses of language were as broad as Derrida's, and who, in literary works, succeeded in directing our attention to the action of language use. His time in history corresponded more to Wittgenstein's than to Derrida's. The juxtaposition of Joyce to the materialists suggests that what philosophy has finally come to has always been practiced in literature: the use of language to indicate what language does, can do, or should do is in plain sight but not acknowledged by law and science.

His writings suggest that his attention was taken by Austin and by speech-act philosophy. In reading his commentary[24] on these works, one gets the impression that he spotted his kinship with them, and as a result, spent some significant reflection on them. Cavell, however, raises an important question: "How is it that Derrida misses the extent of Austin's differences from the classical and/or academic philosophers with whom Austin, as much as Derrida, is at odds?"[25] It might be asked—Is this a case on Derrida's part of "there is something to this but I dare not admit it"? Cavell sees both Austin and Derrida as criticizing the same things in the tradition of Western philosophy: "Austin's analysis of the performative may be seen to be motivated precisely as an attack on what deconstruction attacks under the name logocentrism."[26] Perhaps a feature of Cavell's usage suggests an answer to his question: the use of the term "attack"— conventionally used to describe or verbalize the act of disagreement among male philosophers—inhibits a more cooperative predisposition in philosophical discourse.[27] Cavell's reflection suggests that Derrida may not have been familiar with the full range of Austin's work, and that he may not have properly contextualized Austin's concept of the performative as a counter-example[28] to logical positivism. Cavell's critique of Derrida gives the sense that Derrida may have relied too heavily on *some* of Austin's texts themselves, without seeing other of Austin's texts that create the context for reading the texts, or even entertaining the thought that Austin had philosophical pathways similar to his own. Cavell's essay implies that Derrida has a presumption of opposition that overrides more cooperative stances that could have been taken.[29]

---

24. Jacques Derrida, "Signature Event Context," *Limited, Inc.,* trans. Samuel Weber (Evanston, IL: Northwestern UP, 1988), 1–24.

25. Stanley Cavell, *Philosophical Passages: Wittgenstein, Emerson, Austin, Derrida* (New York: Blackwell, 1995), 48.

26. Cavell, *Philosophical,* 49.

27. Walter Ong describes this as the intrinsic male need for agon or struggle (chapter 9, section 5). Janice Moulton, "The Adversary Method in Philosophy," *Discovering Reality: Feminist Perspectives on Epistemology, Metaphysics, Methodology, and Philosophy of Science,* ed. Sandra Harding and Merrill B. Hintikka (Dordrecht: Reidel, 1983), is discussed in chapter 10 as part of her critique of language and knowledge.

28. Cavell, *Philosophical,* 50.

29. Pedagogical purposes usually encourage the noticing of similarities among different collections of writings. But because academic research usually ignores the pedagogical function of scholarship itself, the adversarial function ends up being what is actually taught to young scholars, and that is partly how agonistic and oppositional styles limit both learning and teaching. It also ought to be remembered that several idioms likely occupy Derrida's language use, in addition to the academic ones: Jewish speech habits and French intellectual ones. Additionally, the repetition, permutation, recombination, and variations on themes in Derrida's writing reach obsessive levels, so that the foregoing features of his writing must be entertained as part of his edifice. This issue is discussed further in section 5 of this chapter.

Cavell addresses the issue of materiality by noticing the connections between Wittgenstein, Austin, and Derrida.[30] Of Derrida, he observes that "he likes Austin's theory of performatives for its refusal of the view of language as the transferring of a something called a meaning from one place to another (communicating) place. And he likes Austin's instinct in relating writing to speaking by way of the idea of the signature."[31] Both Austin and Derrida emphasize the palpable in language, and each finds ways to reject the emphasis on the metaphysical (or, perhaps, the spiritual or transcendentally symbolic) sense of what language is. There is, for both, no essential meaning passing through the conduit of words: the words themselves are exchanged and are, therefore, not different from what they communicate. Wittgenstein rejects the appeal to the metaphysical also through his nominalist stances: the false essentializing of abstract concepts, identified by Cavell as "our wish for super-concepts."[32] By seeing ordinary usage as the limit of language, and by viewing ordinary language as available through its *Sprachspiele,* Wittgenstein belongs with Austin and Derrida as language materialists.[33]

Readers of Derrida cannot fail to notice that his texts communicate the feel, the phenomenology, of speech action, the feeling in our responses that the thinking and the speaking or writing are happening at once to us. I might put it this way: noticing that the texts are meant to act on me in a certain way—something I don't notice, for example, in reading Dickens, but that I might observe in reading Jorge Luis Borges or Ursula K. LeGuin—I start to reflect on what action that speaker/narrator is taking by speaking or writing in just that way. This is not that difficult a question, because I and many of my conversation partners are given to just that play of language we find presented by Derrida in so-called serious academic contexts. What about this change in context?

---

30. Henry Staten's discussion had raised this issue earlier to a limited degree, but his perspective is not the same as Cavell's, which is more interested in making philosophical connections that are motivated by an affective kinship among thinkers that philosophy usually overlooks. Henry Staten, *Wittgenstein and Derrida* (Lincoln: U of Nebraska P, 1984).

31. Cavell, *Philosophical,* 60.

32. Cavell, *Philosophical,* 61. Or Whitehead's "Fallacy of Misplaced Concreteness," cited in chapter 1.

33. Henry Staten approaches this view, but neither elaborates on its radical consequences nor sees Derrida's response to Austin as one of recognition of a kindred view. Staten does not associate materiality with the ubiquitous uses of language by all people in a total social ecology, playing a role analogous to the atmosphere's support of life. His notice of the importance of "scenes of use" points subsequent discussions in this direction (*Wittgenstein and Derrida,* 26). However, the way philosophers approach scenes of use remains a problem today, as the discipline has not overhauled its self-placement outside these scenes and replaced themselves inside, as would be done if the writings of Wittgenstein and Austin were themselves taken as material.

There is a helpful group of studies on Derrida's critique of logocentrism.[34] There is perhaps less discussion regarding the changes in the subjectivity of speakers if our sense of the use and feel of language becomes more like Derrida's, more like Wittgenstein's. Here, also, Cavell has made a start:

> Say then that the price of having once spoken, or remarked, taken something as remarkable (worth noting, yours to note, about which to make an ado), is to have spoken forever, to have entered the arena of the inexcusable, to have taken on the responsibility of speaking further, the unending responsibility of responsiveness, of answerability, to make yourself intelligible. It is recognizing *this* abandonment to my words, as to unfeasible epitaphs, presaging the leave-taking of death, that I *know* my voice, *recognize* my words (no different from yours) as mine.[35]

Here is a result of Derrida's early discussions in *Of Grammatology*. To speak is to mark and to remark. This is the writing of the voice, which in classical Western metaphysics lives in a radically different zone from that of the written letter. Derrida says/writes that the voice and the letter are in the same language category—that they are the same genre:[36] palpable semiotic actions. I don't know if Cavell's "forever" accurately characterizes Derrida's sense of iterated markings, because the markings, spoken or written, are equally permanent, equally transient, or as variably transient as any material things from gluons to mountains. But Cavell's "forever" does say that the voice is as material as the text, and in his passage above, he says that the voice delivers an equivalent (to that in writing) level of ethical responsibility, an equivalent level of commitment, of movement within interpersonal space, of going on the record and having it count, of putting the word there and expecting it to stay there, of presenting something that could and—more often than not—does outlive the individual speaker.

---

34. For example, Gayatri Chakravorty Spivak, "Translator's Preface," Derrida, *Of Grammatology* (Baltimore: Johns Hopkins, UP, 1974), ix–lxxxix; Christopher Norris, *Deconstruction: Theory and Practice* (London: Methuen, 1982); and Jonathan Culler, *On Deconstruction: Theory and Criticism after Structuralism* (Ithaca, NY: Cornell UP, 1982).

35. Cavell, *Philosophical*, 65. Notice the similarity of Cavell's last sentence to Derrida's more radical and cryptic formulation: "My death is structurally necessary to the pronouncing of the *I*. That I am also 'alive' and certain about it figures as something that comes over and above the appearance of the meaning." Jacques Derrida, *Speech and Phenomena and Other Essays on Husserl's Theory of Signs,* ed. David B. Allison and Newton Garver, trans. David B. Allison (Chicago: Northwestern UP, 1973), 96. Although the two statements may be read as consistent with one another, Cavell's additional element is that he is aware of the kind of social scenes in which such thinking makes sense: responsibility for and to others is both now and over and above the meaning of my present pronouncements.

36. A use of a vocabulary broached in chapter 3 and discussed again in this chapter.

The speaker's being abandoned to his or her words is the path to knowing his or her own voice, which is a figure for self-awareness. Cavell says that any words are attached to a speaker, that there are no words which are not so attached, regardless of the anonymity of the authorship of most texts, as the words do not themselves acquire viability (or legal tender) until overtaken by living people in the presence of others: your and my words are no different from one another, yet they are different words.

This sense of the intimacy of speech, of reading, of hearing, of immersing oneself in any textual event, is a change in the phenomenology of formal academic work, a change that follows from what the theory is claiming as well as from what it is doing. The volume of output of Wittgenstein and Derrida implies how much trouble is involved in articulating, at once, a change and a need for change in the fundamentals of thoughtful discourse, not to mention the change in the mores, practices, and habits of Western civilization. This volume of output bespeaks a level of urgency sometimes found in those who seek to formulate what seems important and vital. In these two writers the energy may also be understood as a degree of gender-marked agitation; each says repeatedly how their thoughts aim to revise twenty-five hundred years of thinking in the West.[37] Cavell (among others) has begun the process of disseminating both of their works, and of speaking with a casual fluency different from traditional academic writing. He has engaged different topics, and especially topics of popular culture, that can work with the discourses introduced by Wittgenstein and Derrida. And perhaps more importantly, as a result he has, by his own example, lowered the pitch of argument and dispute in a way that has made academic projects more visibly useful to other social and cultural interests.

Wittgenstein's discourse style is interrogative and subjunctive. Imagine if Freud wrote in that style: it would be someone else. Wittgenstein in his later work did make declarative statements, but many of them are relatively brief and aphoristic, a radical difference from the relentless declarations of the *Tractatus*.[38] His keynotes in the *Philosophical Investigations* are his questions, his stipulations

---

37. Stuart Chase said this of Whorf (see chapter 3, section 4), but Whorf did not say it of himself. Freud said it of himself—he imagined that he was "disturbing the sleep of mankind"—and it is also reflected in his twenty-volume collection. The agitation at work in many thinking men's need to produce constantly also is responsible for the academic speech conventions that characterize criticisms as attacks. Not every scholar has a large-scale revolutionary purpose such as those of Wittgenstein and Derrida; yet to become nervous about such a purpose is characteristic of other forms of male anxiety that appear in combative contexts. Ong's discussion of male psychology (see chapter 9, section 5) does not refer to this aspect of oppositional behavior—nor, as a result, to its emotional accoutrements.

38. His informal writings in philosophy resemble similar formulations in Kafka that comment on situations of his protagonists. Each has a certain playful irony that chal-

of scenes, his imagination of conventional situations that could take unexpected turns. His writing characterizes at once the adequacies, comforts, and uncertainties of ordinary usage, claiming that philosophy has grossly exaggerated the degrees and significance of the limits of reference and communication. The discourse has a relaxed bearing, an openness to associations that are appearing through a certain mood, but that pertain to several different topics. Formal writing conventions do not accommodate such peremptory changes of topic and interest, and yet in reading a work like *Culture and Value* or *On Certainty*,[39] it is not alarming to see that the titles are not indicative.[40]

IV. Contradiction, Neologism

If you read Derrida just after reading Wittgenstein, you see a different form of play. It is plausible to call it a more serious play, but it is only less relaxed or more intense, carrying with it the same ironic sentiment found in Wittgenstein, and not found, for example, in Husserl or Merleau-Ponty, or even Russell; it is certainly not found in Locke or Hume or Condillac. In the beginning of his essay "Différance," Derrida writes, "The verb 'to differ' [*différer*] seems to differ from itself."[41] A few paragraphs later, he writes, "*Differance* is neither a

---

lenges the solemnities of their respective genres. In the words of Ludwig Wittgenstein, "Philosophers use a language that is already deformed as though by shoes that are too tight." Ludwig Wittgenstein, *Culture and Value*, (1929) ed. G. H. von Wright and Hekki Nyman, trans. Peter Winch (Oxford: Blackwell, 1980), 41. Kafka writes in "A Country Doctor," "To write prescriptions is easy, but to come to an understanding with people is hard." Franz Kafka, *Complete Short Stories,* trans. Tania and James Stern (New York: Schocken, 1999), 223. This sort of connection moves Wittgenstein's work away from the self-importance of traditional philosophy and toward, in addition to ordinary language, ordinary experience and its literary readings. This style of serious thinking in ordinary language is a path to language access for the majority, but it is pushed aside and sometimes censored in academic and other contexts.

39. Ludwig Wittgenstein, *On Certainty,* ed. G. E. M. Anscombe and G. H. von Wright, trans. Denis Paul and G. E. M. Anscombe (New York: Harper, 1969).

40. In spite of this relaxed bearing, there are references in Ray Monk and Norman Malcolm to Wittgenstein's frustration at not being understood. He was always recognized for his intelligence, but he was not wrong to claim that he was not understood. However, his feeling "not understood" can have a different sense: he was understood well in the sense that thinking as he advocated it would have overturned the careers of many of his colleagues and peers; they felt the force of his messages, and so did not react, leaving the false impression that they did not understand him. Ray Monk, *Ludwig Wittgenstein: The Duty of Genius* (New York: Penguin, 1990), 499–504; Norman Malcolm, *Wittgenstein: A Religious Point of View?* (Ithaca, NY: Cornell UP, 1994), 80.

41. Derrida, *Speech and Phenomena,*129. "Différance" was first published in 1968; the version in this volume has a few pages of discussion before "I will speak, therefore, of a letter," the sentence that begins the version of this essay found in Jacques Derrida,

word nor a *concept.*"[42] Usually, the response to such locutions by those starting to study Derrida is to try to decipher them. Who would say such things seriously? Derrida follows up on these sentences, but the comments don't clarify the remarks in the conventional sense. Students must wait until they achieve an extended familiarity with several of Derrida's texts to get the sense of his apparent contradictions or nonsense statements. At that point, and not before, their playful aspect becomes visible. His "play" is that no word, no usage, no meaning can be relied upon come what may. Play shows why this is so. There is nothing in the verb "to differ," cited *unused and with no antecedent context,* to suggest a comprehensible meaning, nor is the neologism "différance" a word or a concept: *it was just made up.*[43] Derrida's writings present a few new words and a few new contexts for a few old words newly used—such as "trace" and "supplement"—and then he waits for the novelties either to sink in to other readers, or to disappear with him: his usage takes account of his living status by carrying the view of his own transience.[44] But such moves, in their provisionality, their playfulness, and yet also their scripted character being repeated in print and then repeated by readers, are part of his *Sprachspiel*—which, in this case, may also be appropriately translated as "language game," as we are learning the rules of translation. In addition, there is a wide context of other works—writing, playing, and so on—that must be permitted its effects in order for the neologisms to be given a chance to speak. Yet this is no different from familiar, ordinary language-learning processes—the gradual getting used to new thoughts through simultaneous playful, serious, and semi-serious actions, until they become part of a collective stock of recognized language.[45] But becoming aware, during these

---

Margins of Philosophy, trans. Alan Bass (Chicago: U of Chicago P, 1982), 1–28, quotation on 3.

42. Derrida, *Speech and Phenomena,* 130.

43. That is, when the talk was first given and the term was not heard by that audience. Now that it is no longer just made up, rereading this passage has a new value: the appearance of contradicting the law of non-contradiction: the word "to differ" is itself and also has another sense, and that's that; "différance" remains a word and a concept. Derrida lets the unconventionality of the words provoke the interaction between himself and readers.

44. Wittgenstein writes, "A new word is like a fresh seed sewn [*sic*] on the ground of the discussion" (*Culture and Value,* 2).

45. Wittgenstein asserts, "I still find my own way of philosophizing new, and it keeps striking me so afresh; that is why I need to repeat myself so often. It will have become second nature to a new generation, to whom the repetitions will be boring. I find them necessary" (*Culture and Value,* 1). Even though Derrida did not make this observation, it may as well apply to him; he is equally repetitious—and for the same reasons. Derrida does refer to his own repetitiousness in *Monolingualism of the Other, or The Prosthesis of Origin,* trans. Patrick Mensah (Stanford, CA: Stanford UP, 1998); this is discussed in the next section of this chapter.

processes, of their playfulness and provisionality is new, as we are not used to acknowledging how the materiality of language is the basis of our learning it to begin with.[46] Rather, because we are not aware of the materiality of language, we attribute stability to the experience of continuous usage, while longer periods of stable, reliable usage tempt us toward the false generalization of permanence; this assumed essential feature of the usage is then appropriated as an instrument of authority. The uses of secret, sacred, standard languages depend on their artificial, *declared* permanence. Such declarations are rarely direct performatives, but appear through other official documents issued by governments: the language of biblical commandments, of constitutions, or of laws of science, or of papal bulls, are illocutionary speech acts, part of whose action is to *declare the permanence of their own language.*[47] But if the society functions with a sense of the transience of the language, the institutions associated with official language are more eligible for change without violence.

In his discussion of Claude Lévi-Strauss in *Grammatology,* Derrida engages the important anthropological observation that, contrary to Enlightenment rationalism, literacy is not the key to liberation but is a party to governmental exploitation (and, often enough, enslavement) of the population.[48] Lévi-Strauss's investigation led him to the view that literacy (in the sense of learning the technologies of reading and writing) is hoarded and controlled in any case by authoritarian or even democratic rule.[49] Derrida's critique of Lévi-Strauss,[50] however, derives from his (Derrida's) version of the materiality of language, the shorthand for which in his works is *écriture,* "writing." This is, of course, his principal neologism (that is, a new *usage*—the use of the term *writing* to apply to deliberate, systematic symbolic markings, and not just alphabetic visual recording of spoken language), which takes its time dissolving into formal discussions. In English, *writing* and *scripture* are not cognates; in French *écriture* means (among other things) scripture. So what would read as "holy writing" in

---

46. This is elaborated in chapter 5 with regard to the study of the acquisition of language: when infants acquire language, the words feel permanent, a feeling that justifies the term "acquisition" for the use of language.

47. For the foregoing list, how many will say, "Yes, I know they are laws, but they can change at any time, easily"?

48. Jacques Derrida, *Of Grammatology,* trans. Gayatri Chakravorty Spivak (Baltimore: Johns Hopkins UP, 1974), 101–140.

49. This point is consistent with Talmon's description of totalitarian democracy and its cousin, liberal democracy. J. Elspeth Stuckey transposes Lévi-Strauss's thesis to contemporary democratic contexts of writing pedagogy. The argument of this work, effective as it is, might be even more effective if it accommodated Derrida's exception to Lévi-Strauss. J. Elspeth Stuckey, *The Violence of Literacy* (Portsmouth, NH: Heinemann Boynton-Cook, 1991).

50. Which is that the oral uses of language may also become instruments of enslavement (Derrida, *Of Grammatology,* 133).

English reads "Holy Scripture" in French. Translating Derrida into English loses that important connotation, although other English usages, such as "inscription," have moved closer to the French set of connotations. Yet assuming the French-language community to be a primary readership of Derrida leads us (more quickly than it does assuming an international audience) to the radical secularization of his usage. The converse is equally significant, especially in view of Hamann's discussion of language and thought as having been *given* by sacred texts: using the term *écriture* lends ordinary secular writing a holy or special status—which, given Derrida's total project, *materializes* the ordinary writing, points to its materiality, its importance, its irreducible relevance, and its availability for a variety of iterations and incremental changes (as well as fixings) by the *authority of ordinary people*. Here the terms "holy" and "sacred" mean something like "mattering to speakers in the most urgent way."

Thus, of Lévi-Strauss's argument, he observes, "Yet once again,[51] I do not profess that writing may not and does not in fact play this role [as a tool of authoritarian rule], but from that to attribute to writing the specificity of this role and to conclude that speech is exempt from it, is an abyss that one must not leap over so lightly."[52] The warning is somewhat understated, given his elaborate effort to make this point repeatedly in different contexts. Writing, scripting, and the letter refer in Derrida's work to any sign—that is, any coherent usage of an articulation, a marking that accompanies other behaviors, other gestures, or other words or works. Speech has the identical function. It fixes the language, more and less provisionally, depending on the context, and inhibits language growth that happens among speakers and writers not being coerced by social institutions. Derrida's interest in Austin derives from the fact that the latter also had a way of saying that speech was no different from other gestures or behaviors. Utterances/texts necessarily appear in context, serving functions, acting, or doing, as is done by any script, any ritual, any trope, any *Sprachspiel*. However, Derrida was impatient with Austin for the same reason he was impatient with Lévi-Strauss: he saw in both figures a tacit underlying presumption of a principle of Western metaphysics—the stability of speech in Austin's case,[53] and the separation of writing and literacy from speech in Lévi-Strauss's case. Derrida's sense of writing is that of *marking*, which is also achieved by speech,

---

51. As in the case of Austin, Derrida is sympathetic to what Lévi-Strauss is claiming, and has said so a number of times.

52. Derrida, *Of Grammatology*, 133.

53. Derrida said that Austin's stipulation of "felicity" in speech acts betrayed an underlying commitment to traditional concepts of transparency and language stability ("Signature Event Context," 323). To Derrida, felicitousness of speech acts might apply only in trivial cases, or perhaps even no cases, as it is not possible to determine that the *speech* created the felicitous outcomes; the contexts through which felicity must be tested are ever widening.

writing, pictures, dance, and so forth. This marking is a limit and is itself, relative to Western metaphysics, a deferral from the presumed essence of thoughts and experiences. Yet it is the locus of human action—material in its palpability, its relevance to its occasions, in its fragility, transience, or even its stability. The markings are subject to the same destiny available to everything else material, which to Derrida as to Wittgenstein is everything else that we say exists. If there are no essences or no inner meanings, however, the markings are movements we make with our bodies from one experience to others. The movements are simultaneously orderly and uncertain,[54] A and not-A: names identify and multiply possibilities for identification. They create categories, laws, and groups as they participate in every behavior that is collectively shared, viewed, experienced, and relied upon. It is this genre function of language in particular—contested as it has been since the days of the sophists, the nominalists, the heretics of early modern Europe, and the empiricists of the eighteenth century—that renders the disclosure of the materiality of language consequential. Derrida reflects on this issue in his essay "The Law of Genre" (1980).

The essay is one of several of his that are suitable for engaging the classical nominalist issue: How referential are class nouns such as law and genre? If their reference is less than fixed, how are people to read the written law, and how seriously are genres of law and laws of genre to be taken?[55] Some may read Derrida's essay as denying the connection of materiality and genre, given its insistence that all genres are mixed, but this statement hardly renounces the term "genre"; instead, like all Derrida's other uses of familiar terms in new senses, the statement brings it under closer consideration, makes it more available for new readers to examine, though not necessarily to arrive at a stable sense of these terms: only to the understanding that the terms themselves—the writings—are the most stable phenomena.

The path to seriousness with Derrida (and in a different sense with Wittgenstein) is through play. "Genres are not to be mixed," he starts; "I will not mix genres" comes next, followed by "I repeat: genres are not to be mixed. I will not mix them."[56] A page or two later he writes, "If a genre is what it is, or if it is supposed to be what it is destined to be by virtue of its *telos*, then 'genres are not to be mixed'; one should not mix genres, one owes it to oneself not to get mixed up in mixing genres. Or, more rigorously: genres should not intermix."[57] Who

---

54. As Ralph Cohen described genres, "necessary and loose" (see chapter 3).

55. As suggested earlier, these are the usual issues in the study of the Hebrew law by observant Jews. Each new Talmudic case reviews the concept of law and genre, and no decisions revoke either category.

56. Jacques Derrida, "The Law of Genre," trans. Avital Ronell, *Critical Inquiry* 7.1 (Autumn 1980): 55.

57. Derrida, "Genre," 57.

will not recognize the (speech) genres of each of these grammatical permutations? There are different kinds of laws; there are oaths, promises, statements of position, vigorous commitments of self and intention, and who knows what else. But they are all characteristic of the way law lives in our society, our civilization. If you announce the law of anything, the declarations of commitment go with it, the oaths of allegiance (to the United States Constitution: "to the flag and to the republic for which it stands . . . with . . . justice for all"). At the end of *Limited Inc.,* Derrida jokes or exaggerates or speaks seriously, "[T]here is always a police and a tribunal[58] ready to intervene each time that a rule [constitutive or regulative, vertical or not] is invoked in a case involving signatures, events, or contexts."[59] Genres and laws are speech action rules, and Derrida explains his exaggeration (the police) by describing how laws bring transgression and violation. He writes in "The Law of Genre," "What if there were, lodged within the heart of the law itself, a law of impurity or a principle of contamination? And suppose the condition for the possibility of the law were the *a priori* of a counter-law, an axiom of impossibility that would confound its sense, order, and reason?"[60] Yes, what if there were? Just suppose. Notice how interrogatives and subjunctives that are similar to Wittgenstein's sound different when Derrida uses them. Yet are they different? Isn't it true that Western law, derived from Roman law, presupposes a principle of contamination, of rebellion of the ruled against the rulers, an uprising of the "primal horde"? Do we not understand the law to be coercive, and aren't there social institutions (police and tribunals—inquisitions) that protect the law's protectors, and not the population? And don't we feel that this coercion is the fundamental principle of civilization? Didn't Freud imply that this was the case (see chapter 7)? Didn't the Church "police" itself and the behavior of "unlawful" members of the university communities (see chapter

---

58. Notice how even saying these words "police" and "tribunal" change the atmosphere of Derrida's writing, regardless of whether this usage is lighthearted: in reading, we don't quite know, as we probably would not know if we heard them used in a talk. Because they are figurative, they are both comic and serious, referential and metaphorical. It is difficult, but possible, for traditional academic thinking to accommodate this rich, material feature of usage.

59. Jacques Derrida, "Limited, Inc a b c . . . ," *Limited, Inc.* (Evanston, IL: Northwestern UP, 1988), 105.

60. Derrida, "Genre," 57. Derrida rearticulates the speech action of the law. Catharine MacKinnon makes a similar point: "[B]ecause law is backed by power, so its words are seen as acts." Catherine MacKinnon, *Only Words* (Cambridge, MA: Harvard UP), 40. Pornography is also action, and becomes a certain kind of police action because, as both MacKinnon and Andrea Dworkin argue, it serves and trains men in supremacy in our society. Dworkin asserts, "[P]ornographers are the secret police of male supremacy." Andrea Dworkin, "Against the Male Flood: Censorship, Pornography, and Equality," *Feminism and Pornography,* ed. Drucilla Cornell (New York: Oxford UP, 2000), 29. Also a figuration, it nevertheless articulates the speech action of much pornography.

8)? Didn't the Church avoid the police by transferring the criminal priests? Didn't the administration of Pennsylvania State University avoid the police by permitting the assault of children to continue? Were these trusted custodians of language not placed outside the law? Didn't the Inquisition ask the state to execute heretics and witches and thereby enforce the law (see chapter 9, sections 3 and 4)? Does the law protect anyone but those who can afford to use it? And in language pedagogy, is grammar not equally protected by classroom police and tribunals that deny participation in educational institutions unless grammatical laws are upheld?[61] Is this "only kidding"? Is this as true as it is untrue?

The discussion of law in Derrida's essay seems as if it may be in the background, as the essay appears in literary journals and spends most of its space discussing a short story, a *récit*. But it cannot be denied that the law—its variations, its status, and its active effects on people's lives—as Patricia Williams has noted,[62] exhibits the materiality of its several languages and genres: their weight changes depending on which classes of people they affect. The law of genre, given as a literary matter by the kind of journal that prints it, is also a law matter, which is a brief way of repeating in yet another genre what Derrida wrote to begin with. One may understand Derrida to be following Wittgenstein's instructions and *showing* what genres, laws, and changes do in the use of language, rather than trying to explain what they do in declarative, referential terms.

Derrida reflects on the terms "law," "genre," and "language" as they are involved in the issue of what is meant by natural categories, the issue that started with Plato and Aristotle and which animated the opposition of nominalism to realism. Derrida holds genres to have been naturalized in philosophic discussion. He then observes that the term "natural" is "this difficult word whose span is so far-ranging and open-ended that it extends as far as the expression 'natural language,' by which term everyone agrees tacitly to oppose natural language only to a formal or artificial language without thereby implying that this natural language is a simple physical or biological production. . . . What however seems to me to require more urgent attention is the relationship of nature to history, of nature to its others, *precisely when genre is on the line.*"[63] Language and genre both have been characterized in Western history as natural, which renders both terms transparent—that is, as *referring to* received, given, and known entities,

---

61. Diane Ravitch compiles a list of terms and usages (not poor grammatical usages) that different sources in the United States have found socially, politically, and personally offensive. Diane Ravitch, *The Language Police* (New York: Knopf, 2003), 171–202. This also is not new: it performs the service, however, of raising our awareness of how seriously the usages are taken by all parts of society.

62. Patricia Williams, *The Alchemy of Race and Rights: Diary of a Law Professor* (Cambridge, MA: Harvard UP, 1990). Williams, herself revising academic discourse, explores how the same laws affect blacks and whites differently.

63. Derrida, "Genre," 60.

rather than their being material marks that have been traded and changed in the distributions of social authority. As used by Derrida the term genre summons the nominalist debates which highlight the wordness of *genre,* so to speak, as the feature that matters most to us. Derrida articulates the unarguable "hypothesis"[64] that "a text cannot belong to no genre, it cannot be without or less a genre. Every text participates in one or several genres, there is no genreless text; there is always a genre and genres, yet such participation never amounts to belonging."[65] The last clause of this citation warns against assuming any *necessary* generic identity or any single factor defining the genres of texts.

This sense of genre is cognate with Wittgenstein's sense of *Sprachspiele* and Austin's sense of speech acts. To wit: an utterance/text (to Derrida, a swatch of writing) cannot belong to no play, act, or game; it cannot be without or less a play, act, or game. Every utterance participates in one of several plays, acts, or games; there is no play-/act-/gameless utterance/text; there is always a play/act/ game and play/act/games, yet such participation does not fix an utterance/text as necessarily part of a play/act/game. All texts (language, languages) are contingent on use, on the context of use, and the social relations of use. The translatability of Derrida's hypothesis into English, and then into Wittgenstein and Austin, helps to describe it (by inscribing it) in a context that makes it clearer and articulates the terms of the materiality of language. Derrida's formulations in this essay, along with Bakhtin's and Todorov's,[66] decisively link considerations of language to considerations of genre, considerations of genre to issues of language, and both to the necessity of recognizing the living constituencies that are associated with language and genre.

In some criticism, deconstruction has been mischaracterized as advocating a nihilistic uncertainty about the use of language, and as having instigated approaches to literature that are in some sense absurd: all literary works deconstruct or deny themselves.[67] Yet Derrida's discussion of Maurice Blanchot's *La*

---

64. Derrida, "Genre,"65.

65. Derrida, "Genre," 65. Compare the use of the term "belonging" to its similar use in Derrida's *Monolingualism,* discussed in section 5, below. The principle involved is that being a member of a genre has no dimension of necessity, nor does the connection of a person to language have such a dimension. By denying the coercive aspect of "belonging," Derrida underscores the customary, the habitual, but not the lawful.

66. In *Genres in Discourse,* trans. Catherine Porter (New York: Cambridge UP, 1990). Derrida's discussion of genre contrasts with Todorov's smooth, rational presentation that continues Bakhtin's earlier formulations. However, the contrast also points up the difference between a language user who is deliberately exploiting the materiality of language and one who is not.

67. Gerald Graff complains about Jonathan Culler, "Having demonstrated the uninterpretability of the novel [Flaubert's *A Sentimental Education*], its refusal to lend itself to thematization, Culler proceeds to read the novel in the thematic way which he declares inapplicable." Gerald Graff, *Literature Against Itself: Literary Ideas in Modern Society*

folie du jour (The madness of the day) shows the opposite tendency: the desire to immerse oneself in texts so fully as to have them throw open the widest possible perspective on language and society, to admit the literary work, finally, to speech action rather than just to fiction.[68] One of the reasons Derrida's work had been distorted into an academic fad is that the academy, following its traditional values and paths of detachment, did not (and perhaps was not able to) recognize Derrida's materialist stance on language as a basis for the integration of literature to social discussion and action. Academic literary criticism exploited Derrida's unorthodoxies to create a boom in literary theory, but one that rarely noticed and did not value the materiality of his language use and his sense of what language is. Critics mistakenly viewed his own playfulness as the result of a trait in language instead of it being a trait in people. The phrase "play of language" was read as if language without speakers were living, thus becoming an absurdity. Many students went along with this way of reading deconstruction. Derrida's prolific output, his work in writing, and the physicality and palpability of this effort became stimulus for cultic behavior in the academy; had it been recognized as a realistic, even pragmatic respect for the use of language no such drift into absurdity would have been possible. Those who read and write may also play as part of their contribution, as this play reminds us of the flexibility of language, of its adaptability to the change within which we all live our lives.[69]

A salient feature of Derrida's reflection on the Blanchot account affects French readers differently from how it affects non-French (and, in the present case, English-speaking) readers. This feature also affects how the generic sense of law is bound up in the local characteristics of language, and how the law is

---

(Chicago: U of Chicago P, 1979), 159. Another familiar answer to deconstructive criticism by respected critics (Meyer Abrams, oral presentation, Modern Language Association, December 1974) is to claim derisively that that critic's own language undermines itself and therefore we don't have to listen to it. Critics who were educated by Western metaphysics had no means to cope with Derrida's claims. Some critics born into grammatology more than with it—such as Barbara Johnson—produced compelling readings of classic works without fearing the end of literature. Barbara Johnson, *The Critical Difference: Essays in the Contemporary Rhetoric of Reading* (Baltimore: Johns Hopkins UP, 1980). The fact that Johnson is a female reader may be germane: there is an attempt to extend the new perspective, not falsify it. This issue is taken up in chapter 12.

68. In Johnson the essay "Melville's Fist: The Execution of *Billy Budd*," is especially noteworthy (*Critical Difference*, 79–109). Billy Budd was executed because his violent action took the place of his failure to speak. Johnson, fully immersed in this text, shows at once the text's action and her own verbal interactions with the text. Rather than showing this literature as "against itself," Johnson emphasizes how much it is itself a social action, as well as the senses in which her effort is a social interaction. Chapter 12 further discusses Johnson's perspective on the materiality of literary language.

69. Given this situation, one might want to say that Derrida was as misunderstood as was Wittgenstein.

a different genre in different languages.[70] One could confine such matters to the one Blanchot story and Derrida's treatment of it, but considerations of linguistic relativity are not far removed from this treatment in this essay.

Toward the end of the essay, Derrida writes, "Even though I have launched an appeal against this law [of genre], it was she who turned my appeal into a confirmation of her own glory."[71] Had the story been written in English or in German, one could not have made this claim, nor could one have said, "It was *he* who turned. . . ." English does not have gender inflections, and in German "the law" would be *das Gesetz* or *das Recht,* gendered neutral. After having paid homage to the law and her glory, he writes, "The law is mad.[72] The law is mad, is madness; but madness is not the predicate of the law.[73] There is no madness without the law . . . Madness is law, the law is madness. There is a general trait here: the madness of the law mad for me, the day madly in love with me."[74] The law being referred to as female, then mad, and then the day "in love with" him, raises issues not considered by Derrida in this essay but relevant to understanding the materiality of language. The Christian West, based on Greek idealism and related values, divided the mind and the body in a gendered way—the mind gendered male, and the body female—and this tradition can be found in European writing into the twentieth century, in the work of George Bernard Shaw, for example, in his fantasy of humans ultimately evolving into pure minds.[75]

---

70. Examples of this difference in the present volume would be how canon law was presented through the Latin-speaking hierarchy, and how Talmudic law was disseminated by Hebrew-speaking rabbis.

71. Derrida, "Genre," 80.

72. The French is the title term, *folie,* which translates into "madness" in English. Both languages include the connotation of pathology, as in the term "insanity," and both have a more figurative sense—as in the phrase "that way lies madness." An additional connotation in French is that of extravagance—a wildness or indiscretion, usually given by the term "crazy" in American English, a term that appears in Derrida's *Monolingualism* to describe the mother tongue, discussed below in this chapter. The "madness" of the law may thus also be read as the "extravagance," or the "excess," of the law—a phrase that, for Europeans, would describe a host of familiar events (associated with the world wars), that, perhaps, Americans would not easily recognize. The term falls into a different group of terms in French from that in English.

73. In the preceding sentence, madness is the grammatical predicate. Derrida's negation of this fact again is an instance of the materialist suspension of the traditional rules: one is not constrained to read or hear a grammatical predicate as a strict equation or equivalence. Just as "participation never amounts to belonging" to a genre, predication never dictates equivalence, and, rather, leaves open to circumstances the actual application of the togetherness of law and madness ("Genre," 65).

74. Derrida, "Genre," 81. Here, also, "madly in love" can be read as "crazy about."

75. Bernard Shaw, "Back to Methuselah: In the Beginning," in *Complete Plays: With Prefaces* (New York: Dodd, Mead and Co., 1963), 2:6. Contemporary scientific work in cognitive science begun in the 1950s falls into this category: the radical separation

The French traveled the path of other Western cultures in separating the mind from the body and maintaining the principle of their duality, their separation. The writer (culturally designated sayer, teller, poet, *dichter*) Blanchot "noticed" this gendering and, safely within the genre of fiction, played it out in his *récit.* The reader (Der Rida or De RRida[76]) notices, by citing it in his essay, how "the law" (*la loi*) and "the truth" (*la vérité*) cleave, so to speak, to the protagonist: "Let us be attentive to this syntax of truth. She, the law, says [to the narrator/ protagonist]: 'The truth is that we can no longer be separated. I shall follow you everywhere, I shall live under your roof. . . .' He: 'The truth is that she appealed to me.'" Derrida notes at this point that both the truth and law are female and concludes in his reading, "One cannot conceive truth without the madness of the law."[77] The indirectness of the narrator's response is something like, in the film *Casablanca,* the indirectness of Rick Blaine's response to Ilsa's repeated declarations of her love for him: "Here's lookin' at you, kid." In each case, she commits herself; he drinks to his own scoptophilic pleasure. Conscious of not escaping Western metaphysics, Derrida is less conscious of his non-escape from global androcentrism.

The male writer and reader, tucked safely in the fiction and then in academic discourse, projects the troubled character of gender relations onto the question of law, the truth, and the validity of categories. Both men see the materiality of the law[78]—the linguistic basis of truth, of the law of truth, and their implication in this materiality—marked by its femininity. The problem posed by their access of awareness is in the genres of their writing. How will such thoughts, appearing through genres that lawfully fulfill a different referential function that is consistent with the history of philosophy and of the academy, change the genres, regardless of the intensity Derrida's challenges to the law of genre? In fact, the challenge seems so intense ("the law of the law of genre . . . is precisely a principle of contamination, a law of impurity, a parasitical economy"[79]) as to distract from the thought that is nevertheless affirmed—the fundamental necessity of genres, civil laws, truths, and so forth.

---

of the knowing functions of the mind from feelings, passions, and so on, and scientific experiments being conducted with this separation considered axiomatic.

76. For those remembering the 1970s jokes.

77. Derrida, "Genre," 80.

78. It is perhaps worth noting that in Hebrew, in which the law is treated as a relatively flexible, material entity regardless of its divine status and origin, its grammatical gender is feminine. The Mosaic Law, Tor*ah,* has a feminine ending (ah) and is treated with the same deference that men, in some contexts, offer women. Traditionally men gather to study and honor the law, while "she" teaches the population at large—in the religious service in the synagogue—after the Sabbath Queen has arrived each week.

79. Derrida, "Genre," 59.

This is a crossing point for the issue of materiality. Historically, material things are associated with feminine things, especially since femininity and bodily awareness have been associated with one another in male-governed culture. The male-coded myth of the evil of women helps to push men toward the excessive, fatuous valuation of spiritual entities, and particularly toward the claim of the spiritual essences of language and the need to exercise dominion over the access to language. The minority position of the materiality of language is related to the minority status of women. Toril Moi writes in connection with Julia Kristeva's approach to language (discussed below), "Femininity and the semiotic do, however, have one thing in common: their marginality. As the feminine is defined as marginal under patriarchy, so the semiotic is marginal to language."[80] (Kristeva's distinction between the semiotic and the symbolic—discussed below—is germane, but Moi's remark remains consistent with the characterization of language presented here.) All cultures have been androcentric, and so there is no direct correlation between the status of women and the materiality of language, nor, obviously, is the recognition of materiality a full, reliable solution to the burdens of gender inequality. Only this much can be said: in the West (and possibly in other societies) the entry of women into authoritative positions weakens the strict upholding of the mores of referential language as the standard, an issue discussed further in chapter 5.

V. Translation

In the process of Derrida's performance of the materiality of language, a struggle is taking place between the sense of the obsoleteness of Western metaphysics and the need to present this sense in genres respected by readers who have not agreed that there is a problem with the genre of Western metaphysics. The introduction of gender in his essay puts an accent on the struggle: the categories, the genres of Western thought/writing cannot be revised unless the social categories associated with these genres are likewise revised, and this shows only the faintest signs of happening. Yet in most of Derrida's work, one does not find, except in the abstract terms suggested above (*la loi, la verité*, and so on) a path from the readings of the texts to the historical institutions that may be affected by these readings. However, his 1996 *Monolingualism*[81] departs significantly from his earlier idioms by combining aspects of his autobiography with his reflections on the topic of language in multicultural contexts. This discussion is so suggestive as to render many of his earlier abstractions—ones that had caused trouble for traditional thinkers—familiar: the categories represented by the previously

---

80. Toril Moi, *Sexual/Textual Politics: Feminist Literary Theory* (New York: Routledge, 1985), 166.
81. Derrida, *Monolingualism*.

confounding terms become recognizable as historical, social, cultural, and in play in our daily lives. The assumed academic reference of deconstruction as an analytic process is counteracted by Derrida's autobiographical presentation, which shows processes of language combination—the mixing of languages and genres—on occasion having a "local habitation and a name." This new work of mixing, and the reporting of the mixing that had taken place as historical events in the writer's life, relates Derrida to Johann Hamann's sense of language on the one hand, and on the other hand to traditions of Hebrew, Jewish, and Jewish-French, Jewish-German, or Jewish-English handling of language across the gamut of sacred and secular texts, genres, dialects, and registers of speech and writing.

The law and the truth are female and language is maternal (the mother tongue). Referring back to the population groups of Algeria during World War II, Derrida reports: the schools had "French nationals," "French citizens of Algeria," and "indigenous Jews,"—"for all these groups, French was a language supposed to be maternal, but one whose source, norms, rules, and law were situated elsewhere. . . . As for my family, and almost always elsewhere, we used to say [to refer to this "elsewhere"] 'France' among ourselves."[82] France was the locus of French, Derrida's mother tongue, and Algeria was not the locus: his own French, therefore, was "of the Other": "[N]ever was I able to call French, this language I am speaking to you, 'my mother tongue.'"[83] At the same time, he writes, "I cannot bear or admire anything other than pure French."[84] Then, "I feel lost outside the French language. The other languages which . . . I read, decode, or sometimes speak, are languages I shall never inhabit."[85] These are the documentations of his opening statements: "I only have one language; it is not mine."[86] And then, "1. *We only ever speak one language. 2. We never speak only one language.*"[87] In these sequences, all the sentences are to be read as true. They are, as we come to understand while reading the rest of the volume, all shorthands, like any other use of language. During interpretation we say, "This is true in one sense, that in another"; but put them together and remove the contexts, and they become a contradiction. The same reading strategy applies to the other of Derrida's contradictions mentioned earlier. Once the whole text is assimilated, there are neither contradictions nor paradoxes in the propositional formulations that look confounding by the reading habits deriving from the expectations of transparent language. However, the source of their confound-

82. Derrida, *Monolingualism,* 41.
83. Derrida, *Monolingualism,* 34.
84. Derrida, *Monolingualism,* 46.
85. Derrida, *Monolingualism,* 56.
86. Derrida, *Monolingualism,* 1.
87. Derrida, *Monolingualism,* 7.

ing appearance is the same source as Wittgenstein's unorthodox presentation of a point of view: the conscious use of the materiality of language. The classical logical forms in which premises are presented, then facts, then conclusions are replaced by forms that might well be called "poetic" as Hamann had discussed this term, which includes prominently, perhaps principally, the choices deriving from poetic license. The forms of argumentation and reference are so thoroughly ingrained in academic expectations that the kinds of play seen here (which are often erroneously justified as being the play of the signifier) are deemed positively occult.

Derrida's *Monolingualism,* however, presents historical and autobiographical material that documents each phase of the various contradictions, especially the one that says he has only one language and it is not his. The feature of his writing that demands commentary is his thorough change of academic register, a move identical to Wittgenstein's—both being consistent with the eighteenth-century theorist Hamann's insistence on the unity of language and thought. Each writer's changing the register makes it clear that that thought has changed with the register, just as Whorf's changing of national languages shows that thought has similarly changed with the language. Once the terms of the change—the register, the language, the difference of cultural context, for example—are invoked they are considered part of one picture in this language—one picture, in that there is no need to think either of unity or of separation of thought and language. I have already suggested how deeply Wittgenstein depends on the German, as much as Derrida on the French—and neither on some abstract meta-language that would count as thought: "there is no metalanguage, . . . *a* language shall always be called upon to speak about *the* language—*because* the latter does not exist."[88] The texts and language are the locus of a discussion in which any reference to a distinction between language and thought is nugatory.

In the phrase "untranslatable translation"[89] (itself a shorthand for "nothing is untranslatable; but *in another sense,* everything is untranslatable"[90]) we hear the terms of membership in a multilingual civilization. The annoying sense of contradiction comes only from a tacit reliance, a faith, a presupposed belief in the referentiality, the primacy, and the clarity of the spoken voice speaking to the hearing ear. Once it is understood that language continues to function in translated and untranslated ways at the same time, once it is understood that new translation may always be needed, and once it is understood that the way *this* language lives in *this* culture is like the way *that* language lives in *that* culture, one may remove the compulsion to place the search for the accuracy of translation ahead of the search for its purposes and contexts.

---

88. Derrida, *Monolingualism,* 69.
89. Derrida, *Monolingualism,* 66.
90. Derrida, *Monolingualism,* 57.

Translation is sometimes accurate, sometimes not, and never accurate, never not. The Sapir-Whorf hypothesis caused a similar sense of consternation as its critics sometimes implied that it meant that translation was not possible. Yet if that were so there would have been no means for Boas, Sapir, and Whorf to present in English any instances that would have communicated the contested hypothesis to begin with. Our ordinary knowledge (of what is in plain sight) of total contexts, rarely recognized as salient or fundamental, ratified the terms of the Sapir-Whorf hypothesis beforehand, just as Derrida's movement between contexts ratifies the truth of each of his contradictory propositions. This movement overturns the rule of the law of non-contradiction. Now we may allow that: sometimes, it is A and not-A at once. Yet this small change from being totally in effect to being partially in effect also repeals the law of, and the automatic reliance on, transparency, and the primacy of referential function as the essence of language.

Writing is opaque and is a metaphor for the varying degrees of the opacity of language, of all forms of symbolic behavior. As Cavell began doing in his readings of Wittgenstein and Austin, Derrida has begun to affiliate writing with passionate action and motivation: "Yes, by this word *écriture* we would indicate, among other things, a certain mode of loving and desperate appropriation of language and through it of a forbidding as well as forbidden speech (for me, the French language was both)."[91] As he explains about his school experience, one can get so-called pure French in a written text, because it is read and not heard, but not through the great variety of French speech—the formal Parisian "forbidding" French and the vernacular Algerian "forbidden" French. The use of the now-established term *écriture* sacralizes all signifying, all use of symbolic and figurative material, in just the sense described by Hamann. Writing (language and symbolic forms understood to be material) is what people grow into as part of the terms of being alive. Derrida's attachment to language had come about through a "loving and desperate appropriation," in a community (the indigenous Jewish community) first marginalized and then (during World War II) actively endangered. Understanding *écriture* to refer to all forms of language use (before its use as a descriptive category for Derrida in the 1960s) was an access to social affiliation with the less marginal, less endangered, and less fully identifiable.[92] Derrida describes the Jewish community and his own mentality in Algiers as already having been "contaminated" by Christian culture, and thus, in a sense, on the run before the war began. Notice the terms in which he describes this negative effect: he and other Jews had begun to acquire "the respectful belief

---

91. Derrida, *Monolingualism*, 33. Derrida here enacts the revocation of the sacredness of the received language through his articulation of its sway on his uses of language.

92. It was not lost on the Germans that Jewish men were already marked as such; the circumcision was clearly a part of Jewish *écriture*.

in inwardness, the preference for intention, the heart, the mind, mistrust with respect to literalness or to an objective action given to the mechanicity of the body, in short, a denunciation, so conventional, of Pharisaism."[93] One can see in this list the principal terms of the Greek approach to language and mind— marked, perhaps, by Locke's phrase "cheat of words," words that had come to be superseded in value by experimental knowledge on the one hand, and the inner authority of conscience and intentionality on the other hand. Derrida's turn to writing, to literalness, to the importance of bodily gestures, and to physical marking as the fundamental legal tender of social existence is, in this description, a recuperation of historic Jewish uses of language and bodily marking, a revocation of Western metaphysics and its belief in the "presence" of the intention and in the authenticity of "the heart."

The dependence on the inanimate and the ineffable is the collective psychological circumstance that represses people's recognition of the materiality of language and represses this recognition's capacity to act, to play a role in feelings and social relations. In assimilating Derrida's uses of language we cannot fail to feel their exaggerated urgency; their excessive uses of extreme terms like always, never, ceaseless, endless, and impossible; and the dozens of contradictory sentences, phrases, clauses, and so on. I have seen no formal commentary on these habits of writing, much less on their relation to what critics have usually referred to as his project. In *Monolingualism,* Derrida becomes his own reader. He characterizes his taste for purity in the French language as "hyperbolic,"[94] a trait he "contracted" at school: "The same goes for hyperbole in general. An incorrigible hyperbolite. A generalized hyperbolite. In short, I exaggerate. I always exaggerate."[95] It could not be the case that this is an idiosyncratic trait, regardless of the account given for it. The hundreds of contexts and audiences that overlook this trait without complaining speak to its being a common trait in academic discourse, and certainly in French academic writing. What is a good context for understanding its action?

Some of the personal circumstances reported by Derrida augur the intellectual style of a responsive adolescent in a French territory during and after World War II. Regardless of what "contamination" may have been affecting Derrida's community at that time, one Jewish value came through: learning and study.[96] For

---

93. Derrida, *Monolingualism,* 54.

94. Derrida, *Monolingualism,* 48.

95. Derrida, *Monolingualism,* 48.

96. Critics have already noted the fundamental role of Jewish life and values in Derrida's achievements. Readers interested in pursuing this theme might review Susan Handelman, *The Slayers of Moses: The Emergence of Rabbinic Interpretation in Modern Literary Theory* (Albany: SUNY P, 1982). Gideon Ofrat's *The Jewish Derrida,* trans. Peretz Kidron, (Syracuse, NY: Syracuse UP, 2001), is a comprehensive, up-to-date, and provocative review of Derrida's various connections to Jewish writings and values.

most readers, Derrida's exceptional erudition outweighs his exaggerated usages regardless of what problems have resulted. However, that exaggerated diction is also a mixed genre, as it is characteristic of Jewish vernacular discourse as well as French academic discourse. Viewing exaggerations as a *Sprachspiel,* a specific (and in some cases culture-specific) speech/writing genre, gives them referential value. Although Derrida did not identify these tropes and genres in a wider sense than has already been cited, it is strongly suggested in other parts of this text that his total language package—the combination of the provocative styles with the provocative pronouncements *about* language and philosophy—the critique of Western metaphysics combined with the contradiction of Aristotle's law of non-contradiction, has this specific cultural dimension. Derrida's writing, its repetitions, its permutations and recombinations, its language that turns back on itself to refer to new things and to undo references just asserted bespeaks both play and struggle[97] that mark two fundamental aspects of diasporic Jewish life over a period of twenty centuries.[98]

As in Kafka's work,[99] the Jewish identity of the play/struggle has been, mostly, concealed in Derrida's many texts, as his readings have derived from a wide range of Continental philosophers. *Monolingualism,* however, joining the postcolonial and multicultural discussions that have developed, demands attention to language, which necessarily includes *one's own language.* Regardless how fully the issue of "one's own" is reconsidered, regardless of how active are Derrida's characteristic permutations, he is nevertheless forced, in a sense, to *want* to return to an "absolute idiom." "There are speakers who are competent in more than one language," he writes, "But do they not always do it with a view to an absolute idiom? and in the promise of a still unheard-of language? of a sole poem previously inaudible?"[100] This formulation is at once Hamann

---

97. Some might say that two so-called cultural parties of European Judaism, the Chasidim and the Mitnagdim, represent, respectively, play and worship through joy and dance, and struggle and worship through solemn study and serious devotion to practices.

98. Typically, hyperbole "will have rushed a French Jewish child from Algeria into feeling, and sometimes calling himself, down to the root of the root, before the root, and in ultra-radicality, more *and* less French but also more *and* less Jewish than all the French, all the Jews, and all the Jews of France" (Derrida, *Monolingualism,* 49).

99. As described by Ernst Pawel, "Kafka's world [was] dense with hate. But he had never known any other. . . . Understanding, when it came, turned out to be as toxic as the air itself." Ernst Pawel, *The Nightmare of Reason: A Life of Franz Kafka* (New York: Vintage, 1985), 44. Evelyn Torton Beck writes, with regard to Jews' response to the toxic atmosphere, that they recognize "the essential absurdity of [their] situation even in the most dangerous or tragic circumstances," and "this humor survives in the work of Kafka." At the same time, Beck observes, "Kafka's narratives are entirely devoid of specific references to Jewish themes." Evelyn Torton Beck, *Kafka and the Yiddish Theater* (Madison: U of Wisconsin P, 1971), 29, 181.

100. Derrida, *Monolingualism,* 67.

(the born-again Lutheran theist Pietist), Derrida, and other diasporic Jews, as well as, perhaps, all people in their feeling the deep comfort and confidence in their effortless access to the mother tongue. To speak at all, to "write" at all, Derrida offers, is itself a messianic promise, and as such, a *speech act,*[101] because of this longing for the "poem" of the absolute idiom, which is out of reach because there is no transcendent "metalanguage." This feeling does describe the deep Jewish attachment to speech, to language, and to text as the single tangible in an otherwise uncertain political weather map in Europe. When Hannah Arendt declares that the *"Muttersprache"* remains after the Holocaust,[102] Derrida takes pains to show that this also is not so, because, he claims, the German language *must* have been implicated in its mad use. He sees Arendt as disclaiming responsibility for the German language on the grounds that a language cannot go "mad":

> Arendt is not willing or able to think of this aberration: in order for the "subjects" of a language to become "mad," perverse, or diabolical, evil with a radical evil, it was indeed necessary that language have a hand in it; it must have had its share in what made that madness possible; a non-speaking being, a being without a "mother" tongue cannot become "mad," perverse, wicked, murderous, criminal, or diabolical. . . . And we will understand less than nothing in something like Nazism if, along with language and speech, we exclude everything that is inseparable from it: it is not nothing, it is almost everything.[103]

This is one of Derrida's most explicit statements regarding the inseparability of language from the living political context. Arendt had been criticized for naturalizing the Eichmann phenomenon, suggesting her movement toward denial in her claims. Here also Derrida finds her trying to salvage a feature of a (temporarily) diabolical society—the very feature that must have been, and must still be, a hallmark of its actions: the language, the mother tongue.

Derrida further observes that Arendt "did not perhaps *wish* to see . . . that it is possible to have a demented mother."[104] This phase of his critique of Arendt recalls the "madness of the (female) law" in Blanchot, in French (*la loi*). Having described his own deep involvement in the mother tongue that is "not his"—that is, recognizing Arendt's attachment to the mother tongue[105]—

---

101. Derrida, *Monolingualism,* 67.
102. Derrida, *Monolingualism,* 85.
103. Derrida, *Monolingualism,* 87.
104. Derrida, *Monolingualism,* 87.
105. "As the Heideggerian she remains in this respect, but like many Germans, Jewish or not, Arendt reaffirms the mother tongue, that is to say, a language upon which a virtue of originality is bestowed. 'Repressed' or not, this language remains the ultimate

he now indicates the necessary involvement of the language *in* the law, as was shown in the Nazi perversion of ordinary language in its various laws, pronouncements, and proclamations. Derrida offers that there is no escaping, through mothering, through the lasting power of the mother tongue, the collective effects of the law and the language, and no safe place when the total society falls into the diabolical vein, as the law and the language both, regardless of their loving approach to each individual, are enablers and accomplices of the violence and killing. In this context, Derrida's introduction of messianism (the saving of the total society)[106] as being part of the promise of language use, says that the recovery from the perversion is in the *écriture* of the survivors rather than in the claim that the *Muttersprache* was not implicated in the degenerate society. The significant scale of post-Holocaust literature, history, film, drama, and poetry has created the grounds for recovery of all peoples involved in the machinery of destruction.

In connection with the madness of German society during Nazism, several of the uses of madness by Derrida include—but also go beyond—pathology, as one must do when confronting the mass normalization of madness. The term also has the sense of "crazy" as in "crazy about you"—in love, silly with love, devoted to a fault: *distracted*. "When a mother loses her reason and common sense, the experience of it is as frightening as when a king becomes mad. In both cases, what becomes mad is something like the law or the origin of meaning (the father, the king, the queen, the mother). . . . [O]ne is always crazy about a mother who is always crazy about that of which she is the mother without ever being able to be uniquely that."[107] We experience mother as a unique figure, perhaps permanently: *my* mother. This experience creates the feeling of the "origin of meaning" that is subsequently abstracted under the guidance of male group psychology as the transparency of language, the fixed and reliable meanings of familiar terms. By calling this origin a "prosthesis," Derrida reduces to ordinary dimensions the overwhelming authority granted to "my mother," but also the overwhelming authority we have conferred, erroneously, on the transparency of language. Later in life, some understand the non-uniqueness of mother, but hold on to the sense of the origin of meaning as a process of adaptation to the terms of Western metaphysics: not, in other words, a necessary development, but one encouraged by traditional habits of separation of thought and feeling, mind and body, male and female, spirit

---

essence of the soil, the foundation of meaning, the inalienable property that one carries within oneself" (*Monolingualism*, 91).

106. This feeling seems related to Vivien Law's thinking of the inquiry into language as the human effort needed to revoke the threats of destruction by "the Bomb" (see chapters 1 and 2).

107. Derrida, *Monolingualism*, 88–89.

and letter that have become established as standard, traditional, normative, in Western values, created by centuries of teaching that men are the normative gender.[108]

VI. Julia Kristeva and the Struggle with Gender

There is a kind of madness in Derrida's writing, the reading of which feels like paralysis. His writing welcomes in its richness, and excludes in his repeated conversations with himself. There are many intimations as to how to read it, and they start with the matters of genre and gender, the discussion of which in "The Law of Genre" strikes the notes of recurring unrest, doing and undoing, a habit of throwing every ingredient into the same pot. Different as it appears in Derrida's writing, his restlessness participates, as he himself often observes, in traditional Western ways of establishing dogma and ideology. There is pain in this long struggle to speak so-called pure French, to reach the interdicted language, the abstraction of the forbidden languages (including Hebrew) of his Algerian childhood. But as certainly as he has forged a decisive *oeuvre* performing the materiality of language, he shows only an indirect connection with the *value* of women's custodies of language and their exclusion from the traditions of Western writing. The main absence in Derrida's presentations is not the philosophical abstraction of unending deferrals of meaning and faith, but an ignorance of the rootedness of language as much in the bodily experiences of menstruation, conception, gestation, parturition, lactation, and nursing as in the markings of circumcision, wounding, initiation rituals, endurance of pain and humiliation, and other typically masculine ways of expressing the bodily existence of women as well as men.[109] In women's lives these bodily experiences are bound up with the intimate, devoted attachments to partners and children, attachments whose physicality is equally a feature of (mostly) women's responsibility. So that when the words, the sounds, the music, the poems of childhood

---

108. The understanding of language through knowledge of the details of infantile language acquisition has only been undertaken seriously in the past few decades. There were studies in infantile language acquisition in the nineteenth century, but it was not until late in the twentieth that researchers sought connections between the philosophical and historical study of language development and the ontogenesis of language in infants and children in social contexts. This issue is considered in chapter 5, as it is associated with the larger-scale entry of women into this field of research and into the study of language more generally.

109. Freud, for example, speaks of the vagina as a wound (it bleeds) when, in fact, it is men who prove themselves, in puberty, and often enough throughout their lives, by their ability to withstand wounding. This mythology of false imagery is a staple of the thinking of men, not unlike Freud's claim that sons wish to kill their fathers while, in reality, the fathers have always sent their sons to war (an issue treated in chapter 7).

make their ways from mothers to children, these other experiences of women having a reduced social value are passed along to children, just as clearly as the Nazis' German went bad along with their gang of secret police. Derrida's writing shows a struggle to find this missing language, a struggle that he did not resolve—in much the same sense that Husserl's struggle for intersubjectivity, as Derrida had shown decades back, could not be resolved given the axioms (the "metaphysics of presence") of his ways of analysis.

One of his approaches is in his 1993 essay, *"Khōra,"*[110] which is considered by Gideon Ofrat.[111] Two features of this idea are noteworthy: its proximity to mysticism, and its having been used two decades *earlier* by Julia Kristeva in her attempt to relieve philosophy of its masculine avoidance of facing the living person's experiences.[112] In what seems like an attempt to face the meaning of the mutual dependence of men and women, Derrida, in his usual style of iterated contradiction, summons from Plato the image of a mysteriously empty "metaphysical" zone that holds some secret beyond the familiar binaries of Western philosophy. Ofrat writes,

> It is a third species transcending the great Platonic categorical dualities of essence and appearance, idea and matter, spirit and body, and so on—the third metaphysical element. . . . There are [in Plato's *Timaeus*] as many definitions of the term as there are interpretations. All the same, the Platonic concept is plainly connected to the metaphor of mother, or nanny, or vessel, or—place; the feminine place.[113]

Ofrat, noting Derrida's viewing of this "place" in exclusive terms—a living absence—shows its likeness to the Hebrew *Makom* (meaning "place" or sometimes "room," as in "room to live comfortably") often used as a synonym for God (because God must not or cannot be named directly), and to the other Hebrew (mystical) term *Shekhina* (meaning "presence"; it is feminine in grammatical gender) for God. Ofrat follows this path to Derrida's reading of Blanchot in *Demeure* ("dwelling") as confirmation of, perhaps, a syndrome of traditional female loci: a woman's "place" is in the "dwelling." The verbal appeal and adroitness of this chain of references, however, do not conceal this familiar de-meaning of women. Derrida departs from his materialist location in this regard: in the last paragraph of this essay on the *khōra*, he notes that "Plato never used" the

---

110. Jacques Derrida, *On the Name,* ed. Thomas Dutoit, trans. David Wood, John P. Leavey, Jr., and Ian McLeod (Palo Alto, CA: Stanford UP, 1995), 89–130.

111. Ofrat, *Jewish Derrida,* 63–68.

112. Julia Kristeva, *Revolution in Poetic Language,* trans. Margaret Waller (New York: Columbia UP, 1984).

113. Ofrat, *Jewish Derrida,* 65.

word *hyle* ["material"] "to qualify *khōra,* let that be said in passing to announce the problem posed by the Aristotelian interpretation of *khōra* as matter."[114] This female entity, the receptacle of stories, this zone of primordial neitherness, so to speak—neither presence nor absence, "neither generative nor engendered"[115] seems to be an exaggerated, hyperbolic description of a familiar feminine locus. Except insofar as Derrida is following Plato, why would this female entity be additionally characterized as a third species? As the ancient Hebrew interdiction against naming God yields the substitute names of *Makom* and *Shekhina,* Derrida's habits of language play and philosophical permutation produce this excessive effort to come to terms with a material fact of life in plain sight: all people are born of women, and are yielded up to civilization on the semiotic foundation of which women have had custody.

One of the principal reasons for the barrenness of Western metaphysics is its lack of attention to, and its frequent outright denial of, the processes of the life cycle. Each phase of it is abstracted toward mysticism—birth, sex, and death— and virtually none of it is recognized as a locus of female attention, female thought, interpersonal relations, or self-other differentiation—all the contact zones of growing infants, children, youth, and adults.[116] Academic, philosophical uses of language, like the thinkers themselves, move with alacrity away from the infant, "mewling and puking in the nurse's arms." Infantile speech is known as "baby talk" or "cooing." Scholars as recent as Walter Ong patronize the woman-centered world in which most children learn to think, behave, and, of course, use the language.[117] Several centuries after the established success of empiricism and experimental observation, the animus against using these scientific procedures to look seriously at the roles of language in the total life cycle has barely abated.

Julia Kristeva entered the mostly male French academic world at first as part of it, although she gradually shifted her perspectives and then moved toward articulating the issues in the study of language from a point of view that consciously departed from orthodoxy. The opening sentence of an early work reads "To work on language, to labour in the *materiality* of that which society regards as a means of contact and understanding, isn't that at one stroke to declare one-

---

114. Derrida, *"Khōra," On the Name,* ed. Thomas Dutoit, trans. David Wood, John P. Leavey, Jr., and Ian McLeod (Palo Alto, CA: Stanford UP, 1995), 89–130, quotation on 127.

115. Derrida, *"Khōra,"* 126.

116. It is not that men were not aware of how women's attention was oriented, as evidenced by the perverse response to this awareness during the witch-hunting period in the medieval and renaissance periods (chapter 9). It is, rather, that men did not cope with this awareness in a civilized way: all refinements of culture were lost in recrudescent panic each time men needed to be responsive to the roles and work of women.

117. Discussed in chapter 9, section 5.

self a stranger (*étranger*) to language?"[118] From the beginning of Kristeva's professional life, the materiality of language was an explanation for the marginality of the subject matter as well as the marginality of those who approached language with that sense of it. She announced her own location in this enterprise as a stranger, something Derrida, who had similar views, did not do until his 1996 monograph, *Monolingualism of the Other* (discussed earlier this chapter). In the 1974 published version of her dissertation, Kristeva continued, "Despite their variations, all modern linguistic theories consider language a strictly 'formal' object—one that involves syntax or mathematicization. . . . [M]odern linguistics' self-assigned object—lacks a subject or tolerates one only as a *transcendental ego* . . . and defers any interrogation of its . . . 'externality.'"[119] Despite the fluctuation in and final abandonment of her early Marxist interest, Kristeva was steadily motivated by the academically unorthodox insistence of placing a living subject—that is, living people—into the study of language, and she approached the issue from a variety of contexts.[120] She characterizes the academic study of language as being "removed from historical turmoil" and as "formalizing utterances that hang in midair." Scholars, she writes, listen to a "narrative of a sleeping body—a body in repose, withdrawn from its socio-historical imbrication, removed from direct experience."[121] She includes among these scholars Saussure and Chomsky[122] (and perhaps also Derrida), and those who remove language from its historical and social contexts for purposes of study, on the tacit assumption that this removal is the most responsible and scientific way to proceed. She calls their approach "an embarrassment."[123] Throughout her career, Kristeva continued to write in what

---

118. Julia Kristeva, *Semeiotike: Recherches pour une sémanalyse* (Paris: Seuil, 1969), cited and translated by Toril Moi (*Sexual/Textual Politics,* 150).

119. Kristeva, *Revolution,* 21. "Interrogation of its 'externality'": facing the fact that no mind or self is outside the use of language. When she introduces the idea of the *chora* (the same term as Derrida's but spelled with a C), she observes, "our theoretical description of the *chora* is itself part of the discourse of representation that offers it as evidence," a thought similar to Derrida's recognition, in his discussion of translation, that one cannot reach beyond the languages involved in the translation to some transcendental thought-language that is the same for all people (26).

120. The works of sociolinguists Robin Tolmach Lakoff (discussed in chapter 6), Deborah Tannen, and philosopher Naomi Scheman (discussed in chapter 10) may also be described as having the same purpose and orientation toward candor about human experience in the study of language.

121. Kristeva, *Revolution,* 13.

122. Kristeva refers to the "Janus-like behavior of a prominent modern grammarian; in his linguistic theories he sets forth a logical, normative basis for the speaking subject, while in politics he claims to be an anarchist." Julia Kristeva, *Desire in Language: A Semiotic Approach to Literature and Art,* ed. Leon S. Roudiez, trans. Thomas Gora, Alice Jardine, and Leon S. Roudiez (New York: Columbia UP, 1980), 23.

123. I have omitted (in the main text) her claim that this dehumanization derives from capitalism. However, later in her professional life, her Marxism left her and she

might be called a conventional academic idiom. Her struggle is comparable to Derrida's, but has a different emphasis. Being female, it was necessary that she enact compliance with the academic discourse, but that was not a guarantee of recognition; for Derrida, being male, departing from the academic idiom was a violation loaded with ambivalence, as his traditional kinds of erudition and standing in the academy brought him attention from the beginning.

The somewhat similar struggles of Kristeva and Derrida also appear in their uses of Plato's *khōra,* taken from his dialogue *Timaeus,* although Kristeva reflected on and made practical use of it two decades before Derrida did. Each tries to locate a zone and a terminology to recognize the historic claims of women, and each came upon the same figure for that purpose. In her inclusion of the living person in the study of language, Kristeva relies on the distinction in psycho-analysis, used in describing mental functioning, between primary and secondary processes. Freud referred to prelinguistic infantile thinking, dream thinking ,[124] and other forms of peremptory ideation[125] under the umbrella term "primary process," which was presumed to characterize the workings of the unconscious mind. Secondary process thinking is deliberate, "rational," and ratiocinative, and considered to be under the aegis of the conscious mind (assuming that "minds" are so divided). Kristeva translated this division into two "orders," thus, perhaps, avoiding localization in a living mind: the semiotic, which is loosely equated with primary process; and the symbolic, associated similarly with secondary process thinking. Language as we use it (according to Kristeva) resides in the symbolic order, but its groundwork, its foundation, and its mental preparation take place in the semiotic order that establishes the movements of signification as a general capability during the infantile period before language acquisition:

[T]he *chora,* as rupture and articulations (rhythm), precedes evidence, verisimilitude, spatiality, and temporality. Our discourse—all discourse—

---

followed a similar humanistic understanding of language on different grounds. Her early claim is nevertheless consistent with her later views, although the grounds changed.

124. In the *Timaeus,* the *khōra* is a "third nature" (the other two being mind and true opinion), "which is space and is eternal, and admits not of destruction and provides a home for all created things, and is apprehended, when all sense is absent, by a kind of spurious reason, and is hardly real—which we, beholding as in a dream, say of all existence that it must of necessity be in some place and occupy a space, but that what is neither in heaven nor in earth has no existence." Plato, *Timaeus,* trans. Benjamin Jowett, *Plato: The Collected Dialogues,* ed. Edith Hamilton and Huntington Cairns (New York: Pantheon, 1961) 52b, 1178–1179. Plato's description of the chora is on a cosmic scale, but Kristeva, coming from a Freudian direction, uses the dream-perception language in her rereading of the description, thus using Freud's having brought dreams back into categories of discussable experience.

125. A term I take from the work of the late George Klein of New York University (personal communication, 1971).

moves with and against the *chora* in the sense that it simultaneously depends upon and refuses it. Although the *chora* can be designated and regulated, it can never be definitively posited. . . . Neither model nor copy, the *chora* precedes and underlies figuration and thus specularization, and is analogous only to vocal or kinetic rhythm. . . . The theory of the subject proposed by the theory of the unconscious will allow us to read in the rhythmic space . . . the process by which significance is constituted. Plato himself leads us to such a process when he calls this receptacle or *chora* nourishing and maternal, not yet unified in an ordered whole because deity is absent from it.[126]

In introducing the living subject into discussions about language, Kristeva found in Plato a thought that may correspond to psychoanalyst D. W. Winnicott's "transitional space,"[127] which describes the state of mind of infants moving from pre-linguistic to linguistic existence. From birth to the acquisition of language, infants accumulate, cultivate, and establish a series of muscular moves and gestures, including vocal gestures that are assembled in interaction with mothers and other caregivers. Some of these gestures, noticed by observers such as Freud and Piaget, seem more clearly to be precursors to language acquisition than others (but much more observation is needed); contemporary researchers have identified more, including early organization of eye movements that, in later life, accompany speech. Kristeva's aim to establish a semiotic phase of development identified with nourishment and interactions between infants and mothers[128] provides a different philosophical vocabulary for the psychoanalytic descriptions. In the consideration of the materiality of language, the significance of this vocabulary is more that it resembles Derrida's appropriation of the same term for similar purposes, than that it enriches the psychoanalytic descriptions. In the discourse communities occupied by both Kristeva and Derrida, first Kristeva and later Derrida come upon the same term from the same source to cope with a key issue in the understanding of language—the processes of its early acquisition in cooperation with mothers. Heretofore these processes have been in plain sight yet unseen, remaining, it might be fairly claimed, in the "unconscious" minds of male philosophers—that is, part of the not-A of language.

---

126. Kristeva, *Revolution*, 26. Kristeva's reading of the *chora* is more decisive than Derrida's. Whatever textual uncertainty there may be in the classical text, Kristeva reads (translates) it as a description of a stage in the development of the human subject.

127. D. W. Winnicott, "Transitional Objects and Transitional Phenomena," *Playing and Reality* (New York: Basic, 1971), 1–25.

128. The matter of physical nourishment and nurturing is also essential to the process of language acquisition, and is discussed in chapter 5. In psychoanalytic terms, there is a great deal of oral preparation for speech, related to nursing, eating, and the in-and-out modalities of how the mouth works as a part of the body.

Kristeva's and Derrida's uses of this term *chora* bespeak the awkwardness of philosophy trying to face something fundamental yet always being denied, reduced, diminished, or rejected. At the end of his discussion of the term, Derrida observes, "Philosophy cannot speak philosophically of that which looks like its 'mother,' its 'nurse,' its 'receptacle,' or its 'imprint-bearer.' As such, it speaks only of the father and the son, as if the father engendered it all on his own."[129] Derrida does not reflect, however, on this philosophical stoppage or propose reasons for it. His closest pass at this issue is his discussion of the *lack* of nurturing during his unusual autobiographical account that reintroduces the "living subject" (himself) as one not at peace with his own contested acquisitions of language. Kristeva, however, obviously had considered women as much speaking subjects as men, and she approaches this issue from women's axiomatic lack of access *to* the symbolic order, to philosophy, and to the language of the public, of society, of the academy. Her fundamental task was to start at the point that, as Derrida finally admitted decades after Kristeva had begun her enterprise, philosophy had failed: to begin to provide a vocabulary, a discourse, a way of approaching the issue that has always been in plain sight for students of language—the participation of non-men.

In explicating Kristeva's work, Toril Moi observes that "she believes with Freud that the body forms the material basis for the constitution of the subject."[130] For Kristeva, as for Erik Erikson,[131] the bodily basis refers to modalities of bodily functioning, modalities being the ways the erogenous orifices lead a person to respond with *figurative* socialized conventional behaviors to the passing of food and excremental matter, and to the pleasure in several bodily functions. These modalities, however, are not ways of predicting social functioning. In psychoanalytic practices and in related research in biography and society, the relation of social figuration to bodily development is interpreted backward, so to speak—in retrospect, after the text of socialization is written, or inscribed in public.[132] Kristeva's simultaneous attention to the individual and social bodies identifies her sense of the materiality of language. The infantile semiotic period that is also symbiotic is a way of insisting that the term "speaking subject" must refer to all subjects who speak, as well as to the individual's interactive and social histories that produce the speaking subject. The concept of the semiotic functioning in early infancy also emphasizes, as Moi indicates[133] that for Kristeva

---

129. Jacques Derrida, *On the Name,* 126.

130. Toril Moi, *Sexual/Textual,* 166.

131. Erik H. Erikson, *Childhood and Society* (New York: Basic, 1949).

132. This is a variation of Wittgenstein's reading of Freudian dream interpretation (discussed in chapter 3), in which the written text is the narrative of the dream and the free associations. The interpreter (analyst or patient) creates a context from the knowledge of individual history in which the text "ceases to be puzzling."

133. Moi, *Sexual/Textual,* 165.

this early period is genderless, yet also socialized through the mothering relation. Kristeva aims not to emphasize femininity or to suggest a positive association of women with nonverbal semiosis, but, on the contrary, to create a story of language development that cancels the polar arrangement of genders and that leaves room to recognize the language fluidity that serves all members of society. For Kristeva, Moi observes, "The *chora* is a rhythmic pulsion rather than a new language. It constitutes, in other words, the heterogeneous, disruptive dimension of language, that which can never be caught up in the closure of traditional linguistic theory."[134] This formulation is close to Wittgenstein's rejection of the possibility of finding a theory of language. Kristeva adds a reason for this claim with her reference to how language develops in the particular space of infantile life, a kind of space that, perhaps, actually provides an open-ended, unstructurable space for the use of language. The source of this provision, in the formulation, is the social relation: infant and mother or caregiver.

However, the one shared element between the infantile semiotic and femininity, Moi notes,[135] is their common marginality in androcentric society: as women are a subaltern class in society, the non-referential and nonverbal are in the subaltern semiotic. Here again the material foundations of language and their inextricability from the socialization process are, in childhood and adult life, considered to be forgettable and associated with a (female) population that is repressed by society. The repression of the materiality of language is part of the androcentric repression, by and in men, of women and children.[136] It could not merely be a feature of language in isolation that is repressed. To repress a feature of language must also be a suppression of a class, a genus, a constituency of living people, and this fact emerges as those heretofore repressed now join the discussion and produce genres of language that are distinctly other than the traditional referential genres. At the same time, genres previously expected to be read referentially may now be reread with other assumptions (that is, by populations previously without access to these genres), and thereby acquire a continued, if less coercive, role in academic discussions.[137]

---

134. Moi, *Sexual/Textual*, 162.

135. Moi, *Sexual/Textual*, 166.

136. Moi emphasizes that Kristeva's effort is not to point to the repression of women, but to the repression, by and in men, of motherhood (*Sexual/Textual*, 167). One need not argue this point. There are enough cases to show the repression by and in men of women as a class, of children, and of the perversion of the institution of parenthood through radical definitions of parental roles.

137. This is what has happened to Freud's work, which is often dismissed on the grounds of its androcentrism. The readings of his works, the psychoanalytic practices, and the assumptions regarding a person's need for psychotherapy have been changed radically from their early forms. But certain thoughts of his, such as infantile bisexuality—and thus, perhaps, the bisexual potentiality of all adults—are now entertained in

Kristeva's formulations bring a greater reference and a greater rationality to Derrida's viewing the "metaphysics of presence" as the sign of a benighted civilization. By viewing infants' first paths of socialization as residing in a semiotic atmosphere that can be reasonably likened to Winnicott's "transitional space," she proposes a common, universally known part of experience—infantile habits and growth—that accompanies us into adulthood, as a way of understanding why presence is always in a state of change, and thus deferred, as Derrida described it.[138] Growth is unstable, even though it seems as if it is not happening, and that we are staying the same. Why say "continuous differing" when growth processes, always in plain sight, both describe and explain the surprises of change as well as the stabilities of life? The advantage of Kristeva's description is that it removes the feeling of gratuitous intellectual provocation that Derrida's abstractions created and perhaps still do create. Even in reading Derrida's texts, their intensity, we may now entertain, helps to obfuscate the value of his thinking. But when his texts are read alongside Kristeva's, as well as the other texts we considered and those that are reviewed in subsequent chapters, his own struggles become helpful in our effort to understand how frustrating these matters of language have been, and how difficult it is to establish the sort of open discussions that have, at least, some chance of letting the use of language help more in the processes of the human species' surviving its repeated movement toward self-destruction.

VII. Materiality, the Offspring of Maternality

Derrida and Kristeva share the sense that Christianity has perpetuated for many centuries the Platonic metaphysics of presence. Kristeva's sense of the materiality of language is similar to Derrida's from the standpoint of the ways language

---

a variety of individual cases. Another factor is the continued viability of talk therapy. This was an early mark of Freud's and it has grown and changed, all the while continuing its effectiveness and social desirability. Furthermore, the early openness of the psychoanalytic enterprise to women was a factor, from the beginning, that allowed for increasing numbers of women to help revise the earlier offensive features of psychoanalysis. See, for example, Kate Millett, *Sexual Politics* (New York, Doubleday, 1970); Juliet Mitchell, *Psychoanalysis and Feminism: A Radical Reassessment of Freudian Psychoanalysis* (New York: Basic, 2000); Dorothy Dinnerstein, *The Mermaid and the Minotaur: Sexual Arrangements and Human Malaise* (New York: Harper, 1976); Nancy J. Chodorow, *The Reproduction of Mothering: Psychoanalysis and the Sociology of Gender* (Berkeley: U of California P, 1978) and *Feminism and Psychoanalytic Theory* (New Haven, CT: Yale UP, 1989); and Jessica Benjamin, *Shadow of the Other: Intersubjectivity and Gender in Psychoanalysis* (New York: Routledge, 1998).

138. Recall (in chapter 3) the preference Whorf seemed to have for "earlier and later" rather than "past, present, and future" to refer to the passage of time. The rejection of

functions. However, Kristeva's inquiry into maternality contributes a dimension (related to her attention to speaking subjects) that Derrida handled with abstractions that obscured the interest of his *khōra* discussion. Kristeva observes,

> [Christian] theology defines maternity only as an impossible elsewhere, a sacred beyond, a vessel of divinity, a spiritual tie with the ineffable godhead, and transcendence's ultimate support—necessarily virginal and committed to assumption. Such are the wiles of Christian reason (Christianity's still matchless rationalism, or at least its rationalizing power, finally become clear); through the maternal body (in a state of virginity and "dormition"[139] before Assumption), it thus establishes a sort of subject at the point where the subject and its speech split apart, fragment, and vanish. Lay humanism took over the configuration of that subject through the cult of the mother; tenderness, love, and seat of social conservation.[140]

Whether mothers were idealized or demonized in Christian doctrine, they were cordoned off from the rest of civilization. The extreme constructions of mothers and women limit their existence to iconographies and the third-person discourse of clerics, whose authority defined the kind of subjects mothers were to be: separated from speech, a revocation of the very terms of mothers' existence as mothers with offspring. These were the same figures, who, during the witch-hunting periods, were executed because their comfort with and understanding of the life cycle was the occasion for churchmen's paranoid fantasies.[141] Their speech, however, as derived from the open-endedness of the *chora* (the mother's social behavioral space), includes all gestural and figurative actions in infancy, participating in a rapidly changing process of growth that, Kristeva suggests, is beyond the reach of science as now practiced. Kristeva further notices, however, that increasing secularization of culture in more modern times has not so much changed as transferred such classifications of women. Her revisions of these namings begin with a sense of the consequence of recognizing, under present assumptions, how women as custodians of early lives discredit the traditional view of individual identity:

---

presence, familiar in twentieth-century philosophy, could also be read as a wish to find a language, a vocabulary, or a discourse that can work with our wish to recognize change, transience, and temporality without recourse to the superstitions or other declarations of a transcendental force that superintends our destinies. By moving away from the nominalization of time, we stop imagining that we can stop it.

139. Kristeva references the Virgin Mary's "sleep" after her death and before she was taken to heaven (*Desire*, 269).

140. Julia Kristeva, "Motherhood according to Giovanni Bellini," *Desire*, 237–270, quotation on 237.

141. See chapter 9, section 4.

So, if we suppose that a *mother* is the subject of gestation, in other words the *master* of a process that science, despite its effective devices, acknowledges it cannot now and perhaps never will be able to take away from her; if we suppose her to be *master* of a process that is prior to the social-symbolic-linguistic contract of the group, then we acknowledge the risk of losing identity at the same time that we ward it off.[142]

Motherhood is a threat to and a source of individual identity: a threat in its insistence on the open-endedness of language, on the embeddedness of language in other figurative and gestural behaviors commonly used by speakers; and a source in its role as a sustainer of life and society. The "woman-subject," Kristeva says, is "a thoroughfare, a threshold where 'nature' confronts 'culture.'"[143] The mother is a place (*khōra, Makom, Shekhina*)[144] of constant change: "Heraclitus' flux, Epicurus' atoms, the whirling dust of cabalic, Arab, and Indian mystics, and the stippled drawings of psychedelics—all seem better metaphors than the theories of Being, the logos, and its laws."[145] Whereas Heidegger struggles with *Sein,* and Derrida with the uses of the term "law" and the implications of its grammatical gender, Kristeva overrides (but does not censor)[146] these terms; like Wittgenstein, she rejects formal theory as a preferred approach to inquiries into language.[147] The uncertainty of self, rather than being an occasion of fragmentation, is redefined in terms of the relationship that begins the processes of socialization—a clear, known relationship, yet one that no formal way of thinking is in position to predict or otherwise fix.

In her focus on the infantile symbiosis, Kristeva's formulation recalls those of Hamann, especially his insistence on poetry as the mode of the givenness of language.[148] Although she announces an interest in discussing the foundations

---

142. Kristeva, *Desire*, 238.

143. Kristeva, *Desire*, 238.

144. Kristeva does not entertain the Hebrew terms used by Derrida. The last two terms—themselves displaced names for God—would function intelligibly, if secularized, as additional versions of the Kristeva's readings of the *khōra*. The mother's unnamable place is always there, in plain sight, and immanent in human society.

145. Kristeva, *Desire*, 239.

146. She continues to use the term "law" routinely, as in the term "grammatical law," cited below.

147. In her commentary on Kristeva, Moi cites Wittgenstein's rejection (in section 28 of *Philosophical Investigations*) of Augustine's approach to language acquisition as a simple process of referential naming: "The attempt to *fix* meaning is always in part doomed to failure, for it is of the nature of meaning to be always already elsewhere" (*Sexual/Textual*, 160). This is Moi's formulation; Kristeva, more like Wittgenstein, stresses variability of reference over more radical deferring of the sense of names and nouns.

148. Kristeva shows some sympathy with Lévi-Strauss's thought that "language could only have been born in a single stroke" (*Language: The Unknown*, 46). But she

of poetic and artful work, she proposes no deep distinction between poetry and other arts. Her sense of the primacy of language—something, unlike other art forms, that is shared by all people—leads to the implication that poetry and other gestural "arts" acquired in infancy (by all people) bring a more appropriate set of associations to the discussion of language developments than law, science, or theory. Western thought has repressed the poetic character of language—its so-called poetic license, perhaps—which, Kristeva suggests, undergoes a "primal repression within the mother's body": "the artist speaks from a place where she is not, where she knows not."[149] In society, artistic work is separated rigidly from direct involvement in the changes of the life cycle. This separation produces extreme images and values of both art and motherhood—extremities that may describe Bellini's paintings of Madonnas and infants: "aesthetic practice makes clear that the Mother as subject is a delusion, just as the negation of the so-called poetic dimension of language leads one to believe in the existence of the Mother, and consequently, of transcendence."[150] Poetry finding itself in a transcendental status in Western culture is the formula of its segregation and part of the groundwork that sustains the repression of materiality.

In her 1981 treatise *Language: The Unknown*,[151] Kristeva presents the history of linguistic science on the basis of its materiality. She indicates the idleness of searching for an origin of language because regardless of which guess one makes, one cannot expect ever to find tangible scientific evidence that could decide the question.[152] Her stance relates the use of language to the total socialization of the human species: the use of language "is a social function overdetermined by the complex process of exchange and social tasks, produced by it, and incomprehensible without it."[153] The early parts of *Philosophical Investigations* give instances of the embeddedness of language uses in ordinary social tasks. These so-called ordinary instances cited by Wittgenstein relate to familiar social activi-

---

distinguishes the human awareness of signification from the development of knowledge, which is overseen by history and the overall development different peoples. Although Lévi-Strauss has no more evidence for this claim than do other speculators on the origin of language, Kristeva is emphasizing the point that awareness of signification is a part of the species, and that however it is conceived, it cannot be understood as a separate attribute. Knowledge, however, while also not separate, follows a different developmental path, and is not in plain sight and therefore not subject to swift collective agreement.

149. Kristeva, *Desire*, 242.

150. Kristeva, *Desire*, 242.

151. Julia Kristeva, *Language: The Unknown: An Initiation into Linguistics*, trans. Anne M. Menke (New York: Columbia UP, 1989).

152. "[W]e have little of the information needed to judge an 'origin' of language" (*Language*, 23). She indicates, subsequently, that some linguists have abandoned the "ambition of constructing general theories [of the origin and history of language] for which no scientific proof can be furnished" (*Language*, 45).

153. Kristeva, *Language*, 20.

ties. Kristeva argues against trying to localize language biologically, because both physiological and social manifestations of language participate in what we understand as language.

Kristeva proposes two general senses of materiality: the "phonic, gestural, or graphic"[154] appearance of language and the grammatical "laws" that are a shorthand for "the objective relations between the speaking subject and external reality"; these grammatical laws "reflect as well the connections that govern human society."[155] The latter claim refers to grammatical categories such as "person," "case," and "tense," which mark the social situations in the exchange of language—situations that can, in turn, be observed through the grammatical usages. The stipulation of these two parts of language experience amounts to claiming that the two aspects of materiality are in the individual (body), and the collection of persons (bodies) that gather to exchange language and other material things. Additionally, indirectly acknowledging Derrida's sense of the term "writing" as a part of recognizing the materiality of language, Kristeva entertains the plausibility that certain kinds of graphic representation may have preceded oral representation. While no conclusions can be reached, the thought that there was likely a *cooperative* or *coordinated* development of speech and writing gains credibility once one surveys the broad range of ancient graphics in the archeological record—going back perhaps thirty-five millennia. Her discussion of prehistoric writing does not decide the question but gives an account of a social scene of earlier (not primitive) human social development that includes the elements we now recognize as part of an organized, orderly society.

Kristeva presents various aspects of contemporary linguistic science as supporting the view that the material action of language gives knowledge of what is real, and whose truth is "confirmed by social practice."[156] The fundamental terms of traditional science and philosophy are retained and reread, not censored or rejected. This has been part of the strategy of feminist critique of language and knowledge that has emerged in the contemporary period. The concept of the materiality of language facilitates a pragmatic[157] approach to truth that starts with a small T and that focuses on the social practices. Wittgenstein's "slab, block" *Sprachspiel* is a case in point: if the practices proceed smoothly with a given vocabulary, those involved know the practice, even, for example, if new vocabulary is introduced to explain a practice to strangers. It would not be possible to distinguish whether knowledge of the language was separate from

---

154. Kristeva, *Language*, 18.
155. Kristeva, *Language*, 18.
156. Kristeva, *Language*, 30.
157. An approach beginning in the nineteenth century, and one that perhaps, if Wittgenstein can be understood as an earlier linguistic pragmatist, may be considered a philosophical preparation for the more consequential approaches to language that followed.

knowledge of the practice, whose mere existence suggests that the knowledge of the practice is true. Similarly, Austin's set of felicitous speech acts also are based on a social efficacy that is considerably deeper than the words themselves, and it is hardly possible to distinguish words as speech acts from practices. Rather than accepting the Saussurean *langue* or the Chomskyan "competence" as independent signifying systems that are conceptualized without reference to the social practices, Kristeva rereads knowledge, truth, and language as constituents of a social cycle of speech and writing and behavior.

The eighteenth-century conundrum of whether thought precedes language or vice versa finds in Kristeva's work a different form that has a family resemblance to the earlier puzzle: (taking the role of what she opposes) she asks if there is an abstract "system" of language, *la langue,* which creates categories such as "subjectivity," "dialogue," "history," or "present" (for example), then do they create their real-world referents, or merely reflect them? Kristeva, demonstrating her impatience with accepting traditional premises and traditional ways of posing problems unsusceptible to practical solutions, rejects the question: "This is an insoluble, metaphysical problem."[158] That is to say, it doesn't matter. Her alternative formulation bypasses the grammar of the question as well as its semantics. She calls attention to

> the *isomorphism* of the two series (the real/language; the real subject/ the linguistic subject; experienced temporality/linguistic temporality) of which the second, language and its categories, would be both the *attribute* and the *mold* that arranges the first series, extralinguistic reality. It is in this sense that we can speak of a "materiality" of language by not allowing ourselves to posit language as an ideal system closed in upon itself (such is the "formalist" attitude) or as a mere copy of a regulated world that exists without it (such is the "realistic," mechanistic attitude).[159]

Material language is at once an attribute of "the real" *and* a means of molding it. The principle of her formulation is that there is *no separating the two categories from one another,* even though they can be separated grammatically. Language is material because it is part of the real; there is no sense in which language is removable from experience. Derrida, with regard to translation, offered a similar principle: one can move back and forth between languages, but there is no realm of thought that is common to the two languages, or that will guide one toward a correct translation relative to that realm of thought. Thought and language, experience and language, are one. This is not a claim that language stands alone as a force. On the contrary, Kristeva's phrase "by not

---

158. Kristeva, *Language,* 36.
159. Kristeva, *Language,* 36.

allowing ourselves to posit" notes affirmatively that these approaches to language do not confer initiatives onto language, but keep such initiatives where they have always been—among people. Nor does it say that people are masters or rulers of the language. Rather, language that is shared was born and nurtured from a source that no person remembers, but which all persons experience. *Some* of this experience is remembered by parents and caregivers, but then given back in a new language—adult language we identify as the mother tongue. Derrida may wish to say that this is the sense of the endless deferring of meaning. But there is no need for such an extreme and abstract description of such common, flexible experience. Rather, there is always access, through social relations, to the mother tongue(s), but the scope of such access is indefinite, and may always grow through socialization. What one cannot identify is a locus of finality with regard to the use of language. Such places are created mendaciously by masters and rulers, and by academics who serve these overseers, who, understanding the materiality of language—the universal access to it of all people—then narrow the language into its transparent form, give the law, restrict, censor, and inhibit use and interpretation, limit authority to what can be heard or read in the officially authorized texts, and divide a population from its language. Kristeva's focus on the indelible action of maternity reminds us of the corrupt character of this division, of the price civilization has paid for maintaining it.

CHAPTER FIVE

Materiality and the Contemporary Study of Language

I. The Stubborn Nativist Premise

Transformational linguistics has come to be a reference point for researchers of language and language acquisition. Psycholinguists, sociolinguists, anthropological linguists, and language evolutionists each announce responses to the nativist premise (that there is a biologically discoverable language acquisition device) of transformational linguistics. Since the late 1950s the study of language has been stalked by this premise.[1] Although many recent researchers do not accept the premise, there has been a strong pull to compromise with it even by those inclined toward an interactionist approach.[2] For other researchers, the nativist premise has changed

---

1. For a long time few were willing to say that the nativist premise is false, unproductive, or not what should be asked about language. Early challenges to Chomsky include Hubert L. Dreyfus's in *What Computers Can't Do: A Critique of Artificial Reason* (New York: Harper and Row, 1972), 238–241. This is still a forceful refutation of Chomsky's attempt to separate competence from performance. In 1973 Robin Tolmach Lakoff began her career-long challenge to Chomsky in *Language and Woman's Place* (New York: Harper, 1975). Her work is discussed in detail in chapter 6. Rudolf P. Botha's *Challenging Chomsky: The Generative Garden Game* (Oxford: Blackwell, 1989) is a point-by-point attempt to discredit Chomsky's theory. It is placed inside an ironic framework that could be read as a satire of all academic work; the book makes Chomsky's arguments resemble medieval scholasticism.

2. "Our aim is to reach a compromise between what have traditionally been called the nativistic and interactionist theories of language acquisition." Kathy Hirsh-Pasek and Roberta Michnick Golinkoff, *The Origins of Grammar: Evidence from Early Language Comprehension* (Cambridge, MA: MIT Press, 1996), 11. Alison Jolly takes a similar stance: "[G]rammar has an innate basis. . . . Children have a strong innate program for learning language, but of course they learn it from others." Alison Jolly, *Lucy's Legacy: Sex and Intelligence in Human Evolution* (Cambridge, MA: Harvard UP, 1999), 310–311. It is noteworthy that some of those seeing the locus of research in language acquisition have settled on interaction as a fundamental, but still add the concept of instinct, with an eye to biologize that principle. Chapter 4 of *The Interactional Instinct* "provides behavioral evidence that human infants have an innate drive to attune to, imitate, and

into a "language instinct"[3] that seeks, in spite of its evolutionist sound, inside-the-body sites for the secret of language. The nativist premise rejects the use of language as eligible to explain language; rather, logic must explain it.[4] Even though transformational grammar began with an emphatic rejection of a prematurely dogmatic Skinnerian behaviorism,[5] proponents of nativism have moved toward positivist attitudes that enlarge hypotheses into dogma prematurely and look for proofs: they are guessing that there is something more real underlying the descriptive and ethnographic science styles that are increasingly used by researchers in language and language acquisition. To nativists, the words given as explanatory descriptions are "only words" because there must be something clearly material and mathematically articulable that would provide a tangible explanatory basis for language. The performed language for nativists remains—as it has been traditionally—intangible, immaterial, and therefore inaccessible by real science.

An interesting kind of compromise with nativism can be found among some researchers in language evolution, a perspective which seems not to hold a nativist premise. They see language in the wider area of symbol making and using; they treat language as a form of species-specific adaptation, which means that language is taken as developing according to principles true of species in general; and they

---

interact with conspecifics. This bias is a powerful developmental precursor to the ontogeny of symbolic formation and referencing in humans and, therefore, for the acquisition of language. The interactional drive essentially motivates infants to achieve attachment and social affiliation with their caregivers." Namhee Lee, Lisa Mikesell, Anna Dina L. Joaquin, Andrea W. Mates, John H. Schumann, *The Interactional Instinct: The Evolution and Acquisition of Language* (New York: Oxford UP, 2009), 9. Here, as in other uses of innateness and instinct, an abstraction, "innate drive," is attached to a process to name what is *not* being studied. See also note 11, below.

3. Steven Pinker's *The Language Instinct: How the Mind Creates Language* (New York: Morrow, 1994) and *The Blank Slate: The Modern Denial of Human Nature* (New York: Viking, 2002) argue for a scientific orientation toward the study of language and mind promoting the assumption that only wired-in phenomena count as scientific explanations. But some reject this path altogether; see Michael Tomasello, "Language Is Not an Instinct," *Cognitive Development* 10 (1995): 131–156. Christine Kenneally notes that recently Pinker has suggested that language is a "polygenetic" adaptation. Christine Kenneally, *The First Word: The Search for the Origins of Language* (New York: Viking, 2007), 224. A favorite term of those who wish to identify a biological site for language and that interaction is "hardwired," a term used by both Lee et al. and Pinker.

4. The need for explanation is itself partly a function of Enlightenment rationalism: Wittgenstein's substitution of description for explanation signals his change of the sense of what language is and what it can do from his approach to language in the *Tractatus*. If there is no demand for explanation, the tasks of studying language move toward more useful and achievable ends.

5. Noam Chomsky, review of B. F. Skinner's *Verbal Behavior, Language* 35 (1959): 26–58. According to Kenneally, "At the time, people spoke about Skinner in the terms they would later use to describe Chomsky" (*First Word*, 28).

dedicate their efforts to proposing, within the framework of evolutionary reasoning, how this adaptation might have started.[6] Several of them make reference to Chomsky's division of the study of language into competence and performance as categories that must be reckoned with even though their own work takes a different tack.[7] In spite of their relatively wide context of observation, language evolution researchers do not question the nativist premises of transformational grammar.[8] Most of them do not report doubt about the LAD (the language acquisition device said to be biologically locatable in the brain and/or genes). Some refer to "the language faculty,"[9] implying that it is a discrete ability separable from gestures and movement as well as from relationships and values.[10] They continue to try to define, understand, and search for so-called language universals as the likely key to finding the LAD. Nevertheless, the language evolutionists have enlarged the context of

---

6. Terrence W. Deacon, *The Symbolic Species: The Co-evolution of Language and the Brain* (New York: Norton, 1997), is a case in point, discussed in the next section.

7. Maggie Tallerman, ed., *Language Origins: Perspectives on Evolution* (New York: Oxford UP, 2005); Morten H. Christiansen and Simon Kirby, eds., *Language Evolution* (Oxford and New York: Oxford UP, 2003); Brian MacWhinney, ed., *The Emergence of Language: Social Function and the Origins of Linguistic Form* (Mahwah, NJ: Erlbaum, 1999); Robin Dunbar, Chris Knight, and Camilla Power, eds., *The Evolution of Culture* (New Brunswick, NJ: Rutgers UP, 1999); James R. Hurford, Michael Studdert-Kennedy, and Chris Knight, eds. *Approaches to the Evolution of Language: Social and Cognitive Bases* (Cambridge: Cambridge UP 1998); Robin Dunbar, *Grooming, Gossip, and the Evolution of Language* (Cambridge, MA: Harvard UP, 1996). These studies take features of language—such as diversity, vocalization, grammar, gestural versus conceptual communication, and fitness—and entertain a variety of comparisons among different species. Most of the contributors to these volumes are empirically oriented and want to test the extent to which specific regularities fit into the widely accepted stories of evolution. The different statements add up to new arrangements of known data, and they are useful especially in encouraging others to raise issues of communication among members of a species by comparing the full range of observable species.

8. Robin Lakoff, a critic of Chomsky, reviews Terrence Deacon's *The Symbolic Species,* and observes that in spite of his claims to the contrary, his idea of "innateness" is more or less the same as Chomsky's. Robin Lakoff, "The Growth of Little Gray Cells," *Washington Post* 23 November 1997: X06.

9. Ted Briscoe, "Co-evolution of the Language Faculty and Language(s) with Decorrelated Encodings," *Language Origins,* ed. Maggie Tallerman (New York: Oxford UP, 2005), 310–333; Marc D. Hauser and W. Tecumseh Fitch, "What Are the Uniquely Human Components of the Language Faculty?" *Language Evolution,* ed. Morten H. Christiansen and Simon Kirby (Oxford and New York: Oxford University Press, 2003), 158–181. The latter essay notes that many of the subsystems that enable humans to recognize speech are found in other species. However, a welcome conclusion of this empirically oriented essay is that the authors do not know how unique the language faculty is.

10. This would hold true more strongly of Steven Pinker's explanation of why language is an instinct. Although he is evolutionary in his orientation toward the issue of

the study of language.[11] They consider factors such as bodily and brain processes, small-muscle articulation and coordination of senses and actions, and comparisons to a variety of primate communities and socialization practices. They respect the need to study both cultural evolution, which pays attention to how the many languages may have come about; and to biological evolution, which, they believe, is the fundamental context that could reveal the origin of the alleged language acquisition device. It might be said that in the work of those studying language in the context of the evolution of the human species, the matter of the wired-in language acquisition device is an open question. But it might also be claimed that these researchers assume that something physically identifiable related to language capability is innate. Few, if any, reject the implied goal of either choosing between innate and learned or identifying what is innate and what is learned. Few, that is, understand the evolution of language as not requiring attention to the premise that the essence of language is innate. The majority of language evolutionists wants to pay some degree of attention to this possibility. Furthermore, few among language evolutionists are deterred by the likelihood that the fossil record will never be able (or will never be complete enough) to yield convincing conclusions about the path of language development in isolation from all other development.[12]

II. Terrence Deacon and Evolutionary Explanation

Terrence Deacon's comprehensive study *The Symbolic Species* seems as if it does not require attention to the nativist premise.[13] However, the premise comes in through the back door, so to speak, as his theory derives from the cognate premise that a historical origin of language can be found, a premise held by

the distinctiveness of language as part of the human species, he holds the view that the wired-in status of language is the only way to explain its rapid acquisition by children. This was Chomsky's principal early contribution that changed linguistics toward its current majority status. The term "instinct" poses its own problems, in that it is used almost always to identify behaviors of living things that observers have assumed were not learned. This reliance on instincts and drives as explanations (rather than just as arbitrary names for things that are not understood) has characterized biological and psychological science since Darwin. Deacon refers to Pinker's "instinct" as "a formal redescription of what remains unexplained" (*Symbolic*, 39). A discussion of the use of the concept of instinct and of rejection of this use is presented in chapter 10.

11. Credit for opening discussion of studying language through evolutionary considerations is usually given to Steven Pinker and Paul Bloom, "Natural Language and Natural Selection," *Behavioral and Brain Sciences* 13 (1990): 707–784. See also Chris Knight, Michael Studdert-Kennedy, and James R. Hurford, "Language: A Darwinian Adaptation?" *Approaches,* ed. Hurford et al., 1–15.

12. This stance of observing that evidence for innateness *cannot* be found is taken by Julia Kristeva, chapter 4. Additionally, what value can such a project have?

13. Christine Kenneally's *First Word* favors the evolutionary theory without insisting on either innateness, cultural learning, or both. Kenneally's full review of "the search

the eighteenth-century philosophers (chapter 2). Deacon makes a strong effort to replace the search for a specific LAD in the brain by linking the question of the evolution of language to the evolution of the characteristically larger human brain; he envisions a long calendar for the development of language and, beyond the matter of the capacity of the brain as an organ, he aims to link language, brain size, and social or adaptational development of the human species in a single explanatory narrative.[14] In spite of the considerable length (over five hundred pages) of the treatise, the narrative outline is clear, and its recounting brings out its assumptions. Deacon speculates that at some point about two million years back, the primate-like human species started to eat meat due to the scarcity of foods that could be gathered. Both males and females could gather food adequately for the whole community. When, due to shortages of gatherable foods, meat was needed to sustain the species, humans started to hunt. However, reliable hunting could not be carried out by both males and females equally: males were better fit to hunt as they did not have pregnancies. In this way, meat-eating led to the gender-marked division of labor: the necessary separation of the male work of hunting from female work of gathering and care of offspring that remained dependent for a period of years. Hunting needed to be done by groups of men and for periods of time longer than a day.[15]

This separation of sexes posed a challenge to social stability.[16] Although the food supply was adequately maintained by hunting, some group cohesion was lost: both sexes could beget and bear children with partners not in their own groups. Deacon proposes that language started to develop as a device that helped humans adapt at once to the need to secure food supplies and to maintain stable social arrangements. The brain gradually began enlarging toward this adaptive project, thus encouraging the growth of the capacity *to secure by symbolic means* the bond between parents who produce children together, as well as the bonds among all parents wanting and needing a stable group.[17] Deacon's speculation

---

for origins," represented with some irony in her book's title, seems ready to be surprised by findings yet to come.

14. Chomsky has already rejected such efforts—the speculations of evolutionary biologists—on the ground that they are merely stories that cannot be documented. See Rudolf P. Botha, *Unravelling the Evolution of Language* (Amsterdam: Elsevier, 2003), 179–187.

15. Deacon does not speculate about why he did not consider groups of non-pregnant women to be capable of hunting during the times that men might have practiced child-care. The lack of such speculation already suggests the political marking of his reflection. This marking emerges with little ambiguity in the discussion later in this section.

16. Deacon, *Symbolic*, 393–401.

17. It is not really clear, however, why symbolic means were needed; other species, such as ducks, remain bonded without the use of symbols (this is acknowledged by Deacon). Furthermore, is the task of incubation performed by both ducks and drakes?

is that the language that we know was urged into the evolutionary process by the collective need to make contracts between the sexes, contracts aimed to preserve both social stability and activities necessary for universal daily survival.

In addition to his assumption about meat eating and the gendered division of labor, Deacon's narrative depends on the conception of language as a symbol-making and symbol-using function, a conception that was similarly described by Ernst Cassirer and Susanne K. Langer.[18] Although Deacon takes pains to spell out how the use of symbols is qualitatively different from signaling and indicative reference, his complex description is not very different from the simpler ones given by of Langer and Cassirer, who, like Deacon, use the term "symbol" rather than "sign" (as some semioticians prefer) to designate, identify, refer to, or name what language marks are. As Langer discussed,[19] the difference between the symbol using of humans and the (albeit advanced) sign using of primates, is that a symbol may be uttered and comprehended with an indefinitely long period of delay or of spatial distance between its use and the experiential presence of its referents. If a primate understands the word "banana," this means that the utterance of the word leads the animal to look for its appearance, or otherwise to relate the hearing of the sign to the appearance of its referent. One needs a brain larger than the primates' for symbol using because each symbol depends on a very large accessible store of memories, not just one or a few, to render the viability of the various symbols. Secondly, there cannot be merely one symbol. Each user must know tens of thousands of symbols—each of which has references and cross-references in memory—in order for any one of them to function as symbols. Thirdly, the symbols relate to one another through the use of grammar, and so the ways of relating are also stored in the large brain and accessible at every moment for inserting into experience. Finally, the word "symbol" is preferred by Langer and Cassirer because media other than language are describable in this way—especially the languages of art, mathematics, music, dance, or any form of denotation that contributes to and helps to sustain the stability of civilized life. Symbols are material marks that at once depend on their relation to environmental objects and events and depend on their relation to one another.

Deacon seems aware of this perspective in his attempts to say that ritualization was an essential part of the movement of the human species toward language. One contributor to the evolutionary-biology study of language, Robin

---

18. No mention of these sources is made in this treatise. Although this omission is not necessarily a problem, the similarity between the older sources and Deacon is salient in the present discussion.

19. Ernst Cassirer, *The Philosophy of Symbolic Forms,* trans. Ralph Mannheim (New Haven, CT: Yale UP, 1953); Susanne K. Langer, *Philosophy in a New Key: A Study in the Symbolism of Reason, Rite, and Art* (Cambridge, MA: Harvard UP, 1942).

Dunbar, has related the rituals of primate grooming to human gossip. As Dunbar details, primate grooming resembles the common rituals of gossip in their appearance of spontaneity and emotional involvement as well as in their ubiquity across cultures.[20] Deacon and other researchers are alert to the comprehensiveness of the use of symbols and the constant combination of different zones of symbolization (such as language, music, dress, and dance). From most present indications, the project of relating the evolution of language to the evolution of the larger human brain seems plausible, sensible, and worth continuing. One wonders, however, what will count as evidence for this theory.[21]

Additionally, no one knows whether meat eating played this role in human evolution, and it does not seem likely that such a fact can be discovered.[22] More importantly, no one knows whether the separation of male hunters from female gatherers even took place—or, if it did, whether it was enough of a factor to support contemporary researchers' views of the evolution of language. Of conspicuous interest in Deacon's account is his stipulation that the need for a promise of loyalty between men and women—a promise of being exclusive partners to each

---

20. Dunbar, in spite of his cultural approach, shows something of a gee-whiz feeling about language: "Language makes us members of a community, providing us with the opportunity to share knowledge and experiences in a way no other species can" (*Grooming,* 7). Dunbar recognizes the very strong influence of popular culture, particularly romantic fiction, and he relates this fact to what his book aims to show as fact: "Our much-vaunted capacity for language seems to be mainly used for exchanging information on social matters; we seem to be obsessed with gossiping about one other" (6–7). If, provisionally, this fact is true, Dunbar's conclusion is significant (although no more supported by evidence than any other speculation about the origins of language): "If females formed the core of these earliest human groups, and language evolved to bond these groups, it naturally follows that the early human females were the first to speak" (149).

21. Dean Falk draws a different conclusion in considering Dunbar's proposal. Admitting that "humans use language to 'groom' each other," Falk suggests that "social intelligence *per se* probably was not the prime mover of human brain evolution. Language was. . . . [N]o amount of training has ever resulted in a chimpanzee who could read, write, or talk anything like a human does. . . . Unlike the brains of other primates, human brains *do* language." Dean Falk, "Brain Evolution in Females: An Answer to Mr. Lovejoy," *Women in Human Evolution* ed. Lori D. Hager (New York: Routledge, 1997), 130. Falk's view is consistent with the view of language as a way of life for humans. Furthermore, he writes based on his studies of brain lateralization, "it is best to abandon the assertion that one sex or the other is more 'intelligent' or that one sex should take more credit for the unique evolutionary history that made us 'human'" (133). Falk's view is also consistent with Philip Lieberman's view that language is a total brain activity.

22. Chomsky uses this fact to *rule out* any speculation about evolution in order to support the assumption of innateness, to keep it as the axiom for linguistics. The assumption of innateness, relative to ongoing thinking about language, is unimportant, however, if one continues to entertain the thought that language evolved as part of the total human species. If innateness became unimportant, Chomsky's edifice of transformational rules becomes less important and the nature of linguistics changes radically.

other, in fact—was a major instigating factor in the evolution of language.[23] In effect, Deacon suggests, language came about because men and women needed a means to establish mutual trust in a context of food scarcity. Again, no one knows how true this speculation is or will turn out to be. Yet, considered in the context of some of Darwin's terms and formulations, it suggests a certain perspective that must be entertained in connection with Deacon's provisional explanation. For example, in Darwin's work, phrases such as "struggle for existence" and "survival of the fittest" remain presumptions of evolutionary theory, and they are, more or less, held by Deacon and others doing related research and speculation. The common assumption is that a harsh and hostile nature provokes a response from species toward adapting to those challenges. Darwin's work established the axiom of competition as a scientific given—a premise that is generally taken to be obviously true and that few question. Consistent with Darwin's vocabulary, Deacon adds in monogamy as a response to the "struggle for existence."[24]

This single move of viewing the need for mating and marital loyalty as the grounds for the evolution of language is one of the most curious in his treatise. Deacon justifies this move, in part, by claiming that males need to know who their offspring are.[25] Why this need should be characterized as biological is not comprehensible except from the point of view that, in the past and often

---

23. According to Deacon, "Marriage, in all its incredible variety, is the regulation of reproductive relationships by symbolic means, and it is essentially universal in human societies. It is preeminently a symbolic relationship, and owing to the lack of symbolic abilities, it is totally absent in the rest of the animal kingdom. What I am suggesting here is that a related form of regulation of reproductive relationships by symbolic means was essential for early hominids to take advantage of a hunting-provisioning subsistence strategy" (*Symbolic,* 400–401). This argument makes use of the fact that both marriage contracts and language are characteristic of human social relations, and are not found among other living things. Deacon's opinion seems to be that they must have evolved together, and toward the *same adaptive purpose.* Deacon acknowledges exclusive partnering in other species, such as birds. He does not explain why these species did not develop language: he may wish us readers to remember that brains of other species were much smaller than ours. The research strategy of Deacon and others thinking about evolution is linear: find one key factor and relate all others to it. Given the variety of possibilities, it seems clear that many factors worked together. What cannot be known is the path of combination.

24. Some critiques of knowledge and language have challenged these terms. To wit: it is not necessary to the theory of evolution to consider nature to be harsh and hostile, or that there is a "struggle for existence" or that "scarcity" is a necessary part of nature, rather than an accidental or contingent development. Michael Gross and Mary Beth Averill, "Evolution and Patriarchal Myths of Scarcity and Competition," *Discovering Reality: Feminist Perspective on Epistemology, Metaphysics, Methodology, and Philosophy of Science,* ed. Sandra Harding and Merrill B. Hintikka (Dordrecht: D. Reidel, 1983), 71–96. These issues are considered as functions of the use of language (see chapter 10).

25. He offers a few instances in which human observers of primate societies drew this conclusion about male behaviors. But imagine basing an explanation of the evolution of

enough in the present, biological reasons are given to justify social purposes and prejudices; for example, an alleged larger brain size was long used to document (erroneously) the claim of males' superiority to females. It is fairly well established that men want to know who their children are mainly for purposes of the passing of wealth and property—of kingdoms, perhaps—and not because of a psychological need: this need is social and not biological. Sex and life can assume a variety of arrangements in which adults care for other people's children.[26] Thus, consider what it could imply if the theory of the evolution of language rests on this need. It could imply that for humans exclusive sexual partnering is an innate biological element rather than the social preference it usually appears to be. It could imply that sexual discipline is wired in, and that those who do not have enough of this discipline are maladaptive, biologically diminished, a runt of some sort. It could imply a connection between sexual discipline and the capability to use the language or to exercise one's symbolic talents.[27] Deacon did not make any of these claims. But it seems bizarre to find this sense of social relations appearing in a study whose contexts are measured in millions of years, and where the social formations that took place between two million and eight thousand years ago are totally unknown. Just as Darwin's terms (such as the "struggle for existence") may not discredit the theory of evolution,[28] Deacon's speculation does not annul the interest of studying language and brain evolution together. However, Darwin, Deacon, and several of the other researchers studying the evolution of language are led to omit or reduce attention to what

---

language on the specifically *male* need to know. This issue suggests that we review other aspects of Deacon's speculation—such as men doing the hunting—to decide how male coded they are. Deacon sees marriage as a means of biological survival. The males must bring meat to the females with children: "Females must have some guarantee of access to meat for their offspring. For this to evolve, males must maintain constant pair-bonded relationships, and yet for this to evolve, males must have some guarantee that they are provisioning their own progeny." Therefore symbolic means—the marriage contract— were used in order to stabilize this system. The false note in this explanation is that males would hunt only to feed their own children. This is a projection of contemporary androcentric values. (*Symbolic*, 396–401).

26. Deacon cites Lévi-Strauss's discussion of the wide variety of social purposes served by marriage as evidence of its prominence in almost all human societies . Regardless of what Lévi-Strauss may have intended, the ways social institutions have been used cannot be cited as evidence for biological species specificity in the same sense that gaits and opposable thumbs can be thus cited.

27. If this line of reasoning obtained, men who have had many partners, such as Pablo Picasso, may belong in this category.

28. Gross and Averill ("Evolution and Patriarchal") have objected to this and other Darwinian terms, such as "scarcity": they claim these terms rest on the premise of competition, where it could be assumed with equal justification that there is "plenitude" and the search for food is only rarely competitive among species.

must be the richest source of information (or data or facts)—the interaction of infants and their caregivers, the bearers of the mother tongue.[29]

However, before looking into this latter context, which is perhaps the most accessible source for the understanding of language and its place in human life, one further point may be made about Deacon's own sense of what language is. Repeatedly in this treatise, perhaps dozens of times, Deacon refers to the singularity and uniqueness of language as a phenomenon of nature. Deacon refers to the "savantlike language ability of young children."[30] This phrase, in addition to his use of Chomsky's premise that the speed with which children acquire language would be miraculous if the acquisition device were not innate, implies that this speed, without it being programmed in some way, would be an anomaly. Even the large size of human brains does not offset his perception of the miraculousness of language acquisition. Furthermore, he is at pains to say that human language cannot be considered contiguous with the communication practices of other species: "nonhuman forms of communication are something quite different from language."[31] Although Deacon rejects the "miraculous accident" explanation of children's knowledge of grammar, and he does not think the knowledge of grammar in children is the "crucial mystery"[32] posed for scientific understanding, he poses another question that marks the question of the uniqueness of language: the absences of what he calls simple languages in other species. In this regard he is disputing Derek Bickerton's speculation that language as we use it arose from protolanguages that are like pidgins and creoles.[33] The comparison of human language to the communication behaviors of other species makes the case for human uniqueness for Deacon. Repeatedly Deacon emphasizes the vast distance between human language and the communication techniques of other species, such as whales, birds, primates, or bees. He insists that language is a different genre of communication because of its intrinsic features.[34]

In emphasizing the radical difference of language from other species' socially oriented gestures, sounds, warnings, cries, or other ritualized vocalizations, Dea-

---

29. This fact is not unrelated to Walter Ong's reference to the undisciplined nature of baby talk (see chapter 8) and its emotional character (see chapter 2). Is it accidental that men working in male-coded contexts tend to devalue the emotional developments of infancy, where the human brain grows from its nonlinguistic condition into the linguistic stage?

30. Deacon, *Symbolic*, 13.

31. Deacon, *Symbolic*, 33.

32. Deacon, *Symbolic*, 39.

33. Derek Bickerton, *Language and Species* (Chicago: U of Chicago P, 1990). It is also doubtful that there are any simple languages: there are only different ways of life that could include a variety of interaction techniques.

34. This implies that human language is superior, not just different.

con continues the tradition, discussed in chapter 2, that language is the most decisive and most clearly identifiable mark of the uniqueness of human beings. For him, human language sets human beings apart from everything else in nature. This is the same tradition that viewed language as a divine spark, a special transcendental contribution to single out humans from the rest of life. Now, however, a scientific theory is used to authorize this specialness, and at the base of that theory is the axiom of the social marriage contract, entered into because men—*men* and not *men and women*—needed to know that they were the fathers of the children claimed to be theirs by the mothers. In its philosophical orientation, therefore, Deacon's scientific speculation is not terribly different from the religious speculations of the humanist period in the early Renaissance: a social premise from relatively modern times (not identified by Deacon as such) of men's needs is projected back two million years and suggested to be an originating force for the gradual coevolution of language and the human brain. Deacon's overall project must be evaluated on the basis of the viability and collective coherence of its details, but it is quite significant that this theory, like Chomsky's, is based on premises that follow a tradition of knowledge claimed in the interests of all, but which serves only some.[35]

Susanne Langer's concept of the symbol and her means of differentiating symbol using from nonhuman signing follow in the nominalist more than the realist tradition.[36] Her stance is materialist in that she gives symbols no status beyond their functions of handling feelings and thoughts in social activity. Exchanges of symbolic material are constituents of human physicality and have no meaning outside of the context of their use. The human distinctiveness of these contexts resides in part in that the exchanges need not be present in space or time. This capability for delay renders the symbols' action contingent, but does not affect the fact that both symbols and their circumstances of exchange are material. Because exchanges evoke what could be an expectation of experience, say, "tomorrow" or "next year" or "in China," symbols give the illusion of independence from material action, but this is not the case any more than it is when an unseen shift in the jet stream changes weather patterns. Deacon's explanation of symbol using, as when he stipulated a need for symbols in order to maintain loyalty in sex relations, assigns a historical origin to an adaptive

---

35. Yet without the innateness presupposition or the male-need-to-know stipulation, Deacon's thesis about the connection between brain size and the evolutionary development of language use can contribute to the views of language acquisition presented in the rest of this chapter.

36. The realist aspect of Langer's perspective is that she sees concepts, which are mental constructions, as mediating between the physical symbols and their referents. But these concepts have no role in her discussion of the use of the symbols. Rather, they are a stipulated stopping place for the symbols that, in her theory, permits the discussion of delay of use that differentiates symbolic from signific or indicative behavior.

function (acquiring certainty about one's paternity) that cannot be identified as adaptive in the behavior of living people.[37] By contrast, the explanation of the delay characteristic of language use in people is observable as a change in behavior, and is in any event not part of an attempt to account for the phylogenetic acquisition of language. One can see in the short period of time (which could be a week or less) during which infants move from one-word "sentences" to multiple-word constructions how their behavior changes. Both Langer and Deacon do speak about processes that must be going on inside an infant's brain. Langer's references to "inside" are provisional rather than essential, and are in some sense unimportant; we all *say* that when we speak, our brains are doing various sorts of arranging of memories, responses, sensory impression, and so on. The scientific question is whether anything practical is discovered by matching brain activity with symbol using, or whether the attempt to describe language and symbol use should look at different data. When considering what counts as an explanation, we hear from increasing numbers of research sources that "language itself" is no longer a credible entity: it is not an entity susceptible to the traditional scientific strategy of isolating the object in a neutral zone apart from everything else, and examining its essence.[38] The evolutionary study of language has adopted one possible wider view—yet, as Deacon's treatise suggests, the results are still distracted by claims of origins that are not verifiable.

III. Studying Infantile Language Acquisition

One kind of origin of language is available for extended research: the developmental process through which infants learn to speak.[39] As suggested by Ong's description of baby talk as occurring outside contexts of formal scholarship, and because women were the custodians of infants, there had been no basis in scholarly life for imagining that dedicated study of infantile language acquisition would provide insight into language.[40] An early attempt at comprehensive obser-

---

37. But if attention is removed from the origin of language, it is more likely the case that language considered as an adaptive function is a means toward any form of social conflict resolution: it is not necessary to guess what happened in the past to notice its adaptive actions today.

38. This is an important reminder from Christine Kenneally: language is not a "monolithic thing." (*First Word,* 289).

39. Some language evolutionists have entertained the issue of how to relate knowledge of how infants come into language with that of how the human species may have evolved into language. See Michael Studdert-Kennedy, "Introduction [to part 2]: The Emergence of Phonetic Structure," *Approaches,* ed. Hurford et al., 123–129; and Peter Macneilage and Barbara L. Davis, "Evolution of Speech: The Relation Between Ontogeny and Phylogeny," *Approaches,* ed. Hurford et al., 146–160.

40. The suggestions by Wittgenstein, Austin, and Cavell that encourage the observation of children and infants were taken up in formal, professional, and funded ways only in

vation was published by Clara and William Stern in 1907.[41] At the beginning of the twentieth century Freud and Piaget revoked the Victorian idealization of childhood; Freud saw it as the phase in the life cycle during which passions, personalities, and relationships develop; Piaget saw it as the key to discovering how knowledge and understanding develop. In their formulations, each disclosed salient aspects of infantile behaviors that, in contemporary observations of infants, have continued to be useful premises.[42] Yet traditional philosophical approaches to the study of language, including that of transformational grammar, have reached that point of frustration experienced by Wittgenstein after the completion of his *Tractatus,* and which led to his change in perspective: formal quantitative logical theory, as used by physical sciences, is inapplicable to the study of language.[43]

The study of infantile language acquisition instead demands observation and verbal description: the choice of what to observe and how to describe the

---

the latter half of the twentieth century. The opening of *Philosophical Investigations* presents Augustine's account of how he acquired language as part of an erroneous tradition of belief about language and its acquisition, one that is reconsidered in the present study.

41. Clara und William Stern, *Die Kindersprache: Eine psychologische und sprachtheoretische Untersuchung* (Leipzig: Johann Ambrosius Barth Verlag, 1928). It has not been translated into English. Infants' speech is difficult to translate because it is more dependent on the gestural context than the speech of older persons.

42. In his "Little Hans" case, Freud observed the "*fort-da*" (language?) game that subsequent researchers and most parents have documented in infants: their attention to, and pleasure in, disappearing and reappearing objects and people. Piaget used the term "reciprocal assimilation" of sensorimotor schemata to describe how infants assimilate learned schemata to one another, thus creating a new schema, redefined as such by the new occasion which motivated the reciprocal assimilation. One researcher, Annette Karmiloff-Smith, credits Piaget with being one of the earliest contributors of data that could counter the nativist premise. She outlines how Piaget placed language in the broader context of cognitive and symbolic functioning (as did Langer and Cassirer) and claims that children's access to language is, in fact, access to a more comprehensive machinery of knowing, of which language is one part. Annette Karmiloff-Smith, *A Functional Approach to Child Language: A Study of Determiners and Reference* (New York: Cambridge UP, 1979).

43. A pertinent work in this regard is Richard Rorty, *Philosophy and the Mirror of Nature* (Princeton, NJ: Princeton UP, 1979). This influential reflection identifies Heidegger and Dewey, along with Wittgenstein, as key revisionists of language philosophy. Its "anti-foundationalist" thesis leads him to view the writing of philosophy as participation in the "conversation of mankind." He, like a group of sociolinguists, favors pragmatism as the most useful research philosophy to approach question of language. However, Rorty, like Wittgenstein or Derrida, writes about philosophy in ways that maintain its separation from other forms of inquiry. Philosophy has reached its limits only because it remains discipline bound. In part, this paralysis is related to the department system in universities. However, it is also due to something Janice Moulton discussed in her essay on adversariality: the failure to acknowledge an unspoken premise, which, in this

observations are the keys to identifying salient phenomena.[44] New descriptions place the infantile phenomena in different contexts; in the literature, the variety of descriptions and contexts have started to add up to a picture of how infants develop and acquire language. This picture supersedes the approaches of trans-formational grammarians and other approaches that are not inclined to use the overwhelming volume of material accumulated by observers of infants in both contrived and naturalistic settings. The issue of what to observe is still a matter of choice for researchers, but one thing is clear: the contexts of observation have been widening since the Sterns first recorded what their children said. Infants speaking various languages have been observed,[45] and the full speech community and environment of infants is increasingly considered to be a part of the process of language acquisition for each child. Gradually in this century, the living contexts of speech and language have become a necessary site of investigation, and their results move the presuppositions of research toward recognition of the materiality of language.

Interactionist researchers have challenged the assumption that a child gets too little stimulation to bring about the use of language.[46] They have shown that the level of stimuli for infants is enough to account for their acquisition of

---

case, is the assumption by philosophers of an authoritative role played by their subject matter among the variety of approaches to language. Rorty himself may or may not be traditional, but he participates in the traditional self-regard of those practicing philoso-phy. A figure such as "the conversation of mankind" may be welcome, but the question of local purposes in such conversations remains the repeated test of this figure. These purposes or uses, such as conflict resolution, are not part of Rorty's address.

44. In the several contemporary approaches to the study of infantile language acquisi-tion, there is still considerable debate on the vocabulary and the means to describe the behavior of infants themselves, as well as the interactions of mothers and infants. Anat Ninio and Catherine E. Snow note that "there is a surprising lack of agreement among the different investigators about the nature of the earliest speech uses. . . . [T]he studies use disparate systems for categorizing speech act types or functional uses, with categories of widely varying scope." Anat Ninio and Catherine E. Snow, *Pragmatic Development* (Boulder, CO: Westview P, 1996), 59–60.

45. Dan Isaac Slobin, ed., *The Crosslinguistic Study of Language Acquisition* (Hills-dale, NJ: Erlbaum, 1985). This sort of study has been rare. Botha observes the casuistry needed for transformationalists to hold that inferences about universals may be made from examination of only one language, a procedure characteristic of the Chomskyan search for universals (*Challenging*, 187). A more recent collection of essays seeking universals docu-ments the complexity of explanation noted by Botha: Morten H. Christiansen and Simon Kirby, eds. *Language Evolution* (Oxford and New York: Oxford University Press, 2003).

46. Clark cites a series of studies that found that the subtlest and most complex grammatical forms are heard repeatedly by children during their frequently practiced rituals of feeding, changing, dressing, playing, and getting attention from adults. Eve V. Clark, *First Language Acquisition* (Cambridge and New York: Cambridge UP, 2003), 428–430.

grammar as folded into a total entity of sound, gesture, vocabulary, and social responsiveness; and some have described how it takes a decade for a child to show a fully developed grammar.[47] They have also shown how to observe the infantile experience of what Kristeva and Derrida referred to as the *khōra:* starting with Piaget's observations of pre-linguistic sensorimotor experience, researchers have recorded a body of data that suggests how schemata learned in earlier phases (starting from birth) combine to form new schemata of motion and behavior that are used and presented in interpersonal situations, and thus become behavioral templates for the use of first words.[48] It is a process of construction and adaptation to the immediate social and physical circumstances, any one element of which cannot be considered crucial. The data collected by the many researchers identifying themselves as developmental, cognitive, pragmaticist, or interactionist—and combinations of these—strongly suggest that the child's syntheses of experiences and interactions moves toward a comprehensive social, interpersonal function of which language is a key element.

There is no single interactionist theory of infantile language acquisition. The field as a whole may be described as having an orientation that treats the acquisition of language as Lev Vygotsky and George Herbert Mead had proposed in the 1930s: that an individual's language is internalized dialogue. The language a child uses emerges from his or her having been socially stamped or initiated, so to speak, a process through which each usage was heard or used in relation either to direct conversation or to the overhearing of the conversation of others.[49] George Herbert Mead uses similar reasoning to move away from

47. Robbins Burling, "The Slow Growth of Language in Children," *The Transition to Language,* ed. Alison Wray (Oxford: Oxford UP, 2002), 297–310.

48. I have discussed this issue in some detail in chapter 2 of my book *Subjective Criticism* (Baltimore: Johns Hopkins UP, 1978), and before that in my essay "New Considerations of the Infantile Acquisition of Language and Symbolic Thought," *Psychoanalytic Review* 63.1 (1976): 49–71, especially 52–53 and 56–57. I return to some of these thoughts in section 5 of this chapter.

49. David Bleich, *The Double Perspective: Language, Literacy, and Social Relations* (New York: Oxford UP, 1988), 69–71. In this section I review the correspondence between the proposals of Vygotsky and Mead regarding their consideration of social experience as the datum prior to individual development. Like Piaget, Vygotsky presents persuasive observations that show how infants arrive at verbal and behavioral gestures of indication through their interaction with adults who channel, for example, a grasping movement toward a pointing movement. In this phase the child, who is about one year old, demonstrates how a supposedly more animal movement like reaching *for* something turns into a *similar gesture,* but one that now necessarily involves another person: the pointing could be read as asking. In this sense socialization is a necessary action that *converts* sensorimotor behaviors into social behaviors. The child's ever-enlarging brain is a participant this conversion. When the pointing becomes *verbal asking,* the child has fully acquired symbol-using capacity and is behaving according to recognizable social conventions.

the longstanding habit of Western thought to consider the individual mind the primary locus from which general understanding of human beings may be taken. If the principal achievement of infantile life is self-objectification— seeing oneself as the same kind of object as others appear to be—this came about as the *result* of a process of socialized sharing. A person's conceptualiza- tion of self is a perceptual separation from the insidedness of communion with another. At the moment of experiencing separateness and togetherness at once in that relationship, it becomes possible to see oneself also as separate.[50] Some of the researchers have seen both Vygotsky and Mead as sources for their own styles of investigation.[51] The interest in the materiality of language that began in the twentieth century emerged from a sense of language not being eligible for abstract or logical formulation, but instead requiring a verbal description related to the unmeasurable—but identifiable—social circumstances in which each individual develops.

Language by itself cannot be seen as an adaptive capability. The total move- ment toward socialization, carried by the uses of language, looks more like what might be identified as a species-specific process of adaptation. Here adaptation should also be taken to mean survival, and we go no further than this standard: survival as a teleology attributed to living things does share something with Darwin's sense of evolution, but changes it somewhat from emphasizing that the so-called fit survive toward emphasizing that the species survives without reference to who is fit for this future. When language is viewed in this social context its materiality is also more visible, since it is more subject to the use and fate of other material things: if the language is not used, it dies, and disappears from the mouths of people.[52] When the language is used, even if only in print

---

50. G. H. Mead, *Mind, Self, and Society*, ed. Charles W. Morris (Chicago: U of Chicago P, 1962), 225–226. This passage about self-objectification (also discussed in some detail in my *The Double Perspective*) provides an additional basis for Wittgenstein's rejection of the possibility of a private language. If there is simultaneity of the acquisition of both self-awareness and language, they must both be derived from the long experience of sharing, mutuality, and—finally—reciprocity in infantile development.

51. For example, Michael Tomasello, *Constructing a Language: A Usage-based Theory of Language Acquisition* (Cambridge, MA: Harvard UP, 2003), 28; Lois Bloom, *The Transition from Infancy to Language: Acquiring the Power of Expression* (Cambridge: Cambridge UP, 1993), 17; John L. Locke, *The Child's Path to Spoken Language* (Cam- bridge, MA: Harvard UP, 1993), 103; and Michael Lewis and Louise Cherry, "Social Behavior and Language Acquisition," *Interaction, Conversation, and the Development of Language*, ed. Michael Lewis and Leonard A. Rosenblum (New York: Wiley, 1977), 227–242.

52. This point is made by Daniel L. Everett, who has studied dying languages in Brazil. In 1995 Everett spoke with the "five remaining speakers of Oro Win [who] now find that not only are they unable fully to recall their own language, but they cannot speak any other language as native speakers. They have lost their history and their

as some languages now appear, it is part of a living, physiological situation, regardless of how many people are present and regardless of how great the spatial and temporal separations from the site of articulation. The use of language is always material, as are its effects. The usual references to meaning or thought or ideas as underlying language or being its essence are extraneous to any analysis of particular speeches, texts, or contributions to conversations.

In a recent effort to stipulate a larger cultural scene for the acquisition and function of language, Michael Tomasello observes,[53] "It seems significant also that linguistic symbols have a materiality to them, in the form of a reliable sound structure, because this is the only way in which they could be socially shared. These public symbols—which the speaker hears herself produce as she produces them—are thus available for perceptual inspection and categorization themselves."[54] This observation is significant because Tomasello seeks to describe a broad social context that will hold the study of language, and like others already cited in this discussion, he says that only whole cultures are wide enough entities to identify the full context of language. He tries to show, in the citation of his own several studies of infants, how the study of the infantile acquisition of language must include awareness of how cultural factors such as usage and behavior customs are communicated to infants acquiring language. In this attempt, Tomasello notes in passing the materiality of language, but his discussion of it goes no further. To him, it "seems significant." From the standpoint of the present discussion it *is* significant. Noticing the materiality of language gives a decisive push toward recognizing its role in the adaptation and survival of the human species.[55]

---

community . . . within the next decade or so the Oro Win language and all vestiges of the Oro Win as a distinct people will be lost to them and to us. . . . We will have lost their knowledge of the jungle, a philosophy of life, paths to happiness. We will have lost their literature, art, and scientific knowledge. . . . When they go, they are gone for ever." Daniel L. Everett, *Language: The Cultural Tool* (New York: Pantheon, 2012), 304–305.

53. Michael Tomasello, *The Cultural Origins of Human Cognition* (Cambridge, MA: Harvard UP, 1999), 127.

54. Compare this with Julia Kristeva's statement, "[W]e can speak of a 'materiality' of language by not allowing ourselves to posit language as an ideal system closed in upon itself (such is the 'formalist' attitude) or as a mere copy of a regulated world that exists without it (such is the 'realistic,' mechanistic attitude)." Julia Kristeva, "The Materiality of Language," *Language: The Unknown* (New York: Columbia UP, 1980), 18–42, quotation on 36. Kristeva implies that the conception of language derives from collective "attitudes," a term which seems to tone down the traditional dogmatisms of "theory" or "system" or "ideology."

55. But it is no more decisive than are dam building for beavers or nest building for birds: all are ways of life for those species and cannot be isolated from those species' total behavioral repertoires that sustain their lives. As Dean Falk observed, "human brains *do* language" (see note 21, above).

Tomasello's use of "seems" has an additional connection to my argument herein: it suggests that materiality has crept into the researcher's awareness in spite of himself. This path toward awareness helps to confirm the repression of materiality in the past. Historically, it is clearer that the depth and scope of social behavior, rather than its materiality, was repressed. Plato's reasons for considering the banishment of poets from the Republic involve a caution about permitting space for the emotional life of the total population. It did not seem to matter how the population became aroused: the danger was in their arousal.[56] Plato may have been aware of the "material cause" potential of public speaking and widely heard verbal artworks. At the same time, the articulation of the eternal life of ideas as the hidden essence of words is one of the earliest versions of what became the realist orientation toward language discussed earlier in this book.[57] Plato's dialogues show the connection between social, collective repression and the repression of linguistic materiality.

IV. Recognizing Affect in Language Acquisition

This historical tradition of repressing the social or material sense of language emerges in a more emphatic way in the contemporary study of infantile language acquisition: the almost uniform failure to include infants' affective lives in the presentations of how cognitive faculties grow.[58] As cognitive psychology developed from Piaget's documentation of how reasoning and understanding develops in children, researchers considered the language strand in this process to be particularly interesting, but something that ought to be studied by itself. One of Piaget's students, Annette Karmiloff-Smith, has attempted to reread Piaget by emphasizing how important the role of language is in the development of intelligent behavior.[59] Another contemporary researcher, Eve Clark, broadly documents the central roles of mother-infant interaction, and she includes study of the mother's language as part of the scene of investigation. Aware as these

---

56. Yet if one remembers that Plato lived in a society in which slavery and war were the rule and not the exception, what non-slave, non-soldier would advise anything other than to fear the enlightenment of the total population?

57. See chapter 1, section 4.

58. Lois Bloom states, "In linguistics, the historical emphasis on spoken words and sentences has meant that emotion was ignored in studies of language. . . . When language and affect have been considered together in psychological research, the emphasis is generally on words that name the emotions and not on the cognitive connections between speech and affect" (*Transition,* 17).

59. In *A Functional,* Karmiloff-Smith wants to compromise and consider both Piaget's and Chomsky's works equivalent contributors. Her later work *Beyond Modularity: A Developmental Perspective on Cognitive Science* (Cambridge, MA: MIT P, 1992) includes nativist claims by using terms such as infantile "predispositions" and "sensitivities," thus implying that both Chomskyan and Piagetian perspectives contribute to understanding: this is less a compromise than a synthesis.

researchers (Tomasello included) have been of the wide context needed for the study of language acquisition, little room has been found for the discussion of children's affective lives. The tradition of separating cognition from feelings and passion has continued intact in the otherwise progressive developments in the study of language acquisition. The name "cognitive science" correctly reflects the focus of researchers on the processes of language acquisition in the development of intelligence and reasoning. This separation, although not entirely inimical to the project, remains a sign of repression: no researcher on human social life can afford to overlook the emotional behavior of any person, much less infants and mothers, whose emotional bonds are discernable because they are so familiar. Knowledge and data about infants' emotional lives are as valuable as the other kinds of knowledge and data that have been developed.[60]

Few researchers have taken this position.[61] John L. Locke observes,

> Cognition and affect are so intimately interrelated that it is impossible to say which comes first and which is more likely to drive the other into additional elaborations. The evidence suggests that each capacity influences the other, and I take the position that cognition and affect must work together if infants are fully to experience the urge to convey, and therefore to learn and use spoken language.[62]

---

60. In some research recognizing the role of affect in infants' lives, the language used to describe it inhibits comprehension of the total scene of affective expression. For example, Marc D. Hauser writes, "[P]rior to the onset of communicative utterances, human infants produce a number of sounds that are mere expressions of changing affective states, including pain, hunger, and joy. Such sounds are also accompanied by facial expressions. . . . Eventually, however, some of these sounds are coopted for use in intentional communication, as occurs when infants use grunts to indicate their desires." About these grunts, Hauser later writes, "before they begin to communicate about objects and events in the external environment, infants convey information about their affective state." In this regard adults also make sounds that "provide the infant with direct information about its caregiver's emotional state." Marc D. Hauser, *The Evolution of Communication* (Cambridge, MA: MIT P, 2000), 482, 488, 489. Sounds are "mere expressions of changing affective states." To a mother or caregiver, decisions about what each sound means is consequential. Not including the total scene and using the term "affective state" does not describe the continuous action of caregiver and infant; rather this description isolates "states." Similarly, caregivers are said to "convey information" about their own "affective states." But isn't it truer to say that infant and caregiver are interacting with each other, gradually familiarizing themselves with the sounds and gestures of their relationship? Is information transfer the best way to describe the exchange of gestures in a living relationship? Because of the conventions of "scientific" description, we do not get an accurate picture of the scene of language interaction.

61. And I have found only two, although both of these cite other sources. See Locke, *Child's Path*, 328–329.

62. Locke, *Child's Path*, 324.

Having cited other sources that claim the necessity for including affectivity as part of the study of how intelligence develops, Locke observes that linguists and psycholinguists have not taken up this path of study: "we seem to have thrown everything into theories of language *except* affect."[63] He says that "affect does for language acquisition what motivation does for learning. Affect moves infants to socialize and to assimilate the behavior of others; it gives them important personal information to convey before they have language and complex thoughts. . . . Affect drives and is sustained by cognition."[64] Finally, Locke considers, "it is unlikely that language will develop without a felt need to communicate."[65]

Although he approaches recognition of a critical role for the child's emotional life in the acquisition and use of language, Locke does not reach the point stipulated by Freud and other psychoanalytic researchers early in the twentieth century: that affect and people's emotional lives are bound up with specific, identifiable interpersonal relationships.[66] There is no need to accept such things as the Oedipus complex, penis envy, and other of Freud's androcentric hypotheses in order to credit psychoanalytic thinking with placing on the research table the fact that our emotional lives develop through our relationships with our parents and others (siblings, grandparents, friends) who are invested in our growth, health, and daily behavior. Although Locke did not follow the research implications of his observation, his recognition of emotional development in language acquisition is noteworthy. Few other researchers within the disciplines of cognitive or developmental language have viewed the infantile acquisition of language as being tied to the combined affective and cognitive life within living and cultural relationships. Perhaps the most developed work—a career-long enterprise—comes from Lois Bloom.

Bloom's work from the 1970s continues to be cited because of its comprehensive collection of data (a wide variety of examples of infantile speech in a variety of interpersonal contexts), and because of its movement toward an empirically grounded description of language acquisition. In the course of compiling this data, she moved steadily toward a position regarding the fundamental roles of affective development, the Intentional Model, outlined in 2001 but not yet taken

---

63. Locke, *Child's Path*, 329.

64. Locke, *Child's Path*, 329.

65. Locke, *Child's Path*, 330.

66. This term "relationships" can also apply to situations in which children are raised by "villages" and extended families. The so-called family romance conventions that are used (but increasingly challenged) in the West are not essential interpersonal structures for language or anything else. Even in trying circumstances infants are raised by groups of people who care about their welfare; when this is not the case, as when there is extreme poverty, the society itself is in danger, and the acquisition of language is not the matter of greatest consequence.

up by other researchers.[67] It is likely that the immediate reason for this caution is related to the disciplinary style in cognitive psychology, but other explanations may well apply.[68] It has not been a priority to study people's emotional lives in connection with the development of cognition. Bloom seeks more than simple inclusion of affective behavior; the Intentional Model suggests that the child's affective life is integrated into cognitive and interpersonal development, and Bloom emphasizes that the acquisition of language is fundamentally tied to the child's regular, continuous attempts to coordinate (inner, subjective, mental) intentions with those of the adult interlocutors. Bloom sees the child as facing a series of "discrepancies"—misunderstandings between child and caretakers— and that, to a significant extent, the effort of acquiring language is made up of many attempts to resolve miscommunications.[69] She cites Roberta Golinkoff's earlier essay[70] that called attention to the prominent role played by this process of misunderstanding, and attempts to overcome it, taking place between child and caretakers—a process that begins in the sensorimotor period, when communication involves not words but the exchange of the child's gestural deixes for the caregiver's verbal responses. Both Clark and Tomasello also emphasize the importance of the social, exchange-marked relations between infants and adults but they do not place a great deal of emphasis either on the resolution of misunderstandings or on the expression of affect. Their main attentions are on accounting for how a large inventory of vocabulary and syntactic combinations come to be constructed by the child out of previous schemata, in a style of reasoning resembling Piaget's work, but with a richer store of data. As were Piaget's formulations, their results are mostly taxonomical and persuasive; and perhaps more than Piaget, their aims are to create an empirical basis for reducing the credibility of both the innatist hypothesis and the belief that the logical description of language provides explanatory insight into what really happens during our countless fluent uses of language.

---

67. Neither Eve V. Clark (*First*) nor Michael Tomasello (*Constructing*), each of whom has presented comprehensive descriptive discussions (theories) of infantile language acquisition, has discussed Bloom's theory, although they cite much of her data.

68. For instance, there was not enough time to respond within the treatises that were being written. However, it is also the case that Bloom's attention to the affective life of the children is a minority interest among cognitive psychologists—regardless of Bloom's tendency to follow the standards of statistical research in cognitive psychology in most of the research she has reported.

69. Bloom's orientation is consistent with the conception of language as a species-wide adaptive function: if from infancy language solves misunderstandings and thus stabilizes relationships, that function of language stays with us.. This raises the question, posed in the present book, of why it fails so often in adult lives and society (see chapter 11).

70. Roberta Michnick Golinkoff, "'I Beg Your Pardon?' The Preverbal Negotiation of Failed Messages," *Journal of Child Language* 13 (1986): 455–476.

There are affirmative casts to the presentations of both Clark and Tomasello: their developmental and constructionist perspectives include collectively held sources such as cultural styles, habits, mores, and conventions as essential features of the language-acquisition process. Bloom, while open to these being likely sources, seems to seek a comprehensive framework through which any one instance of a child's acquiring language should be describable as well with an Intentional Model: one that includes an account of the mutual perception of intention on the part of the child and speaking partners. I do not think she has achieved this goal, but she presents "explanatory principles"[71] that want to go beyond description toward identifying the child's initiatives. But if intentions or intentional states are not perceivable and if, similarly, feelings are not perceivable directly, but are presumed on the basis of subjects' behavior,[72] there seems to be no basis, on first consideration, on which the intentional model can be used empirically.

Yet Bloom's intuition about the situation seems to make more sense than to do without any locus for the inclusion of both feelings and interpersonal purposes or intentions (on the part of both infants and caregivers). In this matter, the separation of academic psychology from psychoanalytic psychology[73] is a handicap. However, neither the psychoanalytic description of child development nor the several cognitive descriptions are enough by themselves to account for the acquisition of language. A psychoanalytic perspective, especially insofar as it has developed beyond the androcentric presuppositions with which it began, is in position to describe the relationships between caregivers and infants in a way that would complement the plausible, promising descriptions given independently by Piaget, Clark, Tomasello, and Bloom.

Evolutionary anthropologists and language researchers have noticed, alongside the large brain of human beings, the long period of childhood dependency.[74] Children become self-aware[75] and cognizant and psychologically autonomous before

---

71. Lois Bloom, Erin Tinker, and Ellin Kofsky Scholnick, *The Intentionality Model and Language Acquisition: Engagement, Effort, and the Essential Tension in Development*, Monographs of the Society for Research in Child Development, vol. 66, no. 4 (Boston: Blackwell, 2001).

72. As Wittgenstein discussed.

73. If psychoanalysis is included as part of academic psychology, it has its own clinical zone in universities' psychology departments. But it may be just as true that psychoanalytic practitioners have believed that their views of the body-zone theory of child development (oral, anal, and phallic), and its traditional Freudian vocabulary that stipulated "an unconscious mind" created a sense of territorial sovereignty in which cognitive considerations were unwelcome.

74. Several language evolutionists refer to this fact, including Deacon, Knight, Dunbar, Hurford, and Studdert-Kennedy.

75. Some might say intelligent.

they become socially independent.[76] Yet this long period of dependency is rarely cited as being as significant in relation to language acquisition as is the large human brain.[77] It could be of interest to ask why the study of language acquisition was not strongly linked to socialization sooner, and why there is still reluctance to view the acquisition of language and children's long socialization period as being the same process.[78] In psychoanalytic thinking, this dependency is a fundamental consideration: psychoanalysis was noticed to begin with because it placed importance on what happens to people during their long period of dependency, during which their caregivers (families, usually) turn into their loved ones. Without sentimentality, Freud proposed that the "bond of love" formed for many, if not most people, in infancy was a key to understanding civilization, a theme later taken up by Erik Erikson.[79] Even if academic cognitive psychologists acknowledge that language acquisition must be studied by observing infants interacting with caregivers, they still do not describe the infants' behaviors as if the relation between infant and caregiver were of compelling importance to both parties. Lois Bloom's introduction of intention to the rich data of language acquisition is a step in this psychoanalytic direction, although she does not describe it that way. It seems that this term is at least partially in keeping with the tradition in academic psychology, where, on the one hand, it is commonly believed that people have intentions that are "conveyed" by language, and, on the other hand, one can use the term "intention" to describe observations without confusing others. It would be better if this term were not used, and it would be better if the exchanges of conversation were less frequently described as "communication," as this term also suggests that the uses of language are conveyances of something deeper—that is, meaning or intention.

From a psychoanalytic perspective, intention is a reference to what follows from a relationship, in which people depend on one another for a wide variety of attentions and contributions. The language of casual relationships may also be described as partaking of some intentionality.[80] The terms "desire" and "love"

---

76. One might say that newly linguistic infants have recognized their own agency.

77. Yet there is also a clear connection between the long period of dependency and the way societies are formed; each makes provisions for the children and values them greatly.

78. This perspective would be consistent with Falk's observation that humans "*do* language."

79. Several of Erikson's works continue the theme he introduced in his first work, *Childhood and Society,* which discussed how the understanding of the childhood of prominent adult leaders gives insight into the nature of the rest of society. Attention to the collective approaches to childhood has led to the thought that the beating of children is one source of the adult tendency to violence. Alice Miller, *For Your Own Good: Hidden Cruelty in Child-Rearing and the Roots of Violence,* trans. Hildegarde and Hunter Hannum (New York: Noonday P, 1983). Once collective practices are taken into consideration, awareness of them affects how to interpret any individual's path of development.

80. In *The Double Perspective,* I describe how Husserl remained frustrated to the end of his life because of his not being able to describe the intentionality of intersubjective

are too strong to apply to all relationships, but they do apply fairly well to the relationship between infants and parents. It is thus not simply the dependency of childhood that affects the acquisition of language, but it is the strength of that dependency that must be playing a role in the total process as described by Clark and Tomasello, for example. Bloom's intuition is like Husserl's: a child's intention is a deep and serious matter because of the dependency of child on parent (and the reciprocal attachment of parent to child). Furthermore, our putative intentionality is bound up in our sense of self-awareness: for Husserl, this awareness was fundamental to our existence, and it was not possible for him to continue to claim its fundamentality yet describe relationships without reference to it; the latter is the sort of description Wittgenstein's reflections exemplified.

Psychoanalytic description is compatible with Wittgensteinian description,[81] and for this reason it is helpful to link it to the empirical or materialist thinking of the researchers in infantile language acquisition. In psychoanalysis, interpersonal dependency does not require proof: it is a fact in plain sight. At least this is the case in the post-Freudian world of psychoanalysis, which began by stressing object relations (that is, interpersonal relationships) and developed further to address some of the fundamental gender issues and inequities in Western societies.[82]

The understanding of psychoanalysis regarding the process of infants' separating themselves from their caregivers is still accepted; at about the time of language acquisition (including syntax), the child enters the so-called terrible twos, where attempts at autonomous behavior, when they first fail, result in tantrums and frustration for caregivers as well as the infants. The period of language acquisition (the two-word combinations that follow the initial "vocabulary spurt"[83]) is a period whose emotional life can be plausibly described as the pain of separating from bodily dependency on the mother or other caregiver. One can see the differences in scope among, for example, Golinkoff's description of misunderstanding, Bloom's description of "discrepancy,"[84] and the violence of infantile behaviors during the terrible twos. The set of cognitive emphases alone

---

experience. I also suggest that Derrida's critique of Husserl amounted to his explaining Husserl's frustration because he did not get, so to speak, how the materiality of language prevented the success of such a project.

81. Psychoanalysis did not start out this way; several abstract (imaginary) entities were considered to be part of people's minds. However, object-relations psychology, which emphasizes how people relate to one another, does not depend on the stipulation of abstract entities that are acting on their own.

82. Instances of this further development are found in Kate Millett, Juliet Mitchell, Nancy Chodorow, Dorothy Dinnerstein, and Jessica Benjamin. For full references, see chapter 4, note 137.

83. Bloom, *Transition*, 189–199. The claim of a "vocabulary spurt" referred to as "VS" is not challenged by any researcher.

84. Bloom and Tinker assert, "According to the principle of discrepancy, development is enhanced when children act to resolve a mismatch between what they have in

does not seem commensurate with the actual behaviors of infants at this age. Bloom repeatedly wrote that the acquisition required "effort" on the part of the child. But that too is not strong enough to apply to the maximum release of bodily energy by the child either in frustration, or need, or anger, or confusion. Parents also have their patience tried, and while guidebooks on parenting may help, it is difficult to remain patient with a newly autonomous child. The turbulence of the transition to language must be accounted for, since it is recognized as part of this process in all children; it cannot be cordoned off to some other area and assumed not to play a role in the child's total active growth. When Tomasello noticed that the language "seemed" to be material, he might also have noticed the materiality of the process of the child's separation from bodily dependency: that "other" voice that had become so familiar now has a different meaning or status to the child.[85] The sound and use of those words are marking the relationships of great importance or value to the child. To the child, it is a unified perception and the language that he or she has just acquired plays a major role in the process, as much in instances when the language is abandoned in favor of crying, kicking, and screaming as in those when the language is itself used to restore the understanding between him- or herself and caregiver, when it is used to resolve discrepancies, when it *brings back the loved one that the child feels is more distant than had been comfortable.*[86] This is then read as a *verbal restoration* of a social relationship that was previously dependent on a different

---

mind and what is already evident from the situation" ("Intentionality Model," 19; italics in original).

85. Tomasello's definition of symbolic communication is valuable for its clarity, but also as a sign of what is left out—the emotional behavior of the child that signals the importance of the change. Here is his description: "[S]ymbolic communication is the process by which one individual attempts to manipulate the attention of, or to share attention with, another individual. In specifically linguistic communication, as one form of symbolic communication, this attempt quite often involves both (a) reference, or inviting the other to share attention to some outside entity (broadly -construed), and (b) predication, or directing the other's attention to some currently *unshared* features or aspects of that entity (in the hopes of sharing attention to the new aspect as well)." Michael Tomasello, "On the Different Origins of Symbols and Grammar," *Language Evolution,* ed. Christiansen and Kirby, 94–95. Tomasello's definition, which seems to apply as far as it goes, omits the urgency of these events for the toddlers taking the step to language. My discussion in section 5, this chapter, further considers that for each child the affective bases for catching on to both words and grammar are the same, and that if this were the case one need not stipulate different sources in culture and history for symbols and grammar.

86. If this role for language achieves credibility, it contributes to an account of the role of language in human adaptation; adaptation in this discussion means something like "ways of functioning that facilitate survival as a species." This issue is elaborated further in section 5 of this chapter in connection with the specific narrative of Helen Keller.

sort of bodily behavior. The acquisition of language moves the bodily relation more fully to speech, but *it is no less a bodily relationship.*

Because the bond with the recovered loved one is so strong, it is hard to study on a statistical basis. The cultural data Tomasello seeks may be accessible to researchers, but the presumed intentionalities[87] of child and caregiver(s) are not perceivable at all, and the terms of the relation between them are also generally not shared with the researcher. The close relationships that could account for the special character of each child's acquisition of language—and that would, if understood in a suitably large number of instances, become a basis for a full general account of language acquisition—can be observed only with an extended narrative collaboration of caregivers, researchers, and children.

For most researchers, the phases of language acquisition are generally agreed upon. Holophrases or single-word usage last from about one year of age to about eighteen or twenty months when there is all at once a "vocabulary spurt" and the formation of two-word combinations that sound like sentences when heard in a living context. By and large, researchers have credited a process of construction to account for both the ability to acquire the names of things rapidly as well as the ability to put these words together in sentence-like verbal gestures in interpersonal situations. Lois Bloom has attempted to show that emotional, expressive behavior is integrated into the child's acquisition of both vocabulary and grammar.[88] Her statistical results do suggest confirmation of a principle she formulated in her 1993 study:

> The core of development that brings an infant to the threshold of language in the second year is in the integration of affect, cognition, and social connectedness to other persons. Children learn language in the first place because they strive to maintain intersubjectivity with other persons—to *share* what they and other persons are feeling and thinking. Affect expression has been in place as the vehicle of intersubjectivity since birth and is well established by the end of the first year.[89]

Bloom's description is an integrated or unified vision of language acquisition. In this view, language as the path to intersubjectivity is a fundamental

---

87. Although in informal discourse, there is nothing unusual about discussing each other's intentions.

88. Both her 1993 and 2001 studies cite and describe several experiments that try to measure the levels of affect in the children. The statistics themselves are not doubtful, but the meaning of the terms "affect" and "expression" without a sense of their specific function in the relationships keeps them distant from Bloom's aim to demonstrate their importance.

89. Bloom, *Transition*, 245–246.

achievement of infantile development. She seems to hold intersubjectivity to be as important as have object-relations psychologists; this relationship is the site of a strong bond that motivates the language development process.[90] She does not report specifically how this bond works in the child's achievement of language, but John Dore does present such an outline. Although Dore's work is cited by Bloom, she, like other researchers, has not taken up his formulation—which outlines a hypothetical explanation that is close to Bloom's formulation and consistent with the views of Clark and Tomasello.[91]

One element in his discussion is different from the work of most of the other researchers in this group of cognitivists studying language acquisition: Dore tries to describe the detailed sequence of exchange that shows how the affective relationship between adult and child (in his essay, A for adult, B for baby) *motivates* the child to overtake the symbolic forms proffered by the adult. Like Susanne Langer, his fundamental sense is that the capacity for symbol making and using is part of a coordinated or unified set of schemata in which there is no separation between affect, cognition, and language use. His discussion, like Bloom's, uses the idea of intent to refer to a moment at which the child seems to have made conscious, deliberate choices to make a gesture or say words: the child seems to want to do something or have something done. As tempting as it may be to want to locate an "origin of intention,"[92] most of the data from several researchers suggests not that intention is a momentary origin tied to specific gestures, but that what researchers are calling intention is something that also existed in early infancy but gradually became similar to the adult sense of wanting something and seeking it. Discounting Dore's search for a beginning of intent, his discussion does suggest in a plausible way how affect enables the child's overtaking of specific language forms in a way that will be remembered. Dore writes, "I hypothesize that A's interventions in B's affect expressions *transform* them into

---

90. In the 1993 study, Bloom touches on the issue of the child's perceptions of self and other, but in this discussion there is a presentation of frequencies of verbal and emotional reference as opposed to narrative descriptions of the bond or attachment of mother and child (*Transition*, 152–153). Elizabeth Bates has also stressed the importance of the mother's participation in the relationship with the child. This relationship strives for "an interactive style in which harmony and affective synchrony predominate," and in which "the mother stimulates and challenges her child." Elizabeth Bates, et al., *The Emergence of Symbols: Cognition and Communication in Infancy* (New York: Academic P, 1979), 268. Bates's focus is on the quality of the relationship rather than on its role, regardless of quality. Neither Bloom nor Bates entertains self-other differentiation on the affective scale proposed by psychoanalytic thinking.

91. John Dore, "Feeling, Form, and Intention in the Baby's Transition to Language," *The Transition from Prelinguistic to Linguistic Communication*, ed. Roberta Michnick Golinkoff (Hillsdale, NJ: Erlbaum, 1983), 167–190.

92. Dore, "Feeling," 169.

intents to express those affect-states."[93] This process is less mysterious than this abstract description suggests; it is common behavior between caregivers and infants. As Dore describes in this section, suppose a year-old infant laughs and seems happy about something; the mother then claps her hands and smiles. Dore describes this event as the mother providing a conventional gesture for the feeling of the moment. Dore does not say the following, but it is consistent with his reasoning: suppose the child is happy about having taken a first step. There may then be not only a clap, but also a verbal usage, such as "Yes, come to Mommy." Suppose the child is happy about being held, or swung, or kissed: there is *always* a verbal response, often a characteristic one (that is one that that mother repeats, according to the customs of her culture and personal language use style). The verbal usage is also a conventional *gesture* that becomes associated with the child's behavior. Dore does say that words come to play the role of conventional gestures that the child is motivated to remember, reproduce, or change. This link between sensorimotor and verbal behavior was described by Piaget, but without reference to the affective premium it pays both child and adult.[94] The Piagetian processes of assimilation and accommodation account for the incremental changes in gesture that carry over into language use, which would be usefully described as oral gestures that continue the longstanding process of gesture exchange begun at birth between infant and caregiver. When the child reproduces the gestures given by the adult, "when feeling the same affect," this allows "both B and A together to 're-cognize' and share the same affect state."[95] Dore acknowledges how this description follows those given by Vygotsky, Mead, and later figures: individual acquisition follows from earlier involvement in a process of mutual exchanges of language. Put another way, individual language acquisition is derived from and motivated by collectively used tropes of language use.

He then offers the following formulation:

> [W]e assume that word meanings are consequences in B of what AB feel and do. The dialogue they engage in is the interface between his functional intents and her formal requirements for interpretation. Though A cannot give B his needs, motives and intents, she does supply him with the forms necessary to express them.[96]

This passage describes the acquisition of language as the *gestural materialization* of feelings and intents. No matter how Dore and other researchers describe the

---

93. Dore, "Feeling," 169.
94. I made a similar point in "New Considerations."
95. Dore, "Feeling," 169.
96. Dore, "Feeling," 171.

child's behavior, any citations of intents and affect states do not finally have a palpable referent: such states are inferences that facilitate a certain kind of conversation or discourse. But when a voiced form—rendered by the mother or caregiver, reified by convention, and commonly heard in similar interpersonal circumstances—is overtaken by the child as described by Dore, the inner states of both adult and child have been *materialized by the language.* The *use* of the language has become the actual locus of whatever inner states have been provisionally inferred.

Dore repeats that through several possible means, the action of the adult *transforms* affect states into intents and inchoate intents into conventional words. But he also suggests that "dyadic partners match, analog, complement, imitate, and mismatch each other's affect, but express themselves in different forms. Adaptation to each other's affect and form constitutes the dyad's very identity (from which B derives his identity . . .) . . . Mismatches of both kind and intensity abound in every dyad. After intentionality emerges the only solution to mutual comprehension in dialogue is a shared system of linguistic symbols."[97] The adult does not herself transform the child, but the *relationship* between the adult and the child is a negotiated one in which each party adjusts to (or adapts to, if the evolutionary vocabulary may be applied) the gestures and verbalizations of the other. There is at least a family resemblance between the "mismatches" of word and gesture mentioned here, the "discrepancies" described by Bloom, and the "misunderstandings" noticed by Golinkoff. There is an assortment of situations of understanding and the striving to reach understanding that characterize the actions between adult and child, the negotiations of which eventuate in a *shared language* and an identity for the child. This identity could also refer to the agency or intentionality achieved by the child when language becomes a principal means for the child's interpersonal initiatives.

Dore offers that the child is *motivated* "to maintain some intimate state of communion" and uses the term "identity" to describe what the child derives from this "communion with the adult."[98] The term "identity" has long been a part of the psychoanalytic object-relations perspective.[99] An underlying affective attachment helps to promote the individual events of gesture overtaken by the child. Such motivation is impossible to translate into behaviors that are observed, recorded, and counted. Yet it is a commonplace of all cultures that infants are

---

97. Dore, "Feeling," 172.

98. Dore, "Feeling," 169.

99. In *Childhood and Society* (1949), Erik Erikson used the term "identity" to name the result of a successful adolescence. In his scheme, identity has counterparts in earlier and later stages of development. The achievements of each of Erikson's seven stages of the life cycle become part of an accumulating identity for each person. In this sense the use of the term "identity" for an infant is consistent with its object-relations usage.

attached to their parents (and most often to the mother) in a serious way and they behave as if they like being attached. This is not a bond that requires any further proof, as it is in plain sight. This may be less often a certainty, but mothers and parents are also attached to their infants, and this, too, is not something that requires statistical documentation. The assumption of the bond between parent and child is so reliable that few would call it an assumption at all.[100] From the psychoanalytic object-relations perspective, the assumption of this bond is behind its stipulation that during the same period identified by cognitive or developmental psychology as the acquisition of language, the child is integrating body, self, and society into an identity that depends on language.

V. Language Acquisition and the Integration of Body, Self, and Society

In the cognitive or developmental studies of language acquisition that acknowledge the social and interpersonal aspects of this process, the matter of self-other differentiation is only infrequently treated. Dore's description is consistent with this idea but does not use the psychoanalytic category. Many of the examples of infantile speech are also consistent with it, such as the child's pleasure in the "disappearance" games—"Now you see it (or her); now you don't," "Mommy gone!"—usages found in many of the studies; as well as "all gone" and "more" holophrases and sentences. And I have not found reports of child language that refer to the child's attention to excremental functions and how they are to be regulated, although these also would be relevant with regard to matters of bodily integrity and social adaptation. In discussing the child's development, attention simply to affect or to emotional states does not adequately characterize the full picture, especially the child's growth into fluent orientation around various bodily functions. The fact that body parts are mentioned by the AB dyad, that they are referred to, and that the child feels their functions distinctly— sometimes with pain or other discomfort that then is responded to promptly by the mother—are also part of the language acquisition context. Mothers and caregivers have a much richer picture of child development than has been given by the language acquisition researchers.[101] Because our bodies are such a promi-

---

100. Wittgenstein's critique of philosophy is, in part, a critique of discussions about assumptions that require no proof or further verification than consensus within the relevant contexts.

101. In *The Interactional Instinct*, Namhee Lee et al. try to say that language is a "complex adaptive system" with nodes and connectors: "In the system of language, the nodes are probably human individuals, the connectors are the social web of human relations, and the resources are the linguistic information that flows over the network of individuals and their social web" (25). Following the convention of describing people as

nent source of what we understand to be material, it is hard to imagine bodily awareness not playing a significant role in the acquisition of language. During the acquisition of language bodily functions located in some zones of our bodies are transferred to other zones: because of this development, gesturing usually occurs with speech.[102] The process of self-other differentiation is dramatic because we do not distinguish between our bodies and our selves until we learn to. There is no so-called life of the mind that is separate from the life of the body. Some may want to deny that the body matters much, but one is hard pressed to forget it. Self-other differentiation refers at once to a bodily separation of the child from the mother and to an emotional and social separation: there is only one separation taking place, and the various parts of each individual's body are bound together in the same process.

It is perhaps not well known how psychoanalytic thinking presupposed the materiality of language to a significant extent (but not altogether). A familiar instance of this assumption is given by the phrase "the talking cure," which refers to how symptoms sometimes are relieved when patients go through the verbal psychoanalytic processes of free association, self-observation, and collaborative interpretation.[103] Wittgenstein described this process as placing the dream (or the symptom) into a new context in which it ceases to be puzzling.[104] As Jessica Benjamin discusses, Freud thought that simply giving utterance to the symptoms would make it possible for them to disappear, and to enfranchise the patient to become a collaborator in his or her treatment.[105] She further observes that Freud stuck to this talking cure throughout his career as part of his "effort to remove the analyst from the position of coercive authority and to enfranchise the patient."[106] The path to this status, writes Benjamin in her description of psychoanalysis, is "[f]rom body to speech . . . [t]o make the inarticulate articulate, to translate the symptomatic gestures of the body into language."[107] Although Benjamin's overall

---

being hardwired, this work abstracts social relations as something to be deciphered and described as electronic devices are. The problem is less whether this description is right or wrong, but that it omits the common and rich social contexts of child development. Applying the presupposition of instinct enables this reduction to count as science.

102. Imagine the same gesturing that accompanies speech occurring without speech. The person would seem psychotic; the gestures make no sense by themselves.

103. Post-Freudian therapies are more dependent on talking and especially, speaking collectively either in dyads or in groups, about self-presentation. There are support groups for almost every possible trauma and complaint, over and above those that give counseling.

104. Ludwig Wittgenstein, *Lectures and Conversations on Aesthetics, Psychology, and Religious Belief*, ed. Cyril Barrett (Berkeley: U of California P, 1967), 45.

105. Jessica Benjamin, *Shadow of the Other: Intersubjectivity and Gender in Psychoanalysis* (New York: Routledge, 1998), 11.

106. Benjamin, *Shadow*, 11.

107. Benjamin, *Shadow*, 9.

characterization of psychoanalysis has a political valence ("enfranchisement"), the fundamental idea of rearticulating the body in speech is a reenactment of the process of language acquisition. Infants are not prisoners in their bodies, but the growth process, the long period of dependency, is a host to the *transference to speech* of many of the bodily dependencies with which one cannot cope without care from others at first. The bodily dependency undergoes a decisive change with the child's acquisition of language: bodily functions that were simply dealt with by caregivers now begin to get the child's collaboration, and a clear instance of such collaboration would be toilet training, for which most infants are ready during the period of language acquisition. The many studies of the actual usages during AB interactions bear out in a general way the larger process described by Dore: the mothers' substitution of articulate speech for the infant's gestures and verbal efforts. During the critical periods of language acquisition, the gestures, the experiences, and the bodily actions that may produce pain are *assimilated* (in the Piagetian sense) *to another part of the body: the muscles and organs of speech.* One form (genre) of our material lives—our bodily and interpersonal experiences and interactions—are translated *into another material form, speech.* We do not translate our experiences and relationships into a spiritual or incorporeal meaning. Although experiences are often remembered, they do not become Ideas. Wherever memories may be located in our brains, they might as well not exist if they are not articulated: What would a memory be if it were encoded into electronic patterns and not accessible by using language? Psychoanalytic practices—the various talking cures—repeatedly show that the articulation of these memories activates them, and often enough enables individuals to overcome their coercive and injurious effects and then convert them into life-enhancing (adaptive) practices.

A dramatic demonstration of the action of the materiality of language, and of its decisive role in child development, lies in the story of Helen Keller and Anne Sullivan. I have returned to this story repeatedly; others who have cited it have not considered it as valuable as I do.[108] It was first brought to my attention by Susanne Langer's *Philosophy in a New Key*.[109] Langer's use of the Keller story

---

108. Lois Bloom cites it in *Transition*, 102–103. Mainly, Helen Keller's own account and Anne Sullivan's are used to give evidence of the vocabulary spurt. Generally, for Bloom, the different accounts of this event show that "observations we make today [referring to observations by psychologists during experimental studies] often ring true when we encounter them in other contexts" (103). Bloom notices that many have reported the observation of children's discovery that "everything had a name." She does not, however, discuss much further what role this discovery plays beyond its place in the vocabulary spurt.

109. Langer and Ernest Cassirer were two of the pioneers in raising the issue of the status of symbolic forms, or semiology as it is sometimes known in Europe. Like Johann Hamann, Langer argued for an affective basis for language, but she was not deeply concerned with an origin of language as much as with how to see all symbolic forms as helpful to understanding our emotional lives and their contexts.

is part of her (Langer's) exploration of the broad scope that symbolization has in our society and our behaviors. "Everything had a name" for Langer referred not exclusively to applying new words to new things, but, more generally, to the fact that a child discovers and can feel the characteristic human means to social integration and understanding at once. It was not meaning that was so important to Keller and to Langer, but the feeling of trustworthy connectedness to others that the reacquisition of language had restored to the previously unsocialized child. Is it not plausible to say that the feeling that Keller reported, the feeling emphasized by Langer, and the affect noticed by Bloom and stressed by Dore refer to experiences that happen to all people in infancy? While is it not possible to assign meanings to feelings, can there be a feeling whose meaning is not already formulated by an interpersonal relationship?[110] Any feeling that can be cited (outside those of pleasure and pain), has to have a connection to *interpersonal* relationships and usually has physiological markers such as laughter, crying, sweating, tumescence, secretion of vaginal mucus, heart-rate and blood-pressure changes—bodily arousals. The feelings are not inner states because they, too, are material and therefore are observable only in physiological and social terms.

The feeling that can be hardly identified in infants, but one that the relationship between Anne Sullivan and Helen Keller shows clearly, is the feeling of insight (the light bulb; the I-get-it feeling) into what the acquisition of language achieves at once cognitively and interpersonally.[111] This story is important partially because its helpfulness is fortuitous: If Helen Keller had not gotten sick at the age of nineteen months,[112] when she already had a word for water, her story of acquiring language could have looked more like the stories

---

110. Naomi Scheman, *Engenderings: Constructions of Knowledge, Authority, and Privilege* (New York: Routledge, 1993), especially "Anger and the Politics of Naming" and "Individualism and the Objects of Psychology." Citing Wittgenstein, Scheman argues that feelings ought not to be understood as inner states, but as functions of interactions and relationships. The belief that there are inner states at all, she suggests, derives from the ideology of individualism (37).

111. The term "insight" can be used to identify adult insight, infantile accession to grammarized language from holophrases, or simian insight that the stick over there can be used to get the banana over here. Such distinctions, while relevant to other aspects of psychology, do not need to be applied to the comparison of Helen Keller's language acquisition to that of infants. Lois Bloom's observation that Helen told her story in retrospect suggests that what was insight to the twenty-two-year-old may have been simply a very pleasant and useful discovery for the six-year-old (*Transition*, 102). Helen's change of behavior, the documentation of which is in Anne Sullivan's letters and on which I will comment further, tells enough for us to discern its connections to the effort to describe how people grow into language.

112. Joseph P. Lash, *Helen and Teacher: The Story of Helen Keller and Anne Sullivan Macy* (New York: Delacorte P, 1980), 43–44. Helen Keller developed normally until she got sick. Lash reports that she had several words, including "water," and that she

of infants presented by several researchers—a gradual and seemingly unremarkable accession to the use of language. However, the five years of Helen's living in a liminal status in which her gestural language—the many signals that counted as words, requests, instructions—continued to be understood at a nineteen-month level placed her achievement with Anne Sullivan in much greater relief: it was, relative to ordinary infantile development, exaggerated in the event itself and in the shortening of the build-up period with Anne Sullivan—about a month. What takes many months for an infant took only a month when Anne Sullivan "mothered" Helen into language. The swiftness and unexpectedness of this achievement made it seem like a "miracle," as Anne Sullivan first described it. With small adjustments, the great majority of examples and principles adduced by the researchers on infant-caregiver interactions is consistent with the events leading up to Helen's success and with those behaviors that followed immediately. It was not miraculous, owing to Helen's early normal development, but it was lucky: Anne Sullivan was able to recreate the usual means for Helen to continue her acquisition of language, and that process of recreation discloses new dimensions of the achievement of language, the materiality of the language, and finally its appearance of immateriality; the appearance of immateriality is one of the grounds on which religious claims for its impalpability and its spirituality have been based. Even Anne Sullivan's use of the word "miracle" (and its subsequent reification in William Gibson's dramatic retelling of the story in *The Miracle Worker*) to describe her success with Helen casts it in a religious light.

Anne Sullivan was something of an intrusion into the Keller household and in Helen's life. An Eastern Irish "spitfire," raised in poverty and in orphanages and then sent to the Perkins School for the Blind after a trying childhood caring for her sick younger brother (who died in the orphanage), entered a middle-class Southern farm whose patriarch fought for the Confederacy in the Civil War. Sullivan came as an employee—a paid, live-in teacher for Helen. Having herself been blind, but then cured until her blindness returned in old age, Sullivan was more in position to read Helen than most of her family members, who loved her, but who had no choice but either to indulge her or to restrict her radically. Sullivan, although not necessarily in a place she wanted to be, knew how lucky she was to get a job—and a serious, challenging one at that. It greatly mattered to her that she succeed with Helen.

Helen was not required to observe dinner table decorum. She was permitted to take food from others' plates and to eat without utensils. Her "appalling" table manners were established in the Keller household, as were other demands she

---

imitated others' words. Anecdotes he includes suggest an awareness and an intelligence that had no means of reaching others. Thus she was at once socially unattuned and unable to use the conventional machinery of communication.

made that were "unconventional."[113] Sullivan thought that her first priority was to discipline Helen, to teach her "obedience and love." To do that, however, she had to get Helen entirely under her supervision, which she did by moving herself and Helen into separate quarters on the farm, the proximity of these quarters to the farm having been concealed from Helen. Sullivan also brought Helen the finger-spelling technique, which she put into effect immediately: she spelled into Helen's hand the word "doll" to tell her that she brought it as a gift from the students at the Perkins School. Anne describes the stages of Helen's response to her. In early March 1887, she was violently resistant to Anne's attempts to discipline her eating habits. Helen had temper tantrums that included pinching Anne and getting slapped in return. Each new demand, such as the one to use the spoon, was violently rejected with more kicking and screaming. It was a continuous test of wills, but in two weeks Helen was subdued. Anne described it as a miracle in her account of 20 March 1887: "A miracle has happened! The light of understanding has shone upon my little pupil's mind, and behold, all things are changed!"[114] There is something faintly humorous about this description, since the term "understanding" refers at this stage to a voluntary obedience. The description says that Helen is now peacefully cooperative with Anne, suggesting that Helen accepts this new relationship. In the description, Anne says, "The great step—the step that counts—has been taken. The little savage has learned her first lesson in obedience, and finds the yoke easy." The term "obedience" is not just descriptive. Here, as in Victorian times, it is a principle of child behavior.[115] Perhaps it did not apply to infants of eighteen months, but as children got older and could speak, obedience was the standard that families tried to attain. In its most benign sense, obedience meant understanding that the adult mores were how things were done and that children needed to observe these behaviors

---

113. These included getting up at midnight and demanding to get dressed and start the day, since she could not distinguish that it was still night (Lash, *Helen,* 47). I am summarizing here what I cited in full in "New Considerations" and in chapter 2 of *Subjective Criticism.* I have retold the story of Helen and Anne several times, each with a somewhat different emphasis. In the present account, I include keynotes of the previous discussions, and add the present interest in how this account, in the context of the most recent research in infantile language acquisition, relates to the materiality of language.

114. Helen Keller, *The Story of My Life* (Garden City, NY: Doubleday, 1954), 268. The most reliable account of Helen's development is printed in the letters written by Anne Sullivan to Mrs. Sophia Hopkins in Massachusetts, and these letters appear only in Helen's first autobiography. In the index of Joseph P. Lash's biography, under "the writings of Anne Sullivan Macy," these key letters are not listed. Instead he paraphrases them. Since I have already cited them twice, I am referring to the citations in Helen Keller's first autobiography.

115. Alice Miller's study *For Your Own Good* presents considerable documentation from parenting manuals about the key value of getting children to obey parents.

and make them their own.[116] Because Anne applied the principle of obedience in its more benign senses, she became another parent for Helen, hence, her excitement at Helen's cooperative mien. Anne Sullivan's accounts show how fully Helen had to learn bodily self-control as a key part of the language acquisition process. Perhaps the "miracle," to Anne, was that Helen accepted her "mother-hood," or Anne's mothering presence, her authority, her supervisory place. This matters because a mother is also the one who brings the mother tongue.[117] In this case, Anne was the only member of the household who could have this role, and the so-called miraculous moment (at this first stage) was Anne's success in distinguishing from everyone else's her role in teaching bodily self-discipline to Helen. It would be inaccurate to conclude that Helen was simply overpowered, although she was at first. Rather, Anne's new power was accepted as benign and not one that induced fear arbitrarily. Helen was dependent on Anne as infants are dependent on their mothers.[118] "She lets me kiss her now, and when she is in a particularly gentle mood, she will sit in my lap for a minute or two; but she does not return my caresses."[119] Here, the permitting of physical, bodily gestures of love repeats the situation in her home, in which her mother was permitted this role. The permission is, on the one hand, particularized, but on the other hand, it is, more or less, universal: the child does not just *permit* herself to be loved, but considers it part of the usual atmosphere.

This anecdote also speaks against the use of the term "communication" to describe the principal use of language, and it seems especially incomplete when describing the exchanges between infants and caregivers. For most children, a condition of trust and intimacy between themselves and adult caregivers is an essential feature of the mobilization of their awareness and willingness to converse. When the sense of adult care is missing, the growth process is slowed, or sometimes permanently stopped if conditions are severe enough. One may put the issue this way: children feel and recognize their dependent attachment

116. In its most threatening sense, the standard of obedience implied bodily beatings and pain in the event of disobedience. Anne Sullivan did apply the more benign sense, a fact that accounts, in part, for the lifelong bond the two women developed.

117. Understanding, of course, that any intimate caregivers can assume this role. Lash observes, on the basis of Anne's reflection ("I like to have Helen depend on me for everything and I find it much easier to teach her things at odd moments than at set times") that "Annie [was] a substitute mother, the child's alter ego. Helen now slept in her bed. Mrs. Keller had wanted to get a nurse, but Annie decided she would be the nurse" (*Helen*, 54).

118. Helen's aunt, Ev Keller, disagreed with her brother's impatience with Anne's withholding of breakfast from Helen until the latter got dressed: "Miss Annie is going to be Helen's salvation. . . . Helen must learn obedience and feel her dependence upon her" (Lash, *Helen*, 53).

119. Lash, *Helen*, 54.

before they start the process of individuation that requires the use of language. The recognition of their dependent condition, as suggested by the research in language acquisition, is indeed sensorimotor, and the acceptance and recognition of dependency is gestural; no child says, "I now know you are in charge." The gesture is with the body—making it available for touching, hugging, kissing, and so on: a process for which there have been hundreds of practice runs since birth. The long period of human dependency always involves such physical interaction with the caregivers, and while each of our bodies does have individual zones and foci of attention, in the matter of being loved by family members, we, in principle, entrust our bodies and selves to these present and valued others. The "basic trust," described by Erik Erikson as the feeling that governs our earliest months, derives from our having successfully entrusted our whole selves and bodies to our loved ones. Although the term "communication" is not erroneous, it tends to diminish the fullness of exchange between infant and caregivers on which the trust is based. However, this term continues to be used, again not erroneously, to describe every use of language and to give more weight to the use of language as various ways to transfer information from one to another. But could one describe the interactions of mothers and children, of lovers, of good friends, for that matter, as people transferring information to one another?[120] Conversely, can misunderstandings of what has been said be described as people not getting along? If we are studying the use of language among people, a part of which is the exchange of information, the total engagement of each relationship is in play during conversation, and the information-exchange dimension cannot, as a rule, be separated out as more, or less, important than other aspects. Stipulating the full relationship between Anne Sullivan and Helen Keller makes clear the depth of engagement that each had with the other, a depth that begins in ordinary cases in infancy and is an essential foundation for the growth process into language that follows.[121]

In the first two weeks of contact with one another, this bodily bond was established. In this case, however, it is different from the usual bodily bond, because from her first day in Tuscumbia, Alabama, Anne Sullivan was spelling words into Helen's hands—speaking to her as any parent would speak to a child.[122] In retrospect, it seems plausible that Helen would not associate the

---

120. When lovers are not getting along, they often say that they are "not communicating," and the phrase is usually understood to be a euphemism. But does it mean in such cases that information is not being exchanged successfully or "felicitously"? Or does it mean that the fundamentals of the relationships have been forgotten?

121. On the basis that Anne Sullivan required that Helen be under her complete control, it is likely that she (Anne) understood her task in just this full sense.

122. She wrote, "I asked myself, 'How does a normal child learn language?' The answer was simple. 'By imitation.' The child comes into the world with the ability to learn, and he learns of himself, provided he is supplied with sufficient outward stimulus.

manual activity with the long-forgotten experiences with language. On the one hand, although the auditory and visual experiences were in memory storage, they were inactive for five years; on the other hand, the infant who spoke a few words and imitated others had no sense that that was language activity separate from the general activities of relating to others. No child is conscious of such a separation. Helen's was unlike the situation that exists for the seeing and hearing, in which language involves touching only secondarily: it could take place with speaking and hearing, as a different aspect of the exchange. For Helen, the new task was to distinguish the roles—the genres—of the *two kinds of touching*. While one may be tempted to distinguish an emotional from a cognitive touching, this would not describe the problem. Rather, the problem for Helen would be to discern how the finger spelling fit into or was a part of the existing relationship of trust and, perhaps, love.

Here again, the matter of discord, discrepancy, and failure of communication plays a significant role. The relationship is tried by the confusion of the words "mug," "milk," and "drink." Anne Sullivan wrote that "She didn't know the word for 'drink,' but went through the pantomime of drinking whenever she spelled 'mug' or 'milk'" (5 April 1887).[123] At this point, she asked for the word for "water," by pointing to it and patting Anne's hand. Anne spelled the word for her, and the matter dropped until later, when Anne tried to solve the mug-milk confusion with the help of the word "water." This was the moment when "Helen [had] taken the second great step in her education. She learned that *everything has a name, and that the manual alphabet is the key to everything she wants to know*" (italics in original). This moment, enacted in William Gibson's play almost exactly as it is narrated in Anne Sullivan's letter, is Helen's resumption of her previously socialized childhood: she related the new touch-words with the long-ago-used heard words she had before her illness came: "Suddenly I felt a misty consciousness as of something forgotten—a thrill of returning thought; and somehow the mystery of language was revealed to me."[124] Anne Sullivan

---

He sees people do things, and he tries to do them. But long before he utters his first word, he understands what is said to him. . . [She would talk into Helen's hand] as we talk into the baby's ear. . . I shall use complete sentences in talking to her, and fill out meaning with gestures and her descriptive signs when necessity requires it; but I shall not try to keep her mind fixed on any one thing" (Lash, *Helen,* 56). The sense of "imitation" for Anne Sullivan was different from what it was for Augustine: Sullivan's imitation was unspecified; the child chose what to imitate and repeat, taken from the widest context. This philosophy seems to resemble Bloom's emphasis on the action and behavior of the child, pursuant to its interests and inclinations.

123. Keller, *The Story,* 273.

124. This is Helen's narrative from *The Story,* quotation on 34. Distant though it may be from the moment it happened, it corresponds well with the on-the-scene report by Anne Sullivan. Of course, one might well be skeptical of any such reports, especially since the language of Anne and the language of Helen corresponded extremely well

described the achievement of "obedience" as a "miracle," and now Helen Keller describes her enlightenment as the resolution of a "mystery." These terms, like Aunt Ev's use of "salvation" to describe Anne's longed-for success, are part of the traditional discourse for referring to heavenly, transcendental experience. However, in Helen's case, there seems to have been only the sense that a frustration had been overcome, and not that she had reached anything beyond her now highly complex tactile experience.

In ordinary children, there is a long period in which there is continuous practice in vocalization, articulation, and the use of the voice in ways that constantly refine the global crying or grunting. The muscles in the mouth and tongue and throat are all practicing sounds, most of the time within a socialized context. Piaget's experiments had shown that sometimes the child uses its mouth or other parts of its body (like finger pointing) to teach itself something about, for example, things that open and close, or things that are out of reach. Early noisemaking by the infant (who must be hearing these noises) brings attention and relief; gradually, new noises—words—are made that accomplish similar and more refined levels of satisfaction. The child can finally speak the noise without abandoning the sense that its own body is functioning.[125] The identical process was set in motion for Helen by Anne. But in this case Anne had to teach Helen that the bodily dependent relationship had to continue its growth through Helen's and Teacher's hands, and not through their mouths and voices. The acquisition of language requires this ability to transfer sensorimotor behaviors, which are complex in their own right, to another medium capable of the refined distinctions in vocabulary and grammar needed for the use of language. Helen had begun the process in the usual way. Five years later, she had to learn to transfer the still-remembered infantile socialization apparatus to the tactile forms of language, which now included many of the gestures she had used during her interim, pre-linguistic period. Like other children, Helen developed from a state of almost full bodily dependency (on Anne) to a state of both autonomy and initiative (to use Erikson's terminology) in which the language had become the principal source of the growth of their relationship, whose mutuality became more and more apparent. Anne Sullivan came to see it as her vocation to attend Helen's complete development into adulthood. Because this full transformation is so visible, and because it corresponds so fully to how children usually acquire language, it is much easier to use its terms to account

---

throughout their lives. Yet can one strongly doubt the other claims made by Anne— that, for example, "she had added thirty new words to her vocabulary" (274) in a few hours, claims that are consistent with the vocabulary spurt acknowledged by all language acquisition researchers?

125. Why this bodily sense is abandoned in the adult world is a key issue of this book: social authority is harder to maintain with language understood as material.

for the many salient factors mentioned by the psychologists: affect, relevance, pragmatic utility, and—most difficult of all—the connection between the learning of words as names and the learning of grammar and syntax, the latter still posing the most difficulty for researchers.

VI. The Mutual Dependency of Naming and Predication

Much of the extant data, but especially Dore's, describes the child's acquisition of words in a way that takes account of its dependent status: the dependency of both parties, actually, motivate each to continue to work together, as is clear in the case we are considering. It is especially important in this connection to understand the term "dependency" in a non-pathological sense. The child is physically and emotionally dependent on the mother and caregivers, while mothers and caregivers see their efforts toward the child as labors of love in which they feel their own value as individuals and as social figures. This mutuality accounts for the great (Lois Bloomian) "effort" on the part of both figures to bring the child into language. "Dependency" is the term that describes how the child feels and understands at once that the relationship between the word and the thing, the name and the object named, *depend* on each other. If the word merely corresponded with an object or action or person, it would not be a word or a symbol; many animals have the ability to observe the correspondence and work it into their behaviors around people. But when the word and thing depend on one another, or when we feel or otherwise sense that they depend on one another, they are symbols.[126]

The traditional term for the formal, regular dependency of some words on other words is predication, which describes a mutual or reciprocal relationship between two principal parts of a sentence. The noun (phrase) and verb (phrase) are predicated on one another. Each gives the other a specific value in the specific situation in which they are used. Part of the problem of grammar is that this reciprocity is not recognized. Instead, the predicate is taken to modify the subject, but not vice versa. Together subject and predicate make sentences or other provisionally discrete constructions. *The recognition of what a word is is at the same time the recognition of what a sentence is, as both require the mutual,*

---

126. In *The Double Perspective*, I discussed Saul Kripke's idea of a "rigid designator" to describe proper names: one feels a certain necessity in the connection between word and person, a necessity that could just as soon apply to other *particular* things. The case is different for class nouns and abstractions, as nominalists claim: no necessity is felt because the designation is not rigid; what belongs in the class cannot be assumed or predicted and can be decided only in retrospect. Nevertheless the word and class depend on one another but in a more provisional and flexible way. One can put it this way: a particular name is committed to a person or specific thing; a class name is professionally related to a class of things and, thus, is more contingent on local contexts.

reciprocal predication of one experience on another. To use a word as a word and not as a sign is already to have used a sentence. The action of reference as *mutual predication* is similarly unrecognized. We say, "The word refers to the thing," but we don't say, "The thing refers to the word." Yet in experience, the word and thing can toggle their mutual dependency. In infants, it is hard to tell how the holophrases are used, though the researchers seem to want to say that the word is predicated on a gesture that the child makes at the same time, such as pointing. The infant is working out their mutual dependency. The word and the pointing focus on a total behavior of sharing a perception with another person. Conversely, the gesture is predicated on the word, since without the word, less "communication" would be apparent: in Dore's and Bloom's terms, "intent" could not as readily be exchanged.

In Helen Keller's case the mutual predication of the touch-word and the water was clear. Less clear, however, was the mutual predication of the touch-word and the remembered oral word, the earlier predication that was assimilated to the present predication: the schema of using the oral word now fit onto the schema of using the touch words, as the infantile experience corresponded to the new childhood experience of the water. Several layers of *cognitive stereoscopy*[127] preceded the events at the wellhouse that then motivated Helen to ask for the names of things, and to proceed in her version of the characteristic vocabulary spurt. Because Helen was six years old and not twenty months old, her perception of the touch-words as a *class* of behaviors with a specific function was more rapid than the corresponding perceptions of the infant, who more likely feels the rituals of naming as a series of successful social initiatives enabled by the oral muscular ability, as Helen was enabled by the tactile muscular skills and memories. It looks as if the ability to use a name (a particular symbol), a class name, and a sentence *arrive at once* and result from the same ability to use two different gestures, two different experience genres, working together. However, there is no reason to try to specify the actual moment.[128] For Helen Keller the only reason it is tempting to do so is that the texts recording her achievement seem to localize it at one moment. But for the infantile acquisition of language, it does not seem necessary or possible to identify a specific moment of change. Behaviors of infants seem intelligent for a period of perhaps a year,

---

127. This is the term I used in *Subjective Criticism,* and discussed further in *The Double Perspective,* to describe the "depth" created when an old schema (or trope) is reciprocally assimilated to one another in a new usage. One may also identify this effect as "insight" as Piaget had already done.

128. The issue here is this: How necessary is it to look beyond plain sight in regard to this matter? If every child goes through this process, and one can discern a full set of circumstances in any one child that is observed, what will count as proof that all three abilities arrive at once, where "at once" may well mean over a week's time?

yet only over a short period does the vocabulary increase rapidly and the word combinations begin.

The underlying emotional process for the child is the growth away from the mother or caregiver toward doing things on his or her own, and, in Helen's case, doing things on her own as well as *together with a loved one.* Helen seemed to know that Anne Sullivan had a specific name and asked for it, something an infant likely would not do; the speed of her grasp was rapid as compared to that of an infant. At first Anne Sullivan was an alien and hostile presence; then she was a benign disciplinarian. But when Helen learned that the words she used were used in the identical fashion by Anne in an impersonal way, it followed that the words themselves (the use of language in its adult forms) were the *way back* to Anne from the discrepant experiences of that same day and of the previous month. The mutual dependencies of word and experience, of word and gesture, of word and word, and of word and classes of related words are instances of the *same* behavioral schema or trope: different levels or forms of predication, applicable as regulated by present-time social experience. When mothering works smoothly, the way back to mother is not felt as a great event. Rather, the child's behavior changes and the rapid increase in talk and skill with talk clearly create the socially demanded means of relating to other people. As time passes, the body gets larger, and social intelligence grows, the way back to mother and the way into the rest of the world become the same way.

The connection between the long period of childhood dependency and the acquisition of language is that the learning of words and of grammar transforms the condition of dependency into social capability, and the means of this achievement is the use of language. Within language use both words and sentences appear on the foundation of gestural (sensorimotor) interaction[129] within a relationship of interpersonal dependence. The words are first dependent on the gestures and interpersonal circumstances of use, and then dependent on one another. The latter phase is usually referred to as predication. The branching tree diagrams introduced by transformational grammar presuppose that each word combination is the transformation of a predication; for example, the phrase "the red apple" is a transformation of "The apple is red." If one removes the transformational requirement that predications take a propositional form, "red apple" and "apple red" would be both predications, whereas in English the *custom* is to put the adjective first and in French to put it second.[130] Without the propositional axiom, different grammatical rules can be seen as accidental at

---

129. Kristeva's *chora* is discussed in chapter 3.

130. Sometimes transformationalists' attempts to establish "rules" as innate take on a propagandistic cast. In a 1995 television presentation about language, the voiceover narration says something like, "Why would we consider 'the red big balloon' incorrect and insist on "the big red balloon'?" Because the first version is so strange, the false

first, but stabilized due to social needs for mutual understanding. In this light, the search for universals in language that has been an academic conundrum for centuries was not entirely fanciful; it was, rather, a characteristic exaggeration of an intuition that nevertheless has some basis in common, so-called universal human experience, but not in genetically determined biology. The exaggeration is the obsessive and sometimes vindictive arguments devaluing the category of "performance" as awkward approximate approaches to a mathematically pure ideal.

Language performance is all there is. Ideals that are applied and rules that are stipulated must be treated as provisional tools for thinking and discussing, and not declared to be existing unless there is a material basis, unless there are collective experiences whose consensus suggests reality. The same reasoning would hold true for such thoughts as "the unconscious mind" or "the ego and the id." The many teams of researchers in infantile language acquisition have disclosed the richness, complexity, and eligibility for research of the family's or "village's" experience in bringing their children into language. These experiences have discredited decisively the argument for a poverty of stimulus. Those who claim that the stimulus for language is impoverished have also refused to identify and authorize what the stimulus really is: the bodily and social contexts through which language is acquired. But more importantly, the aggregate of work by researchers of all stripes, considered together, enumerate necessary features and stages in the acquisition of language, and provide the basis for understanding the acquisition of language from social sources, as suggested by Mead and Vygotsky during the earlier parts of the twentieth century.

Dore and Bloom both observed pleasure and satisfaction in infants' use of words and in their acquisition of grammatical language: the relationship with the teachers is reaffirmed. On the one hand, the infants grow apart from the loving teachers of childhood, the bringers of the mother tongue. On the other hand, the children's access to language enables and motivates them to return to those same people, and subsequently to all the other people who are becoming common figures in their lives. Any use of language makes connections between and among people. This affirmative, invigorating process is often forgotten when language is thought of simply as a conveyance of information or even of meaning. The sentences that are gestures of return and affiliation are actually bringing people together—not in a fictional or spiritual way but actually—in living circumstances for specific purposes, no matter how small or local. If these gestures are not considered to be part of human adaptation and survival,

---

impression is given that the rule is more than just an arbitrary convention. A great deal of transformational grammar depends on reading conventional usages as being deeper than convention.

they remain mysterious curiosities.[131] The return to others that language enacts renders the concept of language a characteristic process of human adaptation, a way of life, a viable means to work with our ways of life, a way to work in society, and certainly, a way to teach it. All of these descriptions add up to Falk's description: "Humans *do* language."

Once the collective, social, and interpersonal foundations of language are allowed, the materiality of language becomes a sensible, useful way to guide responses to a wide variety of language experiences. The repression of language is the repression of its social character, the impoverishment of its infantile mother or family roots, the attempt to idealize language into a spiritual, incorporeal entity that transcends bodily existence in some mysterious and miraculous way. Regardless of how many or how few texts survive the rampant destructions of history, their survival is the proof of their and our materiality.

---

131. A similar claim may be made about penguins huddling together in the winter: it is mysterious until it is understood as a means of adaptation and survival.

CHAPTER SIX

Recognizing Politics in
the Study of Language

I. Language, Politics, Gender

The materialist description of language includes combinations of several tropes of mutual dependency—speech and other bodily gestures, subjects and predicates, language and personal relationships, and speech communities and societies. Changing configurations of these several political relations constitute the uses of language. Because mutual dependency characterizes local, individual interactions as well as the broader relations of communities, societies, and nations, relations of dependency guide the political identification of those relations. In personal relationships, each person has, at once, individual interests and a share of the mutual interest. The use of language in such relationships negotiates those interests. The broad range of language uses, from ordinary everyday formulations to the public uses, all take place in political circumstances. But, more than that, political movement describes the minutiae of language use, the total buildup of reciprocally dependent schemata learned in the pre-linguistic sensorimotor period of infancy leading to the combinations of words dependent on one another, the sentences dependent on one another, and the overwhelming frequency of mutual trading in words and feelings and gestures; all of these must be understood as a politics of bodily and social self-regulation.

Recent Western language philosophy shows a struggle to recognize the political character of language. The works of Wittgenstein, Bakhtin, Austin, and Whorf each, in different senses, indicates that uses of language are regulated by different interests. For example, it is a political gesture to correctly identify which *Sprachspiele* are in effect, which speech acts may be used, what sort of behavior is referred to by languages one does not know well, and when to judge that someone's utterance has ended and it is your turn or right to take the floor. Political errors of language use under these circumstances are usually self-regulating. But similar decisions—in intimate relationships, in business dealings, in public venues of newspapers and courts, and in international relations—are equally about which language one should use or has been used; all have political weight but cannot be said to be self-regulating. The failure of negotiation often results in violence and bodily harm. The political character of language uses in all circumstances demands that mutual dependencies and individual interests be part of considerations of how to use the language.

Derrida's *Monolingualism of the Other* is an attempt to fold the wider political circumstances of his biography into his sense of the materiality of language. He refers to historic political issues that, for example, Jews, Algerians, and colonized people faced long before he was born. Furthermore, he struggled with the political consequences of the gendering of the law and of truth, as given by the French language. Derrida strove to understand how, in a political cause, the contradictory character of the uses of language in his own life can be recognized. Political understanding led him to say just how the Aristotelian principle of non-contradiction is revoked. Our language is ours and not ours. What we say is part of us and part of others, but belongs to no one.

A theme of Derrida's text, clearly present though not prominent, is World War II. His reflections on Hannah Arendt in *Monolingualism* led him to consider whether the spillover of madness from Germany affected the status and understanding of languages more generally; he observed that the mother tongues, contrary to Arendt's feelings and claims, cannot have survived unscarred from the mass perversion of speech and law in European societies. This intuition in Derrida was also experienced by others in Europe, as they, too, began to write about how language itself had been implicated in the trauma of the two world wars and the rise of authoritarian governments in many nations. These writings are significant for the understanding of the materiality of language because they represent the struggle of men and of male-coded styles of thinking to understand the political character of language use without including reference to the political roles of gender. Their struggle would be less painful and perhaps more hopeful had the actual claims of gender politics entered into their reflections.

Gilles Deleuze and Félix Guattari's *Anti-Oedipus*[1] seeks a rationale to dispose, finally, of the recurrence of despotic rulers as well as the tendency of great numbers of people to sustain it. Their style of writing suggests that the West suffered a mass affliction of total mediation that has made language an accomplice of tyranny: "It is curious, therefore, that one can show so well the servitude of the masses with respect to the minimal elements of the sign within the immanence of language, without showing how the domination is exercised through and in the transcendence of the signifier."[2] They are noting the phenomenon of censorship, domination, and even enslavement of the total population to the total

---

1. Deleuze and Guattari, *Anti-Oedipus: Capitalism and Schizophrenia*, trans. Robert Hurley, Mark Seem, and Helen R. Lane (New York: Penguin, 2009).

2. Deleuze and Guattari, *Anti-Oedipus*, 207.

mediation of the immanent law without people noticing that for the despot the "signifier"—the language, the law, the truth—is transcendent.[3] Their long meditation on the necessity of ending such tyranny and the wars it inevitably produces, even followed up by a second volume,[4] simply does not make the connection given by Virginia Woolf in a footnote in *Three Guineas*,[5] namely that the devastation—she cites photographs of human destruction in wartime—caused by public tyranny is traceable to the almost universal practice of private tyranny in every home, where children are taught that tyranny and its enforcement by corporal punishment and abuse are normal—the way society, even life, is and must always be. Who but women and children are the millions of people denied access to their own language and forced to accept the "transcendence" of the masculine "signifiers"? Similarly, many ordinary men struggling to sustain families also accept the transcendental signifiers, yet they often see no path other than violent opposition to achieve access to language. Deleuze and Guattari's volumes reflect their impatience and their struggle to articulate a solution: they are long, abstract, distant, needlessly figurative and allegorical, and difficult to understand because they do not consider that the rule of men has stolen and despoiled the mother tongue from the beginnings of each person's life, has established a "symbolic order"[6] that prepares us to expect the next tyranny.

A comparable sense of the monolithic rule of language is given by Michel Foucault's meditations on the tyranny of "discourse" on the one hand, and on its self-nullification on the other:

> Whether it is the philosophy of a founding subject, a philosophy of originating experience or a philosophy of universal mediation,[7] discourse is really only an activity, of writing in the first case, of reading in the second and exchange in the third. This exchange, this writing, this reading never involve anything but signs.[8] Discourse thus nullifies itself, in reality, in placing itself at the disposal of the signifier.[9]

---

3. As it is in George Orwell's *Animal Farm* (New York: Harcourt, Brace, 1946), in which there are peremptory changes of the constitutional language.

4. Gilles Deleuze and Félix Guattari, *A Thousand Plateaus: Capitalism and Schizophrenia,* trans. Brian Massumi (Minneapolis: U of Minnesota P, 1987).

5. And discussed in chapter 11 at greater length.

6. Kristeva, discussed in chapter 1, section 2, refers to the symbolic order as "the signifying venture of men" that overrules the semiotic learning in the earlier developmental stage of infancy. French poststructuralist work has, generally, taken it for granted that this symbolic order is male coded.

7. Possibly read as "total mediation" (chapter 1, section 3).

8. This is the usual French or Continental usage, and it corresponds to my use of the term "symbols" in several other discussions in this book.

9. Michel Foucault, *The Archeology of Knowledge and The Discourse on Language,* trans. Rupert Sawyer (New York: Pantheon, 1972), 228.

Discourse is at the center of Foucault's several explorations of the institutions that govern contemporary Western civilization. He depends on his access to public discourse, his fluent handling of it, and his energy in presenting it to those eager to hear it. But he concludes that it is self-nullifying, and he understands formal education to be the instrument of self-nullification: "What is an educational system, after all, if not a ritualisation of the word; if not a qualification of some fixing of roles for speakers; if not the constitution of a (diffuse) doctrinal group? . . . What is 'writing' . . . if not a similar form of subjection? . . . May we not also say that the judicial system, as well as institutionalised medicine, constitute similar systems for the subjection of discourse?"[10]

What is creating this apparent paradox, this thoroughgoing reliance on uses of language that are, after all, self-nullifying? Foucault's emphatic expressions of frustration and passion place him confronting the extreme positions found in authoritarian societies similarly characterized by Deleuze and Guattari as the only choices available in this civilization. Foucault explores sex without gender and power without people. His overarching strategy leads him to consider institutions in abstract terms without specifying host societies, without attention to the living people and their different national languages occupying those institutions. His own discourse therefore also would not say that men run the education system, the judicial system, or the medical profession. Yet the gendered power structure is a principal basis of history's recursive tyranny, as well as of authoritarian behavior in smaller contexts. Without finally acknowledging the bases of the tyranny he opposes, his writing remains unable to escape its own paralyzing paradoxes—his admirable, generous passion notwithstanding.

When Deleuze, Guattari, and Foucault were writing in the late 1960s and early 1970s focusing on how language has been overwhelmed by authoritarian international politics, the materiality of language as a political idea was recognized by Kristeva, and some other public discussions were in evidence. In 1980, a different sort of synthesis was attempted by two British researchers from the standpoint of the sociology of language.[11] Like the French writers just considered, Silverman and Torode are responding to the need for a new understanding of language to be responsive to the proliferating scenes of social trouble that, historically, the uses of language have been unable to affect.

Silverman and Torode sense the materialist turn, but do not, like Wittgenstein and Derrida, insist that two millennia of confusion and struggle with the contested subject of language must now give way to a clearer, more active, more realistic sense of what things to do with the material words. Part of their caution is in their continuing search for a comprehensive critical theory of language,

---

10. Foucault, *Archeology of Knowledge*, 227.

11. David Silverman and Brian Torode, *The Material Word: Some Theories of Language and Its Limits* (London: Routledge and Kegan Paul, 1980).

something Wittgenstein eschewed as part of his attempts to create a realistic understanding of language use. They are persuaded that the turn to language materiality involves the rejection of transcendent ("capitalized"[12] terms such as Being, Language, and God) language categories: "The overcoming of transcendence is as much a task for everyday life as for philosophy."[13] Their perspective is similar in this regard to those of Deleuze and Guattari and Foucault.

In addition, like other researchers discussed in the preceding chapters, they reject the competence model as a path toward a comprehensive critical theory.[14] However, for Silverman and Torode, the faith in finding a critical theory is encouraged by the work of the Frankfurt School of philosophy, especially the several efforts by Jürgen Habermas to establish a basis for an intersubjective theory of language. His ideal of communicative competence is politically motivated, egalitarian in its frame of mind, rational in its approach to social life, and generous in spirit. In their turn toward Habermas, the term "material" reacquires its earlier association with Marxian discourse. Although such an association is not intrinsically disabling, it nevertheless calls to mind the androcentrism of the Marxian vision as well as its fluent insistence on revolutionary violence as the only path toward justice for all.

In this regard, Silverman and Torode show no more inclination than Deleuze and Guattari or Foucault to consider the political, material, or linguistic consequences of the subordination of women. The political function, role, weight, and influence of gender subordination in history and of the researchers themselves do not enter into the search for the theory of communicative competence as derived by Silverman and Torode. Their combination of sources leads toward the materiality of language. But egalitarian idealism includes gender equality. If politics is brought to the forefront in language studies without reference to a principal historical basis for large-scale social domination, that does not remove us from the recursive return to authoritarian, military bases of government. If the materiality of language is to be recognized in the forms that can have effect, the use of political considerations must begin with the acknowledgment that the study of language is itself a political subject. The use of the word politics must refer to all members of society.

An American effort that may be characterized in terms similar to those I used for the foregoing researchers is the work of James Boyd White,[15] who presents

---

12. Silverman and Torode, *Material,* 43.

13. Silverman and Torode, *Material,* 43.

14. "We have implied . . . that a critical theory of language cannot develop from a competence model" (Silverman and Torode, *Material,* 337). They include Jonathan Culler's competence model in *Structuralist Poetics: Structuralism, Linguistics, and the Study of Literature* (Ithaca, NY: Cornell UP, 1975), in addition to Chomsky's among models that would not lead to a viable theory.

15. James Boyd White, *Justice as Translation: An Essay in Cultural and Legal Criticism* (Chicago, U of Chicago P, 1990).

a critique of the legal profession that is cognate with Foucault's critical citation of the law as an institution. White observes,

> [O]ur words get much of their meaning from the gesture of which they are a part, which in turn gets its meaning largely from the context against which it is a performance. . . . little of what happens in any real utterance is reducible to the words uttered, let alone to the "propositions" they are supposed to express, and . . . much lies in the gesture, in the relations between speaker and auditor, in their material context, in the understandings they share. . . . Instead of thinking of language as a code into which nonlinguistic material is translated, or of language use as the manipulation of that medium for the expression of ideas, we can imagine languaging as a kind of dance, a series of gestures or performances, measured not so much by their truth-value as by their appropriateness to context.[16]

In his several books, White has tried to humanize law practice by viewing language and the language of the law as locked in the principle of language transparency. His understanding of the gestural character of language, his rejection of the coercive habits of binary thinking, his emphasis on the total context of language usage, and his perception that a *principle* of language transparency is repressive[17] all resemble the general direction taken in the work of the five researchers considered earlier in this chapter. But he also resembles them in his almost exclusive reliance on texts—judicial opinions—written by men who write for an audience of other men. As a result, his effort sounds more like a plea for generous, helpful common sense than recognition of the political circumstance that nullifies what is otherwise a welcome formulation.[18]

II. Linguistics' Second Opinion

In the 1970s, when Deleuze and Guattari, Foucault, and Silverman and Torode made different cases for the roles of language in politics, Robin Tolmach Lakoff's slim volume *Language and Woman's Place* was published.[19] This work has played

---

16. White, *Justice,* xi–xii.

17. White, *Justice,* xii.

18. Joan Wallach Scott, writing about how male historians lose their claim to authority, observes, "Many of these historians, writing from a position that supports the democratic and socialist goals of past labor movements, uncritically accept masculine concepts of class and rule out feminist demands for attention to women and gender as so many bourgeois distractions to the cause. . . . By refusing to take gender seriously, labor historians only reproduce inequalities that their principles commit them to ending" Joan Wallach Scott, *Gender and the Politics of History* (New York: Columbia UP, 1999), 67.

19. The latest edition of this work is Robin Tolmach Lakoff, *Language and Woman's Place: Text and Commentaries,* ed. Mary Bucholtz (New York: Oxford UP, 2004). Many

a role in the academic discussions of language and linguistics that Wittgenstein's informal presentations played in the profession of philosophy in the 1930s. The observations are modest, personal, informal, reflective, and brief. Lakoff, like Wittgenstein, held an established, respected place in her profession. But her writing, her language use, her discourse, and her way of greeting the academic public were all fresh, relative to the existing conventions of scholarly work.

She started in the kitchen. Is it not clear, she asked, that a woman usually says, "Oh dear, you've put the peanut butter in the refrigerator again," and that a man would more likely say, "Shit, you've put the peanut butter in the refrigerator again."[20] Such ruminations were met with academic skepticism because they were "unscientific." There were no statistics, no experiments, no logical arguments, no imaginary competence, and, of course, no scientific method in sight. But humanists also were doubtful, for it was called "essentialist": How could one claim that language, which is "only words," be tied to the sex or gender of the speaker? Anyone can use words, and to claim that some words are used regularly and differently by one gender and others by another gender must be guessing.[21] Regardless of how much complaint there was about such work, Lakoff relied on certain kinds of recognizable personal and public experience—speech that was familiar, easily observable, and commonly used—to reach understanding, the same sources of authority, *experience,* preferred by the Wife of Bath over Church authority.[22] Lakoff examines what is already observable, and then describes the language animating those experiences in political terms.

Lakoff uses a humanist or critical technique of trying to identify trends or loose patterns and then inviting comment on them. This humanist aspect of her scholarly discourse was not recognized for what it was, and was patronized regardless, because it is based on lived experience rather than on formal sources.

---

women participated in the political initiative represented by 1975 edition: they were in all disciplines as well as in public venues. Lakoff is virtually alone, however, as a linguist who valued and respected academic, humanistic research, and for a long while she was certainly a lone voice challenging the hegemony of transformational linguistics.

20. Lakoff, *Language and Woman's Place* (2004), 44.

21. Deborah Tannen addresses this complaint in *You Just Don't Understand: Women and Men in Conversation* (New York: Morrow, 1990). Lakoff's reflections on gender and language helped to make it possible for Tannen to reach millions of people with her forceful study, which identified many contexts that showed the different patterns of speech used by men and women when they speak with one another.

22. "The Wife of Bath's Prologue and Tale" was written at the end of the fourteenth century. Chaucer was not exceptional as a male author in recognizing the basis of women's ways of joining society. However, such recognition by literary figures had the same subaltern intellectual status as nominalism had in the academies of the day. Regardless of how fully Chaucer was able to ridicule clerics and the Church, their hegemony—and men's hegemony—remained in place until recently, when there have been signs of their abatement.

Lakoff's work showed that it was not necessary to interview the not formally educated as Luria did, or to go into the Amazon as Everett did, to notice just how experience, recorded for our society in centuries of Western humanities, is a key foundation for our ways of life, for our uses of language. Furthermore, Wittgenstein's caution, discussed in chapter 3, applies. Because of the multifariousness of the contexts of language use, he urged that explanation and formal theory were not useful approaches to the study of language, and, instead, that recursive description, always retrospective, according to the contexts of use and need was a more viable approach to understanding language as part of social experience. This is the technique used by Lakoff in 1975 and it characterizes her subsequent work.

When Lakoff started writing, the discipline of linguistics, as well as other academic attentions to language, excluded experiential contexts of language use and their political circumstances as likely sources of understanding. The main perspectives in language research had to be scientific, cognitive, evolutionary, or brain-physiological. This exclusion began to abate with the publication of *Language and Woman's Place* in 1975. From that time until the present, Lakoff has urged forcefully that the study of language and the uses of language *both* take place in a political atmosphere, a bath of often-conflicting interests and dependencies that cannot be considered in isolation or as separate from each manifestation of language—spoken or written, individual or collective.[23] Readers of her work will notice that she has continued to identify it as "linguistics," and sometimes as "linguistic pragmatics"; she has thereby insisted on broadening the academic locus of the study of language: she has insisted and demonstrated that uses of language affect, in a political sense, every consequential aspect of society and of personal life.

She has not identified her work as addressing the materiality of language. Rather, she understood issues of language to be political gestures based on observations about gender relations reported in *Language and Woman's Place*. Women's experience and gendered experience more generally were not considered to be factors in the study of language until the twentieth century. Similarly, the fact that, until the twentieth century, language philosophers and researchers were men has not been considered salient in the study of language. In her review of the history of transformational grammar, Lakoff observes that the formal character of transformational theory (hierarchical), the social character of the group (almost all males who follow a male leader without question or opposition), and the style of work (adversarial), add up to an intolerably exclusive political scene of work. At once dismayed yet not surprised, Lakoff observes

23. "All language is political; and we all are, or had better become, politicians." Robin Tolmach Lakoff, *Talking Power: The Politics of Language in Our Lives* (New York: Basic, 1990), 2.

that work on Chomskyan linguistics followed "the academic perspective [that] is inextricably masculine, as it has been for the last couple of millennia in the west."[24] As an academic move, Lakoff's principal theme that language use and gender were politically joined and must be discussed with that circumstance in mind was unprecedented. Her book staked the claim that the uses of language and the study of language must include reference to and examination of the political circumstance in which each usage takes place. Her case in point was the political relation of women as a class to men as a class. It became clear how the acknowledgment of either gender or politics in the understanding of language showed that both factors were bound up with one another, and not separable: if gender was discussed, it was necessarily a political factor; if political circumstances were discussed, gender factors had to be recognized.

Understanding language as political gestures presupposes the materiality of language. If language is fundamentally spiritual, mental, ethereal, otherwise incorporeal, or a vessel for the impalpable inferred abstraction called thought, then language has already been dissociated from the behaviors of living people; it has been fixed, made permanent in an imaginary way, just as Plato suggested that ideas were permanent. This point of view is necessary to those in political ascendancy—to tyrants, kings, or popes, but also to institutions, such as governments, the corporate community, and universities: when language is accepted

---

24. Robin Lakoff, "The Way We Were; or, The Real Actual Truth About Generative Semantics," *Journal of Pragmatics* 13 (1989): 939–988, quotation on 973. As described by Lakoff at least twice, this was not her early opinion because the atmosphere was ebullient—overflowing with confidence that language, a riddle of the ages, could be understood in ways that were exciting in themselves, and seemed to promise an explanation of the less-understood features of language, such as its swift acquisition by infants in all societies. There were some researchers—those who advocated generative semantics—who had their doubts, she reports. They used many of the notation techniques that came with the reporting of theoretical transformational generative grammar—they retained a good deal of the vocabulary, such as "deep structure," "phrase structure," and asterisks to mark ungrammatical sentences—but they did not revise the perspective that held that the reference of each word was separable from and independent of its context. Transformationalists and generative semanticists drew conclusions from sentences that had no actual context of use in real life: sentences whose only context of use was the discussion of the grammar of their sentences. The most comprehensive account of the departure from transformational generative grammar is in "The Way We Were"; this is also the most no-punches-pulled account. Lakoff offers another account in her "Author's Introduction: *Language and Woman's Place* Revisited" in the 2004 reprinting. A third brief, accurate account of the beginning of the shift away from transformational generative grammar (by those who were early adherents) is given in Kira Hall and Mary Bucholtz, eds., *Gender Articulated: Language and the Socially Constructed Self* (New York: Routledge, 1995), 2. Hall and Bucholtz mention five figures who tried new pathways, only one of whom was female—Robin Lakoff.

as fixed by the majority, it is those in the ascendancy who fixed it.[25] But if it is understood to be dependent on the human bodies that produce speech and writing and thus materialize whatever it is that seems internal to us, if the common bodily humanity of members of all social classes is recognized, then language must be linked to how these bodies—these people—relate to one another in actual observable experience. Language has to be understood as a function of people's *membership* in a common species.[26] Language must be neither more nor less fixable by any one segment of the society. The fixing of language—the establishment of common conventions of usage and truth—thereby depends directly on the politics of collective action of speakers and writers.

To recognize the materiality of language, itself a new political gesture, is also to recognize the political action of individual uses of language. Before the movement of the disenfranchised—women and societies ruled by imperial nations—in the twentieth century to free themselves from "domination,"[27] politics conducted mainly by men was usually a power struggle whose military solution was tolerated, accepted, and—more often than not—sought. Men who held power have accepted as a "rational choice," the move toward attempted total subjugation or destruction of their enemies. Freud's "primal horde" narrative, found in *Totem and Taboo* and in several of his later works on civilization, is also descriptive of the ordinary power-struggle politics present throughout history.[28] Men with various jealousies and interests participated in a cycle of revolution and stability and, if possible, kept a peace punctuated by violent revolution and the installation of a new order. The dominated, the disenfranchised, and the subaltern classes were not considered to be active participants in the politics of governance. Women are the largest group of people taken as subaltern. This largest group is also the last group in our time whose political claims have won at least some recognition.[29]

---

25. This fixing is referred to by the European researchers discussed earlier in this chapter as the establishment of the "transcendental signifier" and of the "symbolic order."

26. Perhaps the term "membership," with the sense that one can cancel one's membership, can be related to Derrida's sense of "participation without [necessarily] belonging."

27. The term used by Herbert Marcuse and other members of the Frankfurt School to describe what we now refer to as the hegemony of a ruling class. Herbert Marcuse, *Eros and Civilization: A Philosophical Inquiry into Freud* (New York: Vintage, 1962).

28. Freud's "primal horde" hypothesis and its implications are considered in more detail in chapter 7, section 3.

29. Some may doubt even this modest claim. The reports from around the world of trafficking in women, gang raping of children and girls, and the surgical removal of sex organs say to some people that nothing has changed. See, for example, Nicholas D. Kristof, "One Girl's Courage," *New York Times* 12 October 2011, as well has his several years of reportage on this topic. Kristof details how a teenage rape victim in Sierra Leone was stopped from going to school, while authorities ignored the forty-one-year-old pastor who was the perpetrator.

Gender is politics that challenges the politics of power struggles and war.[30] Introducing gender to the study of anything means changing its politics in such a way that equality, rather than victory, is the aim. Lakoff's several works move carefully toward these goals, but without introducing an unrecognizable academic jargon, notation, or discussion. Lakoff writes in ordinary language about ordinary experience. Yet the subject is always language as it appears in publicly acknowledged experience—the movement of conversations from issues of personal concern to collectively held values, public formulations, and names and usages that are taken for granted. Two of her earlier works are about beauty and about psychotherapy.[31] Each of these zones is part of her lived experience and that of her collaborators. In the earlier work, she and Raquel Scherr demonstrate how women's actual talk about beauty is censored by the domineering public languages of beauty given by, for example, the cosmetics and entertainment industries. The later work, merely by recounting the events of Freud's analysis of "Dora," shows how several older men and some women closed in on the eighteen-year-old girl so that she lost all access to language: she simply was not heard. The issues given academic attention in these works grow from life situations experienced by the books' authors and recounted in the books. Lakoff's own language is material in its having been taken from her experience and resubmitted as collective experience, without laws, instincts, or biological necessity having been stipulated. The language of her claims is a challenge to science as it is now practiced, yet it also *is* science in a sense similar to what the language of psychoanalysis was when it was first introduced: it is a *tertium quid,* a third choice of discourse that is *both* humanistic and scientific.

The vector of application of Lakoff's language is radically different from that of psychoanalysis, the materiality of whose language was placed firmly in

---

30. This point is made dramatically by Virginia Woolf in her 1938 *Three Guineas* (New York: Harvest, 1966), in which she demonstrates that "war is men's activity" and that it is supported by territoriality; by elaborate and excessive military clothing, medals, and other gratuitous decorations; by the collection of more taxes than most people can afford; and by denying women access to education. The narrator of this volume hesitates when asked to contribute to the prevention of war, showing that a man's solicitation of support from women adds up to the characteristic hypocrisy of gender tyranny: men assume the right to be tyrants domestically over women and over other men, but are outraged at the likelihood of a tyrant in another society claiming the same right over them. Furthermore, I would draw a link between Woolf's observations and Vivien Law's characterization of language as an *alternative* to "the Bomb" (see chapter 1, section 1). Woolf's book is considered in greater detail in chapter 11, section 3.

31. Robin Tolmach Lakoff and Raquel L. Scherr, *Face Value: The Politics of Beauty* (Boston: Routledge and Kegan Paul, 1984); Robin Tolmach Lakoff and James C. Coyne, *Father Knows Best: The Use and Abuse of Power in Freud's Case of Dora* (New York: Teacher's College Press, 1993).

individual contexts by Freud and by the subsequent practices of psychoanalysis in the decades after him. Freud struggled greatly when he tried to understand civilization as if it were a socially privileged individual patient trying to cope with abstract forces such as aggression and libido. His final explanation rests doubtfully on his reliance that instincts exist as a collective phenomenon and must account for the frustrations and destructions characteristic of all civilizations. By thinking of civilization as if it were an individual, he tacitly reestablished as a presupposition the traditional androcentric claim that there is no way to overcome the recursive instinct-driven movements toward war.

Lakoff moves between individuals and different zones of society. To her, there is no one aspect of civilization whose problems demand solutions, but there are several zones, in plain sight through the public media, whose language is taken up by individuals and whole constituencies through a variety of uses. The various local discourse samples show what the civilization is like in each area. From her perspective, the work of the linguist is to observe every aspect of society in which she lives, indicate the salient uses of language at those times and places, cite the sources of use and the means of repetition, and to use the multifarious citations to show the political action of language in each venue. Some may want to say that the language documents the politics, but this is not Lakoff's way of viewing her materials. Her project is to show that *the language is the politics, the politics the language.* Once that identity is understood, the various scenes she studies reassume their common appearance, but now they are understood in revolutionary ways: they have been placed in a context, like Wittgenstein's dreams, in which they "cease to be puzzling."

III. Interpreting the Present

One of the most challenging purposes of academic effort, which insists on respecting the histories we have received, is to relate the edifice of our reconstructions of the past to the requirements of the moment. When this effort is not made, academic claims reduce to jargon, guesswork, posturing, and abstraction. Noteworthy features of Lakoff's writing over the past forty years are her references to the Latin language and literature—her familiarity with "the foundations of Western civilization"[32] and with classical philology—and her ability to work her humanistic style of understanding into her rational and pragmatic characterizations of language use. The perspective she brought to the study of language emerges from her own experience with the so-called feel of the Latinate tradition of academic work. In her description of academic work today, she reports that the "tribal sweathouse" of male colleagues in the linguistics depart-

---

32. The influence of Latin is discussed in some detail in chapter 9.

ment washed over her own voice "like the ocean enveloping a pebble. It was as if I had not spoken—in fact, did not exist."[33] In the political scene of the department meeting, the unbalanced population that passed along the humanistic, language-oriented tradition led her to identify the politics of language use as the key factor in linguistics. The perception of present-day academic experience as a function of academic history is uncommon. The discussions in part 2 further document the path Lakoff took from dedicated academic membership early in her professional life to the critical task of identifying the politics of language.[34]

Four senses of history appear in Lakoff's cumulative work: common understanding of so-called Western civilization with respect to the received texts of Greece and Rome, the humanistic tradition since then, the history of modern linguistics, and the capability of extant, present texts[35] to show the action of gaining access to language. The connection of this last factor to the other three gives Lakoff's work its distinctiveness, sets it apart from other academic work, and provides a glimpse of how political thinking derives from the conception of language use given in other parts of her work. Although she does not describe language as material, her descriptions of various uses of language show a family resemblance to other instances of the materiality of language discussed in this book. If Kristeva's term "materiality of language" is taken as the name of a Kuhnian paradigm, Lakoff's approach to language is a principal part of this paradigm.

In *The Language War*,[36] Lakoff considers the question of hate speech. As others have done,[37] she seeks a principled way of opposing it without subordinating the search for political equality (treated in the fourteenth amendment to the Constitution) to the principle of free speech (articulated by the first

---

33. Lakoff, *Talking Power,*143, 149.

34. Perhaps, to understand any cumulative scholarly commitment, one needs to wait until late in a scholar's life to see how it adds up.

35. These include texts in public media, such as newspapers, television, or anything—for that matter—released to and for the public.

36. Robin Tolmach Lakoff, *The Language War* (Berkeley: U of California P, 2000), 86–117.

37. These citations also appear in chapter 3's discussion of J. L. Austin. Judith Butler, *Excitable Speech: A Politics of the Performative* (New York: Routledge, 1997), reflects on the actual damage done by hate speech or name-calling. Catharine MacKinnon, *Only Words* (Cambridge, MA: Harvard UP, 1992), makes a related point regarding pornography. Kent Greenawalt, *Fighting Words: Individuals, Communities and Liberties of Speech* (Princeton, NJ: Princeton UP, 1995) is relevant and useful. Stanley Fish describes how no speech can be free because of its ever-present interpersonal contexts in "There's No Such Thing as Free Speech, and It's a Good Thing, Too," *There's No Such Thing as Free Speech, and It's a Good Thing, Too* (New York: Oxford UP, 1994), 102–119. The global reach of this issue is treated in Mari J. Matsuda et al., eds., *Words That Wound* (Boulder, CO: Westview P, 1993); and in Michael E. Brown and Sumit Ganguly, eds., *Fighting Words: Language Policy and Ethnic Relations in Asia* (Cambridge, MA: MIT P, 2003).

amendment).[38] She asks how fully is speech to be considered an action. Avoiding the conventions of abstract binaries, she observes, "Language is intermediate between thought and action: it is thought made observable. It straddles the line between the abstract and the concrete, the ethereal and the corporeal."[39] Remembering the humanistic separation of words and action,[40] she observes that when civil laws were made, there was no public doubt about the difference between words and action. But in the preceding century, as psychology was taken more seriously, it became widely acknowledged that words have palpable, bodily effects. She cites Austin's speech act theory[41] to move *toward* a more comprehensive view of speech *as* action, citing hate speech as a familiar, clear instance of generic speech action. Yet one genre of speech is just that, one genre. How far can the sense of speech as action be taken? Continuing to respect the view that "words are not the same as actions," she considers Franklyn Haiman's view that "language is 'mediated' action."[42] But she is not ready to describe language this way either: "To say that speech is not action is to fall into the logical error of drawing a sharp distinction between mind and body."[43] Here Lakoff is in accord with figures like Johann Hamann[44] and well as with contemporary feminist figures who have argued to revoke this historic way of speaking altogether. However, she does not say there is *no* distinction between mind and body, just no *sharp* distinction. This, too, counts as a revolutionary usage: she honors the received tradition and opposes it only incrementally, as if she does not want to debate *whether there is* a distinction, but only to leave room for *referring* to mind and body as different from one another. She is not concerned in a final way with whether they are rigidly and permanently different, but leaves open the possibility for different uses, depending on the context of discussion. Through such lines of reasoning, binaries are removed as coercive standards in the use of language.

At junctures like this, acknowledging the materiality of language becomes salient: if language is taken to be material, one no longer demands absolute consistency of usage,[45] and one consciously grants the speaker the latitude to

---

38. Her approach to this constitutional binary is this: "the deal has to be both-and, not either-or." Lakoff, *Language War*, 114. This expectation is also a gesture that revokes Aristotle's principle of non-contradiction.

39. Lakoff, *Language War*, 104.

40. Discussed in chapter 2.

41. As discussed in chapter 3.

42. Lakoff, *Language War*, 107.

43. Lakoff, *Language War*, 108.

44. Discussed in chapter 4.

45. "A foolish consistency is the hobgoblin of little minds." Ralph Waldo Emerson, "Self-Reliance," *Ralph Waldo Emerson: Essays and Lectures* (New York: Literary Classics of the United States, 1983), 257–282, quotation on 265.

use received language in different senses. What matters is how the usage fits into the overall movement of her discussion, and how this movement can affect our own ways of approaching language. Our relation to the writer or speaker determines the weight we give to her usages: what kind of action do *we* take in consequence of our immersion in this discussion? We don't ask whether *she* is consistent. We ask how we let the text act and how we let the text lead us to action. I describe this circumstance by calling any use of language, spoken or written, a *political gesture*.[46] This term, "gesture," usually refers to what we do with our bodies, and is always used that way in the theater. A language gesture in everyday life is both physical and metaphorical, meaning that the fact that it was made to begin with adds an initiative to it in a political way. But the term also refers to the fact that speech gestures are dependent on previous gestures, on others' gestures, and on the *Sprachspiele* of mutual responses. Exchanges of language gestures are bodily ways for people to mark the relationship that lives in the present moment, changing it personally and politically. Recognizing the materiality of the language of the text passes along to us political capability.

An important characteristic of Lakoff's writing is that she often offers several terms, formulations, and liminal judgments to represent her claims. She does not claim the role of the transcendental signifier or of a builder of the symbolic order. Each local (that is, chapter-by-chapter) investigation is an element in the enactment of her overall program of demonstrating, as a matter of historical responsibility, the necessity for understanding the political, gendered weight of language usage. Some discussions assume a forceful position in the disputes over which amendment (the first or the fourteenth) shall take priority in any one case. She states that equal protection of all by the law is our first priority, but that it is not now an actuality. So "[u]ntil that goal is achieved, the First Amendment guarantee of free speech merely serves to protect the interests of those who are already protected by the Fourteenth Amendment: those with traditional power."[47] The study of language has this political responsibility—to achieve a trustworthy enactment of the principle of equal protection of all citizens. This principle is the same as equal access to the law and to language.[48]

The end of the matter is this, Lakoff says: "Members of groups that know viscerally that meaning-making is power and are watching their unilateral and

---

46. White, *Justice*. White does *not* characterize language gestures as political, although different political weights can feature in a respectful reading of his work and of his various citations of judicial opinion.

47. Lakoff, *Language War*, 109.

48. As suggested by Kafka's parable "Before the Law," cited in chapter 1. The work of Martha Fineman, discussed in chapter 11, also emphasizes mutual interdependency as the ground for describing principles of justice.

absolute access to meaning-making erode"[49] try to "diminish . . . the importance of language" in their own minds and in the minds of others. As her discussion proceeds, her usage changes slightly: "As long as the narrative [of who has power over whom] continues uninterrupted and unquestioned, language can be used . . . by those with language-making power against those without it" to do "word-harm."[50] Ultimately, Lakoff shows that the language, rather than meaning, may be harmful; language may do just what actions do. Both words and actions can be benign, and both can do harm. Because both are material, each speaker or person has a political choice to make as to what to use and how to use it.

Lakoff notes that conservatives have backed the first amendment in their defense of hate speech. This is the political choice of those who are "already protected" by the fourteenth amendment. Their support of free speech is "a last desperate attempt to hold on to their power by denying the potency of language at the moment when the right to control it is slipping from their grasp."[51] Yes, this is a reading of American society in the year 2000. There is no question but that access to language is growing, and those who speak variations of so-called standard English are heard more frequently and with more consequence. "Potency" is no longer the term used to describe ordinary male sexual function, thus dissociating this function from connotations of power. Here Lakoff uses the term to describe a point of view that is still defined by the reliance on gender-marked view of male sex as power. Advocating the priority of free speech over equal access to language—something shared by all people—remains part of the political agenda of many. The traditions of sex/gender language uses continue to exercise political influence. In describing the politics of language use, Lakoff also shows how bodily involvements enter every context, and how inextricable these involvements are in the descriptive analysis of the language.

IV. Struggles for Access to Language

Starting with the secret acquisitions of literacy by slaves,[52] African Americans have struggled for access to the language of white America and for respectful recognition of African American Vernacular English (AAVE). Lakoff describes three contemporary instances in *The Language War*: the testimony of Anita

---

49. Lakoff, *Language War*, 116. Also, how shall we take her use of the term "meaning-making" and its variants? I used the term "access to language" instead because meaning makers are those whose own *usage* becomes authoritative by virtue of their placement in society (those constructing the symbolic order and the transcendental signifiers). I translate the term in this context to be read to mean those whose language counts.

50. Lakoff, *Language War*, 116.

51. Lakoff, *Language War*, 117.

52. A commonly taught account is that of Frederick Douglass, *Narrative of the Life of Frederick Douglass, an American Slave* (New York: Dover, 1995).

Hill, the jury's acquittal of O. J. Simpson, and the public disputes over the role of Ebonics (an obsolescent term for AAVE) in school curricula. Placed in the historical perspective of the interdiction against literacy, Lakoff's narratives show incremental strides overcoming the weight of custom, habit, and precedent deployed to discredit that language, and thus also the social and political standing, dignity, and equality of African Americans.

The experience of Anita Hill suggests ways that misogyny is at once a model for race bigotry and an almost acceptable means of concealing that bigotry; the common interest of men, black and white, overrides the specific interest of African Americans. At the confirmation hearing in Congress for Clarence Thomas, Anita Hill, a black law professor who had worked with him, testified that he had spoken to her about viewing pornography and also had asked her if a hair on a Coke can was a pubic hair. She described interactions she had with Thomas that suggested his behavior was improper and thus cast doubt on his suitability for the Supreme Court. Anyone who followed this story understood, more or less, its role in national politics: the Republican nominee, Thomas, was being discredited by testimony that pitted women's integrity in professional contexts against men's presumption that women may be assumed to be primarily sexual objects. The outcome was that Thomas was confirmed by the 85-percent-male Senate. The white men who confirmed his nomination found it easy to overlook Anita Hill's sworn testimony. Thomas had angrily denounced the acceptance of her testimony as a "high-tech lynching," using the history of violence against black men to override the grounds for accepting Anita Hill's testimony. However, insofar as the story of Anita Hill's language gestures remains on the record, it may perhaps usurp in consequence the confirmation of Clarence Thomas.

Lakoff understands this hearing to be one of several national turning points marked by language-use events. The key to the matter is that established men's authority and power are challenged when "historically weaker and voiceless parties [acquire] autonomy and the power of speech."[53] Furthermore, it was sexual speech by someone black and female: "Traditionalists" were "horrified" by the uttering of the word "penis" by a black woman "in the sanctum sanctorum of the Senate Caucus Chamber."[54] More generally, these hearings "gave women and others the interpretive power they had lacked and gave it to them publicly in front of everyone at the very highest level of public discourse."[55]

Lakoff repeatedly refers to the total national discourse in her analyses of events such as this. She reviewed the many comments on the hearings in order to present a comprehensive new narrative that shows the role of language in

---

53. Lakoff, *Language War*, 150.
54. Lakoff, *Language War*, 157.
55. Lakoff, *Language War*, 157.

the exchanges of political fire. This approach is required because citation of Hill's language alone does not reveal its action. Lakoff adds up the reactions to her Senate appearances before concluding that Hill's language conferred interpretive power to a specific constituency, women, as well as to a more specific group, black women. The materiality of Hill's language—the political action it took—requires placing it as fully as possible in the context of other actions: the nomination of Thomas and the congressional debate surrounding it, including the immediate intimations by senators that Hill was lying.

A question arises about Hill's action because the same hearing suggested that Clarence Thomas never did have public access to language, as has been suggested by Toni Morrison. In her preface to a collection of essays on the Thomas hearings, Morrison characterizes Thomas as one who, like Friday in *Robinson Crusoe,* has lost his native language:

> Both Friday and Clarence Thomas accompany their rescuers into the world of power and salvation. But the problem of rescue still exists: both men, black but unrecognizable at home or away, are condemned first to mimic, then to internalize and adore, but never to utter one single sentence understood to be beneficial to their original culture, whether the people of their culture are those who wanted to hurt them or those who loved them to death.[56]

By virtue of his "rescue" into mainstream society, Thomas lost his access to his native language, Morrison observes. Her observation proved truer than anyone might have imagined at the time, as the *New York Times*[57] details how Thomas has said nothing for the past five years (2006 to 2011) during Supreme Court hearings. The report says that no other justice has been silent for a whole term during the last forty years, "much less five [terms], without speaking at least once during arguments." The contrast between Thomas and Barack Obama makes the point even more dramatically. Obama was elected U.S. president in part because of his overwhelming facility with the language, his ability to bring it to others, and to have this constituency overtake it as its own. His access to language translated fluently into political power, and his hold on his office rests on the speech action of his periodic public formulations.

Both Lakoff and Morrison take access to language and to political standing to be part of the same asset for any one individual. But all three cases—of Hill,

56. Toni Morrison, "Friday on the Potomac," *Race-ing Justice, En-gendering Power: Essays on Anita Hill, Clarence Thomas, and the Construction of Social Reality* ed. Toni Morrison (New York: Pantheon, 1992), xxix.

57. Adam Liptak, "No Argument, Thomas Keeps Five-Year Silence," *New York Times* 12 February 2011.

Thomas, and Obama—are more easily intelligible by members of the public by observing how they use language habitually. This point is not emphasized by Lakoff, but it characterizes her approach to the study of language. Language gestures that are the basis of news events are reported and observable by everyone but are rarely identified as political. The commentary on such events by a broad range of observers is an equally salient part of the total political scene of action.

The jury's verdict after the trial of O. J. Simpson is an individual language gesture given collectively in public. Lakoff reads this judgment as a moment when members of the African American jury gained access to language by "framing" Simpson. Lakoff changes the familiar colloquial metaphorical reference of "framed"[58] to refer to the jury's having *contextualized* Simpson's crime by identifying it as having taken place in circumstances that highlighted the history of unequal justice—actually, no justice—for African Americans. The jury's acquittal of Simpson is the articulation of this frame: its words, "not guilty," framed the "repugnant" action of a "murderer [going] free"[59] with a counter-conventional usage. Such actions are a version of "the antithetical sense" of some words observed by Freud.[60] "Not guilty" applied to one who actually committed the crime changes the reference of "not guilty" *on this occasion* to the reference Lakoff suggests: the guilt of this defendant can only be assigned in a system of justice "trustworthy" to *all* of its constituents. Because the system of justice has proved untrustworthy during the trial and at the many previous trials in which *innocent* black men were convicted of murder, the jury used its access to language—its authorization to render judgment—to say, of O. J. Simpson, "not guilty." The common description of the jury's action is that a judgment was given and it is uncommon to consider the language of the judgment to be as central as Lakoff says it is. Yet every judgment in every court is a language gesture, a speech action: defendants are pronounced guilty or not guilty. Lakoff's description renders the language intelligible only in the context of the whole

---

58. The chapter is entitled "Who Framed 'O. J.'?"

59. Lakoff, *Language War*, 226.

60. Sigmund Freud, "The Antithetical Sense of Primal Words," *Collected Papers*, trans. Joan Riviere (New York: Basic, 1959), 4:184–191. It is cited in chapter 7. Freud followed the practice of calling words from ancient languages primal. The essay is a review of a book on ancient Egyptian usages, which showed many words to have a variety of opposing references; there were also words that were made up of parts having opposite references, and Freud offers examples in English and German. Although there are no "primal" words, Freud understood the simultaneous assertion of opposites to be a common characteristic of dreams, and he was pleased to learn that it is a common feature of languages. The gestural function of language describes this feature of usage: if we assume that the context teaches how to understand an individual word, it would not be strange that the same word could have several senses. This is the case for very many words that have multiple uses, if not always opposite ones.

narrative, the series of events that led to the verdict, as well as the history of African American men on trial for murder of white people.[61]

Lakoff's reflection on Ebonics is part of her reading of the long history of African Americans seeking the American ideal of equal justice. She reflected on the controversy about teaching Black English (African American Vernacular English—AAVE) in Oakland, California, schools. In keeping with her reading of language-use cruxes as the site of political action, Lakoff sees this dispute, reported nationally and echoed in a few other school districts across the country, as reflecting the struggle of the "majority community . . . to maintain its right to control language: in this case, to determine what form of language is 'good' English, the form that is suitable for public discourse. Since the powerful have always had the right to make their form of language—the standard—the only publicly valid form,"[62] the white community wanted to keep their language standard in order to hold power.

Geneva Smitherman has made it a career project to inquire into the history and use characteristics of AAVE from the era of slavery to the present.[63] Her work is a comprehensive collection of investigations of the history and grammar of AAVE, and her work is the basis for Lakoff's discussion: AAVE is the language of a large national constituency who can teach as well as learn from speakers of standard English. Its speakers' eligibility to teach it to others counts as having access to public language. It has not sought to be a formal public language, or to be counted as an alternative to standard English, but even as a minority language, it suffered humiliations and condescensions not visited on other local dialects or immigrant languages: it was considered an incomplete or erroneous language, the language of people who could not develop a language. In this sense the disputes over Ebonics were not a struggle for power. They were a marker of white claims of superiority that were characteristic of a slave society. The wish to study Black English was simply a wish to immerse oneself in one's own culture, and to have that language and that culture count as one

---

61. Compare Lakoff's technique of writing about the law with that of James Boyd White (discussed in section 1 of this chapter). Most of his discussions reflect on the speech action of judges and justices. Lakoff's focus is on the witnesses and the jury. Both matter, but as actions of gender politics, the choices are consistent with Lakoff's sense of how language authority is distributed.

62. Lakoff, *Language War*, 249.

63. Smitherman's books include *Black Language and Culture: Sounds of Soul* (New York: Harper and Row, 1975); *Talkin' and Testifyin': The Language of Black America* (Boston: Houghton Mifflin, 1986); *Black Talk: Words and Phrases from the Hood to the Amen Corner* (Boston: Houghton Mifflin, 1994); and *Talkin' That Talk: Language, Culture, and Education in Black America* (New York: Routledge, 2000). The last work especially details the subtleties of the political battles that took place when African American school boards wanted to formalize the study of Black English.

of those languages or dialects counted as eligible to be taught or for interaction with other speakers and dialects.

V. The Materiality of a Subaltern Dialect

As Smitherman's several studies show, Black English is not well described as the subordinate language of a subaltern in society, although its having been taken as subordinate has also been the case. While white society has actively overtaken the music, dance, and clothing mores of African American culture, it has suppressed the social and political character of Black English, which has been a constant reminder of the repressive tropes common in European Christian white cultures. June Jordan's essay "Nobody Mean More to Me than You and the Future Life of Willie Jordan"[64] is a presentation of Black English that shows how its uses carry political and social conventions repressed in mainstream white society. This critical essay takes liberties with critical writing that are similar to the liberties taken by Lakoff—and for similar reasons. Jordan records the personal and collective *experience* of Black English and then discusses how its pedagogy is problematic, because students who speak Black English consider it erroneous when they see it represented in literature. In this essay, her students actually try to gain access to public venues through the use of Black English, and are rebuffed. At the same time, however, Jordan's descriptions of several of its characteristic features point up how these features present a political challenge to mainstream English.

Jordan describes features of Black English that place the struggle of the critics and philosophers discussed in this book in a different light. Wittgenstein, Bakhtin, Derrida, Austin, Whorf, and Kristeva sensed that something was wrong in the language of Western philosophy and metaphysics, but more often than not they backed into difficult and obscure language in order to present their search for a more satisfying take on language. Here is how Jordan describes Black English:

> Our language devolves from a culture that abhors all abstraction, or anything tending to obscure or delete the fact of the human being who is here and now/the truth of the person who is speaking or listening. Consequently, *there is no passive voice construction possible in Black English.* For example, you cannot say, "Black English is being eliminated." You must say, instead, "White people eliminating Black English." The assumption of the presence of life governs all of Black English. Therefore, overwhelmingly, *all action takes place in the language of the present indicative.* And

---

64. In June Jordan, *On Call: Political Essays* (Boston: South End P, 1985), 123–139.

every sentence assumes the living and active participation of at least two human beings, the speaker and the listener. . . . If your idea, your sentence, assumes the presence of at least two living and active people, you will make it understandable because the motivation behind every sentence is the wish to say something real to somebody real.[65]

In trying to demonstrate how this sense of language looks in real life, Jordan develops several guidelines that, relative to those of formal English speech and writing, can be understood as playful, a trait which is conventional in Black English and it is taken up fluently and with enthusiasm. For example, "to say something really positive," like "he's fabulous," "try to formulate the idea using emphatic negative structure": "He bad." Or "use double or triple negatives for dramatic emphasis": thus, "Tina Turner sings out of this world" becomes, "Ain nobody sing like Tina."[66] It is a convention, in fact, to decorate ordinary conversation with a variety of dramatizations: "Do not hesitate to play with words, sometimes inventing them: e.g. 'astropotomous' means huge like a hippo plus astronomical and, therefore, signifies real big."[67]

In contrast to this guideline, we are reminded of our extended inquiries into *Sprachspiel* in Wittgenstein, the "play of difference" in Derrida, and the "carnivalesque" in Bakhtin.[68] These writers did, indeed, observe and use the

---

65. Jordan, "Nobody," 129. Compare Jordan's description of Black English with Everett's description of Piraha (as reported by John Colapinto): "[T]he Piraha perceive reality solely according to what exists within the boundaries of their direct experience— which Everett defined as anything that they can see and hear or that someone living has seen and heard." John Colapinto, "The Interpreter," *New Yorker* 16 April 2007: 118–137, quotation on 130. I read the three instances of subaltern language use already cited (Luria's peasant, the Piraha, and Black English) as having something to teach us citizens of Western metaphysics: there is something excessive about our historic willingness to disrespect the moment and to use our language to underestimate the present, and pretend that we can transcend it with our imaginations—the sacralization of our abstractions. Well-educated African American critics have made this same observation, and have shown how our intellectual life has been impoverished by this long-held custom of thinking that we are able to transcend the present moment, whether the moment is measured in hours or lifetimes.

66. Jordan, "Nobody," 130–131.

67. Jordan, "Nobody," 132.

68. This is Bakhtin's term, only briefly mentioned in the present study, in his discussions of literature, for the "heteroglossic" character of literary language: a flow of usages that combines a wide variety of tropes and speech genres so that it comes to us in the rich colors and actions of carnivals. Here, James Joyce's two novels, *Ulysses* and *Finnegans Wake*, are instances of a writer recognizing and using heteroglossia in his work. Two germane discussions of the carnivalesque appear in Susan Miller, *Textual Carnivals: The Politics of Composition* (Carbondale: Southern Illinois UP, 1993); and Christine Iwanicki, "The Materiality of Language," Ph.D. diss., Indiana University, 1995, 276–316.

playful qualities of language gestures, their theatrical and dramatic character, but the academic tradition heavily informed the ways they must write about their observations. Although Wittgenstein may be said to have resisted the academic tradition to an extent, he was nevertheless deeply into a work mode of individual contemplation that, combined with his moves away from traditional philosophy, resulted in books made up of a collection of related thoughts rather than a planned, constructed edifice of argument. Lakoff, also in an academic tradition, takes some of the liberties described by Jordan, but she, too, is clearly within the boundaries of the Western academic posture.

Especially salient in Jordan's comment is the claim that Black English "abhors" abstraction. This is the issue of the ages that appears in the history of nominalism.[69] Now, once again, a subaltern language rejects the habit of abstraction by using metaphors sooner than generalizations. Placed in the context of Black English, we get a sense of why, perhaps, people have continued to insist on the value of nominalism throughout Western history: the conduct of everyday life becomes somewhat humbler and more respectful of the value of the present moment; there is uncertainty in using a linguistic abstraction to anticipate the future. It is neither right nor wrong that Black English is spoken mostly in what white English calls the present indicative, but in view of the fact that all people live their lives necessarily in the present alone, the present moment may indeed reflect Martin Luther King's "the fierce urgency of now"; If not now, when? "Carpe diem." Slaves, former slaves, or the terminally ill *must* seize the day in order to survive. However, *any* person's life is enhanced by the ability to recognize the value of the present and not presume on the future or long for an unrecoverable past. If language usage, our habits of abstraction and nominalization, push us toward assuming what is eternal, toward assuming that we know what will take place tomorrow, toward thinking that we can recover the past in a sense beyond the surviving material artifacts, we lose sight of the palpable, material pleasure of the moment as it is assimilated wastefully into fantasy and illusion.

Putting Jordan's sense of Black English alongside the philosophical efforts discussed in this book suggests, perhaps, that my lengthy analysis might be viewed as redundant but for the fact that I, unlike Jordan, do not have another dialect or another language that can make the argument Jordan makes. I have access to the hegemonic, standard-setting languages, tropes, and traditions that are legal tender in Western civilization.[70] Yet we arrive at the same conclusions: that language is something we can and should play with in the cause of enrich-

---

69. Discussed in chapter 1, section 4.

70. At the same time, I do have access to Yiddish, which began and has continued to be a subaltern dialect of a hegemonic language, gradually acquiring a full literate status. Usages in Yiddish have some of the double-voiced characteristics (discussed again in chapter 12 in connection with the materiality of literature) of Black English, and my

ing, deepening, and decorating our social relations; that the language gestures emerging from such play represent a political stroke that seeks at once inclusion in society as equal and that claims pedagogical authority to teach thoughts similar to those our struggling philosophers tried to teach; and that language is part of our bodies and the main means of connecting with others that surround us, nearer and farther from us both.

Barbara Christian's essay "The Race for Theory"[71] speaks directly to those of us in the academy who have relied on our interest in revising our own traditions but who were not born with the "dissatisfaction" with which she was born. Christian writes,

> These writers [poststructuralist, postmodernist, and French feminist critics] did announce their dissatisfaction with some of the cornerstone ideas of their own tradition, a dissatisfaction with which I was born. But in their attempt to change the orientation of Western scholarship, they, as usual, concentrated on themselves and were not in the slightest interested in the worlds they had ignored or controlled. Again I was supposed to know *them,* while they were not at all interested in knowing *me.* Instead, they sought to "deconstruct" the tradition to which they belonged even as they used the same forms, style, and language of that tradition, forms that necessarily embody its values.[72]

Christian's viewpoint is clear: the authors that are discussed in several of the preceding chapters are themselves struggling with language problems whose solutions were self-evident to Christian and Jordan by virtue of their native (mother) cultures and languages. "I lived among folk for whom language was an absolutely necessary way of validating our existence."[73] This meant for her that theory is something presented through narrative, the technique used by Lakoff to re-present linguistics to the public and to the academy. Christian writes that "people of color have always theorized—but in forms quite different from the Western form of abstract logic. And I am inclined to say that our theorizing . . . is often in narrative forms, in the stories we create, in riddles and proverbs, in the play with language, because dynamic rather than fixed ideas seem more to our liking."[74] In academic life as we are used to it, it is hardly

---

knowledge of Yiddish led me to the present understanding of Jordan's description of Black English.

71. Barbara Christian, "The Race for Theory," *Feminist Studies* 14.1 (1988): 67–79.

72. Christian, "The Race," 72.

73. Christian, "The Race," 72.

74. Christian, "The Race," 68. Like the eighteenth-century philosopher Johann George Hamann (see chapter 4), Christian attributes a substantive function to poetry

conceivable that literature, which has its own edifice of professional validation, should present itself as theory. Its reference to reality is figurative, yet it is a genre of theory in that it presents responses, readings, and interpretations of experiences that demand such attentions. For Christian, herself immersed in a feeling for language materiality from childhood, there is no problem in moving back and forth from understanding the figurative as history, as literature, and as theory, as understanding in the same authoritative sense that we now view the understanding given by science.

Christian's discussion understands any literary speech action, oral or written, as play, as a *Sprachspiel,* and sees in it the same decorative functions given to language by Jordan's description of Black English. In playing with the term "theory," Christian recontextualizes it through reasoning similar to Lakoff's concerning the term "not guilty." Christian affirms the right to create a new reference for "theory," as for any key term in common use. Never having been asked to participate with European critics on a mutual basis of exchange, but asked only to adapt to a received and presumably established standard, Christian further affirms the necessity for authentic language exchange between African Caribbean and African American and European American cultures. She demands that the paths of mutual cultural dependency be exposed as such, and that the conversation involve two or more fully enfranchised perspectives.

Theory for Christian is where the language is appropriated as the means of survival, as a means to answer the "assault on our bodies, social institutions, countries, our very humanity."[75] It was "pithy language that unmasked the power relations" of the colonial world in which she lived. She understands language to be connected to the survival of all bodies in the culture, and she implies that speakers of her language understood the same thing. Yet beyond its status as an instrument of collective survival, language, which includes as subgenres theory and literature, was a path to "grace and pleasure," a form of (Derridian) writing that is "both sensual and abstract, both beautiful and communicative."[76] This is the material language-in-use that today increasingly seeks, even demands, recognition in every part of society.

Christian's affirmative claim as well as her expectation that the respect for one another's language go in both directions emerges forcefully in Jordan's essay. Like Christian, Jordan brings out what few advocates of full emancipation for all people usually do not even mention—namely, the assumption that those holding hegemonic status have more privileges and more access to everything, not just language; and that many sympathetic advocates see their mission as sharing

---

and literature. Although she does not speculate about the origin of language as Hamann does, she reports from her experience its material collective functions.

75. Christian, "The Race," 68.
76. Christian, "The Race," 68.

the riches that they have, as if they were saying, "You can be more like us." Christian and Jordan both contest this self-understanding of even sympathetic members of the hegemony: "I was supposed to know *them,* but they were not at all interested in knowing *me.*" Christian and Jordan both notice that this attitude, presented as generous, continues the narcissism endemic to Western thinking about philosophy and the philosophy of language.

VI. Recasting the Study of Language

In the work of Wittgenstein, Derrida, Bakhtin, Austin, Whorf, Cavell, and Kristeva, we understand that their many writings are given in the cause of breaking out of the narrow, self-oriented thinking that was constraining understanding of the ubiquitous manifestations of language. However, the acrobatics of their own uses of language urges the view that the standing and expectations of academic language were obstacles to achieving a consensually endorsed paradigm. For these writers, the political context proved antagonistic, and perhaps coercive. Yet all were dependent on it. Kristeva's work, different from that of the others in her choices of subject matter, still reflects a high degree of academic abstraction and a usage style that requires understanding of a wide range of her work in order to consider that her usages are more like inhibiting academic tropes than markers of her membership in the male academic tradition, although her usages may be characterized both ways. Women in predominantly male contexts do adapt to the usages of the majority.

The work of these figures and reflection on their importance in the study of language also suggests that, more generally, academic conventions have limited the access to language of even those who presumably have access through the writing of many books. These scholars are immersed in perhaps hundreds of received tropes, gambits, and postures of academic usage. Many people with credible access to ordinary language complain about the obscurity and difficulty of academic formulations such as those studied and cited in this book. The reduced access to language for all people is a feature of the hierarchical, political shape of societies.

The insistence on the political action of both language and the study of language is Robin Lakoff's move in a new direction. Possible changes are augured by the work of Lakoff, Christian, and Jordan; several other major researchers on language and literacy have tacitly adopted assumptions like the materiality of language and who presuppose the political orientation of the study of language.[77] Many contemporary researchers fall into this category. Some of them, researchers on infantile language acquisition, are considered in detail in

---

77. One cannot predict whether this new population of researchers and teachers will eventually affect more general attitudes toward language. What can be said is this: this

chapter 5. Some should be noted now. Shirley Brice Heath's *Ways with Words* (1983) is an ethnographic study of three communities in the Piedmont—black, white, and integrated. Heath studied literacy acquisition in each community by living there and developing relationships with community members. She showed how literacy styles and values are embedded in the collectively held language-use conventions and social relations. Her work is understood to participate in at least three disciplines: anthropology, education, and English. It has helped to revolutionize the study of literacy. Deborah Tannen has written several volumes, many published through trade rather than academic venues, studying the language uses found in everyday domestic and work situations. Her 1990 *You Just Don't Understand* was a popular success that led many women to get their male partners to read and discuss issues of gender politics as reflected in their speech to one another. Tannen is often hired to advise businesses on how to develop gender-egalitarian styles of discourse. Her study *The Argument Culture*[78] is discussed in chapter 7 as a critique of academic writing. Marilyn Sternglass's *Time to Know Them* (1997) is a longitudinal study of six university students of different ethnic backgrounds over a period of six years, showing the total contexts of their acquisition of literacy. It reveals the complexity of all social circumstances in which we strive to teach language and literacy. Deborah Brandt's *Literacy in American Lives* (2001) is based on comprehensive interviews of people of all ages, highlighting how economic factors create sponsors of literacy acquisition. Like Heath, she pursues understanding of all of her informants' vocational, social, and family lives, and she shows the roles language-use mores play in the acquisition of literacy for a broad range of people in the American Midwest.

Largely based in the discipline of professional education, the Whole Language movement, founded by Kenneth and Yetta Goodman in the late 1960s and early 1970s and taken up by many teachers, advocated a form of language immersion to teach language and literacy to students of all ages through secondary school. Some university faculty members, such as Constance Weaver,[79] have advocated forcefully for this approach to language education, but many more, especially school boards, have eschewed such communally based efforts to teach language and literacy. A good number of these researchers are men working along similar

---

new population has taken up an old minority tradition in its contemporary forms in the causes of social generosity and political emancipation.

78. Deborah Tannen, *The Argument Culture: Moving from Debate to Dialogue* (New York: Random House, 1998).

79. Constance Weaver, *Reading Process and Practice: From Socio-Psycholinguistics to Whole Language* (Cambridge: Winthrop, 1980); Constance Weaver, Diane Stephens, and Janet Vance, *Understanding Whole Language: From Principles to Practice* (Portsmouth, NH: Heinemann, 1990).

lines.[80] The change in how the study of use of language might proceed is this: language observed in living experience is the principal source for the understanding of language; the idiom of reporting is primarily narrative and ethnographic. All of these researchers follow Wittgenstein's principle—description instead of explanation. They report on language conventions. They take account of the broad contexts. By reporting on so-called forms of life, they also communicate the roles of language in different ways of life.

The Exodus trope of Moses not reaching the Promised Land could be used to describe the fate of the mid-twentieth-century male philosophers studied in this book. Moses was told by God to speak to the rock to extract its water, but Moses struck it instead, and so was denied access to the Promised Land. It is tempting, isn't it, to project today's view back onto the past and say that because Moses, experienced in "striking" rocks for water (as he had previously done) did not "hear" the instruction to speak, to let his language sustain his constituency? Like Moses, the scholars treated in some detail in previous chapters spent their forty years struggling in the desert circumscribed by the disciplines they received from the history of the university, only to die before a new generation understood the value of their journey in ways they did not anticipate. It might be said that the earlier generation did not know where their understanding pointed.

This later generation, comprising Robin Lakoff, Barbara Christian, and many other women—and many who bring new styles of understanding from other societies and cultures—have, like Lakoff and Christian, lived with political awareness all their lives. Being in a subaltern circumstance offers no way to separate oneself, or to urge escape into a protected academic self-rarefaction. If university enrollment figures are to be trusted, more women than men are now studying. Some like Robin Lakoff and Deborah Tannen have understood that women may have a characteristic, if not exclusive, set of usages urged by their political interests, habits, and conventions drawn from the politics of having to cope with their placement in society. At professional academic meetings, some of the adversariality has diminished because of the presence of women and their fluent upholding of politeness conventions.

---

80. These include figures such as Michael Tomasello, Philip Lieberman, and Dennis Senchuk, mentioned in earlier chapters. In anthropology figures such as Clifford Geertz have carried forth the politically responsive practices of humanistic anthropology; as have Anne Ruggles Gere, Elizabeth Long, and Joan Shelley Rubin. See Clifford Geertz, *Local Knowledge: Further Essays in Interpretive Anthropology* (New York: Basic, 1983); Anne Ruggles Gere, *Intimate Practices: Literacy and Cultural Work in U.S. Women's Clubs, 1880–1920* (Urbana: U of Illinois P, 1997); Elizabeth Long, *Book Clubs: Women and the Uses of Reading in Everyday Life* (Chicago: U of Chicago P, 2003); and Joan Shelley Rubin, *Songs of Ourselves: The Uses of Poetry in America* (Cambridge, MA: Harvard UP, 2007).

In the cause of anticipating, or perhaps only hoping for, change in academic life, part 2 of this book considers problems in the history of academic language and social institutions; and some of the practices of scholars, researchers, and scientists and how they present their understanding. There are reasons to think that assumptions sympathetic to the materiality of language are enlarging their purview, their population of interested students, and their influence. Will such developments be enough to overcome the historic atmosphere of frustration with the contested subject of language?

Part Two:
Language in the University

CHAPTER SEVEN

Frustrations of Academic Language

I. Sacralization and Abstraction

Every university subject depends on exchanges of language. Fluency with specific discourses and gestures is the only way to know any subject matter. Since universities were founded, students' qualifications first for study and then for employment was facility in the use of language. Within the university the use and study of language has been contested. The general public had limited access to the language of knowledge and authority. University faculty members had custody of language, taught it, spoke it and immersed themselves in it, kept it away from the general population, and were reluctant to use their own access in courageous and imaginative ways. They established their own usages in different subject matters and discouraged their discourses' interaction with those used by other subject matters. An atmosphere of self-protection was present in individual disciplines, and peace was maintained mainly by keeping the boundaries between disciplines relatively rigid. Over the centuries of university life uneasiness within the community of privileged scholars and teachers has been perpetuated by the disparity between the conventions of university language uses and the freer, inventive uses of vernaculars outside each university.

It is customary to think that the problem of limited access to the language of universities no longer exists. But today's version of limited access is not a significant departure from how things were when Latin was the only language that counted and when most people outside the university were illiterate. Deborah Brandt's comprehensive study of contemporary literacy in the United States provides a vocabulary for seeing this similarity. She sees literacy as "a valued commodity . . . a key resource in gaining profit and edge."[1] She says, "[T]he powerful work so persistently to conscript and ration the resource of literacy." As a result, people have to compete to become literate, and "[i]t is this competition that has made access to the right kinds of literacy sponsors so crucial for political and economic well-being."[2] Brandt describes the struggle of the majority

---

1. Deborah Brandt, *Literacy in American Lives* (New York: Cambridge UP, 2001), 21.
2. Brandt, *Literacy*, 21.

to achieve both elementary literacy and the complex literacy of extended education. It is something one has to compete for because it is controlled by the economically and politically powerful. This same atmosphere of competition and struggle surrounds the striving of the public for access to language, which means—in addition to literacy—the ability to reach and hold the public floor, to have their voices heard and respected, and to have authoritative dominion over the language they bring to others.

This struggle has been ongoing during the eight centuries of the university period (1155 to the present), and its political shape has been produced by the locations of the university in society. One might expect that the purposes of universities as schools would lead them actively to disseminate language and access to it to the greatest possible extent, but this has not been the case. Those in universities understood just how politically comfortable it can be if one limits access to language to those in the university culture. This understanding was the same on the part of American slaveholders, who always limited the access of slaves to literacy, radically reducing their chances to win their own freedom, let alone self-determination.

In thinking about access to language, one may be inclined to consider that the humanities have been the principal sites of language cultivation and use. Several recent studies of the university relate the "ruins" of the university to the shrinking of language and humanistic study.[3] But this is only part of the picture. Language uses in science are not often studied and reconsidered, but participate just as much in the limiting of public access to the language and subject matters of science. Both the humanities and (social and physical) sciences use jargons and a host of obscure formulations. It remains a mark of distinction today to use a language that few can understand; Latin played that role for perhaps six centuries in university life. In universities today there are "experts" rather than teachers and scholars. We anticipate that each expert will choose to retain his or her own zones of epistemological privilege rather than to find ways to remove the boundaries between his or her own discourse and the language uses of other disciplines as well as of everyone else. So for a variety of reasons the access to language for most people remains as limited as it was during the times of almost universal illiteracy, while the experts limit their own access to language by binding themselves to an underlying set of rigid abstractions and conventions in the cause of maintaining professional authority.

Part 1 describes how access to language has been limited by the persistence in academic writing of the customs of Platonic realism as the governing principle

---

3. Frank Donoghue, *The Last Professors: The Corporate University and the Fate of the Humanities* (New York: Fordham UP, 2008); Alvin Kernan, ed., *What's Happened to the Humanities?* (Princeton, NJ: Princeton UP, 1997); and Bill Readings, *The University in Ruins* (Cambridge, MA: Harvard UP, 1996).

of language use. Deriving from the tradition of nominalism that dates back at least two millennia, a materialist paradigm that rejects Western metaphysics has been growing since the mid-twentieth century, and some have begun to respond to its perspective. Scholars in humanities and sciences have discussed this development.[4] Their work shows how the growth of gender awareness and the entry of women into academic life have given the materiality of language a greater visibility in most academic disciplines.

Before modern times, the university as an institution grappled with language that was entangled with religious beliefs and practices. Often matters of religious doctrine could not be recognized as issues with language because language was thought to be transparent. Those who claimed it was not transparent, and that the choice of language affected the substance of the issues being considered, were usually ostracized and sometimes executed because such a claim, if it won general assent, would compromise or dissolve religious authority. Attached to this struggle is an additional salient fact: language was a contested subject because only men were in the university. Men's preoccupations and styles of work limited imaginative exploration of language and created an atmosphere, ethic, and default strategy of mutual opposition. Adversarial styles aggravated the political anxiety created by a dogmatic adherence to Platonic realism and by a fierce, mean-spirited opposition to nominalism, a precursor to materiality and a language philosophy held by several prominent figures who did not renounce their faith. Until recently, there was no language to present androcentrism as having an active political effect on the ways language was studied and universities were run. If we think now of the early history of the university as a site of gender problems, this history becomes more comprehensible, more visible as a sequence of events resulting in the university system into which we were born.

Certain peculiarities of academic work follow from the fact that intellectual life and its different discourses were conducted only by men. Men in all-male groups had to agree not to face (that is, agree to repress[5]) their awareness of some of the implications of their homogeneity as well as of their exclusivity. This repression, serving the solidarity of these groups, led to the taboo against challenging assumptions and premises of beliefs and language uses that have sustained their official identities. The result of this taboo has been that disputed

---

4. Chapters 10 through 12 discuss the approaches of those in academic work who reject traditional realist academic language uses as well as those who have, consistent with a sense of the materiality of language, introduced new considerations of the ways language is chosen, used, and taught in several different disciplines.

5. Another way to think of collective repression is that the repressed material is an open secret. Certain situations or behaviors are not eligible for discussion and so they are secret in that sense. Because people know that these situations are there, the secret is open. However, in the case of individual repression, usually the person seems actually unaware of the secret—so the repression is characterized as being unconscious.

issues (that were not problems in religious practice) that could be resolved with flexible assumptions about language instead went unsolved, prolonging debate over centuries, and were at best understood to be paradoxes. These habits (or customs or traditions) of repression established debate, argumentation, and an overall agonistic atmosphere for as long as universities functioned: because the all-male groups separated themselves from the material and social realities of society at large, competitive agonism was received as a fact, a necessity, and an unquestioned set of practices that perpetuated the culture of power struggles and hierarchical functioning. It was understood that intellectual validation could come only through oppositional tropes. Certification in the university came when a student won or performed well in a disputation. But in modern times, the conventional understanding of science holds that one arrives at a valid scientific theory by falsifying competing hypotheses or the prevailing theory.[6] This view contrasts with the view that a good theory is one that works, with the understanding that in some cases it may not work. Throughout academic history, men's unquestioned allegiance to hierarchical social organization required a winning theory, a winning viewpoint, and tended to eschew finding value in understandings that are approximate—not rigid—regularities, effective some of the time but not others. In modern times, the entry of women to academic work and to scientific practice has made it easier to identify male collective repression and the inflexibilities of thought and practice associated with men's social organization, and have begun to change the substantive conclusions that men's groups of humanists and scientists have taken for granted as universal knowledge.

Two particular language gestures have inhibited the recognition of the materiality of language and have collaborated to limit the access of people to their own and others' languages: abstraction and sacralization. The habit, trope, gesture, or gambit of academic abstraction[7] came from the Platonic tradition, which held that ideas were higher than words. Only certain men were permitted to identify ideas, and they held the most intellectual authority. When universities were founded in the twelfth century, churchmen took and held this authority: they identified the abstractions that were then taken to have references in reality as the key ideas. The stabilization of abstract terms through the exercise

---

6. This is Karl Popper's description of how science arrives at a true theory. Karl Popper's 1935 *The Logic of Scientific Discovery* (New York: Harper, 1965) is a fundamental text in twentieth-century positivism. Why doesn't he say that one arrives at a more satisfying explanation, that science proceeds by achieving understanding rather than by defeating a competing point of view?

7. Any speaker practices abstraction. The difference between ordinary or common abstraction and academic abstraction is that the former is usually understood to be provisional and contingent, whereas the latter is rigid and taken to have a fixed reference: it is often sacralized.

of religious authority is sacralization—giving the reference the transcendental status of sacred texts.[8] Many sacralized abstractions have remained more or less stable until the present. Although the use of any abstraction involves a certain degree of distortion or falsehood, any speaker of a language knows how to use this distortion or falsehood purposefully. But because of the political placement of universities as wards of the church, distinct uses and habits of abstraction developed. Theology having been the main university subject in terms of importance (but not in terms of enrollments), abstractions that had no tangible reference in anyone's experience frequently were created, contested, and replaced by other nonreferential abstractions. In addition, the disputations that certified graduates made special use of these abstractions and their logical manipulations, so that both the abstractions and the logic that bound them together could not be related to the experience of living people outside the university. Yet this combination played a major role in the certification of new figures of authority. These uses of language—the sacralized abstractions and their logical presentations—retained over several centuries the highest level of authority. They were challenged successfully only in the nineteenth and twentieth centuries. Similar challenges to the authority of clerical or academic discourse before modern times were turned back with charges of heresy, and proponents of such challenges were excommunicated and sometimes executed. As a result, academic discourse as we now use it had become embedded in the certification processes of all students because the style of language use and the language that bore it, Latin, were sacralized.[9] Thus, only a small minority of men was permitted access to any text of consequence.

In the twentieth century, universities have grown into a position to change their handling of language as a result of two social changes: the population of universities began to include women and others who were not previously eligible for admission, and materialist conceptions of language[10] have affected how

---

8. Nonreligious sacralization, which happens now in science as well as other areas of academic life, is done by secular authorities such as scholars and scientists, who today enjoy a standing similar to what church standing was in earlier times. William Clark uses Max Weber's term "charisma" to describe the enhanced standing of members of the academy: "In short, as vested in clothing, books, furniture, titles, and so on, charisma at the traditional university served to uphold authority by sanctifying traditions and differentiating academics as a group from other groups in society." William Clark, *Academic Charisma and the Origins of the Research University* (Chicago, U of Chicago P, 2006), 18. As Clark discusses it, charisma describes the larger context of sanctification that supported the sacralization of texts and language.

9. The Latin language was once a vernacular. The Church sacralized it. The sacred texts were originally written in Hebrew and Greek. But then the Church took Latin (from the Romans) for its official use, thus sacralizing it.

10. Materialist senses of language are variously associated with "poststructuralism" and "postmodernism," two abstract terms that include reference to language, but do

abstractions represented claims of knowledge. The grounds on which knowledge is both claimed and contested have changed. Processes of sacralization of language and texts have been challenged and often discredited. Although the ability of the Church to sacralize language and texts has been radically curtailed, the customs of textual sacralization and of binding abstraction have continued, and are in effect today in the humanities and the sciences. In addition, medicine and law, whose official terms remain in Latin, are inhibited (although not altogether constrained) by the habits of reified abstraction and by their caution about changing their usages even when experience suggests change makes more sense than continuing traditional usages: both of these subjects took their language usages from the earliest universities.[11] Often physicians and attorneys are responsive to the circumstances of individual cases and their choices are not limited by abstract constraints. However, few who are educated in universities assume that all abstractions are provisional and contingent. Because of this inhibition the perception of contingency is repressed, and people, unthinkingly, become rigidly committed to terms and texts that might easily be changed and improved.

Pursuant to the tradition of sacralizing texts and abstractions, this chapter considers the social and political factors involved in the frustrations with academic language. There are several contexts for this consideration: the proliferation of academic writing over the centuries; the reasons for men's collective

---

not specify its various behaviors. My use of the term "materiality" aims to specify how postmodernism and poststructuralism have changed classical senses of language.

11. Because professional writing in law and medicine is no longer subordinate to the authority of universities, professional initiatives reviewing received practices and usages have appeared. In the field of law, a few critical sources are germane. I have already cited Catharine MacKinnon's observation that free speech is more accessible to the wealthy. Chapter 12 cites her materialist reading of pornography. A similar materialist-oriented reading of the law is found in Patricia J. Williams, *The Alchemy of Race and Rights: Diary of a Law Professor* (Cambridge, MA: Harvard UP, 1991). Williams reviews several laws and usages, which, when read and applied by different groups, yield different results. For example, one can read the law with a "rhetoric of certainty" (rights) or a "rhetoric of context" (informal rules) and come up with different judgments in a variety of cases (158). James Boyd White tries to describe how justice is achieved by the process of translating legal language into the language of "our experience of ordinary life and from our reading of literature." James Boyd White, *Justice as Translation: An Essay in Cultural and Legal Criticism* (Chicago: U of Chicago P, 1990), xi. Each of these legal studies focuses on finding new principles of reading legal language and then rewriting it for future laws. This approach recognizes the materiality of the language. An analogous example in medicine could be Nancy Ainsworth-Vaughn's *Claiming Power in Doctor-Patient Talk* (New York: Oxford UP, 1998), which recognizes and evaluates the weight of the language use of doctor and patient. In medical schools, new courses in medical humanities aim to teach physicians the different results of different language choices when speaking to patients.

repression; the use of paradox as the explanation of problems in real life; the recursive reliance on argument and intellectual agonism; and the consequence of academic comfort with the protection of more powerful institutions. Each of these factors has, in the past and now, become a part of one or more of the other factors, and in different forms has played a role in the resistance to recognizing and using the materiality of language. All of the foregoing factors could continue to cause frustration in the study of language; this book seeks to minimize those roles and to contribute to a new turn in academic work.

II. The Writing of Many Books

Toward the end of Ecclesiastes, the presumed author—the "preacher" or Koheleth—perhaps the Israelite King Solomon, observes, "[T]he making of many books would have no end; and much preaching [or study] is a weariness of the flesh" (12:12). How this sentence is translated already poses an issue of scholarship: is it preaching, or study? Both translations might be considered today. Any original copy is unknown. When this text was written, books were handwritten and expensive; the law was read aloud in public; most people were illiterate. Why did the writer say that there would be "no end" to the "making of many books"? Why is the making of books unrelated to cost and popularity? And why is much study or preaching weariness of the "flesh" and not of the mind? The Hebrew *davar*[12] answers that question: language is "always already" material. The work of preaching, study, and writing is corporeal, material, difficult, and important. To Koheleth—a speaker to and for a congregation, yet who is still a member of it—involvement in books is a bodily function, at once a challenge to physical life and a necessity. Giving weight to both translations is that study and preaching are similar: they involve careful attention to the language, to the bodily action of the uses of language.

This text, Ecclesiastes, is unlike other texts of the Hebrew Bible. God's role in it is not prominent: at the end, the speaker declares God to be the judge of all things, and urges young people to fear God and keep his commandments. But God's work and power are not mentioned, extolled, praised, blessed. The text is not about God; it is mainly about which choices to make in life, emphasizing how throughout generations the developments of events are similar, cyclical, and lead to the same ending for all people. The writer observes that regardless of what choices one finally makes in life they can have no bearing on how one's life ends up. This is a preacher who suggests that righteousness, strength, and study does not lead to good results: "I turned about, and saw under the sun, that the race is not to the swift, nor the battle to the mighty; and that also the wise have no bread, nor yet the men of understanding riches, nor yet men of

---

12. As discussed in chapter 1, *davar* in Hebrew means both "word" and "thing."

knowledge favor; but time and chance will overtake them all" (9:11). One can say nothing is rational or predictable.

This declaration suggests a principal theme in the text: the fruitlessness of wisdom, understanding, and knowledge—and the writing of many books in spite of this vanity. In chapter 9, verse 16, he observes, "Then said I, Wisdom is better than might: although the poor man's wisdom is held in contempt, and his words are not heard." His words do not matter because he is poor. However, in the previous verse, he observed that a poor man delivered a besieged city with his wisdom. Is this a contradiction? Are both formulations true? The latter choice is more compelling, yet the speaker's frustration is as strong as in the first verse: all is vanity. The speaker claims to have searched for wisdom for a lifetime without, however, neglecting the accumulation of riches and the pursuit of comfort. He claims to have failed to find either satisfaction or wisdom, but he wrote this book. And if no one person wrote it, is it enough to say that it is part of a larger sacred text because people thought it was interesting and important? The text, riddled with disillusionment and despair, was nevertheless written and compiled. In understanding this text, it might be reasonable to say that the speaker was perplexed and was forced into a place where the "end of the matter" is to "[f]ear God, and keep his commandments" (12:13)—the solution, perhaps, to the conundrum of the previous verse, the writing of many books. The preacher has experienced every good thing there is and discovered only emptiness. From one standpoint, his despair cannot be gainsaid. The race is definitely not to the swift. Books are written because there is no answer, not because there is one. The writing of many books is the substitute for an answer to the fact that there is no explanation for the riddles contemplated by Koheleth and by the many academic thinkers after him. Books, therefore, are not sacred; as they are written for their own sake by anyone who can write. Writing books is a customary response to the riddles of existence and civilization.

Is this practice gender marked? Are *men's* books written for this reason? Is there a connection among the cosmic perplexity of Koheleth *referenced* by the text, the practice of producing texts to cope with this frustration, and his reflections on women? In chapter 7, verses 25–26, the preacher said, "Then I turned myself about together with my heart to know, and to search, and to seek out wisdom, and the reason of things, and to know the wickedness of folly, and the foolishness of madness. And I find as more bitter than death the woman, whose heart is snares and nets, and whose hands are bonds . . ."; and in verse 28, "What my soul constantly sought, but I found it not; one man among a thousand did I find; but a woman among all these did I not find." But later, in chapter 9, verse 9, the preacher says, "Enjoy life with the wife whom thou lovest all the days of the life of thy vanity, which God hath given thee under the sun."

Koheleth is a male figure with access to many women, yet who is aware of the transience of this privilege and of his kinship with those who seek it themselves: their common subordination to "time and chance." Nevertheless, is the riddle itself a men's riddle, and the writing of books a men's solution—especially if the writing of any book in an illiterate society renders that writing sacred? Koheleth's phrase "Live out the days of thy vanity with the wife whom thou lovest" shows his recognition of women's "claims of love"[13] as a path to continued civilized life for men, in spite of the incomprehensible mysteries of life and the remoteness of social peace. Koheleth's observation that the writing of many books would not end, in spite of the toll it takes on the flesh, is also an oblique statement regarding the permanence of men's hegemony. In this regard we may relate him to Freud: a man of understanding, yet not enough understanding to extricate himself through his serious writing from the frustration of recursive social failure, war, and arbitrary fate. The question this poses is how far this perspective of the rich, powerful, literate men of understanding in antiquity shall be considered a male-coded perspective, given that there is no extant female-coded perspective with which to compare it. Is it the case that this perspective on life, society, gender, and the writing of books has remained the same since Koheleth said that there was "nothing new under the sun"?[14]

III. Freud's Repression and Other Limits

The university as an institution as we know it began in the twelfth century in Bologna.[15] There preachers and students from all over Europe became men of understanding, who sought wisdom and knowledge. They confirmed Koheleth's prediction that there would be no end to the writing of many books. They established a tradition of book writing that we immediately recognize in today's universities as having been continued from the time of medieval Europe and earlier. Freud, despite having gone through university training, is not known for his academic affiliation, but his writing style as well as his "writing of many books" and essays places him in the tradition cited by Koheleth: one whose

---

13. Discussed shortly in regard to Freud's similar sentiment.

14. Compare Koheleth's view of books to that of Anthony Grafton: "I am a lover of old libraries. . . . [As a student] I lived in what felt like a bibliomaniac's paradise and in retrospect still seems to have been an idyll. . . . I prowled the vast open-stack collections at the University of Chicago where I studied, and Cornell and Princeton, where I taught, pulling books off the shelves by the dozens." Anthony Grafton, *Worlds Made by Words: Scholarship and Community in the Modern West* (Cambridge, MA: Harvard UP, 2009), 290. Grafton was in contact with the historic charisma described by Clark. How shall his love of books and awe in their presence be described? Is it new information that touches him, or are there other factors, such as the "loneliness and freedom" of libraries mentioned by Humboldt? (289) Are Koheleth's and Grafton's feelings equally present in academic life?

15. A good short introduction to the history of the university is Charles Homer Haskins, *The Rise of Universities* (Ithaca, NY: Cornell UP, 1957). This work is further cited and discussed in chapter 8.

writing of books is a response to the riddles of existence. Most would consider him to be like Koheleth also because he was given to announcing facts about human behavior regardless of how unpleasant they were. He is the figure who introduced the term "repression" into our vocabulary. Repression is what we do with unpleasant facts or perceptions about ourselves and our society: we put them in some part of our memory with which we have only minimal contact, so as to keep the more affirmative parts of our lives before us. Freud described how it worked in individual psychology, and he envisioned how, through the use of language, individuals might shed the burden of repression. But then when he tried to say how civilization might escape the consequences of its repression, he could not say how it might be done. While he did not say that one should fear God and keep his commandments, he did say that the only hope for civilization is to trust science.[16] For many, science does, indeed, play the role that God once played for individuals and society.

Freud considered the use of language to be a scientific instrument. Through his reliance on talk and free association to produce tangible changes in people's lives, he helped bring the materiality of language into view in modern times.[17] Yet it is also well known how frustrated he was with this effort, how inconclusive psychoanalytic therapy often was in spite of the appeal of and public fascination with the theory. He seemed to have a rigid hold on his own uses of language in therapy, and he did not reflect on how better to bring to bear the use of language in the treatment of psychological and psychosocial complaints. Freud's frustration within his own area of innovation is related to his frustration[18] with how to understand civilization,[19] repression, and recursive war and violence.

---

16. "No, our science is no illusion. But an illusion it would be to suppose that what science cannot give us we can get elsewhere." Sigmund Freud, *The Standard Edition of the Complete Psychological Works of Sigmund Freud,* trans. James Strachey and Anna Freud, with Alix Strachey and Alan Tyson (London: Hogarth P, 1957), 21:56.

17. Both Wittgenstein and Derrida credit Freud with a new view of language that is sympathetic to their own views. One of Derrida's contributions is "Freud and the Scene of Writing," *Writing and Difference,* trans. Alan Bass (Chicago: U of Chicago P, 1978), 196–231. Derrida discusses Freud's (figure of the) "mystic writing pad" as a way to describe how forgotten memories were "written" in our minds and remain there as "traces." This pad presents an image of both the lasting power and the transience of what has been written, which in turn suggests that verbal or material-symbolic articulation is the last stop in understanding experience.

18. In this regard, Freud, like the figures discussed in some detail in part 1, could be described as having Moses's frustration (also cited at the end of chapter 6): finding himself unable to consummate his achievement. Moses was prohibited from entering the Promised Land because instead of speaking to the rock to bring water, as God had instructed (Numbers 20:8) he struck the rock. Is Moses's frustration the result of "male violence"? As elaborated below, Freud was not able to see his being implicated in the hegemony of men.

19. *Kultur* was translated as "civilization" in the book title in the following note, but it is not the only choice. The German word implies a process of cultivation, which

Freud wrote with confidence about how civilization had failed. His accounts are found in *Totem and Taboo, Group Psychology and the Analysis of the Ego, The Future of an Illusion,* and *Civilization and Its Discontents.*[20] What follows is his originological explanation. Once upon a time there was a "primal horde."[21] It was ruled by one powerful man who got all the pleasure he wanted, especially sexual access to all women, while everyone else had to repress and suppress their wishes for pleasure. After a while, these other males formed a social contract to kill the ruler. Although change may have temporarily taken place, the group members felt guilty. This recursive process of rule and revolution continued indefinitely, perpetuating the guilt and the orderly civilization. At one point, the slain ruler was converted into a symbol, the Christ, and the gang or mob became worshippers, symbolically (and for many, miraculously) eating the ruler and drinking his blood in a religious ceremony at regular intervals. When translated into more secular terms, this is how the story looks, as Freud tells it:

> Human life in common is only made possible when a majority comes together which is stronger than any separate individual and which remains united against all separate individuals. The power of this community is then set up as "right" in opposition to the power of the individual, which is condemned as "brute force." This replacement of the power of the individual by the power of a community constitutes the decisive step of civilization. The essence of it lies in the fact that the members of the community restrict themselves in their possibilities of satisfaction, whereas the individual knew no such restrictions.[22]

Freud used the primal horde story to interpret the logic of civilization given above, its wish to use collective solidarity to reach stable and peaceful circumstances, and renouncing violence ("brute force"). He used this story also to present civilization's perpetuation of the feeling of discontent, which he traced to the collective repression of erotic desire and the supervening demands of instincts, including what he called "death instincts." He considered this generationally repeated repression to be a fundamental paradox—an irrational, unsatisfactory situation from which there is no escape—that marked the beginning of civilization and accounted for both erotic and violent behavior.[23]

---

includes education and nurturing. Civilization in English tends instead to imply cities, industry, buildings, and money.

20. All in the *Standard Edition: Totem and Taboo* (1913): vol. 18; *Group Psychology and the Analysis of the Ego* (1921): vol. 18; *The Future of an Illusion* (1927) and *Civilization and Its Discontents* (1930): vol. 21.

21. This account is from *Totem and Taboo,* and references Darwin.

22. Freud, *Standard Edition,* 21:95.

23. Commentary on the wider and more general use of the term "instinct" is given in chapter 10.

Freud expressed a clear sense of the difference between illusion and reality. The belief in the involved, caring God was the illusion; his scientific explanation the reality. The progress of civilization, Freud implies, involves accepting the limited authority of scientific explanation—his own—because it is real as a replacement for the absolute authority of fantasy, the abstraction of God's existence.[24] As a scientist, Freud is an advocate, a comprehending protector of the collective character of culture and civilization, and a person committed to transforming it from its foundation of primitive and childlike forms of thought to, presumably, modern and mature forms such as science. It might be argued that Freud wanted to transform unconscious discomfort to conscious discomfort, or as he formulated in a different context, to transform neurotic suffering into ordinary human sadness. The premium, obviously, is not so much a gain in the quality of life, but in a sense of control over our lives. Thus far in this account, Freud is focused firmly on the eschewing of vain abstraction and the amelioration of daily experience. But now *his* sense of *Kultur* begins to take on too great a sense of abstraction. Civilization is supposed to "protect men against nature and to adjust their mutual relations."[25] If people can enact these purposes consciously and rationally, it would be a gain over reaching these ends through dependency on false beliefs, he argued. An axiom of psychoanalysis is that more conscious control over our lives is better than less control, especially because there is no hope of getting complete control over unconscious forces, instincts, impulses, and so on.

Freud's elaborates his pursuit of control in an early passage in his 1927 *The Future of an Illusion:*

The decisive question [about civilization] is whether and to what extent it is possible to lessen the burden of the instinctual sacrifices imposed on men, to reconcile men to those which must necessarily remain and to provide a compensation for them. It is just as impossible to do without control of the mass by a minority as it is to dispense with coercion in the work of civilization. For masses are lazy and unintelligent; they have no love for instinctual renunciation, and they are not to be convinced by argument of its inevitability; and the individuals composing them support one another in giving free rein to their indiscipline. It is only

---

24. Freud did not exaggerate the power of science. He did not claim that psychoanalytic explanation was lawful in the sense that physicists claim nature is lawful. His citation of science as a reliable authority is juxtaposed with the autocratic abstraction of God, used by the Church in his time to affirm its authoritarian identity. Yet his sense of the reliability of science did not yield any new understanding of the discontent of civilization; he left the matter in the category of paradox.

25. Freud, *Standard Edition*, 21:89.

through the influence of individuals who can set an example and whom masses recognize as their leaders that they can be induced to perform the work and undergo the renunciations on which the existence of civilization depends. All is well if these leaders are persons who possess superior insight into the necessities of life and who have risen to the height of mastering their own instinctual wishes. But there is a danger that in order not to lose their influence they may give way to the mass more than it gives way to them, and it therefore seems necessary that they shall be independent of the mass by having means to power at their disposal. To put it briefly, there are two widespread human characteristics which are responsible for the fact that the regulations of civilization can only be maintained by a certain degree of coercion—namely, that men are not spontaneously fond of work and that arguments are of no avail against their passions.[26]

This passage presents what is usually taken to be a peripheral feature of psychoanalysis, the main focus of which is on the individual psychology of members of privileged classes. After he became established, Freud tried to apply what he thought he understood about individuals growing up in families to the whole of Western civilization. From the vantage point of his own social class, Freud judged that the "masses" were intractable, lazy, and undisciplined. Leaders are supposed to establish for everyone else the means of self-control and then to hold, themselves, the *"means to power"* necessary to civilization, even when the rule of law, or the community, overtakes the individual. The leaders act to establish the best illusion for all to accept and to force everyone into orderly lives by hoarding the means to power. Freud claims his rationality to be superior to illusions that enhance the sense and feeling of individual self-control. Over and above the principle that unconscious forces can overtake an individual at any moment is the principle that the majority of people *must be controlled by a minority:* that is, "maintained by a certain degree of coercion." His social fears have to do with the fickle mob and the possibility of a malevolent leader or oligarchy coming to power. His best-case view of civilization is that leaders like himself provide guidance to those having trouble with "instinctual renunciation."[27] In view of his personal experience as a prospective leader, one should not be surprised at his continuing pessimism. At the moments of his writing these later works, the mobs were gathering and the malevolent leader growing in power next door to him.

---

26. Freud, *Standard Edition*, 21:7–8.

27. Freud's attitude could be compared with Humboldt's during the founding of the University of Berlin a century earlier: that of the benevolent philosopher-king (discussed in chapter 2).

In reviewing Freud's work today, it is helpful (and increasingly common among those who read his works analytically and politically) to think more deliberately of his gendered identity.[28] As a man Freud may have been in an untenable position. His opponents were other men. His friends were other men. As a member of the masculine gender, he had to have remained within its social, psychological, political, and cultural boundaries. In his views on the fundamental bisexuality of people; his interest in women; and his having inspired and welcomed many women, including his daughter, to his line of work he was—perhaps—different from most men. But he nevertheless participated in the ways of thought that had the historical momentum of as many millennia back as we may go. His work shows his habitual, regular, automatic return to the male-identified mind as his point of reference for his psychological considerations that were in principle meant to apply to all people. His interest in and movements toward women and non–heterosexually identified people suggest his responsiveness to the overwhelming presence of these others in human society. But in each of these moves, the masculine perspective was a worldview for which no alternative could be imagined, much less put into practice.

As a man, he was one of countless figures who would not associate the character, purpose, style, or feeling of his work with a gender identity that might be other than it was.[29] It is possible to interpret Freud's sense that a minority of people must rule the majority as something deriving from his cultural position in Europe. It is also possible to interpret his stress on control and personal renunciation from moral considerations that are shared by many cultures and genders. But it is essential to bear in mind that the minority that Freud described as possibly hoarding the "means to power," coercing the masses, and providing leadership has been, without exception in history, men.

It might be surmised that Freud did not forget this fact. In *Group Psychology and the Analysis of the Ego* (1921), the only two specific groups he considers are the church and the army. He notes the involuntary and coercive quality of

28. In addition to the works of Dorothy Dinnerstein and Nancy Chodorow, Jessica Benjamin's *The Bonds of Love: Psychoanalysis Feminism and the Problem of Domination* (New York: Pantheon, 1988), belongs among other feminist analyses valuing talk therapy while rejecting the masculine orientation of his family romance and phallic orientation. A strong critique of Freud's androcentrism appears in Robin Tolmach Lakoff and James C. Coyne, *Father Knows Best: The Use and Abuse of Power in Freud's Case of Dora* (New York: Teachers College P, 1993).

29. His response to Mill's *The Subjection of Women* (Cambridge, MA: MIT P, 1970) shows that when given the chance, he rejected that choice. See note 33, below. However, Julie Nelson suggests that Mill's wishes for a quantitative economics may also be described as derived from an assumed male worldview. Julie Nelson, *Economics for Humans* (Chicago: U of Chicago P, 2006), 23.

membership in these groups. He notes their hierarchical organization and their overarching dependency on the total authority of the leader and the god figure. He characterizes the leader as "a kind of elder brother; he is their substitute father."[30] He explores at some length the "libidinal" ties among the members and he inquires into the psychology of the "panic" that can destroy a military group. All of these issues bear directly on the fact that the members are men. Freud, however, does not consider the gender constituencies of the groups as part of his problem. Rather, the assumption of their masculine makeup is so ordinary *that it does not call for scientific or scholarly scrutiny*. The assumption of male leadership of society is an element in the total mediation achieved by the language and laws created by men. Closely related to this issue, in respect to the masculine constituency, is the ordinary character of coercive measures used to maintain group integrity. But after acknowledging the presence of "severe punishment" and "persecution" within the group, he offers this: "It is quite outside our present interest to enquire why these associations need such special safeguards."[31] Again, Freud's own political placement accounts in part for this purposeful omission. But it seems to be the case that, in view of the historic illusions of men's gender discussions, Freud's perspective did not include a priority for taking account of the consequences of *political* gender identity, consequences such as gang rape, assassination, and war. What makes this a reasonable judgment is the following passage from *Civilization and Its Discontents*:

> Furthermore, women soon come into opposition to civilization and dis-
> play their retarding and restraining influence—those very women who,
> in the beginning, laid the foundations of civilization by the claims of
> their love. Women represent the interests of the family and of sexual
> life. The work of civilization has become increasingly the business of

---

30. Freud, *Standard Edition*, 18:94.

31. Freud, *Standard Edition*, 18:93. However, Pierre Bourdieu has filled in some of the blanks. He reflects on the guilt and shame felt by the gang: "Like honour—or shame, its reverse side, which we know, in contrast to guilt, is felt *before others*—manliness must be validated by other men, in its reality as actual or potential violence, and certified by recognition of membership of the group of 'real men.' A number of rites of institution, especially in educational or military milieu, include veritable tests of manliness oriented toward the reinforcement of male solidarity. Practices such as some gang rapes—a degraded variant of the group visit to the brothel, so common in memoirs of bourgeois adolescents—are designed to challenge under test to prove before others their virility in its violent reality. . . . [These practices] . . . dramatically demonstrate . . . their dependence on the judgment of the male group." Pierre Bourdieu, *Masculine Domination* (Palo Alto, CA: Stanford UP, 2001), 52.

men, it confronts them with ever more difficult tasks and compels them to carry out instinctual sublimations of which women are little capable. Since a man does not have unlimited quantities of psychical energy at his disposal, he has to accomplish his tasks by making an expedient distribution of his libido. What he employs for cultural aims he to a great extent withdraws from women and sexual life. His constant association with men, and his dependence on his relations with them, even estrange him from his duties as a husband and father. Thus the woman finds herself forced into the background by the claims of civilization and she adopts a hostile attitude towards it.[32]

Although one may want to pay attention to Freud's acknowledgment of the *involuntary* exclusion of women from civilization, a comprehensive reading cannot overlook the transcendent role played by civilization. From the beginning, women's contribution to civilization has been to lay its foundation "by the claims of their love." These claims are pushed into the background,[33] along with the claims of family, childrearing, and domestic life in general. Thus, while "the work of civilization has become increasingly the business of men," this is so only in the respect that civilization's work has demanded more and more of men and thus can spare less and less attention to women's claims of love and family. Freud is getting to a point he has made repeatedly: civilization has been purged of erotic and domestic life as if it were proceeding along this necessary path. Women as a political, gendered class could not be included in progressing civilization only because civilization could not accommodate the erotic and the domestic. Freud's notice of the increasing association of men with one another is also subordinate to the transcendent march of civilization, and in any case something for which men as a class could not possibly be held responsible.

Freud did not describe women as a gendered class in society. *The Origin of Species* was published in 1859, but John Stuart Mill's *The Subjection of Women* was published in 1869.[34] Freud translated this work about "the legal subordina-

---

32. Freud, *Standard Edition*, 21:103–104.

33. As they are in *Ecclesiastes*.

34. And was possibly written by his partner (and wife from 1851 to 1858), Harriet Taylor—or at least with her, according to Peter Gay, *Freud: A Life for Our Time* (New York: Norton, 1988). However, Susan Moller Okin, in her edition of *The Subjection of Women* (New York: Hackett, 1988) says that the book was written in 1861, three years after the death of Harriet Taylor, and was withheld from publication until 1869. Okin assumes that this is Mill's work. See also Susan Moller Okin, "John Stuart Mill's Feminism: The Subjection of Women and the Improvement of Mankind," *Mill's The Subjection of Women*, ed. Maria H. Morales (Lanham, MD: Rowman and Littlefield, 2005), 24–51.

tion of one sex to the other"[35] in 1883, while he was courting Martha Bernays. He complained about its humorlessness, its error in thinking that women were seriously oppressed, and its failure to acknowledge that "nature" has destined woman, "through beauty, charm, and sweetness," to stay out of the competition in public life and remain an "admirable ideal."[36] Peter Gay observes that this conservative opinion is remarkable given how revolutionary psychoanalysis had subsequently become, but it is actually consistent with Freud's never-abandoned view that public society is a place for men: he could not see why people claimed otherwise.

In this way, Freud's arrival at a paradox of how civilization is perpetuated becomes a masculine paradox, a paradox only because men alone are overseeing the repression, suppression, coercion, and enslavement of other men and women. By "finding" the Oedipus story saturating the stories, myths, families, and societies of Western civilization, Freud provides a description of *masculine* civilization, and not just civilization. Whether or not the story of the primal horde is established with the evidence of relics, bones, or other materials—How could it ever be?—it is clearly a story of what takes place every day in every society: the gathering of men—sometimes boys—into clubs, gangs, groups, mobs, armies, teams, taskforces, parliaments, congress, and so forth, in the service of either opposing those above (less frequently) or coercing those below, and always, always in the name of justice, social order, or civilization. Because civilization is so decisively constructed with men's institutions, the figure of the primal horde is regularly and profoundly true. And because it is so true, albeit in an unanticipated sense, it has been discredited as science. Freud himself, honoring science, could not pursue it too far, could not announce it without hedging and apology, even though its gang psychology spoke quite loudly to describe the common experience of women, Jews, dissenters, heretics, and others who spoke up in Central Europe. The primal horde is a description of the *politics of civilization now,* rather than the evolutionary science of how civilization began.

This reading of the primal horde account suggests how the Oedipus complex is also the scene of Freud's and civilization's repression, although not in the sense explained by Freud. What seems overwhelmingly true in human history is not that little boys wish to kill their fathers and marry their mothers, but that older men—fathers—gather into groups and send their sons off to die in wars.[37] Powerful men and ordinary soldiers in war (and often enough in societies

---

35. Mill, *Subjection,* 3.

36. Gay, *Freud,* 38–39.

37. As is dramatized in Arthur Miller's play, *All My Sons,* in which Joe Keller learns that his selfishness is responsible for the death of the aircraft pilots fighting for his country, his way of life. Several of Miller's plays present this reversal of Freud: the fathers, not the sons, want to do the killing and want to demean women sexually. The sons then learn this way of the world and perpetuate the cycle. If the sons wish to break the

not at war) gang rape the conquered women. Contrary to Freud's insinuation that the Oedipus complex is "instinctual"[38]—a term used to pretend to identify what is not understood—the fathers' killing of their sons is a historical fact, well documented, even commonplace, and reported—if obliquely—through the provocative story of Abraham and Isaac in Genesis: "God" told Abraham to sacrifice Isaac. Freud, like other men, used his sense of implication in men's behavior as the ground for tracing aggression, violence, and killing to the imagination of little boys rather than showing that men, not boys, teach and learn killing throughout history. It is noteworthy that the abuse of women is not a category that Freud applies to men. Freud's insight into language and society was paralyzed by his not having emerged from the rules of Greek, Latin, and German academic rationalism and its support system.[39]

Freud had introduced into cultural discussions a process by which the use of language ameliorated psychological suffering and depression in individuals. When he turned his attention to groups and the aggregate of cultural groups, he no longer seemed to have confidence in the efficacy of language: "arguments are of no avail against [men's] passions."[40] Because of this belief, he comes to advocate what Plato is claimed to have advocated: the coercive rule by an elite. Freud's sense of hierarchical androcentrism prevented him from extending his therapeutic experience with language to groups and to society as a whole. When he refers to the angry mobs and lazy, ignorant masses, does he include women? Freud came to his pessimism about civilization partly because of World War I and partly because he thought the "claims of love and family," which were not part of the war-making apparatus, were also not a part of civilization. Freud's estimation of the fate of human societies is strongly connected to his sense that the foundations of civilized life are superintended by men who themselves need to be ruled by even more powerful men. There are few, if any, signs in these writings that Freud thought that war was a male-coded enterprise—and that it was *men,* and not *men and women,* who are unable to renounce violence. In spite of the fact that his own technique of dealing with suffering was verbal, this technique was discarded in his discussions of the fate of civilization. Freud's rootedness in male psychology occulted the possibility that the same media that would ameliorate personal unhappiness, language and conversation, could play a

cycle, they are excluded from the club. Arthur Miller, *All My Sons: A Play in Three Acts* (New York: Reynal and Hitchcock, 1947).

38. A term discussed critically in chapter 10.

39. Bourdieu's comments, cited above, also help to persuade us that the Oedipal problem lies with adult men, and not with the wish fantasies of children: adult men are usually in position to exercise choices of violence and coercion.

40. Freud, *Standard Edition,* 21:8.

role in the collective tasks of avoiding war and violence and help the processes of human survival in nature.

Freud was one of the first to bring the materiality of language into collective awareness and to use it toward what he thought were therapeutic purposes.[41] He showed how the articulation of dream experiences, and subsequently of interpersonal experiences more generally, could lead an individual to a different conduct of life. Psychoanalytic treatment, talk therapy, presupposes and has come to depend more elaborately on the materiality of language. Freudian orthodoxy was radically revised over the last century because the uses of language that seemed to work for some individuals had little value when applied to collective, social situations, particularly those that included both men and women and that included families and communities. Androcentrism kept Freud focused on the family romance. But the culture at large could not see, as much of today's culture does not see, that treating the family as the erotic and affective foundations of civilization also places men as a class as the government of civilization. Freud's social struggle can be traced to his considering male supremacy to be axiomatic.[42] As a result, his insight about the efficacy of a materialist use of language could not reach a more general or universal applicability.

IV. It's a Paradox

It is acknowledged by critics and scholars that Freud's writings on civilization derived from the collective depression in Europe after World War I. His *Beyond the Pleasure Principle*, which speculated about a "death instinct," began this series of writings.[43] He did not seem troubled by the absurdity of calling death an instinct. Like other abstractions given as explanations, the inference of a death instinct is authorized by an accepted body of understanding—a lore of some kind—in this case Darwin's evolutionary formulations. Within the idiom of scientific authority, stipulating a death instinct alongside a life or love instinct had a certain comforting, plausible symmetry. Who does not want understanding of why our lives are ultimately surrendered? By offering this explanation, Freud steps into the role of medium, as this thought—the stipulation of a death instinct—is a response to the war and not a feature of individual psychoanalytic treatment.

Freud's paradox is this: all human behavior is governed by instinct; war behavior brings death; therefore war making follows the death instinct, *and must*

---

41. However, as has been perceived by several critics, his conduct of therapy depended on the autonomy of the therapist and the compliance of the patients, not an egalitarian circumstance.

42. Notice his lack of generosity toward Mill (see p. 275, above), who had different premises about gender.

43. *Totem and Taboo* excepted.

therefore be inevitable. If the term "instinct" were not there, or if there were no habit of searching for a universal principle of behavior, Freud would not have reached the point of paradox.[44]

Men who have meant well and who have tried to understand the road to peace have more often than not reached a point of paradox: the recursive resort to war and killing is a "paradox" when it is assumed that all people are "good" and want to do no harm. Often, paradox as a final explanation seems honest, but the same people who arrive at paradox with regard to war have not considered what Virginia Woolf wrote, directed toward men: "[T]o fight has always been the man's habit, not the woman's."[45] If Woolf's reading of history is folded into the discussion of war making, there is no paradox. When a paradox is advanced as a conclusive description of a social problem, those examining the issue are missing something. More likely, they already know that men, rather than men and women, are making war, and put this thought out of discussion: they are repressing it. Claiming that a paradox exists in reality (rather than only in logic) is a false invocation of logic when accurate perception is needed. In logic, one can say that a premise is true in all possible worlds. But if we are speaking of people's experience, there is only one world, the real world, where there are no premises, and no universal assumptions, that apply all the time. Academic language has followed Freud in its reliance on paradox to cope with repressed understanding of actual experience.

Most theodicy falls into paradox as it faces "the problem of evil." Often what people call evil takes the form of disease and natural disaster, which leads some to ask why God permitted such things to happen. The same sort of questions arise about men's violence against others, especially against those weaker than they are. Referring to the latter case as the problem of evil is an abstraction without a referent. The obfuscation provided by the phrase's abstract reference is deliberate. More specific and accurate phrases might be "the problem of natural

---

44. R. M. Sainsbury's *Paradoxes* (Cambridge: Cambridge UP, 2006) is a useful starting point that could speak to my several citations of paradoxes in this book. Sainsbury claims that paradoxes "are associated with crises in thought and with revolutionary advances. . . [leading us to] come to grips with key issues" (1). Yet in each case that this study examines, the simple question Who cares? easily casts doubt on the admirable effort made by this author to take paradoxes seriously. Try this answer to the barber paradox: If the barber shaves everyone who does not shave himself, who shaves the barber? If paradoxes are, as a result, understood as jokes, this conclusion casts a different light on those writers who rely on paradox to conclude their analysis of urgent social problems. The ease with which the universalist premises of paradoxes are accepted is the source of all the time wasted entertaining them outside the field of formal logic. Believers of such premises also believe in Chuchad (see chapter 1, section 3).

45. Woolf, *Three Guineas* (New York: Harvest, 1966), 6. Woolf's discrediting of paradoxical explanation is discussed in chapter 11, section 3.

disaster" and "the problem of men's violence." The problem of evil often uses another all-purpose category, God, to be a transcendental space into which the alleged paradox is unloaded. If you believe in God, the paradox is deferred into God's will; if you don't believe in God, it remains a paradox. Repeatedly in discussions of war, violence, and other "evils," scholars struggling for insight ultimately shrug at the terrible paradox they encounter when they try to find a solution.[46] Alternatively, they become solemn, as God's mysterious purposes are thought to be beyond the limits of the comprehension of human beings.

The text of Koheleth is an archetypal response to this search for understanding, and he provides none but the religious solution. The problem of evil is cited: one good man in a thousand and no good women are to be found. People labor in vain. Effort does not produce success. Understanding and wisdom are unrecognized. Knowledge increases pain. But the solution is to follow God's commandments and love your wife. "Vanity" is how things are. Whether or not Koheleth really meant his conclusion about serving God could qualify as one of the two traditional solutions to the paradox of the vanity of civilization. What is relevant is that the writing of this book, one of "many," is "man's" response to the frustrating paths of people's lives described by the author.

The structure of the reasoning toward paradox depends on Aristotle's principle of non-contradiction: for example, either there is free will or determinism. The debate continues to show how supposedly paradoxical it is that both can exist, and there is thus plenty of work for scholastics or anyone else who takes pleasure in examining extended logical permutations or who believes that hairsplitting brings credible results. Abandoning the universalist premise—insistence on God's omniscience—makes the paradox go away, and the matter of free will is entertained in contexts of living people who make choices. The gesture of the solemn authoritative thinker is to stipulate a contradiction that coerces the uninformed into an adherence to the universal premise, while their (the thinkers') correct observation of how things are—people have free will but need to learn how to use it in social relations—is pointed toward the casuistical argument that ends in paradox. The correct perception of how people use free will is therefore not ignored, but removed to the context of those in a position to say "which [meaning or person] is master"—in a position to provide a single authoritative reading. However, if figures such as Freud are found to make the same gestures with language as have been made historically by the perpetrators of what Freud referred to pejoratively as illusion, perhaps it is worth considering that what Freud has in common with the superintendents of superstition is the masculine gender and its presumption of supremacy.

---

46. This issue is elaborated in chapter 11, especially in the discussion of Konrad Lorenz's *On Aggression*, trans. Marjorie Kerr Wilson (New York: Harcourt, Brace and World, 1966).

Paradoxes are characteristic of uses of language that accept the universal applicability of an abstraction. In ordinary experience, some things are not understood and then identified as paradox. Calling them "mysteries" has been one way of identifying them, but even that term suggests that there is a solution somewhere, sometime. Paradoxes are identified and announced by those with access to language, people who can formulate the language in such a way that attracts attention and appeals to our continuous need for understanding. But if paradoxes are taken to be material rather than verbal or mental, if they are understood to be descriptive only of *logical* formulations, if they function as specific political gestures, this function must have been undertaken by specific individuals or groups whose political interests are served by that function. Identifying the political function makes it possible to examine the mutual implication of language gestures and social context without resorting to an imaginary spiritual status of language or to the unknown reference of abstractions. The political gesture of those who declare paradoxes about social life is to place themselves in the position of saying, "I don't really know" and "I am not responsible."

The university as an institution has supported its scholarly membership in order to supplement its curtailing access to language through its declaration of paradoxes at key junctures of potential insight. Because in the early university, logic played such an influential a role in the study of all subject matters, explanation by paradox played a prominent part in the development of the institutional entity we now recognize as the university. This institution is not simply a place or a context. It is the source of understanding which languages are to be used on which occasions, of the power to use language at all or to be silent, and of the power to judge the uses of language by all people, especially its own constituents.

V. Agonism

In the early university, the Greek rhetorical tradition combined with Aristotelian logic in the formal disputation that certified degree candidates. This was how men were prepared for public life as churchmen, lawyers, or political leaders. In *Orality and Literacy*, Walter Ong extols this tradition,[47] partly because it was in Latin—a learned language that took men out of their native vernaculars and its domestic feelings—and partly because it was active, vital, and manly. Ong suggests that there is something valuable about competition,[48] fighting, win-

---

47. His characterization is considered at greater length in chapter 9, section 5.

48. Valerie Miner and Helen E. Longino, eds., *Competition: A Feminist Taboo?* (New York: Feminist P, 1987). Competition is a practice, a premise, and a common expectation about "how things are." It is contested on the ground that it is male coded. Chapter 10 discusses of its role in evolutionary thinking.

ning, and character building.[49] He also finds it *natural* for men. As far as can be discerned today, verbal agonism was a fundamental identifying characteristic of university life until perhaps the nineteenth century.

Deborah Tannen, characterizing contemporary American society as an "argument culture," says that "[o]ur schools and universities, our ways of doing science and approaching knowledge, are deeply agonistic." She relates this agonism to the academic tradition and training in debate.[50] It is so common to teach through argument and learn to argue that other ways of academic functioning are unknown.

Arthur Brittan observes that arguing in the contemporary university is embedded in an elaborate hypocrisy that shows an alternating disclosure and repression of competition, hostility, and jealousy:

> Take the university as an example. Here reason is supposed to be the supreme value. The Western liberal university is theoretically built on the bedrock of open scholarship, supposedly available to all. They are supposed to be free of gender and race discrimination. . . . [T]he point I am making is what we all know, namely that the university is not a community of democratic scholars disinterestedly pursuing the question for truth. . . . [I]t is a morass of petty jealousies and betrayals. Those of us who make the grade, who get to the top of the academic pile, spend a great deal of our time denigrating the work of others. We compete with each other in ways which are no different from the cut-throat world of business . . . Moreover, we resent some of [students'] abilities. We see them as potential rivals in scholarship, as possible threats to our academic reputation. . . . [W]e [men] have not recognized our masculinism, our commitment to gender inequality, our sexual objectification of women. The university is no different in this respect than any other institution, except that it glosses violence more successfully. Violence is often hidden behind a rhetorical smokescreen—it is couched in the language of academic "one upmanship,". . . [whose] aim is to hurt and diminish its object.[51]

---

49. As discussed in chapter 8, this was often far from the case. Frequent violence broke out, and the responses to it were kept within university walls. Sentiments were often of a fighting sort, if actual behavior usually stopped short of killing.

50. "Students at [medieval] institutions were trained not to discover the truth but to argue either side of an argument." Deborah Tannen, *The Argument Culture: Moving from Debate to Dialogue* (New York: Random House, 1998), 257–258.

51. Arthur Brittan, *Masculinity and Power* (New York: Blackwell, 1989), 203–204.

Brittan's description of today's university is similar to the extended accounts[52] of the early university, accounts which do not include hypocrisy[53] as a behavioral feature: early universities took the competitive style as well as its misogynist orientation in stride as part of its homogeneously male culture. Instead of habitual physical violence in today's agonism, repressed violence emerges indirectly through local backbiting and through elaborately phrased attacks and counterattacks in journals and book reviews. Brittan urges men to recognize their automatic implication in these combative styles; he understands them to be androcentric ("masculinist") gestures.

Agonism in universities has affected uses of language and has depended on the assumption of language transparency. Because winning an argument in which the two sides held a common premise was more important than deciding on which were the most desirable premises, disputes removed the uses of language—the phraseology choices, the diction, the vocabulary—from the processes of evaluation of assumptions.[54] Since many of the arguments were about the Eucharist and the Trinity, considering either of these an abstraction (by a nominalist) and therefore not transparent would yield the conclusion that *one cannot tell* what their reference in actual experience is, beyond the reference to another verbal formulation—a conclusion churchmen found unacceptable. Universities and the language they used, Latin, limited access to language of any but those who were committed to the fraternal formulations of Latin speakers and other supporters of the church organization. Neither the curriculum nor the means of certification was neutral, as the church discourse was official and thus not tolerant of alternative ways of speaking and writing, or of usages in other languages. That language problems are repressed is also a key factor: when there is only one category of anything, this means as a practical matter that other possible categories are not seen: the single category is a total mediator.[55] If it is not given in the official discourse, it is not relevant.

---

52. Discussed in chapters 8 and 9.

53. Men's hypocrisy about violence is a principal way of concealing the continuation of the culture of combat and violence. Often, in male-centered films, a male protagonist is depicted as committed to rejecting violence altogether. In *From Here to Eternity* (dir. Fred Zinnemann, 1953), Pruitt "will not fight"; in *First Blood* (dir. Ted Kotcheff, 1982), Rambo will not fight; in *History of Violence* (dir. David Cronenberg, 2005), Tom Stall will not fight. Ultimately all three prove to be the masters of violence, and all three films show the provocation as having justified the protagonist's heroic violent retributions.

54. This is Janice Moulton's main point in "A Paradigm of Philosophy: The Adversary Method," *Discovering Reality: Feminist Perspectives on Epistemology, Metaphysics, Methodology, and Philosophy of Science,* ed. Sandra Harding and Merrill B. Hintikka (Dordrecht: Reidel, 1983), 149–164.

55. Discussed in chapter 1, section 3.

Total mediation is something akin to the way argument as a mode of discourse works in academic life today: if it is not an argument, it does not really count. The fact that argument is quietly an agonistic style—one that requires competition, combat, and winning and losing—is repressed, or if not repressed, rationalized as being both reasonable and exciting. This, too, is a relic of the all-male institutions in which it was normal to fight and produce winners and losers. The mores of competition and contest are so common today that few people think we can do without them.[56] In economics, market competition is the ideological foundation of today's economic style, even though every competitor actually strives for circumstances in which all competition is eliminated—monopolies; if there is only one source for a product or service, it is a total mediator.[57] Even though no competition—a monopoly—is the unspoken goal of all economic competitors, the ideology hypocritically and mendaciously maintains competition as the publicly announced ideal for economic activity. Total mediation in language takes place when there is only one acceptable form of creating texts, or only one form of achievement that will win certification in the university (disputation in earlier periods, and argument today).

Premises were understood to be given in transparent language to begin with. This was the language of men, the only authoritative language there was.[58] In this language, in order to facilitate good standing among men, members repressed tendencies of sympathy and kinship by invoking Aristotle's not-A or the excluded middle. Men usually knew that A may not be A, that both A and not-A may be taking place at once, and that the middle may not be excluded. Male scholars also knew that they must not admit this as they take their places in the cohort of other men.[59] Usually the not-A has to be repressed. Sometimes the not-A represents a different but interesting belief; sometimes it is a different nation, race, or family; sometimes it is a different custom of eating or praying; sometimes it is a different language, or a different subject matter. But most often,

---

56. In every academic department I have known, the proposal to eliminate competition for prizes has drawn howls of outrage, partly because of the likely offense given to the prize donors. Their economic leverage censors any attempt to change the political *Sprachspiele* of recognizing students' achievements. Increasingly, however, the sharing of prizes among two or more students has become accepted.

57. Economic theories and their alternatives are discussed in chapter 11.

58. This fact was recognized by Walter Ong in *Orality and Literacy: The Technologizing of the Word* (New York: Methuen, 1982). However, neither Ong nor anyone else has claimed that the language of men was a dialect or something with an independent identity. Rather the phrase "language of men" refers to how men speak and interact with one another when in all-male groups.

59. Ruth Hubbard, discussed in chapter 9, gives a modern example of men on the brink of admission, then noticing, then pulling back.

most decisively, most loudly, the not-A is women, as well as traits that have been
associated predominantly with women—some of which are feeling and passion;
dependency; need; care of the body; and candor about sex, childbirth, death, or
other bodily processes.[60] To express doubt about this universal assumption is to
jeopardize membership in the men's community. It is almost impossible for a
male group member publicly to eschew the Aristotelian gesture yet still retain
membership in the community of men.[61]

That violence is just below the surface of university agonism becomes more
apparent when we remember that violence has always been used to teach boys
from the earliest grades onward. In teaching young boys Latin, as Augustine[62]
and others have reported, the *use* of language is suspended in the teaching of
language and bodily pain, instead of language, is inflicted in order to force
obedience. Corporal punishment was also a way of communicating the sacredness of the language. It was supposedly teaching how obedience is related to the
holiness of the language. The justification given by teachers usually was this: it
worked for me, so it will work for you.[63] Because it worked up a point, its cruelty
was rationalized and people deceived themselves into describing such practices
as generous contributions to the child's education. In modern universities, the

---

60. Classical Greek antiquity, which had an acknowledged place for male same-sex
activity, was no less prone to war and violence. Same-sex behavior did not, as it may
today, imply greater kinship with the not-A or the excluded middle. Eva Cantarella
quotes H. I. Marrou: "In my view, love between men is a recurring feature of military
societies," but says that women were segregated by law, rather than accidentally through
military socialization of men. The common factor in those times and ours is male
supremacy as the foundation of gender identity for both sexes. Eva Cantarella, *Bisexuality
in the Ancient World* (New Haven, CT: Yale UP, 2002), 5.

61. Most men probably do not like to fight, but few men would say that they reject
fighting under any circumstances. This feature of men's communities emphasizes how
high the stakes are and shows why the repression of tendencies to reject violence has continued. Poverty and shame are possible, even likely, results of the loss of status in men's
groups. Because of the willingness to move to violence on the part of some men, most
men and women would sooner collaborate with those willing to use force than resist.

62. "[O]bedience to my teachers was proposed to me, as proper in a boy, in order
that in this world I might prosper, and excel in tongue-science. . . . [A]nd yet, if idle in
learning, I was beaten. For this was judged right by our forefathers; and many, passing
the same course before us, framed for us weary paths . . . multiplying toil and grief
upon the sons of Adam." *Confessions of St. Augustine,* ed. Charles W. Eliot (New York:
Classic Books of America, 2009), 11–12.

63. In the Augustine citation, "this was judged right by our forefathers." This is an
example of a false inference: by any measure, it does not follow that what worked for me
will work for you, especially if pain was involved. In order to maintain a masculine style,
the punishing teacher represses the obvious: that there is no need to inflict pain in order
to teach. The practices of corporal punishment in education are related to the supposed
right of parents (fathers) to harm household members as part of upholding their authority.

process of gradually, incrementally cultivating young people is subordinate to teaching that winning a competition—for admission, for support, or in tests taken by many—is the truest sign of learning. Early universities had taught that learning is winning a disputation and that winning a disputation is learning. Such practices, born of men's repression on a collective scale over the centuries, have undercut intellectual life and cast it in terms that do not serve even the men who rely on these practices. The result of these mores and violent practices and the repression that supports them has been the exclusion of women and most men from access to language, from study, from having authorized opinions,[64] and from cultural and political initiatives that could benefit many. These exclusions were marked by outbursts of scapegoating, paranoid hunts for heretics, and three centuries of European (and American) witch-hunting. The authors of the continuously reprinted—over a period of three hundred years—official manual[65] for witch-hunting, trial, and execution were university-trained bishops authorized by the pope to create this manual. Such action was enabled by ecclesiastical custody of an official language that overruled others' language.

Given this history, universities today nevertheless have re-embraced argument, the culture of argument, and the view that everything is an argument.[66] The proliferation of argument practices in contemporary universities in the United States has intensified the use of argument today to such an extent that every piece of academic writing seeks to be understood as an argument.[67] In this approach to writing and academic usage, the ordinary practice of exchanging language gestures is replaced by the learning of a ritual gesture having a comparatively fixed structure. At one point in the recent past, academics ridiculed "the five-paragraph essay" that ninth graders brought to the university as their writing skill. Now so-called college writing is equally reducible to the ritual of a thesis sentence, a claim, a warrant, and a conclusion. In writing pedagogy, students are urged to identify each of these elements of argument specifically. In almost every university, essays in all subjects are expected to be presented in this form. The textbook cited above counts this as a fundamental principle and

---

64. In the words of Koheleth, "the poor man's wisdom is held in contempt, and his words are not heard." (Ecclesiastes 9:16).

65. Heinrich Kramer and James Sprenger, *The Hammer of Witches: A Complete Translation of the* Malleus maleficarum, ed. and trans. Christopher S. Mackay (New York: Cambridge UP, 2009).

66. This is the title of a best-selling textbook for writing courses, first published in 1999. Andrea A. Lunsford, John J. Ruszkiewicz, and Keith Walter, *Everything's an Argument: With Readings* (New York: Bedford St. Martins, 2007).

67. For at least the last three decades, in the application of almost every academic job candidate, there is a sentence that reads, "In my dissertation, I argue. . ." They do not discuss, explore, consider, suggest, research, evaluate, compare, estimate, test, speculate, or imagine. They argue.

teaches that the students' presentations of their understanding have to be in that form or a minor variation of it. It teaches that understanding and arguing are the same thing in academic writing.[68]

Universities, by teaching competition and coercing its practices through grading, periodic inspections of classrooms, questionnaires for students, as well as other actions it considers necessary to everyday functioning, achieve this ideological victory for its protectors and its sponsors. Students *believe* that competing through arguing prepares them for the market. Perhaps, to a degree, it does. But it also censors their ability to see economics or perhaps any human activity as being able to function without competition. Most people could consider alternatives, but the hegemony of competition forces repression: for any person to suggest that competition is harmful, futile, or unproductive, endangers their standing as a so-called team player.

Gerald Graff[69] accepts this principle when he declares that "summarizing and making arguments is the name of the game in academia." The many university subjects, he says, obfuscate what is "in plain view": "learning the moves of the underlying argument game that gives coherence to it all." Believing that making arguments is the main purpose of learning in the university is not different from using the adversarial debate in the medieval university to certify students. If you succeed in learning how to debate (or make arguments in subject-matter courses), that becomes your credential: yet it is the case that no department or discipline has the principal goal of learning to make claims about the subject matter; rather, learning the subject is the goal, and knowing how to use its specific language gestures and discourse styles is considered an essential part of this learning. Among these gestures are reporting, describing, narrating, presenting possibilities, or speculating—depending on what subject matter it is.

The premise that argument is what students should be taught in writing classes is fearful; but it is also doubtful and at least questionable and needs to be examined. Graff contests Deborah Tannen's discussion suggesting there are more than two sides to every question. Here, too, Graff rejects Tannen's perspective, which holds, among other things, that the airing of three or more

---

68. Heather Dubrow has observed that a thesis should be "one important aspect of many essays, not the most important characteristic of all essays." Heather Dubrow, "Thesis and Antithesis: Rewriting the Rules on Writing," *Chronicle of Higher Education* 49.15 (2002): B13. It might be germane to remember that Dubrow is the author of *Genre* (New York: Methuen, 1982), and that that subject teaches us to observe that any writing is—to one degree or another—a mixed genre, as discussed by Bakhtin, Todorow, and Derrida (see chapter 4).

69. Gerald Graff, *Clueless in Academe* (New Haven, CT: Yale UP, 2004), 3. This patronizing title seems to represent among faculty a widely held and comfortable attitude toward students: they are not considered likely to know that they are students who have come to the university to learn about how it functions while learning the subject matters.

points of view are gestures that are socially and politically more productive than the viewing of all issues as having only two sides. Graff's earlier work[70] viewed the conflicts themselves as having only two sides, left and right. Graff took a position above these political disputes, implying that a true academic perspective transcends politics. But the politics he did teach, perhaps without trying, was that two views, left and right, were the *only* ways to articulate issues.[71] The actual effect of such binaries in serious discussion is to present political work as a matter of choosing sides rather than of identifying interests and respecting the interests of several or many parties. University debate teams also boil issues down to two sides, and although debaters may know it is only a debate, the practice is a widely promulgated structure of thinking that communicates its authority through the unquestioned acceptance of this format, just as medieval disputations certified university degree holders. It is a male-coded initiation rite.

The near worship of argument as a solution for teaching the use of language in universities reflects the action of a political use of language that serves a sponsoring authority just as disputation served Church sponsorship of university curricula and certification. Argument is a way that the use of language (speaking and writing) is embedded in the *political* role of the university as an institution protected by established powers.[72] The fact that universities are protected institutions indicates that it is in their interest to limit debate and to limit access to discussion of those with a wide variety of opinions. A situation in which all students—members of the academy—may contribute different points of view is not controllable by university

---

70. Gerald Graff, *Beyond the Culture Wars: How Teaching the Conflicts Can Revitalize American Education* (New York: Norton, 1993) and *Teaching the Conflicts: Curricular Reform and the Culture Wars* (New York: Garland, 1994).

71. Graff includes an autobiographical segment in his book that recounts how his youthful reading about sports laid a foundation for the "heavyweight" books in which he later became interested. In this account, and in the account of Mark Edmundson he cites, no mention is made that the early reading was about *sports*. Many people, even today, consider sports to be a neutral subject, and not an industry and an ideology dedicated almost exclusively to men. Here, too, competition is considered to be the lifeblood of its activity—even though, as the public today is becoming increasingly aware, the actual competition is between franchises for markets and championship players who bring in money. Graff does not mention whether his youthful interest in sports could well have stuck in his perspective to this day and transformed itself into an involvement in the mores of competitive arguing and (should it be said?) *winning*. Mariah Burton Nelson observes that in men's sports, the "last bastion of male domination, . . .[M]ale bonding is based on the illusion of male supremacy, and where all of the visible women are cheerleaders, manly sports set the stage for violence against women." Mariah Burton Nelson, *The Stronger Women Get, the More Men Love Football: Sexism and the American Culture of Sports* (New York: Harcourt Brace, 1994), 6, 7. Many of us in academic life have entered it with such youthful involvements, and it takes some doing to recognize the extent of men's sports culture's effects on us.

72. Discussed in chapter 8.

sponsors. In the early university, logic was used to regulate which arguments were to emerge to begin with; later, science and mathematics were used to that end; today, in addition to technological commitments, economic considerations regulate which issues may be argued; to wit: it is much easier to resist or make friends with the winner of a two-sided argument than it is to manage a complex set of decisions from independent sources. Economic sponsors of universities—corporations—are in a position to manage any result, just as Church sponsors of early universities were in position to regulate (through censorship and repression) the several results that came from academic debates, about, for example, theology and canon law.

Teaching argument as Graff proposes instructs students how to comply with these unseen constraints. Students and many others are not actively informed (by those who *can* tell them) about the politics of protection and sponsorship of the schools they attend. They are not informed about the regimenting purpose of teaching argumentative writing that distracts students from concentrating on the principle of telling the truth regardless of its actual uncertainty and complexity. Graff beats his own breast[73] about silently complying with so-called intellectual behavior—talk— that intimidates others and makes him pretend to understand when he actually does not. Such behavior on the part of intellectuals is a form of bullying that is common in academic life. Those who seek recognition find it necessary to appease such bul- lying even in informal conversation with senior figures in the hierarchy. But rather than identifying this behavior for what it is, Graff frets about his own inability to explain to friends and relatives outside academic life what he does.

In this autobiographical segment, Graff's account also shows the key element of repression in the academic tradition: the knowledge that academic mores were developed in all-male societies for their own use and benefit, and which functioned for centuries to maintain this exclusivity. For people today, access to language means recognizing its materiality and the history of the academic repression of materiality. Our responsibility as teachers and scholars is to present the subject matter of language in ways that speak to all people.

VI. Protection as a Principle of Academic Governance

Some have been alarmed about corporate influence in American universities.[74] Eyal Press and Jennifer Washburn discuss[75] how corporations have come to use

---

73. Graff, *Clueless*, 4.

74. For example, Richard Ohmann, "What's Happening to the University and the Professions? Can History Tell?" *Politics of Knowledge: The Commercialization of the University, the Professions, and Print Culture* (Middletown, CT: Wesleyan UP, 2003), 85–123. See also Bill Readings, *The University in Ruins;* Stanley Aronowitz, *The Knowledge Factory: Dismantling the Corporate University and Creating True Higher Learning* (Boston: Beacon P, 2000); and Frank Donoghue, *Last Professors.*

75. Press and Washburn, "The Kept University," *Atlantic Monthly* March 2000: 39–54.

universities for their own ends, how universities have come to think of themselves as corporations, and how faculty members and researchers have behaved in society just as corporations do.[76] This essay and its suggestive title may be startling if one assumes that universities are dedicated to disinterested research and teaching.[77] Press and Washburn say that a university is like a rich man's mistress: living well but only if cooperating with the keeper and agreeing to be used in demeaning ways that must never be announced. Universities' preoccupation with patents and ownership of so-called intellectual property turns their attention from the needs of students and from the pursuit of research projects whose success is not anticipated primarily in commercial terms. Most universities are nonprofit, but they nevertheless pursue research projects that could yield a revenue stream to be shared with the corporate sponsors of those projects. The universities may be satisfied with lower return than are corporations, but the psychology and economics of developing new products are similar in each institution. Both are involved in gaining ownership of medicines, processes, technologies, and even certain biological entities that, if sold to the public, would bring in significant wealth. Thus, Press and Washburn suggest, the universities have been kept—protected—and are, therefore, in a compromised and exploited situation.

The protection of universities provided by corporations is a contemporary form of custody that emerges from a tradition of university protection that began during the period of their founding when they acquired a royal charter and Church sponsorship. The Western university has never been autonomous or governed by institutions that follow the ideals of eighteenth-century German *Lernfreiheit* ("freedom to learn") and *Lehrfreiheit* ("freedom to teach")—or, as we refer to these items, "academic freedom."[78] It is unheard of that a university should function independently of the influence of national governments and Church oversight. Even when state sponsorship became more influential than Church sponsorship, the traditions and privileges of the Church-run academy

---

76. In 1918, Thorstein Veblen described how the purposes of competitive business had made their way into curricula and university management styles. Although his reflection is germane, he views American universities as outside the tradition of the European university. However, the European university was as much a servant to the Church and crown sponsorship as American universities have been to business and corporate institutions. Thorstein Veblen, *The Higher Learning in America: A Memorandum on the Conduct of Universities by Business Men* (Stanford, CA: Academic Reprints, 1954).

77. The ideal articulated by Brittan, *Masculinity and Power.*

78. Sheldon Rothblatt, *The Modern University and Its Discontents* (New York: Cambridge UP, 1997), 24. Academic freedom derives from four Enlightenment values sought by German neohumanist university reformers: *Bildung,* comprehensive education; *Wissenschaft,* the formal scholarly or scientific knowledge established by disinterested research; *Lehrfreiheit,* "the right to teach one's competence"; and *Lernfreiheit,* "the right of students to have open access to knowledge."

remained in effect. Corporate "keeping" of today's American universities is more of the same: corporations work in tandem with governments just as the church once did to found, sponsor, and protect universities. Nonprofit private universities run on endowments donated by corporate members of boards of trustees. State universities also accumulate endowments. The historical sequence of protection went from the church to monarchies, to democratic states, and to corporations. Some universities, under the influence of Enlightenment ideals of liberty—such as those in Germany at the beginning of the nineteenth century—moved toward autonomy, but university life, until very recently and because admission was restricted to the sons of privileged families to begin with, had no problem with being protected and sponsored by wealthier institutions—benefactors, or in Press and Washburn's terms, keepers. Today, because people start school as small children and proceed through postsecondary education in relatively fluent fashion, it occurs to few university students that they are in a protected institution.[79] Even less frequently, university students today feel the effects of protection in their studies and career preparation. Finally, and most pertinent to the issues presented in this book, few notice how the university as a protected institution affects our common language—and through that medium influences how, more generally in society, we conduct our social relations. The fact that universities are protected is one of the most enduring means of perpetuating longstanding hierarchical and androcentric social arrangements. This perpetuation takes place through the teaching of language values and styles of discourse that date back to Plato and Aristotle.

On our postsecondary diplomas, it says that our degree entitles us to "rights and privileges": we are ready to go to something like a next stage, or we are qualified in some formal sense in a subject matter or a professional competence. However, its reference is broader and more substantive, and, while concealed in contemporary society, it marks a key role played by scholars in society from antiquity, through the Middle Ages, to the present. In various formal ways scholars have been protected by emperors, popes, and kings. Their rights and privileges were formally declared in edicts and bulls, and enforced by state and Church authorities. Being protected is a tradition, a set of habits and values that, having acquired the momentum of history, is not treated critically but taken for granted. The central issue in this book is the use of language. The presupposed status of the site of its teaching tells about the history of the use of language in the university.

---

79. This is less true of male fraternity members, whose flouting of underage-drinking rules, hazing practices, and cavalier views of date rape are routinely overlooked. However, such behavior must more accurately be identified as entitled, which is a close cousin of protected. Other students, however, are not likely to be aware of the scope of protection by large influential corporations.

CHAPTER EIGHT

The Protected Institution

I. Protection in the Early University

Pearl Kibre traces the tradition of scholarly privileges granted in medieval universities to classical times; the Roman emperors thought that masters of liberal arts "were the chief instruments by which Rome could accomplish her mission to preserve, in the face of the barbarian threat, the civilization and culture which had become largely synonymous with the classical literary tradition."[1] Teachers and scholars were, therefore, formally exempted from a variety of civic duties and obligations, and they were freer than most others to buy certain foods, for example. They were protected from taxation and civil harassment. When power shifted from Rome eastward to Constantinople, similar privileges obtained. They existed for Charlemagne. For seven centuries after Rome, there had been an informal tradition of protecting scholars, and although the rights and privileges often waned or could not be enforced, the tradition remained and was fundamental in the process of establishing the earliest medieval universities and the dozens that followed in early modern Europe. We are perhaps less aware of these privileges today. But when political change threatens these protections, we notice them: political attacks on tenure, a typical scholarly privilege, alert us that scholarly protections are in the hands of others outside the university.

There are many treatises that attempt to identify the origin of universities. Historians agree that there was an originating period for Western universities. During several decades at the end of the twelfth century, groups of scholars in Italy, France, and England were transformed from informal and local associations to publicly recognized bodies of students and teachers, who were referred to at that time as scholars and masters. The key to this change is that public recognition meant that local and national sovereigns, combined with bishops and popes, issued formal documents of recognition. The earliest was the *Privilegium scholasticum* or the *Authentica habita,* issued by Frederick I Barbarossa

---

1. Pearl Kibre, *Scholarly Privileges in the Middle Ages* (Cambridge, MA: Medieval Academy of America, 1962), 4.

for the University of Bologna in 1155.[2] This was a form of constitution issued in response to the demands by students in Bologna for personal security in their studies.[3] Paolo Nardi writes that Frederick "affirmed the pre-eminent value of scientific knowledge, and recognized as praiseworthy and deserving of protection all persons who in pursuit of it were obliged to live far from their own country."[4] The background effects of this order were that students could be tried for offenses by either masters or the bishops—their choice; by inserting the *Habita* into Justinian's *Codex,* Frederick helped to further secularize[5] the Holy Roman Empire; and the masters at Bologna who taught Justinian law were pleased with its having become, so to speak, more official.[6] This was an improvement in the circumstances of learning because the protection and support of the emperor was new and reassuring. A century before Frederick, it was understood in Bologna that "precedents from Roman and canon law could be used to defend papal claims."[7] Marcia Colish notes that Matilda of Tuscany (1045–1115) founded the law school at Bologna because of its usefulness to the pope. Similarly, there was papal and imperial recognition for the University of Paris and Oxford University early in the thirteenth century.[8] The *Authentica* represented civil or secular oversight of the university, an oversight embodied several centuries later in the U.S. Constitution, which delegates education to state governments. Similarly, in Europe national democratic governments now oversee universities.

---

2. Hastings Rashdall, *The Universities of Europe in the Middle Ages,* vol. 1: *Salerno, Bologna, Paris,* ed. F. M. Powicke and A. B. Emden (New York: Oxford UP, 1997), gives the date as 1158 (143). Paolo Nardi, "Relations with Authority," *A History of the University in Europe,* vol. 1: *Universities in the Middle Ages,* ed. Hilde de Ridder-Symoens, gen ed. Walter Rüegg (Cambridge: Cambridge UP, 1992), gives the date as 1155 (78). See also Gabriel Compayre, *Abelard and the Origin and Early History of Universities* (New York: Scribner's, 1893); V. A. Huber, *The English Universities,* vol. 1, trans. Francis W. Newman (London: Pickering, 1843); S. S. Laurie, *Lectures on the Rise and Early Constitution of Universities with a Survey of Mediæval Education, A.D. 200–1350* (London: Kegan Paul, Trench and Co. 1886); Damien Riehl Leader, *A History of the University of Cambridge,* vol. 1: *The University to 1546* (Cambridge: Cambridge UP, 1988); and J. I. Catto, ed., *The History of the University of Oxford,* vol. 1 (Oxford, Clarendon P, 1984).

3. Friedrich Heer, *The Medieval World: Europe 1100–1350,* trans. Janet Sondheimer (London: Phoenix, 1998), 196; Rashdall, *Universities,* vol. 1, chapter 1.

4. Nardi, "Relations," 78.

5. Kibre, *Scholarly,* 11. Kibre notes that the *Habita* applied to students of grammar as well as to law students. She considers that the emperor wanted to protect loyal law students at Bologna, but also to protect the many scholars traveling there from Germany, across the Alps.

6. Nardi, "Relations," 78–79.

7. Marcia L. Colish, *Medieval Foundations of the Western Intellectual Tradition 400– 1400* (New Haven, CT: Yale UP, 1997), 269.

8. In about 1215 the Paris Statutes were instituted, but de facto university existed earlier as a cathedral school.

Just what does state and Church recognition imply about how the institution functions? There are two principles of coherence that operated at once to create the university, and perhaps to keep it in stable form for eight centuries.[9] The first is the association of students and teachers. During the eleventh and twelfth centuries, students had been coming to Bologna from all over Europe to study law, a discipline revived by the new attention to the Justinian code of civil law and by the twelfth-century renewal, often called a renaissance, of culture and mercantile activity in Europe after the Crusades. Similarly, students came from all over Europe to study theology in Paris and Oxford and medicine in Salerno.[10] The students were outsiders and thus considered an alien group by the

---

9. Rashdall observes that "the universities of all countries and all ages are in reality adaptations under various conditions of one and the same institution" (*Universities*, 1:4). Charles Homer Haskins wrote in 1923, comparing the first medieval universities at Bologna and Paris to those in the twentieth century, "The fundamental organization is the same, the historical continuity is unbroken. They created the university tradition of the modern world, that common tradition which belongs to all our institutions of higher learning, the newest as well as the oldest, and which all college and university men should know and cherish." Charles Homer Haskins, *The Rise of Universities* (Ithaca, NY: Cornell UP, 1957), 3. It is widely documented that the 1215 Paris Statutes defined most of the curriculum of universities for the next two to three centuries. Olaf Pedersen suggests how the Church takeover kept the universities stable after early "town and gown" battles toward the end of the fourteenth century: "in the dispute with the professors of religious orders, the pope had gained a position of supremacy over the universities. In the time to come, these submitted one by one to the authority of the Holy See by accepting the statutes that the pope had issued or at least approved. . . . [I]t became more and more common for the statutes not only to define the university structure and form of government, but also the curriculum and textbooks." Olaf Pedersen, *The First Universities: Studium generale and the Origins of University Education in Europe*, trans. Richard North (Cambridge: Cambridge UP, 1997), 187. Documentation of the stability that followed is found in Martha Bronfenbrenner: "No change was made from 1570 to 1858 in the statutes of Oxford; no essential change from 1558 to 1830 in the organization of the University of Leipzig; and no change from 1360 to 1783 in the laws of the theological faculty of Bologna." Martha Ornstein Bronfenbrenner, *The Rôle of Scientific Societies in the Seventeenth Century* (Chicago: U of Chicago P, 1928), 259. Of eighteenth-century Europe, Notker Hammerstein writes that there were "common features of the sciences and the continent-wide predominance of certain academic theories and methods, and of particular methods of teaching." Although the universities developed distinctively, "they became no more than variants of a common European university pattern. This development was inherent in the rationale of their own practice and outlook." Notker Hammerstein, "Epilogue: The Enlightenment," *A History of the University in Europe*, vol. 2: *Universities in Early Modern Europe: 1500–1800*, ed. Hilde de Ridder-Symoens, gen. ed. Walter Rüegg (Cambridge: Cambridge UP, 1996), 630.
    10. A. Lecoy de la Marche, *La chaire française au moyen âge: Specialement au XIIIe siècle* (Paris: Renouard, 1886), 450.

local communities. They were referred to as "nations,"[11] since they organized in groups from the same parts of Europe or spoke the same vernacular. They were "organizations of convenience based on like interests ranging from the welfare of members to a share in the government of the overall university . . . brotherhoods, associations, congregations, corporations, or colleges . . . the living communities in the university towns and cities . . . [in] an unknown, alien environment."[12] As such they were exploited by local landlords and other businesses. In order to curtail these practices, the students formed themselves into an interest group and appealed to local authorities to exercise their civil authority (which included courts and police) to stop these practices. The local government agreed that it was to the advantage of everyone that the students remain to study without being harassed. Rules were thus enacted to control, for example, rent gouging, and the "*universitas*" of students became recognized by Frederick as a more formal collective, as opposed to simply a group with common vocational activities.[13]

As a result of Frederick's edict, their union became viable, with an affirmative purpose—and not that of functioning as an opposition group or an irritant. The students modeled their organization in part on the craft guilds of Europe.[14] As university members, students and teachers functioned as an apprenticeship system (as they do now in graduate education). Rashdall takes some pains to explain that the term "universitas" does not refer to something like "a place for all knowledge" but to the social practice of collectivizing the economic interests of a de facto constituency, as takes place in unions today. After a while, in Bologna, the teachers—the "masters"—came to be included with the students

11. Pearl Kibre, *The Nations in the Medieval Universities* (Cambridge, MA: The Medieval Academy of America, 1948). Jacques Verger writes, "In many universities, especially those with a fairly large recruitment, the students were divided up in terms of their geographical origin, into 'nations.' Thus, there were some twenty nations at Bologna, ten at Orléans, four at Paris, and four also at the main universities of the Holy Roman Empire and of Eastern Europe (Prague, Vienna, Leipzig, Louvain, etc.) and at Salamanca." Jacques Verger, "Patterns," *History*, ed. Ridder-Symoens, 1:39.

12. Rainer Christoph Schwinges, "Student Education, Student Life," *History*, ed. Ridder-Symoens, 1:211.

13. Alan B. Cobban, *The Medieval English Universities* (Berkeley: U of California P, 1988), 2. Jacques Verger indicates that the formal name for the early groups was "*universitas magistrorum et scholarium* of such and such a place" ("the university of masters and students" ["Patterns," 1:37–38]). "The medieval universities were . . . organized communities of individuals responsible, in certain towns, for higher education" (38).

14. Laurie, *Lectures*, 95. Cobban says that the "essence of the medieval university was the academic guild organized for the mutual defence of its members and for the supervision of the teaching regime" (*Medieval*, 8). Ruegg describes a law teachers' strike at Oxford in 1209 that in 1214 led the municipality, with the possible cooperation of the papal legate, "[to grant] the scholars liberties and privileges like those which were provided in Paris." Walter Rüegg, "Themes," *History*, ed. Ridder-Symoens, 1:13.

as belonging to the university; in Paris, the students remained separate and the university identity was relatively magisterial—or, in contemporary terms, identified by the corporate faculty. In Bologna the students and other people assisting in learning and study secured the support of local authorities who came to guarantee more comprehensive formal protections against arrest, prosecution, confiscation of funds, and other actions that would affect local citizens. Thus two salient features of the university at its beginnings are that it is a creature of students' economic and political initiatives and that it is formally protected. Cobban suggests that the archetypal models for the European university, Bologna and Paris, emphasize distinct organizational templates: Bologna being the craft guild model, as it was student initiated; Paris being the corporate or "magisterial" model, in which the teachers were the authoritative figures.[15] The protection from above and outside gave the university what, in contemporary terms, could be called an autonomous corporate identity. Because universities were protected by state and Church,[16] certain immunities and exemptions, in addition to those granted locally, applied; and certain levels of autonomy were granted to universities that were not granted to craft guilds, especially immunity to prosecution in civil courts. Tax breaks also applied to universities, although they did not apply to guilds.

Because these two forms of collective identity, union and protected corporation, are needed to describe the university, there is reason to say that universities from the beginning were in an institutional class by themselves. These are grounds for the plausibility of Rashdall's claim that the *Studium* might stand alongside the *Sacerdotium* and the *Imperium* as the three principal institutions of medieval Europe.[17] Universities became so widespread by the beginning of the sixteenth century—and so similar to one another in form and means of teaching

---

15. Cobban, *Medieval*, 16–17. Verger writes, "A *studium generale* was an institution of higher education founded on, or, at any rate, confirmed in it status by, an authority of a universal nature, such as the pope or (less frequently) the emperor, whose members enjoyed a certain number of rights, likewise universal in their application, which transcended all local divisions (such as towns, dioceses, principalities, and states). These rights concerned . . . the personal status of teachers and students, who were placed under the immediate safeguard of the supreme authority, be it papal or imperial, which had founded the university in question . . . they received from the pope the right to enjoy the revenues from ecclesiastical benefices" ("Patterns," 1:35–36).

16. Olaf Pedersen uses the term "corporations of scholars" to identify the student groups—thus avoiding the union/management binary we Americans might slip into unconsciously (*First*, 78, 213). An example of how state and church worked together before the Reformation to back universities is the founding of King's Hall in Cambridge. Edward II petitioned the pope in 1317 for recognition of its *Studium generale*, and it was given that status in 1318. (Leader, *Cambridge*, 1:78).

17. Rashdall, *Universities*, 1:2.

and certifying students—that in terms of scope, involvement in society, public respect, and practical effect, the network of European universities was indeed comparable to governments and church networks.

There are two fundamental differences between the universities and the other two institutions: universities were *dependent* on church and state; and they had no armies, few independent sources of income, and a jurisdiction that was limited to themselves and even then was subject to church oversight. Although church and state worked with one another—even if they were often at odds—universities depended on the economic and legal support of both. Universities' relationship with church and state was analogous to adolescent boys' relationship with their parents: they could do a great deal on their own, but they needed the family car; they might do well in school, but they needed those checks from Mom and Dad to come in on a regular basis;[18] they may be brilliant on the athletic field, but few could acquire wealth and influence as a result. They misbehaved and cut up, sometimes to a criminal degree, but their loyalty to one another kept them out of trouble; often one of their parents, the Church, would pretend crimes didn't happen, while the other, the state, didn't care. As occurs in other exclusively male institutions, the values of adolescence remained as the values of adulthood and are then identified as manly.[19]

The other difference between universities and church and state is universities' actual powerlessness and their presupposed servitude to their protectors. These features are so fully part of university life that they are not noticed.[20] Many

---

18. Charles Homer Haskins reports a genre—"a much copied exercise"—of the letter home for more money. A medieval Italian father reports, "[A] student's first song is a demand for money, and there will never be a letter which does not ask for cash" (*Rise*, 76–77). Peter Moraw offers this more general observation: "One of the paradoxes of the universities and their components is that they tried to claim social autonomy in many detailed respects without being socially autonomous at all, let alone socially powerful. . . . [T]he governing principles were patronage, privilege, and inheritance." Peter Moraw, "Careers of Graduates," *History*, ed. Ridder-Symoens, 1:246. Charles McClelland writes, "[T]hroughout all of its history . . . the university has required two almost contradictory things: to be supported by society and to be left alone by it." Charles McClelland, *State, Society, and University in Germany, 1700–1914* (Cambridge: Cambridge UP, 1980), 4. According to Guy Fitch Lytle, "The universities of medieval northern Europe were nurtured originally within the culture of international Christendom, as the special children of a centralizing papacy." Guy Fitch Lytle, "Patronage Patterns and Oxford Colleges, c. 1300–c. 1530," *The University in Society*, vol. 1: *Oxford and Cambridge from the 14th to the Early 19th Century*, ed. Lawrence Stone (Princeton, NJ: Princeton UP, 1974), 112.

19. Kibre gives a basis in antiquity for one fight always on the hands of scholars: that their work was unmanly. She cites how "Teutonic warriors" said that "letters, . . . are far removed from manliness" when the mother of a courtier wanted her son to become educated (*Scholarly*, 5).

20. Paolo Nardi observes that "[i]n reality the authorities founded the new universities [in the fourteenth and fifteenth centuries] for their own political and religious

interested in study, interested in learning the history of texts, their writing, their influence, do not in fact want political or military power or ownership of land that national governments and the Roman church routinely had. Sometimes, among scholars, the interest in texts and civilizations of the past, in the workings of nature and the universe, is so great that in order to protect this interest a false, vain claim must be made: that knowledge should be sought for its own sake. This claim becomes a publicly endorsed ideal that allows scholars and researchers to continue working toward what people will accept as a universal good. Yet as the Roman emperors already knew, there is no knowledge to be sought for its own sake. The history of the university suggests that the knowledge sought within the university was for the sake of its protectors—and only indirectly, and usually accidentally, for the sake of the total population.[21] The ideal of knowledge for its own sake was a rationalization of how the knowledge was actually used, even knowledge we now consider to be superstition. Knowledge is always sought in a political context.

Here is an example. The university at Bologna was the premier spot in Europe in the mid-twelfth century to study Roman and canon law, according to Paolo Nardi:

> It has been roundly denied that the Bologna school was an ecclesiastical foundation; but the bishop of Bologna was unquestionably the only authority to be given jurisdiction over scholars by the emperor himself. Later the conflict between the emperor and the commune of Bologna strengthened Bologna's links with the papacy. The Holy See had its own lively interest in promoting the teaching of law, as may be inferred from the great output of canon law rules at the time, and from the appointment to high office of many prelates trained in law.[22]

The structures of canon and civil law both derive from the Roman Empire. The Church and crown, in the twelfth century, actively used and shared this legacy. Both institutions could collect money, while secular sovereigns, additionally, commanded the military, using taxes for that purpose. The university as an organized institution could better do what Church and crown needed done, namely, find and articulate sources from history and provide logically articulated reasons for administering religious and secular laws at that time. The university

---

ends" ("Relations," 1:103). Furthermore, many, like the well-known university at Prague, consciously followed the models of Bologna and Paris.

21. Haskins writes, "By the thirteenth century the mediaeval church was a vast administrative machine which needed lawyers to run it, and a well-trained canonist had a good chance of rising to the highest dignities. No wonder canon law attracted the ambitious, the wealthy, even the idle" (*Rise*, 37).

22. Nardi, "Relations," 1:80.

was both a think tank—a supplier of reasons *and language*—and a training institution for ruler-managers.[23] By chartering and underwriting the university, both
Church and crown could expect and demand loyalty to its actions and its doctrines. After the Reformation, Church control receded slowly toward Protestant
and state control: in the twentieth century, mercantile and industrial interests
became sponsors with their own stake in what the universities taught; at this
time religious organizations were no longer the main protectors of universities.

The servitude of the university was not noticed because there were no choices
until humanism started to activate the feeling that the search for the understanding of texts, nature, and life required a certain degree of autonomy—jurisdiction
over what to study, or academic freedom. But even when it was noticed, its
loyalty to its "parents" could not change in any fundamental way. Usually those
who wanted to learn, read, and study were ready to serve the Church—or if they
were lucky or wealthy, the crown. The social value of the university, for at least
seven centuries, was that it trained church leaders, courtiers, and some other
royalty, and more university teachers. It also trained lawyers—needed by both
church and state—and doctors, the latter needing degrees to teach but not to
practice medicine. When Protestantism overtook northern Europe, universities
continued to found their work on religious education. Modern experimental
science, today a common university enterprise requiring expensive laboratories,
started outside the university and gradually worked its way in. As discussed in
section 7 of this chapter, the history of modern science suggests that it too served
the Church, and as Church influence receded, it has served industries and the
great corporations that support it within universities.

A student in early universities may have felt a certain freedom in the practices
of study, but he was destined to serve; to be part of the university community, he
assumed that he would serve more powerful constituencies and agree with them
on what the truth is. In return for this service, he was protected in society.[24] He
had privileges; he was not subject to civil law, he did not have to pay certain
taxes, he had access to food supplies that others did not have, and he was treated
as a learned and holy person no matter how he behaved out of public sight. Two
other factors were essential: you had to know Latin, and you had to be male, as

---

23. Rüegg writes, "[T]he popes looked upon the university as an institution which,
under their direct jurisdiction and protection, could organize and control studies and
could as a result deal with the three tasks in which the papacy was so interested." These
were strengthening doctrine, strengthening power against feudal interests, and recruit-
ing new staff. Furthermore, "The entire material existence of the academic institutions
depended on the prebendal provision [the salaries] for their members by the church"
("Themes," 1:16–17).

24. Kibre, *Scholarly*, 7–8. Another way to say this is that no student questioned his
place in an assumed social, political, and economic hierarchy, nor was the hierarchy itself
questioned.

the foregoing pronouns indicate.[25] More than other factors, these two most clearly show the stability of the university as an institution over its past eight centuries.[26]

II. The Men's Association

It can no longer go without saying that only men made up the university populations.[27] It must be said and considered. Women were admitted very rarely.[28] But in contemporary discussions, the social psychology of all- or mostly male groups has become a factor in itself. Reviewing the history of the university, bearing in mind that it is an all-male institution, yields a different understanding of this history. Every aspect of the university may be reviewed in this light. Hierarchical protection and male population are closely bound to one another as part of the social psychology of men in groups.

David Noble presents a detailed discussion of this phenomenon going back to the New Testament, the Church fathers, and the monastic traditions of the early Middle Ages.[29] His account suggests that misogyny was always a prominent feature of medieval European society, and that, in consequence, the attempt to exclude women from ecclesiastical work was constant, but it was not always successful, and there were periods during which nuns and monks worked side by side through paired nunneries and monasteries.[30] However, he suggests that

---

25. Olaf Pedersen notes that the statutes of the University of Naples announce that the university was there "for the general good of all who may wish to study," and suggests that many thirteenth-century universities followed this principle. But then he notes that "[t]he only restriction lay in the clerical status of students, which implied that they had to be Christians" (*First*, 213–214). They had to be Latin-speaking men as well.

26. The different roles played by Latin, and subsequently by vernacular languages in universities, are considered in the next chapter.

27. Schwinges observes that "[t]he world of the medieval student was thoroughly masculine. For the girl or woman student this world had no place . . . even with the increasing declericalization of the *universitas* nothing changed in this respect" ("Student Education," 1:202). Some women were educated and became accomplished, but not in the university. Those who did work in the university were helpers—wives, maids, and cooks. Alan Cobban is the most recent of those to mention the "masculine character" of university life. However, he offers no analysis of what it may mean for the character of the university. Alan B. Cobban, *English University Life in the Middle Ages* (Berkeley: U of California P, 1999), 2.

28. On one occasion, they were permitted to be examined for and awarded a degree, but only by passing the disputation without having attended the university (Colish, *Medieval*, 268). And whether science was practiced inside or outside the university, women were unwelcome in scientific circles, as David Noble has discussed in *A World without Women: The Christian Clerical Culture of Western Science* (New York: Oxford UP, 1993).

29. Noble, *World*, 108–137.

30. This collaboration led to the growth of opposition in doctrine and practice to the Church—to heresies.

the revivals of learning in the eleventh and twelfth centuries (the "awakening" identified by Heer[31]) were accompanied by a papal reform movement that helped to restore ecclesiastical authority to a centrally controlled European network of bishops rather than locally controlled networks of monasteries that worked closely with secular rulers. In the early part of the twelfth century, the prestige of the Bologna law school helped the papal effort to use the courts to reestablish papal law, an element of which was the "law of celibacy."[32] During the previous, more relaxed period, sexual austerity was always an ideal, but room was found to accommodate clerical marriages (and concubines) without considering them religiously illegal. Abelard (discussed in the next section) lived in the midst of this change of ecclesiastical orientation and was punished, partially as a result of his involvement in this change. Noble sees the change as directly affecting the character of the medieval university:

> The revival of learning in the cathedral schools of Europe, which spawned the medieval university, was itself an instrument of the reform movement. Indeed, it was no accident that the new universities emerged at the very moment when the clergy was finally forced to become celibate, when the ecclesiastical world without women had at last been secured. . . . It is hardly a wonder, then, that, as Frazee has pointed out, "the legislation of the Latin church remained unchanged from the twelfth century to the twentieth." Thus was created the most powerful and enduring men's club in history.[33]

Noble's reflections require further contextualization. First, while it is essential to think about the church as a men's club that has sponsored the Western university for eight centuries into our own time, it is equally important to remember that just about every powerful or governing social institution should be described as a men's club. Only recently have people started to ask why history itself seemed to have been only about men. This fact is related to a second issue in Noble's presentation: the role of gender identity. There is a clear sense in his narrative that the fact that "the exclusively male educational enclaves at Paris and Bologna became noted centers of homosexuality"[34] was also a way of discrediting the male rule in the sense that this form of sexuality was a basis for excluding women. As considered in greater detail in chapters 9 and 10, the

31. Friedrich Heer, *Medieval*, chapter 5.
32. Christopher Brooke, *Europe in the Central Middle Ages* (London: Longman, 1975), 242; and Charles Frazee, "The Origins of Clerical Celibacy in the Western Church," *Church History* 41 (1972): 160 (Cited in Noble, *World*, 296).
33. Noble, *World*, 131.
34. Noble, *World*, 155.

exclusion of women has taken place *regardless* of the sexual practices of men. Classical Greek society practiced bisexuality and still excluded women from the main institutions of society. The institutions of androcentrism, in fact, become more clearly domineering and dangerous when viewed as invariant with respect to sexuality, and this applies to the history of the university.[35]

The danger I refer to is physical violence: the reliance, consciously and unconsciously, on ultimate weapons: the transcendence of verbal interaction through the resort to threats of physical violence, actual violence, or removal of employment rights—a host of actions that endanger the physical existence of others. As is well acknowledged and considered at length by Virginia Woolf in *Three Guineas,* historical and social narratives show that men have usually resorted to physical violence to resolve disputes that, in their judgment, did not respond to verbal and other peaceful means of negotiation.[36] The option of doing harm, even verbally, is significantly more common among men than among women. This characteristic of the androcentric rule of society has been as present in religious and intellectual contexts as it has been in statecraft and national political histories.

A good example of the practical consequences of male supremacy in the university is found in Heer's account of the relation between the papacy and the University of Paris, which was for a long time the European capital of theological studies. As a general matter, he observes, "For the Popes the universities were the object of their highest hopes and the occasion of their deepest disappointment."[37] The masters at the university were French bishops, who opposed a papal bull permitting mendicants to hear confessions. A papal legate (later to become pope himself) speaking to the faculty in 1290 said this:

> At Rome we account them [the mendicants] more foolish than the igno-
> rant, men who have poisoned by their teaching not only themselves but
> also the entire world. You masters of Paris have made all your learning
> and doctrine a laughing-stock. . . . It is all trivial. . . . To us your fame
> is mere folly and smoke. . . . We forbid you, on pain of losing your posi-

---

35. Today's universities, which are making some progress toward gender equality in some areas, have many members of a variety of sexual orientations. Yet the procedures for professional advancement and success are still geared more for men's success than for women's. It is not sex alone that is dirty or contaminating; it is the bodily, or material, character of human beings that, in matters of faith and knowledge, had been avoided, denied, hidden, repressed, suppressed by male groups, who say that the search for understanding is something spiritual, mental, *geistig,* something not material.

36. The point given by Virginia Woolf in *Three Guineas* (New York: Harvest, 1966) is considered in some detail in chapter 11, section 3.

37. Heer, *Medieval,* 195.

tions, your dignities and your benefices, to discuss the privileges of the Mendicant Orders, whether in public or in secret. . . . Rather than revoke the privilege [of the mendicants to hear confessions], the Roman Curia will utterly destroy the University of Paris. We are called by God not to acquire wisdom or dazzle mankind but to save our souls.[38]

This was a response to a dispute over who may grant the power to hear confessions. It is an exposed instance in verbal form of the underlying relation of the papacy to the university and its male social psychology. On the one hand, Paris had been a stronghold of theological studies in Europe, an institutionally identified subject the papacy needs to have in the forefront of public consciousness. On the other hand, in this very role it stood to become an alternative (a choice, a heresy[39]) to the authority of the pope. Mendicants had a history of pursuing alternative religious lifestyles, and often collaborated with groups of women who had also taken vows of poverty. The sense that another authority would replace it sent the papacy to extreme positions; the first authority might not try to replace by force or coup, but it likely thinks itself more authoritative. The principals were eager to threaten to make the fantasy of destruction into a reality, and all parties to the dispute believed that such radical measures would be tried.

Consider the elements of this speech. First, the legate discredits the mendicants' intelligence. Then he says they are dangerous, even lethal to themselves and others. Then he says their work is unimportant—trivial. Next, an order is given: "We forbid you," disobedience of which will result in firing and loss of salaries (benefices, the term describing how the Church supported faculty members in universities). Finally, the legate says that rather than back down, he would sooner "destroy the University of Paris." And this destruction is a calling from God, done to save souls. Even if the papacy does not finally destroy the university or fire its faculty, this is not blustering or rhetoric or bravado. Such talk represents how things are: in cases of dispute and differences of opinion, where real disagreement exists, the more powerful party precipitates a test of who can win. One can also call this verbal gesture a disingenuous either-or social psychology: we are bigger, better, and stronger, and we do not need to find a solution that satisfies both our interests.

The papacy did not visit to negotiate and the French bishops did not ask permission to oppose the papal bull. Both parties were ready to fight. But it was not likely that the pope would destroy a university faculty that had in its preeminence in theology highlighted the Church's commitment to understanding God's will. Both parties' bypassing their understanding that it is not really

---

38. Heer, *Medieval,* 196.
39. Further discussion appears in chapter 9.

in their interest to fight left the power principle of political behavior as the only way to cope with disputes. The ante is raised from the practical issues on the table to the issue of who is stronger; neither party can get out of the situation without elaborate rituals designed to save face in addition to settling the dispute.

According to Jacques de Vitry (d. 1240), there was chronic hostility among the "nations"; each group of young men gathered at the universities viewed other groups as inferior. He wrote,

> They wrangled and disputed not merely about the various sects or about some discussions; but the differences between the countries also caused dissensions, hatreds, and virulent animosities among them, and they impudently uttered all kinds of affronts and insults against one another. They affirmed that the English were drunkards and had tails; the sons of France proud, effeminate, and carefully adorned like women. They said that the Germans were furious and obscene at their feasts; the Normans, vain and boastful; the Poitevins, traitors and always adventurers. The Burgundians they considered vulgar and stupid. The Bretons were reputed to be fickle and changeable, and were often reproached for the death of Arthur. The Lombards were called avaricious, vicious, and cowardly; the Romans, seditious, turbulent, and slanderous; the Sicilians, tyrannical and cruel; the inhabitants of Brabant, men of blood, incendiaries, brigands, and ravishers; the Flemish, fickle, prodigal, gluttonous, yielding as butter, and slothful. After such insults, from words they often came to blows.[40]

This account describes the atmosphere among the student groups: at each other's throats, or more mildly, competitive, jealous, and ready for a fistfight. The circumstance accompanies the administrative ethic of authoritative bullying; these two features are almost always found together in men's groups, but it also describes athletic teams, armies, and whole societies.

Jacques de Vitry actively encouraged the women's religious movement in the early thirteenth century. He was an itinerant preacher who gave vernacular sermons and achieved significant popularity in northern Europe.[41] He worked at the same time that the University of Paris was being established and other universities were in the early stages of formation. He is described as the "representative of this female religious movement in Belgium."[42] In his 1935 *Religious*

---

40. Cited in Haskins, *Rise,* 17–18; also by Hilde de Ridder-Symoens, "Mobility," *History,* ed. Ridder-Symoens, 1:282.

41. His popularity with ordinary people might be compared with Abelard's popularity a century earlier with young scholars.

42. Herbert Grundmann, *Religious Movements in the Middle Ages: The Historical Links Between Heresy, the Mendicant Orders, and the Women's Religious Movement in the*

Movements in the Middle Ages, Herbert Grundmann uses the term *Bewegung* ("movement") to describe both heretical and non-heretical groups: those who lived in monasteries and convents were not members of the Church's administrative structure. The movement of women toward a religious life was a significant counterpoint to the university movement. Women took vows of poverty and chastity as part of choosing this way of life.[43] Grundmann and others have documented that women from all social classes made this choice. Women who might have had prosperous material lives if they agreed to arranged marriages rejected this path for the religious life. According to Grundmann, James of [Jacques de] Vitry "stressed that he saw many women among [the Cistercians] who renounced their parents' wealth and rejected marriages with wealthy and prominent men in order to live in poverty by the work of their own hands, humble in food and clothing, dedicated totally to their religious goals."[44] Such women were members of heretical sects as well as non-heretical ones.[45] When the papal legate came to the University of Paris demanding that mendicants not be allowed to give sacraments, the female affiliations of mendicant orders might also be counted as having provoked the exaggerated outrage of the legate. Repeatedly, women had been critics of the Church's authoritarianism and greed. What would universities have been like had women been members of those communities, if they had been able to choose university life over vows of poverty and chastity?

There are many aspects to the gender dimension that made it a tacit but ever-present element in disputes among churchmen. This issue plays a prominent role in the life and work of Peter Abelard, the scholar who is widely believed to have set in motion the social machinery that established the medieval university in Europe. He did so in the life he led, in his style of teaching, in his ways of presenting his thoughts, and in the substance of his theology.[46]

Twelfth and Thirteenth Century, with the Historical Foundations of German Mysticism, trans. Steven Rowan (South Bend, IN: U of Notre Dame P, 1995), 76.

43. This was not a "lifestyle" in the sense the term is used today, but a vocational choice meant to sustain them and give them a known place in society.

44. Grundmann, *Religious,* 83. Specific instances are described on 85.

45. Most accusations of heresy were not clear-cut and had to be tried. One political role that Jacques de Vitry played was to assure church authorities of the non-heretical status of many who chose humble religious lives. At the same time, charges of heresy were used for other purposes: "A Cistercian chronicler of [the late twelfth century] reports the burning of a maiden in Reims who was held to be an adherent of the *Publicani* [a heretical sect] because she had not permitted herself to be seduced by a cleric" (Grundmann, *Religious,* 79–80). There is further discussion of heresy in chapter 3.

46. Gabriel Compayre, *Abelard;* also Rashdall, *Universities,* vol. 1. All of the histories of the university already cited have credited Abelard with a strong influence on the development of universities, which began only a decade or two after his death. How-

III. Peter Abelard's Effects

In presenting the twelfth century "awakening" in Europe, Friedrich Heer reflects on how in the early part of that century in France, the itinerant scholar Peter Abelard—who had an idiosyncratic, upbeat, optimistic style of learning and study—attracted a great following of students.[47] He made public an enthusiasm for learning and study that was rarely seen or practiced—joy and celebration that included a surprising level of candor about emotional life. From Abelard's correspondence with his student and lover Hélöise, Heer observes the following:

> Abelard presented his monastic and masculine contemporaries, whose minds were obsessed with power, honour (in Heaven as well as on earth), war, violence, and "their right," with the idea that the type of the new Man was to be found in Woman: hers was a higher form of manhood, refined in soul and spirit, capable of conversing with God the Spirit in the inner kingdom of the soul on terms of intimate friendship. Abelard stressed the point that Christ's women disciples, his dear friends, his "apostlesses," stood closer to him than any of the men; . . . Abelard elevated Mary Magdalen, the patron saint of women sinners, above the militant saints of the feudal Middle Ages, and so initiated a Magdalen cult; this peculiarly feminine form of spiritual eroticism can be seen depicted in the full flower of early Italian Renaissance art in the Bargello at Florence.[48]

Although Heer kept the traditional (in 1961) usage of "manhood," he understands Abelard to be a figure who had given an alternative to what a man was thought to be—the alternative being an affirmation of men's kinship with women in regard to learning and scholarship. This alternative identity did represent "heresy,"[49] a term that originally meant choice, but in the second century had come to mean a particular choice: the choice of not following the orthodox

---

ever, he is understood to have prepared the ground for the ideals of learning and study that characterized scholasticism and formal reasoning. A recent comprehensive study of Abelard is M. T. Clanchy, *Abelard: A Medieval Life* (Oxford: Blackwell, 1997).

47. Heer, *Medieval*, 74–95.

48. Heer, *Medieval*, 85.

49. Noble, *World*, 44–45; Peter Brown, *The Body and Society: Men, Women, and Sexual Renunciation in Early Christianity* (New York: Columbia UP, 1988), 104; Alain Le Boulluec, *La notion d'hérésie dans la littérature grecque, IIe–IIIe siècles*, vol. 1: *De Justin à Irénée* (Paris: Études augustiniennes, 1985), 36–91. (Further details of Le Boulluec's discussion are in chapter 9, section 3-1. He argues that Paul changed the use of "heresy" from "choice" to "seditious choice.") Shannon McSheffrey cautions against any too-simple association of women with religious opposition and heterodoxy. Her study does suggest, however, that women who were called heretics were not unlike men (like

line, which very often meant following a female choice.[50] Among orthodox male Church leaders, there was a perception of the heretic male seditious of the Church as similar to women as a class. Heer observes, as Bernard of Clairvaux did try to brand Abelard a heretic, that Abelard "enrage[d]" "monkish school-masters" for whom God had to be masculine and for whom "impure woman-kind" could not interfere with "mind and thought."[51] The monastic culture was overtly misogynistic; Abelard was a leader of youth and women, and his lifestyle became a model that urged men especially not to be ashamed of passion for learning or for people.

Heresy had been a useful category for the established church since its refer-ence was changed from "choice" to "seditious choice" by Paul. Before and during the early university period, when the Church was occupied with suppressing heretical groups, many members of these groups were women. Although it is not possible to separate definitively declarations of doctrinal heresy from the sociopathic fear of women, the androcentric practice of scapegoating women fit very well with the paranoid style of heretic hunting. The association of women with heresy was a major component of the three-century witch-hunting period (about 1400 to 1700), and the authors of the bible of witch hunting (the *Malleus maleficarum* of 1487), Heinrich Kramer and James Sprenger, were both bishops and faculty members (masters) of the University of Cologne acting in response to a papal bull.

Abelard is an exemplary figure because his experience still represents some of today's endemic struggles in academic life. Although Abelard was defeated and humiliated by this struggle, the record of his achievements tells a more enabling story. After Abelard universities generally suspected the imaginations and popular appeal of enthusiasts of all sorts and brought harm to them repeat-edly. Abelard's social and intellectual independence showed that in universities, there were struggles among men that weakened them, weakened the institu-tion, and led us to ways of learning and study that we take for granted today, unaware that their effectiveness is questionable even for those who take them up with conviction. In his personal life, Abelard's challenge to some customs of traditional misogyny through his relationship with Héloïse led to his castra-

---

Abelard and Ockham) who were thus identified—they were observant Christians who sought varieties of religious expression: "Heretical sects drew women more than men because such groups provided women with more opportunities for religious activity and expression than they could find in orthodoxy." Shannon McSheffrey, *Gender and Heresy: Women and Men in Lollard Communities* (Philadelphia: U of Pennsylvania P, 1995), 2.

50. In Protestant contexts, in which heresy might have been thought to be less of a factor, witchcraft was a comparable accusation, with similar punishments—banishment, shunning, or execution.

51. Heer, *Medieval*, 85.

tion and the retaliatory castration of the culprits by Abelard's defenders. These events, and his being caught up in this exchange of mutual mutilation, suggest the social psychology of his role in society, and show that his style challenged the exclusion of women from the male community of students.

Abelard and Héloïse were an academic couple who violated the culture by letting their passions for learning and for each other present an academic stance that put in relief, beyond the monkish tradition, the endemic fear of women among churchmen, a fear whose Christian forms date back to Paul.[52] The challenge emerged through Abelard's enormous popularity as a teacher: people discovered and rediscovered where he secluded himself and insisted that he continue teaching. Several of Europe's popes and bishops were taught by Abelard. Given this level of influence, he was a threat to the traditional austere mores in learning; if permitted, his ways might have taken root. Some of his academic gestures did work their way into the universities, but it has taken centuries; the process of teachers having access to the general population and becoming popular leaders still has a long way to go. Because those of his values that did get through were sifted by the Church, their partial appearance may not be recognizable as having been articulated by him or by others who shared such an approach to academic life.

Abelard's gift was his ability to make humane change and innovation plausible within existing traditions. He was a theologian who studied secular philosophy first,[53] and like many at that time he sought ways to integrate the "pagan" thoughts coming from classical Athens into the Christian view of life and the universe. Rashdall observes that "the tendency to introduce dialectical distinctions and methods of argument into theology became more and more irresistible."[54] Abelard had a talent for secular logic and dialectic and had the élan of the precocious student. He made it seem reasonable that *reason* (usually logic in Aristotle's sense) should be used systematically and enthusiastically in the study of theology. He also had views that promised change.

Perhaps the most prominent continuing theological issue of the Middle Ages was that of transubstantiation: Did the body and blood of Christ really exist in the wafer and wine people took during communion?[55] The prevailing doctrine in

---

52. Discussed in some detail by Brian Easlea, *Witch-Hunting, Magic, and the New Philosophy: An Introduction to the Debates of the Scientific Revolution, 1450–1750* (Sussex, NJ: Harvester, 1980); by Noble, *World;* and by Brown, *Body.*

53. Compayre, *Abelard,* 20. Roscelin's critique of universals is understood here to be secular.

54. Rashdall, *Universities,* 1:49.

55. Referring to times around the year 1000, Rubin writes, "The Church through its administrators and intellectuals was forging a language of religion which enhanced embryonic claims to clerical privilege. . . . Now the unifying grace was being claimed

Abelard's time dated back to the ninth century, according to Rashdall: the body and blood of Christ was in the wafer. As always this doctrine posed problems for many. Abelard used this debate to supplant his teacher William of Champeaux in Notre Dame in the second decade of the twelfth century. He reported in his autobiography how he persuaded William to weaken his realist advocacy of universals.[56] Abelard had two sources: Aristotle and his earlier teacher Roscelin, the nominalist. The latter philosopher had a doubtful view of universals, a view that embodied the perceived difference between Plato and Aristotle. The Platonic view, which was the more orthodox one in Abelard's time, was that the essence of an item, its ideal form (the universal), inhered in each instance of that item in reality. The Aristotelian view is that each item was divided into substance and accident. The Aristotelian explanation of transubstantiation was that the physical wafer was accidental and its substance was Christ. Abelard said (according to Rashdall) that "if the whole 'thing,' i.e. the whole of the universal, were 'essentially' present in each individual of the genus or species, none of it was left to be present in any other individual at the same time."[57] This argument prevailed, and William, his teacher, was forced to retract his orthodox view, at which time he was supplanted by Abelard.[58]

What is the doctrinal, philosophical, and religious significance of this event? It was a new doctrine, but it did not really disturb the belief in transubstantiation; it just provided a fresh and somewhat unanticipated account of it, one in keeping with the growing influence of Aristotle. But also, and this is not as clear or as palpable, it took a stand on this old problem of universals and nudged this problem's influence away from the epistemology of the day.[59] The fears

---

and disposed of through sacerdotal mediation. . . In a complex world brought together through its language of religion, the eucharist was becoming a focus for claims to universality and efficacy which had to be made stronger, more uniform and applicable everywhere and at every time . . . Within this symbolic order the claim was made that through sacerdotal ritual action matter could be transformed into something quite different, a repository of supernatural power, and that only such sacerdotal action could effect this change." Miri Rubin, *Corpus Christi: The Eucharist in Late Medieval Culture* (Cambridge: Cambridge UP, 1991), 13.

56. Clanchy writes, "Abelard was particularly proud of making William change his position on the meaning of universals. On the technical point of logic Abelard was doubtless right. What he does not explain is that he was arguing from a Nominalist point of view similar to Roscelin's" (*Abelard*, 83). Abelard likely omitted this source of his view because when he was writing his autobiography he was already accused of heresy.

57. Rashdall, *Universities*, 1:51–52.

58. The debate is itself casuistic and derives from magical assumptions, but that matters less than the fact that Abelard's was the more progressive voice.

59. That this happened in 1120 is of interest in the present discussion, as the Platonic view of universals is found in the twentieth-century work of Noam Chomsky as well as in the twenty-first century work of several linguists. Morten H. Christiansen, Chris Collins,

felt by orthodox clerics were justified on several grounds, but one of them was that Abelard was supplying the leadership to those who wished to overtake the new learning and use it in new ways—the strengthening of the role of reason (logic and dialectic) in the authorization of theological doctrines. Moreover, that Abelard's teacher was the nominalist Roscelin was an additional ground to treat Abelard's thought as seditious. Nevertheless, from the standpoint of theology, Abelard was not revolutionary, except with respect to the *social* character of his approach to learning and religion. Compayre and Rashdall both suggest, in fact, that the orthodoxy that held in the Church for two centuries of scholasticism (the thirteenth and fourteenth) came from Abelard. The church appropriated the logical and dialectical technique and installed it in all university curricula,[60] but successfully suppressed those features of Abelard's style of scholarship that led to his being accused of heresy and forced to burn his own book.[61] Abelard's history represents the recursive events in Western university life until the Reformation: challenges were overtaken and rendered orthodox by the powerful, protecting church, while true changes were avoided.

A prominent feature of the Reformation's changes was also present in Abelard's approach to scholarship. Abelard "freely expressed his surprise that educated men should not be able to study the Scriptures for themselves without any other aid than the text and the gloss. The unheard-of doctrine was received with derision, and Abelard was jestingly challenged to make the attempt."[62] When the attempt succeeded, Abelard's teaching was seen as unauthorized, and he had to stop teaching in this style in Anselm's territory, Laon. Because of Abelard's lifestyle and teaching style, his views, as fully Christian as could be, were more often than not construed as heresy for most of his mature life, and he had to battle this charge through cross-examinations and callings to account. His actual challenge, however, had not to do with doctrine or with faith, but with

---

and Shimon Edelman, eds., *Language Universals* (New York: Oxford UP, 2009). In the period between Abelard and Chomsky, the Platonic doctrine has had many adherents; the one of interest for Chomsky was Descartes, although some have said that his use of the adjective "Cartesian" does not apply.

60. Compayre writes that in the middle of the thirteenth century, "[t]o reason well had become the whole duty of the studious man. There was no thought of knowing the history of humanity, still less of observing the phenomena of nature" (*Abelard*, 180). According to Charles Thurot, "La logique était d'abord l'objet exclusif de l'enseignement dans la Faculté des arts. La logique étant un art autant qu'une science, les maîtres faisaient pratiquer à leurs élèves les préceptes qu'ils leurenseignaient, et les exerçaient à l'argumentation" Charles Thurot, *De l'organisation de l'enseignement dans l'Université de Paris au moyen-âge* (Paris: Besançon, 1850), 42. Compayre paraphrases thus: "Logic was regarded as the art of arts, the science of sciences" (*Abelard*, 180).

61. Rashdall, *Universities*, 1:57.

62. Rashdall, *Universities*, 1:53.

how he articulated both doctrine and faith—and particularly that he brought
his own good news with passion, personal conviction, and enthusiasm. In the
university, his way of life continued but was split into two zones with a rigid
boundary between them. Logic and dialectic became the university's scholastic
practice; off campus, so to speak, students and scholars definitely enjoyed life,
yet with less discipline and dignity than was characteristic of Abelard. The
university structure cordoned off any enjoyments and sexual practices and then
looked away from the trouble they caused because they were not permitted on
the record.[63] The university structure aggravated doctrinal separations of knowledge from passion for authorized people, students, and clerics; and insisted on
a rigid separation of male sex activity and emotional life from scholarship. This
syndrome is a feature of university life today.[64] In retrospect, how Abelard lived
and what he advocated could reasonably be understood to have eventuated first
in Protestantism—the "rights of private judgement,"[65] and subsequently in secular humanism. In the university, attitudes toward language[66] were the principal
influence to slow the process, and they continue to inhibit it.

Heer also describes what could be identified as a cyclical process with regard
to the public admission of women to intellectual and cultural life. Starting in

---

63. A full account of student life is found in Rashdall, *Universities,* 3:339–459.
Rashdall discusses initiations, drinking practices, writing home for money, as well as the
universities' governance (or lack of it) of crimes and misbehaviors that resulted. Anonymously written, the *Manuale scholarium* is presented in Latin as a dialogue between two
students and shows adolescent males learning the discourse of students, leading to the
discourse of misogyny: "[N]or do I care to look on women. Much more beautiful is the
sight of wisdom, which is acquired by the study of letters. For the joy of paradise rests
where the reward is gained by abundance of virtues and disciplines. Now in the dance
hall, if you weigh it well, there the thing is devilish; not prudence, but passion, not
learning, not justice, not truth, but sham. The roses seem to blossom on the cheek and
there is all that beauty on the surface but inside there is an ulcer, full of madness, and
foulness, and poison." *The* Manuale scholarium: *An Original Account of Life the Mediaeval University,* trans. Robert Francis Seybolt (Cambridge, MA: Harvard UP, 1921),
90. If the presumed date of publication (1481) is correct, this dialogue was compiled six
years before the *Malleus maleficarum* was published.
64. In spite of flexible hours and a measured teaching pace, university women are still
not comfortable attending to both scholarship and family, whereas men continue to give
priority to academic and professional demands. Mary Ann Mason offers results from a
recent study of doctoral students' career goals: "Women . . . said they didn't have time
in graduate school to have children, and they also feared that doing so would mean they
would no longer be considered serious scholars by their professors." The traditional overt
segregation of women is now often underground. The enduring value is the unwelcome
status of family life in the university "club." Mary Ann Mason, "A Bad Reputation,"
Chronicle of Higher Education 6 February 2009.
65. Rashdall, *Universities,* 1:65.
66. Discussed in the next two chapters.

the awakening of the twelfth century, there were several prominent and powerful women as rulers and as influential members of kings' courts. There were also religious and church women. The twelfth-century abbess Hildegard of Bingen, for example, "held that the decadence of Church and society was chiefly caused by masculine weakness: women therefore must act where men had failed; this was the *tempus muliebre,* the era of women."[67] Women's initiatives came in heterodox and heretical contexts during the twelfth century, and many died in these causes. According to Heer, "the Church continued to distrust women who were spiritually restless, suspecting them all the time of heresy."[68] In the literal sense of the term, they were heretical, as they brought alternatives for common practices and behaved generously toward petitioners in the exercise of political power. Heer writes that "[t]he growth of the vernacular languages owed much to feminine influence, as is clear enough from religious and literary sources."[69] The shift away from Latin as a formal, official, written language to the various vernaculars in Europe began at the same time as the formation and then the expansion of universities in the fourteenth century. During this time, however, Europe was racked with war and plague; Jews were expelled from most western European countries and migrated to eastern Europe. And finally at this time, the church took over universities and women's influence was opposed and revoked.[70] The French court banned women from succession to the crown.[71] Heer observes that "the great mass of homilectic [*sic*] literature is still pervaded with hatred and distrust: woman is portrayed as 'sin,' without qualification. The tradition is an ancient one, going back to Augustine and the early Fathers, above all to St. Jerome, the patron saint of misogynists: 'woman is the gate of the devil, the path of wickedness, the sting of the serpent, in a word a perilous object.'"[72]

However, even during the twelfth century, a relatively relaxed moment in Europe with regard to women in society, the university was completely male. A few women became learned, but not through formal university study. The spirit of Abelard was only faintly present in the intense activity of the thirteenth and fourteenth centuries, the founding and spread of universities throughout Europe. Abelard's open and generous style was mostly opposed, and the fraternal, military, hierarchical styles of functioning characterized the growth of the universities. Women may have played a role in the increasing use of the vernacular, but it was not until the seventeenth century—five hundred years after universities began—that Latin was no longer the exclusive language of learning and study.

---

67. Heer, *Medieval,* 264.
68. Heer, *Medieval,* 264.
69. Heer, *Medieval,* 262.
70. Pedersen, *First,* 78.
71. Heer, *Medieval,* 263.
72. Heer, *Medieval,* 265.

Historians have characterized the influence of science as progressive in helping to democratize university study.[73] However, women did not enter the university in any significant numbers until the mid-twentieth century, three hundred years after the scientific revolution.

IV. University Formation as a Reaction against Abelard

Although the spirit of Abelard and of his student, John of Salisbury, was taken up by Renaissance humanism two centuries later, his values were inhibited and permitted to obtain only in a very slow, piecemeal progress, as Church authorities and other groups—such as monasteries—considered them threatening. In spite of the fact that threats from women or from male friends of women were not about to displace the church hierarchy, fearing them was common among powerful men and the institutions that sustained them. As a result, at the time of Abelard's death in the middle of the twelfth century, there was an air of conflict in response to Abelard and his values. This atmosphere had an effect on the gradual move of groups of scholars and teachers toward more formal study and learning in a recognized, officially constituted university. People traveled to different centers of learning as Europe in its awakening was becoming more cosmopolitan. The younger students that followed Abelard were mobilized and began to search out other teachers and schools.

As described earlier in this chapter, groups of university students were called "nations" because of their coherence around their shared vernaculars and ethnic affiliations. Such groups began the universities' colleges[74] that localized the gathering, learning, eating, and playing in one place: campus. Before the formation of colleges, their status as a confederation of clubs was the *universitas* that secured some protections from economic exploitation. But by the time the colleges were formed early in the thirteenth century, the universities had more elaborate and formal protection from the Church or, less often, other well-endowed sources from local or larger governments. For example, the Sorbonne, founded in 1257, was characterized as "a study community organized in the form of a brotherhood and living together in regulated and moral fashion."[75]

---

73. As considered in chapter 10, science, to a great extent, overtook the style and influence of Latin in its own cause, and continues, to the present day, to use Latin as its official terminology in law and medicine.

74. Pearl Kibre writes that in Bologna at the beginning of the twelfth century "the foreign students had formed *collegia* or nations according to the land of their birth, primarily for mutual benefits, fraternal association, and amity. These early nations in turn appear to have coalesced to form the larger associations, the *universitas ultramontanorum* for students from outside Italy, and the *universitas citramontanorum* for students of the Italian peninsula and the surrounding islands" (*Nations*, 5).

75. Schwinges, "Student Education," *History*, ed. Ridder-Symoens, 1:214.

Because of the high-minded character of these fraternity-like groups, especially of the colleges, a large degree of repression and suppression took place, which was evident in the lawlessness that frequently resulted when students and other college members let off steam. What was unified in Abelard's life was bifurcated as his enthusiasms for learning became institutionalized in the university. Specifically, there was a monastic austerity regarding learning on the one hand and a tacit permission to release one's ungainly impulses on the other. Colish reports that "[t]avern brawls in university towns were frequent, bitter, and sometimes fatal. The tension between town and gown based on the economic dependence of merchants on students who were frequently foreigners and who enjoyed legal privileges often exploded into violence."[76] Rashdall details a series of initiation rituals in which first-year students were subjected to extended humiliation.[77] If they survived mentally intact, they were subsequently welcomed into the club of university or college members. Sometimes university students were themselves victims of egregious crimes at the hands of what might be called rival gangs: members of monasteries who also studied and prayed, but who lived a simpler, unmonied existence. The initiations involved rituals of the sort now depicted in films about the military—verbal insults, bodily beatings, smearing with unpleasant foods or oils, and mock removal of body parts. Like any initiation, these were done one student at a time, so that the feeling of being overwhelmed and helpless was jubilantly promoted and intensified. After the initiation was over there was a drinking fest paid for by the initiate, whose money was confiscated for that purpose even if that was the only money available for the duration of his stay at the university. If it seems that there was no law or local rules protecting the newcomers, this would be accurate. The so-called privileges of the university included oversight of all internal activities, which meant, in this case, permitting the adolescent male tradition wide latitude.

By the same token, there was no real protection for the very students who performed these initiations. Rashdall gives several accounts of university students murdered by the gangs of monks acting on the pretext of a boundary dispute between the monastery and the university. Students were assaulted with various weapons, seriously injured, and sometimes killed. One case reported by Rashdall involved the provost of Paris hanging a scholar in public. These were not treated as crimes, and justice was done on an institutional level: the provost had to found chaplaincies for the university—a pecuniary punishment for the exercise of brutality and murder. Rashdall observes, "It is significant of the lawlessness of the times that the ordinary course of justice seems to have been quite incapable of reaching ruffianism of this kind when committed by such offenders as the

---

76. Colish, *Medieval,* 271.

77. Rashdall outlines hazing rituals that are not all that different from those in twenty-first-century colleges (*Universities,* 3:376–382).

abbot and convent of S. Germain."[78] Yet the insularity of the university to civil authority exists today. Although the crimes are not the same, and violent crime is subject to civil justice, courts are reluctant to hear complaints given by members of university communities, especially in cases where jobs are lost: there is an expectation that local justice needs to be honored in the university community. Whether this is a result of the masculine population of the university and of the civil authorities is not provable directly. But the principle seems to be that *this* men's club is going to respect the rules of *that* men's club. It was assumed, strangely, that violent disputes between the abbey and the university emerged in a just result. It is likely that while these were understood to be crimes, their wholly masculine zone of action permitted the "boys will be boys" treatment of the crimes—the assumption that the law does not have to protect weak boys from strong ones.

It may be true, as Rainer A. Müller observes about university life in the early modern period, that "drink, gaming, and love," did not and do not overtake academic life for the young men at universities.[79] It was an ongoing battle between regulations about behavior, the need to study, and the need to enjoy life that marked the daily existence of university students. It could be that there were more positive aspects than negative ones, as for many there now are. However, the style of recreation as well as the constancy of drink, gaming, and love as the traditional amusements of academic young men signaled an underlying structure in the university that resembled the ethic of military organizations: there is a strong boundary between the responsibilities of study on the one hand and the license to indulge on the other. The responsibility to study contributed to the buildup of the institutions that supported the university—the Church and the crown. The forms of indulgence involved tolerating harm to others—often to women, but to men as well—damage to property, and the waste of monies hard earned, often, by the families of the majority of students. From the standpoint of which groups in society are served, the amusements and the extracurricular crimes of students are continuous with the service they are preparing to do when they leave the university to be employed by the Church, for example, or when they remain in the university to train a new generation in the same ethic.

V. The Unchanging Curriculum

Acknowledging the unity of this institution across the cultures of Europe and North America involves recognizing an underlying social logic of how the pursuit of individual intelligence functions in the West. It should not be surprising to

---

78. Rashdall, *Universities*, 3:428.
79. In *History*, ed. Ridder-Symoens, 2:352.

learn of such an institutional unity of form, given the similarity of habits and culture in societies overseen by the Roman Church. Nor is it remarkable that at the University of Paris, Europe's leading center of theological study, the curriculum changed only slightly, and always from without, until the mid-fifteenth century. Pedersen observes that curricula remained stable because "[t]he statutes and privileges were too precious to be tampered with, lest rights already obtained were lost, chief among them being the right of the universities to govern themselves."[80] That faculty attempts to govern amounted to anything under these circumstances is doubtful. Today, faculty governance is a rubber stamp for boards of trustees and/or legislators, and faculties are supine—even in regard to curriculum development—lest their small scope of authority over the university be further diminished.[81]

The European universities developed the *Studium generale,* a term that refers to what some have thought of as universal knowledge. Most universities offered a comprehensive range of subjects to study, and they have in common an almost complete dependency on the Church and the crown. This dependency is hidden by the history of how the *universitas* was formed by students' initiatives; very few historians explore the consequences of this dependency of the university, in the long term, on higher authority.[82] Rather historians admire the health and vigor of the institution on the basis of the intrinsic energies and motivations of its constituents, where "parental" support (that is, supervisory sponsorship) may have been necessary but not definitive or coercive. However, there can be no mistaking the fact that the success of the *universitas* initiative in the twelfth century was predicated on the establishment of a contract between unequal parties. What happened to Abelard—his being accused of heresy—was an event that led, very slowly, through the Reformation and further changes in the German universities in the eighteenth century, to concepts such as "academic freedom" today.[83] Yet that, too, is undercut by the condition of dependency on superior funding and force; it can be and is routinely overridden;[84] in authoritarian

---

80. Pedersen, *First,* 300.

81. In this chapter, there is further discussion of how Galileo actually taught Ptolemaic astronomy, believing it false, when he worked at the University of Padua, since that was its curriculum (Bronfenbrenner, *Rôle,* 218); he then left to work under patronage to write his two main treatises.

82. Sources cited in this chapter show that historians have criticized male supremacy and Church bullying. Dependency is a different issue affecting social and psychological assumptions about conducting one's life. However, men's embarrassment about their dependency on others, men as well as women, is the basis of the bravado of academic autonomy to pursue knowledge wherever it may lead. This issue is further considered in chapter 11.

83. See chapter 7, note 74.

84. These complaints are common today, as described by Press and Washburn, "The Kept University," *Atlantic Monthly* March 2000: 39–54. When private funding sources

societies, it is canceled with impunity. Only with great difficulty today can scholars pursue truly independent pathways; in such cases the scholars may be honored, but have no tangible influence on public policy. Very few roads to influencing society independently of government and corporations are open.[85] However, total scholarly independence is not a reasonable ideal. Because it arose in response to coercion and repression, that is where it is pursued. Scientists and scholars, as individuals, are responsible to society's interests, just as institutions are. The issue is this: In what contexts are scholarly autonomy and independence to be exercised?

Colish's account of the origin of modern universities differs from Rashdall's in one respect: she claims that because the curricular requirements in medieval universities were identical across universities and unchanging over hundreds of years, this represents a significant difference from the varieties present in modern universities. However, in a relative sense, it is not a key difference: the unchanging curriculum of the medieval university served purposes similar to those promoted by the more varied curricula in modern universities: the preparation of students to serve the sponsoring institutions. Corporate interest includes the need to sell their products and services locally, and the need to expand corporate markets. This interest is today's analogy to Church interest (which could include being an ordinary priest, a bishop, a monk, a canon lawyer, or a theologian). The educational standards in both historical periods prepare students to run the foundational institutions. The custom might have been, then and now, that university education was used to create choices and differences in social values.

---

are supporting basic research, especially in medicine, for example, the fundamental purpose of the university is controlled by the interests of external parties rather than by the collective interests of society. A scientist may have an entirely different sense of what research should be done, as opposed to the research a drug company will want done to improve economic performance of the company. Chapter 2 (this volume) considers how Humboldt tried to found the University of Berlin in order to secure such freedom, but slowly in his lifetime and more quickly after his death, the state overtook the university and made and administered its own rules. Willis Rudy, *The Universities of Europe, 1100–1914: A History* (Cranbury, NJ: Associated UP, 1984), 103. In general, scholars sometimes taught and studied things of their own choice, but once they became both popular and independent, their views were examined for heresy. In the nineteenth and twentieth centuries, it was common for students to become politically active and, thus threatening, to the governments that sponsored the universities (107). A contemporary instance of political overriding is mentioned in chapter 2: Linda Brodkey secured overwhelming departmental support for a change in the required writing curriculum, but the University of Texas considered this change politically threatening and overrode the department's vote, canceling the change. Linda Brodkey, *Writing Permitted in Designated Areas Only* (Minneapolis: U of Minnesota P, 1996), 211–227.

85. Some would reasonably claim that government, including both political parties, is itself in the pay of corporations and their mendaciously identified "political action groups."

But then, as now, those with more progressive views were considered heretical: advocates of choices that serve the general population have not been welcome in the university, the Church, or corporate culture.

This conclusion may seem doubtful in view of the fact that disputation, challenge, and logical questioning was at the heart of the scholarly (scholastic) experience. But this form of arguing is not what ordinary real-life arguing is about, which is the admission of *differing premises* and the *search* for common ones.[86] In medieval disputation, a common premise was assumed, and the winner of debates was the one who was judged to be closest to having upheld the common premise. Logic was important because the premises were the same on both sides. When this is the case, as, for example, that transubstantiation is the true description of the communion ritual, the path to conclusions can be more, or less, logical. Skill in the use of logic is important when disputants engage in discussion with the same presuppositions. But logic is only marginally important if the disputing parties are trying to agree on the premises of their discussion. Such premises necessarily include empirical considerations. Yet as was the case in the many arguments about transubstantiation, the empirical situation stayed the same: people took communion thinking that this ritual validated their membership in the Church, without attention to whether, logically or otherwise, the wafer and the wine could be the body and blood of Christ. The miraculous premise was in play regardless because it was a matter of faith and not fact. The debate would have consequences only if someone said that since the wafer and wine were not really the body and blood of Christ, we ought not take communion. The dispute would then be over what to do rather than what to think, and logic would not apply. Practical considerations would instead be brought to bear. Of course no such substantive challenge to the ritual was made. Taking communion happens in some Protestant denominations as well.

The rigidity of the curriculum resided largely in its use of Aristotle as the source to be studied and mastered, and on that basis students learned the practice of logical disputation. Rashdall notes the "entire omission of the poets, historians, and orators of ancient Rome"[87] from the 1215 statute-prescribed curriculum

---

86. Janice Moulton, "A Paradigm of Philosophy: The Adversary Method," *Discovering Reality: Feminist Perspectives on Epistemology, Metaphysics, Methodology, and Philosophy of Science*, ed. Sandra Harding and Merrill B. Hintikka (Dordrecht: B. Reidel, 1983), 149–164. Moulton shows that the tradition of academic argumentation, which derives, partly, from the tradition of certification through disputation in the medieval university, is a specific genre: the argument from a common premise. She suggests that such arguments are casuistical, as premises are assumed but not themselves subject to examination or revision. Thus, non-logical (non-Aristotelian) arguments are ones that debate premises, which require rationality, but do not require formal logical techniques. Additional commentary on Moulton's essay is found in chapter 3, note 90.

87. Rashdall, *Universities*, 1:440.

at the University of Paris. It is not possible to distinguish Church authority in the matter of university curricula from the authority of Aristotle's works and the Christian uses of them. As Thurot described, logic and reasoning were primary in universities, and they were taught through the use of Aristotle. Even grammar was taught as a logical, rather than practical, subject. For example, we might ask how one explains this structure, or this rule, rather than just in which cases this rule applies. The process of establishing theological truth—that is, doctrine—involved the use of logic; students learned the Christian premises—the various elements of received doctrine—and derived the various acceptable results from their logical disputations. The proficiency in logic and disputation was barely distinguishable from proficiency in canon law or theology.[88] In universities where civil law was the main interest, logic was also essential. One reason many physicians did not get university degrees is that medical practice did not depend on intimacy with texts, but on traditions of cures and treatments: medicine was a craft, and did not consult formal scientific research as it does today. One could learn anatomy without help from the universities. Physicians who did win degrees were recognized for their achievements and were permitted to teach in the universities, but they were not especially more authoritative as physicians. Therefore, as long as canon and civil law were the main subjects of the university curricula, there was hardly any change in the canon of curricular texts.[89] Even in civil law, where precedents are a factor, the reasoning skill was still paramount. The universities functioned in a society in which there were only two kinds of authority: Church and state,[90] but the latter was not as influential in universities. Textual authority was created by readers, or clerics who were the constituency of the Church. Thus, the curriculum was stable, and the universities served their benefactors conscientiously.

VI. Changes in Reading Practices

This situation began to change with figures such as Copernicus, who introduced a thought about the universe which, heretofore, had no standing at all: that Earth was not the center. The subject of astronomy, which studied the heavens, was like

---

88. Today, a similar situation applies in a discipline like economics: one can plausibly claim that proficiency in economics is hardly separable from proficiency in mathematics, although many doubt that this should be the principal way to understand economic processes. This issue is discussed in more detail in chapter 11, in connection with critiques of the discipline of economics.

89. The cost of reproducing texts was likely also a factor in the rigidity of the curriculum. When printing became available, it helped to expand the curriculum. It is of greater interest to consider why literacy and education did not grow faster than they did, even with the advent of printing, an issue discussed in chapter 9.

90. Peter Moraw observes that before and "well into" the university era, "the church was culturally and socially the *prima causa* and chief base of the groups and concerns

the study of written texts. One had to read the sky to determine how things were, to determine the reference of the visual presentation. It took perhaps a century and a half before the Copernican idea was generally recognized to be true, but only after a telescope was used to read the text as given more closely and determine salient facts, such as the revolution of moons around distant planets.[91] The Copernican and Galilean revolution on Earth might be understood as a revolution in *reading*. Yet it was also a different kind of revolution, as the book in this case was not a text written by people: in astronomy, the application of logic (mathematics) to technologically enhanced empirical observations yielded new premises, which posed an authoritative threat to views derived from naked-eye reading. Universities understood this and perceived, correctly, that this new kind of reading was a serious threat not simply to the universities, but to the authority of the Church.[92]

The other threat to the Church, approximately contemporary with Copernicus, was a challenge to its reading practices with received written texts. Just as Copernicus had direct access to the heavens without Aristotle's official mediation, Martin Luther claimed direct access to the Bible, a palpable, real text anyone could, in principle, read. Luther said that mediation was no longer needed. People could learn to read; the Bible could be read in the vernacular; copies could be printed, and the Church (meaning in this case priestly authority) was not needed. The Church had depended on its role as a total mediator. But now, the possibility of direct popular access to the cosmos and to texts stood ready to change the most stable of social institutions, the Church and the university.

Perhaps the earliest large-scale result of the emerging changes in reading is the recognition that languages other than Latin could refer to things that were different from what could be referred to in Latin: the vernaculars, Greek, and Hebrew.[93] Vernaculars were increasingly used in universities, and chairs in Hebrew

which were important for the social history of the universities" ("Careers of Graduates," 1:245). State meant, usually, either city-states or smaller municipalities.

91. Although this was recognized as true, Galileo still had to renounce his commitment to this understanding, not unlike his having to teach Ptolemy in Padua under institutional coercion. As this case suggests, the mid-seventeenth century had still not moved science into an authoritative position.

92. Copernicus did not try to publish his theory because "he was vulnerable to disdain from university professors and his superiors in the Church." When it did come out, "little serious attention was given at first to the heart of the book, the new theory." Marie Boas, *The Scientific Renaissance, 1450–1630* (New York: Harper, 1962), 73–74. Boas also indicates, however, that Einstein's relativity could not be "heard" by most people in modern times. Copernicus's theory that Earth is mobile was so distant from almost everyone's common knowledge that in a sense it was not possible for the theory to affect traditional practices and beliefs.

93. For example, the reference of *love* would be different in Latin, Greek, and Hebrew. In Hebrew "love" is used mainly as a verb. In Latin it is *amor*, and in Greek *eros*. So alternative vocabulary would be a choice for readers and could in turn be read as heresy.

and Greek were established in Wittenberg, which was at the forefront of the change in perspectives on Christianity. The Reformation, taking place at the height of Renaissance humanism, was enhanced by the latter movement's placement outside the Church and by its emphasis on the importance of *several* languages at once playing a role in learning.[94] Although most accounts of Renaissance humanism stress the recovery of texts and the production of new literature in the vernaculars and in classical literary Latin, it is not as clear, in these accounts, that the proliferation of language consciousness was the locus of novelty that spurred enthusiasm in contexts outside the Church-protected universities.[95] Humanism, a term that probably comes from Cicero, emphasizes certain subjective inner values such as aesthetics, individual conscience, and interpersonally derived moral principles that were absent from university curricula in the thirteenth and fourteenth centuries, but were very well represented in the vernacular *Divine Comedy*. The immediate effect of humanism was to call attention to such values that, by and large, could only be considered outside formal Church contexts—and certainly not in university lectures. As a result, it was perhaps not obvious that the proliferation of languages (ancient and vernaculars) and new uses of old language was such a fundamental factor in the change of public consciousness at the beginning of the sixteenth century.[96] As a rule, as Simon observes,

> Humanist scholars usually met with opposition at the universities, of whose scholarship they were very critical, but found their services much in demand elsewhere as diplomats and advisers; while those who continued to concentrate on scholarship found patrons among leading statesmen, both lay and ecclesiastical, and employment as tutors.[97]

The humanists (such as Thomas More, who advised Henry VIII) were Catholic Christians, but not orthodox churchmen or academics. In this identity, they

---

94. "Both Erasmus and Vives tirelessly demonstrated that Latin, combined with Greek, was the most suitable and desirable medium of learning, as also the gateway to literatures comprehending the accumulated wisdom of mankind." Joan Simon, *Education and Society in Tudor England* (Cambridge and New York: Cambridge UP, 1966), 104–105.

95. Simon maintains that the "pre-humanists" in Italy in the fourteenth century were "lawyers, trained in university schools where the professors of civil law were married laymen active in affairs, or the sons of legal families which in the conditions of city life easily built up fortunes and attained a predominant position" (*Education,* 60).

96. "This classical influence began as an inspiration where the vernacular writers borrowed words, figures of speech, subject matter, and general structure from Greek and Latin literature, and ended as an age of literary rules based on classic practice and ancient literary criticism." Frederick Artz, *Renaissance Humanism, 1300–1550* (Kent, OH: Kent State UP, 1966), 90.

97. Simon, *Education,* 65.

represented the values that led to the rejection of the papacy, even though they did not reject it themselves. During the humanist period their values were sometimes identified as combinations of pagan and Christian values, and sometimes just pagan values. Yet they did not advocate for any purely secular perspectives such as are common today. Nevertheless, the Church-backed universities could not allow the characteristic humanist literary and historical subjects into the curricula. Their having permitted ancient languages other than Latin to be taught was a big change.[98] Yet the special combinations of language, literature, history, and concern for individuals[99] could not be recognized in university curricula until the eighteenth and nineteenth centuries. Even Protestant universities drew a rigid line between religious education and humanist values.

VII. Empirical Science and Other Troublemakers

Where new ideas about the planets and stars on the one hand and languages and texts on the other hand added up to a curriculum alternative to the traditional seven liberal arts, the growth of empirical science was an entirely new factor that posed a challenge to what universities considered to be knowledge. Institutions of humanistic study provided a model for study in empirical science: academies and patronage outside the university. In Italy in the fourteenth and fifteenth centuries, humanists formed associations of scholars whose members had temporary stints in universities, but were not primarily associated with them. The beginning of the sixteenth century showed the humanities as the primary extra-university study, but by the end of the century advances in astronomy, mechanics, and the technology of measurement and observation turned attention to physics, its mathematical handling, and its availability for experiment. Arts and sciences as we know them today were resisted by the universities until the eighteenth century, but their slow entry into university curricula[100] coincided with the shift of principal custody of the universities from the churches to central governments and municipalities.

---

98. Simon observes that the biggest step taken by the university was the "profound study" of Hebrew and Greek (*Education*, 135).

99. Simon describes the wide change augured by humanist values thus: the "transition from the medieval to the modern world, from an ecclesiastically dominated to a lay culture" (*Education*, 61).

100. According to Roy Porter, "many universities remained supine. The combined effects of religious orthodoxy, censorship, and their prime role as training grounds for clergy and lawyers, certainly left the Spanish universities indifferent to science." Roy Porter, "The Scientific Revolution and the Universities," *History*, ed. Ridder-Symoens, 2:556. Generally, "most historians have agreed . . . that the part played by the universities [in the Scientific Revolution] was small" (532–533). Willem Frijhoff writes, "Indeed, the great revival of science largely bypassed the universities, although not to the same

The beginning of the seventeenth century saw university curricula for most students unchanged from their form in the thirteenth century. Martha Ornstein Bronfenbrenner's description of curricula emphasizes how every subject, especially scientific ones, was studied by reading one or more of Aristotle's treatises and commentaries on them.[101] The scientific works were thought to be mastered just as, earlier, the Latin treatises were—through disputations that, Bronfenbrenner observes, "were never supposed to bring in new subject matter; they were only to give the student a chance of combining and recombining . . . what he had acquired from Aristotle or other authorities."[102] Thus, even if empirical science were taught, the fixed method of student certification, disputations regulated by the professor, could not accommodate the subject itself. In this deep sense, universities were not ready to accept empirical science as a formal subject. Bronfenbrenner describes the sense of sufficiency of classical view of science as the "most pernicious feature of the [university] system [of certification]."[103]

Italian universities were the most liberal, sustained as they often were by private wealth and secular public backing, a tradition of city-state autonomy. Yet here, although there were incipient uses of equipment like scales and thermometers, there were still no formal laboratories established; at the end of the seventeenth century, the University of Bologna was bequeathed an amateur laboratory. Anyone seriously interested in scientific research had to have his own laboratory, independently financed, and this was not related to the formal training of students for university degrees. The University of Paris was the most conservative. The new statutes of 1600 stipulated that only Catholics be admitted; repeated the program from the thirteenth century, with, perhaps, more attention to Aristotle; and continued attention to obsolete Greek treatises of Galen and Hippocrates. In addition, "[t]he use of the vernacular was suppressed wherever possible" and "[t]he death penalty was prescribed if the book [by a faculty member] were printed without authorization."[104] There was censorship of any teachings not in the formal statutes, under the threat of the revocation of the teaching license. Teaching of chemistry other than Aristotle's (of the four elements) was forbidden.

extent everywhere. The universities had correctly seen that the new learning threatened the established order of their disciplines, for the work of the seventeenth-century philosophers and mathematicians was so important that it far exceeded the narrow limits of those disciplines *stricto sensu*." Willem Frijhoff, "Patterns," *History*, ed. Ridder-Symoens, 2:45.

101. Bronfenbrenner, *Rôle*, 215.
102. Bronfenbrenner, *Rôle*, 214.
103. Bronfenbrenner, *Rôle*, 214.
104. Bronfenbrenner, *Rôle*, 221.

Descartes tried to negotiate with the university and the Church. He promised a way "to demonstrate the truth of the existence of a God and the immortality of the soul"[105] such that there would no longer be atheists. Lynn Nelson characterizes this effort as a "covenant to leave the business of values to something *other than* science," which enabled science to "go about the business of finding out 'how things are' without interference."[106] Nelson observes that at the time "it was a good bargain," but it split the world in two, declaring, as many have after Descartes, that knowledge of the material world was fundamentally "different in kind" from knowledge of values and that science need concern itself only with material knowledge. Although this division may seem harmless in some senses, we are so used to separating questions of fact from those of value that we do not see how this is not a necessary separation but one that is applied, like any doctrine or principle, selectively by those authorized to establish doctrine. In addition, this attempt to placate the Church failed. His formulation about the identity of matter and extension were found to oppose the doctrine (again) of transubstantiation, and thus Descartes's work could not be taught, and his writings were placed on the Church's *Index librorum prohibitorum*. The 1671 proclamation against Descartes's works by the archbishop of Paris "was accepted by the faculties without a dissenting voice."[107]

Today, Descartes is understood to be a rationalist in the Platonic tradition that underwrote Church doctrine during the first millennium and until Aristotle's work was taken as the main Church orthodoxy, after Abelard. However, Descartes was not rejected on the basis of his handling of Greek sources, but rather on the basis of his attempts to find philosophical certainty through individual thought processes that would be consistent with faith and inoffensive to the French religious apparatus. The so-called crime of Descartes was similar to the crime of Galileo. Each considered himself unambiguously faithful. But each wrote in the vernacular and attempted to reach constituencies outside orthodox boundaries. The substance of their thoughts was unfamiliar and correctly perceived as a challenge (although not so intended) to the Church-run religious apparatus and the Church-run university. Both Galileo and Descartes were independently protected by patrons, but not by the university's protector,

---

105. Bronfenbrenner, *Rôle*, 222.

106. Lynn Hankinson Nelson, *Who Knows: From Quine to a Feminist Empiricism* (Philadelphia: Temple UP 1990), 305. Although Descartes is known for his "rationalism," this attempted deal is similar to the attitude of nominalists, whose ability to recognize when faith was needed let them turn attention to the uses of universals, which they treated as empirical questions. Additional discussion of Nelson's view of Descartes is found in chapter 10, section 2.

107. Bronfenbrenner, *Rôle*, 223; cited in Charles M. Jourdain, *Histoire de l'Université de Paris au 17e et au 18e siècles* (Paris: Hachette, 1862–1866), 235.

the Church, which viewed them as heretics. Consequently, these practitioners of science and philosophy stayed, mostly, outside the university. The church resisted efforts to establish bases of learning outside of its purview.

Almost all members of the British Royal Society were educated in the university. When they began to gather informally in 1645[108] they held university appointments. Yet their meetings were extracurricular and interdisciplinary and without royal pecuniary sponsorship. The group met for perhaps fifteen years before the king's formal recognition and charter converted it into the Royal Society. In addition to the wide representation of interests, including those of industry and business, the distinctive interest of this group was empirical observation and experimentation as promoted earlier by Francis Bacon. Oxford and Cambridge were already Protestant, and this difference from the University of Paris could account for the slightly looser hold on curricula by the British universities. But the latter were similar to those of the rest of Europe in the seventeenth century in that there were few or no laboratory facilities for organized, planned experimentation.

The Royal Society had a different rationale for its existence from that of the formal, enduring universities. It was something like a free market of scientific investigation, and it solicited interest from the public, emphasizing that there were no requirements of wealth, social standing, or available time for research that disqualified potentially interested people. Thomas Sprat wrote,

> It suffices if many be plain, diligent and laborious observers who though they bring not much knowledge, yet bring their hands and eyes incorrupted. . . . Men did generally think no man was fit to meddle in matters of consequence but he that had bred himself up in a long course of discipline for that purpose. . . . Experience . . . tells us greater things are produced by free way than the formal.[109]

Because it was recognized and chartered by the king, but not financed, the Royal Society, in retrospect, turned out to be the most independent of any group of scholars in Europe at that time. Its attempts at vocational inclusiveness attracted many individuals willing to contribute funds, laboratories, and equipment needed for careful experimentation and measurement. Only one university in Europe rivaled the open-mindedness of this enterprise: the German University of Halle, founded by Frederick, King of Prussia, in 1690, which functioned in the vernacular and rejected the hegemony of Aristotle. Bronfenbrenner observes

---

108. After the death of Galileo and five years before Descartes's death.

109. Thomas Sprat, *The History of the Royal Society of London for the Improving of Natural Knowledge* (London: n.p., 1667), 72–73. Quoted in Bronfenbrenner, *Rôle*, 111.

that it "became the model of all other university reform."[110] Another German university, at Altdorf, was the first to establish (also at the end of the seventeenth century) professional-scale laboratories specifically dedicated to research in physics, chemistry, and biology.

There were learned societies in several European countries toward the end of the seventeenth century, but they were supported by the state, and thus were not as flexible in undertaking research and, in retrospect, not as prolific as the Royal Society, whose distinctive characteristic, beyond its financial independence, was its combination of researchers from inside and outside the university. In addition, the scientific societies helped to weaken considerably the custom of presenting learned work in Latin: there were no language constraints for members who published their work.[111]

However, the Royal Society retained an insularity that is still in evidence in today's universities, even as the use of Latin in science education has all but disappeared: the gender constraint. David Noble, citing several sources,[112] writes,

> As Bacon had earlier heralded "the Masculine Birth of Time," so now Oldenburg, first secretary of the Royal Society, announced that the purpose of the society was "to raise a Masculine Philosophy . . . whereby the Mind of Man may be ennobled with the knowledge of Solid Truths."[113]

Noble cites other statements such as churchman Joseph Glanvill's observation that "the case of Truth is desperate . . . The Woman in us, still prosecutes a deceit, like that begun in the Garden; and our understandings are wedded to an Eve, as fatal as the Mother of our Miseries"; one of the Society's founders, Walter Charleton, characterized women as "traitors to Wisdom: the impediment to Industry . . . the clogs to virtue, and goads that drive us all to Vice, Impiety, and ruine. You are the Fools Paradise, the Wiseman's Plague, and the grand Error of Nature."[114] Whether such sentiments are ideology, propaganda, venting, principle, or authentic belief, their function among Society members is the same: the conservation of the male group's bond of superiority. They put a more specific accent on Bacon's reflection that knowledge is power. They imply that the substance of scientific knowledge now pursued with such

---

110. Bronfenbrenner, *Rôle*, 234.

111. The publications of the Royal Society, which have been continuous since the seventeenth century, have been in English, with the proviso that work in other languages may be submitted.

112. Evelyn Fox Keller, *Reflections on Gender and Science* (New Haven, CT: Yale UP, 1985); Easlea, *Witch-Hunting*, further cited in chapter 9.

113. Noble, *World*, 229.

114. Noble, *World*, 229–230.

326 LANGUAGE IN THE UNIVERSITY

vigor and conviction has kinship with comparable movements in the earlier history of the university that converted useful approaches to knowledge, such as Abelard's and Aristotle's, into rigid dogmas enforced by groups of men in privileged clubs.

In the Rüegg and Ridder-Symoens history of the European university, Roy Porter says that the slow entrance of science into the universities is more understandable than previous scholars have allowed. The conventional view had been that modern science began outside the university, a view generally accepted in the present discussion. Yet Porter's view remains valid, although he does not take into consideration the exclusionary psychology represented by the use of Latin and the absence of women. Both the conventional and Porter's view obtain, however, by taking into account the wider sense of male group psychology: the "primal horde" formulation given by Freud.[115] It is a psychology of group hegemony followed by insurrection followed by periods of stability and the installation of new leaders. Each phase of this process is characterized by strong intragroup hostility and sometimes terminal fighting. Male groups develop a style of behavior that requires the permanent subordination of some to others, that requires power struggles, that leads to extreme measures such as violence, which in turn is accepted to be a necessary ongoing risk or threat in order to ensure regular civil collective behavior. The dependencies that develop among men seem to get infected with suspicions that challenge people's fundamental sense of safety. Elected governments have depended on this social psychology only slightly less than monarchical and totalitarian governments have. Enlightenment types of idealisms are undercut by the continuous recrudescence of men's group psychology.[116]

Some of the effects of this psychology on the work of male historians are considered in chapter 10, but it is enough to observe at this time how the influence of Abelard, Aristotle, Luther, Calvin, Descartes, and Galileo (among others) worked into the university in ways similar to the ways experimental science worked into it. At first the new material is deemed heretical and thus a threat to the existence of traditional university customs. Over time, the "insurgent" set of ideas gains support until it reaches the threshold of widespread acceptance, and then the universities overtake the new thinking, bureaucratize it, and, often, turn it into a dogma and treat it as the Final Truth. There are

---

115. Outlined in chapter 7, section 3.

116. Two men who have looked into this issue (before the insistence of feminism) are Lionel Tiger, in *Men in Groups* (New York: Vintage, 1970), and Konrad Lorenz, in *On Aggression* (New York: Harcourt, Brace and World, 1966). The latter is considered in some detail in chapter 10. Both books, straining for candor, end up describing the incomprehensibility of this recursive destructive way of functioning. They conclude that men's group behavior is paradoxical.

then dogma fights, as there were between Calvinists and Lutherans in Germany in the late seventeenth century,[117] whose dimensions, as in the previous battles, become violent and murderous.

VIII. New Values, New Languages

By the eighteenth century, science and the vernaculars had worked their way into Catholic and Protestant universities, although women had not. Science was tested by its relative consistency with certain religious cosmologies: are the heavenly bodies "perfect"? Are the paths around the sun perfect circles (as Galileo believed) or are they ellipses (as accurately measured by Kepler)? Is the human body as "mechanical" as the solar system, or does science need to account for its spirit? Can one separate the soul from the body and faith from science, or should one seek a single sense of how humans are in the cosmos? As such questions have occupied the thoughts of university professors and other philosophers, the protection of the universities by powerful institutions continued and worked more or less as it did during the church's custodies in the medieval period. In England, Henry VIII had taken command of the universities and, along with the Church of England, sponsored them and oversaw their curricula. In France, the king had sponsored both the University of Paris and the French Academy.

The secular values that govern contemporary society—commerce, industry, science in their service and in the service of medicine and pharmacology—were developed outside the university and made their way in during the eighteenth century. Founding figures such as Galileo, Descartes, and Newton—like Abelard—modeled values that subsequently became orthodoxies of higher education. In retrospect and in spite of the expectable complexity of how societies developed, the university's adoption of science was connected to the secularization of temporal power: churches were now secondary to monarchies, and when monarchies receded at the beginning of the nineteenth century, nationalist governments had the same interest in the universities as centers of "intelligence."

The ideal of the free pursuit of knowledge was also tied to the break from Church orthodoxy and from the Latin language. The founding of the University of Halle is an early scenario of how most European universities adopted secular values and new organizations to teach and learn under those values. This also provided the machinery for the switch of sponsorship from mainly church backing to mainly state backing. At the end of the seventeenth century (in 1679), Christian Thomasius, a law professor at Leipzig, announced his lectures in German instead of Latin, causing an uproar. He eschewed the professorial

---

117. Andrew Dickson White, *Seven Great Statesmen in the Warfare of Humanity with Unreason* (New York: Century, 1910), 116.

gown and actually gave the lecture in German. He considered the knowledge of Latin to be "useless," and wrote in 1687,

> It is a principle of politics that the ruler must accustom his subjects to the language of the ruler. This principle the Pope has adopted and requires all priests to use the Latin language as a sign of their subjection to him. Ever since the time of Charlemagne this superstition has been introduced into universities, and in order that they should be withdrawn from the supremacy of temporal rulers, all professors and students were included in Holy Orders. Thus Latin became the language of the learned only because it was the language of the parsons (*Pfaffen*).[118]

Thomasius further wrote,

> Foreign languages are of use in order to understand what has been written in them; but in those things which are realized through the intelligence which is innate in all nations, knowledge of foreign language is not at all necessary. Worldly wisdom is so easy a matter, that it can be understood by all people; Greek philosophers did not write in Hebrew but in their mother tongue.[119]

Thomasius's explanation of the use of Latin as a sacred language is not an originological one: there was no moment when one pope decided to subject everyone else to his rule through the use of Latin. The explanation does correspond to the *function* of Latin in the church and in the university. As considered in the next chapter, the use of Latin established a ruling class, and this class being hierarchically organized makes the use of Latin an aspect of service to the pope. In Germany in the late seventeenth century, rule of the total society had shifted to secular figures. Without this shift, without the action of the scientists in the air of Europe, and without the spreading authority of the newly founded, secularly supported academic societies, Thomasius's moves might have resulted in his execution. However, the time seemed hospitable to this move (we think now in retrospect), as it could work with the nationalism that was rising in Europe.

Thomasius's challenge to the language in authority for many centuries resulted in his winning the favor of Emperor Frederick of Prussia, who soon (in 1690) founded the University of Halle. As a faculty member, Thomasius rejected

---

118. "Hodermann quoting Thomasius" (Bronfenbrenner, *Rôle*, 233 [no other source given]).

119. Bronfenbrenner, *Rôle*, 233, citing Ludwig Salomon, *Geschichte der deutschen Zeitungswesen von den ersten Anfaengen bis zur Wiederaufrichtung des deutschen Reiches* (Oldenburg: n.p., 1900–1906).

the rule of Aristotle as well as that of Latin. This university, Bronfenbrenner observes, "became the model of all other university reform."[120] In addition, Thomasius's vision foresaw the chance for the increasing presence of women as university students, and Thomasius was himself a strong opponent of the witch trials, which ended several decades later, in the eighteenth century.[121]

Thomasius helped to lead the West toward the Enlightenment individualism now usually associated with John Locke. Thomasius interpreted public law into a zone separated from received traditions of Roman and Church law, and consistent with the secular government of society. This vision suggested the values of individual religious freedom as well as individual political freedom—and Thomasius helped to create, at the end of the seventeenth century, the legal discourse that would make it possible to enact such laws. But to treat religion as a freedom for individuals also took its influence away from public institutions such as universities. Subsequently even the Catholic University of Göttingen, founded in 1737, nine years after Thomasius's death, "enjoyed special fame in this tradition of public law."[122] From this time on, the principal protectors of universities were state governments—though Church influence, especially at Oxford and Paris, continued to hold theological training in a privileged place.

Neither secularization nor the recognition of individual human rights, however, had a serious effect on the tradition of androcentrism that continued to govern universities even as the changes of custody from church to state took place. These traditions are in effect today governing the distributions of power and influence in universities; androcentrism (or, as some call it, male supremacy) is still the underlying form of university protection. In part, it can be read as self-protection in the following sense: under the assumption that men's associations protect one another in hierarchical contexts or structures, universities could count on governments not to question male supremacy in learning and knowledge, just as governments assumed that universities will pursue no subject capable of challenging existing regimes and that the universities will not protect those who opposed the incumbent political ideologies.

---

120. Bronfenbrenner, *Rôle*, 234. Similarly, Notker Hammerstein writes that with regard to the influence of the Enlightenment on university reform in the eighteenth century, "we should refer above all to Christian Thomasius and the University of Halle. The movement then spread to the other universities" ("Epilogue: The Enlightenment," 2:633).

121. According to Brian Easlea, in "the middle of the eighteenth century," men had "brought witch hunting to an end and eliminated educated belief in the possibility of Satanic witchcraft" (*Witch-Hunting*, 196).

122. Wilhelm Schmidt-Biggemann, "New Structures of Knowledge," *History*, ed. Ridder-Symoens, 2:515.

Universities have participated in censoring heresies throughout their history, and they have persecuted scholars for discovering facts that contradict religious dogmas. However, it is not the new ideas or facts alone that were responsible for various churches' fears of what these scholars were doing: subject matter alone did not pose a strong enough threat. Rather, the new subject matters, which included those now considered false or superstitious, as well as those now accorded transcendental respect, amounted to changes in language use, new vocabulary, and often elevated the vernacular to the highest academic status. The potentially heretical subjects were challenges to the Latin language as well as to Church dogma. The special language was always needed to enact hegemony over learning and study and to retain the traditional style of protection.

CHAPTER NINE

The Sacred Language

I. The Ascendancy of Latin

The language of the Church and of Roman civilization is Latin. The Church's language is not Greek, Hebrew, or Aramaic, the original languages of the sacred texts.[1] There were many centuries during Church rule in which few scholars knew Greek, whose study in the universities began in the early fourteenth century but did not become established until the fifteenth.[2] Greek was the language of pagans, but also, partly, that of the early Christians who, if they were Roman citizens, may have spoken Latin and several other languages—Coptic, Amharic, and Armenian.[3] In the early centuries of the first millennium, "the task of transmitting the arts fell to the agencies of the Roman church."[4] In the fifth century, Latin became the official language of the royal courts in Italy, Spain,

---

1. The complexity of the various languages used in antiquity is described by Françoise Waquet: "Without going back to the first Christian community in Jerusalem, which probably celebrated the liturgy in Aramaic, we can say that the spread of Christianity inside the Roman empire would have been accomplished in the language that was known everywhere: Greek. Latin did not replace it even in Rome until quite late, after the Greek language had fallen from use, probably at some time during the third or fourth century." Waquet says that Latin was adopted by the Church for convenience: "The prime reason [it was adopted] was to ensure communication by using the common language of the Empire." Françoise Waquet, *Latin, or, The Empire of the Sign,* trans. John Howe (New York: Verso, 2001), 41–42. That was one reason; this chapter considers other reasons.

2. Rüegg describes how in the early fourteenth century the pope authorized chairs in Hebrew, Greek, Arabic, and Aramaic, but the universities did not start actually teaching them until the beginning of the fifteenth century. Walter Rüegg, "The Rise of Humanism," *A History of the University in Europe,* vol. 1: *Universities in the Middle Ages,* ed. Hilde de Ridder-Symoens, gen. ed. Walter Rüegg (Cambridge: Cambridge UP, 1992), 455.

3. As listed by Waquet, *Latin,* 42.

4. Pearl Kibre and Nancy G. Siraisi, "The Institutional Setting: The Universities," *Science in the Middle Ages,* ed. David C. Lindberg (Chicago: U of Chicago P, 1978), 121. But Harvey Graff suggests that at least some schools continued to function. *The Legacies of Literacy: Continuities and Contradictions in Western Culture and Society* (Bloomington: Indiana UP 1987), 38.

and France.[5] There was no doctrinal connection between Latin and Christianity; historical development led it to become a sacred language between the sixth and eighth centuries; it has remained sacred since then. Because the pace of language change is slower than the turnover of individual lives, Latin lost its vernacular status on its own, acquiring the status of a superior or elite second language in schools, universities, and the Church.[6] In stages and steps over several centuries Latin became confined to the Church and the universities, to civil and canon law, and was spoken in universities until the seventeenth century.

It became an official language partly because it was written. Oral Latin grew and developed on its own, but its authority diminished as a formal medium, and in the university, it was used informally to practice, and then formally in the disputation, the final examination of students getting their degrees. Becoming the language of the sacraments and theology encouraged—perhaps coerced—the belief that it was intrinsically sacred. The written language was the authoritative one, in no small part because writing was expensive, and only the wealthy could afford to write and to learn to do it.[7] As with androcentrism, it can no longer go without saying that literacy was a privilege of wealth. Within Christianity in the first centuries, "Writings . . . attracted fascination as the vital, living monument to the spoken word of the Creator and the Savior. They took on the power and mass appeal of magical sacred texts."[8] To an illiterate population, the written text can seem to have a special power, to have been produced in a social location forbidden to most people, and thereby imbued with supernatural power beyond its weight as authoritative.

After printing became common at the beginning of the sixteenth century, the great majority of the European population remained illiterate, which meant that written documents retained their implied special power. Because writing was at once so expensive, visual, and seemingly permanent, the transparency of words (the presupposition of mutually understood unambiguous references) taken for granted in conversation might be intensified for one who can read. However, the relationship between the parties—writer and reader—is no longer fluently

---

5. Graff, *Legacies*, 37.

6. Brian Stock, *The Implications of Literacy: Written Language and Models of Interpretation in the Eleventh and Twelfth Centuries* (Princeton, NJ: Princeton UP, 1983), 19–20. Stock says that in the second half of the third century we find the first signs that spoken and written Latin were different. He speculates that this difference is the forerunner of the humanist idea that a "second language," spoken by all, transmits, according to Marrou, a "tradition generally recognized as having an essential superiority over all others." H. I. Marrou, *A History of Education in Antiquity,* trans. G. Lamb (London: Sneed and Ward, 1956), 342.

7. According to Graff, "Most buyers [of books in early Christian times] were libraries, schoolmasters, and wealthy patrons" (*Legacies,* 29).

8. Marrou, in Graff, *Legacies,* 29.

mutual, and the language of the writer (speaker) gets the credit for transparency as a result of the dialogic presumption of the use of language: if the language is shared, you accept as a given that each usage is also shared by the writer (speaker) and you. When you don't understand a speaker, you can often clarify on the spot, but if you don't understand a writer, the text has to be interpreted, and a reader different from you but reading the same words may understand something other than what you understand.[9] The social relations of speaking and writing are different from one another, although the materiality of the language and the social character of the exchanges obtains in both contexts: one might say the two materials (the two media)—speech and writing—are different.

The social and political status of writing and literacy has been a continuing issue in modern scholarship. For the most part, but with exceptions, it has been studied outside the contexts of language philosophy, linguistics, literature, philology, psychology, political science, economics, sociology, anthropology, and other implicated fields.[10] Literacy has been often studied as part of the curriculum in professional education, but usually with the idea that achieving literacy is a necessary *preparation* in modern society.[11] This separation is a problem because writing is part of speaking as much as it is part of reading. As many aspects of contemporary life suggest, visual and oral recording are closely connected, and brought even closer by new technologies. Writing is predicated on speaking as much as it is predicated on reading, and both predications are bound up in specifiable social relations.[12] As some of the recent socially oriented studies of literacy suggest, literacy conventions change with the subject matter and local

---

9. The same sort of misunderstanding does occur in oral situations; it just is treated differently, depending on the actual circumstances.

10. Both Harvey Graff's several comprehensive studies of the history of literacy and William V. Harris's review of classical literacy, *Ancient Literacy* (Cambridge, MA: Harvard UP, 1989), concentrate on presenting the evidences of literacy and of which groups of people achieved it. Because such inferences are speculative, they have not related their findings about the degree and spread of literacy to the uses of language in those societies. The evidence of the actual use of language in any bygone society is hard to find or identify to begin with.

11. Shirley Brice Heath's *Ways with Words: Language, Life, and Work in Communities and Classroom* (New York: Cambridge UP, 1983), Marilyn S. Sternglass's *Time to Know Them* (Mahwah, NJ: Erlbaum, 1997), and Deborah Brandt's *Literacy in American Lives* (Cambridge: Cambridge UP, 2001) begin to relate, in comprehensive and critical senses, the degree of literacy and the processes of achieving it to various uses of language and various aspects of society. These studies do make use of understanding achieved in the disciplines listed above.

12. Grammatical predication also grows out of social relations—those developing in infancy, a perspective considered in chapter 5. Deborah Tannen's early studies of sociolinguistic behavior moved back and forth between literary and real-life examples. It is clear from such discussions how fully literary and conversational uses of language are continu-

circumstances of use. Latin today retains its historic privileged status in law and medicine. This ascendancy has been recently reviewed and is discussed in this chapter.

II. Literacy and Access to Language

In studying literacy, Western scholars have assumed a radical distinction between it and orality:[13] they are two different modes, following different rules, and most susceptible to study as contrasting states of language. But if language is recognized as material, its oral and literate uses share a gestural materiality, and their differences are not radical, but are those of context, usage, and social arrangement. Lévi-Strauss emphasizes that writing has been used to maintain and promote political power—to build and rule civilizations; he recognizes the materiality characteristic of the language uses of office holders and political leaders:

> The only phenomenon with which writing has always been concomitant is the creation of cities and empires, that is the integration of large numbers of individuals into a political system, and their grading into castes or classes. . . . [I]t seems to have favoured the exploitation of human beings rather than their enlightenment. . . . My hypothesis, if correct, would oblige us to recognize the fact that the primary function of written communication is to facilitate slavery.[14]

This "hypothesis" is not susceptible of a proof, but the evidence of history suggests that the literate class is also the slave-holding class.[15] Writing is an enabling technology, a luxury, a form of access to language and salient social relations that those who are ruled don't have.

---

ous with one another: their common features are usually the literary tropes and speech genres. This closeness is a basis for Derrida's reference to all uses of language as "writing."

13. Walter Ong's *Orality and Literacy: The Technologizing of the Word* (New York: Penguin, 1982) is based on this premise and is discussed in section 5 of this chapter. This work, which considers orality from several points of view, is something of departure from earlier scholarly treatments of oral literature, which was not considered in the total context of language use. Ong is aware that this total context is essential for his discussion, but his distinctions rely on the classic assumptions of radical differences between orality and literacy.

14. Claude Lévi-Strauss, "A Writing Lesson," *Tristes tropiques,* trans. John Weightman and Doreen Weightman (New York: Atheneum, 1973), 299.

15. As discussed by Harris, *Ancient.* Although classical Greek societies are often cited for their enlightened political and social conventions, they were slave societies. Some slaves became literate, but *access* to literacy was available to very few. As is commonly

William V. Harris acknowledges, "Over and over again 'divine' ordinances have assumed written form; Moses is simply the most famous 'intermediary.' Zeus acquired writing-tablets soon after the Greeks. . . [M]en who claimed religious authority employed the reality or the image of the written word to enhance their authority."[16] However, Harris's hesitation about the hypothesis is connected with some salutary consequences of literacy:

> [W]hat is hegemonic or exploitative merges imperceptibly into what is
> an instrument of social discipline, and that in turn into what is benign.
> Writing makes empires possible, indeed . . . Writing was also vital to the
> development of the city; but are we to say that the city has been mainly
> a source of exploitation?[17]

Posing the issue of literacy as an instrument of exploitation in this way implies that one cannot be confident about the connection between literacy and the access to social privilege. However, if literacy were associated with a more general access to language and its technologies, the issue would no longer be whether literacy is a weapon or a tool, or a question of what would have happened in the past, or whether cities are good or bad, or whether civilization is good or bad. The question would become empirical and political—a question of the total population's access to language, and not whether the various types of access are harmful.[18] If the scholarly study of language focuses on this question, it studies how the access to language affects the success and failure of whole societies, nations, empires, city-states, and civilizations. Universities have played a significant role in determining which populations get access to languages, literacies, texts, and documents. Most people have been illiterate and have had little access to language, and the situation is not very different today. Furthermore, literacy by itself does not create access to language.

---

known from the history of American slavery, a principal means of perpetuating slavery is enforcing the illiteracy of slaves. In cases of heresy and witchcraft, leaders (sometimes called "heresiarchs") who made social choices not approved by the Church facilitated the group's acquisition of vernacular literacy. Such developments were the grounds for the Church's fears of socially and politically enabled rivals to its own dominion over religion, the law, and medical knowledge.

16. Harris, *Ancient*, 39.

17. If the city is to be taken as a reliable simulacrum of civilization, the answer to Harris's question is yes. If, in the city, women are illiterate and men run it based on their access to writing, it may well be justified to view cities as a "source of exploitation." This description might be contrasted with Freud's (see chapter 7), which overlooks the exploitation on the (false) ground that women's own initiatives take them away from civilization.

18. This issue is similar to an issue raised in chapter 1, comparing statements by Vivien Law and Roger Cohen. Inquiries into what language practices do social harm are

The idea of access to language distinguishes among the various cases of literacy as a weapon or a tool, as those with most access can decide on how to use the language. Such decisions may then be promoted on a public, collective scale. The question then becomes how to distinguish between the use of language by those with the most access to it and the use by everyone else. This issue renders the question of materiality and transparency of language germane, and it necessitates political thinking. If one continues to think of the language itself or literacy itself as items manifested by the documents preserved in the historical record, it is hard to conceptualize the different uses of language embedded in the different places of society. But because the access to language and literacy is also observable in the historical record, it is less difficult to identify different uses in terms of different levels of access: what was the social standing of the authors and the audiences of these texts? Lévi-Strauss's view emerges from the comparison of access to use. At this juncture, the distinction between transparent and materialist senses of language becomes a salient factor in the search for productive ways to study language. This is the value of the study of total mediation by Rosalind Morris discussed in chapter 1. There are practical consequences of assuming transparency and materiality in order to describe specific uses of language—those uses that have been documented and recorded. The transparency of any one use of language is necessarily provisional, as it depends on collective acceptance: all members of society assume the same reference for specific words or larger texts and usages. Materiality is a description of language regardless of which usage is in effect, whereas transparency is a specific usage for only some occasions. Recognizing materiality provides a ground for distinguishing genres as parts of social scenes in which references can (and do) change as part of changes in social arrangements and initiatives by people in the ordinary conduct of life.[19]

The histories of the church and of the universities present the Latin language as the total mediator. Informally, it was the language of knowledge because

---

often distracted by the need to locate a cause in a specific practice, such as pornography or violence in films, both of which are as much responses to public demands as they are entrepreneurial initiatives. If one is to search for causes at all, the habits and tastes of the society generally have to be a part of the picture. The degree of political access to language, which in these cases is access to mass markets, is almost never a factor in such studies.

19. Many familiar terms make this fact clear. In some situations, "God" has a fixed reference, but in other situations, it does not, such as, perhaps, in "Thank God it's Friday." "Love" is also a good example. There are some senses in which everyone accepts certain references for both terms; but there are also so many circumstances in which the reference of the two terms is contested, to the point of violence: "All is fair in love and war." Such variation takes place because the language is material—attached to living people and used as a social, conversational gesture. In the case of the Eucharist, the dispute is over which things are material to begin with.

any authoritative knowledge had to be presented in written Latin.[20] Today, for example, even when Latin does not play that role in most instances, it is more "accurate" to say one has a broken *femur* than a broken thighbone.[21] The physicians' records still carry the Latin names. The different language inserts contextual factors that change the signification, partly by calling attention to the social status of the user of the word. When the user is the authoritative figure or party, the language becomes transparent, giving the official (that is, "correct") reference. A non-authoritative user saying "thighbone" is using a substitute that interferes not with the reference of *femur,* but with its authority and its political status, which is necessarily a part of any use of language.

The situation is similar with a sacred usage and with uses of language within sacramental rituals, a familiar and important instance being the Eucharist and the centuries of dispute about it. Within the sacred context, the priest's Latin words transubstantiate the bread and wine: a translation from the Greek that has been placed into the mass and put to a use different from its use in the New Testament, where it is not clear that the phrase "this is my body" is literal. But in the Mass it is not questioned by those taking communion. The language is sacred, and its Greek or English versions are irrelevant: the Mass is said in Latin, and each person partakes of (eats) the body and blood of Christ. Although Latin is not the sole factor leading to the successful performance of this ritual, it was one of the factors without which the ritual would lose its validity.[22] Another factor is that a priest has to say the words (and the communicant has to have been confessed, and so on). This ritual was troublesome because, repeatedly in history, some people insisted that the priest's words had to make a truthful reference. When this standard is applied, things said about the Eucharist could be construed by Church authorities as unorthodox references, which were unacceptable. Thus the authority of the ritual, residing in the language as used by those authorized to perform the ritual, would be compromised if the language were questioned. Questioning sacred language necessarily questions sacred authority.

---

20. Peter Goodrich considers the historical misuse of Latin. Using Françoise Waquet's text, cited earlier in this chapter, he offers this sense of how Latin functioned after it stopped being a vernacular: "Teaching Latin had to be the sign of something else; it was a code, a secret encounter, a politics by other means." "Distrust Quotations in Latin," *Critical Inquiry* 29.2 (Winter 2003): 193–215, quotation on 199. Both Waquet and Goodrich emphasize the apparent paradox that Latin retained a high status even though only a minority of the population could use it (Goodrich, "Distrust," 199). In the present discussion, the emphasis is on the fact that Latin retained its sacred function both before and after printing: it continued to have the same social effects of preserving an elite and of limiting the general population's access to official formulations.

21. Which language used to describe the injury tells who is speaking and in this way identifies the political and social situations of use.

22. That is, until other languages were permitted to be used in the Mass.

Given these two common uses of Latin in the Church and in the university, it also is a secret or encoded language, as others have noted. If people asked for the vernacular translations of the Latin, they could be told. If people wanted to learn the sacred language, they may have been able to learn it.[23] However, most people commonly could not afford to go to school to learn it. Those few boys who did go to school did learn Latin grammar.[24] For centuries the main purpose of going to "grammar school" was to learn Latin grammar. Those vocationally pointed in specific directions could learn enough Latin to go to universities and pursue the trivium and advanced professional studies. Although the language was available for study, its locus of use excluded most people: almost all women, and most men not pursuing clerical, legal, or medical subjects. In addition, its secrecy was maintained by literacy: because it was so expensive and so difficult to write, few could do it. Those who did learn to write got jobs as scribes, notaries, or other official writers. Still others who did pursue clerical vocations wrote (or dictated) the texts we are now studying and reading as representative of the history and society of Western civilization. The Latin language was secret in that it was not accessible to the vast majority of the population.[25] Although Latin vernaculars were used, there were, as John Fisher describes, "standards"—special efforts were made to standardize them as, it was argued, any written language needs standard orthography and punctuation as well as standard usages and styles.[26] Latin was official, holy, authoritative as knowledge, separated from the ordinary lives of the vast majority of the population, and—with few exceptions—confined to an elite group of men. The Latin language was a key instrument establishing the political structures of European societies.

Latin was a secret language in additional critical senses.[27] Early in the sixteenth century, humanist educator Juan Vives wrote that "it is also useful that there should be some language sacred for the learned, to which might be consigned

23. But they also often could not. The 1229 Council of Toulouse prohibited the possession by the laity of both Old and New Testaments, and it strictly forbade the laity "having any translation of" the "Psalter or the Breviary." How fully this canon was enforced, however, is not possible to say. Edward Peters, *Heresy and Authority in Medieval Europe* (Philadelphia: U of Pennsylvania P, 1980), 195.

24. As discussed in section 5, learning Latin could be compared to a fraternity initiation: punishment was a regular part of the process of remembering tenses, verb forms, and vocabulary.

25. According to Waquet, "From soon after the beginning of print, written Latin was inaccessible to all but a small pan-European elite" (quoted in Goodrich, "Distrust," 199).

26. "[I]n the Middle Ages the official language was Latin, and unofficial speech and writing was in local dialects." John H. Fisher, *The Emergence of Standard English* (Lexington: UP of Kentucky, 1996), 67. Fisher distinguishes between Imperial Latin, which is always written, and vulgar Latin dialects, which became the Romance languages.

27. Walter J. Ong, S.J., *Rhetoric, Romance, and Technology: Studies in the Interaction of Expression and Culture* (Ithaca, NY: Cornell UP, 1971), used this phrase "secret language"

those hidden things which are unsuitable to be handled by everybody, and thus become polluted."[28] This statement refers to the tradition in Catholic theology that avoids exposing those without proper preparation to material that could not be understood without it, although the thought about pollution is unnecessary for the practical purpose and given for other reasons. Vives, loyal to the Church, was also a leading Renaissance figure advocating the enlargement of the university humanities curriculum to include the study of other languages. In his view, people had to be properly prepared to study material given in the sacred language. In this cause he advocated the principle of making other languages, including Hebrew,[29] available to scholars. In the latter case, he suggested the grounds for concern with his warning that learning Hebrew exposes the student to "corruption" of understanding because things have been "falsified in Hebrew writings by Jews." Perhaps this position is germane enough to be considered, but what about this other position: Jews "so often change their abodes, and have not leisure to bestow due labour on literature. Certainly if you consult two Jews as to the same passage, rarely do they agree. I would wish the Latin language to be known thoroughly, for this is a benefit to society and to the knowledge of all the sciences."[30] This view may be compared to earlier suspicions of Greek as being a pagan language and a potential danger to church orthodoxy. Other languages may be considered essential, but they are also viewed as possible rivals.[31] This danger is further represented in his view of the Jews—and their habits of holding several opinions of the same text. Jews joke about this feature of Jewish culture. The collective acknowledgment of there being more opinions than people is considered by Jews a point of pride.[32] Even though Vives' passage about Jews looks biased in one sense (that is, saying that itinerancy compromises study), in another sense it has a common ground with ordinary Jewish approaches to texts: Jews in serious contexts, including non-rabbinic readers, entertain several readings of sacred texts, particularly insofar as these texts are treated as sources of law governing daily life. Readers study differ-

---

with an immediate sense identical to mine, although not with the same critical purpose. I return to this matter in the last part of this chapter.

28. Foster Watson, ed. and trans., *Vives, On Education: A Translation of* De tradendis disciplinis *of Juan Luis Vives* (Cambridge: Cambridge UP, 1913), 93.

29. Watson, *Vives*, 95.

30. Watson, *Vives*, 95.

31. There can only be a rival language if one is considered to be better than another. If each language has something distinctive or characteristic to say, it would not be possible for one to rival another.

32. It is also an indication that the materiality of language, approached by study styles in learned Jewish contexts, is likely the basis of the proliferation of opinion. However, Daniel Boyarin, in *Unheroic Conduct: The Rise of Heterosexuality and the Invention of the Jewish Man* (Berkeley: U of California P, 1997), describes Jewish life as being less hierarchical than Catholic life, although I would not read his description as amounting to separate but equal: men in Judaism always have had the final say as to how the law

ing opinions in the Talmud—for example, Shammai and Hillel, conservative and liberal schools, respectively.[33] But the Church authorizes only one opinion. For even the progressive Vives, the need for a single reading of sacred texts, and for an uncorrupted language and an unpolluted understanding, suggests the high level of conscious constraint of the function of Latin, and especially the need to confine it to the small group of authoritative men in whose custody it becomes a secret language. Protecting sacred languages from contamination creates a standard of social purity that is maintained by the secrecy of the language.

III. Heresy and the Opposition to New Language

III-1. CRIMES OF LANGUAGE USE

The secrecy of the sacred language that sustains church orthodoxy is connected to two virulent phenomena that have resulted from the active protection of orthodoxy: the fear of and continual testing for heresy and the campaigns of witch-hunting,[34] both of which drew the involvement of university figures, sometimes as alleged heretics (John Wyclif and Jan Hus[35]), sometimes as inquisitors (Heinrich Kramer and James [aka Jacob] Sprenger[36]). The preoccupation

---

was to affect social action. It is worth noting that recognition of language materiality does not necessarily come with gender equality.

33. In early Christian times, Gnostics occupied a position similar to that of Jews: "To the bishops . . . [Gnostics], even when they seemed to be sincere Christians intent on striking out on their own spiritual paths, were dangerous to the movement. The bishops may have been right; as Tertullian said, gnostic Christians agreed only to disagree." Elaine Pagels, *Adam, Eve, and the Serpent* (New York: Vintage, 1988), 77. Pagels described how these Christians had varying interpretations of the new faith, and they were therefore feared.

34. There is no need to assume a strong boundary between the two practices: scholars have generally settled on "dissent" as the term that describes their comparable positions in society. In the words of Jeffrey Russell, "Orthodoxy defines heresy." Jeffrey Russell, *Dissent and Order in the Middle Ages: The Search for Legitimate Authority* (New York: Twayne, 1992), 4. Similarly, in Edward Peters, "Heresy [exists] only in relation to orthodoxy" (*Heresy*, 14). Like Russell, Norman Cohn understands witchcraft to have been considered a more heinous crime that includes heresy, one that requires an inquisition even more than heresy. Norman Cohn, *Europe's Inner Demons: The Demonization of Christians in Medieval Christendom,* (Chicago: U of Chicago P, 1993). The two offenses were connected in an insidious ritual: a suspect would be asked if she believed in witchcraft. If she answered no, that would be heresy, as the doctrine held that witchcraft existed. If she answered yes, she would be further interrogated as to her own and others' involvement. Paul Tice, "Foreword," *The* Malleus maleficarum *of Heinrich Kramer and James Sprenger,* ed. and trans. Montague Summers (Escondido, CA: Book Tree, 2000), n.p.

35. Faculty members at Oxford and Prague, respectively.

36. "First published in 1486, and reprinted thirteen times before 1520, it was the work of two Dominican inquisitors, Heinrich Kramer or Institoris (his Latin name) and

with both of these issues, in turn, served to shore up the strength of orthodox university curricula and standards of knowledge and faith, and by creating an atmosphere of fear, they communicated the authority of the Church.[37]

In the histories of heresy and witchcraft, the status of the language was a key factor. The control of each practice was sought through inquisitions—organized searches by the Church for offenders, accompanied by the demand that offenders individually declare their beliefs and identify others—and often by executions, which were carried out by secular authorities at the request of the Church.[38] Because of the theocratic aspect of the state, challenges to religious orthodoxy were received as political challenges as well (Wyclif and Hus both had royal support) and were dealt with as such. The punishments for both crimes were often the same, burning alive at the stake (Wyclif, but not Hus, escaped this fate). These organized assaults, tortures, and cruel punishments took place because of *what people said* (part of which was the use of the vernaculars), and not because they committed felonies. The alleged crimes were those of *contradicting,* usually, but not necessarily, in print, a known doctrine or authority.[39] Medieval heresies[40] were usually found in living groups rather than in isolated manuscripts or speeches, but they were behaviors concealed by "a shield of words."[41] It would be also true that the uses of the words themselves were offensive behaviors. Bishops and royal advisors understood that things said were never *just* things said and were linked to various practices and social events; consequently, to say these words was treated as a criminal act on that score. Lambert observes in addition that "[f]ears of heresy were aroused by the work of scholars and their discussions; accusations circulated, could be, and

---

Jacob Sprenger. Kramer, the principal author, was an elderly and perhaps emotionally disturbed theologian who had been appointed as an inquisitor for southern Germany in 1474. Sprenger, a professor of theology at the University of Cologne, had received a similar appointment as inquisitor for the Rhineland in 1470." Brian P. Levack, *The Witch-Hunt in Early Modern Europe* (New York: Longman, 1987), 54.

37. According to Peters, "universities emerged in the early fifteenth century as bastions against heresy and treated even intellectual dissent among their members very roughly" (*Heresy*, 219).

38. Norman Cohn, *Europe's Inner Demons: An Enquiry Inspired by the Great Witch-Hunt* (New York: Basic, 1975), 23.

39. In other words, choosing the wrong item in the list of A and not-A. Inquisitors, tacitly recognizing the materiality of language, treated the wrong speech choice as a seditious social gesture.

40. Cathars, Waldensians, Albigensian, and Hussites all formed living groups with their own religious practices, and some clear language denying the divinity of Christ but not rejecting Christianity.

41. Malcolm Lambert, *Medieval Heresy: Popular Movements from the Gregorian Reform to the Reformation* (Cambridge, MA: Blackwell, 1977), 14. The phrase is cited from an eleventh-century account.

were, used in politico-ecclesiastical battles."[42] Because the Church could both criminalize language (on the one hand) and give it the power of miraculous transubstantiation (on the other hand) only *its* language could be counted as material. The materiality of the language was presupposed, and it was artificially confined to the sacred language, while presupposing and recognizing materiality was denied, by convention or decree, to speakers of vernaculars, who were not permitted to materialize their language.

Norman Cohn observes that at the end of the twelfth century the "intellectual elite," which included "learned clerics who stood at the very centre of affairs," believed that the Devil, in the form of a cat or other animal, "presided over the nocturnal orgies of heretics."[43] Witches were accused of collective practices and collectively held beliefs, and part of the response to such accusations was to extract through torture (imaginary) information about the collective scope of the alleged practices. Both sets of practices were considered to be diabolically motivated. Lambert details this background for heresy[44] and Cohn shows the demonization of heresy and the application of the same diabolical explanation to the witch-hunts.

The Greek term *haeresia* for "heresy" changed under the influence of the growth of Christianity.[45] As discussed in chapter 8, Alain Le Boulluec describes how the original meaning of the word was *choice* (of philosophical schools) with a brief discussion of its uses by two Jewish sources, Josephus and Philo, each of whom use it to refer to schools of thought or sects—the Essenes, the Pharisees, and the Sadducees. Boulluec further suggests that Paul gives the Greek word "heresy" an unfavorable connotation by saying that the Jews call his faith heresy: "But this I confess unto thee, that after the way which they call heresy, so worship I the God of my fathers, believing all things which are written in the law and in the prophets."[46] Paul identifies Christianity as the true way, as other schools (Jews) are said to use the term "heresy" to discredit Paul's faith. Paul also distorts how the Jews used the term. Le Boulluec suggests it plausible to conclude that Paul gives the term a negative connotation.[47] Such changes, occurring spontaneously over time, are common for many words. This change

---

42. Lambert, *Medieval,* 16.

43. Cohn, *Europe's* (1993), 40.

44. In the words of Lambert, "Heresy . . . is 'depravity,' 'poison,' 'the path of error,' 'depths of wickedness,' 'madness and devilish error.' The heretics are enemies of all truth,' 'doomed and wretched'" (*Medieval,* 13).

45. Peters has an account of the transformation of the term toward its present pejorative meaning (*Heresy,* 14–17), agreeing with Le Boulluec (note 47, this chapter) and with Russell (*Dissent,* 2).

46. Acts 24:14. Le Boulluec's discussion is first cited in chapter 8, section 4.

47. Alain Le Boulluec, *La notion d'hérésie dans la littérature grecque, IIe–IIIe siècles,* vol. 1: *De Justin à Irénée* (Paris: Études augustiniennes, 1985), 37–38.

marks the establishment of categories of thought by their relation to one creed, a narcissistic definition that measures other thoughts and judges their value relative to its own presumed superiority. The significance of this different sense of heresy is its new reference and in its use as the basis for excommunications and executions. The term "heresy" itself might be and sound less offensive had not so much brutality and killing resulted from its having been become a crime of language use.

Christianity eventually acquired imperial status when the emperor Constantine converted in the fourth century. This was an enormous achievement for Christianity in that his conversion, along with the efforts and writings of the Church fathers, allowed the Church to see itself on the Roman scale.[48] Having reached this place, it stayed there for thirteen centuries, until well after the Reformation. Europe lived during this long period under a series of analogous loose theocracies, with two branches of government—church and state—each collecting taxes.[49] While not formally allied to one another, and acting often on behalf of opposed interests, such hegemony would nevertheless feel a threat from expressions of collective religious independence or individuality. In the fourteenth century, the Wycliffite heresy was connected socially and politically to the crown's opposition to the Church. To speak (and write) heretical thoughts also necessarily implied a threat to temporal power. Heretics proposed a new sense of sacred language or different references for the existing language of the Church. The threatening language initiatives found in the heresies, viewed alone, have been discussed and studied as if they were just thoughts, but few were. Both Church and heretics understood that the new formulations, which were a function of different mores of living and religious orientation, were connected to challenges to Church social organization and dominion and were created for the purpose of mounting these challenges.[50] Such challenges would more likely be directed against the Church than the state because the former

---

48. Overtaking, that is, the status of the Roman Empire. As Goodrich discusses, both canon and civil law were already overtaken from the Roman Empire. James Carroll suggests that the later Augustine, cognizant of the imperial identity of Christianity, "justified the use of coercion in defending, and spreading, the orthodox faith." James Carroll, *Constantine's Sword: The Church and the Jews, a History* (Boston: Houghton-Mifflin, 2001), 211. Jeffrey Russell notes that in the eleventh century, under Pope Gregory VII, the Church identified itself with its hierarchy of bishops and proclaimed its dominion over temporal monarchs as well (*Dissent*, 3–4). This move provoked schisms and eventually led to the Reformation.

49. If this were not the case, the Church schisms of the eleventh, fourteenth, and sixteenth centuries would not have been such important events. In retrospect, both the schisms that succeeded and those that failed mattered greatly in that many were affected.

50. This was true of all the well-known medieval heresies. People gathered regularly, had different practices, and did not recognize the supreme authority of the pope.

had no army, but as historians have recorded, the state was often an eager ally, especially in the execution of dissidents.

The ability to withstand the results of heretical speech action seemed to have stayed with the Church until the sixteenth-century Reformation, when most of northern Europe went on a different path with respect to how Christianity was governed. The Church regarded its political, rather than its doctrinal, authority as the measure of its health, even though publicly it, like the heretics, used a shield of words to represent a stance that held religious belief—faith—to be the fundamental value. The changes of religious doctrine in northern Europe were more successes of secular over ecclesiastical authority than the salutary arrival of enlightened values, although the latter effect was part of the picture at the time, and enlarged in subsequent historical periods. In both England and Germany, the universities were a key factor in the shift of religious authority: Henry VIII took control of Oxford and Cambridge, while the German emperors founded new universities in Germany, many of which eventually established world standards of scholarly practice.

III-2. WYCLIF AND THE LOLLARDS

In England, the change of political and cultural authority was augured by its history of production of vernacular literature,[51] and then by the Wycliffite heresy that switched the focus from the sacred language to the vernacular as the language of God and the language of the people: one language was enough for sacred and secular functions.[52] Anne Hudson speculates that the Wycliffite challenge might well have become a formal reformation in England had printing been available to it.[53] It had important features of a full-fledged religious revolution, including significant royal backing and a large number of lay enthusiasts. But because the word could not get out fast enough, the Church could rally its own adherents. At the time (between 1350 and 1450) there was a growth of universities and especially of theology faculties in European universities. Along

---

51. In Italy, there was also a vernacular literature, and a group of influential, enlightened city-states whose population and universities became independent (as they had previously been) of Church influence. Perhaps there was no reformation there because it was not needed: there was already an independent secular tradition, without formal opposition to the Church, in Italian humanism (discussed in chapter 2). Furthermore, the original charter for Bologna was given by a secular monarch and only later assumed by the Church.

52. It may be worth comparing the use of Hebrew in contemporary Israel: it is now a full vernacular, yet it remains the historic sacred language of law, prayer, and worship. The whole society has access to the language. Still, English is a required second language in Israel. Its function is to establish a continuing connection with other Western societies.

53. Anne Hudson, *The Premature Reformation: Wycliffite Texts and Lollard History* (Oxford: Clarendon P, 1988), 510. The pope could not stop the presses.

with Paris, Oxford and Cambridge came to be considered leaders in theology. These new centers of theology helped to counteract dissident movements. During this period of theological enrichment, Wyclif and his group were the "best organized attempt to provide a corpus of religious instruction in English."[54] Whatever doctrinal variations Wyclif may have presented, the use of the vernacular and its popularity could not be rendered a heresy.

Norman Cohn said that early millenarian heretic leaders were usually semi-intellectuals,[55] men who, more often than not, were not formally within the studious professions but who read enough to challenge established doctrines. In the case of Wyclif, the heretic was a university scholar supported by a Church benefice. During his lifetime, he was controversial, but he escaped direct persecution.[56] His vernacular translation of the Bible was not considered heretical, although his readings of transubstantiation were, perhaps, just about heretical, but somehow couched in a strong enough shield of words to escape excommunication and execution. Twenty-five years after Wyclif's death, however, Archbishop Thomas Arundel of Canterbury drew up rules that censored the study of Wyclif's work in the universities, ordered his books burned, prevented anyone from teaching about his efforts, and required oaths from the existing faculty that they would not speak about Wyclif's views.

The fact that Arundel's censorship of Wyclif took place before the Papal Schism ended (in 1417) suggests why such an action would seem belated: it was a response to a Church crisis outside England, an attempt at a Church restoration. Anne Hudson's assessment that printing was needed to facilitate the reformation seems correct in light of the fact that heresies had been building in Europe in the twelfth and thirteenth centuries, whereas the fourteenth-century heresies of Wyclif and Hus were different in that they enjoyed royal support. Hus was supported by the Holy Roman Emperor, and Wyclif by the English King Edward II. Because Wyclif was a "propagandist paid by the English royal family to write anti-papal tracts,"[57] his heresy was more clearly a preliminary move toward the Protestant structure of national churches. The change in doctrine was not just a matter of belief; it was related to a vision of major change in the society. The status of the language of the Eucharist was related to this anticipated change in society.

---

54. J. I. Catto, "Wyclif and Wycliffism at Oxford 1356–1430," *The History of the University of Oxford* ed. J. I. Catto and Ralph Evans (Oxford: Clarendon P, 1992), 2:175.

55. "In the main such men [the millenarian prophets] came from the lower strata of the intelligentsia. They included many members of the lower clergy, priests who had left their parishes, monks who had fled from their monasteries, clerks in minor orders. They included also some laymen, who unlike the laity in general, had acquired a certain literacy." Norman Cohn, *The Pursuit of the Millennium* (New York: Harper, 1961), 70.

56. Perhaps because of quiet royal sympathy.

57. Marcia L. Colish, *Medieval Foundations of the Western Intellectual Tradition, 400–1400* (New Haven, CT: Yale UP 1997) 254.

Wyclif's vernacular Bible was one of many European initiatives toward vernacularization. However, this gesture said to the public that the Bible is for them.[58] Wyclif's heresy also derives from a conscious policy that held sacraments be explicable to all people, not just to theologians or other clerics. Conversely, Wyclif "regarded the layman's belief as highly relevant to scholastic interpretation of the sacrament."[59] Wyclif's religious stance demanded a correspondence between Church doctrine, Church liturgy, and popular belief. His interpretation of the Eucharist is consistent with the scriptural words of Christ, that in eating the bread and drinking the wine, one should remember him. This is how Aston explains Wyclif's view: "Again and again, Wycliffe remarks that in the mind of the faithful, consideration of the nature or quiddity of the host is obliterated or suspended . . . at this central moment, when the words of consecration are pronounced. Complete concentration on the person of Christ removed the spiritual understanding from worries about the perceptions of the senses."[60] This view is heretical because the orthodox (official Church) reading of scripture had an Aristotelian basis. Perception of the senses meant that one felt and saw bread and wine, but that they were accidents appearing with the substance that was "the whole body of Christ, blood and spirit . . . complete in every point of this sacrament."[61] According to Aristotle, substance and accident could not exist apart from one another. The Thomist (orthodox) reading of Aristotle upheld this view, but said that the priestly words converted the substance to the body and blood of Christ. Wyclif's heresy converted the knowledge that the substance of the host was Christ's whole body to the knowledge that partaking of the host brought the communicant's mind away from what the substance was, and toward Christ himself. Wyclif, it was read by his accusers and followers both, naturalized the Eucharistic event. For his followers, this naturalization promised a new integrity in social and religious life; to his accusers, it was seditious of the Church.

In fact, as Miri Rubin[62] writes, Wyclif's was a new form of a series of challenges to the sacrament. A typical formulation is found in this version of the Albigensian heresy:

---

58. Again, this fact supports Hudson's guess: if it had been immediately printed, it would have spread so rapidly as to have evaded Church authority.

59. Margaret Aston, *Faith and Fire: Popular and Unpopular Religion, 1350–1600* (London: Hambledon P, 1993), 56.

60. Aston, *Faith*, 59–60. Another formulation is Colish's: "Wycliff rejects the orthodox view that the bread and wine on the altar change into the body and blood of Christ when the celebrant says the words of consecration. His reason is that bread and wine, like everything else, are reducible to their essential, archetypical natures, natures not subject to change. Thus, no substances, Eucharistic bread and wine included, can change into other substances, under any circumstances whatever" (*Medieval*, 255).

61. Aston, *Faith*, 58.

62. Miri Rubin, *Corpus Christi: The Eucharist in Late Medieval Culture* (Cambridge: Cambridge UP, 1991), 321.

They teach that the host of Christ's body does not differ from lay bread; instilling such blasphemy in the ears of simple folk, saying that even if Christ's body was as large as the Alps, it would have already been consumed by those eating it, and would have been totally annihilated.

Rubin comments that "If sacramental bread were like any other bread, then the priestly function, the particular sacerdotal efficacy which justified priestly privilege, and ultimately the whole ecclesiastical structure, was put into question."[63] The priesthood took for itself—through an authorized reading of the Gospel—the power to convert the bread into the body of Christ. This is a magical power, but when placed into the hands of a recognized authority, it becomes merely a sacred and secret power exercised through a particular use of its sacred and secret language. This power is enabled, perhaps decisively, by the mendacious transparency of the priest's language, and functions identically to how the magician's language functioned in Rosalind Morris's account of Chuchad (see chapter 1). The challenges to the veracity of the sacramental conversion of substance was by any measure a challenge to this supreme, widespread authority, and it was correctly read by the Church as such. It was called heresy and punished with torture and a slow death by fire, which was meant to purge the community of the diabolically motivated spirit.

The heretical view of this sacrament was accepted by many before the vernacular became important in the Wycliffite movement: the naturalization of the ceremony did not require the vernacular.[64] Yet the vernacular was one of the ingredients necessary to effect the social change implied by the challenge to the ritual. Had the Church taken a more positive view of the vernacular it (the Church) might have been strengthened earlier and less vulnerable to radical change: "Fear of the vernacular tended to check rather than foster the struggles of the medieval Church to raise the standards of the humble parish clergy."[65] The topic of the Eucharist, represented by terms such as *transubstancio, substancia, accidens,* always remained untranslated as the "convention was that such matters were not to be ventilated before the laity."[66] It was considered to be a heretical practice, furthermore, to read the Bible without Church mediation.[67] After Wyclif's death, the Lollard movement continued for a century as a dissident movement. Rubin continues,

---

63. Rubin, *Corpus,* 328.

64. The previous heresies, Catharism, Albigensianism, and Beguines, for example, all challenged the central element of the doctrine—that the substance of the Eucharist was the *actual* body of Christ.

65. Lambert, *Medieval,* 270.

66. Lambert, *Medieval,* 234.

67. Lambert, *Medieval,* 233.

Lollardy was confined neither to a particular social group nor to a specific cultural milieu. The centrality of vernacular reading for persuasion, conversion and maintenance of the Lollard world-view is striking. Lollards created social and "textual-communities," to use Brian Stock's phrase, which were heterogeneous but which necessarily combined reading, sociability and mutual support. The texts as sources of knowledge and The Text, scripture, as the authority for all knowledge, are here linked.[68]

The conversion of a sacred language to a vernacular is as much a materialization of language as the declaration of the bread to be bread in a situation in which communicants decide to think consciously of the bread as a *reminder* of the transcendental, not as the actual transcendental. The Eucharistic declaration is the gesture that performs the action of turning the communicant's attention to Christ. This thought—which prevents the ecclesiastical change of reference—when collectively practiced and acknowledged, is what makes it dangerous to the existing institutions and practices. Such trading of views among ordinary people and such a text-centered communitarian social life suggest what had been denied by the confinement of religious life to a privileged language: a devoted, learned, religious population that came up with different translations of sacred texts in the common language of everyday life, the mother tongue, the vernacular.[69] The ordinary population, by using the vernacular, could overtake the religious life practiced by the formally educated elite. Yet often enough, ordinary people had to keep their religious practice a secret, repress it collectively. Sometimes meetings were concealed behind trade or other kinds of gatherings; sometimes family members were in the dark about the membership of relatives in Lollard groups. The secrecy and repression that described the sacred language applied in a different sense to the social and religious life of the Lollards.[70]

There were three keys to this Wycliffite change. The first is a conscious return to the original text, to the words as they were read before formal interpretation, "Take, eat; this is my body" (e.g., Matthew 26:26). Readers now with direct access to the text can see the path from the account in the sacred text to the ceremonial reenactment of the events related in that account; even if a priest does it, direct access to the Bible teaches its figurative, metaphorical status, and shows that the new bread, like Christ's bread, is *figuratively* his body. The second is the rendition of the original text as well as sacraments and liturgy in the native language of the population. This move highlights the change of the sacred text from the Greek to the Latin, suggesting that the use of Latin by the Church was one human choice (heresy?) among many, and not something heavenly. Third

---

68. Rubin, *Corpus*, 332.
69. Rubin, *Corpus*, 333.
70. Lambert, *Medieval*, 271.

was the mutualization of the hermeneutic process—the beliefs of the laity should contribute to the readings of the priesthood as much as orthodox readings guide the laity. Clearly, such a move also makes it unnecessary for a special class of readers and priests to provide an authoritative sense of the texts and prayers, as they now speak for themselves. But the foregoing added up to heresy, and although Wyclif was not executed, others were. These humane developments were understood to be diabolically motivated. They were cast as evil and their opposition was backed up with physical violence and murder. The continuing privileged use of Latin by universities bespoke their overtaking of the repressive actions of the Church against those who sought (and achieved) collective variation of status and uses of Latin.

The fear of the devil was also part of university life and was considered as a temptation that endangered the use of dialectic as the highway toward truth. Dialectic was manifested in the final examination for all degree candidates, so it was ordinary and based on the use of Aristotelian logic. However, sophistry was the bad sibling, so to speak—a corruption of the disputation from the search for truth toward the mere wish to persuade, and this sibling was considered diabolically oriented.[71] Wyclif and the Lollards, like other critics of the practices of disputation, considered sophistry to have corrupted academic study fundamentally. Ghosh writes that "for Wyclif and the Lollards, contemporary scholastic endeavour is reduced to a sterile game of vanity and power. . . . Most disturbing for them was the extent to which the Bible was implicated in such an academic milieu. . . . Lollardy was . . . taking on not just the disputative practices of medieval academia and the place of the Bible within such practices, but more generally, received notions of textual *auctoritas* and of accepted uses of biblical exegesis."[72] Recalling that Wyclif was himself an academic, his views did challenge the Church, but they also were the basis of a critique of the university. At the same time, Wyclif and the Lollards also participated in this psychology of purification. Although there was a doctrinal departure from orthodoxy, the Lollard movement shared a tendency with the universities and the Church: the need to expel a taint of evil, to purify practices and communities.

III-3. SERVETUS AND THE TRINITY

Working alone within the new Protestant culture and without royal support, Michael Servetus (1511–1553) was not as lucky as Wyclif. He was burned alive as a heretic, possibly through the instigation of John Calvin, for his opposition

---

71. Kantik Ghosh, *The Wycliffite Heresy: Authority and the Interpretation of Texts* (Cambridge: Cambridge UP, 2002), 218n12. In chapter 6, the citations from Deborah Tannen's work implied a similar thought by viewing the argument culture being more about persuading others to win a competition rather than a mutual search for the truth.

72. Ghosh, *Wycliffite*, 5.

to Trinitarian Christian theology. University educated, and likely overestimating the intellectual latitude available from the schisms of northern Europe, Servetus was an itinerant theologian who took a strong stand on perhaps the second-most-worked issue of Catholic orthodoxy—the basis for maintaining a tripartite reference for God. Was God one or three? Some heretics challenged the godliness of Christ; others the godliness of the Holy Spirit. If monotheism was the foundation of Christianity, why are there three different components of God?[73] Servetus's treatises are now claimed by Unitarians[74] to be some of the movement's founding documents. Servetus considered the word of Christ, but not his body, to be eternal; he viewed the Holy Spirit as representing the "breath of life" described in Genesis as what God instilled in human bodies—the air that sustains all living things. These simplifications led him to assert the unity of God.[75]

In earlier forms this heresy developed on the basis of the movements to install Aristotle's logic as the basis of theology. In Servetus's time, however, a new reading of the world, the sky, and nature had begun, and Servetus was acquainted with it though his medical studies, which he undertook, in part, to support himself because of establishment opposition to his theology. Galen's explanation of anatomy was still established as the standard knowledge. "Galen had been of the view that the human body possessed a triadic hierarchy of physiological functions . . . the vegetative . . . the animal . . . and the nervous";[76] with each of these functions was associated a specific fundamental fluid. The three functions were sustained by three "spirits": the vegetative function, seated in the liver, was governed by venous (dark red) blood; the animal function, seated in the heart, by arterial (bright red) blood; and the nervous function (moods and emotions), seated in the brain, by nervous fluid. Mason observes that triadic models

---

73. Lawrence and Nancy Goldstone trace this issue to Constantine, who convened the Council of Nicaea in 325 CE, which declared the common divinity of all three parts of God. Lawrence and Nancy Goldstone, *Out of the Flames: The Remarkable Story of a Fearless Scholar, a Fatal Heresy, and One of the Rarest Books in the World*, (New York: Broadway, 2002), 65–67.

74. A Unitarian presentation of Servetus is Roland H. Bainton, *Hunted Heretic: The Life and Death of Michael Servetus (1511–1553)*, ed. Peter Hughes (Providence, RI: Unitarian Universalist Historical Society; Blackstone Editions, 2005).

75. Standford Rives, *Did Calvin Murder Servetus?* (Charleston, SC: Booksurge, 2008), 93. Several accounts say that Calvin had him arrested when he came to Geneva because of insulting remarks Servetus was said to have written on a copy of Calvin's book. Rives said Servetus denied having done this. Regardless, Servetus was clearly anti-Trinitarian. Calvin's behavior toward Servetus—executing a heretic—was identical to Church behavior toward heretics. Similarly, Protestant treatment of witches was essentially the same as the Church's treatment of them.

76. Stephen Finney Mason, *Main Currents of Scientific Thought* (New York: Abelard-Schuman, 1956), 172.

such as this were common in "later antiquity and the middle ages."[77] Various combinations and permutations of three categories made up the taxonomy of material things in the world—both living and nonliving things in nature.[78] In other words, there was a culturally established conceptual connection between the explanatory paradigms of nature and of God.

When Servetus examined the human heart the prevailing explanation of how it worked held that the blood passed from the right to the left ventricle through the septum—the muscular wall separating the two chambers. Servetus decided that it was not possible that anything could pass through that septum, let alone so much blood, so quickly. In this way he inferred, correctly, the process of pulmonary circulation: the blood emerges from the right ventricle, enters the lungs, becomes enriched with "breath," turns bright red, and enters the left ventricle, which pumps it to the rest of the body.[79] This description led Servetus to stipulate a generic change in the conception of blood. Now it was one thing, not two or three: "Servetus suggested that the single spirit of the blood was the soul of man, or rather, as he put it, 'The soul itself is the blood."[80] Obviously, this was also a theological change that challenged the thought habit of tripartite descriptions of fundamental categories of existence. As a result, Mason writes, "One of the charges brought against Servetus, when he was caught by Calvin at Geneva and tried for heresy, was that he held the soul to be the blood, for it implied the unorthodox view that the soul perished with the body."[81] Probably the greater thought or language crime , however, was the radically different idea based on a single empirical doubt: that blood cannot pass through the septum of the heart. Servetus changed the use of language: "the soul itself is the blood." There were no longer three fundamental fluid spirits: there was only one. This thought, and the disrespect felt by Calvin at its communication in a theological commentary, led to Servetus's being burned alive as a heretic. Because of this judgment and execution, his writings also were ordered to be burned. Few manuscripts actually remain to tell his views. Only because some are extant can this account be given now.

The execution of Servetus for a language crime deriving from an accurate perception of the human body took place when the witch-hunting of Europe began

---

77. Mason, *Main*, 172.

78. For example, for any one large category tripartite sets of subcategories were inserted, such as material things, material and spiritual things, and spiritual things.

79. This description of pulmonary circulation was published about thirty years before William Harvey (1578–1657), now credited with the discovery of blood circulation, was born. In the thirteenth century, Muslim physician Ibn al-Nafis put forth a model of pulmonary circulation identical to Servetus's, and it, too, was not noticed until after Harvey. Howard R. Turner, *Science in Medieval Islam: An Illustrated Introduction* (Austin: U of Texas P, 1995), 137.

80. Mason, *Main*, 172–173.

81. Mason, *Main*, 173.

an intense and widespread phase that did not end until the eighteenth century. Among other things, the execution of Servetus announced that the Reformation had actually overtaken the approaches of the Church it had pushed aside. The witch-hunt practice, evidence for which existed in pre-Christian times, began its most virulent modern period during Servetus's lifetime and about a century after Wyclif's death, with the papally authorized *Malleus maleficarum* of 1486. One of the common practices in the treatment of suspects was the examination of their bodies, which were said to show diabolical connections.

IV. Witch-hunting and the Fear of Mothers' Tongues

The Reformation fulfilled the purposes of the heretical groups to some extent. Individuals could seek direct access to the sacred text, and they could use the vernacular in prayer and worship. As a result of the rejection of a central Church administration, there was a variety of local religious communities that created practices from these principles. One of the earliest results of the growth of Protestantism was the appearance of new and converted universities. They remained interested in theology and retained disputation as the means of degree certification. However, scholastic theology with conclusions answerable to a single judge of orthodoxy was gone.[82] Henry VIII's takeover of Oxford and Cambridge between 1535 and 1553[83] was analogous in its effects to the growth of universities on the Continent. The local church was a national church, but that was still more local than a church whose leadership was in a different society and spoke a different language yet could affect local lives and procedures. Furthermore, this was the height of the Renaissance: there were geographical discovery, new texts, new translations, new literature, new knowledge, new languages, and printed texts. The question thus arises why in this period there was a sudden proliferation of one of the cruelest, most virulent practices in Western history: witch-hunting, witch trials, and executions by fire throughout Europe. These practices became most intense in Scotland[84] and Germany, sites at which some of the most progressive universities were founded and established.

---

82. A full account of post-Reformation growth of universities, including their changeover to Protestantism, is found in Willem Frijhoff, "Patterns," *A History of the University in Europe*, vol. 2: *Universities in Early Modern Europe: 1500–1800*, ed. Hilde de Ridder-Symoens, gen ed. Walter Rüegg (Cambridge: Cambridge UP, 1996). Frijhoff includes various tables and statistics showing the distribution of universities as well as the years of their changes in sponsorship.

83. Willis Rudy, *The Universities of Europe, 1100 to 1914: A History* (Cranbury, NJ: Associated University Presses, 1984), 66.

84. Christina Larner gives accounts of the burning of witches alive in Scotland. Christina Larner, *Enemies of God: The Witch-Hunt in Scotland* (Baltimore: Johns Hopkins UP, 1981), 113–115.

The history of witch-hunting has been a source of fascination for scholars and non-scholars alike.[85] The term "witchcraft" acquired a referential status, although it was an imaginary practice claimed to be real by those who were hunting witches, not by those supposedly practicing it.[86] It is an abstraction with no reference. The term "witch" is traceable back to the King James Version Exodus 22:18 (this verse is translated even in some Jewish versions as "Thou shalt not suffer a witch to live"). But the Hebrew word *m'cha-shay-fah,* means "sorceress," or "female magician."[87] In pre-Christian biblical times, when magic was practiced by Egyptians, women were prohibited from this activity. The accounts in Exodus of Moses's confrontation with Pharaoh involved a magic contest, won by Moses, which enabled him to escape Egypt, under the guidance of God's "strong hand and outstretched arm," with the Israelite slaves. Accounts of magic or sorcery could be compared with contemporary forms of occult knowledge—such as is found in science: making drugs or manipulating technological equipment—to which only some people have access. When such knowledge is used to produce incomprehensible effects, it looks like magic. If the effects are harmful or tragic, one might understand them to be diabolical.[88] The question of interest for the medieval and Renaissance periods, and for the

---

85. Norman Cohn, *Europe's* (1993), 144. Some contemporary feminists have tried to appropriate the history of *witchcraft* and, by reusing its vocabulary from a position of agency, recuperate it from its reduced status; one such example is Starhawk (pseud. of Miriam Simos), *Dreaming the Dark* (Boston: Beacon P, 1982). One recent scholarly account is Walter Stephens, *Demon Lovers: Witchcraft, Sex, and the Crisis of Belief* (Chicago, U of Chicago P, 2002). Probably the most comprehensive scholarly account is Stuart Clark, *Thinking with Demons: The Idea of Witchcraft in Early Modern Europe* (Oxford: Clarendon P, 1997).

86. Cohn's discussion, cited above, shows how easily even twentieth-century academic researchers conferred credibility onto the fantasy that there were secret night meetings of witches at which all copulated with the devil. See especially Cohn, *Europe's* (1975), chapter 8. In the words of Russell, "witchcraft was largely an invention of inquisitors— and of later historians. . . . The erroneous conviction that large numbers of witches were engaged in a conspiracy to betray Christian society to the Devil was almost universal in the sixteenth and seventeenth centuries among academics, clergy, rulers, and other dominant groups as well as among the ignorant" (*Dissent,* 100). According to Stephens, accusers claimed that an established ritual was to desecrate the host by spitting out secretly at communion and then urinating on it at the "Sabbat" (*Demon,* 253).

87. Jeffrey Russell gives a good account of the non-diabolical meaning of sorcerers in Exodus, and suggests that James I of England insisted on translating the Hebrew erroneously as "witch," given the European hysteria about witches. If occult knowledge is used for welcome ends, it does not require a paranoid explanation. Jeffrey Russell, *A History of Witchcraft: Sorcerers, Heretics, and Pagans* (New York: Thames and Hudson, 1980), 32–35.

88. Again, Morris's story of Chuchad (chapter 1) is relevant: the "magic" of both the conjuring of the dead and the sales of Amway products depends on occult knowledge,

secrecy of sacred languages, is this: Why were women suspected of having gained access to such languages—of the body, of sex, of the life cycle—and why was the possibility of such access treated as an extreme threat? It is in the context of this question that the exclusively male population of the Church, the university, and the inquisitors becomes obvious. Why were these men so panicky, spooked by women who had occult knowledge?[89]

The Inquisitions[90] were conclaves (or cells or gangs) of men, usually urged on and supported by the pope. They wore robes and were dedicated to seek out heretics, and then individual witches thought to be articulating heretical thoughts, and then groups of witches who promulgated collective practices that involved transactions with the devil. The pope was the background support for the local inquisitor, who instilled public fear. Not all witches were women, but most were, and this demographic corresponds to the usual objects of mob scapegoating violence: few are exempt (that is, gang members themselves are eligible to be bullied and murdered), but usually the violence is focused on one weaker group.[91] Many of the recent studies of the witch-hunts and of demon consciousness in Western history recognize the misogyny of witch-hunting; but some are not persuaded that misogyny is the underlying factor in this practice.[92] The records do show that the witch-hunt period of almost three centuries singled

---

which in these cases are common confidence schemes. A male seduction is a confidence scheme that assumes women don't know the game. If women were sexualized—that is, they knew sex—it was read as sex with the devil. Female desire was considered diabolical. This thought remains in our own culture as depicted in a litany of tales of femmes fatales in which, invariably, a woman who takes sexual initiatives is also a murderer or thief—and diabolically motivated. This fantasy, in turn, is an instance of Angela Carter's characterization (cited in chapter 12) of women in an unfree society as "monsters."

89. Two reviewers of Walter Stephens's study, Ingrid Rowland and Anthony Grafton, compliment Stephens for "shrewdly avoid[ing] making obvious remarks about the prurience of a celibate clergy," and emphasizing that the clergy's concern was "not pornographic, but metaphysical." Ingrid Rowland and Anthony Grafton, "The Witch Hunters' Crusade," *New York Review of Books* 49.14 (26 September 2002): 68. Not emphasizing the obvious in this case is an error that overlooks normalized viciousness in the name of scholarly detachment. The diminution or avoidance of the item that requires the most discussion in the history of witch-hunting has enabled men, more generally, to refuse to face women's desires, sexualities, and bodily actions.

90. Edward Peters, *Inquisition* (New York: Free P, 1988).

91. Erik Erikson's discussion of Hitler, in *Childhood and Society* (New York: Basic, 1949), uses this same model—the bullying gang—to explain the conversion of German society to one that abided the mass murders. Confirming statistics on the gender of witches may be found in Brian P. Levack, *Witch-Hunt*, chapter 5.

92. The most notable of this group is Stuart Clark, whose massive *Thinking* seems to have investigated every aspect of the medieval and Renaissance obsession with witchcraft, included the earlier history of magical practices. This work is necessary for anyone wanting to look into this issue. But because of the work's extraordinary comprehensiveness, it is all the more challenging to ask why it does not accept the central role of

out women for trial and execution for the crime of witchcraft; often women in large groups were thus tried, and then tortured in order to get them to name other women (or men) who were also guilty of the same crime.

As germane as the studies of Western demonology are, it would miss the point to decide that specific fantasies, which are different from one another, motivated witch-hunts (or similar outbreaks of murderous violence against individuals and groups). The social shapes of such outbreaks are similar to one another (i.e., the gang effect), and as a result the fantasies' generic function as pretexts is the main interest of the present discussion. The fantasies provide novel formulations that then justify the recrudescences of violence in the cause of religious exercises of power. Neither is this violence traceable to an instinct for aggression—as is believed by Lorenz and, it seems, by Freud.[93] Rather, collective bullying rampages are erotically and sadistically tinged and they reappear in history largely because only one thing is considered eligible to stop it: superior force. Gang violence such as witch-hunts always has pretexts: always there is an imaginary danger stipulated, and violence—killing—is the only way to be rid of it with certainty.

This mechanism—the focus on a weak constituency as posing a lethal threat to the commonwealth, and the need to eradicate it—is the normaliza-

---

misogyny given by critics such as Christine Larner and Marianne Hester to the practices of witch-hunting. The answer is this: Clark does not give any explanatory status to the history and experience of misogyny. It is noteworthy how he strives to read the history of witch-hunting as a function of language, especially because he notices that in contemporary language philosophy "[t]here has, indeed, been a fundamental shift away from the realist assumption that truths are discovered lying around in the world [that are then represented] in language, and towards the anti-realist idea that they are made by language-use itself and then commended by members of speech communities who find them good to believe" (4). But rather than understanding anti-realist to be materialist (or even nominalist), he adopts what is (in my view) an incorrect reading of the poststructuralist sense of language: language "should not be asked to follow reality but be allowed to constitute it. Here, the object of attention would become language itself, not the relationship between language and the extra-linguistic world" (6). This reading follows the view of language as a "prison house." The latter view depends on assuming a binary between language and the extra-linguistic world. The materialist view, discussed in chapters 1, 3, and 4 (and in several places in subsequent chapters), has no such binary because the materiality of language considers language to be a gestural practice that is continuous with the rest of existence—another material among many in our experience. Clark uses the principle of the separation of language from other experience to continue a purely academic consideration of witchcraft and witch-hunting, which, later in his discussion, permits him to make the argument against the fundamental misogyny of the witch ideology. Women were accused of witchcraft because those who were accused were the opposite of saints (132–133). By staying within the religious discourse and stressing this binary, Clark is able to overlook the overwhelmingly male-coded erotic sadism in the experiences of many women and in the Church-motivated practices of hunting witches.

93. The term *instinct* has no agreed-upon reference. It is considered in chapter 10.

tion of paranoid thoughts. The signs of threat are always verbal. People begin to say things that depart from the usual rituals and conventions.[94] Although it is possible that any one person accused of being a witch actually murdered someone or caused the death of a newborn and it could not be proved, it is not possible that large groups of women were doing this all the time and concealing it under the guise of witchcraft. It is not known now what the accused actually admitted, or whether someone accused at such a trial would ever recount what really happened, if anything. However, because the records of what was said come from trial records, the confessions are now understood to have been coerced.

Norman Cohn's discussion of witch practices cites Livy's account of Bacchanalian feasts at which there were sexual orgies.[95] Blood was drunk, people were killed, the law was broken, and those refusing to go along were sacrificed. Gradually the Romans began to fear the Christians, whose numbers were small at first, but grew over the course of the first two centuries after Jesus's death. The Romans then accused the Christians of practices that were just about the same as those Livy described. Cohn characterizes this as a smear, but Christians were persecuted nevertheless: they were thrown to the lions. The orgies were also imagined to be some kind of worship, sometimes of male genitals—not that farfetched if genital worship is only a figure for fellatio, which could be just as characteristic of a Roman orgy as of a Christian one.[96] Gradually the Christians became an estimable force in late Rome, and then Constantine converted as Christianity acceded to imperial status. Now the Christians were the rulers, and Paul's early warnings about heretics began to seem more and more credible. There was a need to correct the error of those who said things differently from the way Church leaders said things, especially during the sacraments—as these were the religious nodes, or benchmarks of religious and civil identity. Heretics could be pagans, Jews, Gnostics, or Muslims, but they were all threats, sunk in error and particularly susceptible to approaches of the devil.

---

94. In Henry James's short ghost novel, *The Turn of the Screw,* there is a long delay before it is announced why Miles, the presumably diabolical boy, was dismissed from school. The only reason given was that he "said things." Henry James, *The Turn of the Screw* and *The Lesson of the Master* (Amherst, NY: Prometheus, 1996). This style of simultaneous emptiness and mystery is the prologue to witch trials. Perhaps the accused may have said something; perhaps the accusers may have suggested something. The verbal exchanges then culminate in the interrogations (and frenzy) of the trial.

95. Cohn, *Europe's* (1975), 10–11. Will we ever be able to know what actually took place? In fact the value of these descriptions is almost completely narrative or linguistic, as is their role as recycled accusations.

96. Contemporary pornography routinely depicts heterosexual fellatio with men standing and women on their knees, appearing to admire and worship. The relevance of pornographic depiction to the materiality of language is discussed in chapter 12.

R. I. Moore says that while heresy was feared and persecuted in the early centuries of Christianity, the record shows little sign of it until after the millennium, at which time "the persecuting society" was established by the Church, and remained in that identity until the present.[97] In the twelfth and early thirteenth centuries, the Lateran Councils decreed the Inquisitorial structures and gave direction to local bishops on the search for heretics of all sorts. The Church no longer waited until heretics were found spontaneously. Now, and repeatedly until the eighteenth century, they searched for such dissenters, tried and tortured them, and then turned them over to secular authorities for execution.

Moore and other historians agree that the eleventh and twelfth centuries were good times: social and cultural renewal or reawakening in Europe as the classical Greek heritage was rediscovered, translated into Latin, and promulgated, culminating in the systematic blending of Aristotle with scholasticism to create the university and its curriculum for the next four or five centuries. This was when Abelard's scholarly spirit exercised its influence, and his work was declared heretical and then taken over by the universities. Until the fourteenth century, there were periodic witch trials, since the fear of heresy was steady and the fight against it constant. Heretics such as the Cathars and Waldensians in the south of France at the end of the twelfth century were thought to participate in orgies with incest and animal worship. Why did this aspect of the fear of heresy attach itself to the witch-hunts, expand to inquisition, and focus on women just before the Reformation, to continue on into the eighteenth century? Perhaps putting the question in terms of both periods clarifies it. The first period of persecution, from the eleventh to the fifteenth century, had witch trials but focused on heresy; the second period of persecution, from the fifteenth to the eighteenth century focused more on witch-hunts and trials, during which Protestants as well as Catholics persecuted individuals and groups of witches.[98] If one imagines a trajectory of increasing enlightenment and secularization from Abelard to the eighteenth century, a period of continuously expanding new views, this trajectory is marked by the increasingly violent attempts to exterminate and terrorize dissenters. New views became new orthodoxies, so that, as the number of orthodoxies increased, violent suppression of challenges to them increased accordingly. This fact may be accounted for by remembering that this trajectory represents the usual path of men acquiring power, suppressing dissent, and finally succumb-

---

97. R. I. Moore, *The Formation of a Persecuting Society: Power and Deviance in Western Europe 950–1250* (Oxford: Blackwell, 1987).

98. According to Russell, "One of the curiosities of the witch craze is that the concept and idea of witchcraft passed unchanged from the Catholic fourteenth century into the Protestant sixteenth and seventeenth centuries, and that the prosecution of witches was equally strong in Catholic and Protestant regions; no significant statistical difference has been found" (*Dissent*, 100).

ing to the new group—the primal horde motif. The additional question about the witch-hunts is this: Given the underlying misogyny of androcentric rule, why would it be aggravated during a period of increasing enlightenment? Why wouldn't enlightenment ameliorate rather than aggravate misogyny?

Enlightenment involves the movement toward the development of new genres and new language. This means new forms, new vocabulary, and new sets of references, which include new access to language by new populations.[99] The heretical groups in the first period of persecution had a set of new uses some of which included denial of the Eucharist, of the Trinity, and of other features of Christian doctrine. Along with this, they lived differently, in addition to their rejection of the pope's rule. In the second period of persecution, as Cohn has described, there were no colonies of witches or secret night meetings, but there were practices of women whose work often had to do with healing, childbirth, childcare, and food preparation—all activities concerning how bodies work, develop, deal with illness and adversity, survive, and die.[100] Ordinary women living ordinary lives must have had the same sexual feelings as they do today, just as men do; the change has been in the socially acceptable forms of sexual behavior.

The Reformation and Renaissance involved changes in how the cosmos was understood, first, but also, as exemplified by the discovery of the circulation of blood, in how the body was understood.[101] Illness was a threat at all times, but the outbreaks of the Black Death certainly made anyone with medical capability particularly valuable.[102] The history of this period cannot, therefore, be boiled

---

99. In Waquet's study of the history of Latin use, it is very clear how regularly the moves away from Latin were resisted. Some who wrote in the vernacular reserved Latin for other works. Because anyone aspiring to scholarly or scientific work had to learn Latin early in school, the Latin tradition established itself and collaborated, or even blended, with other aspects of androcentric social practice, an issue discussed in the next section of this chapter.

100. Richard Kieckhefer, *Magic in the Middle Ages* (New York: Cambridge UP, 1989), 3. One of Kieckhefer's example texts of magic, written anonymously in the fifteenth century, is a combination of science, religion, and magic, addressing all of the issues stipulated here: household management, pest control, preparation of medicines and foods, as well as specific procedures, prayers, incantations, and writings that accompany the practical procedures. Marianne Hester shows that women's occupations were not listed in court records of witch trials; if they were married, only their husband's occupation was shown. Marianne Hester, *Lewd Women and Wicked Witches: A Study of the Dynamics of Male Domination* (New York: Routledge, 1992), 164–165,

101. Michael Servetus's interest in blood circulation suggests a connection between respect for the materiality of the living body and opposition to dogmatic abstraction. Westerners credit William Harvey with discovering the total body blood circulation in 1628 through experiments with live animals and cadavers.

102. In addition, as reported by Russell, women seemed to have survived the Black Death at considerably higher rates than men. This became grounds for suspicion of witchcraft (*A History*, 115).

down to great intellectual advances; the places where women worked continued to be dangerous. Mostly, cures were derived from informal sources—folk
knowledge and doctors who were part of craft guilds. Those trained in the
university were not necessarily those with knowledge of cures and treatments as
they are today; they knew mainly the history of how human bodies were understood—the theory of humors, which now, to us, appears to be superstition.[103]
Whatever status university-based knowledge may have had, it was not better or
more practical than the medical knowledge of practicing doctors, midwives, and
older women with years of experience in treating physical ailments.[104] It was thus
recognized that women had access to medical knowledge at a level equivalent
to that of men. If university-trained men were protected by the Church and by
kings, and if these authoritative figures were feeling uncertain in their authority,
they would perceive women's dominion over human bodies as a threat: "Behold,
the man is become as one of us" (Genesis 3:22).[105]

Marianne Hester observes that the medical theory is not enough to account
for the comprehensiveness of the witch-hunts, and especially not their sadism
and virulence.[106] Healing was one of several callings in which women's access to
language took on a new authority during this historical period. In the past, wom-
en had been involved in similar practices (accounting for the violent response,
commanded in Exodus, to female magical practice), but the present scale of
female practice, combined with the inherent doubt about nature, the cosmos,
and religious authority among the authorities themselves, especially urged the
serious recognition of the Exodus commandment. Historically, medical knowledge had been connected to knowledge of magic—a private knowledge of herbs,
drinks, or foods that have unusual effects, yet that do specifically ameliorate
some pains and illnesses. Alchemy was on the borderline of magic and science,
as was astrology. That there was doubt in the culture at large about the authority

---

103. At the beginning of the sixteenth century, medics feared "that translations of
their textbooks would harm their incomes by encouraging self-help among common
people. Moreover, they faced effective competition from the informal practice of medicine by cunning folk and folk healers." Bob Scribner, "Heterodoxy, Literacy, and Print
in the Early German Reformation," *Heresy and Literacy, 1000–1530*, ed. Peter Biller and
Anne Hudson (Cambridge: Cambridge UP, 1994), 270.

104. Historians generally agree that a disproportionate number of those accused of
witchcraft were over forty, widows or single women who were not involved at the moment
in child raising, or past the period of birthing. Levack, *Witch-Hunt*, chapter 5, has age
statistics.

105. I assume that the androcentric structures of society predate the historical record.
The thoughts of Genesis represent collective social orientations that were present millen-
nia before it and before the civilizations that have come to us through other documents.
Gerda Lerner, *The Creation of Patriarchy* (New York: Oxford, 1986), 209.

106. Hester, *Lewd Women*, 118.

of these subjects is documented by the superstitious beliefs of mainstream figures such as Boyle and Newton, as well as the errors of Galileo and Copernicus due to superstitious beliefs. When orthodox knowledge is called into question by authorities themselves, the knowledge of the unorthodox becomes a credible alternative and possible rival. And when that knowledge, such as that of the life cycle—including sex, nursing, and childbirth—has been the very knowledge obsessively avoided by men, especially those in the university whose main task was to master texts and announce the law on that basis, such palpable bodily knowledge may well appear to be threatening.

The characteristic text of the witch-hunt period was the *Malleus maleficarum*, a dialectically organized volume commissioned by Pope Innocent VIII in 1484 and published in 1486. This one was reprinted many times until 1530, and then republished a century later.[107] The authors were a pair of bishops whose effort in this cause was exceptionally intense. The doctrinaire quality of institutionalized misogyny has been documented. This work was one of many to provide reasons that were meant as a basis for the persecution, torture, murder, and collective extermination of certain classes or groups of women deemed threatening and identified as heretical. A policy of direct extermination did not arise because women were understood to be a "necessary evil."[108] This term signaled the repressed understandings that men, celibate or not, are implicated in the sexual passions, embedded in the life cycle, and mostly, perhaps, guided by the common language of both sexes during infancy and childhood. It is expectable that those in authority might want to deny or repress knowledge of their attachment to and involvement in the lives of those they dictate. The consequence of such repression is the reemergence of that sense of implication in displaced contexts and an exaggerated scale of action—finding and punishing in others the traits one conceals from oneself. It is particularly germane that a document of this nature (the *Malleus*) directly represented the pope: these writers were part of a bonded group of men holding sacred authority.[109] As a result, inquisitions were further empowered, and an atmosphere of profound fear was established, as denouncing others and exposing them were the aims of torture.[110]

---

107. There were several other manuals like this one that had similar sentiments. A recent version of the *Malleus* is Heinrich Kramer and James Sprenger, *The Hammer of Witches: A Complete Translation of the* Malleus maleficarum, ed. and trans. Christopher S. Mackay (New York: Cambridge UP, 2009).

108. *Malleus maleficarum,* quoted in Russell, *Witchcraft,* 116. Having committed the "first sin," and having led men into sin as well, it is not surprising that they are called evil themselves, now because of having sexual relations with the devil.

109. There was a normal status to writing this sort of a book.

110. In this case (as in the cases in the news in 2009), the most likely purpose of torture was to force individuals to implicate others (and not to confess their own crimes).

Materials found in the surviving magic books show the mixtures of magic, religion, and science—mixtures not terribly different from those honored by official authorities. Writing and prayers were called for in the use of remedies, medicines, or spells, which often were no more than wishes for something good or bad to happen. Certainly the use of animal products as medicine is as familiar as the use of animals as food. The idea of worshipping (or copulating with) a goat and eating a child is the reverse of what anyone caring for a household might do: treat the child as especially precious (holy) in a bodily, admiring, and social way; and slaughter and eat the animal. Furthermore, the projection of this fantasy onto imaginary groups of crazed women reflects centuries of debate and official concern, perhaps also revulsion, about the Eucharist (eating a human body), and the involvement of these debates in the Inquisitions against heretics. The Eucharist sacrament is a combination of the goat/child accusation. The god is worshipped, then killed and eaten, his blood imbibed in a formal, regularly repeated ritual that is the culmination of the process of moral cleansing for each faithful person. The nub of the long dispute about the Eucharist was whether words uttered by priests can perform the apparent miracle and thus validate the cleansing process by causing verbally (magically) action from beyond. It could be claimed that when one took in the actual body and blood it was fully spiritual, in contrast to the full physicality of the alleged witch's alleged behavior. This could only happen if the words were not recognized as material—that is, recognized as being accidental vessels of Godly meaning transmitted from God through the priest to the scenes at hand. The same is true for the bread and the wine. If the words, bread, and wine themselves were understood to be material, they would be like any other material things: capable of being reread, used figuratively, discussed, and applied in a wide variety of contexts. In this context, however, all three items must be understood only to be insubstantial, incorporeal vessels ("accidents"), containers of a heavenly substantive essence that can be summoned only by the official priest.

The witch-hunts represent a practice spanning four or five centuries that boiled down to punishing a class of people for special knowledge that depended on the flexibility of received tropes and rituals, on the fluent appropriation of their texts (actual texts and the text of the human body), of the use of texts, of their new texts (the magic books), and their invention of alternative magic words. The hunters feared the knowledge of the text communities of those who were not members of the lawgiving text community. The transition from the fifteenth to the sixteenth century may well be described as one of growing panic when the pope commissioned the *Malleus maleficarum*. The changes taking place included the discovery of the Americas, the movement from the geocentric to the heliocentric universe, followed by successful departures from the Church in England and in Germany. These are changes in a world picture held by most in Europe for a millennium, since the imperialization of Christianity in the fourth century. But because the social and political structure of civilization had been grounded in the social psychology of groups of men in this period, the changes would seem more threatening to men—as it was men's structures, especially authority structures, that changed shape. Rulers in ordinary times were fearful that their dominion would be challenged (by other men). Circumstances brought changes of unprecedented scope that few could assimilate and rationalize fluently. Men could not blame the explorers, the scientists, or the reformers, and could not execute heretics as a response to uncertainty about the cosmos any longer. But they could, with the help of the increasingly popular devil folklore, blame the class of people who were already to blame for the Fall—the first disobedient figures, the first to lead men into temptation. New knowledge, new faith, and a new world picture gave a new sense to the various choices women had made all along, choices that had always puzzled men. To cope with this change, an even greater effort must be made by both religious groups of men, Catholics and Protestants,[111] to extirpate the diabolical influences in society—those with knowledge of and proximity to the body, of the life cycle, of households, and those who combine this knowledge with a sexual interest similar to that of men. This form of coping, because of its basis in fear and panic, is then converted, as an act of collective self-stabilization, into traditional symbolism and ritualization: the female magicians are causing men's panic, and they must be discovered and removed from society. The Inquisition was already established, and it was appropriated to fight the chthonic roots of heresy—the original choosers, the original alternative to men, the original "helper as if opposite" (*ayzehr k'negdo* in Hebrew)—women.

It is an action that shows repression through the collective psychological self-abuse of churchmen. Secular authority was willing to carry out the sentences of the Inquisitions, which meant only that two different men's associations were willing to collaborate with one another to fight a common fear. Most people, including many or perhaps most men, would not engage in the humiliation of

In such paranoid assaults, the torture aims actually to *create the conspiracy* that would document what the inquisitor already knows to be imaginary.

111. According to Bob Scribner, "it quickly became a dictum of the new evangelical [Protestant] church that ordinary lay people could not be relied upon to derive knowledge about the way of salvation directly from their own reading of scripture" "Heterodoxy," 275. Protestant church leaders began to feel about "direct access" much as Catholic bishops felt about it: there must be a formally authorized reading. See also note 84, above. The common involvement of Catholic and Protestants in becoming possessed by the witch fear involved the universities: Levack writes, "The entire process of transmission [of witch fantasies] was abetted by the universities, which exposed future judges to the growing body of demonological and inquisitorial literature and which also advised local jurisdictions how to conduct witchcraft prosecutions" (*Witch-Hunt,* 53).

and violence against women urged by the Church. But when the gender of the governing men is forgotten by men, they become formal, pure, essential authorities, and the figures of both the rulers and the ruled have been abstracted from society, removed from it and viewed simply as good and evil, safe and unsafe, or healthy and diseased.[112] Such abstraction of people depends on a radical reduction of language that is then announced through scholastic thinking and disputation practices as a radical refinement of it. The removal of authoritative language from general access was understood to be a process of sanctification and declared to be the highest, purest, most accomplished form of thinking. The removal of language to its secret place authorizes the rule of men by that class of men popularly recognized as learned and wise. The approach to language now practiced in academic institutions and representing the values of abstract thought is a fundamental collaborator in the systematic occulting of language,[113] which the use of vernaculars in modern times has barely curtailed, while such collaboration is understood to be a virtue, a strength of the human spirit.

V. Learned Latin

Until the eighteenth century, Latin had a clear, elaborate location and status in Europe. To many, it was an austere, fearful entity, perceived as such from its introduction in "grammar" school: the purpose of going to school at all was first to become familiar with Latin.[114] Several historical sources give accounts of the commonness of flogging in grammar school.[115] Errors in comprehension

---

112. Russell, *A History*, 32, 63. Early heresies were dualistic religions in which the devil or evil principle was a force equal to God's. These declined until the eleventh and twelfth centuries, when the devil seemed to return as a factor in the moral cosmologies. The rise of witchcraft is due to this recrudescence of devil fear in popular culture and in some zones of Church and university thinking.

113. Occulting occurs when academic language is deliberately and conventionally obscure, jargonized, pedantic, overgeneralized, simultaneously overassertive and hedged, and exclusive. Such unwelcome results remain today because the social psychology in which they became normalized has changed so little. See chapter 6, section 5.

114. Joan Simon writes of English schools in the fifteenth century: "Even merchant benefactors did not require teaching of any specific kind beyond instruction in grammar." Joan Simon *Education and Society in Tudor England* (Cambridge and New York: Cambridge UP, 1966), 50.

115. However, Rashdall says there is no evidence for it in the university. In book 1 of *Confessions*, Augustine wrote of his strong fear of flogging in grammar school. John of Salisbury wrote in 1159, "And because memory is strengthened and talent is sharpened by exercise, [Bernard of Chartres] urged some by admonitions to imitate what they heard and others by blows and penalties." John of Salisbury, "How Bernard Drilled the Boys in Grammar at Chartres," *University Records and Life in the Middle Ages*, ed. and trans. Lynn Thorndike (New York: Columbia UP, 1975), 7.

of Latin grammar, rather than misbehavior alone, led to whipping. Corporal punishment thus communicated the special status of this language. Because of the pain, however, the bodily locus of the language had to be repressed once the language became an autonomous skill in the boy's repertoire. This practice seems to have been so fully normalized that the association of pain and humiliation with grammatical error exists in contemporary society and is part of popular culture.[116]

Suzanne Reynolds describes the psychology of Latin literacy pedagogy.[117] Literacy meant Latin literacy, and it was also automatically the road to authorized religious status or membership. Citing the sermons of Jacques de Vitry, Reynolds observes that the *puer* "learnt . . . [the] correct pronunciation so that he might be able to voice correctly the Latin words of the divine office. This is a correctness that extends from the linguistic into the spiritual sphere." Vitry's (thirteenth-century) sermons presented the figure of the devil with a "burden . . . made up of syllables mispronounced by the choir. These mispronunciations are a kind of vocal sin and, so the devil explains, mean that the choir have in effect stolen the prayers from God." The sacral status of the language and the fear of error are communicated at once. To learn Latin was to embed simultaneously fear and social status in young boys, the combination that defines the continuing atmosphere of normal church membership and functions.

Walter Ong's several discussions of Learned Latin in the Renaissance acknowledge the gendered identity of academic culture from medieval times to the present. He observes that "the only academic world the West had ever known at all until three centuries ago, was never anything other than an all-male enterprise."[118] "Earlier groups of learned men," he writes elsewhere, "seem never to have achieved the close-knit, jealously guarded internal organization of the university. It seems not irrelevant that they did not have a secret language to nourish their *esprit de corps*."[119] This theme is articulated repeatedly in his studies of academic values, and shows the continuity between the strong-armed

---

116. "Oh, you're an English teacher? I better watch how I speak."

117. Suzanne Reynolds, *Medieval Reading: Grammar, Rhetoric, and the Classical Text* (New York: Cambridge UP, 1996), 8–9.

118. Walter J. Ong, S.J., *Interfaces of the Word: Studies in the Evolution of Consciousness and Culture* (Ithaca, NY: Cornell UP, 1977), 26–27.

119. Ong, *Rhetoric*, 121. However, the groups listed by Ong, like the Athenian Academy, did have a tool that was inaccessible to others: literacy. Today specialized writing practices, which include knowledge of computer discourses and languages, in and out of the academy have the excluding (gatekeeping) function once played by the Latin language. Ong unceremoniously refers to Latin as a "secret language." By and large this concept is taken for granted in today's societies and is not viewed as especially significant. This is one of the most common facts about language-in-use that is generally not studied by students of language: discourse styles, dialects, and languages that

techniques of Latin pedagogy (for boys) of the fourth century, the literatures of war and individual glory in battle, and the roles of Learned Latin in universities and in Western culture. Ong considers that the seventeenth-century "interest in the epic . . . in Western Europe amounts almost to a frenzy [that is] not unrelated" to the way Latin was taught.[120] The witch-hunt frenzy occurred during the same period. Ong's reflections describe how essential Learned Latin was to the maintenance of orthodoxy, and how fully it identified the social structures eschewed by heretics, by many women who joined them, and, later, by learned and religious leaders of the Reformation. More than this, however, Ong credits this language with laying the foundation for the best achievements of Western civilization:

> Devoid of baby-talk, insulated from the earliest life of childhood where language has its deepest psychic roots, a first language to none of its users, pronounced across Europe in often mutually unintelligible ways but always written the same way, Learned Latin was a striking exemplification of the power of writing for isolating discourse and of the unparalleled productivity of such isolation. Writing, as has earlier been seen, serves to separate and distance the knower and the known and thus to establish objectivity. It has been suggested [by Ong, in 1977] that Learned Latin effects even greater objectivity by establishing knowledge in a medium insulated from the emotion-charged depths of one's mother tongue, thus reducing interference from the human lifeworld and making possible the exquisitely abstract world of medieval scholasticism and of the new mathematical modern science which followed on the scholastic experience. Without Learned Latin, it appears that modern science would have got under way with greater difficulty, if it had got under way at all.[121]

In his earlier work, Ong asked why the connection between eating and language use did not find more attention in the scholarly literature, as he has an acute sense that the mother tongue is strongly connected with mothers' care of infants, their nursing (breast feeding), and their wiping of infants' mouths.[122] He is also cognizant of how baby talk is part of everyone's language acquisition process, and that it must play a role in the language we use as adults. He then distinguishes this ordinary process of language acquisition from the acquisition

---

are peculiar to specific groups serve political purposes that affect how social relations proceed. Imagine sitting at a dinner table at which all others are speaking a language we do not know.

120. Ong, *Rhetoric,* 134.
121. Ong, *Orality,* 113–114.
122. Ong, *Interfaces,* 23–24.

of Learned Latin, which is "insulated" from the "emotion-charged" depths of
the vernacular. Because of this insulation, because of the learning of the language in the exclusively male environment of Latin teachers, an abstract (or
removed-from-home) foundation for Western civilization was created. Although
he appears to recognize the influential roles of infantile emotional life for men
and women, Ong also says that abstract thought and insulated language are
essential for the achievements of civilization. He observes that in other cultures
that have had an official written language, such as Sanskrit, classical Chinese,
classical Arabic, and rabbinic Hebrew, these languages have been "much more
important than any mother tongues."[123] Literacy is a necessary accomplice in
these achievements, he continues, whereas "orality," though basic, is too rooted
in emotion and bodily needs to be suitably segregated. Ong makes no connection between Learned Latin and the Renaissance witch-hunts, but it is not a
coincidence that his sense of how language has functioned in society and in the
academy shows a connection to the obsessions of the inquisitors in the witch-
hunts: the body-oriented enterprises of most women in that society—infant
care, sick care, feeding, and household management, to name a few. Learning
Latin was another way to distance oneself from those who have custody of our
bodily lives.

To learn Latin is a process of separation from the mother tongue. Of course,
no one forgets the mother tongue, but as Reynolds observes, "[T]he vernacular
is always subsidiary to Latin."[124] Bearing in mind that the great majority of
women spoke the vernacular and did not learn Latin, the structure of society
was such that Latin-language pedagogy was a principal means of societal self-
maintenance. Civilization meant Latin-speaking religious civilization. As considered in chapter 5, language development in all societies gradually separates
children from infantile dependency. But as is seen in the uses and teaching
of Latin during the university period we are examining, the processes of placing men in superior positions takes place, from childhood onward, through
Latin pedagogy.

In the more recent work *Orality and Literacy* Ong mentions the change in the
academy's populations—the entrance of large numbers of women—but he does
not discuss this change or evaluate it, except perhaps to imply that a new orality
is making its way into the academy. His earlier work, however, presents several
factors that strongly imply his sense of the superior value of a literacy-centered,
male-trained and populated academy. He did write without attributing causality
that "[a]s girls and women came into academia, Latin declined."[125] He goes to

123. Ong, *Interfaces*, 28.
124. Reynolds, *Medieval*, 64.
125. Ong, *Interfaces*, 26. How true is this? The vernacular entered German and British
universities in the seventeenth century, but women did not enter until the twentieth century.

some lengths to justify the social mores of the male academy and relates these mores to the acquisition of Learned Latin.

One principal justification, already cited, is this: abstract thought on which the Western intellectual tradition is based, was propelled by the social and intellectual separateness of the pedagogy of Learned Latin. But Ong is also very interested in the individual psychology that results from the processes of separation, and sees particular virtues in it: the male initiation value and the habits of oppositional argument of Learned Latin. In turn, the development of these virtues rests on the belief in the fundamental biological difference between men and women, and on justifying male academic values on that basis. Whatever else may be said of Ong's discussion, there is no place in it that considers in an affirmative way that an academy that includes both women and men is to be desired or is an improvement over the traditional academy. Ong's view reflects what R. I. Moore described as the values of Latin literacy that became established in the twelfth century, when the universities were founded, and when "western Europe was changing from a warrior into a clerical society." Latin literacy was "coming to be regarded, with celibacy, as a defining attribute of the clerical class which provided not only spiritual but administrative and governmental services and leadership, at a time when the power and status associated with those functions was growing rapidly."[126]

This moment, when literacy, celibacy, Church influence, and the academy all advanced together may also be related to Ong's observation that Latin had "become a sex-linked language, used only by males . . . exclusively a tribal language."[127] Its learning "took place in the physical hardship setting typical for puberty rites."[128] There was corporal punishment (in the Renaissance, as there had been for Augustine), early hours, compulsory Latin conversation in private, and competitions and disputations. It was taken for granted that an all-male population needs to be initiated and tested, just as it is in military groups. The texts that were learned and taught were also about war and violence, recounting the adventures of the hero and his own variety of "agons": "The academic world . . . was profoundly agonistic, and its agonistic structures registered masculine needs."[129] The learning of Latin was characterized by such a surfeit of male culture that the sense of how things are as male supremacist was beyond all questioning by the boys—and likely by girls, who learned this sense from other sources.

126. R. I. Moore, "Literacy and the Making of Heresy c. 1000–c. 1150," *Heresy and Literacy, 1000–1530,* ed. Biller and Hudson, 22, 23.

127. Walter J. Ong, *Fighting for Life: Contest, Sexuality, and Consciousness* (Ithaca, NY: Cornell UP, 1981), 130.

128. Ong, *Fighting,* 131.

129. Ong, *Fighting,* 135.

Ong does not question this social alignment, and tries to justify it on a biological basis. He views women's "lower articulatory volume" of voice to be a "disadvantage" in the academy and in public contexts because being an orator is "crucial to academic success" and to politics in the contemporary United States.[130] Ong traces fundamental biological difference to the womb, where "the male mammalian organism must from the start react against its environment."[131] Such facts are as imaginary as those that rendered women less capable because of smaller skull size, yet they are given as facts in justification of a vision of society. What is of interest in Ong's work is not so much a matter of how right or wrong he may be; his scholarship will likely help students of these subjects. However, his struggle is remarkable and similar to Freud's in their common rootedness in androcentrism. The struggle reflects the inability of his personal humanism to overcome the momentum of men's history. Although he is a gentle man, he says that agonism is necessary; although he is a person who learns from and teaches many, he says that Latin is best; although he is interested in other cultures and other societies, he says that no other has achieved as much as ours. Striving to recognize the meanings of women's entry into the academy, he cannot find the language to renounce the orientation around the presumption of male superiority—to come out and say, finally, that the unpredictable changes that will come to the structures of learning due to the changes in university populations are desirable for us and for future generations, and that we have been paying an overwhelming price for an institution of learning addressing only the interests of men.[132]

Latin, not just a language, is the sign of a certain kind of society in which we still live:[133] one that values secret, sacred, transparent uses of language. As Ong has shown, the academy—Western universities as a group in which there are variations—has been the foremost advocate for this kind of language, and today, even if Latin no longer rules, the rules of Latin's influence remain as an academic legacy. This legacy has guided how language has been studied in modern times and has helped to keep the study of language a relatively narrow, even mysterious project again and again evading our ability to transform its study, as was done with other subjects, into central influential, rich zones of research.

---

130. Ong, *Fighting*, 140, 141.

131. Ong, *Fighting*, 65.

132. Like Freud, Ong sees correctly the surface manifestations of how gender values are juxtaposed, yet neither man is able to infer correctly their political meaning!

133. This is the burden of Peter Goodrich's discussion, cited above. Although he does not blame Latin for specific problems in our society, he shows clearly how Latin remains pervasive, yet unconscious to most of us. His discussion makes it easy to decide that because of this continuing presence of Latin, we are also overly influenced by the culture and social psychology that we are trying to overcome in other venues.

CHAPTER TEN

Language Uses in Science, the Heir of Latin

I. The Heir of Latin

Science is the heir of Latin. Biology and medicine retain Latin as their formal vocabulary. What Latin did in medieval and early modern Europe, science does now, worldwide: it provides a most trusted language to which all, in principle, have access, but which, in reality, few have access. Science has enabled technology, perhaps an even more trusted language because of its material output. It has provided medicines and practices that prolong life. Academic work in science is considered more important than any other academic work, just as works in Latin were the only authoritative works before the advent of modern science. The pursuit of so-called pure science is better supported than other academic pursuits, even when the practical value of such pursuits is not clear. Most people associate scientific work with secular values. Yet its style of functioning resembles the practices of those studying and teaching Latin texts: science is a higher pursuit in this society, and its language has been sacralized as the Latin language was. Universities are protected by corporations who rely on work done in university science laboratories in every scientific discipline.

When social and psychological disciplines entered the university in the twentieth century, each developed techniques of study that emulated the older quantitative sciences. These techniques are still a matter of dispute, as a substantial minority pursues social science through various descriptive and narrative forms of explanation and practice. For the majority, physical science is the standard in the following sense: results that are presented verbally but not quantitatively are considered to be less scientific, and therefore less authoritative. At the same time, the humanities are "feminized." Where once the exclusive male access to humanistic texts coded such study masculine, the same subjects today, studied through vernaculars by majority-female student populations, play a subordinate role in universities and have a lower status in society. The social ethic and reach of science renders it the heir to standing of Latin in the earlier universities.

369

Because of this status, most scientists consider their work not eligible to be challenged on social or political grounds. Those who have presented such challenges have been sometimes attacked with a surprising degree of indignation and contempt. Paul Gross and Norman Levitt refer to feminist critics of science as "a coven of hierophants signaling to each other in an arcane jargon impenetrable to outsiders."[1] Aren't scientific and other academic findings presented in jargon understood only by other members of that discipline? Is this word "coven" an echo of the centuries of witch-hunting? Isn't the figure a paranoid projection of scientists' own behavior?

Some scientists are feeling the political weight of the criticisms. In parts of this political critique the uses of language are addressed, but scientists have not responded to the challenges to these uses. The language uses of science still have the role of total mediation, as Latin once did. Science and scientists still overwhelmingly assume either that scientific writing is transparent or that the verbal language—the discourses presenting science to the public themselves—does not matter.

II. Objectification and Gender Identity

The use of language is built up with cumulative levels of mutual dependency,[2] first of *chora* or sensorimotor (prelinguistic, bodily) gestures (schemata) with one another, then of the sensorimotor gestures with verbal gestures,[3] then of verbal gestures with one another, and finally of language use and social relations, in which objectification (the process by which the child recognizes the analogy and the difference between self and other and is able to name things) is a collective process. The path of Helen Keller's acquisition of language shows how the ability to objectify things and experiences is embedded in a social and political scene that enabled her to learn to objectify ("everything has a name"). Similarly the practices of objectification in science, often referred to as "objectivity,"[4] emerge from political scenes and collective interdependencies.

With social gender development in mind, consider how people are both autonomous and dependent while growing into adulthood. We all are born of women and are dependent on them and other caregivers for several years.

---

1. Paul Gross and Norman Levitt, *Higher Superstition: The Academic Left and Its Quarrels with Science* (Baltimore: Johns Hopkins UP, 1994), 73.

2. As discussed in chapter 5.

3. Verbal gestures *are* sensorimotor gestures, but involving, in addition to other bodily movements, the oral and aural parts of the body.

4. This abstraction, familiar to most readers and broader in reference than objectification, also refers to the ideology through which science, scholarship, and law are presumed to be practiced.

Socialized, independent children are dependent on adults for another several years. When men become sexualized, society urges them (generally) to renounce dependency and conceal feelings of dependency from public view or exclude them from a positive male identity. Socially, men start to value and perhaps cultivate distance from women, who become "objects"[5] for them: the role of women in men's lives tends to narrow to courtship and sex rather than friendship and partnership; men start to value individual independence in society over mixed affiliations with those on whom they depend. On becoming sexualized, women's understanding that they can carry, bear, and nurse children teaches them to remember their stake in dependency and their need for autonomy.[6] This mixture of dependency and autonomy, of attachment and self-other differentiation (objectivity), obviously not contradictory in people's lives, is a reality principle learned by women. Although men acknowledge the claims of this reality, they start to think of themselves as not in it, and overvalue the benefits of autonomy, independence; the mixture is itself otherized or objectified as not-me. Men follow a different reality principle, which includes the priority of providing, the need for competition,[7] fighting in the service of providing, and very often power over other people; these traits lead to repeated tests of strength and dogmatic ideals of loyalty to other men (either you are with us or against us; either we win or you win). Adolescent boys, having already objectified women as a defensive action,[8] learn that sex is easily used as a form of political and social power, although if girls use it this way they are stigmatized. Because dependency is considered a shameful value among heterosexual men, they have learned to separate sex from their modes of dependency and arrive at the thought that they can buy sex when it is desired or needed, or, less frequently, that it is not a crime to take it with the use of drugs or violence. If these values reside in men as a group, this group is like Freud's "primal horde," following its "pleasure principle" and then civilizing themselves by making deals among themselves—one of which is to immerse themselves on an exaggerated scale in providing, or accumulating wealth, or inflated ambition.

---

5. This word itself may be male coded in the psychoanalytic usages: "love object" and "object relations." To heterosexual men, the object status of women may be more literal; to heterosexual women, the object status of men may be more metaphorical.

6. This description does not vary with regard to sexual orientation: men separating public and private is not determined by sexual orientation: women valuing the mixture of public and private is similarly invariant with regard to sexual orientation. One may say that both paths of gender development have been assimilated through the guidance of the collective culture.

7. The term "breadwinning" metaphorically connects providing with competition. But the term "providing" itself does not imply competition.

8. Chapter 8 cites an example from the fifteenth-century *Manuale scholarium*, showing the psychological proximity of objectification of women and misogyny.

Freud's binary of reality and pleasure is sustained by individualism. Putting Freud aside, if the empirical reality is taken to be individual and societal inter-dependency, then the not-reality is war, excess, exaggeration, false abstraction of moral virtue, isolated heroes, and the pursuit of pleasure regardless of risk and consequences.[9] Although one could consider this collection of activities to be self-indulgent, can it be said that self-indulgence follows a *pleasure* prin-ciple? Freud said the unconscious affirms everything. But isn't it truer to say that reality affirms everything (including the not-reality cited above), and that the fact of universal and reciprocal human dependency includes the ability to affirm different views and follow different paths at once? Like women, men need both dependency and autonomy, but men repress the awareness of their dependency, overlooking the fact that there is only one reality.[10] The struggle between two principles[11] in people's minds is an abstraction that might describe people's experience in some cases. The articulation of these struggles becomes inflated into paradigmatic assumptions. When people say they try to avoid, for example, "temptation," this term is a temporary identification of feelings to be applied differently in different cases, rather than a stable real feeling that appears in all people in the same way.[12] Because different people are tempted by different things, it is misleading to say that temptation is a universal nemesis. People hear and recite the Lord's Prayer repeatedly; some might say that it is only a prayer. People repeating the prayer privately presupposes their sense of temptation in order to keep our understanding of the word stable. Yet when you repeatedly,

---

9. Such as participating in sports that are physically dangerous like football or automobile racing.

10. "There is only one world, the 'real' world" was Bertrand Russell's response to the "possible worlds" philosophy. Russell comments, "Similarly, to maintain that Hamlet, for example, exists in his own world, namely, in the world of Shakespeare's imagina-tion, just as truly as (say) Napoleon existed in the ordinary world, is to say something deliberately confusing, or else confused to a degree which is scarcely credible. There is only one world, the 'real' world: Shakespeare's imagination is part of it." Betrand Rus-sell, *Introduction to Mathematical Philosophy* (London: Allen and Unwin, 1919), 169. The "one world" view may also be attributed to Spinoza (1632–1677), whose work was taken to have denied the transcendence of God by saying that God and the world were one. Rebecca Goldstein's reads Spinoza thus: "Nothing outside of the world—no transcendent God, in other words—explains the world. Its explanation is immanent within itself." Rebecca Goldstein, *Betraying Spinoza: The Renegade Jew Who Gave us Modernity* (New York: Schocken Books, 2006), 53. Spinoza's formulations show a diminished role for "explanation" for reasons similar to those given by Wittgenstein. Chapter 1 cites Stuart Hampshire's reading of Spinoza's logic as "thoroughly nominalist," a judgment consistent with the syndrome of perspectives discussed in this chapter and this book.

11. Similar and related to the "good and evil" frame of mind.

12. Chapter 1 references Stuart Hampshire's citation from Spinoza's *Ethics* that has made this point.

ritually, ask not to be led into "temptation," temptation is understood as a fixed thing that should be avoided in *every* instance, a behavior that would serve few.

The practice of reifying the reference of temporary general objectifications utilizes the ability to objectify learned early in the acquisition of language. In the process of repressing dependency and keeping up the appearance of certainty and authority, people learn to bet, so to speak, on ever more fixed objectification. Because the process of language acquisition is founded on a buildup of mutual dependency relationships, its early achievement is the ability to objectify things, people, actions, behaviors, and phenomena that require special identification. Simply to identify something by name is an objectification, and the use of language has no sense without this gesture. Objectification and predication are parts of the same action of combining, for example, an observation with a verbal (oral) behavior. To make a predication and to identify something are both acts of objectification.[13] These actions are common to all gender identities. A question entertained in this chapter is this: How does the materiality of language—through the range from two-person relationships to whole language communities—help to use collectively the practice of temporary general objectification without rendering objectivity into a dogma?

III. Science and Objectivity

Modern science is in the business of objectification of experience gained by deliberate experimentation and investigative research. Its achievements are acknowledged to be a result of its having found ways to improve and prolong life. Such tangible benefits have helped science attract collective support for its findings. People were gradually persuaded that it is better to think of the planets moving around the sun than of the sun and planets moving around the Earth: the solar system was differently objectified and mathematically described (identified and named). This understanding created an atmosphere of change, novelty, and perhaps revolution in how the cosmos is perceived. The time became hospitable to Descartes's reification of two genres of experience—the subjective and objective—and how they are related to one another in a scientific, coherent system of thought.[14] Lynn Nelson's account of Descartes's practical philosophy of objectivity provides a motif of how

---

13. This view of language is held even by transformationalists who have said that predication is a universal feature of language. They have also suggested that because it is universal, it must be innate. Some have reasoned similarly about androcentrism and marriage: because they are universal, they must be innate.

14. Subjective and objective have always been there. Descartes put them in a scientific discourse. Another way to put this fact is that Descartes "legalized" (made lawful) the provisional binary—treated it and other regularities as laws of nature. Edgar Zilsel, "The Genesis of the Concept of the Physical Law," *The Philosophical Review* 51.3 (May 1942):

modern science became a collective project of Western civilization. Because social, moral, and sexual knowledge were already admitted provinces of the Church in the seventeenth century, Descartes mapped out a different territory for science that Nelson characterized as having appeared as the result of "Descartes' Covenant," a *de facto* deal made between him and the Catholic Church[15] that would allow him to continue to work in science and philosophy:

> The relationship between the ideal of a "value-free" science and the view of knowers and evidence we are considering is neither extraneous nor accidental. Descartes' compromise with the church—in effect, an agreement to cleave the world in two, separating values and facts in its severance of mind and body, the spiritual and material—is, at its core, a covenant to leave the business of values to something *other than* science. The covenant and the compromise it facilitated were made to enable science to go about the business of finding out "how things are" without interference, and at the time, it was a good bargain.[16]

But in order to enter into this particular covenant to facilitate the compromise, Descartes had to issue a blank check: that knowledge of the physical world is different in kind from knowledge of values and that science would concern itself only with the former.[17]

Like marriage arrangements, peace treaties, and corporate mergers, Descartes's covenant is a deal between men that presents itself as applying to all:

---

269. Further discussion of the legal vocabulary is given in section 5. Lynn Nelson's take on Descartes is introduced in chapter 8, section 7.

15. He was nevertheless considered a heretic and his books censored.

16. Lynn Hankinson Nelson, *Who Knows: From Quine to a Feminist Empiricism* (Philadelphia: Temple UP, 1990), 305. There are several useful accounts, pertinent to the present study, of Descartes's having provided a coherent vision of how to divide experience into the material and the spiritual. One is in Brian Easlea, *Witch-Hunting, Magic, and the New Philosophy: An Introduction to Debates of the Scientific Revolution 1450–1750* (Atlantic Highlands, NJ: Humanities P, 1980), 113. Easlea also gives an example of what would be part of the covenant: "Descartes thought he could agree with both Copernicus and the Church. For Copernicus is correct in stating that the earth orbits the sun while the Church is correct in stating that the earth is stationary—stationary that is, Descartes explains, with respect to the aetherial vortex!" (116). Another is in David F. Noble, *A World without Women: The Christian Clerical Culture of Western Science* (New York: Knopf, 1992), chapter 9. A third is Susan Bordo, ed., *Feminist Interpretations of René Descartes* (State College: Pennsylvania State UP, 1992), especially chapters 2 and 6.

17. If this covenant is taken as true, it could also be said that the Church forced Descartes into holding a mendacious philosophical position simply in order to do his work without interference. However, the Church is but one of several sources of authority that would require this sort of intellectual compromise.

as far as one can tell historically, the public presentation of any authoritative knowledge has followed a similar path.[18] Such a deal segregated knowledge accumulated by women, unacknowledged knowledge about how human bodies work and how men conducted their lives. Since men knew that women did have authoritative knowledge based on their presence in all people's personal lives, this part of men's knowledge must also be repressed; women could not use their knowledge without taking risks. Those women who had practical medical knowledge, such as midwives and nurses, were often accused of being witches.[19] As Easlea has described, the success of science at first intensified the practices of witch-hunting.[20] Orthodoxy, which protected both the Church and the ruling classes, was threatened for perhaps a century following Copernicus's first announcement. As churchmen (including Protestants) became more aware of the significance of secular knowledge, the persecution of witches, through the long-established Inquisition, intensified: women were the scapegoats because, on the one hand, the male scientists could not be hunted and executed, and on the other hand, public ignorance of women's medical knowledge and medicines made it easy to view them as occult figures or magicians.[21] If one understands Descartes to have been participating in the traditional

---

18. According to Dalia Judovitz, "we have come to equate what was a highly specific Cartesian epistemological process with a culturally generalized process of representation as objectification, with all men (particularly men) applying the Cartesian maneuver to an endless range of circumstances." Dalia Judovitz, *Subjectivity and Representation in Descartes* (New York: Cambridge UP, 1988), ix. Quoted in James A. Winders, "Writing Like a Man (?): Descartes, Science, and Madness," *Feminist*, ed. Bordo, 114–140, quotation on 135.

19. A longer discussion of this circumstance is found in chapter 9. Easlea notes that this suspicion is documented in the early fourteenth century when Jacqueline Félicie was "deprived of the right to practise medicine" even though she "conclusively demonstrated to her Parisian judges that she had cured patients given up as lost by physicians qualified at the Sorbonne." Brian Easlea, *Science and Sexual Oppression: Patriarchy's Confrontation with Woman and Nature* (London: Widenfield and Nicolson, 1981), 86–87.

20. According to Easlea, the Church associated science with natural magic whose proponents, like Giordano Bruno, were judged to be heretics and were executed (*Witch Hunting*, 90–116). In the revolutions "not only was the sexism of Aristotle preserved in its essential features but a new and very powerful ingredient was added to it." Seventeenth century philosophers "agreed with or acquiesced" with the view that men were "intellectually superior to women"; "[w]hat the seventeenth-century natural philosophers added to the sexism of Aristotle was the quest for power over the natural world" (Easlea *Science*, 88–89). This view of men's approach to science also helps to explain the intensification of witch-hunting during the period of more rapid enlightenment, the question posed in chapter 9, section 4.

21. If the warning in Exodus about not suffering female magicians to live is to be taken into account, such beliefs about women's knowledge must be traditional and common among men.

sense of male superiority, it was perhaps a "good" bargain for him: the question of women's knowledge or women's access to knowledge was irrelevant to this arrangement.[22] Ultimately, however, the bargain failed, as the church rejected Descartes's explanation of the Eucharist, and his works were censored. If Descartes is a founder of modern science, and this covenant describes his attempt to survive as a scientific philosopher in the face of Church suspicions, this is one of the reasons why objectivity became fetishized. It seemed to be a path of action that would not be censored by the Church (which was already hunting down women with knowledge of how to oversee critical phases of the life cycle); but it was also a way to match the Church's claims of authority, a new male enterprise, a new ground for describing the other—this time Mother Nature—which was a new way to preserve the separateness of men from women, a new zone of authority for men who were not part of either Church or state. Descartes (and others) proposed language that reified ordinary objectification, inflated it and claimed it to be a necessary intellectual strategy: now, material things—living bodies—were considered mechanical or automatic, requiring a spiritual mind to animate it.[23] In the seventeenth and eighteenth centuries people were persuaded that measurement produces better referents for generalizations: instead of gravity being named with words alone (e.g., the "force" of gravity), gravity was renamed as the product of the mass (weight) multiplied by 32 ft/sec^2 ("the acceleration of gravity"). Motion was similarly described as mathematical laws; gravity and motion were thus objectified differently from the way they were before Galileo and Newton. From there, claims advanced to God's having created an orderly universe, a view endorsed by Einstein in the twentieth century. Objectifications that were grossly exaggerated and mixed with superstition (God made it that way and then left it alone to work)[24] remain today in a prominent, if not dominant, role in our cultural lives.

---

22. Men divided up the contested territory, a division that could take place because churchmen were notoriously uninvolved in scientific investigation and they judged those who were, such as Galileo and Descartes, to be heretics.

23. "Both the pornographic literature and the philosophical treatises of the new science postulate a private space where nothing matters but the force of projectiles, the compulsive pushing and pulling of bodies." Margaret C. Jacob, "The Materialist World of Pornography," *The Invention of Pornography: Obscenity and the Origins of Pornography, 1500–1800,* ed. Lynn Hunt (New York, Zone, 1996), 182. These treatises acknowledged that God, the transcendental spirit, is the force behind planetary movements and the maintainer of the constancy of objects: God hears the tree falling in the unpopulated forest.

24. There was always dispute about whether God was intervening in the mechanical movements of Earth and other celestial bodies—another paradox created by the stipulation of transcendent spiritual forces. This issue is discussed further in section 5.

The strategic objectification and rigid scientific naming that came from ordinary contingent linguistic objectification are today being discredited, piece by piece, in each science and more generally in the humanities.[25] The modern presupposition of objectivity has been treated by Naomi Scheman as a feature of men's psychology.[26] Her description shows how the overvalued positivist sense of objectivity retains its connection with the grammatical dependency found in predication and other language practices, but tries to separate itself from any sense of dependency, deny that dependency is a feature of objectification, and pretend that objectification identifies the autonomy of people and objects. The reliance on objectivity requires repression of dependency, contingency, and other values that acknowledge the temporality of thought, science, and people.

Scheman's analysis applies to the stances taken in the age of modern Western science during the seventeenth century until the early twentieth century, and the practice of quantum physics.[27] During this period, empirical observation

---

25. Philosophical treatment of this change remains bound to its discipline, however. Paul K. Moser, *Philosophy after Objectivity: Making Sense in Perspective* (New York: Oxford UP, 1993), sees new modes of explanation, but, unlike Wittgenstein, sees no problems in the assumed necessity of searching for explanations. In this study, philosophy retains its traditional role as the overseer of all forms of thinking. Peter Novick's *That Noble Dream, "The Objectivity Question" and the American Historical Profession* (Cambridge: Cambridge UP, 1988) traces a steady shift away from objectivity in historiography, moving toward verification of historical accounts with greater reference to local contextual reporting. Loraine Daston and Peter Galison suggest that scientists' increasing use of visual imagery is both a step to change objectivity and a gesture toward a more authoritative "trained judgment." Loraine Daston and Peter Galison, *Objectivity* (New York: Zone, 2007), 307.

26. Naomi Scheman, "Though This Be Method, Yet There Is Madness in It: Paranoia and Liberal Epistemology," *Engenderings: Constructions of Knowledge, Authority, and Privilege* (New York: Routledge, 1993), 75–105.

27. There is no beginning to modern science that one needs to fix, although a favorite starting point is Descartes's so-called method of isolating one's own mind from everything else. Bacon, "often called the founder of the scientific method," is also cited for having placed experimentation as the key scientific practice. Alison Jolly, *Lucy's Legacy: Sex and Intelligence in Human Evolution* (Cambridge, MA: Harvard UP, 1999), 311. Different researchers have different means of describing the movement from, for example, undocumented scientific judgments to experimental science. Here I assume that scientific observation took place in the sixteenth century (Copernicus), but the collective gathering of funds and materials to build laboratories for a program of experimentation did not begin until the late seventeenth century (in the Royal Society); and universities did not begin organized scientific research and teaching until the eighteenth century. It would be reasonable to say that the development of science took three centuries; it would also make sense to say that science is still developing and changing. But if "science" functions verbally as something fixed and definite, it will be hard to recognize both its changes and its needs for change.

meant "seeing and knowing without affecting or interacting with phenomena."[28] Scheman says that axiomatic objectivity is like paranoid illness and that this resemblance is concealed by objectivity's normative status: there are no alternative scientific presuppositions. Science has been built on objectivity and tries to confer on its language the functions of a transparent total mediation: I do not affect what I see; what I see is what there is. We use the *word* "paranoid" to describe an illness. Applying this description to a normal situation may seem extreme, but Scheman's usage raises questions about the connections of science and gender, and, therefore, about science as most people understand it.

Scheman first describes Freud's case study of Daniel Paul Schreber, who suffered from spells of paranoia. Freud thought that Schreber had struggled with the repression of homosexual feelings. The form of repression is that such feelings were split off, forming a part of the not-me for Schreber. The process of compartmentalizing the feelings enabled him to see them in others for whom he then felt contempt.[29] The process of establishing an imagined hated other prompts the subject's imagining of reciprocal feelings: the other hates me. This hating other is generalized to all people, as the word "other" means those who are not me. The paranoia is a constant, urgent fear of others, usually involving the possibility of bodily violence. When the paranoid person goes on a spree of violence, that person feels this behavior as self-defense, as he imagines that he will be killed or persecuted (by other men) for his homosexual feelings.[30] The

---

28. Piaget called this ability when it appears in infancy "object permanence," a capability acquired just before infants acquire language. The difference between this psychological capability and the objectivism of science is that the latter admits of no deviation—it is prescriptive. For the child it can feel certain, but it is limited and flexible. The child entertains various forms of involvement with permanent objects, often viewing them in metaphorical senses and not aiming to rule such objects.

29. For those unfamiliar with this case study, the contemporary film *American Beauty* (dir. Sam Mendes, 2001) dramatizes this process exactly. The protagonist's ex-Marine homophobic neighbor's (Colonel Fitts) own homosexual feelings emerge at the end of the film. When Fitts's homoerotic advances are rejected by the protagonist (Lester), Fitts murders Lester, thus permitting him to continue to see in others his own homosexuality. Even if this murder is read as silencing someone who knows the highly embarrassing truth, this sort of repression then becomes a common basis for men's frequent resort to violence in order to maintain the repression.

30. As can probably be asserted with some confidence today, out gay men are justified in expecting violence to come their way. In Melville's *Moby-Dick* and in Wouk's *The Caine Mutiny,* both captains seem closeted and paranoid. They are on all-male ships, where men are especially close (and are described as such in *Moby-Dick*). Ahab is carrying on a vendetta against a whale, and Queeg (accurately) thinks the crew is ganging up on him after having his solicitation of their support rejected. Herman Melville, *Moby-Dick* (New York: Dover, 2003); Herman Wouk, *The Caine Mutiny* (Boston: Back Bay, 1951). Sergeant-at-arms Claggart, in Melville's *Billy Budd,* behaved violently toward Billy, whose bodily beauty he admired; Billy inadvertently kills Claggart, then is executed

key point of Freud's analysis is that the repression takes place for social reasons, and the male subject becomes antisocial—ill or violent or both—in order to save or protect his individual self.

Heterosexually identified men in a heterocentric culture fear that homosexual feelings amount to having too much woman in them, which can mean secretly feeling too dependent or emotional, or perhaps being attracted to men. The repression takes place because it is considered undesirable to be dependent or otherwise like women. Some have argued that anti-gay feelings among men and women derive in both genders from misogyny.[31] Heterocentric norms urge people to simplify their gender identity into one of two social categories, although many people recognize more than two categories. These social mores can incline people toward illusory and impossible intrapsychic goals; for many it becomes so urgent to remain "all man," that the repression of non-all-man feelings encourages violence or results in illness.

This androcentric psychology is *not* strongly related to the sexual preferences of men.[32] During the Christian era, same-sex activity was further devalued from its already subordinate position in Greek and Roman societies, but in the latter societies, objectivity as an ideal did not obtain. In the relatively common pederastic relationships, it was thought possible that the "insemination" of a younger man by an older one could pass along the knowledge and wisdom of the older male.[33] Aristotle's theory that semen has more "vital heat" than menstrual

---

as part of Captain Vere's application of maritime military justice. Herman Melville, *Billy Budd, Sailor* (Chicago: U of Chicago P, 1962). None of these cases are about people who are identified as gay; the war situations render the punishment for being gay debatable if thoughts of sexual orientation are being censored in society. But, historically, war and collective violence commonly distract both individuals and society from the task of resolving the range of sexual difference and taste present in the human species.

31. Suzanne Pharr, *Homophobia: A Weapon of Sexism* (Little Rock, AR: Women's Project, 1988). In antiquity being like a woman meant being in the passive role in sex. It was all right for a teenager to "receive" sex from an older man, but the older man would be shamed or disrespected if he sought to be the receiver.

32. One of the hesitations one may have about David Noble's characterization of the history of science is that Noble seems to treat movements toward homoerotic feelings that he found in several of the early clerics and of seventeenth- and eighteenth-century scientists as the source of misogyny among clerics and scientists. Noble credibly describes the contrast between Bacon's masculinist attitude toward nature and his having been known as a pederast (*World*, 223). But the narrative also intimates that the pederasty, rather than its concealment and repression, was the source of Bacon's bigoted pursuit of heretics and witches and his misogyny. Gay identity, however, should not be taken to imply androcentrism or male supremacy, both of whose principal references are social and political rather than sexual.

33. William Armstrong Percy III, *Pederasty and Pedagogy in Archaic Greece* (Urbana: U of Illinois P), 1996, 1–2, 186–187. This study presents the thousand-year history of institutional pederasty as a feature of warrior societies. In modern times, as suggested

blood, and was thought of as a kind of essence of blood that contributed the soul to human beings, rendered this kind of sex a feature of elite male social domination. Sex between older and younger men had a pedagogical function, as implied in *The Symposium* and in a variety of sources cited by Percy. Among the elite Greeks, who valued contemplation, learning, and knowledge, there was no separate category of objectivity; people did not try to decide if a claim of knowledge was a fantasy or the figment of someone's imagination; people did try to decide what was true generally. Nevertheless, among the Greeks women did not participate in the formal processes of education and learning, or in the writing of treatises about the natural world. The assumption of male superiority has been constant in history, usually associated with becoming warriors, and regardless of changes in the social status of sexual tastes and practices.[34]

Scheman describes the pursuit of knowledge in connection with homophobia, but the male-coded status of knowledge may be also described as deriving from misogyny in the following observation: "Homophobia thus gets joined to another venerable fantasy structure: the usurpation by men of women's reproductive power. At least as far back as Socrates, men have taken the imagery of childbirth to describe their allegedly nobler, sublimated creative activities. Schreber's fantasies expose the homophobic anxieties that underlie the use of this imagery: you can't give birth without being fucked."[35] In modern times, knowledge and understanding have the same high value and a similar male status that they had for the Greeks, for whom "being fucked" was something that happened to younger, lower-status males and women. But in the modern

---

by the novels of Herman Melville and Herman Wouk (see note 30), acknowledgement of this tendency is repressed. In archaic times young men were educated through their sexual bond with older (elite) men. See also Eva Cantarella, *Bisexuality in the Ancient World* (New Haven, CT: Yale UP, 1988); and Lynda Lange, "Woman Is Not a Rational Animal: On Aristotle's Biology of Reproduction," *Discovering Reality: Feminist Perspectives on Epistemology, Metaphysics, Methodology, and Philosophy of Science,* ed. Sandra Harding and Merrill B. Hintikka (Dordrecht: D. Reidel, 1983), 1–16. According to Cantarella, "[T]he male seed . . . in the reproductive process, cooks the female blood and transforms it into a new being; which means that sperm plays an active part whereas the menstrual blood has a purely passive role. Although it is indispensable, the female contribution is that of matter, with which the woman is identified, whereas the male contribution, given that men are all form and spirit, is of an active type. This biological construction inevitably led to the theory—destined to last throughout the centuries—of the inferiority and necessary subordination of women" (*Bisexuality,* 66).

34. A contemporary example of a new status for an old sexual practice is the use of fellatio among adolescents (and adult men) as a way to sidestep some of the risks of intercourse. Oral sex, unless reciprocal, presents as diminishing women; contemporary pornography often depicts women as performing fellatio as a service to men. Fellatio is assimilated to today's forms of androcentrism. This issue is discussed further in chapter 12.

35. Scheman, *Engenderings,* 83.

periods the exclusively male transmission of knowledge to the next generations
of men is not acknowledged to be a male-exclusive action. Because of cultural
changes, modern men may be more aware of their necessary participation in
womanhood but also more likely to repress this awareness. The Greeks may not
have needed this particular mode of repression because womanliness was held to
be passive more than it was held to be dependent; the lesser, womanly status of
a man was recognized if an adult male actually took the passive position in sex
with another man, as young men did in their relations with older men.[36] The
price of objectivity in the modern period is the caricaturing and repression of
men's psychological and social kinship with women. If objectivity is founded on
language objectification learned by all people, it would follow that, as a dogma
of science, objectivity is a male-coded reification of this figurative practice of
separating oneself from other things and people. Maintaining objectivity as a
foundation requires a repression also required by maintaining realist language
practices. For the Greeks, the processes of male separation took place more
through war than through science or professional work, so that the structure
of repression was different.

Scheman, like other critics of male-coded science, respects the value of objectivity as a provisional starting point.[37] Both she and Sandra Harding[38] have tried
to show that in contexts in which one decides to be objective, objectivity changes
its uses and functions and is flexible. Under such circumstances objectivity is
said to occur when everyone who accepts the same social context agrees that
something is true or is the case. Harding characterizes this kind of objectivity
as strong because it includes both women's and men's experience within specific
historical contexts as the source of standpoints through which objective stances
would be taken. Rather than an objective perspective becoming established as a
matter of automatic prior assumption for scientific work, Harding expects that
a self-conscious collective effort, based on a sharing of experience, decides on
questions to be posed and research plans stipulated among interested parties. She
insists that scientific questions and research projects not be coerced in advance
by an abstract standard of what is objective: that is, by conferring not-me status
on the item or process that is to be studied, and thus radically separating oneself

36. Plato's *Gorgias* says that the "*kinaidos,* which came to mean a much disparaged
adult male, presumed to be extremely effeminate in manner and dress, who took the
passive role in sexual intercourse" (Percy, *Pederasty,* 8).

37. Naomi Scheman, "Epistemology Resuscitated: Objectivity as Trustworthiness,"
Engendering Rationalities, ed. Nancy Tuana and Sandra Morgen (Albany: SUNY P,
2001), 23–52.

38. Sandra Harding, "'Strong Objectivity' and Socially Situated Knowledge," *Whose
Science, Whose Knowledge? Thinking from Women's Lives* (Ithaca, NY: Cornell UP, 1991),
138–163.

from this objective entity. Rather, a *collective agreement to objectify* is needed. One may doubt that the term "objectivity" is the only way to describe this consensus-seeking procedure, however, because the term carries meanings from centuries of use in ways that are rejected by Harding and Scheman. The kind of objectivity Harding describes could also be called pragmatism, intersubjectivity, or interactionism, because a machinery of negotiation and exchange precedes scientific effort.[39]

The term "objectivity," in its local usage, refers to the feature of language acquisition whose role in language practices is fundamental: to have language is to be able to objectify. Access to language for individuals is achieved when their objectifications are collectively considered and possibly accepted. Many parts of science do move from public discussions toward legislation and other forms of public regulation. This is especially true in research in genetics of food and animals. Although scientists are still considered the experts, the issues raised by genetic research (for example) are engaged by public forums. Even before such issues have arisen, it has been generally accepted that the predictability of some medications is uncertain, in that they don't work the same way for all patients.

Scheman asks if there are any social circumstances under which objectivity is trustworthy. First, she allows that if there should ever be social justice for the whole human species, it may make sense to take objectivity as a universal priority.[40] If all interested parties have equivalent access to research in science, which questions to pursue emerge from a cooperative context and are not imposed by supervening interests. *Collective* trust is the necessary basis for the presumption of objectivity: "A sustainable attribution of objectivity serves to underwrite a significant degree of—objectively refutable—authority, and it does so by rationally grounding trust."[41] An important reason objectivity is a value to begin with is that it promotes trust: "Central to what we do when we call an argument, conclusion, or decision 'objective' is to recommend it to others, and, importantly, to suggest that they *ought* to accept it."[42] Scheman similarly observes that objectivity cannot promote trust on a collective scale unless it is founded on trust. No formal techniques, such as those of mathematics that are logically rigid, can

---

39. Increasingly, as biological issues become important, public discussion is preceding scientific effort; some of the issues are the control of pregnancies, research on fetal stem cells, genetic food alteration, food disinfection through radiation, gene therapy, cloning, and so on. There are significant data about public support on these matters. Often these data affect government initiative as well as elections. However, such developments are still informal; there is no consensus as to what procedures are appropriate for each issue.

40. Scheman, "Epistemology," 43.

41. Scheman, "Epistemology," 25.

42. Scheman, "Epistemology," 24. The story of Helen Keller shows that trust between child and teacher was essential for objectification to take (in the acquisition of language).

guarantee trust.[43] Trust is a condition, a feeling that constitutes relationships
and that is tied to how people grow and relate within their social memberships.
As she characterizes the situation of even well-educated members of the population, we are ubiquitously dependent on science and scientists without our being
able to assure ourselves of their reliability. The information we get about the
universe, the technologies of daily life, and the medicines we use, we receive
on trust, where trust means, practically, that we are willing to stake our health
on the claims and behaviors of those we have no reason to trust and several
reasons to mistrust: those to whom we are unconnected in any way and who
may, in their own self-interest, easily abuse the total public that depends on
them. We trust those to whose language we have no access. Scheman asks this:
If we live our lives with such a low level of trust, how can objectivity function,
since it acquires its authority on the basis of universal access to the facts? Collective mutual dependency, with access to the relevant languages, determines
how things are objectified. If persons or institutions are trusted, we believe their
claims and promises: this means that we have access to a common language and
can think of their knowledge as being the same for them as for us, a situation
which we call—in shorthand, so to speak—"objective."[44] This is the same result
arrived at by Saul Kripke in his discussions of Wittgenstein's remarks on private
language: just as only a collective usage can establish a language, only collective
agreement can authorize objectivity.[45] The dependency of collective agreement
on the simultaneous negotiability of language and issues or facts depends on the
materiality of language. Language, taken as a total mediator, is not negotiated,
nor are its usages eligible to be changed locally if needed; transparent language

---

43. Erik Erikson described the infant's first achievement (that appears with the acquisition of language) as that of having established "basic trust" in all the elements of the
immediate living environment. Erik Erikson, *Childhood and Society* (New York: Norton,
1950), 247–251.

44. "Wittgenstein writes of the impossibility of trying to ground or prove much of
what we believe to be true. We hear on authority, accept on authority, and confirm by
our own experience a wide range of ideas that form the substratum of our thought about
the world." Emily Martin, *The Woman in the Body: A Cultural Analysis of Reproduction*
(Boston: Beacon P, 1987), 195. Martin, some of whose work is discussed later in this
chapter, focuses on the fact that the experience that "confirms" "common" knowledge
is different for women and for men.

45. I relate Saul Kripke's having derived from Wittgenstein a collectivist source of
objectivity to Derrida's discussions of language in *The Double Perspective: Language, Literacy, and Social Relations* (New York: Oxford UP, 1988), 103–113. Ruth Hubbard observes
that "in science, as in the arts . . . the stories must be 'true' in the sense that they must
reflect other people's experiences." Ruth Hubbard, *The Politics of Women's Biology* (New
Brunswick, NJ: Rutgers UP, 1990), 3. The common foundation of science and art, in
this view, are stories and social relations, and even though the majority of people do not
hold a consensus of this view, it is presented as truer than the existing consensus.

changes by proclamation, as occurred in George Orwell's *Animal Farm* and *1984*.[46] A principal reference of the materiality of language is to language as part of a network of social relations, all the parts of which contribute to everyone's continuous resocialization. Scheman presents objectivity as a value that requires regular reworking, and reuse in incrementally new ways through the exchange of language: "Objective claims . . . are always disputable, but they are not, without dispute, rejectable."[47]

Like the researchers studying childhood language acquisition through social interaction, Scheman grounds her analysis on her recognition that the long childhood dependency of human beings continues into adulthood. When the child learns that language is the means of return to objectified and autonomous loved ones, the child's identification with close adults starts the socialized growth process. For people, dependency is part of the self-conscious life that is sustained by the use of language in the same sense that air sustains bodily life: it is always there, necessary, and used to maintain our stability as social figures. In adulthood and public life, language remains the means of return, the means of retaining affiliation in the absence of loved ones, the means of promoting the growth of close relationships, and the means of forming connections with institutions having diffuse memberships. The language negotiations that appear in interpersonal affairs are also those that underlie the means for science and other not always immediately personal enterprises to function. These practices keep us aware that abstractions are provisional in their ordinary use, that they function as temporary indicative gestures.

IV. Normalizing Abstractions

One of Kristeva's aims in her study of language is to bring the attention to the speaking subject[48] back into the picture being developed by the French poststructuralist language philosophers.[49] As considered in chapter 4, Kristeva's critique of Derrida was justified because his academic style followed the tradition of philosophical and scientific writing. Some scientists have noticed that an impersonal style may communicate unwanted material; they may doubt the past

---

46. In *Animal Farm* (New York: Harcourt, Brace, 1946) when the pigs consolidate their power, revisions peremptorily appear in the publicly displayed list of core principles: "All animals are equal, but some animals are more equal than others." The "but" clause was added on by proclamation.

47. Scheman, "Epistemology," 24.

48. In Moi's words, "concern to safeguard a place for the subject, albeit a subject-in-process" *The Kristeva Reader*, ed. Toril Moi (New York: Columbia UP, 1986), 16. See also Kristeva's essay in that volume, "The System and the Speaking Subject"(24–33).

49. Such as, for example, in addition to Jacques Derrida, Hélène Cixous, and Luce Irigaray.

virtues of impersonal writing conventions used to report scientific procedures and results. They are considering the consequences of thinking that delivering results in transparent language is not possible on a scale that would retain credibility for science.[50]

Ruth Hubbard[51] reports an instance of how the language-use conventions in science work unconsciously on the scientist. She read a 1965 article in which the male scientist reports, "I had consistently failed to recognize one rather significant general concept."[52] But then she reflects: "But immediately the charm is broken. The second sentence does not go on: 'It is what I have decided to call . . .' It reads: 'This is what may be called . . .' The thinking agent has disappeared . . . not another 'I' in the paper; we are back in science. It was a momentary lapse, a minor declaration of personal independence." The abrupt substitution of the passive after a moment of informal (vernacular) candor means that "we are back in science." The scientist was caught in the midst of his own naming of something while not saying that *he* is doing the naming. It is not just that in scientific language "I" is not there. The language of science creates a *fantasy* that "I am not there"; it pretends that the subject is absent. The habitual use of the passive may not be a pathological delusion, but when it persuades the rest of society to trust this usage, it obfuscates understanding of how science is actually pursued. The reasons for continuing this convention are created by the fantasy that science (which might be translated as "human knowledge") is itself mechanical, automatic, and driven by strictly logical laws. Using the passive voice to report active behavior communicates the false assumption that we are working in and on a part of the universe that is neither responding to us nor influencing what we are doing. This assumption is additionally unwelcome in that it emerged from scientists (like Francis Bacon) who championed the aggressive, heroic mission of the scientist to subdue and conquer (Mother) Nature.[53]

---

50. "Over the past thirty years, the traditional model of scientific language so hopefully aspired to by working scientists has come under a barrage of criticism. Not only is the practice remote from the ideal, but significant challenges to even the possibility of such an ideal language have recently been posed by scholars in the history, philosophy, and sociology of science." Evelyn Fox Keller and Elisabeth A. Lloyd, eds., *Keywords in Evolutionary Biology* (Cambridge, MA: Harvard UP, 1992), 2. Keller and Lloyd mention Thomas Kuhn, Max Black, Mary Hesse, Richard Rorty, and Gillian Beer as being among the critics of impersonal scientific writing.

51. Ruth Hubbard, *Politics*, 13.

52. She observes with reference to the cited essay, "Never before or again has such a sentence appeared in the *Journal of Molecular Biology*," reporting that scientists almost never cite features of their actual experience in scientific reports.

53. Easlea, *Witch-Hunting*, 126–129. Easlea shows how Bacon arrived at his "masculine birth of time" by grounding his view of the investigation of the "bosom" of nature in the Eden story that commands hard work for mankind. In addition and in contrast to the somewhat disreputable magicians of his own time, Bacon insists on the "lawful-

The salient elements of the fantasy assumption are that we are not a part of nature and that we may therefore treat it as something to be conquered.[54] Some women in science have reacted to the assumptions behind this style of writing, and called attention to its unnecessary use in the reporting of research results. These observers say that every science, as well as science as a more general enterprise, continues to report results as if people at the site of observation had no effect on the work. Ruth Hubbard says that science does not even exist: "there is no such entity as science. There are only the activities of scientists."[55] The traditional language of science, the conventional language that is used to report all scientific results *today* uses the passive voice, repressing both the fact of the scientist's involvement and the fact that the scientist's action is part of an enterprise some of whose reasons for having been undertaken have not been acknowledged. It will not do to say that everyone knows that the scientist really did it. The issue is this: because the scientist's reports omit this *fact* about how experiments are done, readers don't know what the scientist really did, and the fact that he did it cannot be scrutinized. Its consequences are not considered to be part of science.[56] The attachment of scientists or of communities of researchers to discovered facts raises the question of the scope of application of these new facts. For example, results may become different as a function of who sponsored the search for these results, or of who conceived of the procedures to find them. The results are usually abstractions or principles whose scope of application is unclear at the moment; further tests often produce greater clarity. In any case, the results are given as an abstraction: this vaccine works against this illness in almost all instances of the test populations. But just what this may mean in practice depends on the extended use of the vac-

---

ness" of both the inquiry and the object of inquiry, nature. In this way, he describes the quest to "storm and occupy [Nature's] castles and strongholds" and to "make [Nature] your slave" as derived from an assumed divine commandment in Genesis. This is how "scientific law" (considered in this chapter) came to be a term rooted in the motif of God's plan for human beings.

54. Scientists overlook the contradiction of these two assumptions: Why does one have to conquer, or acquire dominion over, an inert entity? Science proceeds as if the strange wish to subdue what is inert were not visible to those who study how scientists work. This question is similar: Why does the stronger class of people usually feel the need to subdue the weaker class?

55. Hubbard, *Politics,* 12.

56. Ludwik Fleck, in *Genesis and Development of a Scientific Fact* (1935) (Chicago: U of Chicago P, 1979), did take the risk of describing the involvement of scientists. It took a while to be translated into English; Thomas Kuhn used it as one of the sources of his *The Structure of Scientific Revolutions* (Chicago: U of Chicago P, 1962) which itself caused a stir; but the actual nonrational human involvement in the process of discovering the Wasserman test (described by Fleck) has not been entertained as a factor in the results of such discoveries.

cine over time and population (as scientists know). Similarly, Newton's laws were considered absolute until Einstein said that they should be understood as a limiting case. As Kuhn describes, Einstein's sense of the cosmos changed the reference of Newton's laws. Similar cautions apply to every change of scientific understanding: the scope of application is tied to considerations of the total context and to the interests of the research communities.

Hubbard is one of several figures who have insisted on the provisionality of abstractions that have been given or taken as transparent.[57] Just as physics has changed from the assumption of a clockwork universe of the seventeenth and eighteenth centuries, evolutionary biology has grown out of the industrialization values and vocabulary with which Darwin grew up: Malthus said there wasn't enough of everything to sustain the human race—the principle of scarcity. This principle was derived from a logical rather than factual consideration. If population grew unchecked, it increased exponentially, whereas subsistence for this population grew only arithmetically; it is thus "proven" that soon, living things will run out of food.[58] Darwin's readings of Malthus's hypothesis emerged variously as "the struggle for existence," "the survival of the fittest," "competition," and "scarcity," now part of an accepted total picture of the evolution of life forms. Darwin superimposed on this assumption a collection of facts about the thousands of living species on earth. Although there was almost as little understanding of Darwin's facts as there was about Malthus's lack thereof, Darwin's reading was plausible, since it fit the fossil record into a new "story of the jungle."[59] It tells that there is so little food that all the species must be fighting for it. In this all-against-all fight, those who survive must be the fittest.[60] Since the fittest species survived, they are

---

57. One early critic is Evelyn Fox Keller, whose *A Feeling for the Organism: The Life and Work of Barbara McClintock* (New York: W. H. Freeman, 1983) introduced McClintock's approach of looking at full organisms first in order to understand its parts. Keller's reading of McClintock started to contest the assumption that there was a small key that would unlock the mysteries of whole categories, as this was how the discovery of DNA was characterized by Watson and Crick. Ruth Hubbard was one of the first to tell the story of how Watson and Crick failed to credit Rosalind Franklin with having found the basis on which they claimed to discover the molecular shape of DNA. When closely examined, DNA no longer appears to be the secret of life, nor is Watson and Crick's dependence on the work of others concealed. Nevertheless textbooks credit them alone with the discovery rather than also giving credit to Franklin and others involved.

58. Thomas Robert Malthus, *First Essay on Populations* (New York: A. M. Kelley, 1965). It was not considered that any further empirical research was needed to give this claim credibility. The logic was enough to authorize it.

59. This is comparable in authority and appeal to Freud's "primal horde" story.

60. Fear underlies this vision. If there really is a potential fight of each individual against every other, this implies that the whole population lives in fear. What is paranoia for one person becomes normalized as a general principle.

also more sexually fit to be fruitful and multiply.[61] And within the human race, Darwin wrote, we find that the intellectual distinction between the sexes is that "man's attaining to a higher eminence, in whatever he takes up, than can women . . . man has ultimately become superior to woman"; if men did not also pass on their brains to their daughters, the difference between the sexes would be as great as the visual difference between the peacock and the peahen.[62]

Like all stories, Darwin's is laced with what could be facts, though also as with all stories, some of the facts and fantasies cannot be separated from one another—one being true and the other false—with certainty. What can be said with greater confidence is that the story, because it is so often repeated, *promotes the language* of all against all, places this language on the table, enables it to live in people's conversation, and makes it eligible to name things that people then are in position to test for reality. Michael Gross and Mary Beth Averill[63] reject the premise of scarcity and its co-premise, ubiquitous competition among species and between individual members of any one species. Citing a variety of studies, they show how the premise of scarcity (in Darwin's theory) is not founded on anything anyone knows, but on evidence that could be understood (or read) in a variety of ways, such as two animals trying to get food from one another. There is no evidence that lack of food drove any species extinct, although obviously that might have happened. Scarcity is an assumption traceable to an unfounded logical conclusion and not to a fact, but the assumption

---

61. According to John Beatty, this formulation is discredited by many because it is tautological in any empirical application and thus useless. John Beatty, "Fitness," *Keywords,* ed. Keller and Lloyd, 115–119. This perspective also implies that sexual selection follows the same principle, but as Hamish C. Spencer and Judith C. Masters show, there is no basis for this inference. Hamish C. Spencer and Judith C. Masters, "Sexual Selection: Contemporary Debates," *Keywords,* ed. Keller and Lloyd, 294–301.

62. I am paraphrasing Hubbard's citation of Darwin's *The Descent of Man.* Hubbard, "Have Only Men Evolved?" *Discovering,* ed. Harding and Hintikka, 55–56. In 1875, only a few years after Darwin published the foregoing judgment, Antoinette Louisa Brown Blackwell published *The Sexes Throughout Nature* (New York: Putnam). Her aim was to show that "the sexes in each species of beings compared upon the same plane, from the lowest to the highest, are always true equivalents—equals but not identicals in development and in relative amounts of all normal force" (11). She tried to show that in a wide variety of species that a principle of complementarity prevails when the features of each sex in a species are compared. She aimed to revoke the historic misogyny in men's descriptions of women and to show the simultaneous working of equality and difference. Today, as a result of the work of Niels Bohr (discussed by Karan Barad and cited in this chapter, below) the principle of complementarity is known mainly as a principle describing seemingly contradictory explanations of the physical phenomenon of light.

63. "Evolution and Patriarchal Myths of Scarcity and Competition," *Discovering,* ed. Harding and Hintikka, 71–95.

becomes an unquestioned premise. If so, when one inquires as to who might want to believe such a premise, we ask whose interests it serves to hold it. The premise of scarcity and of the survival of the fittest benefits those people who have survived and who have, at least, enough to continue to survive.[64] If this tautology is not noticed by the majority in society, its practical function is to warn the "unfit" not to change anything, as they would be overtaken by the law of the survival of the fittest, the so-called law of the jungle. As a scientific principle, there is virtually no evidence of the truth of endemic, underlying scarcity of food and water or of the survival of the fittest.[65] Both are politically grounded abstractions whose points of reference are in people's imaginations, rather than in anyone's experience or observation.[66]

Several critics of science's uses of language in evolutionary biology have observed that "competition" appears as part of the foregoing syndrome of usages that also includes "struggle, domination, hierarchy, even cooperation—but only as a competitive strategy."[67] Gross and Averill consider competition to be "a core concept of evolutionary theory" that includes the theory of natural selection and sexual selection.[68]

There are no factual grounds for stipulating that competition is a fundamental principle of how species survive, though local competitions could play different roles in the story. Some hold that competition as a principle was transferred,

---

64. Compare this premise to the observation of Koheleth, the speaker in Ecclesiastes: "the race is not to the swift, nor the battle to the mighty; and that also the wise have no bread, nor yet the men of understanding riches, nor yet men of knowledge favor; but time and chance will overtake them all" (9:11). Quite a different picture from the survival of the fittest, but it is given in response to at least some evidence from history and experience.

65. For example, Gross and Averill observe that that is no reason to expect that less fit members of a non-predatory species are more prone to predation ("Evolution," 85).

66. Anyone following sports knows that Koheleth was more accurate than Darwin in accounting for the outcomes of championship competitions.

67. Gross and Averill, "Evolution," 72. More often than not, the term "cooperation" is taken to be synonymous with teamwork, which is a form of cooperation that differs in that teamwork implies that all agree on the common goal—namely to win, or to maximize profits. But cooperative activity includes the processes through which the goals themselves are always eligible for reevaluation. *Both* the goals and the commonness of the goals are available for cooperative study, negotiation, and change.

68. Alison Jolly writes, "What interests me both personally and intellectually is cooperative organization, not competition. This is a fundamental dilemma for anyone trained in Darwinian evolution, with its emphasis on rampant individualism." Jolly ruminates that the "selfish gene," acting in its own self-interest, interacts with the environment, develops love and trust between friends and kin, and develops societies. This is a feminist (and minority) reading of self-interest: Jolly claims that authentic self-interest *is* affiliation and involvement in others. Presupposing the materiality of the term, she is trying to *change the reference* of "self-interest" (*Lucy's*, 3).

through Malthus, from the ideology of the free market to biology.[69] Although this could be true, it is also true that competition is taken automatically to describe almost any social process. It is a term that links economics with sports, where there must be a winner and a loser. Yet there is doubt that competition describes the free market, especially when there are niches and near-monopolies. A free market could refer to a variable market in which price is not the only factor that sells products. Other businesses are not necessarily competing with a given business, but the other businesses are usually described as "my competitors." Is there necessarily a winner and a loser in the list of so-called competing businesses? Because competition is the premise, people understand doing less business to be losing and those doing more to be winning, but such descriptions are not accurate. In spite of the fact that Malthus has been discredited, people still maintain the premise that all individuals are competing with all other individuals for things that are valuable, including possible lovers and mates. People use the phrase "competing ideas" to refer to several different ideas about, for example, how to solve a problem. Is the process by which a suitable procedure is sought that of competition, or a sorting out of advantages and disadvantages of each proposal? What is added when the term "competition" is used to describe such ordinary yet important situations?[70]

The conventional language of evolutionary theory could be understood as characteristic of military institutions, whose social relations may be described as hierarchical, ideological, and competitive. The drift of Gross and Averill's observations as well as the observations by other analysts is that this language is neither arbitrary nor straightforwardly referential. Rather, this is language embedded in conventionally held, taken-for-granted assumptions governing common public institutions, almost all of which are run predominantly by men. Because of the normalization of competition, both women and men overtake the usage of the word "competition" and use the phrase "competing ideas" to describe a series of *different* ideas.[71] The language that came into use functions

---

69. See Hubbard's account in *Politics* and in the early part of "Have Only Men Evolved?"

70. Valerie Miner and Helen E. Longino, eds., *Competition: A Feminist Taboo?* (New York: Feminist P, 1987). This collection shows that there are different forms of competition in different contexts, and not that competition should be opposed as a matter of principle. The many familiar contexts discussed in this volume remove competition from axiomatic status: the term has been materialized in that each instance of competition can be evaluated for its degrees of either necessity of desirability.

71. Is it a matter of competing ideas to decide about the uses of *scarcity* and *plenitude*? Is it necessary to say that one of them must win? It seems *more accurate* to expect that in some cases one term applies and in other cases the other and in still other cases, both, or yet third and fourth terms. Therefore, it is not useful to imagine that ideas like these, including several theories of the same phenomenon, are competing. This issue is

as normative, as a feature of collective ways of life and "ways with words."[72] But because the gender distribution in the populations of the institutions that produced that language was so lopsided, the language we receive from them is lopsided. Because, in turn, it is the normalized language, it has become a total mediator and we see no choices, although, as Ruth Bleier argues and as Gross and Averill propose,[73] there are plenty of choices. These are not limited to the ones supplied by Gross and Averill, such as "nurturance, tolerance, intention and awareness, benignity, collectivism."[74] There are as many or more grounds for conceiving of nature as a site of plenitude as of scarcity, and for expecting generosity and cooperation as readily as competition. The normalization of such abstractions as competition and scarcity as assumptions about evolution helps to conceal the political policies of traditional biological science. Those critics who succeeded Gross and Averill in the search for new ways to formulate the fundamentals of biology[75] sought more accurate terms that were supported, as Scheman and Harding proposed, by experience and other empirical evidence.

V. Instinct, Intelligence, and Other Placeholders

The terms "instinct" and "intelligence" are common normalized abstractions. How are they used? Terrence Deacon (see chapter 5) wrote that instinct is "a formal redescription of what remains unexplained." Although this is true, the use of instinct as an explanation of last resort remains widespread.[76] Usually, it

---

discussed later in this chapter with regard to the alternative ways to conceive of light: complementarity.

72. This phrase is from Shirley Brice Heath, *Ways with Words: Language, Life, and Work in Communities and Classrooms* (New York: Cambridge UP, 1983), discussed briefly in chapter 6. This work shows language use to be a marker of a way of life, and familiarizes us with what it takes to study the use of language in a broad social context. There are so many purposes for such a broad-ranging study that not all of them can be listed. Her view of language use is pragmatic, material, pedagogical and political, but one of the main achievements of this pioneering study is the clear demonstration that that study of language cannot be taken out of the contexts of acquisition and use in communities and societies and examined in isolation.

73. Ruth Bleier, *Science and Gender: A Critique of Biology and Its Theories on Women* (New York: Pergamon, 1984). It is a matter, they suggest, of human orientation—and ultimately of accuracy.

74. Gross and Averill, "Evolution," 72.

75. Among them Evelyn Fox Keller; Ruth Hubbard; and Bonnie B. Spanier, *Im/Partial Science: Gender Ideology in Molecular Biology* (Bloomington: Indiana UP, 1995).

76. A recent use of the term "instinct" is found in Namhee Lee et al., *The Interactional Instinct: The Evolution and Acquisition of Language* (New York: Oxford UP, 2009), discussed in chapter 5. The interest of this study is unrelated to the concept of instinct. It is one of the clearest instances of an attempt to lend a false authority to findings that

had been used to account for animal behaviors that seem intelligent, but because we human animals have often doubted that other animals have intelligence, we needed to say that something other than intelligence and learning accounts for many interesting, complicated, and useful animal behaviors. Generally, the concept of instinct has been part of a binary (instinct versus either intelligence or learning), in which instinct has been the majority party—now perhaps the party of hardwired versus softwired. Discussions in contexts studying evolution have been of the either-or Aristotelian form, in which the researchers seem to believe that one or the other choice has to be made. A good example is given by Bertrand Russell.[77] He narrates how Hingston cut a grasshopper into three parts, with one part twice the bulk of the first, and the third twice the bulk of the second. Each part was given to an ant of the same nest. The first returned with 28 ants to help carry the food back, the second with 44 ants, and the third with 89 ants. Assuming the truth of this report, doesn't the proportionality of these figures imply the use of intelligence? Hingston includes many examples, such as this one of insect behavior, for which researchers try to account. The question remains, however: Does one require the concepts of either instinct or intelligence to account for such behaviors? Hingston eventually proposed a certain degree of flexibility for instincts, as they must change along with environmental change, but that compromise does not solve the problem of whether instinct and intelligence are substantive things that can be found and identified in themselves. If even it is admitted that they can never be found but only inferred, that, too, is a salient result—for they remain imaginary, as are other things whose existence is declared only on the basis of an inferential guess.[78] As a practical matter, one infers things every day and trusts those inferences to a degree. The problem arises when provisionality of scientific inferences is not sent along with the inferences themselves and they are lent certainty when none exists.

More recently, Dennis Senchuk has surveyed discussion on this topic.[79] The wealth of opinion and argument he brings out suggests that the matter of innate

---

are of interest, but are still not conclusive. There is no need to call human interaction instinctive in order to recognize its importance.

77. In his preface to R. W. G. Hingston, *Instinct and Intelligence* (New York: Macmillan, 1929), x. This work is somewhat discredited because of its acceptance of Lamarckian views that acquired characteristics can be inherited. However, Hingston's accounts of behavior are nevertheless challenging to any theory of evolution.

78. Other examples of such items include *phlogiston* which was supposed to be consumed when things burned, and *ether,* the medium which was supposed to have carried light through space. The discovery of oxygen discredited the phlogiston theory, and experiments with light compounded the challenge when it was understood that space was empty, but that light could be observed to be both waves and particles.

79. Dennis M. Senchuk, *Against Instinct: From Biology to Philosophical Psychology* (Philadelphia: Temple UP, 1991).

behavior has gotten as much attention in modern times, proportionally, as theological issues have gotten in the past. It was important to researchers to show that instincts exist, and that they were prior and more powerful as explanations of behaviors than anything else. In non-Catholic religious discussion it could be enough to say that one had faith in God, but in science, faith did not have the same status. Ultimately, Senchuk rejects the concept of instinct as well as the binaries in which it participates—"social learning" or God being other choices for the second term.[80] In advocating for a concept of "flexible prehension," which emphasizes the contingent status of speech gestures, Senchuk is a pragmatist along the lines of James and Dewey. Like Wittgenstein, he is content with searching for different ways to *describe* what looks to be innate, learned, or intelligent. But he is also in a minority.[81]

In his studies of language, Steven Pinker characterized language as an instinct, a view that might be placed among those who want to compromise with Chomsky's innatist view of language.[82] The term also implies a connection with the language evolutionists (whose work Chomsky rejected as "stories") and away from the more empirical attempts to use what is available for study to determine how much can be understood about the learning of language from both the body (anatomy and physiology) and the interpersonal processes that are bound up with our bodies in infancy and childhood. This latter group of cognitive psychologists[83] is different from, yet complementary with, the interac-

---

80. One of his grounds is nominalist: "Suffice it to say for now that I am mainly against multiplying representational realizations beyond necessity, and that I find much contemporary theorizing in 'cognitive science' and philosophy of mind to be insufficiently parsimonious" (*Against,* xix).

81. Although Senchuk's effort is valuable (and agreeable to me), it also feels like an argument for the most philosophically valid way of approaching matters of instinct and intelligence. Once his formulations are understood, however, the absence of political considerations stands out. In matters such as this where abstractions have a history in the male academy, it is important to bring this fact to bear on why the binaries, which Senchuk rejects, have that form to begin with. And a key reason for this staying power is academic agonism, which anticipates or even demands that a true formulation derive from an opposition.

82. With regard to language, Alison Jolly must be counted as one who wants to compromise with the nativists view: "grammar has an innate basis"; and "[c]hildren have a strong innate program for learning language, but of course they learn it from others" (*Lucy's,* 310, 311). Jolly *speaks* of instincts and innateness throughout her study, yet I could find no instance that approached a conclusive demonstration that instincts exist, in spite of her having cited Pinker's work. Jolly does not seem to have a taste for disputation. Still, it makes a difference how these terms are presented in authoritative works such as hers.

83. This group began in the 1970s. In 1979 Elizabeth Bates and seven collaborators (Laura Benigni, Inge Bretherton, Luigia Camaioni, Virginia Volterra, Vicki Carlson, Karlana Carpen, and Marcia Rosser) brought out a volume entitled *The Emergence of*

tionist research discussed in chapter 5. The dedication of Michael Tomasello's 2003 book[84] reads, "For Liz Bates."[85] Bates led a group of researchers who started in a new direction in the study of language, different, perhaps, from both the humanistic tradition of philology begun by Humboldt and the formalist tastes of transformational grammar; it was in the Piagetian tradition, but it included the growing academic interest in brain science. Bates said that the use of language involved the whole brain, rather than just one zone or one language acquisition device.[86] This approach to the neurobiology of language use made it possible for researchers like Tomasello to argue forcefully for the involvement of the whole culture as a source for infants' acquisition of language. The more holistic and empirical approach to the bodily roles in language use also helped to create an atmosphere in which several researchers could challenge the study of language that followed from assuming it is an instinct.[87] The use of this term "instinct" is

---

Symbols: Cognition and Communication in Infancy, (New York: Academic P, 1979). The dedication reads, "This book is women's work. We dedicate it to our mothers, the women who got us interested in language in the first place" (v). This is a rare declaration that a specific research project has such an explicit political dimension. All research projects have such a dimension, even when it is to separate itself from what is commonly understood as politics, but academic tradition demands that political purposes be concealed.

84. *Constructing a Language: A Usage-based Theory of Language Acquisition* (Cambridge, MA: Harvard UP, 2003), v.

85. Bates died prematurely as Tomasello's book was published.

86. A point of view that has been supported by the work of Philip Lieberman: "The neural bases of human language are intertwined with other aspects of cognition, motor control, and emotion." Philip Lieberman, *Human Language and Our Reptilian Brain: The Subcortical Bases of Speech, Syntax, and Thought* (Cambridge, MA: Harvard UP, 2000), 2. Christine Kenneally presents Lieberman as one of four principal figures in today's firmament of language scientists—the others being Noam Chomsky, Sue Savage-Rumbaugh, and Steven Pinker. Christine Kenneally, *The First Word: The Search for the Origins of Language* (New York: Viking, 2007), 68–82.

87. Michael Tomasello, "Language Is Not an Instinct," *Cognitive Development* 10 (1995): 131–156. In commenting on Steven Pinker's *The Language Instinct: How the Mind Creates Language* (New York: Morrow, 1994), Tomasello is especially impatient that Pinker uses the term instinct as a way of claiming that the referent of the word "language" is a "species-universal computational structure of language that is . . . wholly unlearnable" ("Language," 133). Pinker's work remains an argument whose main drift is to shore up the authority of the wired-in, scientific way to study language. He is derisive of interactionist approaches: " [L]et us do away with the folklore that parents teach their children language. . . . The belief that Motherese is essential to language development is part of the same mentality that sends yuppies to 'learning centers' to buy little mittens with bull's-eyes to help their babies find their hands sooner" (*Language Instinct*, 39–40). This formulation is more insulting to mothers' contribution to language acquisition than Walter Ong's celebration of how Latin brings boys away from baby talk (see chapter 9). Pinker is sentimental about how children acquire language alone: "The same kind of linguistic genius is involved every time a child learns his or her mother tongue" (*Lan-*

a tradition in the study of biological science, one that Freud may have used[88] in a sense similar to Pinker's. Tomasello considers the use of "instinct" a problem of language as well as a problem of substance. He says that the word "language" is misused by Pinker and by transformationalists, who consider its reference to be restricted to the grammar "device" in the brain. As a result of the space opened by this group of researchers—"cognitive developmentalists" pursuing an "alternative"[89] group of theories—as well as by feminist critics of science and language, the conventional use of the term "instinct" suggests that language-use customs in science are both dependent on and independent of the facts to be studied.

It is noteworthy, in any event, that the works of Bates, Bloom, Clark, Karmiloff-Smith, Golinkoff, Ochs, Schieffelin,[90] and Kristeva, as well as of the several male researchers in this subject, show no engagement of the matter of instinct. Their emphases are on finding ways to record the observations of children and of children interacting with parents and adults, and then of examining these observations for regularities. The work of the developmental psycholinguists and sociolinguists tries not to stipulate unseen forces or developmental principles.[91] Claims about the child's construction are made *after* the researchers have presented a developmental path from this usage to that usage, from this gesture to this verbalization. A series of specific constructions that happened during formal observation becomes the ground for provisional principles of construction. Those who are claiming that there are as-yet-unspecified devices working in human brains are closer to stipulating miracles and mysteries than those who study the infantile performance data.[92]

---

guage Instinct, 39); Ong's description of Latin acquisition is similarly sentimental. Yet in spite of such remarks by Pinker, Jolly credits his nativist approach to language. The only reason I can adduce for Jolly's gesture is that she gives credit to many and does not engage in academic disputation.

88. In English. There may be some question about the German term, *Trieb* ("drive") being translated as "instinct." The German word *Instinkt* may have a synonym, *Naturtrieb. Trieb* in other contexts could also mean things like inclination or tendency, and may not automatically refer to the same things that the English "instinct" refers to, especially in biological writings after Darwin.

89. Tomasello, "Language," 133.

90. Elinor Ochs and Bambi B. Schieffelin, *Acquiring Conversational Competence* (Boston: Routledge and Kegan Paul, 1983); Elinor Ochs, Emanuel A. Schegloff, and Sandra A. Thompson, eds., *Interaction and Grammar* (New York: Cambridge UP, 1996).

91. However, their uses of the terms "intention" and "meaning" can become problems if examined too closely. In the work of the cognitive developmentalists, there remains a sense that language conveys meaning and that intention is directly identifiable when language is used.

92. Chomsky's original claims were that the acquisition of language would be a miracle of learning if the key to such learning were not in an innate mechanism for acquiring grammar.

Ruth Bleier presents in earlier, differently contextualized, and plainer talk what is implied by Senchuk's critique of the belief in instinct.[93] Her emphasis is on constructing a picture of human development that is founded on a flexible system of learning emerging from a brain that is born before is it fully functional. In this picture, bodily growth, social dependency, and adaptive learning are part of one process, and the questions usually answered by the concept of instinct are distant and not relevant. Growth processes are observable, and the scientific task is to find the most useful way to describe them—as opposed to explain them—in the various species. In view of the linkage of the foregoing factors in individual development, Bleier sees no role for instinct, which she understands to be an obstruction to the scientific study of life. With regard to her discussion of "the brain and human 'nature,'" she observes that "the notion that there lurks an immutable core of *instinct* or *nature* beneath and outside of these dynamic, constantly changing and interacting relationships between our brain, body and environment, beneath and outside of culture and learning is mystical, undemonstrable, and scientifically useless in that it makes impossible any valid explanation of human cultural evolution, behaviors, and social institutions."[94] Bleier views the term *instinct* as having no reference. Nothing in the experience of either self or other living things corresponds to instinct. The historical use of the term is a means of inhibiting discussion of issues such as gender and sex—which, if discussed without reference to instinct by all interested groups of people, are likely to discredit abstractions on which male-coded biology depends. No behaviors of any animals are, finally, explained by instinct.[95] It is a so-called mysterious force, because there is no account of, for example, the dam building of beavers or the nest building of birds. However, she implies, none were sought because the learning processes of nonhuman species were not eligible for scientific study. Instinct is undemonstrable because no one can say what would count as a demonstration of it. The explanation given by Pinker[96] about the "language instinct" is that brain physiology would count as a demonstration of an instinct. But those who have tried to find it have

93. I have discussed how this term has been appropriated by some researchers in language acquisition. I have also suggested that Freud's use of *Trieb,* which was presented in English as "instinct," may be a translator's error.

94. Bleier, *Science,* 52.

95. The term "explanation" is itself a problem, as Wittgenstein observed. It is noteworthy that its problematical status was recognized by Steven Weinberg, discussed in section 7.

96. Pinker expects to find a unique brain physiology analogous to the uniqueness of the elephant's trunk as a defining trait for language (*Language Instinct,* 342). However, his account is no more plausible than Terrence Deacon's because no one can say what will count as evidence for the evolutionary path of a specific bodily capability. The evidence of how different prehistoric anatomies and physiologies were coordinated in the living

found instead, with regard to language, total brain involvement, and no specific organization that correlates with the use of language.[97] Certainly nothing in any brain was found that could be called instinct or even related to it. And the situation does not seem much different for insects or beavers or birds, as all of their brainpower is organized around their respective species-characteristic tasks, which define the species' ways of life. The term "instinct" is used to override consideration of learning from postnatal environmental, social, and cultural interaction—a set of experiences that all species share in different degrees. Does it make sense to say that having a certain way of life is an instinct? If a way of life is considered instinctive, how does it refine the idea of "way of life" so that something illuminating is given? And if ways of life change and develop, at what level shall it be said that the instinct is "adapting" to the environment? The acceptance of the term instinct depends on assuming a definitive separation of individual organisms from the environment. If an individual or even a whole species is thought of as part of the environment, as an element in the total ecology, what need would there be to identify instincts? If the way of life is seen similarly by all observers, the scientific task could be how to rename, resymbolize, or describe it in a way that leads to better adaptation for us, who describe our experiences to one another in the actions of teaching and learning. The acts of description are themselves our conversions of our experiences—our translations—into language, the placing of these experiences into new contexts. What need is there to *explain* dam and nest building? It can only require explanation, if, for example, we first think that is much too sophisticated behavior for that dumb (non-speaking) animal. How do we justify the sophistication? Instinct. Can this answer count as an explanation? Similarly, is it clear what is meant by an explanation of language use as an independent behavior? If you accept that each child is a genius and that the acquisition of language is too hard to have been accomplished within childcare contexts of infantile life, then, yes, instinct provides an answer. Yet if one says, "Language is the human trait that promotes socialization, collective survival, and peaceful growth," this formulation suggests a specific context for this question: Why has the use of language not socialized the human species against individual violence and war? If you then

species is missing. For example, Jolly describes how different sizes of the hypoglossal canal in different fossils are a clue to the slow speed of language evolution, but how can one discover just how those sizes played a role in the evolution of the whole species? (*Lucy's,* 380).

97. Philip Lieberman gives evidence to show that "language is not an instinct, based on genetically transmitted knowledge coded in a discrete cortical 'language organ.' Instead it is a learned skill, based on a functional language system . . . that is distributed over many parts of the human brain. . . . The neural bases of human language are intertwined with other aspects of cognition, motor control, and emotion" (*Human Language,* 1, 2).

say war is an instinct, you can also say war is a stronger instinct than language, and history would back you up. But the only practical result would have to be to resign oneself to the superior influence of the war instinct. Calling language an instinct and using the term "instinct" for any formal scientific inquiry *censors* the study of language phenomena and keeps access to language repressed. For this reason, Bleier considers instinct a "scientifically useless" concept. If sexual activity derives from instinct, would describing different instances of sex be describing the so-called sex instinct? Would it be describing "varieties of sexual activity"? Would one know that any one part of sexual activity—as observed, for example, by Masters and Johnson[98]—is instinctive as opposed to characteristic, idiosyncratic, or deviant? Unless the idea of innateness gets an entirely new meaning, it is inconceivable that an autonomously formed physiological correlative determines the sexual activity of each individual. The thought of a behavior's being determined is itself nonsensical.

The practice of using the term "instinct" in commentaries on language is an example of repression imposed on society by the combination of an authoritative institution (science) and the use of language. The term, vague and only superficially grasped, becomes established through the common interests in using it, interests that prevent other people's language from entering the description, or other heretical voices from being heard. Bleier's claim that the term is "scientifically useless" is confirmed by the fact that no scientist has uncovered an empirical basis for entities such as instincts and drives: it is an axiom of scientists who, therefore, do not wish to treat the concept as a testable theory.

Similar arguments apply to our understanding of intelligence as a trait that is traceable through evolution. Stephen Jay Gould[99] showed that the "intelligence quotient" that is now used routinely by a variety of institutions is an abstraction—an average, to be exact, of several factors that have been measured in intelligence tests. The factors are themselves culturally defined, but more importantly, there is no actual correlative in the brain or in behavior that corresponds to intelligence that is now represented by a single number: there are only test results. The test was first used during World War I to distinguish soldiers from one another, with the expectation that those who scored higher would become officers. Although the army distinguished between officers and foot soldiers on this basis, it is still not known if the test provided anything other than a measure of privilege, or even if this is a good way to decide on who will become officers. Similarly, the use of intelligence tests in schools tracks students, but the overall distribution of students' performance in school correlates with social privileges regardless of test performance. In practice, one

---

98. William H. Masters and Virginia E. Johnson, *Human Sexual Response* (New York: Bantam, 1966).

99. Stephen Jay Gould, *The Mismeasure of Man* (New York: Norton, 1981), chapter 6.

imagines that there is such a thing as brainpower that is the mental counterpart of muscular strength. The assumption that there must be single referents for our own abstractions makes it possible to accept this false measure of a feature of people's behavior.[100] Nevertheless, intelligence and its measurement are considered real and accepted as legal tender because scientists, military leaders,[101] and psychologists—all depending on language transparency, objectivity, and their traditional use—have authorized them.[102]

Both terms of this binary, instinct and intelligence, are instances of total mediation, transparencies given to the public by science, but which have no reference in common among scientists themselves. They do have many believers; however, scientists do not present themselves as believers, but as knowing authorities.[103] Their reading of these terms, their references, affects the lives of people by limiting their access to how language acquires authority.

Consequential features of science and its language are placed in a new light by the considerations of Naomi Scheman and Evelyn Fox Keller.[104] Keller first raised the issue of inaccurate science that follows from hierarchical assumptions

---

100. In cases like this, nominalism shows its utility. Stephen Jay Gould took many pages to say that intelligence is a false abstraction. One need only ask this: From which experiences is the general intelligence capability abstracted? The answer is can only be the intelligence test, which reveals a tautology similar to the survival of the fittest.

101. See Douglas D. Noble, *The Classroom Arsenal: Military Research, Information Technology, and Public Education* (New York: Falmer P, 1991), part 2, and my *Know and Tell* (Portsmouth, NH: Heinemann, 1998), which comments on Noble's study (178–179). Intelligence testing today is still governed by the military psychology developed almost a century ago.

102. Since Gould's demonstrations psychologists have adduced grounds for viewing intelligence as more in keeping with observation. Howard Gardner's *Frames of Mind: The Theory of Multiple Intelligences* (New York: Basic, 1983) is considered a reasonable step. Richard Nesbitt's *Intelligence and How to Get It: Why Schools and Cultures Count* (New York: Norton, 2009) shows that scores on intelligence tests vary with economic status, suggesting a path away from assuming its innateness. Other works, such as Geoff Colvin's *Talent Is Overrated* (New York: Penguin, 2008) and Daniel Coyle's *The Talent Code* (New York: Bantam, 2009), argue that particularly high motivation accounts for achievement more that anything ascribable to an inborn capacity or skill. Nevertheless, intelligence tests continue to be administered on a national scale.

103. Although many scientists have no trouble describing themselves as believers, corporations that use scientific studies never present their claims as beliefs. The closest they come to avoiding categorical claims is to cite statistics, counting on the public's not reminding itself that statistics do not predict individual events and developments.

104. And dozens of others who have presented similar views: Helen Longino, Nancy Tuana, Donna Haraway, Anne Fausto-Sterling, Sandra Harding, Ruth Bleier, Ruth Hubbard, Lorraine Code, Lynn Nelson, Sue Rosser, and Emily Martin, to name a few. See Anne Fausto-Sterling, *Myths of Gender: Biological Theories about Women and Men* (New York: Basic, 1985); Lorraine Code, *What Can She Know? Feminist Theory and the Construction of Knowledge* (Ithaca, NY: Cornell UP, 1991); and Sue V. Rosser, ed.

in her study of McClintock, and later in her challenge to the stipulation of there being a "master molecule" that issues instructions to the rest of a cell and organism. McClintock treated the cell as a total system, with no one element as the boss. Yet in biology, the habit of looking for ultimate drivers of different systems persists, as, for example, in the treatment of the genome as a decisive final answer to what the human essence is.[105]

As a revision of the loaded term "law," Keller proposes the word "order," which has fewer "political and theological origins."[106] The latter term accommodates the practices of approximation and continues to express a certain expectation of regularity in nature (a fact no one disputes), but, mostly, permits flexibility in identifying and grouping classes of phenomena. The orderliness of nature is consistent with both regularity and divergence within a general sense of how natural phenomena work. It is, in addition, friendly to the nominalist principle of not demanding universal reference from general terms. The critique of science's use of language proposes movement toward a materialist perspective—increasing the number of choices for science, the amount of space for development, and its availability to the many natural languages that could refine its vocabulary.

Specific combined revisions of language and fact follow from Keller's general proposals. Emily Martin has shown that established descriptions of how egg and sperm combine are erroneous because the language was derived from men's expectations and beliefs about nature. Traditional descriptions of egg and sperm considered the egg passive and the sperm active. Martin showed that a more accurate basis for describing the coming together of egg and sperm is interactive.[107] Martin cites a study by Gerald Schatten and Helen Schatten

Teaching the Majority: Breaking the Gender Barrier in Science, Mathematics, and Engineering (New York: Teachers College P, 1995), and *Women, Science, and Society: The Crucial Union* (New York: Teachers College P, 2000).

105. According to Evelyn Fox Keller, "The 'central dogma' of molecular biology . . . depicts DNA as the executive governor of cellular organization, with unidirectional transfer of information." Evelyn Fox Keller, *Reflections on Gender and Science* (New Haven, CT: Yale UP, 1985), 133. Emily Martin, reviewing men's descriptions of how the brain is involved in the menstrual cycle, writes this: "So this is a communication system organized hierarchically, not a committee reaching decisions by mutual influence" (*Woman*, 41).

106. Keller, *Reflections*, 134. Keller has been stalwart in relating the gender issues of science to problems of language. In some cases, her proposed changes are subtle, such as the shift from "law" to "order," but they reflect a fundamentally revised political stance toward science. The present discussion, in emphasizing the nominalist and materialist view of language, also tries to describe the coherent language philosophy that animates her various critiques and proposals.

107. Emily Martin, "The Egg and the Sperm: How Science Has Constructed a Romance Based on Stereotypical Male-Female Roles," *Gender and Scientific Authority*, ed. Barbara Laslett, Sally Gregory Kohlstedt, Helen Longino, and Evelynn Hammonds (Chicago: U of Chicago P, 1996), 323–339, quotation on 333.

that "suggests the almost heretical view that sperm and egg are mutually active partners."[108] However, the language of the researchers remains oriented in traditional ways, as they describe how "a long, thin filament shoots out and harpoons the egg." The details of this description, however, show that "remarkably, the harpoon is not so much fired as assembled at great speed, molecule by molecule, from a pool of protein stored in a specialized region called the acrosome. The filament may grow as much as twenty times longer than the sperm head itself before its tip reaches the egg and sticks." Martin asks why "harpooning" is the metaphorical usage, when "bridge-building" or "line-throwing" would be more accurate, as the connotations of destruction or damage would not be involved. However, it is the metaphor of *penetration* that seems to govern these usages. Other studies cited by Martin show how routinely researchers, while even anticipating a scene of mutuality and reciprocity of egg and sperm, continue to describe the sperm's action as penetration. This term also appears casually in nonscientific discussions, as the *entering* of the penis into the vagina is commonly referred to as penetration. Similarly, Martin discusses, the sperm is routinely assumed to *fertilize* the egg—although, of course, this does not happen. There is neither penetration nor fertilization nor even planting as seeds are planted into the earth, although this latter metaphor is also common. This language comes from social and literary sources; the biological process or sperm and egg coming together is a process of cooperation,[109] the studies show, even as the researchers use language that seems inconsistent with this concept.

The temptation to assign social categories to involuntary processes may be perfectly normal, but it matters which sort of society is doing the assigning. It is plausible that if four thousand scientists speaking four thousand languages all looked into the microscope while sperm and egg were meeting, the range of description would be very great, but it would be interesting to see how the group of observers decided to describe the phenomenon. One need not belabor the point, but so far, only members of androcentric societies have been the ones to identify the processes of conception, of the formation of new life. Even though the facts have changed, the usages in these societies continue to follow Aristotle's vision of sperm and egg, male and female. With regard to the use of language, the inertia among even the more egalitarian frames of mind cited by Martin may be traced to the underlying expectations of the transparency of language, to wit: the scientists think that even if it is not really penetration, the word "penetration" refers transparently to the joining of egg and sperm. There is

---

108. Martin, "Egg," 332.

109. The term "cooperation" may similarly describe sexual activity that is mutually sought. But it is more than cooperation if the social setting of sex is included: it is a complex action of mutual service and care—not to mention enthusiasm, excitement, fantasy, and conversation.

a silent corollary among scientists that says the language does not really matter; we all know what we are referring to. Yet in their inertia about language, the scientists continue to keep science for themselves, exclude other people (Gross and Levitt's "outsiders") by excluding other language, and derogate the language that gives science a respectable public identity.[110]

VI. Laws of Nature

Axiomatic usages whose provisionality is usually unknown to the public abound in science. For those whose work the axioms govern, the verbal articulation of these axioms is necessarily transparent, although if pressed most scientists will allow their provisionality and their contingency. Evelyn Keller, who has presented perhaps the most comprehensive review of the language uses in science,[111] observes, "Confidence in the transparency of language . . . encourages the belief that one's own language is absolute."[112] This formulation describes both the history and psychology of post-Renaissance science: confidence in the transparency of language encourages false confidence that my meanings are the same as all other people's meanings, and that Cartesian autonomy is the basis of individualism. Modern science has found ways to honor Locke's view of language as "the cheat of words," and effectively to discourage any temptation to take the mores and speech genres all people inherit into account in the presentation of scientific understanding. According to Keller, "[M]any, if not all, scientific communities [hold] the widely shared assumption that the universe they study is directly accessible, represented by concepts shaped not by language but only by the demands of logic and experiment. On this assumption, 'laws of nature' are beyond the relativity of language—indeed, they are beyond lan-

---

110. Writes Evelyn Fox Keller, "the very language on which [scientists] must rely, even when apparently strictly technical, can subvert their best intentions for 'objective,' value-free description . . . particular conventions of language permit, even facilitate, the unwitting incorporation of social values into the substance of scientific theory." Evelyn Fox Keller, *Secrets of Life, Secrets of Death: Essays on Language, Gender, and Science* (New York: Routledge, 1992), 127. This judgment may be true in many cases. The present study suggests that in many other cases in which scientists choose their language, they may well be aware of the traditional Baconian value of conquest and dominion of the phenomena they are studying, as well as their dominion over the scientific conclusions themselves. In such instances, the scientists repress the erroneousness of their supposedly objective judgments.

111. Her review spans a variety of essays and books over a period of two decades. Keller's studies have attempted repeatedly to present the necessary syntheses of fact, value, and language in how science studies nature. Her work has touched on all the sciences, and her general references to how so-called science works and how scientists think derives from her identification of analogous research strategies in different sciences.

112. Keller, *Reflections*, 131.

guage: encoded in logical structures that require only the discernment of reason and the confirmation of experiment. . . . the descriptive language of science is transparent and neutral; it does not require examination. This assumption . . . is in fact an inseparable part of an objectivist ideology."[113]

An immediate effect of this approach to language is the establishment of the term "laws of nature" as a fundamental feature of everyone's language. Like "instinct," the term has axiomatic status, and behaviors that are considered instinctive are presumed to follow laws of nature. The *Oxford English Dictionary* cites "those who first used the term" in the seventeenth century,[114] who conceived of laws of nature as God's commands on nature. Keller observes that because of this sense, lawful natural behaviors are considered to be acts of obedience. The vocabulary of obedience remains today, even though there has been some attenuation of the religious meaning of nature's mathematically described regularities. Nevertheless, today's laws share a fundamental trait with the seventeenth-century laws: their status beyond language. Most members of societies that hold science authoritative consider laws of nature to be independent of the ways they are articulated—independent, that is, of their *verbal* formulation. The fact that mathematical formulations in their exactitude are also ideals that never fully correspond to measurements is usually ignored because the actual measurements, in technological contexts, work. The asymptotic relation between real measurements and mathematical formulations is still a fact to be reckoned with in the physical sciences.[115] The meaning of physical laws being ideal is not part of science. But the reason they remain laws is similar to the reason they became laws to begin with: they are considered to be autonomous and independent of how they arise in societies or cultures. Language is declared or rendered transparent by science[116] in the service of this purpose, just as Latin was declared transparent by churchmen in order to authorize miracles.

113. Keller, *Reflections*, 130–131.

114. Keller, *Reflections*, 131. See also discussion of Bacon, above.

115. But, in medicine, the fact that a cure may not work in every case has long been accepted without undermining confidence in the understanding of how it works.

116. Physicist Lawrence M. Krauss claims that the universe "arose through a process . . . whereby the energy of empty space (nothing) get converted into the energy of something." Lawrence M. Krauss, *A Universe from Nothing: Why There Is Something Rather than Nothing* (New York: Free P, 2012), 152. If I read this correctly, I understand that "empty space" has "energy." So I wonder if energy is the same as "nothing." In cases like this, one recognizes how the authoritative figure is expecting recognition of the transparency of his language simply because he presents it as such. It is germane in this connection to mention that Krauss is a strident, outspoken opponent of the religious belief in God's having created the universe from nothing. In his attempt to present a secular view, his assertion that the universe "arose" from nothing presents the identical point of view, with "arose" substituted for "was created." But his words cheat us: he also says that "empty space" has "energy."

Keller observes that scientific laws (like canon laws) "imply an a priori hierarchy between structuring principle and structured matter that suggests a striking resemblance to laws of authoritarian states."[117] In the physical sciences, the assumption of language-transcendent laws leads scientists to "the search for the one 'unified' law of nature that embodies all other laws, and that hence will be immune to revision—in Bacon's language, the 'summary law in which nature centres and which is subject and subordinate to God.'"[118] This search for a unified theory of everything derives from the classical physics of the seventeenth and eighteenth centuries. That this search could be a fantasy or a superstition occurs to few; denying it seems to be as intimidating as it is for ordinary people to appear on television and say, "There is no God." Science is locked into this arrangement between scientists and language, and it is perpetuated by both religious and scientific interests.

Edgar Zilsel reviews how the term "law" developed from the term "principle" in classical times, which had no standardized concept of objectivity. There have been several uses in the Bible and other sources that, if recognized, suggest alternatives for describing the natural regularities now referred to by natural law: boundary, decree, prohibition, trait, and so forth. Likely for theological reasons related to the Jewish and Christian "lawgiver" concept of God, the "juridical metaphor" was applied in the seventeenth century and remained.[119] The sense of the metaphor is that in a political context, the law "asserts how reasonable beings *shall* behave, whereas natural laws, as they are studied by modern naturalists, state and describe as a mere matter of fact how physical processes *do* take place."[120] In modern times, "non-empirical components [of the idea of natural law] fell gradually into oblivion."[121] The laws are treated as predictive as well as descriptive, but the term "law of nature" is a dead metaphor because no commandment is given, nor decisions made, by phenomena.

In light of Keller's considerations, however, the metaphor is not dead at all: laws of nature, she writes, function socially in the same way as laws of authoritarian states. These laws are not metaphorical: they are total mediators in the sense that they deny access to science to those using different language. The only challenge to this approach to science and language comes from those who seek to view science within its different cultures and histories, an undertaking enabled by recognizing the materiality of its language.[122]

---

117. Keller, *Reflections,* 132.

118. Keller, *Reflections,* 132.

119. Zilsel, "Genesis," 246.

120. Zilsel, "Genesis," 246.

121. Zilsel, "Genesis," 247.

122. To say that science is different in different cultures does not prevent either translation or other sorts of sharing of the same regularity or natural order. In recognizing

VII. The Big Bang

Steven Weinberg is credited with having put together in 1977 the currently accepted standard model of the history of the universe, particularly its origin in "the big bang" billions of years ago.[123] This model related cosmology to particle physics: the study of the largest collections of matter along with the smallest collections (subatomic particles), and suggests that the same kinds of energies that hold the smallest particles together have been responsible for the origin of the universe. This connection of the largest to the smallest, bound by the same energies, made it tempting for physicists to have "dreams of a final theory,"[124] to search for the "ultimate laws of nature." Weinberg observes that he was not the first to think such a thought, but that, if Greek science is any guide, those studying the physical universe have habitually searched for the ultimate makeup of matter—the ultimate piece of material that cannot be reduced any further.[125] At the end of the nineteenth century, there was some feeling that physics had ended and that matter was understood, but that guess soon went away with the discovery of radiation, with the ability to observe atomic particles, the theory of relativity, and the mutual transformability of matter and energy. Rather than being critical, as Keller is of this long inquiry, Weinberg sees it as a historic quest filled with surprises, and begs scientists to search ever longer for this secret that nature is hiding. He sees this search as a calling, often taking an aesthetic dimension. Weinberg is duly cautious, but consider such terms

---

the sharability of science, cultural specificity and pan-cultural application have to be considered at once. Sandra G. Harding, *Whose Science? Whose Knowledge? Thinking from Women's Lives* (Ithaca, NY: Cornell UP, 1991); *Is Science Multicultural? Postcolonialisms, Feminisms, Epistemologies* (Bloomington: Indiana UP, 1998).

123. Steven Weinberg, *The First Three Minutes: A Modern View of the Origin of the Universe* (New York: Basic, 1993).

124. "No one knows how galaxies formed or how the genetic mechanism got started or how memories are stored in the brain. None of these problems is likely to be affected by the discovery of a final theory." Steven Weinberg, *Dreams of a Final Theory: The Scientist's Search for the Ultimate Laws of Nature* (New York: Random House, 1992), 239. This assertion suggests that while there are large areas beyond present knowledge, the study of the subatomic must be the path to yield knowledge of the very beginning of the cosmos. Most physicists accept this principle not on empirical grounds, but for reasons that seem rather theological. Lawrence M. Krauss, discussed in note 116, above, seems particularly theological, and in its service, casuistical, in his categorical opposition to theology. Einstein used a theological argument in his dispute with quantum theory, discussed below.

125. I have read no source, ancient or recent, which stated, considered, or wondered about the following: there is no point in looking for ultimate particles; we should do something more useful. The thought did occur, however, to Steven Weinberg—after I wrote the previous sentence in this note! (See the end of this section.)

as "final theory," "ultimate laws," and "theory of everything." It could be that there are playful elements in these phrases. The serious elements follow from the not-at-all-playful term "fundamental particle" (also referred to as "elementary particle") which, early in the twentieth century, seemed as though they would be the last particles to be discovered. However, at the same time these subatomic particles were being studied, quantum mechanics arrived in order to articulate both the limits and the possibilities of measuring the particles' behavior. Quantum mechanics changed expectations of measurement to such an extent that by 1993, Steven Weinberg wrote, "[O]ne begins to suspect that all the deep questions about the meaning of measurement are really empty, forced on us by our language, a language that evolved in a world governed very nearly by classical physics."[126] When quantum mechanics first came along, it had the principle of indeterminacy, which limited the measurement of subatomic particles in that only one parameter—velocity or location—could be measured exactly at the same moment; if one parameter were measured exactly, the other would have to be measured probabilistically. This is what Weinberg refers to as our language coming from classical physics: this kind of language and the values that have attached to it do not permit our comfort with probabilistic measurement. We think of it as not really knowing if we have only statistical knowledge, and we are all familiar with this sort of knowing—it works with insurance companies and airlines. When we know the probability, we still don't know what will happen, only what could or might happen. In classical physics, we could predict what would happen if the right measurements were made to begin with. Quantum mechanics disclosed an area of study whose events could not be predicted with the level of certainty that would apply to events governed by classical mechanics and by electromagnetic theory.

Obviously, Weinberg did not give up on being a physicist, nor did he stop loving physics. But we see, buried in his urgent desire to find something worthy of being called a "final theory," the suspicion that the measurements of elementary particle behavior toward this goal is a vain pursuit *"forced on us by our language."* And it is not simply the language of measurement that predicts (and thus controls) movement. It is that this language is the source of the belief in laws of nature that must be obeyed, that these laws are constraints or commandments rather than descriptions that could apply in unexpected ways, perhaps even "unlawful" ways. Weinberg's sentence might thus be translated to read "One begins to suspect that measurement does not after all yield laws of nature, and that we said that it did only because our language led us there." Isn't this perception a tacit realization that the *realist* sense of language has failed in this new kind of data? Viewing Weinberg's reflection from a materialist

126. Weinberg, *Dreams,* 85.

standpoint leads to the possibility that the combination of realist expectations about language and quantum experimental data is not viable. Rather, to cope with the data, we need to get used to a different sense of what to expect from the use of language.

Weinberg was frustrated by more than quantum mechanics, about which he has no hesitations in actual practice. He spends many pages speculating about the at-the-time uncertain fate of the Superconducting Super Collider, planned for Texas, where he worked, and how there was resistance in Congress to building it. It even seems as though his book was meant to help persuade Congress of its potential for research. As of 2012, it has been cancelled in the United States and the Large Hadron Collider has had trouble getting started in Switzerland.[127] This supercollider, which would have generated energies larger than were produced by all previous such machines, also was conceived by physicists hoping to get data that would permit the construction of the "final theory." Physics had developed into such a state that only machines built on this scale could continue the research. There was no other choice but to make such machines if one wanted to find out where the present data about subatomic particles would lead. David Lindley writes,

> [T]he inexorable progress of physics from the world we can see and touch into a world made accessible only by huge and expensive experimental equipment, and on into a world illuminated by the intellect alone, is a genuine cause for alarm. Even within the community of particle physicists there are those who think that the trend toward increasing abstraction is turning theoretical physics into recreational mathematics, endlessly amusing to those who can master the techniques and join the game, but ultimately meaningless because the objects of the mathematical manipulations are forever beyond the access of experiment and measurement.[128]

---

127. "The biggest, most expensive physics machine in the world is riddled with thousands of bad electrical connections." Dennis Overbye, "Giant Particle Collider Struggles," *New York Times* 3 August 2009. On 4 July 2012, physicists at CERN announced that they had found, from the use of the Large Hadron Collider, what "looks for all the world like" the Higgs boson. Dennis Overbye, "Physicists Find Elusive Particle Seen as Key to Universe," *New York Times* 5 July 2012. Steven Weinberg reports that this particle fulfills a prediction of the "Standard Model," and that it verifies the "Standard Model's account of how elementary particles get their masses," which is by traveling through a certain kind of force- or energy field, accumulating mass in the journey. Steven Weinberg, "Why the Higgs Boson Matters," *New York Times* 14 July 2012. Lawrence M. Krauss says that the Higgs boson "appears to have been discovered." Lawrence M. Krauss, "A Blip that Speaks of Our Place in the Universe," *New York Times* 10 July 2012.

128. *The End of Physics: The Myth of a Unified Theory* (New York: Basic, 1993), 19. Lindley references "Paul Ginsparg and Sheldon L. Glashow, 'Desperately Seeking

Lindley describes how the procedures for research in the branch of physics that is seeking the "final theory" have lost their reference to experience.[129] The relation of the mathematical formulations to things that are actually happening is not really understood. This is not because the mathematics reached a limit, but because the processes of measurement are indirect: "forever beyond the access of experiment and measurement." Forever. This situation alarms Weinberg. He remains able to do physics. But the reference of its laws has disappeared. Whatever is said about the particles and their great store of energy, if their lives are measured in billionths of a second and their size is not even meaningful, what, finally, has been measured? Something that *might* have happened billions of years ago and billions of light-years away? What is the use of this knowledge?[130] Weinberg himself addresses this question: "Even if the particle is the Higgs boson, it is not going to be used to cure diseases or improve technology." He also acknowledges that people may not care about "what was going on in the early universe," but "even those who do [care] have to ask whether learning the laws of nature is worth the billions of dollars it costs to build particle accelerators." He acknowledges in this same report, in fact, that the discovery of such a particle has not answered several other questions, and that of course we have not,

---

Superstrings,' *Physics Today,* May 1986: 7–9. The authors express concern that theoretical physics is moving into a world of unverifiable mathematical invention. Similar concerns are expressed by Glashow and R. P. Feynman, in interviews published in *Superstrings: A Theory of Everything?* (Cambridge: Cambridge UP, 1988), ed. Paul C. W. Davies and John Brown" (257–258n6). However, Lisa Randall, who also finds fault with the "Grand Unified Theory," proposes the stipulation of new dimensions, in addition to those with which we are familiar, in order to avoid a theory that has to "introduce a huge fudge factor" in order to maintain its integrity. Lisa Randall, *Warped Passages: Unraveling the Mysteries of the Universe's Hidden Dimensions* (New York: Harper Collins, 2005), 245. She is looking to the work of the Large Hadron Collider to verify her speculations and, presumably, to avoid fudging.

129. This observation about physics is similar to analogous responses to Chomsky's search for the language acquisition device. The appealing abstraction, under the influence of a gathering chorus of (male) scientists, is gradually seen to imply, necessarily, a missing item, the discovery of which becomes the object of disproportionate expenditures and academic effort.

130. Karen Knorr Cetina gives description similar to Lindley's: "[T]hese objects [subatomic particles] are in a very precise sense "unreal"—or, as one physicist described them, "phantasmic" (*irreale Gegenstände*); they are too small ever to be seen except indirectly through detectors, too fast to be captured and contained in a laboratory space, and too dangerous as particle beams to be handled directly. Furthermore, the interesting particles usually come in combination with other components that mask their presence. Finally, most subatomic particles are very short-lived, transient creatures that exist only for a billionth of a second. Subject to frequent metamorphosis and to decay, they 'exist' in a way that is always already past, already history." Karin Knorr Cetina, *Epistemic Cultures: How the Sciences Make Knowledge* (Cambridge, MA: Harvard UP, 1999), 48.

after all, found a "key to the universe." If the discovery is confirmed, its actual significance is that it was something that was predicted by a still-hypothetical model of how elementary particles behave, Weinberg's Nobel prize for this model notwithstanding.

VIII. Intimations of Language Change in Physics

The language of Newton—the clear, transparent formulations of verbal and mathematical laws—now appears obsolete. Our own human language continues to function, but because its referential actions have been so often exaggerated for so long a period, today's physicists have trouble assimilating this strange fact that the *language was misused*. The so-called mysteries of nature are neither more nor less perplexing than they once were. But now we see how some scientists were fooled by a false sense of the use of language.[131] There are no laws in nature that were not made by people. Until now, people thought that these laws were outside of us. But now some physicists who most believed in such laws wonder if such formulations *may* have been products of our own use of language.

If we consider ourselves within the language, a part of the language, and within it in addition, then within the phenomena to which we commit ourselves through language, we are in a position to ask—when the cost of not asking becomes harmful—what it is we want to know and how final is any theory we are likely to invent. What sort of satisfaction would a "final" theory bring? And to whom?

In the same year, 1993, which saw the publication of *Dreams of a Final Theory*, Weinberg wrote a new afterword to his first book about the big bang, the so-called origin of the universe. In it, he engages this issue of string theory that Lindley had taken up as something so abstract as to have lost its reference altogether. Weinberg says at the end of this afterword, "It may be that our real problem will not be to understand the beginning of the universe, or even to decide whether there really was a beginning, but rather to understand nature under conditions in which time and space had no meaning."[132] This sounds like a new understanding. The classic question of the beginning and end of the universe is reduced in importance, if only subjunctively. From its early forms, questions of origin—like that of the origin of language discussed in chapters 2 and 5—have been mythological, in the sense described by Lindley: "A myth is a story that makes sense within its own terms, offers explanations for everything we can see around us, but can be neither tested nor disproved. A myth is

---

131. This is the same circumstance that Wittgenstein complained about in philosophy: language has obfuscated the most useful purposes of philosophy—finding new descriptions—from the age of the Greeks until now.
132. Weinberg, *First*, 191.

an explanation that everyone agrees on because it is convenient to agree on it, not because its truth can be demonstrated."[133] The key phrase is *can neither be tested nor disproved.* Perhaps from the time of Bacon, testing and falsification have governed science, and these procedures depended on the transparency of language, and perhaps on the trivialization of language—its reduction from its common, ubiquitous, literary, and material character to its use as an indicative, mechanical servant. Weinberg seems reluctantly to be saying that this urgent search for the origin of the universe was after all for something that could not be tested or falsified, let alone made obviously true to most people. However, he poses what looks like a fresh scientific question: If we treat time and space as provisional abstractions, put them on the back burner, so to speak, how are we experiencing nature? This is a real question, and since 1993, it has become increasingly serious from an ecological standpoint: to sustain our lives, we have been poisoning what has sustained our lives.[134] This question seems more germane than those about the origin of the universe and the full complement of fundamental particles.

Lindley notices a connection between the particle physicists and the deconstructionists discussed in chapter 4:

[Theoretical physicists'] use of language is as esoteric and baffling as that of the literary deconstructionists: they seem to speak in words and sentences, but it is a kind of code. The mathematical physicist and the

---

133. Lindley, *End,* 255. Cetina writes, "[H]igh energy physics operates within a *closed* circuitry. In many ways, it operates in a world of objects separated from the environment, a world turned inward, or, better still, a world entirely reconstructed within the boundaries of a complicated multilevel technology of representation" (*Epistemic,* 47).

134. I cannot discern just how Weinberg has revised his conception of nature, and especially if it has become for him less of an object. However, his formulation leaves room for a greater level of reciprocity between the animate and inanimate parts of nature, the living and the nonliving parts. Naomi Scheman noted that non-reciprocity derives from the scientific conception of nature as being inanimate: "A specifically Cartesian feature of the conception of the world as independent is the world as inanimate, and consequently not reciprocally engaged in the activities through which it comes to be known" (*Engenderings,* 99). If nature is passive, thinking about reciprocal cycles and self-sustaining systems does not enter the analyses. If people are part of an active natural world, scientific investigation continues, but with different premises.

Shift for a moment to Jane Smiley's novel *A Thousand Acres* (New York: Ballantine, 1991). Sustaining Larry Cook's farm took insecticides that led to one daughter's death from cancer and another daughter's five miscarriages. When the daughters were teenagers, Larry Cook "beat" and "fucked" them (302). In at least these senses the novel is a figure for the common processes of poisoning what sustains our lives. The source of this behavior, in the novel, and perhaps in much wider contexts, is an androcentric ruthlessness of ambition, callousness, and malice in the service of wanting to be supreme among

deconstructionist share the same popular image: each speaks in a private gobbledygook understandable only to those similarly initiated. It is easy to imagine that both are lost in a world of pointless fabulation.[135]

This observation recalls the functions the secret language of elite groups discussed in chapter 9. Lindley does not refer to the male-coded status of secret languages that are also the standard and authoritative languages. Certainly all of us expect language to grow and change under the new historical circumstances in which today's problems are formulated. And even if we allow that in our cultures it is men's habit to slip into the secret code to maintain exclusivity, elite status, and authority, few would say that the physicists and deconstructionists deliberately created these codes for the political purposes discussed in chapter 9. Yet here they are again. In chapter 4, the discussion of deconstructionist writing showed the incremental hesitations on Derrida's part that are analogous to Weinberg's hesitations about the future of physics.

Recently, Karen Barad has tried to address the matter of language in theoretical physics without assigning it a gender identity, but with awareness of its male codedness. She considers together the inertia in the expectation of the transparency of language alongside the inertia in science textbooks in addressing the consequences of the principle of indeterminacy (sometimes called the uncertainty principle) and of Niels Bohr's philosophy of complementarity.[136] More than the issues in biology discussed earlier, the language connection in physics—as Bohr, Weinberg, and Lindley have noticed—was and is less open to change, more radical, and finally, more invested in received habits of thought and social functioning. Starting from Bohr's early efforts to address the meaning of there being a limit to measuring at once two essential parameters—position and velocity—of subatomic particles, Barad outlines how great the changes would likely be in our ways of speaking and in how we conceive "the universe," nature, reality, or, perhaps, all that we see exists. As was the case after Einstein, "space" and "time" demanded new meanings, but also concepts like "matter"

farmers in Zebulon County. In other words, we can always have avoided poisoning what sustains our lives.

135. Lindley, *End,* 19.

136. It is noteworthy that a particle physicist has taken on this task, engaging the questions posed by a member of an older generation. Yet it makes sense pursuant to the relation of biology to physics. Generally, the hierarchical arrangement of the sciences placed physics on top, then chemistry, and then biology—the latter being the science pursued by more women than have pursued the other sciences. As suggested above, physics is most in need of refiguration, as its principles as well as its population has been unable to cope with the philosophical changes science has been experiencing in response to critiques such as those of Keller, Harding, Longino, and others cited earlier in this chapter.

and "energy,"[137] their ontic status as things, the processes of measurement, and finally the sense of language needed to cope with these changes.[138]

Barad bases her discussion on two issues that occupied physics early in the twentieth century: the indeterminacy principle and the apparent mutual incompatibility of the two concepts of light as a wave and as a particle. Regarding the first issue, Barad considers the name of the principle to be significant. She explains that the use of the term "uncertainty" presupposes the possibility of certainty, which was a feature of the Newtonian perspective, and the one referred to by Weinberg in his hesitations. In the present situation, the entanglement of the measuring apparatus with the process of measuring and with the items to be measured renders the object of measurement *indeterminate, indefinite, or ambiguous*[139] rather than uncertain. The level of indeterminacy in macroscopic mechanics is so small as to be negligible. But in aiming to measure the movement of subnuclear particles, the means of measurement becomes part of what is to be measured: the fundamental procedures of Newtonian mechanics are changed so that measurement has become something different. The key to this issue is that the Cartesian "cut" between the object and the measuring subject is no longer applicable. It is not as if the process of observation and measurement stops; rather, the measuring procedures are now understood to define the phenomena, a principle similar to the "operational definition" discussed by P. W. Bridgman,[140] albeit philosophically more radical and far reaching. It is also the same phenomenon as appears, unacknowledged, in the measurement of so-called intelligence: the test *defines* rather than measures the item in question, and then, erroneously, claims to have measured it.

Before focusing on this scene, consider the situation with the problem of light. Here also is something unacceptable in a Newtonian perspective: a condi-

---

137. The description of empty space by Lawrence M. Krauss as having energy may call into question the status of matter and energy as things. But is anyone saying that, for purposes of understanding the history of the universe, there is no difference between something and nothing? Krauss is not trying to overturn the principle of noncontradiction, but Karen Barad is.

138. Barad announces herself as a feminist. The danger of this identification is that her proposals risk being understood as solely "political" and without reference to the total project of physics and science. In the traditional discourse style, politics is assumed to be unrelated to the other academic categories which apply, such as philosophical, scientific, cosmological, and so on. The advantage of this identification, however, is that it puts traditional thinking into a context that is *not* gender marked, that is to say, a context that includes all genders.

139. Karen Barad, "A Feminist Approach to Teaching Quantum Physics," *Teaching the Majority: Breaking the Gender Barrier in Science, Mathematics, and Engineering*, ed. Sue V. Rosser (New York: Teachers College P, 1995), 57.

140. *The Logic of Modern Physics* (New York: Macmillan, 1927).

tion in which light is corpuscular through one sort of measuring procedure and a transverse electromagnetic wave through another sort. Traditional takes on laws of nature and on Aristotelian logic say that light cannot be both because there must be a single essence to the object, light. Barad remarks, "A student who is trying to come to terms with the subject matter (rather than submitting to some form of brainwashing) wants to know what light really is."[141] Bohr's explanation (as cited by Barad) depends on his transformation of light as an essential object—something observed without being affected by observation—into light as a phenomenon—something experienced without our knowledge of our possible participation in the object.[142] In Bohr's words, "the two views of the nature of light are rather to be considered as different attempts at an interpretation of the experimental evidence in which the limitation of classical concepts is expressed in complementary ways."[143] Barad takes Bohr's emphasis on interpretation to be the key gesture that permits the departure from the Newtonian worldview. If the two views of light are "complementary," then our thinking must follow what is experienced, and not what is inferred to be general or essential.[144] This way of thinking adds up to nominalism. Barad sees Bohr as having developed an epistemology that "rejects both the transparency of language and the transparency of measurement; . . . it rejects the presupposition that language and measurement perform mediating functions. Language does not represent states of affairs, and measurements do not represent measurement-independent states of being."[145]

In Barad's subsequent expansion of the formulations given in the 1995 essay, a significant achievement is her having worked out a way to approach the issue of objectivity by focusing on the uses of the word "matter." She creates a context in which it becomes apparent how the uses and instabilities of the term (matter) in physics are like or comparable to the same term's uses and instabilities in ordinary discourse. In physics, research has gotten to the point at which one recognizes the convertibility of matter into energy, itself a challenge to the Newtonian way of thinking. And if one is ready to say that matter *is* energy, it is only the contexts of use that provisionally separate matter and energy as different entities. However, studies in particle physics, Barad's field, repeatedly

---

141. Barad, "Feminist," 59.

142. I think of asking this: Does my seeing the light affect how I think of what it is? What is light that is not seen?

143. Barad, "Feminist," 60.

144. I might also want to say this: Antoinette Blackwell's sense of complementarity also follows from a sense of participation in the gendering of people.

145. Karen Barad, "Posthumanist Performativity: Toward an Understanding of How Matter Comes to Matter," *Signs: Journal of Women in Culture and Society* 28.3 (2003): 801–831, quotation on 813.

raise questions as to whether particles, whose period of existence is measured in billionths of a second and whose size is equally distant from what is ordinarily called matter, should be identified as matter. Similar considerations could apply to astronomical phenomena such as the sun and stars: Are they concentrated energy, or are they matter converting to energy, or both (or phenomena needing new names)? Although such possibilities do not inhibit, and perhaps encourage, experimentation and measurement of various parameters or any other learning about celestial phenomena, the possibilities do inhibit decisions as to the real nature of the sun and stars. Ambiguity and indeterminacy seem more a part of the picture.

By casting doubt on any assumed nature of matter, Barad arrives at materiality and material phenomena, especially the materiality of discourse. Thinking of matter as something undergoing constant, continuous change at various levels down to its smallest known units, its kinship with discourse becomes more plausible. Along with doubt about traditional boundaries between matter and energy, the distinctions between the human and the nonhuman, and the living and the nonliving, also become less apparent; Barad treats their continuous trading of statuses as a sign of the mutual implication of all parts of the cosmos in all other parts. From the standpoint of language-use mores, the problem she poses is how to speak about *things* (matters) while respecting our experience of their continuing change. Even though many things do not grow, they do change, so that from this standpoint, the provisionality of fixed items requires changes in common discourse. Derrida poses a similar problem with regard to language: even though words don't seem to change and are thus understood across generations, new historical circumstances find the same words in new contexts, and the changes in usages over any increments of time produce new words. How do we cope with this understanding of previously reliable language?

For Barad, these changes involve pursuing as far as possible the performativity discussed by Austin in his speech act theory. She seeks "[a] performative understanding, which shifts the focus from linguistic representations to discursive practices."[146] But going beyond speech act theory, even as it appears in more contemporary revisions, Barad arrives at what seem to her to be fundamentals: "material-discursive practices" and "material-discursive forces."[147] The changeability of matter links discourse (or language use) to nonlinguistic phenomena, the living and nonliving bodies-as-experienced that are traditionally understood to be permanent objects. The materiality of language derives from the fact that our uses of language are so fully a part of the rest of our existences. By stipulating that bodies are understood *as experienced* as opposed to what they may be inde-

---

146. Barad, "Posthumanist," 807.
147. Barad, "Posthumanist," 810.

pendently of experience, Barad converts things (objects) into phenomena and she asserts that "there are no noumena, only phenomena."[148] Phenomena, in turn, are the products of *relations*. The latter term is particularly important because it is stipulated as *not necessarily following* relata (permanent objects): "Why do we think that the existence of relations requires relata? Does the persistent distrust of nature, materiality, and the body that pervades much of contemporary theorizing and a sizable amount of the history of Western thought feed off of this cultural proclivity? . . . [My discussion suggests that] it is . . . possible to acknowledge nature, the body, and materiality in the fullness of their becoming without resorting to the optics of transparency or opacity, the geometries of absolute exteriority or interiority."[149] Phenomena are Barad's reworkings of "relata." Instead of the linear "billiard ball" view of causation, Barad proposes "intra-activity," a term that identifies a total interiority of existence. The materiality of all aspects of existence renders irrelevant talk of transcendental or spiritual zones and assumes a complete space of existence in which relations and change are as likely to create things as the behavior of thing-bodies to create relations; in any circumstance in which two or more people are involved, individuals can *decide* whether they need to see relations before things or things before relations or both at once. The understanding of just what the "intra-actions" are in each case follows the experience. Barad sees traditional experience as the distrust of nature and the body. This view is similar to Scheman's description of objectification as deriving from fear and distrust of nature and of other people, as having paranoid characteristics. A radical basis of Barad's vision is her insistence first on how Western thinking of and in science and society derive from fear, and how the abandonment of this fear requires an unprecedented level of trust, simultaneously in nature and in other people.

Barad's proposals give an idea of the scale on which nominalism and the materiality of language have been repressed, as well as what it could mean if they were not thus repressed. The category of language is itself being questioned: "Discourse is not a synonym for language [and] . . . does not refer to linguistic or signifying systems, grammars, speech acts, or conversations. . . . Discursive practices define what counts as meaningful statements."[150] The term "discursive practice" has a ring similar to *Sprachspiel*, a way of describing the language within a living, familiar, understood context of people. Barad's kinship with Wittgenstein appears to be accidental; there is no mention of his work in her discussion. But the similarity derives from an alarm each shares about the profound limitations placed on language in modern times by a dogmatic cul-

---

148. Barad, "Posthumanist," 817n23.
149. Barad, "Posthumanist," 812.
150. Barad, "Posthumanist," 819.

tural embrace of the radical objectivity (positivism) as well as the traditionally repressive effects of Platonic realism.

Finally, Barad describes how it is not just change to which she is attending; rather, she emphasizes her pursuit of the specific paths of how "phenomena come to matter."[151] This statement is meant to be read both as how "phenomena *become* matter" and as how "phenomena *do* matter." One achievement of this formulation is that it removes the traditional sense of matter mattering because it has a solid or substantive essence. This axiom is replaced by the sense of matter as what is important and possibly (but not axiomatically) what is substantive within a specific context, which could be a specific scientific apparatus, a specific scientific project, a specific program of investigation, or any social or interpersonal scene. This conversion of phenomena into matter, this valuation of experience as important, is the basis for understanding the materiality of discourse and language: "material phenomena are inseparable from the apparatuses of bodily production: matter emerges out of and includes as part of its being the ongoing reconfiguring of boundaries. . . . [T]he material and the discursive are mutually implicated in the dynamics of intra-activity. But nor are they reducible to one another. The relationship between the material and the discursive is one of mutual entailment. . . . [M]atter and meaning are mutually articulated. . . . Neither has privileged status in determining the other."[152] Coming to matter is performativity.[153] When people speak, it matters to others, to nonhuman zones, and to nonliving zones; it is part of those zones in the total interiority of existence.

There is a sense in which people have long since recognized a total connectedness in existence. Usually this recognition has been religious and transcendent. Some, such as unorthodox figures like Baruch Spinoza and Johann Hamann, have taken the immanence of God as a fact or perhaps only a useful defining figure: all existence, not just certain grounds and buildings, is holy, they said. Perhaps they found a way of saying that sacralization is a secular process available to every speaker. Barad's critique of science, and of physics in particular, presents a vocabulary and a discourse style that recognizes the development of contemporary physics and the need for an egalitarian discourse of the physical sciences. She is describing materiality without reference to a binary by stipulating that the relationship of things is as substantive as the things themselves. A total interiority removes the binary without removing the material genres of people, contexts, language, and the physical environment that the Western tradition had viewed as part natural and part transcendental, while it tacitly holds onto the superiority of the transcendental. The sense of the ubiquity of materiality is a gesture toward human survival.

---

151. Barad, "Posthumanist," 817, 822.
152. Barad, "Posthumanist," 822.
153. Barad, "Posthumanist," 823.

CHAPTER ELEVEN

Language and Human Survival

I. Nukespeak

At the end of her treatise on the history of the study of language, Vivien Law places "the Bomb" side by side with language, suggesting that their potential effects on human life were comparable, albeit with language additionally capable of having salutary effects.[1] Language evolutionists (see chapter 5) have placed language in a context that is timely because the long-term survival of life, not just human life, is endangered by the existence of nuclear weapons: if language is both a way of life and an evolved means of adaptation, its studied use could move us away from the possibility of collective self-destruction.[2] A certain kind of talk—threats—has forestalled nuclear war so far, but unless the weapons themselves are renounced—a collective speech gesture—long-term survival remains endangered. In its role as an instrument of conveyance, a vessel for meaning, language has not ensured survival. Its materiality, however, casts it as an instrument of adaptation, like technology, rendering it eligible to become the collective practices that enable survival. Considered perhaps a technology of last resort, it is a path toward creating the trust necessary to renounce nuclear weapons. To recognize language as an adaptive function is to recognize its materiality.[3] Several academic subject matters bear on the issue of human survival, and some of the researchers in these fields have begun to promote such a recognition of the use of language in the service of promoting long-term human survival.

---

1. Cited in chapter 1. Vivien Law, *The History of Linguistics in Europe from Plato to 1600* (Cambridge: Cambridge UP, 2003), 275.

2. A view consistent with Philip Lieberman's in *Eve Spoke: Human Language and Human Evolution* (New York: Norton, 1998), 151 (see also chapter 1).

3. On a local scale, most people in any culture have known the benefits of talking long and well enough to avoid fights and guns. Daily life is full of verbal exchanges that resolve conflicts. International politics shows fewer instances of such success with the use of language, and collective survival has been risked repeatedly. Thus far, there is doubt about whether language can become an adaptive instrument that can ensure an indefinitely long survival of life. The resolutions of discrepancies discussed by Bloom and others (see chapter 5) fit into the category of adaptation as well.

Steven Weinberg's teachers learned their nuclear physics during the development of nuclear weapons in the 1940s. In his 1977 account of the big bang, Weinberg said, "I cannot deny a feeling of unreality in writing about the first three minutes as if we really know what we are talking about."[4] In this remark, he seems somewhat aware of the language issues he faced more fully in 1993 (see chapter 10). Although apparently daunted by the scope of his speculation, he does not make a connection between this name, the big bang, for the origin of the universe and the use of nuclear weapons, although the building of nuclear weapons is the only consequence of particle physics that has affected our lives.[5] Unless one already knows the connections, in physics, between Weinberg's subject and the involvement of leading physicists four decades previously in promoting the development of nuclear bombs, we might think that the two kinds of understanding were unrelated. It is not considered to be within the legitimate realm of physics that the discourse of physics—the way the scientists refer to, identify, name, and describe the phenomena they study—which Karen Barad tries to revise away from the sense of the transcendental—played an influential role in persuading men (rather than men and women) that making and using nuclear weapons should be pursued. Specifically, the belief and feeling among nuclear scientists that they were researching the fundamentals of the universe sustained the fantasy of their own proximity to the transcendental and applied it to the need for an apocalyptic victory over two enemies—Germany and Japan—who were understood to be treacherous and evil.

Although Weinberg inserts adroit caveats, usually personal ones, he uses the traditional discourse of positive science. Those committed to the political supervision of nuclear weapons have also used discourses that seem to deny the concrete human stake in understanding their destructive power. Carol Cohn has studied the discussion of this group of men, whom she calls "defense intellectuals."[6] The discourse of this group continues to maintain energetically a separation between the policies of nuclear deployment and the consequences of the

---

4. Steven Weinberg, *The First Three Minutes: A Modern View of the Origin of the Universe* (New York: Basic, 1993), 9.

5. Some have suggested, plausibly, that many nuclear scientists, feeling bad about having participated in making the Bomb, spent the rest of their lives trying to be more constructive, either through research on the evolution of the universe, or on nuclear power for electricity, on radioactive tracers in medicine, and so forth. However, it is also plausible that entertaining the connection between any use of nuclear technology and the Bomb has been censored. Perhaps both perspectives obtain: simultaneous awareness and denial, the combination of which may be described as repression.

6. One has to doubt the convention of calling people who read a great deal and think things through "intellectuals." Are factory workers "manuals"? In this case, however, it is effective in the following sense: Cohn is calling attention to how this group of defense planners has taken the patina of academic membership as an overlay of their practical

use of nuclear weapons. Those in government who think about nuclear weapons are not physicists, but they think as Weinberg did: hesitations are pushed aside while they proceed vigorously with discussions that border on the absurd. Cohn's accounts of these extended observations show directly how abstractions work into regular usages, and just as dramatically, how she, an observer opposed to the enterprise, can be overtaken by its language. Her account suggests that without a strong political orientation coming in to such a discourse community, anyone can become persuaded of its normality. Her political state of mind, however, led her to find in the abstractions a key source for the otherwise incomprehensible callousness about the prospects of so great a scale of destructive power.

In 1984, Cohn spent about a year listening to a group of virtually all male defense intellectuals, whose purpose was to explain to the forty-eight college teachers in attendance "why it is safe to have weapons of a kind and number it is not safe to use."[7] This is the principle of nuclear deterrence. Cohn was "aghast" not at the images of destruction she entertained, but at "the extraordinary abstraction and removal from what I knew as reality that characterized the professional discourse."[8] Cohn learned to speak the language of the defense intellectuals. She noted, "Learning the language gives a sense of what I would call cognitive mastery; the feeling of mastery of technology that is finally *not* controllable but is instead powerful beyond human comprehension, powerful in a way that stretches and even thrills the imagination."[9] She noticed that the more fluent she became in the discourse (what I referred to as "nukespeak"), the "less frightened [she] was of nuclear war" because "the *process* of learning the language [that is, the abstractions and how to use them in substantive discussion] is itself a part of what removes [one] from the reality of nuclear war."[10] This is also true more generally about learning a style of discourse: no matter what language you learn, many of its metaphors and abstractions no longer

---

job, which is to advise the defense department about how to deploy nuclear weapons. They have overtaken the historic academic abuse of treating provisional generalizations as transparent indicative language.

7. Carol Cohn, "Sex and Death in the Rational World of Defense Intellectuals," *Gender and Scientific Authority*, ed. Barbara Laslett, Sally Gregory Kohlstedt, Helen Longino, and Evelynn Hammonds (Chicago: U of Chicago P, 1996), 183–216, quotation on 183.

8. Cohn, "Sex," 184.

9. Cohn, "Sex," 200.

10. Cohn, "Sex," 200. One is not really removed. Rather, the affect that the men might normally feel in being appalled at the prospect of destruction on such a scale is *displaced* onto the more affirmative task of winning. Because the group of intellectuals is already male, they are predisposed to think of winning sooner than of destruction and the pain of others. In Cohn's case, the displacement was onto the task of "mastering" the discourse. The men, in addition to the satisfaction of mastery, sought the satisfaction of winning, which Cohn did not seek.

appear to be figurative, and we become uncritical of their premises.[11] The official language radically narrows the meaning of words and makes them seem fixed, referential, and indicative. Cohn's experience is that by learning the language of defense intellectuals, she felt what it was like to repress understanding of the results of nuclear war.

As Cohn describes this process, it is not exclusive to a military context, but is tied to a gendered syndrome of values, to habits of thinking referred to by Judith Fetterley as "immasculation."[12] Cohn's documentation of this broad androcentric scope includes religious and homoerotic themes. On the one hand, there is a presumption of objectivity; on the other hand, there is an equally articulated series of values within the discourse that are not part of its formal engagement:

> Much of their [the defense intellectuals] claim to legitimacy, then, is a claim to objectivity born of technical expertise and to the disciplined purging of the emotional valences that might threaten their objectivity. But if the surface of their discourse—its abstraction and technical jargon—appears at first to support these claims, a look just below the surface does not. There we find currents of homoerotic excitement, heterosexual domination, the drive toward competency and mastery, the pleasures of membership in an elite and privileged group, the ultimate importance and meaning of membership in the priesthood, and the thrilling power of becoming Death, shatterer of worlds [Oppenheimer's citation of "Krishna's words to Arjuna in the *Bhagavad Gita*"[13]]. How is it possible to hold this up as a paragon of cool-headed objectivity?[14]

Taking seriously all facets of nukespeak shows the affect that accompanies verbal functioning. The combination of an elite discourse, abstractions, euphemisms, and an elite "priesthood," establishes this group's dominion over other groups and over most other parts of society. Nor is the sense of priesthood an

---

11. This is the case with the phrase "laws of nature," discussed in chapter 10.

12. In her study *The Resisting Reader: A Feminist Approach to American Fiction* (Bloomington: Indiana UP, 1978), Fetterley suggests that reading American literature fosters readers' identification with traditional male ideals, especially those that diminish and exclude women. Fetterley describes how curricular choices and styles of pedagogy promote such ways of reading, understanding, and interpreting. Ultimately, it is not that literature necessarily affects readers in certain ways, but that, in Fetterley's experience, the academic uptake of literature has presupposed the normativity of men's experience and men's values. She urges all readers, but especially women, to resist such a confluence of pedagogy and literary translation toward the project of helping to move the university toward more egalitarian practices.

13. Cohn, "Sex," 198.

14. Cohn, "Sex," 213.

isolated metaphor. Cohn observes that the first bomb test was called "Trinity," presumably representing the "male forces of Creation."[15] Some scientists felt as though they were present at the "first day of creation,"[16] much as Weinberg felt as he presented his first three minutes as science: the origin of the universe was a nuclear explosion. Those who worked on the bomb did *refer to themselves* as "the nuclear priesthood."[17] The key terms that created this effect are, ultimately, lies or fantasies. For example, group members spoke as if there were such a thing as a "surgically clean counterforce strike" (referring to the neutron bomb);[18] or, in the case of the attacker having to use two missiles to destroy one of the enemy's, "[t]he aggressor ends up worse off than the aggressed." Cohn observes that this sort of thinking shows that to the defense intellectual the devastation of the attack is not a part of the calculation, but that, rather, "worse off" refers to having been left with fewer weapons after the attack.[19] In considering what it will take to win a nuclear exchange, the loss of life and the overwhelming suffering are not factors in the planners' discussions. A giddiness overtakes them that is understood not to be serious, but which, at the same time, is the affect that replaces other possible responses to contemplating such unbelievable destruction. The state of mind of this group is describable with both Scheman's sense of the connection of objectivity and paranoia and Lorenz's view[20] that both creative and destructive frenzy emerge from the same social and emotional circumstances—*Begeistigung* ("militant enthusiasm"). Both of these ways of accounting for the mood of the defense intellectuals involve the radical narrowing of language reference, in which a preferred sense of the key terms is permitted to overwhelm consideration of all other senses. In practice this is seen in Cohn's discussion: her reading of the nukespeak terms, even if permitted voice in discussions, has no standing as a prospective influence on how nuclear planning should take place.

This narrowing and re-referencing, however, has a specific purpose that is shared when certain abstractions become the ruling conceptual system: the purpose is to hide the involvement of living people in whatever is being considered. In this case, weapons systems, instead of the welfare of nations, were the point of focus. In Plato's case, it was the abstractions "the Good and the Just" instead of people's needs to hear from poets about the violent, painful, and destructive

---

15. Cohn, "Sex," 198.

16. Cohn, "Sex," 198.

17. Cohn, "Sex," 198. Nor can it be ignored that the word "priesthood" also identifies the group of people that protected and constrained universities for centuries. The nuclear priesthood is the heir of the Latin priesthood.

18. Cohn, "Sex, 209.

19. Cohn, "Sex," 206.

20. Discussed in section 2-1.

behaviors of gods as well as of people. But in both cases, whether it is the mass incineration caused by a nuclear attack, or the emotions that are watered by hearing poetry, the groups of men establishing the terms of public discourse are straining to the utmost to conceal the human character, the human feel, in their visions of human society.[21] Certainly, the abstractions of many aspects of science have played this role, as suggested by the phrases "knowledge is power" and "knowledge for its own sake."

As many of us in academic life understand, and as Cohn writes, "[t]here is tremendous pleasure"[22] in mastering an abstract or technical conceptual system. "But as the pleasures deepen," she continues, "so do the dangers. The activity of trying to out-reason defense intellectuals in their own games gets you thinking inside their rules, tacitly accepting all the unspoken assumptions of their paradigms. You become subject to the tyranny of concepts."[23] This model fits well as a description of how Church governance of universities and its use of Latin as a total mediator for about six centuries functioned through a tyranny of concepts that limited the study of language, and that this tacit constraint on imagination is common in academic life today.

Cohn later unpacks some of the individual and social psychology of how nukespeak is maintained as a compelling discourse.[24] Her analysis helps us to understand the linkage between the men in charge, the language they use, and the habitual means of social and linguistic coercion that is embedded in their special discourse; it functions something like the question "Do you believe in God?" does today: regardless of what the true answer is for each individual, the respondent knows by virtue of living in American culture that one can answer only yes if one is to continue to seem normal.[25]

Taking a different view of the same experience she discussed in her earlier essay, Cohn finds that the one thing a male group member cannot show is his kinship with women. One physicist was in a meeting at which the post-nuclear death count, after a new calculation, was shown to be thirty million instead of thirty-five million people. The physicist's expression of disbelief that this difference mattered to the group was greeted with silence. His response: "I felt

---

21. This is why Kristeva aims to reinsert the *speaking subject* in the formal study of language.

22. Cohn, "Sex," 210.

23. Cohn, "Sex," 210.

24. Carol Cohn, "Wars, Wimps, and Women," *Gendering War Talk*, ed. Miriam Cooke and Angela Woollacott (Princeton, NJ: Princeton UP, 1993), 227–246.

25. The hidden and coercive premise is presented as a fact and not as a faith: God exists. A similar process takes place in Congress: "Don't you think we should fund our troops?" Although a minority answers this question no, the majority does say yes. Because the premise of the question—that we must fight this war—is not immediately entered into debate and discredited (it is treated as immaterial), the collective is tyrannized by it.

like a woman."[26] It appears that this man knew from his feelings how to read the silence: he knew the feeling of being a woman in that culture, and he knew that the group response effectively rendered him a woman. This event resembles the report by Ruth Hubbard of how, in a written scientific article, the author caught himself using "I" and then, as if realizing it, abruptly switched to the traditional and official passive voice (see chapter 10).

Cohn looks back at her 1984 experience in the light of the "wimp-factor" narrative when George H. W. Bush was running for office in 1988. Most of the discussion among the defense intellectuals,[27] Cohn observes, was based on the premise that a peace initiative in the form of unilateral arms reduction was "wimping out." Thus, if defense intelligence showed that there were enough arms to retain, even, the "balance of terror," or if there was a weapons system that was of no use, it was nevertheless thought that any pragmatic moves to reduce defense costs by reducing our own weapons systems would be tantamount to surrendering a bargaining chip during arms negotiations. However, it was not considered to be the path to greatest defense advantage, but rather wimping out: the defense intellectuals assumed (understood?) that the Soviets held the same values about strength as they did and would read a unilateral arms reduction as a sign that the Americans were "pussies." In fact, neither side knew just how many nuclear weapons would be enough, as there were enough in any case to incinerate all living things. This latter fact was always forgotten, not taken into account, or repressed in favor of measuring strength by comparing who had the lowest level of womanhood in their posture. Cohn reports that American security specialists who knew their Soviet counterparts who persuaded Gorbachev to withdraw his weapons from Eastern Europe said, "I've met these Soviet 'new thinkers' and they're a bunch of pussies."[28] Similarly, European defense specialists who opposed the Iran-Contra operation or the bombing of Libya were called "Euro-fags."[29] Among the American defense intellectuals there was a broadly understood assumption regarding how to take the measure of international opposition: the macho psychology known to most of us through gang showdowns or individual face-offs on sports fields. The one who comes away with fewest feminine markers wins, and being ejected from the game is

---

26. Cohn, "Wars," 227. As Bourdieu describes it, "Manliness, it can be seen, is an eminently *relational* notion, constructed in front of and for other men and against femininity, in a kind of *fear* of the female, firstly in oneself." Pierre Bourdieu, *Masculine Domination* (Palo Alto, CA: Stanford UP, 2001), 53.

27. Here the term "intellectuals" used as a noun affords this group protection from the cowardly implications of their own placement in the defense process: since their *job* is to think—not fight, but send others to fight—calling them "intellectuals" could identify them as wimping out.

28. Cohn, "Wars," 235.

29. Cohn, "Wars," 236.

a step in that direction. And if the reason for ejection stems from attempts to injure players on the other team, that is also a boost for their gender identity.

The individual confrontations we see routinely in sports contexts enter the defense intellectuals' thinking through the speech usage of reference to a collective enemy as "he" or "Saddam." In the process of reducing an enemy to an individual man, the thinking is simplified through the application of local feelings of not wanting to be pushed around by another individual or a bully. If relative strength of the two warring societies were actually compared, however, it would be hard to say that a nuclear power is being pushed around by anyone. Individualizing the enemy facilitates the assumption of an indignation characteristic of those who feel they are being bullied and thus justified in the use of as much strength as one has in order to "teach them a lesson." Cohn suggests that although this individualized "he" has a psychological function for each individual speaker/intellectual, it is so because it is an abstraction: "[T]he use of 'he' . . . abstracts both the opponent and the war itself. . . . It facilitates treating war within a kind of game-playing model, A against B, Red against Blue, he against me. For even while 'he' is evocative of male identity issues, it is also just an abstract piece to moved [*sic*] around on a game board, or, more appropriately, a computer screen."[30]

As discussed in chapters 5 and 10, abstraction is a gesture common to the use of language by all people because it is the first path toward sentence formation in infancy. Similarly, referring to and thinking of planning as a game is also not necessarily a distorting or mendacious metaphor.[31] The issue, rather, is when and how the abstractions, games, and other linguistic reductions become[32] governing transparencies that users refuse to replace or revise toward other uses and other speech genres, especially discourses given by those with other strategies for the best possible defense. Cohn's description suggests that this has happened for the defense intellectuals because the game usages (such as "bargaining chip") have become identified with the postulate of maximizing the intimidation potential of discourse. Official or accepted usages reiterate the men's distance from women's

---

30. Cohn, "Wars," 241.

31. The translation of *Sprachspiel* as "language game" was, similarly, not necessarily a misleading factor, although it still might be for those reading Wittgenstein in English. "Game" in British culture is not the same as *Spiel* in German culture, and I sought to recover the immediate value of Wittgenstein's term.

32. Authorized agencies declare ordinary and flexible usages official, which means that they have a designated meaning or usage, such as "married head of household." They then become a standard to measure others' usages and behaviors and the concept is an instrument of tyranny. Similarly, the catechism is also a technique for establishing an official language and a means of indoctrinating children. Eventually, most children reject the rigid meanings of many of the early-learned terms, but the price is an adult hypocrisy because membership in the religious community requires honoring its official terms.

lives, from human bodies, and from the collective social welfare. At the same time, the usages try to conceal men's awareness of their own participation in womanhood. This is a process of collective repression.[33] Cohn observes that "gender discourse informs and shapes nuclear and national security discourse, and in so doing creates silences and absences. It keeps things out of the room, unsaid, and keeps them ignored if they manage to get in. As such, it degrades our ability to think *well* and *fully* about nuclear weapons and national security."[34]

The latter point is the urgent and pragmatic issue. The gendered discourse style that is most worrisome is simultaneously a derogation of men's own individual psychologies and of their collective social psychology, both of which, Cohn suggests (as did Naomi Scheman, discussed in chapter 10), are already unconsciously and necessarily implicated in the lives and experience of women. This adolescent-male level of thinking is then presented as addressing the interests of all, yet without it having been derived from the collaboration with women or with other interests not welcomed by the defense intellectuals. In Cohn's account, the anecdote of the physicist is especially instructive: even though the individual feels that he is humiliated by being rendered a woman, he is unable or unwilling to judge the social scope of what happened. He cannot take his own feeling seriously; rather, he believes and feels he must make sure that that feeling does not appear again[35]—it was so unpleasant—and in this way reifies the coercive values carried by the gendered discourse, whose terms and references must not be changed. This situation is analogous to the necessity of members of the church hierarchy to reaffirm official usages. Speaking otherwise would be grounds for excommunication, heresy, and possible execution. In addition to being a "tyranny of concepts," it is tyranny of enforced uses of language.

When the authoritative discourse style, vocabulary, and speech genres come from relatively small groups of men, the language that all people use, have, and need has been sacralized[36] in the service of maintaining male group solidarity: it can no longer be molded or changed and set to purposes other than those

---

33. The abstractions enable men to omit reference to and awareness of several different kinds of factors: "the emotional, the concrete, the particular, the human bodies and their vulnerability, human lives and their subjectivity—all of which are marked as feminine in the binary dichotomies of gender discourse" (Cohn, "Wars," 232).

34. Cohn, "Wars," 232.

35. Cohn, "Wars," 227.

36. Or dematerialized. Someone may ask, "If you can materialize and dematerialize language, how can you say that language *is* material?" This question is challenging if you believe in final proofs of pragmatic knowledge, or if you believe in the finality of any knowledge. However, in the great majority of cases in real life experience, we decide what counts as knowledge, and in some cases, such as medicine, we simply trust what others say they know. In academic life, we try to *propose* different ways of thinking and behaving for pragmatic reasons. In this instance the understanding of language

demanded by the official discourse. In this particular case, human survival seems actually to be at stake. But language other than that which understands nuclear weapons as game tokens, millions of deaths and casualties as acceptable, or unilateral arms reduction as wimping out is not permitted its own set of references; when such language is consciously censored, it puts human survival in doubt. One thing is achieved, however: the discourse and its several constituencies which use it are preserved.

The language of the defense intellectuals is one of many instances of a language double standard; to wit: *they* understand the provisionality of their abstractions, but once others (such as Carol Cohn) begin to recognize the direction of their efforts—that is, to feel the "tyranny of concepts"—the abstractions take on the status of dogma, and are thus no longer treated as provisional: they become the vocabulary that establishes the national defense policy. The defense planners chose the language, but the public's reality is fixed by it. Academic disciplines use a similar language double standard, and are inhibited by similar factors from letting their language have the flexibility it had when it was first proposed and was not yet dogma. In the discussion of the physical sciences in chapter 10, biologists and physicists have also shown an intransigence in their uses of language that derive from being permitted to stipulate that their abstractions have a referent that should be empirically sought: the "fundamental" particle, the "origin" of the universe, the maternal, sex, or death "instincts," the "passive" egg and "active" sperm, the "intelligence" behind the IQ test score: each have motivated scientific inquiries that could have been cheaper, less vexed, or simply not conducted had there been no presumption of a real referent for a stipulated abstraction. Even the term "law of nature," which derives from the religious principle that existence actually has a government (God), helps to inhibit understandings: it is easier to understand exceptions to regular patterns and behaviors when you don't consider them unlawful. It is easier to understand that exceptions to regularities may be as normal as the regularities themselves.

Cohn's several discussions have shown how, in the establishment of social domination in the nuclear weapons communities, the language is commandeered, narrowed in reference, and used as a means to discourage verbal opposition such as the presentation of other premises, considerations, arguments, and perspectives. Language is deprived of its ability to help the non-expert, non-elite majority to resist destruction and to thrive within a generous ecol-

---

as material is analogous to, and a part of, understanding different gender identities as "equal" (the term now applied, as in the phrase "all men are created equal"): it makes more sense and will have salutary social effects. Furthermore, as the history of nominalism and realism shows, both points of view always existed. Yet society was governed mainly by one point of view. I consider it obvious that it did not have to be that way. Yet some say it did have to be that way and that it still does.

ogy. The sacralization of terms and the dematerialization of language, in the process or preserving the men's cohort, is a threat to the survival of all people. Language, the one thing that people with access to it may deliberately use to feel the substance of their lives, is thwarted in its ability to promote human survival or adaptation in nature. In modern times, the custody of vernacular as well as specialized language has been, in large part, in the hands of schools and universities. Yet these groups, owing to their economic dependence on church, state, and corporate sponsorship, have collaborated to inhibit the study and use of language from reaching their capability to insure survival. Science and commercial culture have, during the Enlightenment, supplanted the Church as the principal ruling institutions alongside the nation-state. While, as we have seen, these have been largely secularized institutions, the male demographic they show has retained its traditional character.

II. Instinctive Aggression, Paradoxical Violence

The hoarding of wealth and arms by a small minority of a population has been a fact of political and international life throughout recorded history. The political traditions of elite rule have facilitated the translation of the uses of abstraction from the earlier religious contexts into the languages of science. Some in the nineteenth century and up to the present time presumed that the solution to this political and economic unfairness was a workers' revolution. However, one only has to repeat the main terms of this solution to hear the cost of using them: "dictatorship of the proletariat," "revolution," and "class struggle" show axioms and figures of force and war and lump the great variety of human circumstances into formulaic abstractions.[37] Creating its own standard of scientific rationality, the Marxian contrast between scientific and utopian socialism casts the former as hardheaded and rigorous (and manly), whereas the latter is soft, weak, and deceived by an unrealistic fantasy about the goodness of mankind. Nancy Folbre writes, "Scientific socialism defined class interests largely in terms of the interests of working-class men."[38] Although Marxist discourse does not usually identify this class by gender, the call to revolution appeals to men's individual and collective susceptibility to heroic fantasies. In the societies that have taken up this ideal of revolution, the result has been war, terror, secret police, executions, and purges—actions through which the hero and his "primal horde," his political

---

37. This issue has been played out in George Orwell's two novels, *Animal Farm* (New York: Harcourt, Brace, 1946) and *1984* (New York: New American Library, 1983). As effective as these works are, however, they successfully ignore the matter of gender subordination. Economic injustice remains in his work a problem of (and perhaps for) men.

38. Nancy Folbre, "Socialism, Feminist and Scientific," *Beyond Economic Man: Feminist Theory and Economics,* ed. Marianne A. Ferber and Julie A. Nelson (Chicago: U of Chicago P, 1993), 94–110, quotation on 102.

party, *take* what they believe belongs to them. This was the case in Russia, China, and Cuba. Several of the male revolutionaries[39] have acknowledged the subordination of women and promised to devote attention to it, yet the solution has had no effect in these societies at the most common site of inequality—the bearing and care of children. Women entering the workforce did so in addition to their responsibilities at home. The machinery of governance established single ruling political parties with memberships emerging from the military revolutions, secret policies, and eager bureaucrats, whose populations were like those in the Greek and Roman senates, Roman legions, the Church hierarchies, and dozens of military dictatorships. Usually in the Marxist societies a secret police and military dictatorships terrorized the majority of the population.[40]

Attaching the term "scientific" to socialism takes advantage of science's having taken from the Church the custody of learning, knowledge, and the formal vision of the cosmos. In this role, Marxian thought appropriated the sense of inevitability from science, the feeling that a workers' revolution was a necessary consequence of the so-called dialectic of history. This compulsory sense of history is similar to Church readings of God's will or the supposedly scientific fact that women's brains are smaller than men's and therefore are necessarily inferior. Sometimes such readings are taught to new generations as errors that people made due to ignorance. But the historical repetition of these politically loaded authoritative truths has similar sources and similar results: the concentration of governance in the hands of oligarchies that control wealth and force in the society.

II-1. KONRAD LORENZ

After World War II, Konrad Lorenz addressed issues of war and violence on the basis of his experience as a zoologist who spent a long time studying the habits of animals. The book jacket of the 1966 English translation of *On Aggression* cites Lorenz's introductory comment on his study:

> One particular instinct, which is common to animals and man, and which, for very good reasons, is very much in the center of our interest today, is the instinct of aggression. . . . Is there really a sinister instinct

---

39. Such as Friedrich Engels.

40. An attempt to use Marxist discourse for progressive purposes is found in Rosemary Hennessy's *Materialist Feminism and the Politics of Discourse* (New York: Routledge, 1993). To do this, she has had to ignore the disastrous results of those societies that did take the Marxist calls for revolution seriously, and she had to enlist the most extreme forms of academic abstraction. I read her argument strategy as an unnecessarily acrobatic gesture that resembles the attempt to justify the search for language universals or the use of Ptolemaic astronomy: there is sense in the attempt, but there are simpler and more direct ways to advance the egalitarian purpose of feminist thinking.

of self-destruction which, as Sigmund Freud assumes, is the counterpart to all other instincts preserving the life of the individual and the species, and which threatens humanity with annihilation? Natural science can give answers to all these questions. The insight which it gives into the natural causes of aggression may endow us with the power to control its effects.[41]

Lorenz is confident about providing "insight" from science on the causes of, and "power to control," aggression.[42] Freud's response to World War I influenced how he interpreted the paths to culture and civilization in the West.[43] The death drive (or instinct), Thanatos, is the worst case of what he and others refer to as human aggressiveness. Freud intimated, but did not pursue, this distinction: "[I]t would be unfair to reproach civilization with trying to eliminate strife and competition from human activity. These things are undoubtedly indispensable." But opposition is not necessarily enmity; it is misused and made an *occasion* for enmity.[44] Lorenz does not use this subtlety in Freud's formulation, although he seems to have followed Freud in his use of the term "instinct." Most of his book

41. Konrad Lorenz, *On Aggression,* trans. Marjorie Kerr Wilson (New York: Harcourt, Brace and World, 1966). Lorenz does not simply assume that instincts exist in principle. There are dozens of instances of his use of the word "instinct" as an adjective and a noun. In each case, one should ask, doesn't the usage ask us to accept as given whatever is called instinctive? Ruth Bleier's warning that this usage precludes any local and cultural reading of the behavior in question applies, so that once instinct is stipulated, no further discussion is warranted. Lorenz's discussion of violence does stop at instinct.

42. Lorenz uses the German cognate word, *Instinkt.* He does not use *Trieb* in this context but the German version of the English. Nevertheless, it is noteworthy how interchangeably the terms "wish" and "instinct" (*Trieb*) are used in Freud's writing: a wish is almost always an individual manifestation of the collectively held instinct. A similar point applies to Lorenz's use of the term "aggression." The English translation, however, does not translate the main German title—which, literally translated, could be "The So-called Evil: On Aggression." Including this title would help to highlight Lorenz's euphemistic purpose in his reading of "militant enthusiasm," the English translation of *Begeisterung.* It also might be noted that *Begeisterung* does not imply militancy but only being possessed by a spirit or force. Konrad Lorenz, *Das sogenannte Boese: Zur der Aggression* (Munich: Deutscher Taschenbuch Verlag, 1974).

43. The recursiveness of war led Freud to the "death instinct" or "death wish" he discussed in his 1921 *Beyond the Pleasure Principle* and in several works following it. *The Standard Edition of the Complete Psychological Works of Sigmund Freud,* trans. James Strachey and Anna Freud, with Alix Strachey and Alan Tyson (London: Hogarth P, 1955), 18:7–64. a He also had an exchange of letters with Einstein, presented as "Why War?" *Standard Edition,* 22:199–215. However, war was not a prominent subject in his many writings before this.

44. Freud, *Standard Edition,* 21:112. "Opposition" does not necessarily denote war and violence, nor does enmity, for that matter. It is not antagonism that Freud is addressing, but the willingness to make such feeling have deadly results. Still, there is no place

brings out instances of fighting, rivalry, territorial protection, and even collective fighting (among brown rats) that mark the behavior of several nonhuman
species. He stresses the continuity of human behavior with the different kinds
of nonhuman behavior; by recognizing their kinship with simians and rats that
fight within their species, humans can more easily see, he argues, the natural
causes of aggression, which for Lorenz is a means of adaptation and species
survival. He adduces a wealth of evidence, all attributable to an instinct for
aggression, that naturalizes the phenomena of competition, rivalry, and physical struggles that end in injury and death. Lorenz reads the Darwinian survival
of the fittest as applying more to intraspecies competition than to competition
between species. Fighting to the death among members of the same species is
natural because it redistributes the population on a given territory.[45]

In the book as a whole, an important subtext is the effort to respond to the
Nazi phenomenon. In this cause, Lorenz first examines adolescence, which he
characterizes as a "dangerous period" because of the "instinctive need to be
the member of a closely knit group fighting for common ideals."[46] Like Freud,
Lorenz relates "instinctive" needs to primitive society, whose structure, he suggests, closely resembles juvenile gangs (or primal hordes). The behavior of such
groups, because primordial or archetypically primitive, must be understood as
instinctive and that there is therefore no way to override it. The same youth
that form the gangs also become soldiers in war and the "tragic paradox[47] is
that the danger is greatest for those who are by nature best fitted to serve the
noble cause of humanity."[48] He has thus introduced his principal theme in his

---

in Freud's work implying that the path to violence and war is overwhelmingly male
and rarely female.

45. Lorenz, *On Aggression*, 30–31. According to Gross and Averill, this is the same
evidence that is inconclusive and has emerged from a process of male scientists unconsciously looking for male-coded values. Also, one can see the Malthusian character
of this description of population stabilization. Michael Gross and Mary Beth Averill,
"Evolution and Patriarchal Myths of Scarcity and Competition," *Discovering Reality:
Feminist Perspectives on Epistemology, Metaphysics, Methodology, and Philosophy of Science,*
ed. Sandra Harding and Merrill B. Hintikka (Dordrecht: D. Reidel, 1983), 71–95.

46. Lorenz, *On Aggression*, 267, 268.

47. Here is an important instance of explanation by paradox, or more accurately,
description as paradox (discussed in chapter 7). In this case, if you do not consider
war making to be instinctive, the paradox disappears. In addition, consider the use of
the term "tragedy," especially in its Greek sense, in which a single flaw produces many
murders. Used this way, "tragedy" behaves like "paradox"; either as a description of an
individual action or of a dramatic genre, the term converts unconscionable, destructive
behavior and violence to something merely sad or fearful.

48. Lorenz, *On Aggression*, 267, 268. By the time he reaches this statement, it is clear
that the word "youth" refers only to male youth, and that the entire discussion following
refers to the behavior of male individuals and groups.

penultimate chapter: in young men the forces of achievement and destruction are the same.[49]

In addressing the related phenomena of adolescent gang violence and war, Lorenz says that affirmative gang ideals lose their value as the collective fighting overtakes the group's activity. This view does not refer to the fact that young men usually gather into groups in order to multiply their individual capability for exercising power over other men and over women. As Lorenz moves to the war situation—serving the "noble cause of humanity"—he renders the group-belonging "instinct" more paradoxical.[50] Lorenz does not view either the gang violence or the automatic fitness for war as mainly cultural developments that men as a class have built up over history. However, if he assumed that men were always aiming to consolidate their advantageous circumstances in society it would not be a paradox at all to find that the strongest young men are conscripted, and often actively choose, to become professional warriors, perpetrators of violence—putatively in the "cause of humanity," but tacitly in the cause of keeping masculine identity attached to the exercise of power over others through what Freud called "brute force."[51]

With respect to the Nazi phenomenon, he views gang formation as an instance of object fixation, the object being the single dominating cause announced by the group:

The process of object-fixation has consequences of an importance that can hardly be overestimated. It determines neither more nor less than that which a man will live for, struggle for, and, under certain circumstances, blindly go to war for. It determines the conditioned stimulus situation

49. The context of this identification goes back to Homer. Susan Moller Okin criticizes Alisdair MacIntyre for being "only momentarily puzzled by the paradox" that the heroic actions that bring prosperity to family and community in the Homeric epics end with the death of the hero. Homeric epics, she observes, "depict a society in which most people were perceived as existing for the sake of the male elite, and in which what are presented as 'the virtues' are reserved for these few." Susan Moller Okin, *Justice, Gender, and the Family* (New York: Basic, 1989), 49, 51.

50. As outlined in chapter 7.

51. Nancy Chodorow shows how contrived Freud's view of female development becomes because it insists that the wish for children is a sublimation of the wish for a penis. Nancy Chodorow, *The Reproduction of Mothering: Psychoanalysis and the Sociology of Gender* (Berkeley: U of California P, 1978), 147. One may wish to reverse Freud's thought by saying how men's envy of the ability to bear children causes them to exaggerate the value of the penis, imagining, in the service of this fantasy, that women envy it. Freud, like other male thinkers, necessarily includes terms of thought that at once assume and perpetuate their own hegemony. This is also Lorenz's trope in viewing the warrior ambitions of young men as attaching themselves to the cause of humanity.

releasing a powerful phylogenetically evolved behavior which I propose to call that of militant enthusiasm.[52]

In reality, militant enthusiasm is a specialized form of communal aggression, clearly distinct from and yet functionally related to the more primitive forms of petty individual aggression. Every man of normally strong emotions knows, from his own experience, the subjective phenomena that go hand in hand with the response of militant enthusiasm. A shiver [called "in German poetry . . . a 'heiliger Schauer'" (Lorenz, *On Aggression,* 269)] runs down the back and, as more exact observation shows, along the outside of both arms. One soars elated, above all the ties of everyday life, one is ready to abandon all for the call of what, in the moment of this specific emotion, seems to be a sacred duty. All obstacles in its path become unimportant; the instinctive inhibitions against hurting or killing one's fellows lose, unfortunately, much of their power. Rational considerations, criticism, and all reasonable arguments against the behavior dictated by militant enthusiasm are silenced by an amazing reversal of all values, making them appear not only untenable but base and dishonorable. Men may enjoy the feeling of absolute righteousness even while they commit atrocities. Conceptual thought and moral responsibility are at their lowest ebb. . . .[53]

. . . Without the concentrated dedication of militant enthusiasm neither art, nor science, nor indeed any of the great endeavors of humanity would ever have come into being.[54]

This juxtaposition of ideas demonstrates how paradox is used, with religious weight, as a plausible explanation for men's recursive returns to violence, killing, and sadism. After the long description of how militant enthusiasm overtakes common sense and rationality, how it converts values of decency into the "base and dishonorable," how men are physiologically overtaken to the point that murder and other atrocities become enjoyable and just, how the atrocities themselves seem to be "sacred duty," how German poetry already has a word for this state of being, relating it to religious feeling, Lorenz then asserts that *civilization itself would not be possible without it.* Militant enthusiasm, he declares,

---

52. Lorenz, *On Aggression,* 268. The word is *Begeisterung,* which has a literal sense of "inspirited," which is cognate to the Greek "possessed by a god." However, the English addition of the word "militant" may be adding a thought that is only implied by Lorenz: one would not necessarily call the enthusiasm of a Bacchic ritual militant. Nevertheless, the translator does convey in this adjective some of the contextual material used by Lorenz to describe *Begeisterung.*
53. Lorenz, *On Aggression,* 268–269.
54. Lorenz, *On Aggression,* 270–271.

[l]ike the triumph ceremony of the greylag goose . . . is a true autonomous instinct: it has its own appetitive behavior, its own releasing mechanisms, and, like the sexual urge or any other strong instinct, it engenders a specific feeling of intense satisfaction. The strength of its seductive lure explains why intelligent men may behave as irrationally and immorally in their political as in their sexual lives.[55]

The fact that militant enthusiasm is understood to be an instinct presents a scientific vocabulary for men's long tradition of destructive, murderous self-indulgence and asserts that its devastating results are, finally, necessary. The concept of instinct is essential for this line of reasoning. If in the foregoing citations, including those of Freud, we read the pronoun "men" literally, we have an accurate description of militant enthusiasm as it has appeared in the twentieth century. Like Freud, but more decisively than Freud, Lorenz separates aggressive violence and sadistic cruelty from the rest of human life by calling it an instinct. This separation permits a moral distinction between different kinds of violence—for example, the distinction between sports and war: both aim to defeat the opponent, but one is good and the other bad.[56] The moral perspective supports the act of isolating aggression as an autonomous instinct. If, instead, the underlying perspective took into account the fact that all of the phenomena described by Lorenz, the atrocities as well as the arts and sciences, were overseen, practiced, defined, motivated, and perpetrated by men, it would be less credible to isolate aggression as a true autonomous instinct, which implies that women are equally implicated in militant enthusiasm. It is not possible to adduce instances of comparable scale, consequence, and violence in which women were the principal participants, instigators, inventors, agitators, gun carriers, bullies, murderers, and hate mongers, although some women may warrant these descriptions. Freud's distinction between opposition and enmity corresponds, approximately, to the distinction in the historic collective behavior of women and men, respectively. The militant enthusiasm that is sometimes involved in art and science is also involved in excluding women from these enterprises, for the reasons assumed to be self-evident by Freud: women's interests lay in family and domestic life. So in a fearful sense, Lorenz correctly sees militant enthusiasm in both the self-righteous prosecution of atrocities and in the dedicated pursuit of

55. Lorenz, *On Aggression*, 271. Lorenz does not use *Trieb* in this context but the actual German version of the English: *Instinkt* (*Das sogenannte Boese*, 244). The provisos I suggested that could apply to Freud's usage would not apply in this case.

56. Mariah Burton Nelson's *The Stronger Women Get, the More Men Love Football: Sexism and the American Culture of Sports* (New York: Harcourt Brace, 1994) suggests that in reality, the social psychology of men's sports and war are not very separate, no matter how much one wants to think of them as far apart from one another.

art and science. But rather than entertaining the thought that this is the result of the historical momentum of male supremacy, he understands it to be a paradox not susceptible to resolution.[57] He has used a trick of language and logic, the paradox, upon which to rest his case that war and murder are unavoidable.

II-2. J. L. TALMON

J. L. Talmon (1916–1980) was a historian and an approximate contemporary of Lorenz. He wrote a trilogy of works about how the European Enlightenment of the late eighteenth century contained the seeds of totalitarianism in the twentieth century.[58] The title of his final volume are two terms of the binary he began with in his first volume—the desire of a people for nationhood, combined with the transnational need for revolution that would emancipate the majority of the poor in all societies. Irving Louis Horowitz says in his preface to Talmon's last work, "Talmon came to understand that the 'thesis' [of this book] is itself the paradox: the mutually incompatible claims shoved down the throats of an unhappy and unwilling humanity."[59] The paradoxical and unsatisfying cycle of talk and action is similar for Enlightenment revolutions, Marxism, and Fascism: a revolutionary discourse promising a new age of justice and fairness to the majority appears. Its adherents turn out to have brought a new tyranny marked by terror and murder. Talmon's account shows how abstractions come to

---

57. Suppose you are inclined to be less critical of Lorenz on historical grounds: gender equality was not the acknowledged political task it is today, for example. Charles Tilly does not mention male supremacy or other gender considerations that may acknowledge the disproportionality of participation in violence and war by gender. Here is his conclusion: "[C]ollective violence occupies a perilous but coherent place in contentious politics. It emerges from the ebb and flow of collective claim making and struggles for power. It interweaves incessantly with nonviolent politics, varies systematically with political regimes, and changes as a consequence of essentially the same causes that operate in the nonviolent zones of collective political life. Understanding those causes will help us minimize the damage that human beings inflict on each other." Charles Tilly, *The Politics of Collective Violence* (New York: Cambridge UP, 2003), 238. Tilly's book is a fairly comprehensive review of different sites of violence around the world in the twenty-first century. Yet this paragraph, especially the last sentence, still maintains that it is "human beings" and not overwhelmingly men who preside and run most of public politics and who, as a result, "interweave" war "incessantly" with nonviolent politics.

58. J. L. Talmon, *Origins of Totalitarian Democracy* (London: Secker and Warburg, 1955); *Political Messianism: The Romantic Phase* (London: Secker and Warburg, 1960); and *The Myth of the Nation and Vision of Revolution: The Origins of Ideological Polarisation in the Twentieth Century* (London: Secker and Warburg, 1980).

59. Talmon, *Myth*, xxi. Talmon refers to the uncertain 1981 international roles of the Soviet Union, China, and the United States as "these paradoxical phenomena [that] are the ironical outcome of the fusion of the myth of the nation and the vision of salvationist universal revolution" (554).

undermine the achievement of the European Enlightenment over a period of two centuries. And while he does not use Carol Cohn's term "tyranny of concepts," his analysis shows how this is the case each time political tyranny develops.

His archetype of totalitarian democracy is the French Revolution, which began in philosophy and social idealism and soon moved toward terror and imperialism. Totalitarian democracy is "concrete" and envisions "a state of ideal harmony"[60] regardless of the violence needed to reach this state. A key term he uses to describe revolutionary movements in the two centuries he examines is "political Messianism." The object of salvation is always "the masses."[61] People in the Enlightenment imagined that the rejection of kingship and elite classes would save whole societies, which, if properly educated, would govern felicitously. Talmon notes, however, that the ideal of nationhood replaced rejection of monarchy in Europe: nations were held together by common languages, and therefore nations grew and became ever more imperial without being able to bring universal salvation. However, Talmon locates the problem of messianism within its ideology of incompatible ideals: individual freedom for all along with a "maximum of social justice and security."[62] In his last book, published almost thirty years after his first, Talmon has no further solution to the paradox: "Surely, it could not be just the same eternal and incurable human wickedness or merely a similar concatenation of untoward circumstances that had brought about"[63] both the failure of the French Revolution and the degeneration of the Russian Revolution to a totalitarian disaster. He identifies the sense of nationhood as a myth and revolutions as motivated by illusions. He describes the revolutionary vision of "man" as "Rationalistic abstract universalism"[64] and contrasts this vain idealism with the pre-Enlightenment circumstance in which "[t]here was no abstract man as a lawgiver to himself or to society, no individual person endowed with a right to abstract liberty."[65] His effort, perhaps in keeping with the academic ideal that historians are themselves objective, aims to show that "the fusion of the myth of the nation and the vision of salvationist universal revolution"[66] has produced the "ironical outcome" of "paradoxical phenomena."[67] Here is an example of a paradoxical phenomenon. The Russians and the Germans during World War II are described respectively as "the standard bearers of world revolution at one end, and the guardians of national destiny at the other

60. Talmon, *Origins,* 2.
61. Talmon, *Origins,* 5.
62. Talmon, *Origins,* 2.
63. Talmon, *Myth,* 535.
64. Talmon, *Myth,* 539.
65. Talmon, *Myth,* 539.
66. Talmon, *Myth,* 554.
67. Talmon, *Myth,* 554.

. . . Both creeds adhered to a Manichean view of history. By being convinced of the possession of the all-embracing and all-healing truth, each believed that whatever promoted its goals was right and good, and what hampered its advance was evil. There being no middle ground, what was not Marxist was bourgeois, just as what was not Nordic was Jewish."[68] But are these paradoxes? Talmon's view of ideology is like Carol Cohn's; both see the two sides as slaves to abstraction. Why is it that Talmon sees a paradox in such circumstances? To what extent does Talmon participate in the same logic as Lorenz did, when he viewed war and civilization as having a common source in *Begeisterung*? To say that war making and violence is paradoxical is also to say that the historian himself, after studying for three decades, has not reached an understanding of a pragmatic sort: the moment of paradox is a moment of contradiction and a declaration of the inability to present a discussion that would see the possible terms of human survival. Furthermore, this is a characteristically *academic* conclusion: people studying the processes of society and politics for lifetimes, gathering documents and testimonials, and presenting with confidence analyses of revolutions, ideologies, and struggles for power cannot, nevertheless, understand the recursive destruction that emerges from history. To reiterate: it is an *academic* schema used by people who are as committed to their abstractions as the defense intellectuals are committed to theirs, as civilian leaders who begin wars are committed to theirs, or as zoologists are committed to instinct.

It is endemic to academic language-use habits to rely on mathematical formulations, logical paradox, and abstraction as authoritative descriptions of what is the case. There is a repeated inflated eagerness to make the abstraction stick, to say they refer to something real. It is characteristic in academic analysis to find limitations in one's preferred symbolization mode rather than expecting people, and not symbols, to have created people's problems.[69] Because most academics have been men, such tools are brought to bear to avoid saying "men as a gendered class are prone to violence and make war."

III. Explanation without Paradox: Virginia Woolf[70]

Ten years after the publication of *Civilization and Its Discontents,* and twenty-six years before the appearance of Lorenz's book, Virginia Woolf posed questions closely related to those posed by Cohn, Freud, Lorenz, and Talmon. The reflections she records in *Three Guineas* show, by example, how language can be found to describe the discontent of civilization without deciding that it is a

---

68. Talmon, *Myth,* 549.

69. Which is why, again, Kristeva sought to bring the speaking subject back into the study of language.

70. Virginia Woolf, *Three Guineas* (New York: Harvest, 1966).

paradox. The book is cast as a response to a respected man who is asking the author/narrator to donate to a public fund to help prevent war. In Europe at the time, Hitler was gathering his forces, and war seemed imminent. Woolf's book was published just before the war began. The narrator (speaker) reflects on what it may mean for men to approach women in this cause of preventing war:

> Inevitably we [women] ask ourselves, is there not something in the conglomeration of people into societies that releases what is most selfish and violent, least rational and humane in the individuals themselves? Inevitably we look upon society, so kind to you, so harsh to us, as an ill-fitting form that distorts the truth; deforms the mind; fetters the will. Inevitably we look upon societies as conspiracies that sink the private brother, whom many of us have reason to respect, and inflate in his stead a monstrous male, loud of voice, hard of fist, childishly intent upon scoring the floor of the earth with chalk marks, within whose mystic boundaries human beings are penned, rigidly, separately, artificially; where, daubed red and gold, decorated like a savage with feathers he goes through mystic rites and enjoys the dubious pleasures of power and dominion while we, "his" women, are locked in the private house without share in the many societies of which his society is composed.[71]

In the above, one of several passages in *Three Guineas* that articulate a similar sentiment, Woolf raises the issues of territoriality ("chalk marks" on the earth), violence in men, the ritualized ceremonies of power and domination, and the exclusion of women from public life. The last factor distinguishes Woolf from the male writers who are thinking about some of the same things: Woolf is a member of the excluded—perhaps a member of Freud's masses and Talmon's impoverished workers—now participating in the public discussion. From this vantage point, the "conglomeration of people into societies that releases what is most selfish and violent" is easily identified and is not a paradox. Because she identifies the source of the individual lives of pain and the history of painful lives, Woolf sees no mystery to explain. It is not a problem whose solution could be urged by the listing of four factors at the conclusion of a treatise, as Lorenz offers in his last chapter. The starting point of her thinking is also not the history of women's suffering. The starting point as she gives it—regardless of whether this work is fact or fiction—is in the experience of everyday life for women: a request by a personally benign and established man (a lawyer) for her to advise him on how to prevent war, and to donate money to the institutions that are already trying to prevent war. Because the man is uncomprehending

---

71. Woolf, *Three Guineas*, 105.

of women's perspectives, the requests for money and advice dramatize Woolf's exclusion from the man's, and from men's, society. At the same time, the conversation in the book demonstrates that a rational, coherent understanding of how war comes about poses no problems of either logic or language.

One of the terms of a woman's exclusion from society is that she is not susceptible to the transformations of personality suffered by her metaphorical brother as he enters into society. The violent character of public society is not a paradox because it is a painful fact for a large constituency: half the population. Considered to be a spokesperson for this constituency, Woolf is already in a category different from that of Freud, Lorenz, and Talmon. Yet she shares social position with these men. An acclaimed author and public figure, Woolf moves in her senior years toward issues of global consequence. As Woolf was writing, the war had not yet begun. She cites fact after fact documenting a sense of society not considered by her high-minded masculine counterparts: women are repeatedly asked to support a society that demeans, excludes, and harms them. The request itself is the factor that best identifies men's refusal to see, men's purposeful self-deceit about the fundamental condition of domination under which most people and almost all women are living. Men's request to women for support, both tacit and direct, is presented in this book as the reason for writing the book. In this way Woolf presents a plausible, even likely, explanation of why men feel discontent and express it as a paradox of human life: *lack of collective self-knowledge, and a collective refusal of the language that teaches such knowledge.*

The man's question of how to prevent war seems strange to Woolf because it presupposes her implication in its premise—that women must be with the men and nations who are making war. In the opening pages of the book she rejects this premise, regardless of whether war is instinctive. Although many "instincts" are held more or less in common by both sexes,

> to fight has always been the man's habit, not the woman's. Law and practice have developed that difference, *whether innate or accidental.* Scarcely a human being in the course of history has fallen to a woman's rifle; the vast majority of birds and beasts have been killed by you, not by us; it is difficult to judge what we do not share.
>
> How then are we to understand your problem, and if we cannot, how can we answer your question, how to prevent war? The answer based upon our experience and our psychology—Why fight?—is not an answer of any value. Obviously there is for you some glory, some necessity, some satisfaction in fighting which we have never felt or enjoyed.[72]

---

72. Woolf, *Three Guineas,* 6; emphasis added. Several decades later, during the height of the Cold War, Time-Life Books published *Alternatives to Violence: A Stimulus to Dia-*

In addition to rejecting the man's assumption that women must be with him as loyal supporters, Woolf rejects instinct as a source of men's habitual involvement in and initiation of war and aggression. We cannot know what the history of war would be like had women been equal members of public society. Considered as a group, women associated with war efforts did not do the killing: they did the nursing and other work that supports and maintains life. Regardless of whether they wanted to be soldiers, Woolf emphasizes, women *were not soldiers*.[73] For men, she continues, citing Lord Hewart, "war is a profession; a source of happiness and excitement; and it is also an outlet for manly qualities, without which men would deteriorate."[74] This is a fact of history and a phenomenon true of men living today. Regardless of whether war, the hard fist, and the loud voice are identified as innate (instinctive) or accidental,[75] men in public life seem grossly transformed from the individuals they often are in more private contexts.[76] Because Woolf rejects this condition of society on social and political grounds, the discourse of instincts becomes inapplicable as a path toward finding a ground for women's participation in the prevention of war.

---

logue, ed. Larry Ng (New York: Time-Life, 1968). None of the twenty-two contributors are women. Some, such as Harold Lasswell, Arnold Toynbee, and Abraham Maslow, are well-known scholars. Others, such as Robert McNamara, are experienced in global affairs. The first four lines of Larry Ng's epigraph read, "You are violent. I am violent. We are all violent. This book is about *our* violence." That such a collection should appear, with that epigraph, several decades after World War II and in the midst of the nuclear standoff, suggests that established men, in and out of the academy, continue to lie about which people are involved in war making and violence. The vocabulary of these lies are the abstract ideals with which few would quarrel: "human destructiveness," "the predicament of man," "alienation," "impatience and anger," "the decline of faith," "the purpose of education," "world community," "security," "justice," "law," "science," "mankind's moral malady." Many might well wish to strike the phrase *"our* violence" from the epigraph, but that would change radically the reference of all the abstractions in the essay titles just cited.

73. Ellen N. La Motte, *The Backwash of War* (St. Petersburg, FL: Hailer, 2007). These accounts, first published in 1916 by an American nurse working in Europe during World War I, of the unbearable suffering of wounded soldiers have the same role to play as the pictures alluded to by Woolf in speaking to the man asking her help: the pictures of war, as these accounts, are non-paradoxical answers to the question of war. When the book first came out, it was censored in Europe and in the United States. The 2007 date is the first reissue after the censorship was lifted.

74. Woolf, *Three Guineas,* 8.

75. Here is another reason why instinct remains an abstraction devoid of reference: relative to the issue at hand—the avoidance of war and the survival of life—there is no need to decide between instinct and accident: all want to avoid extinction.

76. However, as Woolf also acknowledges, the violence that characterizes the public life of men also appears in private, first through ordinary social tyranny, but also through the physical violence of beating and rape.

Woolf's final answer to her correspondent, "I will contribute three guineas, but I will not join your society," is an endorsement of the cause of preventing war without her collaboration with this man and his constituency:

And abroad the monster [Hitler] has come more openly to the surface. There is no mistaking him there. He has widened his scope. He is interfering now with your liberty; he is dictating how you shall live; he is making distinctions not merely between the sexes, but between the races. You are feeling in your own persons what your mothers felt when they were shut out, when they were shut up, because they were women. Now you are being shut out, you are being shut up, because you are Jews, because you are democrats, because of race, because of religion. . . . The whole iniquity of dictatorship, whether in Oxford or Cambridge, in Whitehall or Downing Street, against Jews or against women, in England, or in Germany, in Italy or in Spain is now apparent to you. But now we are fighting together. The daughters and sons of educated men are fighting side by side.[77]

Although this is an expression of solidarity in the cause of peace, a moment of unified effort by both sexes, the term "dictatorship" is usually understood by men in its traditional sense—political dictatorship in government. The term "dictator" might be rewritten as "a person whose words rule." The dictator's language is not shared; it is given and is a total mediation. Perhaps "dictator" might be contrasted with the German *Dichter*, "the poet"—the maker of words who does not aspire to rule. Why would one entertain banning the *Dichter* from the republic, when the actual purpose is to ban the dictator?

In order to lay out the sense of dictatorship that she is identifying—hinted at by her allusion to men's mothers' subjugation—Woolf leads her correspondent through a discussion of the Church of England and its masculinization of religion. There, initiatives had been taken to admit women to clerical office and arguments were adduced as to why and why not to admit them. A "Professor Grensted,"[78] who had gathered the evidence, concluded that although the exclusion of women was definitely a "non-rational sex-taboo," also described how, unaccountably, men react with a "strong feeling" to "any suggestion that women should be admitted to the status and functions of the threefold Order of the Ministry." Grensted then reported that it remains "clear that infantile fixation plays a predominant part in determining the strong emotion with which this whole subject is commonly approached."[79]

---

77. Woolf, *Three Guineas*, 102–103.

78. L. W. Grensted, *Psychology and God: A Study of the Implications of Recent Psychology for Religious Belief and Practice* (London: Longmans, 1930). Page numbers are not specifically cited by Woolf.

79. Woolf, *Three Guineas*, 126.

Having placed this formulation on the table—the consideration that men exclude women from an institution in which their presence is invited by the New Testament—Woolf presents a conversation between herself and her correspondent and the feelings each has. For her part, she describes her feeling "an alarm bell within us; a confused but tumultuous clamour: You shall not, shall not, shall not"[80]—perhaps echoing the commandments that are perversely redirected only toward women. Then she asks,

> What are the powerful and subconscious motives that are raising the hackles on your side of the table? Is the old savage who has killed a bison asking the other old savage to admire his prowess? Is the tired professional man demanding sympathy and resenting competition? Is the patriarch calling for the siren? Is dominance craving for submission? And, most persistent and difficult of all the questions that our silence covers, what possible satisfaction can dominance give the dominator?[81]

In the main text, Woolf describes several cases of "infantile fixation"[82]—the presumed malady of men who will not welcome the independence of women—by showing the lengths to which fathers will go to limit, constrain, and keep their daughters in their own control. Men rationalize this behavior by protesting their desire and need to support wife and children. However, the long footnote to this passage makes the point better:

> Evidence of the complex nature of satisfaction of dominance is provided by the following quotation: "My husband insists that I call him 'Sir,'" said a woman at the Bristol Police Court yesterday, when she applied for a maintenance order. "To keep the peace I have complied with his request," she added. "I also have to clean his boots, fetch his razor when he shaves, and speak up promptly when he asks me questions." In the same issue of the same paper Sir E. F. Fletcher is reported to have "urged the House of Commons to stand up to dictators." (*Daily Herald,* August 1st, 1936.) This would seem to show that the common consciousness which includes husband, wife and House of Commons is feeling at one and the same moment the desire to dominate, the need to comply in order to keep peace, and the necessity of dominating the desire for dominance—a psychological conflict which serves to explain much that appears inconsistent and tur-

---

80. Woolf, *Three Guineas,* 129.

81. Woolf, *Three Guineas,* 129.

82. Note the similarity of this term to the one used by Lorenz, "object fixation," to describe the cause animating the destructive violence in the mob action of adolescent gangs and Nazis. It, too, functions as instinct does: an abstraction with no common referent, an inference about something that must be there, but cannot otherwise be identified.

bulent in contemporary opinion. The pleasure of dominance is of course further complicated by the fact that it is still, in the educated class, closely allied with the pleasures of wealth, social and professional prestige.[83]

Woolf puts to the forefront the common institutions—the House of Commons and the household—as the grounds on which to attribute the individually localized feelings to persons in each context. She uses the public bodies to place the conflicting interests and feelings into a single category, and particularly to unite the public and the private.

Cases of "infantile fixation" boil down to the behavior that brought out the diagnosis to begin with: the act of men dominating women. Because of the hypocrisy shown by public opposition to domination and the private practice of it, Woolf suggests that domination yields no satisfaction for men in either public or private actions. For men, public and private are connected by an oppositional relationship: the promotion and practice of domination in private, and the opposition to domination in public—something that may be called a paradox. To oppose domination in public, one can oppose some men's domination over others, but there is no occasion for men publicly to oppose men's domination of women. In private, men practice the domination and develop its language features, such as vocabulary, sentence form, gestures, and tones of voice—features observable today in literature and films about men who batter or dominate psychologically the women who are their intimate partners. The language of dictatorship, Woolf shows, is a common feature of homes, appearing in forms ranging from direct military-style orders to the elaborately nuanced yet relentless denial by fathers of economic freedom for their wives and daughters. Woolf is describing a broad distribution of hypocrisy on which the structure of civilization stands. Ordinary life for men includes normalized lying: eschewing public domination—believing in Enlightenment liberty—but practicing both public and private domination of women, and not permitting themselves recognition of the language through which domination emerges.[84] The result is female suffering and an unidentifiable feeling in men of discontent with civilization that Freud unsatisfactorily understood to be excessive repression for each individual. Woolf's discussion, unlike those of Freud, Lorenz, and Talmon, discloses the premise of the explanation by paradox: the preeminent role of domination in the households of the men as children that then undergoes repression by being

---

83. Woolf, *Three Guineas*, 181n32.

84. Imagine how Talmon's formulations might have changed if such a fact was brought into his discussion. Woolf's discussion is a solution to his paradox: the conflict of values appears to Talmon because the lives of almost all men—liberal and conservative alike—are characterized by this hypocrisy. Similar thought experiments with Freud's and Lorenz's formulations would be equally illuminating.

understood as normative. The discontent of civilization is men's normative lying about what principles are in effect.

Although men are aware of their failure to preserve peace, the language used to articulate this failure stops at paradox because the revocation of the paradox requires a premise of men's own attachment, involvement, and implication in the identity of others. Because of the domination of society by men, women must keep the peace at home and engage in peaceful activities to support war. But men, like women, *prefer* peace to war. Yet because men perceive that adopting the language of life support or unilateral weapons reduction would make them, socially and culturally, into women,[85] that is enough to halt the process of learning short of honoring their own preference for peace. Men are locked into a tradition of sexual separation and heterosexual men are also locked into "compulsory heterosexuality."[86] Woolf's concluding and conclusive point is that "the public and the private worlds are inseparably connected."[87] Men are as connected by the two worlds as women are, but men who rule and govern conceal it from themselves by declaring paradox, whereas women and many men, in presuming the connectedness of different parts of society, view the shortfall in combining liberty with social justice as failure and not paradox.

The more unscrupulous men, such as the political and domestic dictators cited by Woolf, utilize, as Lorenz describes in his discussion of militant enthusiasm, the classical forms of religious and military social organization (Freud's two examples of groups) in two ways: by establishing armies of men to create and maintain law and order; and through propaganda, by sacralizing the texts that fix the traditional language of the inevitability of civilization as it is—creating bibles fixing memory and versions of history, ideals, and social relations. The outbreaks of militant enthusiasm create social institutions that, with ever increasing energy, separate the privileged class from others by forcibly diminishing the nondominant groups, starting with women, and arbitrarily creating new groups of subordinates.

The less unscrupulous men become the genteel fathers described by Woolf; inexorably, these fathers practiced domination through their social relations with other groups of men in the established professions of religion, medicine, and law. If, as Woolf describes, some fathers yielded (to their daughter's wishes and pressure) in private,

> the fathers in public, massed together in societies, in professions, were even more subject to the fatal disease ["infantile fixation"] than the fathers in private. The disease had acquired a motive, had connected itself with a

---

85. As the physicist presented in Cohn's discussion thought.

86. Adrienne Rich describes how rigid sexual separation and necessary heterosexuality go together in "Compulsory Heterosexuality and Lesbian Existence," *Blood, Bread, and Poetry: Selected Prose 1979–1985* (New York: Norton, 1986), 23–75.

right, or a conception, which made it still more virulent outside the house than within. The desire to support wife and children—what motive could be more powerful, or deeply rooted? For it was connected with manhood itself—a man who could not support his family failed in his own conception of manliness.[88]

Thus, the traditional father-governed nuclear family, held in high esteem by pacifists such as Freud, is neither distant nor separate from the manic, frenzied cruelties of the dictators, the disinterested cruelties of the legal system, the greedy cruelties of industry, or the self-righteous cruelties of religious hierarchies. Men, in different degrees and styles thoughtful and ignorant, generous and malicious, share the falsehood of separateness with one another. The male bond takes place through an agreement to remain a separate class of men.[89]

There are no accepted pathways toward safe, equitable conduct of the family and public affairs. There is no consensus about how to integrate two aspects of life whose separation has been taken for granted, or about how to end the separation. Some academic men[90] have studied these issues but with only mixed results—the assumptions of superiority, privilege, autonomy, and individualism,

87. Woolf, *Three Guineas*, 142.

88. Woolf, *Three Guineas*, 138–139.

89. Pierre Bourdieu writes, "What is called 'courage' is often rooted in a kind of cowardice . . . the will to dominate, exploit or oppress has relied on the 'manly' fear of being excluded from the world of 'men' without weakness . . . also [from] the new 'hatchet men' of modern management, glorified by liberal hagiography, who . . . manifest their virility by sacking their superfluous employees" (*Masculine*, 52–53).

90. John Stuart Mill's *The Subjection of Women*, mentioned in chapter 7, was one of the earliest male advocacies. Characteristic of his and some of the later male feminists is a focus on gender equality without calculating how many other features of society would have to change for gender equality to be achieved. This caveat applies to the female advocacies in Marxism. Karl Stern's *The Flight from Woman* (New York: Farrar, Straus, and Giroux, 1965), comprehending of the shape of misogyny, does not discuss the degree to which institutions would have to change in consequence of this recognition (5). A similar caveat might apply to Lionel Tiger's *Men in Groups* (New York: Random House, 1969). Tiger's advice to men is to "'know ourselves.' And here a paradox stares us in the eyes. In order to change how we act, we have to know what we are" (217). Changing the gang effect of men in groups is inhibited by paradox—men don't know themselves well enough to change, but in order to know themselves they need to change. Yet Tiger's book is a useful review of familiar men's groups—clubs and secret societies—whose ubiquity is not well known and needs to be announced recursively in order for their damaging effects to become public knowledge. John Archer's collection *Male Violence* (New York: Routledge, 1994) is a more contemporary survey of the broad ranges of sites of male violence, including family, school, and the explanations of evolutionary psychology. Michael S. Kimmel's *Manhood in America: A Cultural History* (New York: Free P, 1996) and *The Gendered Society* (New York: Oxford UP, 2000) have presented

often enough overlooked by or fostered in us by devoted mothers and sisters, continue to be reproduced on a scale that perpetuates inequality. Both domestic and public violence are tolerated, and a principal means of their reduction is still opposed by those who make and use weapons. Such toleration is still considered normal.[91]

IV. Languages of Dependency and Survival

Lorenz said that *Begeisterung* was a "true autonomous instinct," a "powerful phylogenetically evolved behavior," and "a specialized form of communal aggression." If the instinct was "autonomous," that means it went into action all by itself: a person who followed "his instinct" was not responsible for what he did. In most uses of the term, the autonomous status of instinct is not mentioned, but here it is and it is a sign of either the confidence Lorenz has in its use, or of his lack of confidence in the term "instinct" that requires an extra adjective to make the point.

Lorenz used "autonomous" possibly because the social value of the term has its own connotations in modern usage. Like democracy and freedom, autonomy emerges from the European Enlightenment as one of the human rights each

---

comprehensive views of how the basics of gender understanding are already changing and need to continue. These works are valuable also because they take account of how society actually is, giving information about gender that had not been accessible to the public.

Alice Jardine and Paul Smith's *Men in Feminism* is an attempt by members of the academy to collaborate to face academic androcentrism. Two observations by male contributors are germane. Richard Ohmann's essay therein acknowledges how male supremacy, unlike racism and homophobia, is "maybe as old as the species." Richard Ohmann, "In, With," *Men in Feminism,* ed. Alice Jardine and Paul Smith (New York: Routledge, 1987), 182–189, quotation on 187. This context lets him acknowledge that most men "were dragged into [feminism] kicking and screaming," and that his "very affections" were the "strongest personal incentive" for joining feminism (187, 188). In a similar achievement of self-observation, Cary Nelson writes that for men "[w]riting is at once a mediated form of bodily expression and an externalized encapsulation and rejection of bodily life." Cary Nelson, "Men, Feminism: The Materiality of Discourse," *Men in Feminism,* ed. Jardine and Smith, 153–172, quotation on 157. The political orientations of both Ohmann and Nelson lead them to both feminism and the materiality of language.

91. A point well made by Arthur Brittan in the conclusion to his *Masculinity and Power:* "[W]e [men] have not recognized our masculinism, our commitment to gender inequality, our sexual objectification of women. The university is no different in this respect than any other institution, except that it glosses violence more successfully. Violence is often hidden behind a rhetorical smokescreen—it is couched in the language of academic 'one upmanship,' . . . [whose] aim is to hurt and diminish its object." Arthur Brittan, *Masculinity and Power* (New York: Blackwell, 1989), 203–204. The university style animated the "defense intellectuals" studied by Cohn.

individual has in a just society. Not coincidentally, the term is also a description of the Newtonian universe, which works by itself after its creation. But today as well autonomy remains a key social value—perhaps, in the cause of freedom and control, sought more than any other value: I should be able to do what I want (if others are not hurt). Individuals seek it, institutions seek it, and sometimes ethnic groups seek it. Yet some scholars have tried to say that achieving autonomy without honoring the necessary conditions of people's dependency on one another means that social equality has not been achieved, even relative to pre-Enlightenment societies, and even for men. Autonomy is a foundational value of the defense intellectuals and academic intellectuals, as well as governments and corporations. Awareness of individual and collective dependency, like the awareness of the materiality of language, is repressed, devalued, and even shunned because the mutual dependency of the use of language and the stable functioning of society challenges the priority of autonomy as a collective ideal.

Martha Fineman says that the foundational myth of autonomy inhibits the collective recognition of social mutual dependency: "Foundational myths and the concepts they promote are in fact abstractions. Terms such as autonomy and equality have no independent meaning or definition."[92] As Sandra Harding and Naomi Scheman proposed for "objectivity" (when used as a presupposition), Fineman proposes that abstractions such as autonomy be used in commonly agreed upon contexts that specify their references. Fineman places autonomy in the context of the dependency of individuals and groups on others—of children and of indigent, old, and sick people—and the derived dependency of those committed to care and pay for those immediately in need. However, elite classes are just as dependent; members of these classes are dependent on others in ways that are not distinguishable from the dependencies found in childhood and old age, for example. This fact argues for a broader context of application of the term "dependency" than has been usually assumed. The dependencies she describes are mutual, and everyone's survival depends on others' dependency on them. Autonomy is a myth if sought without reference to this fact. Moreover, both autonomy and dependency contextualize each other: they can both be prior terms, depending on yet other contexts.

"Dependency, through its assignment to the private, marital family, is hidden—privatized within that family, its public and inevitable nature concealed."[93] Institutions are arranged in our society, by the established division of public and private criticized by Woolf, to place whole processes of dependency out of sight. "Privatized"—this term has come to signify an assumed, unquestioned good, especially in economic contexts, to be discussed shortly. It

92. Martha Albertson Fineman, *The Autonomy Myth: A Theory of Dependency* (New York: New P, 2004), 25.

93. Fineman, *Autonomy,* 38.

is relentlessly asserted that if businesses are private and for-profit they must be better than those that are collectively owned or not for profit; but privacy also regularly describes the ownership of the nuclear family by the male breadwinner, the "male head of household": a man's home is his fortress and castle. The term "private" applied to families conceals and protects intra-family behaviors— including harmful and injurious ones—by saying that families themselves are private.[94] The term has reached so far that abortion rights for women have had to be won by claiming a woman's privacy instead of being able to claim her responsibility and equality as the grounds for such a decision. The all-male Burger Supreme Court understood the concept of privacy but misapplied it to justify legal abortion, whose justification is sexual equality. This is a demonstration of the of denial of access to language produced by the total mediation of the term "private." Because "private" is hegemonic, "sexual equality" is censored.

Within the private nuclear family, "There is no autonomy to be found in motherhood. Motherhood is mired in dependency."[95] The mothering relationship is the archetype of dependency because it is treated as pure dependency. The myth is that there is such a thing as pure autonomy in public. In fact, there is dependency in all workplaces, but because they are hierarchical the *mutual* dependencies are ignored in the cause of maintaining the hierarchical structure of order giving and deference. Hierarchical dependency conceals the dependencies of those higher on the pyramid. In the army, it is said that the individual soldier depends on his "buddies" to save his life. This is true sometimes, but the underlying situation is that the soldier is dependent on the command for supplies and support, and this soldier must also obey the commander. But commanders are just as dependent on soldiers. A hierarchical arrangement in the workplace is marked by everyone's fluent use of the term "boss" to describe a member of management whose orders must be obeyed. But consider the dependency of the boss, business owner, or management: "[C]orporations and those who run, direct, and profit from them cannot function without the labor of others. The contributions of secretaries and truck drivers are as essential to commerce as are those of highly paid CEOs and stockholders. Thus, the arguments that began with recognition of caretaking can evolve into a claim for universal provision of basic social goods grounded in basic humanity."[96] Because autonomy

---

94. Fineman quotes MacKinnon: "The existing distribution of power and resources within the private sphere are precisely what the law of privacy exists to protect—the subordination and domination of women" (*Autonomy*, 152). Another challenge to the normative status of privacy is found in Kristin Kelly, *Domestic Violence and the Politics of Privacy* (Ithaca, NY: Cornell UP, 2003). Although Kelly allows that *some things* may be private, she notes that there is no principle of privacy that applies in all cases.

95. Fineman, *Autonomy*, 169.

96. Fineman, *Autonomy*, 289.

is still the foundational myth, this path is not recognized. Fineman's outline of how the workplace and family might change toward sexual equality rests on a public recognition of how dependency relationships, like families, function as public actions. Such recognition is censored. Historic limitations on the use of language are, through a process of reciprocal functioning, the result of and the enablers of female subordination. Institutions associated with women such as motherhood, care of the infirm, and nurturing professions in public participate in these truncations of language-use possibilities. The languages of dependent classes are, willy-nilly, muted.

In the following citation, Fineman traces, as a principle of survival, the path from individual, social, and legal usages and myths toward the related economic issues that are the daily manifestation of the processes of human survival: "[A] just state would provide two different types of subsidies to individuals—lifelong provision of fundamental social goods, which are necessary for individual survival and flourishing, and specific additional subsidies that support the caretaker and caretaking. . . . The second type of subsidy . . . requires the state to . . . oversee and facilitate the restructuring of the workplace so that market institutions accommodate caretaking and, in this way, assume some fair share of the burdens of dependency."[97] Putting aside the issue of just how possible, likely, or desirable such plans are, Fineman considers individual survival to be a public matter. Survival does not stop at such things as helping people through natural disasters. It also refers to the daily survival of all people, to long-term survival of individuals, and to the longevity of the society. The abandonment of the traditional mythological senses of privacy, autonomy, and dependency, if new usages enter the vocabulary of public and academic discussion, implies an overhaul of how this society identifies—names and perceives—its necessary functions. The majority membership of the discipline of economics, however, is disinclined to start thinking in this direction. In the past few generations, academic economists have had influential roles in government, especially insofar as government helps to regulate the distribution of goods and services. Here again we find intellectuals, whose uses of language behave like those of the scientists—exaggerating the range of reference of the "invisible hand" regulating the free market, and the inferred laws of supply and demand.

Contemporary mathematical economics, which is the dominant form of the discipline, began with Adam Smith's concept of an autonomous economy in the eighteenth century which first stipulated the invisible hand that keeps markets stable.[98] Today, instead of a verbal metaphor for the market, there are math-

---

97. Fineman, *Autonomy*, 285.

98. This metaphor, like others that have become axiomatic, is exempt from being researched or documented. Economists have decided that this was a good way to describe market stability, and made it into a fact that few dispute. But since not all markets are

ematical models, which work according to the presupposition of autonomy: the market works all by itself, and no one is responsible if what all people need is not distributed fairly to everyone. Pragmatically, there is no difference between the authority given to the mathematical model and that given to Smith's invisible hand. Mathematical modeling of economies serve the alleged purpose of predicting economic events—general events such as national employment or inflation, and specific events such as how this company will perform this year. It is generally assumed that the "science" of economics is a good way to think about the task of maximizing profits, assuming that no rational person could argue with this goal. Economic thinking is immersed in modeling processes that are given in mathematical formulations.[99] One could also say that different aspects of national economies are named by mathematical models because each aspect has a different model to describe it.

The practices of mathematical modeling in economics and in political science are mainstays of rational choice theory, recently reexamined for its usefulness.[100] The idea of rational choice is an inheritance from Enlightenment individualism. The axiomatic status of reason combined with the assumption that the individual is the fundamental unit of society lead to the premise that individual self-interest will always be in effect for all people: the rationality of the choice is the service to individual self-interest. The premise has a reasonable local application in microeconomics—that all individuals wish to pay the lowest price for whatever they buy. In addition, rational choice theory includes the commonly accepted rule of thumb that all businesses want to maximize profits. When these two applications are combined in the attempt to make sense of the behavior of macro-markets, the markets can be represented mathematically and the models give the false impression that the behavior of the markets can be predicted.

---

stable all the time, the fixed objectivity of the metaphor prevents pragmatic responses to circumstances that endanger people's survival.

99. David Glenn reports on the award of the 2005 Nobel Prize in economics and international relations to Robert J. Aumann for game theory in economics and Thomas C. Schelling for game theory in international relations. Each proposed a form of game theory that was honored by the Nobel committee. Aumann devised a mathematical formula for how business competitors play each other to reduce competition. Schelling devised a mathematically workable formula for how hostile adversaries play each other with threats of annihilation. Although both kinds of games are interesting, their winning of the most coveted prizes implies that the Nobel Committee promotes a form of problem solving that is unreliable in any single case. The use of mathematical treatment of social issues remains a means of avoiding the more difficult but more likely paths of success through verbal, discourse-based social contact. David Glenn, "Nobel Prize in Economics Goes to 2 Scholars Who Developed Game Theory as Analytical Tool in Public Policy." *Chronicle of Higher Education* 10 October 2005.

100. Donald Green and Ian Shapiro, *Pathologies of Rational Choice Theory: A Critique of Applications in Political Science* (New Haven, CT: Yale UP, 1996).

Because the theories are used in this way, they become theories about society that include calculations of both economic and political behavior.

Donald Green and Ian Shapiro approach this issue from their discipline of political science, but they acknowledge that the status of this theory in both disciplines is that it maintains "supremacy."[101] Without expressing a specific advocacy, they view the ideology of individualism as one of the "pathologies" of the theory: "Unlike evolutionary biologists, for example, who have debated for decades over whether the basic unit of survival is the species, the group, the individual, the gene, or some other entity . . . rational choice theorists of politics generally agree that it is by reference to the maximizing actions of individual persons that collective outcomes must be explained."[102] They then show, with a variety of statistically accumulated data, that this assumption does not account for the data of, for example, voting. The data show that self-interest cannot be detected in the voting statistics, nor, of course, can votes be predicted. Perhaps the most important result of their study is, however, that rational choice theory has achieved supremacy *because* of the lack of confirming data: "rational choice theory fares best in environments that are evidencepoor. In subfields like mass political behavior and public opinion, where researchers have accumulated a great deal of data, rational choice theories have been refuted or domesticated by this evidence."[103] Rational choice is an abstraction, like instinct and intelligence, and provides a placeholding assumption for phenomena that the baseline ideology implies does not require close study. New ways to study how people vote and how they buy goods produce data that renders the ideologically motivated abstraction inapplicable. Similarly, if dam building or nest building were studied carefully, the new data could obviate the need for instinct, just as new studies of human learning in various fields have obviated the need for intelligence as an explanatory abstraction.[104] The work of Green and Shapiro suggests that rational choice theory, which governs both economics and political science, is not a useful abstraction. In its role in limiting inquiry, rational choice theory discourages searches for empirical data outside theoretical constraints: it is for academics a total mediator: the language of economics and political science is sacralized.

Another departure from rational choice theory that includes mathematical models but only as one of several strategies of analysis and planning is Elinor Ostrom's effort to say how institutions govern common resources such as fishing waters and grazing fields. She abandons the sole reliance on individual self-interest as the starting assumption and seeks collectivist techniques, which,

101. Green and Shapiro, *Pathologies,* 195.
102. Green and Shapiro, *Pathologies,* 15.
103. Green and Shapiro, *Pathologies,* 195.
104. As discussed in chapter 10.

like those of Green and Shapiro, applies to both academic disciplines.[105] The line of inquiry has expanded and has addressed the wider common resource of knowledge and information that has become available to everyone.[106]

Garrett Hardin's 1968 description of the "tragedy of the commons" refers to the fact that when there is no plan for the use of a common resource, and each interested party tries to exercise "rational choice" on its own behalf, the resource is squandered and becomes available to no one.[107] In addition to this being a "tragedy," it is also a "paradox." Ostrom observes, "The paradox that individually rational strategies lead to collectively irrational outcomes seems to challenge a fundamental faith that rational human beings can achieve rational results."[108] The first approaches to the disciplined study of governing commons led to terms like "tragedy" and "paradox" which expressed the belief that nothing can be done as long as the premise of individual rational choice was in effect. Ostrom showed that rational choice without collective trust among the individual parties and a guiding principle of reciprocity in using common resources usually results in waste and the failure to distribute the resource in ways that benefit all users. If all who need a common resource do not get the maximum benefit from it, the choices that led to loss of resources cannot be understood to have been rational. As a result of Ostrom's work on the use of common resources, researchers began to consider collective trust, mutual dependency, and reciprocity, in addition to individual rational choice when trying to optimize the use of commons. The goal was to achieve the maximum benefit for *all*. Moving away from the initial scholarly fascination with the apparent paradox of rational choice, Ostrom changed the vocabulary and discourse in the political and economic study of how to use common resources. She has reconceived the issue away from a monolithic conception—rational choice—that had been applied to *all* occasions of common-resource distribution. She brought additional collectively oriented strategies into academic consideration of how to distribute common resources. Ostrom showed that each situation of common resource distribution requires different institutional, collective attention. She has desacralized the language into which common-resource problems had fallen and brought flexible ways of identifying problems, with the understanding that consideration of collective interests, trust, and reciprocity are as much a part of rational choice as is individual self-interest.

105. Elinor Ostrom, *Governing the Commons: the Evolution of Institutions for Collective Action* (New York: Cambridge UP, 1990).

106. Charlotte Hess and Elinor Ostrom, eds., *Understanding Knowledge as a Commons* (Cambridge, MA: MIT P, 2007).

107. Garrett Hardin, "The Tragedy of the Commons," *Science* 162 (1968): 1243–1248.

108. Ostrom, *Governing*, 5.

Julie A. Nelson has sought a new vocabulary to replace the use of mathematical modeling in economics. "Nowadays," she writes, "the core curriculum for economics at most American and European (and many other) universities is based on this [Adam Smith's] neoclassical model.[109] Undergraduates study neoclassical theory, usually not realizing that what they see presented as economic knowledge is not based on economists' years of intensive study of actual businesses and households. Rather, the base is actually a set of mathematically convenient assumptions and Smith's image of a mechanically driven economy."[110] As Nelson describes the rule of the neoclassical model, it is a total mediation: "The mechanical image is so deeply ingrained in academic economics that its status as a *particular* image, that is, a *particular* way of looking at things, is rarely presented as open to question. . . . To raise a challenge [to neoclassical theory] would be, after all, to question the 'laws of human nature'!"[111] Here, taken from the physical sciences, the phrase "laws of nature" is used to describe social situations. Nelson, Nancy Folbre,[112] and Diana Strassman propose terms addressed to practical situations in need of action, terms, locally abstract, that can vary in response to expectations of change.

It is not that the use of mathematics is inappropriate, but that economists assume it to be a superior approach and entertain no other possibility of doing economics because of mathematics' apparent promise of predictability. Ostrom's work continued to use mathematical models, but as part of a larger comprehensive approach to provisioning. In certain local situations, such models were useful. But if mathematical models override paths of analysis derived from verbally articulated needs and priorities these models become governing transparencies, and the benefits of using multiple discourses to analyze how the goods and

---

109. The Enlightenment produced values of freedom that are part of the idea of the free market. One cannot say if the wider concept of freedom is a translation from economic values or vice versa. The translation seems reciprocal: it may be enough to say that these two references of freedom serve one another. This concept of economics preserves individual autonomy by not including consideration of anyone's responsibility for others, except through the privacy of the nuclear family. Talmon's inability to solve the riddle of why the promise of the Enlightenment was not fulfilled is also connected to the fact that society ran on this incomplete view of economics, a view that encourages the actions that compromise Enlightenment ideals.

110. Julie A. Nelson, *Economics for Humans* (Chicago: U of Chicago P, 2006), 21.

111. Nelson, *Economics*, 21–22.

112. Nancy Folbre, *The Invisible Heart: Economics and Family Values* (New York: New P, 2001). Folbre is adapting Smith's phrase in the cause of recognizing the widespread social relations of dependency and generosity. The latter value is also found in Erik Erikson's *Childhood and Society* (New York: Basic, 1949) as a characteristic of mature adulthood, although not as an economic principle. Folbre introduces feelings of generosity, even altruism, as grounds for conceptualizing economics. Her discussion is consistent with Nelson's but presented from a somewhat less urgent stance.

services are to be distributed are lost. Nelson bases her critique of economics on the exclusive use of models, the single answer to the challenges of distributing goods and services. She sees the purpose of economic activity to be primarily "the self-preservation of the human species. Self-preservation in turn requires the satisfaction of some basic needs—which are nevertheless subject to evolution."[113] Reference to such fundamentals of provisioning as what sustains life has been absent from academic economics since Smith. Instead, the attempt is recursively made to match economic reasoning with the mathematical exactitude that describes the solar system, following the false assumption that markets have an intrinsic, essential, or autonomous logic. It is fundamentally different to say that economics is the study of collective *provisioning* than it is to say it is the study of individual *rational choice.* In shifting the terms, Nelson also changes the context of naming: "The Greek root of both the words 'economics' and 'ecology' is *oikos,* meaning 'house.' Economics could be about how we live in our house, the earth."[114] The single word thus names two "houses": the local and the collective dwellings.

Changing the understanding of economics to this domestic orientation recognizes the fact of mutual human dependency as part of the purpose and subject matter of economics. Diana Strassman observes that for infants, the old, the sick, and the handicapped,

> all important choices are made by others. . . . Economic theorists, it seems, have formed their conceptual representatives in their own image: autonomous individuals, privileged and free to choose . . . The lack of emphasis on constraints and interdependence stems from the way economic models focus on individual rational choice processes, a focus that deemphasizes (if not ignores) the fact that human beings begin (and often end) life in a state of helplessness and unchosen dependency. . . . [O]ur lives are always a mix of connectedness and separation.[115]

From the standpoint of current economic practice, Strassman observes, to include the study of dependency in the subject matter of economics would be "not economics."[116]

---

113. Julie A. Nelson, "The Study of Choice or the Study of Provisioning?" *Beyond Economic Man: Feminist Theory and Economics,* ed. Marianne A. Ferber and Julie A. Nelson (Chicago: U of Chicago P, 1992), 23–36, quotation on 32. Citation from Nicholas Georgescu-Roegen, *Analytical Economics* (Cambridge, MA: Harvard UP, 1966), 93.

114. Nelson, "Study," 33.

115. Diana Strassman, "Not a Free Market: The Rhetoric of Disciplinary Authority in Economics," *Beyond,* ed. Ferber and Nelson, 54–68, quotation on 62–63.

116. Strassman, "Not," 65.

Nelson identifies the choices of vocabulary and subject matters in economics as unambiguously gender coded. Currently economists are "rigorous and scientific," making "tough assumptions," "use precise math" and "describe mechanisms" in "markets," "industry and government. . . . *We're macho guys.*"[117] This group is *not* "touchy-feely," "humanistic," or "sentimental" in assuming that "people care about each other." They reject connectedness, dependency, and emotion, as well as "vague verbal arguments." Furthermore, they don't study family life, human relations, or ethics. In brief, they say, *"We're not soft, effeminate scholars, like those sociologists and humanists downstairs."*[118]

Most of the time, gender coding is a language gesture that takes place pursuant to conventional usages. These conventions of language use derived from the traditions of scientific discourse. Mathematical calculability is the only factor which could suggest that economists have chosen to study what is easier to study. But that is only true in the sense that it is easier to study what can be counted and calculated than it is to study what needs to be observed in large groups of living people. Because of the similarity of choices such as this one in other fields of social and psychological study, and because of the continuing unwillingness to remember how dependency in human relations plays fundamental roles in each of the disciplines in social science, Nelson's analysis is germane. Those men who may not be reflexively avoiding effeminacy as Nelson described go along with those who do. Nelson, Folbre, and several others stress not that the study of rational choice was erroneous, but that it was considered the only assumption on which to base economic philosophy and research.[119] Nelson, who refers to need and dependency as "material connection," formulates this inclusivist approach:

> Without such an understanding of material connection, we have the scandal of professional economists working out endless theoretical yarns about preferences while a majority of people in the world live in a state of neediness apparent to any observer who has not lost her or his humanity. With an understanding that incorporates both choice and material connection, comes the possibility of abundance and a hospitable nature, if we choose wisely.[120]

---

117. Nelson, *Economics,* 42–43.

118. Nelson, *Economics,* 42–43.

119. A collection showing other choices for economic analysis is Drucilla K. Barker and Edith Kuiper, eds., *Toward a Feminist Philosophy of Economics* (New York: Routledge, 2003). In addition to reconsiderations of empiricism and further reflections on caring in the study of economics, considerations of literature, erotics, and ethics are some of the perspectives brought to bear in the effort to broaden the choices for revising the discourse of economics.

120. Julie A. Nelson, *Feminism, Objectivity, and Economics* (New York: Routledge, 1996), 35. A substantial address to the matter of the majority of human beings living in

So it is an omission of the economic circumstances of the majority of people to which Nelson and the other economists are referring.

In so doing the discipline of economics has followed the tradition established by other academic subjects. In spite of the fact the only men have participated in this tradition in universities, their achievements have taken on universalist reference. Now that other voices are starting to survive, it is quite a struggle to change this established vocabulary of values, strategies, and subject matters. The challenges to the traditional vocabularies, while on the public table, have still not affected those in position to make both public policy and academic curricula.

In reflecting on the effects of androcentrism, can it be accidental that the study of language in the past has not considered the affective life of dependent children, or considered the ubiquitous dependency of words, phrases, and sentences on one another—while, parallel to that fact, the study of society has not considered the mutual dependency of individuals and of individuals on collective institutions? Isn't there a pattern in the several disciplinary approaches to language and society of a correspondence between the dominion of men in civilization and the unwillingness of academics to fold into their inquiries the modes of bodily need and feeling, of interpersonal dependency, and of mutual economic dependency?

In the humanities, the study of language and society has from antiquity taken place through the production of literature. Writers, singers, and other artists have articulated broad senses of social and individual actions, struggles, and fates. Their work, regardless of gender, has not ignored the experiences of dependency at every level, including the use of language. Yet the academic study of literature has found ways to overlook the materiality of language.

---

poverty is found in Daniel Little, *The Paradox of Wealth and Poverty: Mapping the Ethical Dilemmas of Global Development* (Boulder, CO: Westview P, 2003). The study suggests how globally oriented economic thinking affects the traditional forms of local attentions by specific societies. Yet, his use of the term "paradox" suggests not that so many are poor because the well-off have hoarded or are greedy, but that it is not comprehensible that such an imbalance can exist. His book shows that it is quite comprehensible.

CHAPTER TWELVE

The Materiality of Literature and the Contested Subject

I. The Separation of Literature from Language

Language as a means of phylogenetic survival is made up of literary gestures, forms, and genres which appear when language is exchanged. The action of such exchanges, including reading and attending performances, achieves social reattachments and transformed individual autonomy; literary events are occasions of individuals rearranging social relations. As Kristeva and the language researchers observed (see chapters 3 and 5), infants use gestures and have experiences that show a recursive development of mutually dependent metaphorical gestures, usages, analogies, inventions, and playtalk[1] that ultimately find their way simultaneously into language and into new social relations. Recursive (Piagetian) actions of accommodation and assimilation of earlier schemata to new situations may also be described as a continuous process of *translation* that adds up to adult language viability whose schemata then grow as functions of the changing mutually dependent social relations in each person's life. During school years, industrialized cultures try to teach students that referential language has the highest status. Interests in elite rule preserved by these cultures obscure the multifarious functions of language that are at work in literary, figurative ways in the most ordinary conversations as well as in complex texts and performances in elite and popular culture. Literary genres collect the tropes of daily language use as well as the accumulated language gestures of the history of a language.

The university's role in psychosocial translation processes has been to uphold the separation of language understanding from the understanding of other subject matters. Although literature has become a university subject only recently

---

1. This is a neologism that could be translated as *Spielsprache*. Yet I expect that it describes certain kinds of infants and children's speech that never really leaves us. Both these spontaneous forms and the more formal uses of *Sprachspiel* by Wittgenstein (see chapter 3) can be understood as "playtalk" or "talkplay," both of which are different from "language game."

(relative to the eight-century history of the university), literary scholars have followed the academic tradition (followed by scientific researchers since the eighteenth century) of assuming that it is necessary to separate the object of study from its various contexts in order to carry out the study. In the study of literature, literary genres and historical periods are separated from one another and from the different contexts in which they are usually found in order to establish repeatable ways to verify claims. In most cases, these genres and periods are studied without reference to potential ordinary uses of their language.[2] Although not all literary scholars have followed this style, most have and still do. To separate a small piece of the historical literary output from everything else and then to study it in minute detail remains the main technique of scholarly inquiry into literature.

The tradition of isolating texts, genres, types, or historical periods from their several wider contexts shows the deleterious effects of academic handling of texts. Because these texts have been thus sacralized, academic teaching usually bypasses the language actions of literature and, as a result, diminishes literature's ability to teach and motivate its audiences in their own uses of language and social action. This familiar function was suspected by Plato and by many subsequently who have established formal means of censorship.[3] University critics and scholars have claimed dominion over literary texts and assembled them into a sacralized canon. Some literary authorities have treated Plato's anticipation of poets' performances watering the emotions as a real danger in society. They have claimed aesthetic "psychical distance"[4] as an essential feature of critical analysis, and have found a variety of ways, for centuries, to convert literature given as

---

2. When literature is heard or studied in public forums their language effects and relations to ordinary usage are available for study, but they are put aside in favor of the overall reception of the story or the feeling of lyric poetry. For older literature, it is harder, but still possible, to study it in relation to the ordinary language of its time, but when scholars like Lorenzo Valla (see chapter 2, section 2) did just that, he was viewed with suspicion and antagonism.

3. Such as the Roman Catholic Church's *Index librorum prohibitorum*, press and literary censorship in ordinary communities and in totalitarian societies, and film censorship in the United States.

4. Edward Bullough, "Psychical Distance as a Factor in Art and an Aesthetic Principle," *Critical Theory Since Plato*, ed. Hazard Adams (New York: Harcourt Brace Jovanovich, 1971), 754–765. Writes Bullough, "This distance appears to lie between our own self and its affections, using the latter term in its broadest sense as anything which affects our being, bodily or spiritually, e.g. as sensation, perception, emotional state or idea" (755–756). Other criticism before and after Bullough, such as Russian Formalism, has identified the characteristic literary function as the defamiliarization of ordinary experience. Brecht tried to produce a feeling of alienation in his viewers. New Criticism has been successful in teaching a few generations of readers to find the organic unity of literary works as objects independent of the biography and affect of authors and readers.

shared products collectively derived into objects of admiration and worship that are considered to be products of individual genius[5] or other forms of sacralized individual authorship. Because of the elite custody of older works of art, and because of their high prices, these works are honored in exaggerated ways, and, more generally, become isolated from most people's daily lives, whereas popular culture (folklore) is the daily point of access to symbolic materials for most people. In such contexts, aesthetic objects are well integrated into everyday life through song lyrics and a wide variety of entertainments that are found at county fairs, community theaters, and in films.

In 1974, Andrea Dworkin wrote, "Academics lock books in a tangled web of mindfuck and abstraction. The notion is that there are ideas, then art, then somewhere else, unrelated, life."[6] Dworkin describes the academic approach to literature in Platonic terms: ideas, art, and life as hierarchically arranged. Her book, which she describes as a "political action," is about how our culture generally, and not just academic criticism, views literature as uninvolved in the processes of collective survival, growth, and enrichment. As a result, literature (books) does not affect society when placed in academic custody.[7] Working outside the academy, Dworkin considers academic treatments of literature to be unconcerned with truthful writing and unwilling to approach writing as social gestures and initiatives.[8] She views pornography as having material social effects similar in force to those of literature generally, but the effects of pornography are

---

Formal discussions of literature by critics referred to as "experts" or as authorized readers have usually attempted to define literature away from its past popular uses in broadsides, songs, or park performances. Elite social classes have used aesthetics to produce an art reserve for themselves, calling it high art.

5. Christine Battersby, *Gender and Genius: Towards a Feminist Aesthetics* (Bloomington: Indiana UP, 1989), presents a historical survey of the uses of term "genius" as applied to literary authors, shows that geniuses are invariably men, and also that the term is itself understood to be a masculine figure. The habit of noticing or discovering genius is credibly a part of the androcentric custody of literature. Imagine how literature would be treated if authors were not eligible for such characterization, and that they were viewed instead as each having something distinctive to contribute. Wouldn't it be the case that artwork of a similar level of accomplishment has appeared in the humblest contexts, but was not preserved?

6. Andrea Dworkin, *Woman Hating* (New York: Plume, 1974), 24.

7. For Dworkin, "books" includes literature, but also includes all texts available to the public: any text used by people to learn, understand, or reflect.

8. Dale Spender, in *Man-Made Language* (New York: Routledge: 1980), has given similar criticisms, deliberately eschewing membership in the academy because of its male-coded culture. Both writers have been frequently described as going too far and as being personally offensive. Yet few respondents to their works have either asked or answered the question of the real, rational basis for their strong, urgent stand on these issues. As suggested in chapter 2's discussion of Renaissance humanism, there is a tradition of women educating themselves to the point of competence equal to that of their

harmful to women. Dworkin's anger and strong language about the conventional academic treatment of literature and about the collective use of misogynistic pornography are seldom found in academic forums. When her passions are encountered in university contexts, the passions become grounds to discredit her. Yet these feelings and style of writing comprise a key element of her book's substance. Her attitude toward all writing presupposes its materiality, and the absence of this presupposition in the academic treatment of books is one source of her refusal to privilege academic custodians of literature. Because of her sense of the materiality of language, her treatments of literature, pornography, society, and misogyny appear in this early work as a single subject.

Dworkin uses her independence from academic conventions to ask and discuss questions not found in formal criticism. For example, why are literary sources so essential to study established society's historic antagonism toward women? How are the grounds for opposing pornography also the grounds for conceiving of literary readings as material processes that rest on the authors having presupposed the survival and adaptive functions of language? To what extent does the materiality of literature remove erotic writing from its underground location and, as several feminist scholars of erotica have implied,[9] place it back into literary mainstreams, available for all to evaluate? To what extent would the normalization of erotica promote the desacralization of literary texts? Finally, is it possible to expect that literary writing—which any literate person

---

professionally placed male counterparts, a tradition that dates back to classical Greece. Some books by women have survived and have been preserved. Yet it is only in the twentieth century that they have begun to be integrated into university curricula and reread in public media.

9. Two efforts that begin to take pornography texts seriously as part of the uncensored study of gender relations are Angela Carter, *The Sadeian Woman and the Ideology of Pornography* (New York: Penguin, 1979), and Margaret Atwood, "Atwood on Pornography," *Chatelaine* 56 (September 1983): 61, 118, 126. They see a continuum from erotica through pornography; Atwood observes how these genres have been in various forms propaganda and educational tools. Linda Williams, *Hard Core: Power, Pleasure, and the "Frenzy of the Visible"* (Berkeley: U of California P, 1989) is a comprehensive exploration of these different genres and their different purposes. Laura Kipnis, *Bound and Gagged: Pornography and the Politics of Fantasy in America* (Durham, NC: Duke UP, 1996) aims to show that "the differences between pornography and other forms of culture are less meaningful than their similarities," as she provides a social and psychological basis for including erotica and pornography in research plans and curricula (viii).

Nevertheless it is not generally understood how and why erotic genres have remained underground, so to speak. Most will point to religious and moral suppression. But these forces do not account for the circumstances represented by the following fact: police, judges, lawyers, and governors do not crack down on illegal prostitution or pornography because they are the regular consumers of both. It barely needs mention that those shouting most loudly about the immorality of prostitution and pornography are enthusiastic users of both.

can, potentially, assimilate or produce—will move from its present ancillary role in society to one more integrated in small communities, national cultures, and collective action?

Dworkin treats literature as the most reliable record of social values and the most truthful record of how human history has proceeded. Her assumption about the vocation of writers being truth telling[10]—while possibly unfamiliar to modern readers—accords with the history of literacy: those who could write wrote books that people took seriously, such as the Western Bibles. Books have been considered especially valuable mainly because they were material and indispensable to the cultivation of coherent societies. The political value of "many books," recognized by Koheleth as well as by autocrats, led them to use books as material grounds for establishing fraudulent, malignant authority.[11] Dworkin observes, "Many see that the triumph of authoritarian consciousness is its ability to render the spoken and written word meaningless—so that we cannot talk or hear each other speak."[12] Authoritarian interests, which understand the materiality of language and use it deliberately, count on the public's limited access to it. These interests rely on the referentiality of their own language becoming the basis on which the wider population devalues the literary character of its own language—the slang, grammatical departures, figures, tropes, and genres that tell truths without regard to a single code of referentiality.[13] The materiality of books and oral literature has always been an essential feature of their value. Dworkin's claims about what academics do to books could apply to religious custodies of sacred texts and commentaries. Opposing these groups largely because of their historic attachment to unquestioned androcentric principles of living, Dworkin says that "[i]t is the work of the writer to reclaim the language from those who use it to justify murder, plunder, violation."[14] In view of the widespread literacy in our time, Dworkin is especially provoked by universities' continuation of a tradition that still presupposes the elite custody of reading practices. The proposal to banish poets from the republic calls atten-

---

10. "Those of us who love reading and writing believe that being a writer is a sacred trust. It means telling the truth. . . . It means not being afraid, and never lying" (*Woman Hating*, 25).

11. Both the Bible and the *Malleus maleficarum* were printed at the end of the fifteenth century and went through hundreds of printings: they were the most reprinted books for three centuries. If these works alone are considered, it would be hard to draw any conclusion about books but that they have been overtaken and used as instruments of tyranny. Similar but more benign uses of books are made by U.S. presidential candidates to establish a palpable locus of identity and authority for themselves. Once in office, candidates cannot be held to what is in their books.

12. Dworkin, *Woman*, 25.

13. As demonstrated in June Jordan's essay, considered in chapter 6.

14. Dworkin, *Woman*, 25.

tion to the importance of poets: if the poets were not influential, there would be no need for the powerful to fear their influence.[15]

II. The Isolation of Obscene Language

Dworkin's use of the phrase "mindfuck and abstraction" calls attention to a language-use convention that illuminates how the academy inhibits literature from being used in social action. Formal academic criticism, while willing to *cite* any language, is largely unwilling to *use* obscene language as Dworkin uses it.[16] Using obscene language appropriately entails referring to the activities it denotes—bodily functions and actions. Although it is common knowledge—or perhaps an open secret—that so-called street language is used by members of all social classes, a discussion that uses this language routinely is not welcome in academic writing. As George Carlin has repeatedly complained, certain words are not allowed to be uttered on broadcast media, although their meanings and usages are commonly understood by all, including the children who are presumed to need protection from these usages.[17]

Obscene language is street language, and associated with unrefined and impolite—vulgar—behavior and people. What, however, is vulgar? However

---

15. Alicia Suskin Ostriker, *The Nakedness of Our Fathers: Biblical Visions and Revisions* (New Brunswick, NJ: Rutgers UP, 1994), sets tasks that are similar to Dworkin's. Ostriker tries to reclaim the language by rewriting some of the stories in Genesis, saying that the biblical literature itself helped to exclude her from her own traditions, her own culture.

16. The conventions are in fact beginning to change as more women gain access to academic forums and language. Dworkin, Naomi Scheman, Kate Millett, Angela Carter, Laura Kipnis, and others use obscene language in the stride of their formal discussions. Obscene language often appears in high-culture magazines such as *The New Yorker*, although most contributors are not experienced in using obscene language to good effect: the academic principle applies—quotation but little actual usage. Although this is not the first book of its kind, Geoffrey Hughes's *Swearing: A Social History of Foul Language, Oaths and Profanity in English* (New York: Penguin, 1991), provides a rich background and copious instances of how tastes have changed and remained the same at once: "Today an editor is more likely to incur censure for prissiness or cowardice through omitting words which are widely in use (outside the range of ears polite) but nevertheless regarded as not 'fit to print'" (vii). More recent and more comprehensive is Keith Allan and Kate Burridge, *Forbidden Words: Taboo and the Censoring of Language* (New York: Cambridge UP, 2006). In their survey of subject matters with which obscene uses are connected, four of five of these refer to the body, its "effluvia," orifices, uses, and illnesses. The fifth topic is sacred persons and things (1). This study relates the broad variety of behavioral taboos to the verbal censorships and urges the understanding of how verbal taboos are connected to different social means of referring to bodies and bodily functions.

17. Subscriber media do use obscene language and show nudity. This is an important step toward universal access to language. However, only those who can afford subscriber media—computers, cable channels, DVDs, and the like—have access to these language registers in public contexts.

else one may wish to describe it, obscene language makes both referential and metaphorical use of the reference to bodily functions, especially sexual functions, but really including all body parts and functions of both sexes.[18] Furthermore, it will not do for Dworkin to make up an "acceptable" phrase like "mindcoitus" if "fuck" is deemed too offensive.[19] When you convert "fuck" to "coitus" or "intercourse,"[20] it has a new sense, not the sense given by "mindfuck," and it is a term that is not in use. Dworkin's language brings the real human body into view in the way that we experience our bodies—as a source of a wide variety of responses, a mixture of pleasure, inhibition, fear, discomfort, disgust, and fulfillment. "Intercourse" and "coitus" may not be available to all people, but "fuck" is. Because this language so fully recognizes our bodily involvement in the most complex social processes, because it is so familiar to all people[21] and therefore so easily in a position to de-authorize artificial political boundaries, it is censored in the academy, in religious contexts, in so-called polite society, and in the broadcast lanes. There is nothing repellent about obscene language but what has been made so by a specific taboo: one must not call attention to the common human stake in bodily functioning in all social classes and in both sexes. Its censorship and disreputable status are means through which the materiality of language is repressed in the academy and other exclusive contexts. In the various conventions, mores, and rules that repress the language, people lose access to their own bodies, and members of both sexes learn to ignore, despise, or repudiate their physicality and their bodies; we know well how infants are not repelled by feces or other features of their bodies. The repression is not total because there are social spaces for the use of obscene language, and most people use these spaces. The net result is that, in a sense, these words that refer to bodily functions are weaponized, as they suggest the speaker's willingness, or perhaps eagerness, to practice some kind of harm or violation.

---

18. It is polite to refer to tears or saliva, but impolite to refer to snot or even nasal mucus.

19. "Coitus" and "intercourse" include reference to both active and passive roles, whereas "fuck," the transitive verb, places emphasis on the active.

20. As Dworkin did in *Intercourse* (New York: Free P, 1987). The book is an extended reflection on many aspects of heterosexual sex, and continues her habit of changing the registers of the sexual language that is needed.

21. As discussed in chapter 5, the body is the source experience for language that is subsequently used metaphorically on the analogy of bodily functions, including the affectionate functions such as holding and caressing experienced by almost all infants. When adults use adult functions like fucking as metaphors for other behaviors it is an extension of a trope of language acquisition of infancy. For example, the phrase "Fuckin' A!" which means "You're damn right" or, perhaps, "I'm as close in agreement with you as if we were fucking," utilizes people's awareness of the physical certainty that is part of sexual intimacy.

An episode of *Sex and the City* illuminates further the political factors that sustain the category (speech genre) of obscenity.[22] Miranda is in bed with a man who is aroused by so-called dirty talk. He verbally previews his coming sexual activity with and to Miranda, without much effect at first, but they discuss the practice. In their next bed session Miranda learns to emulate the man's verbal tropes, and she notices that she is getting to like it, both for its own pleasures and the stimulating effect it has on her partner. During her explicit verbal foreplay, she includes reference to how she will touch his anus, a practice that was obviously part of their sex together. At that point, her partner shuts down and turns away, they do not have sex at that time, and their relationship ends.

A second relevant vignette in this episode is about Samantha's unsatisfying relationship with her partner. Uncharacteristically, she does not want to have sex with him, but will not say why. They go to a sex therapist, where her male partner forcefully encourages her to explain her behavior, which, as she seems to know, does indeed require an explanation. Exasperated, and ready to end the visits to the therapist as well as the relationship, Samantha blurts out that his penis is too small. This prompts him to walk out of the therapist's office and end their relationship.

In each case the male partner exercised censorship. In the first instance, Miranda learned that sex talk can indeed be sex action,[23] as her partner already understood. But when she accedes to her partner's wishes and begins to use talk as action, she also demonstrates her own independent access to the language, and it embarrasses her partner, who was so badly affected that he could no longer stay in the relationship. Must it not be the case that the male partner already subscribed to a trope of censorship that was violated by Miranda? Might it not also be the case that as a woman, Miranda was not as free as he was to use that talk as action? How else would one view the fact that this gesture by Miranda was sufficient grounds to end the relationship, rather than grounds for further discussion of dirty talk during sex? In this scene it looks as if equal access to language was not available to Miranda, as her partner assumed that his access was definitive.

Samantha's case is related but not the same. Like women's breast size, penis size has also become a factor in, at least, fantasies of sexual fulfillment. But here too, the female partner, after having been implored to speak her mind on an equal basis, is treated rudely for pronouncing that particular judgment. Although men assume the right to discriminate on the basis of breast

---

22. Episode 2, season 2, "The Awful Truth."

23. A key argument made by Catharine MacKinnon in *Only Words* (Cambridge, MA: Harvard UP, 1993), in which she says that because pornographic texts (written and visual) are sex actions, they may be treated by the law as actions accordingly.

size, women are not permitted the same latitude with regard to penis size. If size matters, then both partners should be able to invoke that value and to introduce such judgments into discussion. However, in the vignette, the announcement of the actual judgment was so tortured in advance (Samantha because she expected the result that occurred, and her partner because he did not expect it), that it, too, like Miranda's use of language, was not eligible either to lead to a mutual ending of the relationship, or to be discussed to the point of resolution. "The awful truth," which in these cases may be called "equal sexual candor from women," still causes discomfort for many men. It is similar to the widespread discomfort caused by Andrea Dworkin's repeated uses of obscenity among those who are supercilious toward vernacular references to bodily functions.

Dworkin uses obscene language to write literary criticism of a nonacademic sort. Her use of this language is an instance of sexual candor[24] from women, for the reasons given just above, but also because it is a kind of criticism that, if given by students in contemporary universities, would not be considered acceptable, and students would get lower grades for it, regardless of its coherence, rationality, or substantive interest. Dworkin's having introduced her book as a "political action" followed the principle that writing is one of many conventionally practiced rituals of social self-regulation. Its being about "woman hating" (the vernacular form of "misogyny") and using obscene language as part of the general diction are both gestures not usually found in the critical journals for which most academic critics write.

Men's closer identification with obscene language is related to the assumption of dominion in sexual activity, as well as to the attempt to lend an assumed sexual power to the scene of discussion. Men's writing of pornography has had this function in collective contexts, as in Ovid's *The Art of Love,* and many similar how-to volumes—men's advice to other men about how to get sexual access to women—written on its model to the present.[25] Rarely identified as such, the use of obscene language is also a pornographic gesture, a reminder of the bodily stakes of the conversation or work of literature. However, the use of obscene language alone does not count as a pornographic gesture. Rather its use by men in contexts where androcentrism is in effect—which are almost all contexts—renders that use pornographic.

---

24. By "candor" in this discussion, I mean, generally, "willingness to disclose the full dimensions of their response to the works, in sexual terms."

25. Lynn Hunt and others review the proliferation of such works in the sixteenth century through the Enlightenment. The printing press, like the internet today, licensed men to take ever new initiatives to writing about sex and how to get it. Lynn Hunt, ed., *The Invention of Pornography: Obscenity and the Origins of Pornography, 1500–1800* (New York: Zone, 1996).

D. H. Lawrence's 1928 novel *Lady Chatterley's Lover* shows how the use of obscene language represents a claim of sexual dominion, authority, or superiority. In England and in the United States the work was censored for about thirty years after it was published in Europe. The title of the book names the protagonist, but also names the object of his (and men's) curiosity, the rich, desirable woman who, it is implied, needs to be taught about her so-called animal features. Oliver Mellors, a gamekeeper on Connie Chatterley's estate, becomes her lover. But he also takes the role of her sex teacher. He brings his presumed wisdom from contact with the earth, with ordinary people, and with nature. They do not need a verbal discussion to be drawn to one another, but the narrative puts a great deal of weight on the obscene identification of their relationship.

> "Th'art good cunt, though, aren't ter? Best bit o' cunt left on earth. When ter likes! When tha'rt willin'!"
>
> "What is cunt?" she said.
>
> "An' doesn't ter know? Cunt! It's thee down theer; an' what I get when I'm i'side thee, and what tha gets when I'm i'side thee; it's a' as it is, all on't."[26]

Passages such as this provided grounds for censorship. Yet in spite of the novel's having challenged existing orthodoxies in several ways, it stays with the male fantasy that men know women's bodies and sex better than women do,[27] that even where there is a class difference and the woman is from the privileged class, the man in the lower class has bodily knowledge that Connie Chatterley does not. The use of obscene language thus seems heroic, daring, willing to say the unsaid, and thus lifting both men and women to a new truth. The price of this fantasy is that sex, localized in "cunt,"[28] is separated from the processes of gestation and childcare that are also part of the sexual relation. Lawrence could be credited with an achievement in challenging this language barrier, but this challenge is nevertheless done in the service of the male sexuality that has developed in androcentric societies. Connie Chatterley is portrayed as an ingénue and not as an equal partner. Because Lady Chatterley does not know what cunt is, she must be awakened to her own body by the earthy, earthly man. Yet today, many years after the lifting of the ban on obscene language, people still

---

26. D. H. Lawrence, *Lady Chatterley's Lover* (New York: Signet, 1959), 188.

27. This belief was part of the witch-hunting mentality and was acted out during the examination of the women's bodies, a search for marks of the devil.

28. Later in the novel, Mellors teaches Connie that tenderness "[m]akes 'em [men] really manly": "Ay! it's tenderness, really; it's cunt-awareness" (295). All parts of the sex relation are summed up by "cunt." Dworkin derides this tendency in some men as one of the bases for their use of pornography: "Women is cunt, lustful, wanton" (*Woman Hating*, 57).

wince on hearing "cunt" (the "C word") uttered in public because most of the time it is used in an aggressive, derisive cause.[29]

III. Obscene Literature and the Reading Public

In contemporary times, some widely distributed pornography has been written by women. Dworkin's discussion of Pauline Réage's *The Story of O* and Jean de Berg's *The Image*[30] presents them as a disclosure of what pornography means for women: a portrayal of men's power, "literally over women's dead bodies."[31] Why women undertook to write it, however, bears on what happens when women have access to language.

O's story is told in a deadpan, matter-of-fact style, with the premise that O's suffering comes in the service of her love of René, her first male lover. René's style of speech to O is imperative, often literally, but often presented as a request with an implied threat if not obeyed. O is "trained" at Roissy to accede to any man's request to see, enter, or strike her body. Various instances of such relationships are described. The narrator seems to give just the facts, casting the institution of Roissy as an ordinary school in which O and other women learned to live as sex slaves and who seem willing to accede to being whipped and mutilated: ownership rings are inserted through the flesh of their vaginas. Eventually René gives O away to Sir Stephen, and it is implied that these two men, as well as the groups of men who enter O on any one occasion, are enhancing their connections with one another through the use of O's body. Men's social solidarity is repeatedly cultivated by these events, in which women's bodies are entered, harmed, and scarred. This is pornography in the tradition of Sade, but it is not especially contemporary to either Sade or us. In Ovid's *The Art of Love,* the narrator describes how the gang rape of the Sabine women was made more pleasurable by the resistance of the women and the sense that pain was being inflicted.[32] Dworkin discusses *The Story of O* not because it is

---

29. Eve Ensler's *The Vagina Monologues* (New York: Villard Books, 1998) makes a special effort to change the forbidden status of "cunt" by persuading its audiences to chant the word in unison during performances of the play. Inga Muscio's *Cunt: A Declaration of Independence* (Emeryville, CA: Seal P, 2002) is a serious vernacular discussion whose stress is on the connections between body and society brought to awareness by a willingness to use "cunt" in unselfconscious collective reflection.

30. Pauline Réage, *The Story of O,* trans. Sabine d'Estrée (New York: Ballantine, 1965); and Jean de Berg, *The Image* (n.p.: Wet Angel, 2006). A footnote to Pauline Réage's preface to this text says that the author's real name is Catherine Robbe-Grillet. Both of these works are female-authored texts given within the male pornographic idiom.

31. Dworkin, *Woman Hating,* 63.

32. The narrator, describing the rape, says of the women, "They were carried away, and I dare say their alarm / Gave some of them a piquant extra charm." Ovid, *The Art of Love,* trans. James Michie (New York: Modern Library, 2003), 11.

unique, but because she considers it typical of the androcentric folklore[33] of deciding that in heterosexual sex, women like to be harmed and, generally, take pleasure in pain. "The thesis of O is simple. Woman is cunt, lustful, wanton. She must be punished, tamed, debased. She gives the gift of herself, her body, her well-being, her life, to her lover. This is as it should be—natural and good. It ends necessarily in her annihilation, which is also natural and good, as well as beautiful, because she fulfills her destiny."[34]

Although some are used to characterizing sadomasochism as a perversion and read it as such in this novel, the process of teaching oneself to adapt to circumstances that are harmful because a higher purpose, *love,* is being served, is a common feature of romantic love (and often its basis). It has been taught as such as documented in the history of literature: women who are heroes are patient, await their absent lovers, endure humiliation and pain to prove their love, and accept being separated from their children—generally a series of psychologically extreme sacrifices are routinely demanded of women in situations of romantic love, which is a higher, even godly, purpose subscribed to by all members of society.[35]

This situation is given early in the novel. When O is at Roissy, the school at which she is trained in getting used to being sexually assaulted and whipped, her lover, René, "toying with the leather whip," called her name. "Softly he caressed her hair, smoothed her eyebrows with the tip of his finger, and softly kissed her on the lips. In a loud voice, he told her that he loved her. O, trembling, was terrified to notice that she answered 'I love you,' and that it was true. . . . Rene suddenly ordered: 'Say it again: I love you.' O repeated 'I love you,' with such delight that her lips hardly dared brush the tip of his sex. . . . The three men, who were smoking, commented on her gestures, on the movement of her mouth closed and locked on the sex she had seized, as it worked its way up and down, on the way tears streamed down her ravaged face each time the swollen member struck the back of her throat and made her gag, depressing her tongue and causing her to feel nauseous. It was this same mouth which, half gagging on the

---

33. Freud's view that women are naturally masochistic is not exactly the same value, but it participates in the same androcentric understanding of women.

34. Dworkin, *Woman Hating,* 57–58.

35. In the film *A Price above Rubies* (dir. Boaz Yakin, 1998), the heroine, Sonia, whose access to the language of the jewelry business is admired and coveted by her wily, unscrupulous, and hypocritical brother-in-law, Sender, is invited into the business if she agrees to be his mistress. When taking her for the second time, he says in her ear, "A woman of fortitude who can find? For her price is far above rubies" (a reference to Proverbs 31:10–31: "A woman of valor is worth a price above rubies."). This is a kind of inverse of the pornographic purpose that nevertheless is used as a euphemism for the pornographic moment: "woman of valor" is equated with "woman who is bought, something to which all real women should agree."

hardened flesh which filled it, murmured again: 'I love you.' . . . She received [his discharge] as a god is received, she heard him cry out, heard the others laugh."[36] Many scenes of contemporary pornography show just what was described in *The Story of O*, a woman performing fellatio yet gagging and crying while doing it, obviously in discomfort and struggling both to continue the act and conceal the true dimensions of her discomfort.[37] Dworkin presupposes that the overwhelming amount of pornographic materials is made for men's use.[38] Her formal writings, in collaboration with Catherine MacKinnon, address the normalization of women's discomfort in such scenes and perhaps most male-oriented pornography.

In the text, there is no quotation from René in the form "I love you"—only the foregoing *report* that he declared his love, followed by the quotation from O and the subsequent order from René that she repeat the phrase. A telling phase of the presentation of O is that she is "terrified" that "it was true" that she loved him. Heterosexual sex for O in this work is founded on her fear that her feelings of love enable this depth of interpersonal and bodily humiliation.[39] These are also the grounds for noticing the female authorship of this work. O recognizes the meaning of her feelings in that context and thus poses the issue of romantic love for women: it is a path toward enslavement.

In the earlier, archetypically romantic film, *Casablanca* (dir. Michal Curtiz, 1942), Rick never tells Ilsa that he loves her. When Ilsa says, "I love you," perhaps five times, once with the addendum, "If you knew how much I loved you, how much I still love you!" Rick's response is, "Here's looking at you, kid." At the end of the film, in spite of Rick's having pressed her for her final declaration of love (which is not unlike René's demand for it), he unilaterally declares that they will not fulfill this love, and they will end their relationship. There is

---

36. Réage, *Story*, 18–19.

37. This is the case in the film *Deep Throat* (dir. Gerard Damiano, 1973), but it is also true of today's conventional male-oriented pornographic videos.

38. Several critics (Laura Kipnis, Constance Penley, Linda Williams, and Nadine Strossen) have noticed and written about the increasing address of pornography to heterosexual women, lesbians, and gay males, as well as its production by women. This change has influenced public discussion of the pornography industry. Nevertheless, it remains true today that most publicly available pornography is made by men for men, with women as paid participants. That these women may be exploited is often overridden by the fact that it is one way that many women have come to achieve good incomes as quickly as men can achieve them in non-pornographic industries.

39. Compare this to Freud's view that women "laid the foundations of civilization by the claims of their love." *Civilization and Its Discontents, Standard Edition of the Complete Psychological Works of Sigmund Freud*, trans. James Strachey and Anna Freud, with Alix Strachey and Alan Tyson (London: Hogarth P, 1957), 21:64–145, quotation on 103. Suppose what Freud and others like him thought were claims of love actually were gestures based on the fear that this love would enable the most severe destruction and suffering. What is then to be said about civilization, about *Kultur*?

quite a difference between the mood of *Casablanca* and the mood of *The Story of O*, even remembering that they are about a decade apart. Nevertheless, just as O is rejected in spite of her loyalty to René, so is Ilsa rejected in spite of her loyalty to Rick. How shall the difference between the pornographic story and the romantic film be understood?

In *The Image*, the narrator, a man, is a friend of Claire, who psychologically owns Anne, her sex and whipping slave. With alternate gestures of cruelty and affection, Claire orders Anne to make her body available to her, and subsequently to Jean. Ultimately, Jean "ravages" her anally. Similar to the story of O, the story of Anne is told in a deadpan style, but this story is smaller in scale and involves only the three characters as a opposed to a sort of school run by men teaching women to be slaves. The participation of Claire in this relationship, it is implied, is connected with her relationship with Jean: her mastery of Anne is, in part, a service to Jean. Neither Jean nor Claire is harmed in this relation; only Anne is. This fact leads Dworkin to characterize this work as being about "the [Christian] worship of virginity" combined with the "woman as whore"; Anne represents the "dualism of good and evil, virgin and whore, lily and rose, spirit and nature [which] is inherent in Christianity and finds its logical expression in the rituals of sadomasochism. The Christian emphasis on pain and suffering as the path to transcendence and salvation is the very meat of most sadomasochistic pornography, just as the Christian definition of woman [as whore] is its justification."[40]

Although Dworkin does not consider these works benign, her reading of them is directed toward the subject matter of her book: the attempt to document the tradition and scope of historical misogyny. However, her readings also urge reading the two stories as actions like her own through a feature of them she does not emphasize—their female authorship. In her preface to *The Image*, Pauline Réage wrote, "Even chained, down on her knees, begging for mercy, it is the woman, finally, who is in command."[41] Dworkin takes issue with this opinion and says, instead, that the novel shows that if a "man becomes the master of the master," it "means, despite Reage's assertions to the contrary, that women should serve men, that women are properly slaves and men properly masters, that men have the only meaningful power (in our culture—that power allied to and defined by force and violence), that men created in the image of the Almighty are all mighty."[42]

Jessica Benjamin's discussion[43] of *The Story of O* probes the psychology of O's situation and reaches a formulation different from either Réage's or Dworkin's.

---

40. Dworkin, *Woman Hating*, 73.

41. Berg, *Image*, 5.

42. Dworkin, *Woman Hating*, 70.

43. Jessica Benjamin, *The Bonds of Love: Psychoanalysis, Feminism, and the Problem of Domination* (New York: Pantheon, 1988).

Benjamin's overall subject is "domination," the term used by the Frankfurt School[44] to describe the recursive tyranny in human history. She sees heterosexual relationships as marked by a "necessary tension between self-assertion and mutual recognition that allows self and other to meet as sovereign equals."[45] The term "recognition" is used here in the political and the cognitive senses at once: to assume the other to have standing equal to one's own, as is the case in international mutual recognition. She sees the "necessary tension" as what could replace the customs and mores of domination that now characterize domestic relations as well as collective social and political relations. It might be read as an oblique address to the point made by Virginia Woolf regarding the common male hypocrisy decrying tyranny internationally while practicing it domestically (see chapter 11).

Benjamin reads the story of O as "a web in which the issues of dependency and domination are inextricably intertwined, in which the conflict between the desire for autonomy and the desire for recognition can only be resolved by total renunciation of self."[46] Because O is in love with René, and because she understands the need for this love to survive, she does whatever is necessary to secure the recognition she has already given René. Benjamin intimates that this situation is more than a figure for the ordinary love relation that finds women dominated in one way or another by the men they love, more than that the love itself *means* that women assume the deferential, submissive role. She adds that within such ordinary relationships, submissive roles are often chosen by women and yield satisfaction, whereas fantasies of domination are common among those who do not actually practice it.[47] Like Dworkin, she eschews the circumstances that actualize such fantasies; like Réage, she recognizes the female choice to be dominated as a striving for recognition.

Benjamin describes the behavior of the men as thriving on the fact that O's "will" continues to answer their demands for submission. The rituals of domination are the means by which the men "deny their dependency on her."[48] The narrative shows O always choosing to obey. Then, Benjamin observes, "when her objectification is complete, when she has no more will, they can no longer use her . . . they must perform their violation rationally and ritually in order to maintain their boundaries and to make her will—not only her body—the object of their will."[49]

---

44. And by Pierre Bourdieu in *Masculine Domination* (Palo Alto, CA: Stanford UP, 2001), cited in chapter 11.

45. Benjamin, *Bonds,* 12.

46. Benjamin, *Bonds,* 55.

47. Benjamin, *Bonds.* 55.

48. Benjamin, *Bonds,* 57.

49. Benjamin, *Bonds,* 57.

By stressing O's behavior as a series of choices, by describing these choices as acts of will, by showing that the master men *depend* on the slave women, Benjamin's picture is of women remaining *in conversation* with the men. Their bodily compliances are gestural answers, as linguistic as the affirmative "I love you" that O, coerced in her performance of fellatio, uttered early in the narrative. There is a gestural exchange between the men and O and the other women. The various forms through which O complies with her slave status are also forms in which she continues to strive for recognition. In her case, there is no repression as there is for the men, whose denial of dependency is the same as what Fineman cited as applying to authoritative men in ordinary places of work.[50] The women are choosing pain as the means of perseverance through this intolerable circumstance. But here again, romantic love[51] qualifies as a specification of an intolerable circumstance: women use access to language, which I substitute for Benjamin's "will," to *live through* the machinery of objectification and continue to demand recognition.[52] The story itself does finally imply the destruction of O; but its having been told by women is a salient change from similar stories told by men.

IV. The Double Voice and the Materiality of Literature

Two female authors writing literary pornography at a moment when secular, feminist arguments against pornography (such as those of Dworkin and Mac-Kinnon[53]) have not yet appeared in public discussions suggest a reading different from Dworkin's and perhaps closer to Benjamin's. In view of the overwhelming power of the ideology of religiously derived romantic love (identified as such

---

50. See chapter 11, section 4.

51. According to Benjamin, "O's great longing is to be *known,* and in this respect she is like any lover, for the secret of love is to be known as oneself" (*Bonds,* 60).

52. Reconsider in this context the semiotic (sensorimotor) period in infancy described by Kristeva, and the "obedience" Anne Sullivan evinced from Helen Keller (see chapter 5). None would describe the infant's relation to the caregiver or Helen's relation to Anne as slavery. Instead, each submissive figure uses a gestural vocabulary that also takes part in motivated gestural conversations. If infantile love is understood to be a simulacrum or early template of adult love, one finds nothing strange (or perverse) in the relentless striving of O for ordinary human recognition.

53. Dworkin's and MacKinnon's arguments against pornography appear in (among other sources) *Pornography and Civil Rights: A New Day for Women's Equality* (Minneapolis, MN: Organizing Against Pornography, 1988). The actions they took to try to curtail its production radically are detailed in their volume *In Harm's Way: The Pornography Civil Rights Hearings* (Cambridge, MA: Harvard UP, 1997). These hearings were trying to prepare the way to enact legislation against the production of pornography on the grounds that women were harmed physically by participating in such productions. The legislation did pass briefly, but now it is no longer in effect.

and described by Dworkin), what choices do female authors have in facing the tradition of misogyny in domestic sexual relations and in society at large? Likely the same choice that authors like Herman Melville, Henrik Ibsen, Franz Kafka, Arthur Miller, Angela Carter, Margaret Atwood, Toni Morrison, and many before them who wrote presupposing their oppositional placement in society had. Writing in opposition requires a double voice to be stipulated for the same text: one voice that describes the imaginary scene with fictional reference, and one that has real reference to what authors consider to be social facts.[54] In *Benito Cereno* and *Billy Budd,* for example, the narrative has realistic depositions and accounts of events, creating a documentary feel to the novellas, but they do not present as critiques of military, maritime, or slavery laws. They are, rather, attempts to announce the fundamental uselessness and lawlessness of these laws, attempts to establish the premise that the laws must be opposed on a monumental scale. In the works of each of the writers cited above, some such general reference is present. In Kafka, it is the emptying of the law by collusion of church and state; in Morrison it is the history of slavery in the United States. The double voice appears when the opposition is great, but also where the society has left open a small corridor for writers,[55] still considered potentially seditious, of course, but highly restricted in their potential power by public illiteracy and other more active instruments of censorship.[56] With the receding of illiteracy and women's increasing access to the public language (Kristeva's "symbolic order"), and all people's increasing access to many media, the choices for writers may expand. But in the 1950s, when the two works treated by Dworkin were written, the choices for anyone wanting to approach pornography with the purpose of opening a discussion of gender equality were few. Du Bois's double consciousness emerges in literary works as a double reference—one to one's own group, and

---

54. This is not the same as irony, which is usually more local and more clearly a part of the dramatic situations in the literature. Although writers may be writing in a double voice, one of those voices, the reference to society, is, in Western societies, repressed or rendered secondary in other ways.

55. Society "yields [the Negro] no true self-consciousness, but only lets him see himself through the revelation of the other world. It is a peculiar sensation, this double-consciousness, this sense of always looking at one's self through the eyes of others, of measuring one's soul by the tape of a world that looks on in amused contempt and pity. One ever feels his two-ness . . . two unreconciled strivings; two warring ideals in one dark body, whose dogged strength alone keeps it from being torn asunder." W. E. B. Du Bois, *The Souls of Black Folk* (New York: Bantam, 1989), 3. Du Bois took the permissible small corridor and described the circumstance that could easily also describe O in Réage's novel, as well as the situation of women in any society when they realize how they are placed in relation to men.

56. Dworkin's characterization of academics locking books "in a tangled web of mindfuck and abstraction" describes the complicity of the academy with the more general public fear of the political purposes and effects of literary writings (*Woman Hating,* 24).

the other to the whole group of society, one's own group included. The writings of Réage and Berg begin to make political sense, rather than just pornographic or allegorical sense, if this double reference of their narratives is presupposed.

For women observing that the social choices permitted them often add up to enslavement that is rarely recognized as such, the oppositional gestures of the double voice announces the material role of writing as a challenge to practices and values that jeopardize writers. The more general reference in both the Réage and Berg novellas therefore must be to the ordinary practices and feelings of romantic love—the nuclear family, courtship, marriage, and vows of love for a lifetime (even with new language in the marriage promise marking the equality of status for husband and wife).[57] The necessity of suffering as Dworkin formulated it is part of this ideology as soon as a religious context frames love relationships. Although secular marriages do not always rationalize inequality today, such was not the case when the two novellas were written. Sexual practices still carried with them the sadomasochistic connotation that is preserved by the language of sex—its routine obscenities, and perhaps most of all by the transitive meaning of "fuck": until recently it has been strange to say that a woman fucked a man, or that any so-called passive partner did the fucking.[58] The roles of active and passive in sex—ones that obtained in classical Greek and Roman times—have barely changed, although series such as *Sex and the City* recognize some change. The passive role in sex marked by the grammatical passivity (of being fucked) is also seen as membership in a lower-status social class.[59] Today, moreover, the common word for entry into another body has been "penetrate," which misidentifies the process of entering, especially under consensual conditions. Yet the routine use of "penetrate" still recalls the romantic sense of the male hero having to overcome obstacles to get to his female love object and adds a dimension of strength and force that does not correspond to ordinary conditions during intercourse: there is no need to penetrate another body in order to

---

57. Toni Morrison proposes that any literary work necessarily references, in some way, the whole of society. With this premise, she can reread American literature, enriching it by showing its references to the Africanist presence. If Morrison's premise is transposed to the reading of these works about women's enslavement by men, the reference to the whole society must then point to the abiding ideals and actual practices of romantic love. Toni Morrison, "Unspeakable Things Unspoken: The Afro American Presence in American Literature," *Michigan Quarterly Review* 28.1 (Winter 1989): 1–34; *Playing in the Dark: Whiteness and the Literary Imagination* (New York: Vintage, 1990).

58. As observed by Eva Cantarella and other scholars of antiquity, the enduring sexual categories are passive and active, rather than hetero and homosexual. The figure who is passive, whether male or female, is necessarily the one lower on the social and political hierarchy. Eva Cantarella, *Bisexuality in the Ancient World* (New Haven, CT: Yale UP, 1988).

59. This is one reason for the heroic feeling assumed by Oliver Mellors toward his higher-class lover.

enter it, regardless of which orifice is entered. Whatever fantasies may attach to ordinary sexual activity, its success depends on cooperation between partners or perhaps on ironic playful teasing, but in any case not on antagonism or stubborn resistance. The use of the word "penetrate" perpetuates the traditional androcentric conception of sex as fundamentally violent and harmful—a fantasy attributed by Freud to children. The teaching of violence to children took place in Freud's time more ordinarily through practices of corporal punishment,[60] and, for all we know, adults as well as children throughout history have arrived at erroneous readings of sexual activity.[61]

Female-authored pornography about women's submission to comprehensive social humiliation and bodily mutilation does not fit the androcentric template made by Sade, even if it may seem to include some of his characteristic motifs.[62] The same text is speaking in two different voices to a general constituency and to a female constituency (or any comparable group assumed to be in the subordinate role in society). Dworkin explicated the voices addressed to the public in both novellas. But when she disagreed with Réage's comments in the preface to *The Image,* she may not have considered *herself* part of Réage's readership, although obviously she is. If Réage's and Berg's voices were also understood to be ironic, Dworkin as a fellow protester would be one of those addressed through the more comprehensive reference of the narrative. An emotionless narration, which we can discern in many writers that are familiar, such as Flaubert, is a sign or a clue about a more general reference of the narrative.[63] This style of narrative, when giving accounts of outrageous events, urges the search for a wider supporting context in which these events live. This context is less the ideology of sacrifice and suffering expected of women than it is the recursive sacrifice and suffering that has already taken place in recorded history in millions of people's daily lives—domestic and public, and regardless of which religious ideology is in effect—and then lied about as admirable and desirable: "natural and good." Although Réage's (pseudonymous) voice claims a success for Anne and by implication for O in Réage's own story, the success belongs to the authors

---

60. Discussed in detail by Alice Miller, *For Your Own Good: Hidden Cruelty in Child-Rearing and the Roots of Violence,* trans. Hildegarde and Hunter Hannum (New York: Noonday P, 1990).

61. Since serious talk about sex has been censored in our culture for who knows how long, there is no language context or vocabulary to cope with widespread misinformation and fantasy about sex. There is no language to adapt to this misunderstanding of our bodies, to this "discrepancy," and to create understanding in our intimate relationships.

62. Angela Carter, discussed in section 7, proposes a more complex reading of Sade, with particular attention to the ways women are portrayed, and with the purpose of noticing the political roles such genres played in androcentric societies.

63. Any sort of narration might provide such guidance toward general reference. The deadpan has its own uses.

language, because the context is literary: saying how the society is arranged prevents denial and makes the exposing language available for public use. The language is not given out as an instruction to a privileged group, but presented to the total reading audience as a way of identifying the readership's collective circumstances. The subaltern group will hear and get the double voice. Yet anyone who understands it, subaltern or not, is also in a position to recognize the alarm and to emerge without announcing personal mystification at the events. The political role of the double voice identifies the social gesturing (perhaps in pantomime) and the materiality, rather than the fictionality, of the literature. Its language is a model for describing and opposing simultaneously.[68] Although Dworkin's writing is itself effective as a protest, she does not view the female-authored pornographies as protests, as using the language as a material, gestural social protest and therefore as political actions like her own books.[69] In fact, the two works were so extreme (relative to other contemporary pornography) when presented in public that critics were fooled: they continued to treat the works as aesthetic objects and began to approach the position that Réage offers ironically.

Dworkin cites the 1966 *Newsweek* reviewer (unidentified) who observed that the perversity of allowing the body to be "ravaged, exploited, and totally possessed can be an act of consequence, if it is done with love for the sake of love." This use of love by the reviewer, Dworkin observes in disagreement, derives from the Western religious tradition:

> Any clear-headed appraisal of O will show the situation, O's condition, her behavior, and most importantly her attitude toward her oppressor as a logical scenario incorporating Judeo-Christian values of service and self-sacrifice and universal notions of womanhood, a logical scenario demonstrating the psychology of submission and self-hatred found in all oppressed peoples. O is a book of astounding political significance.[70]

Religious love is an ideology calculated to exploit the impulse of O and women more commonly (although not, as Dworkin implies, universally) to go to extremes of self-sacrifice in the service of love. The language of love, when

---

the men who are supposed to sit in judgment on me.'" Franz Kafka, *The Trial*, trans. Willa and Edwin Muir, and E. M. Butler (New York: Modern Library, 1957), 64–65. Pornography *is* the law, and the sex is depicted, to Josef K., as unattainable. The writer's own language exposes the degeneracy of the law by affiliating it with the sexual failure of marriage.

68. Another recent example of "describing and opposing" is Salman Rushdie's *Satanic Verses* (New York: Picador, 1988), which put him on the run.

69. Except as imitations of male pornographers.

70. Dworkin, *Woman Hating*, 56.

and to some readers,[64] not to their protagonists; it is a successful, social use of language by a minority in a context of overwhelming tyranny.

Here is an analog for the narrative stances of Réage and Berg. In Kafka's one-paragraph vignette "The Vulture," the narrator starts to complain that a vulture was hacking at his feet; a stranger offers to get a gun, aware that it would take too long. The narrator describes how the vulture understands the whole situation and then observes, "[I]t took wing, leaned far back to gain impetus, and then, like a javelin thrower, thrust its beak through my mouth, deep into me. Falling back, I was relieved to feel him drowning irretrievably in my blood, which was filling every depth, flooding every shore."[65] The narrator of "The Vulture" describing his own death enacts his words overcoming the vulture—he has the language—in contrast to the rational but ineffective passer-by, who needs a gun. Repeatedly, the verbal success of Kafka's language is the forthright naming of the outrageous and intolerable circumstances of his own life as a member of the "penal colony"—a society in which he was living in opposition.[66] The execution of Josef K. in *The Trial* belongs in this category: the narration of the endless, pointless search for justice—highlighted by Josef's finding pornography in the law books[67]—is a triumph of narrative language, the deadpan rationality of the

---

64. Benjamin might count as one of these readers. However, because she does not "see" a double voice in these narratives, she describes O's struggle as "paradoxical," briefly likening her fate to those of saints and martyrs (*Bonds,* 60). She also describes the simultaneous wish for autonomy and mutual recognition as also paradoxical, this term, in her usage perhaps pointing to pessimism about the likelihood of overcoming the domination. There is no paradox in wishing for both autonomy and mutual recognition as a formula for just relations between sexes.

65. Franz Kafka, *Complete Short Stories,* trans. Tania and James Stern (New York: Schocken, 1999), 442–443.

66. In discussing the history of language and slavery in antiquity, Deborah Levine Gera observes that "mastery of language and mastery of persons go hand in hand," referring to the naming power of slaveholder. Deborah Levine Gera, *Ancient Greek Ideas on Speech, Language, and Civilization* (New York: Oxford UP, 2003), 208. Kafka's language, as well as the writings of Réage, Berg, Morrison, and the other authors enumerated above, performs the assertion of equality that their characters do not perform: the literature performs a political action opposite to the actions depicted or represented in the literature. The production of literature revokes the subordinate status of the literature's constituencies.

67. Josef K. wants to have a look at the magistrate's law books. He remarks, "How dirty everything is here!" Then "[h]e opened the first of them and found an indecent picture. A man and a woman were sitting naked on a sofa, the obscene intention of the draftsman was evident enough, yet his skill was so small that nothing emerged from the picture save the all-too-solid figures of a man and a woman sitting rigidly upright, and because of the bad perspective, apparently finding the utmost difficulty even in turning toward each other." The second book "was a novel entitled: *How Grete Was Plagued by Her Husband Hans.* 'These are the law books that are studied here,' said K. 'These are

used in religious contexts, references transcendental love, God's love.[71] The self-sacrifice of Jesus is in the name of love, and it is this model through which sexual exploitation is rationalized. Nuns are "married" to God. Priests lead "celibate" lives. The *Newsweek* reviewer follows the guidelines of this ideology—namely, he or she reads the suffering as consequential because it is done both in the name of love and to sustain a particular love relationship. The *New York Times* reviewer of the novel, Eliot Fremont-Smith—who is cited in a blurb on the back cover of a paperback edition of the novel—is similarly deceived by this ideology. He characterizes the pornographic dimension of *The Story of O* as "the deliberate stimulation of the reader as a part of and means to a total, authentic literary experience." The question is, which reader? If the reader is male, one sort of stimulation—arousal—may be expected; if she is female, the stimulation exists only on the premise that women will take pleasure in crying and gagging during sex and in harming each other (and not men) to the same extent that men take pleasure in harming women. Is it plausible that this is true? The reviewer writes as if the reader were male, and not considering that the referencing of this work, like that of many utopian novels (or fantasy or science fiction), is to a non-marginal existing collective state of affairs. The reviewers see no ambiguity or chicanery in the invocation of the ideal of "love," nor do they doubt the pornographic presentation of it by Réage in its political identity. As such, the narrative may be understood to appear through two voices: one addresses those (men) involved in androcentric heterosexuality, and the other addresses those (female readers) most likely to be appalled at being in a position to identify with a figure such as O—"terrified" at noticing the circumstances under which women say "I love you." These readers will see, because it is in their political interest, how the obscene language and sexual explicitness in this work portrays the enslavement of women (and men, for that matter, obsessively denying their dependency) who hold love as an ideal. The value of *The Story of O* is that, more than mainstream pornography written by men meant to arouse and teach men self-interested sexual values,[72] its language and its ironic stance utilizes the

---

71. Dworkin is likely mistaken in identifying this love as Judeo-Christian; it does not appear in Jewish lore or Jewish texts. A discussion of this issue is found in Daniel Boyarin, *Unheroic Conduct: The Rise of Heterosexuality and the Invention of the Jewish Man* (Berkeley: U of California P, 1997).

72. Such as the novels of Henry Miller. Kate Millett finds considerable value in Miller's writing, but as a "compendium of American sexual neuroses, and his value lies not in freeing us from such afflictions, but in having had the honesty to express and dramatize them." Kate Millett, *Sexual Politics* (New York: Doubleday, 1970), 295. Contemporary film and video porn from adult stores and from the internet can be identified as being addressed mainly to men: women presented as and acting completely available to men, merely demonstrating their more general availability with sample performances with the men on the screen. It presupposes the interest (and desire) of the onlooker by

action of the language (which deceived the two reviewers cited) to "stimulate" (that is, arouse). In addition to the stimulation effect, the obscene reporting of the obscene circumstances refers to an equally palpable circumstance among the readership—the continuing willingness of young women and many men to bet their lives on heterosexual love in holy matrimony and on other secular contexts of commitment. This risk continues, in part, because the only public understanding about how sex works comes from pornography. Those who don't view pornography or who conduct sex lives related to their social relationships are not well informed about sex, especially over long periods of time.

Few have read either Kafka or *Story of O* as instances of the social (rather than aesthetic) achievement of language.[73] Unlike the times when historical epics were sung to large audiences, today's epic stories are bought one by one and identified as "fiction," a term that is understood as "not true and meant for amusement." The category of fiction also urges that the story of one or a few figures is exceptional and not conventional. If few are seen to be represented, the individualization by the reader urges viewing the literary figures as imaginary and thus not real. But if the double voice is anticipated, a double reference is implied for the individually identified characters: to themselves and to the class of people in the reader's own society those individuals represent. One way to read the dialogic function of literature would be this: as the fictional reference becomes figurative, the truth function of the literature becomes more palpable. Readers then assimilate the narrative as an interaction of the two voices.[74] The deadpan narrations of Réage and Berg give a studied impression of accurate referential language and individual rationality: only the events beyond the narrators' language seem absurd. Yet, once these events are re-familiarized—placed in the contexts of conventional expectations and, thus, taken as figures of ordinary enslavements of romantic love—neither the obscene language nor the sadomasochistic pornography of these works can be taken as separate or different in social function from the language and references of literature in general.[75] The

---

isolating the sexual activity from all other possible relations that the screen figures may have. Neither Millett's study and assessment, nor Miller's work itself has changed the majority-male audience for pornography or the widely held assumption that the pornography is for men.

73. Some would count literary canonization or other recognition of greatness to be an achievement of language use, but it is not, because greatness judgments are aesthetic. The works are said to be profound or moving, but their *language* is rarely taken as a path to understanding issues that society faces. And the works are usually understood as objects rather than as actions.

74. Presentations of language and literature by Mikhail Bakhtin, Lev Vygotsky, and George Herbert Mead have all recognized the dialogic actions of narrative and the dialogic basis of language in infancy. However, this understanding has remained a minority view.

75. In her comments on Miller, Millett cites Karl Shapiro's 1961 judgment of Miller: "Miller is 'the first writer outside the Orient who has succeeded in writing as naturally

categories "obscene" and "pornographic" cease to be applicable. We *are* dealing with another genre of literature, but are no longer constrained by "mindfuck and abstraction." The literature is using figures from different language registers that describe events barred from public discussion by androcentric protectionism.

The literal reading may be what contemporary men might find in society: those holding a traditional pornographic mindset would read this work just as Dworkin describes: it is "natural and good" that women are enslaved sexually to men because of their love. Furthermore, many could see sadism and masochism as also natural and good, as, at one point, O notices in herself a thrill at hearing the shrieks of pain in other women:

> [A]t Yvonne's first scream O had recoiled and cringed, but as soon as she had started in again and Yvonne's cries had echoed anew, she had been overwhelmed with a terrible feeling of pleasure, a feeling so intense that she had caught herself laughing in spite of herself, and she had found it almost impossible to restrain herself from striking Yvonne as hard as she could.[76]

The narrative describes the bonding that takes place between the women who are whipping each other. Moments like this, which are illuminated by Carol Cohn's descriptions of the pleasure in her having overtaken the detached language of the defense planners,[77] suggests the irony in the narrative voice, as the presumption of androcentrism would urge an estimable degree of credibility. A non-pornographic work such as Margaret Atwood's *The Handmaid's Tale*[78] functions similarly. The presumption of androcentrism might well permit male readers to overlook the figure of the wives overseeing the husband's actual copulation with handmaids as a description of how things *actually* are: men involved in adulterous affairs are usually persuaded that their wives don't know about them, or that they are secret to all except themselves; yet this is usually not the case. The wives are just as likely making silent adjustments and behavior changes in response to the situation.

V. Erotica and Political Action

Historically, erotica has been both androcentric and oppositional in political, social, and cultural contexts.[79] Contemporary approaches to the issue of erotica locate the origin of modern erotica with Pietro Aretino's published drawings

---

about sex on a large scale as novelists ordinarily write about the dinner table or the battlefield'" (*Sexual,* 295). Millett's analysis contests that the sex is "natural" as Miller describes it, but cites Shapiro because she shares a desire for candor in writing about sex.

76. Réage, *Story,* 157.
77. See chapter 11.
78. Margaret Atwood, *The Handmaid's Tale* (Boston: Houghton Mifflin, 1986).

of sexual positions in the sixteenth century.[80] Lynn Hunt's essay collection *The Invention of Pornography* uses this starting point in order to outline a history of how modern pornography may be understood to be part of the slow process of European Enlightenment, with sex writing being used as an instrument of democratic ideology. The connection of sex writing to enlightenment in general became clear in the late eighteenth and early nineteenth centuries. Although it cannot be overlooked that Greek and Roman erotica have played similarly political roles in their own societies,[81] the beginning of widespread accessibility to mass-produced sex writing and images took place during the Enlightenment in France and other sites in Europe. The claims made by several contributors in the Hunt volume about the political character of erotica also apply to classical erotica. In the slave and illiterate societies of antiquity, most did not have access to the erotica that has survived: the images on walls and dishes tell only that the well-to-do had common access.

The critics in the Hunt volume see the use of pornography to oppose tyranny as not automatically androcentric, but, to some degree, as serving and applying to all people. The contemporary studies of pornography and erotica by figures such as Angela Carter, Margaret Atwood,[82] and Laura Kipnis[83] see present-day changes in the uses and status of pornography; these critics see the materiality of pornography in the contemporary emphasis on the body, which, in turn, is a key process in social gender emancipation. A significant group of feminist critics seeks to bring erotic writing to all people, which means, in part, that sex writing could and should assume an active role in general education as well as in literary education. In some societies, the previously disenfranchised are gaining access

---

79. It could be compared to Marxist revolutionaries, freedom revolutionaries, and world terrorist organizations—each of which participates in similar ideologies of power and domination as the institutions they oppose. Further discussion of this issue appears in the treatment of the Hunt and Jacob's essays later in this chapter. Yet as the historical discussions of Hunt and others suggest, a similar seizing point occurs in the political uses of pornography: somehow, when men exclusively are involved in the processes of social amelioration, sooner or later these processes degenerate into violence and authoritarianism.

80. Lynn Hunt, ed., *Invention;* other pertinent volumes are Joan DeJean, *The Reinvention of Obscenity: Sex, Lies, and Tabloids in Early Modern France* (Chicago: U of Chicago P, 2002); Ian Frederick Moulton, *Before Pornography: Erotic Writing in Early Modern England* (New York: Oxford UP, 2000); Walter Kendrick, *The Secret Museum: Pornography in Modern Culture* (New York: Viking, 1987); and Amy Richlin, ed., *Pornography and Representation in Greece and Rome* (New York: Oxford UP, 1992).

81. As suggested by Aristophanes' *Lysistrata* and later by Ovid's *The Art of Love,* for which he was exiled by Augustus. Aristophanes, *Lysistrata and Other Plays,* trans. Alan H. Sommerstein (London: Penguin Books, 2002).

82. Carter, *Sadeian.*

83. Cited above and discussed below.

to literacy, language, and varieties of understanding traditionally kept out of public access by elite social classes. Sex, like language, is the common practice of all social classes,[84] and the reading and viewing of pornography by members of every social class makes this fact obvious.

Margaret C. Jacob characterizes post-Renaissance pornography as a mechanization of sexual behavior, a way of reading sex that resulted from the influence of materialist philosophy.[85] She relates the eighteenth century's interest in pornography to the authority of the newly circulating mechanistic view of the universe. Jacob says that

> [t]he conceptual ability to mechanize and atomize physical nature emerged roughly between the 1650s and the 1690s within a single Northern and Western European generation, the same generation that also invented a new materialist and pornographic discourse. The pornographic novel . . . became the vehicle for explaining and inventing sexual bodies now eroticized . . . The novels postulated for the reader a privatized space occupied only by bodies in motion. . . . [T]he pornographic narratives employed philosophical materialism, which their writers extracted from the new mechanical, scientific reading of nature.[86]

A salient feature of Jacob's discussion is that she views the connections of Christianity to the Newtonian mechanical universe as attempts to Christianize the mechanical philosophy, attempts to "retain spirit or immaterial agents as the source and check on motion in the universe."[87] David Noble[88] has discussed the relatively strange forms of spirituality found in the writings of some of the principal figures of the scientific revolution. Jacob sees this period—the "long eighteenth century"—as intensifying the traditional bifurcation of spirit and matter because of the tacit and repressed conviction that materialism has acquired new authority through empirical and mathematical science. Jacob describes how "[b]oth the materialist and the pornographer were censored, arrested and jailed and their books confiscated because their literature . . . challenged traditional hierarchy, and, frequently, did so intentionally."[89] Also related is the fact that

---

84. A fact in plain sight, yet seldom treated as an issue for comprehensive attention.

85. Margaret C. Jacob, "The Materialist World of Pornography." *Invention,* ed. Lynn Hunt (New York: Zone, 1996), 157–202.

86. Jacob, "Materialist," 158. Also, novels generally offered a "privatized space" that almost asked for erotic uses.

87. Jacob, "Materialist," 161.

88. David F. Noble, *A World without Women: The Christian Clerical Culture of Western Science* (New York: Knopf, 1992), 232; and Elizabeth Potter, *Gender and Boyle's Law of Gases* (Bloomington, IN: Indiana UP, 2001), chapter 10.

89. Jacob, "Materialist," 162.

witch-hunting in Europe was at its height during the period from 1650 to 1790. Although the work of the women who oversaw birth, illness, and care of the dying was highly valued, it was also perceived as a potential threat. Such work had a greater obvious practical value than the traditional spiritual truths that sustained religious authorities.

The materiality of both the inanimate and animate universe moved into plain sight. Churchmen, still fairly influential, understood that if the truth of materiality became a principle overtaken by the total population, religious authority would be reduced. Scientists with ties to religious authority understood that same thing and were reluctant then, as now, to say that no, there is no god. Thus, the everyday-experience understanding of the materiality of life gets suppressed, in part, and mostly repressed. The erotic genres that depend overtly on the materiality of both sex and of language are relegated to a morally diminished, open-secret status, where they may continue to exist but must not be accorded any recognition of value and legitimacy. They must continue to be associated with man's evil nature, with man's inner depravity, with man's desires for a life of unchecked lust. In this connection, it should be repeated that, three centuries earlier, the *Malleus maleficarum* of 1487, commissioned by the pope and authored by two bishops, make the same imaginary yet fearful attributions to women.

Jacob relates the Enlightenment values of individualism, privacy, and democracy to the use of pornography. The urban, mercantile "newly literate public"[90] was a large constituency that had access to printed pornography, regardless of what measures were taken to hide it. Jacob gives some evidence that the eighteenth-century productions of pornography were collective efforts, and women were voluntarily involved. This is also its twenty-first-century social identity: a subversive popular and folk art whose voluntary female involvement has become increasingly a matter of public knowledge. The corporate distribution of pornography—the hotel chains and mainstream cable companies that profit from it—has transformed the United States from a site with a thousand X-rated movie theaters to a site with hundreds of millions of theaters located in the private spaces of homes, hotels, and any internet viewing device one has. Advanced scientific and technological knowledge is associated with the broadening use of pornography, and this is only partly because both the corporations and the computer industry are dominated by men.[91]

A process of socialization exists today in the United States that is also characteristic of eighteenth-century England: a panicky intensification of religious devotion alongside the flocking to, and increasing number of, pornographic

90. Jacob, "Materialist," 191.
91. Frederick S. Lane III, *Obscene Profits: The Entrepreneurs of Pornography in the Cyber Age* (New York: Routledge, 2001).

genres. The same habits of suppression and repression continue as, on the one hand, sex is selling practically every product and service, whereas pornography remains disreputable even as it proliferates. These are the circumstances in which Laura Kipnis undertook her study of pornography, *Bound and Gagged*. She, like several other present-day scholars of erotica, opposes the view of erotica as malignant, and argues forcefully that the contexts of its appearance and use, rather than the material itself, render it a morally diminished enterprise. Moreover, as is shown by some of the citations from her study, she is one of those academics who have become willing to use fluently the obscene language needed to tell the story truthfully. Her own academic standard is different from that of most scholars: even if she does not fully share the views of figures such as Andrea Dworkin, she, like Dworkin, recognizes the academic participation in the devaluation of books and language.

The nub of Kipnis's study is that writers and sellers of pornography are scapegoated in order to continue to conceal male domestic violence, official misogyny, and the inclination, even desire, in official government circles to go to war. Society supports such scapegoating in part because the pornographer is always a member of an out-group, but also, and almost never admitted, because the tradition of the routine use of violence must be concealed and protected.[92] More than most critics, Kipnis takes pains to present pornography as a relatively benign materialization of collective fantasies. She defends anyone's fantasy life as a necessary part of individual and social psychology, and then as something that in no sense can be regulated by law. The case of Daniel DePew is one in which the accused was convicted of a crime about which he had only a fantasy. But the collective social fantasy *about* him enables the violence to be committed against him, even though he himself had not committed a crime. As Kipnis describes, elaborate pains were taken to convict DePew of planning an abduction; the grounds for this effort was the knowledge that his own sex life, consensual as far as anyone had been able to determine, would naturally lead to the abduction and harm of children.

In defending the career of Larry Flynt, the publisher of *Hustler*, Kipnis takes up the line of thinking found in the Hunt collection to show that Flynt's por-

---

92. Kipnis writes, "Although the fact is that children are at far greater risk of abuse, violence, and murder by their own parents than anyone else, cultural panic about child safety attaches far disproportionately to the monster-figure of the pedophile stranger-abductor" (*Bound*, 6). She continues, "The overarching fantasy is that the powerfully monstrous bad thing is somewhere else, that it can be caged, and most crucially, that it's 'other.' Violence isn't here, its *there*. No, over *there*. Not in the family, but in that Satanic cult disguised as a daycare center; not the criminal justice system, but in the psychopathic stranger. Violence never has a history; it's born from itself, residing in the random and the anomalous, not the mundane and the everyday" (*Bound*, 7).

nographic effort is a present-day instance of the political opposition to state and religious hierarchical tyranny, in which academics are participants:

> *Hustler* is simply allergic to any form of social or intellectual affectation, squaring off like some maddened pit bull against the pretensions and the earning power of the professional classes. . . . It's pissed off by liberals and particularly nasty to academics, who are invariably prissy and uptight. (An academic to his wife: 'Eat your pussy? You forget, Gladys, I have a Ph.D.') . . . [I]t smears the rich against the wall, particularly rich women, and dedicates many, many pages to the hypocrisy of organized religion, . . . the scam of the virgin birth, and the bodily functions of nuns, priests, and ministers.[93]

Figures such as Flynt could not sell their wares if its (mostly male) readership were not comprehending of the truth of the sexual derisions offered in the magazine, were not aware that reading *Hustler* is a form of self-examination as well as of self-expression. It is that fact that demands further discussion by those in universities who are in position to discuss and research this fact: why do the men who enjoy such magazines—that is the professionals and the academics, not to mention the judges, police, politicians, and leaders—continue to want such reading? The nudity? The source for sexual stimulation? These could not be the reasons. All people are curious to see others naked; all are interested in observing others copulate. Few do not want to see. But for the men in question—the academics, the professionals, and the public figures—the division between the sleazy and the dignified is essential to the continued privilege of these men. Any hierarchical power structure demands this division, both for its intrinsic pleasures and for its overarching ability to sustain their political power in society. If, as Freud implied, smutty jokes were pointed equally at men and at women, they would no longer be smutty jokes as we know them. They would be only jokes about or with sexual reference. By itself a joke can be local. But as the magazine shows, the jokes fall into a pattern that is simultaneously androcentric and oppositional, allowing the readers to justify the androcentrism with, and perhaps be distracted by, political irreverence and derision.

When female scholars notice this feature of pornography, it is already a new issue, as some of the academic literature cited in this discussion suggests. Even the most vigorous opponents of pornography, such as Dworkin and MacKinnon, did not advocate censorship of either the language or the making of films: on the grounds that women in pornographic films are physically harmed, Dworkin and MacKinnon advocated for these women. Dworkin wrote that "pornographers

---

93. Kipnis, *Bound*, 141.

are the secret police of male supremacy."[94] This claim is true if either women are harmed in the making of erotica or it appears that they are harmed as part of the film convention. The films would then be encouraging the normalization of male heterosexual assault. The "secret police" remark assumes that all pornographic genres are irretrievably heterosexist, an assumption that is no longer reliable. However, she is also referring to the way ignorant adherence to the ideal of free speech has dematerialized pornography, claiming that since it is only symbolic, people, including some women advocating for free speech,[95] don't face its effects on human bodies: the men who derive sexual fulfillment from watching it, and the women who are exploited by the production of it. This bodily identity of pornography actors has long been true of theater actors, who were understood to live in a permissive class and style, and who today are represented by Hollywood celebrities whose bodies are still arguably their main attraction, and who have led the way toward challenging the traditions of marriage and nuclear families. Dworkin's claim is that because pornography is lied about as being "symbolic," it accedes to an unprecedented authority to teach men to continue to demean women by showing that real sex is necessarily demeaning to women. A destructive ideology enforces, in the secrecy of disreputability, an approach to sex that has always been, as far as we know, part of our tradition.

MacKinnon writes, "There is no such thing as pornography, or any social occurrence, all by itself."[96] Yet she shows that only pornography gets the free speech protection, which gives it a false autonomy. This formulation contradicts the present legal justification for free speech, which assumes that speech can exist all by itself, whereas its action as a bodily exchange is neglected, overlooked, or denied. Speech is deemed not to be harmful (although it may not be benign) just because the words are considered separable from the users of the words. If

---

94. "Against the Male Flood: Censorship, Pornography, and Equality,"(1985) *Feminism and Pornography*, ed. Drucilla Cornell (New York: Oxford UP, 2000), 19–38, quotation on 29. Frances Ferguson presents a more abstract yet still related formulation: "[T]he offense of pornography is not its public display of sexually explicit content nor is it the challenge to what we now call 'community values.' Rather, when pornography really deserves to be called pornography. . . it is because pornography constitutes not just a message but an environment, a set of circumstances that succeeds in identifying what one is with what one is worth in an inflexible way." Frances Ferguson, *Pornography, the Theory: What Utilitarianism Did to Action* (Chicago: U of Chicago P, 2004), 156. This statement could be read as an academic translation of Dworkin's complaint that "woman is cunt" in addition to the "male supremacy" statement above. Regardless, Ferguson's viewing pornography as an "environment," a reference not in plain sight, says that we live in a pornographic culture, and she shows that the modern literature of Sade, Flaubert, Lawrence, and Easton Ellis are literary demonstrations that this is the case.

95. Such as Nadine Strossen, *Defending Pornography: Free Speech, Sex, and the Fight for Women's Rights* (New York: Scribner, 1995).

96. MacKinnon, *Only Words*, 18.

you admit that pornographic words are acting, any other words must also be acting in order to be words to begin with. This is the same kind of separation, in a specific context, as the more general assumption that holds thought and language separate.[97] There is only language, which always involves persons whose minds and bodies are just one entity.

MacKinnon and Dworkin opposed pornography on the grounds that the actors are being exploited and harmed. This approach has been successful in the following way: now, the large-scale pornography production companies in California take pains to protect the actors against illness, while the production process is itself no longer underground. Furthermore, this form of advocacy has made room for new creators of erotica that explores women's fantasies, desires, and pleasures in sex to the same degree that traditional pornography had focused on what pleases men who grew up in androcentric societies. MacKinnon and Dworkin succeeded in calling attention to the materiality of pornography, and thus to a potential common and mutual interest in it on the part of all genders. Through their readings and political action, MacKinnon and Dworkin brought attention to the combination of bodies and words that is found in the language and in the sexual activity of all people.

VI. Literature and the Contested Subject

The literature of Marquis de Sade is obscured by the common term "sadism."[98] Masochism, a term whose usage derives from the name and work of a later writer, is commonly linked to sadism, and the combination of the two terms, sado-masochism, identifies the convention of a sexual practice, Bondage-Discipline/Domination-Submission/Sadism-Masochism (BDSM).[99] The words, taken from the names of people who wrote some of the "many books" of which there has been "no end," mark the crossroads of language, the contested subject matter, with people, the "contested" subjects. In general, the works of Sade have not been a part of academic study, and they are seldom part of university reading lists. Recently, in the work of several critics, Sade's writing has been folded into literary and social developments in the post-Enlightenment West.[100] Attention to Sade's writing has changed the subject of language. The works have only

---

97. See chapter 4.

98. Imagine coming upon his work without having heard and used this word.

99. If the length of the history of the human species is in the hundreds of thousands of years, it could not be the case that any one sexual practice is a product of civilizations within recorded history.

100. In addition to the work of Frances Ferguson, see Thomas DiPiero, *Dangerous Truths and Criminal Passions: The Evolution of the French Novel, 1569–1791* (Stanford, CA: Stanford UP, 1992), 333–374; David Morris, *The Culture of Pain* (Berkeley: U of California P, 1991), 224–243; and Carter, *Sadeian.*

come out of censorship in the last several decades. The fact that they have been censored to begin with shows that Plato's hypothesis has remained acceptable: language and literature that is likely to stimulate strong feeling and participate in political action must not be accessible by the public.

The reduction of censorship has coincided with the increased access of women to academic life. In part because of Dworkin's argument that pornography demeans women, and in part because women with access to language have begun to conduct critical exchanges about such material and of Sade's writing in particular, reading Sade's work today shows how broadly access to language has been limited, even recently. His language and his literature have spoken the unspeakable, and his kinship with other writers who have written with similar values has been represented by Ferguson in the same vein. As discussed earlier in this chapter, yet other well-recognized writers may be characterized as such: *affirming the use of language as a means of replacing the conventions of political domination that are so common as to be unspoken.* David Morris observes,

> Rhetoric in Sade's fiction relentlessly sabotages logic: nothing can be left unsaid. At the end of the enormous novel that bears her name, the voracious libertine Juliette states this Sadean ideal with deceptive literalism: "It is necessary for philosophy," she observes, "to say everything." . . . The eroticism he celebrates at such length embraces a horror that ordinarily deprives us of speech. Sade in effect refuses to let us suppress what we cannot speak or understand.[101]

This is an uncommon way of reading Sade: everything must be said. The more common stance on his work is that it promotes the perversions of pleasure in inflicting pain and punishment, particularly on women by gangs of men and by powerful individual men. As with any literature that tells of suffering, pain, and destruction, there is a choice to read it as self-indulgence or as a warning or as a report or as a combination of these.[102] How one chooses depends on the contexts of reading, on the public status of the contested subject. So on the matter of the substance of the work Sade's writing is like any other literature: what it teaches depends on how various social and political constituencies read it.[103]

---

101. Morris, *Culture*, 227. The latter is Morris's translation of "La philosophie doit tout dire." Another translator reads the sentence as "Philosophy must never shrink from speaking out," which rightly suggests the political weight of the original, though not the dramatic and true sense of the more literal reading (327). However, since the common culture of the West censored Sade, there is no need to insist on a best translation, as they each teach something that applies to Sade's work.

102. As the works of Defoe or Melville or anyone else, for that matter, may be read.

103. Frances Ferguson reads Angela Carter thus: "One must inherit things like pornographic texts not to replicate them but to accumulate a range of choices for one's own

The issue is not quite the same with regard to the principle that everything must be said. Although there are many occasions on which circumspect verbal behavior is needed, literature is not one of them.[104] On the contrary, the writing of (many) books is a key aspect of the ubiquitous bath of language in which all persons and societies grow.[105] The discussion of pornography has become a discussion of the extent to which it is fantasy, a prescription for behavior, or a description of behavior. Generally, it is all of these, and scholars have made it their business to identify these different contexts of reading. Because it is all of these, the saying, the speaking, and the writing become the key acts of civilization. Once something is said and heard, people gain access to the language and then are in position to act in other ways. Articulating violence is necessary in order to recognize that people can choose to reject it instead of accepting it as inevitable.

Sade himself did not commit any great crimes, yet he was jailed and then committed to an asylum. He was a rich male aristocrat who wanted to enjoy life, yet was always unsatisfied, as he persisted in the search for a life that was at once provocative of conventional standards, yet differing from the lives of others like him only in its public exposure.[106] His principal difference from other aristocratic men was that he was an obsessive writer, and this is one reason he was taken seriously by Angela Carter.

Carter promotes literature in ways similar to Dworkin's: for its teaching the public about the public conventions of lying and how to identify them. Literature teaches how to read a text and provisionally stipulate its constituency. It teaches which groups' language to suspect and how to answer this language. Sade is a welcome body of work in the same sense that Reage, Kafka, Ibsen, or Morrison are welcome: that is, by calling attention to the process of articulating people's experiences and histories. Gossip falls into this description: the way it is said also teaches what is said, but there is no separating the "way" from the "what."

Carter seizes Sade's work as an occasion to expose the mendacious universalism in the articulation of public mythologies.[107] She reads characters in pornographic

---

'making' of 'history.' One preserves and publishes Sade because writing like his may come in handy, may come to look like an expression of the value of unrepressed sexuality" (*Pornography*, 77–78). This is how Kate Millett reads Henry Miller. Specifically, the censored works give *language* choices, rather than just stories or imagery.

104. This last sentence is my translation of the term "poetic license."

105. Ecclesiastes says, "[T]he making of many books would have no end" (12:12). This is discussed at the beginning of chapter 7.

106. The eighteenth-century picaresque genre, of which several of Sade's works are examples, is a reasonable simulacrum of Sade's life, especially its relentless narcissism.

107. "Mythology" is used here as Martha Fineman describes it. The "foundational myth" is an abstract presupposition, cited in chapter 11. Martha Albertson Fineman, *The Autonomy Myth: A Theory of Dependency* (New York: New P, 2004), 25.

works as "mythic abstractions" devoid of resemblance to real people.[108] She joins the collective identity of the archetype to the individual role of the fantasy: "an archetype is only an image that has got too big for its boots and bears, at best, a fantasy relation to reality."[109] The archetypes under consideration are those of gender, and she reads Sade, himself enslaved by these images and fantasies, as one who explodes verbally to break every known social convention and to record, perhaps as a language/thought-experiment, the feel and weight of this destruction. This verbal proliferation is not the result of forced incarceration. Sade's attitude toward violence is reflected by his having been arrested for opposing the death penalty in the post-Revolution period. As critics have noted along the lines of Jacob's argument presented earlier in this chapter, the exaggerated scope of his verbal output is a response to the Enlightenment itself and its endemic hypocrisy.[110] His work is perhaps an answer to J. L. Talmon's mystification[111] at how the Enlightenment failed to move beyond, then and later, authoritarian rule and war. The gender archetypes, Carter notes, "are culturally defined variables translated in the language of common usage to the status of universals."[112]

The inertia of the gender universals has been an obstacle to realizing Enlightenment ideals. Carter says that the universals of gender "confuse the main issue, that relationships between the sexes are determined by history and by the historical fact of the economic dependence of women upon men."[113] In more recent times, she continues, when women could earn a living on their own, a broad repression set in, abetted by "generations of artists" who have "contrived" to promote the "love-play of the archetypes." "[L]ulled by dreams, many women willingly ignore the palpable evidence of their own responses."[114] Both men and women's subscribing to the false universals of gender is the formula for the perpetuation of androcentrism even as most women know the terms of their

---

108. Carter, *Sadeian,* 6.

109. Carter, *Sadeian,* 6. Here is the theme of exaggeration that appeared in Derrida (see chapter 4), and which is the broader complaint of nominalists about the conventional treatment of language.

110. Koheleth, in his observation about the never-ending flow of books, and in the overall mood of his own "book," could be read as responding to the same things that provoked Sade. Koheleth's style is different, but since, like Sade, he was undoubtedly a highly placed figure, he observes a similar scale of irrationality in the experience of civilization. His aphorisms tell the real rules for surviving civilization. While some of his rules remain androcentric and even openly addressed to men rather than women, the mood of this work can apply to everyone (see chapter 7).

111. See chapter 5, section 2-2.

112. Carter, *Sadeian,* 6.

113. Carter, *Sadeian,* 6–7.

114. Carter, *Sadeian,* 7. Some women respond with disgust to instances of contemporary pornography, but they may not consider this disgust a sign of their implication in the universal pornographic ideal that potentially includes women more generally.

gender subordination. *A universal is a language gesture.* It is made by specifiable people and repeated over generations. If enough energy is given to its repetition, it becomes transparent, received without question by new generations and then repeated as such through the writing of many books. It becomes the unchallenged "way things are."

At this point, Dworkin's warning about pornography being the secret police of male supremacy may apply. Sade, the literary, historical, and linguistic template for Réage, describes the actual terms of ordinary sex—its presuppositions and its prescriptions for how it is to be carried out. Because sex is important to almost everyone, whatever ideology attaches to it carries a dimension of inviolability, and people tend to leave ideology alone at that level in order to participate in sex at all. Carter's description of sex suggests that the pornographic ideal is the actual social ideal, a point made by Ferguson and other students of pornography. The pornographic ideal is the way things are:

At the first touch or sigh he, she, is subsumed immediately into a universal. (She, of course, rarely approaches him; that is not part of the fantasy of fulfillment.[115]) She is most immediately and dramatically a woman when she lies beneath a man, and her submission is the apex of his malehood. To show his humility before his own erection, a man must approach a woman on his knees, just as he approaches god.[116] This is the kind of beautiful thought that has bedeviled the history of sex in Judaeo-Christian culture, causing almost as much confusion as the idea that sex is a sin. Some of the scorn heaped on homosexuals may derive from the fact that they do not customarily adopt the mythically correct, sacerdotal position. The same beautiful thought has elevated a Western European convention to the position of the only sanctified sexual position; it fortifies the mis-

---

115. This remains true in internet pornography. Now, however, he approaches with a video camera, which may or may not be included in the total presentation. Sometimes, the female partner is asked to hold the operating camera during sex and instructed what to photograph. Under the supervision of the male partner, both are having sex with cameras in their hands.

116. Benjamin, referring to O and René, writes, "Her lover is like a god, and her need for him can only be satisfied by obedience, which allows her to transcend herself by becoming an instrument of his supreme will" (*Bonds*, 60). Also, the male kneeling gesture in contemporary heterosexual pornography is the preliminary cunnilingus, which is also the result of complaints by critics about women's pleasure not being considered. As the videos are presented, however, it is clear that the "main event" is the variety of sexual positions in coitus—ending with a male ejaculation, usually on a woman's face and mouth. The cunnilingus is foreplay, and the videos continue to promulgate the imagery of hierarchical heterosexual relations. When the man kneels it is a ritual deception; when the woman kneels, it is worship.

sionary position with a bizarre degree of mystification. God is invoked as a kind of sexual referee, to assure us, as modern churchmen like to claim in the teeth of two thousand years of Christian sexual repression, that sex is really sacred.[117]

Like language and texts, sex has been sacralized in the same cause. This passage describes the phenomenology of total mediation as it appears in conventionally heterosexual sex lives. The reality of sex in a continuing relationship is ignored in order to perpetuate the fantasy of its godliness. One of the verbal universals that constrict sex is love, the object that is said to come, first and foremost, from God. Love and God are *felt* to be universals when they are used. The ritual character of "I love you" may be felt, but it is not acknowledged for fear that relaxing its fixity disturbs stability. The total language of sex—which includes obscenity in a prominent way and does not censor words of love and tenderness—is either censored or kept in the cage of privacy, yet another imprisoning universal. The result is that what Carter describes is not subject to discussion, permutation, or recombination. If sexual activity were thus treated, it would be recognized as both public and private at once, it would be subject to discussion between the principal actors most of the time, it would be part of educational curricula in schools, and it would not be censored in public media—and it would be permissible to use obscene language in front of children. Scholars who are advocating for such enlightenment have been considered in previous chapters: Dworkin, Kipnis, and Carter all fold in the use of words like "fuck" and "cunt" while mounting careful discussions of both sexually explicit materials as well as the social institutions, many centuries old, that have collaborated in the reduction and class enslavement of women.[118] Counting on verbal universals has been a major factor in the machinery of social degradation, as most students of fascism already know.

The interest in universals has been based on another myth: the universality of human experience. Although people's bodies are more or less similar, their differences matter. Because different bodies adapt differently to different cultures, the various differences start to matter more, and the local processes cannot be universalized.[119] Carter writes, "Pornography, like marriage and the

---

117. Carter, *Sadeian*, 7–8.

118. Should scholars such as these achieve further public acknowledgement of the value of their work, think of the response of religious constituencies if such work, as well as Sade's, is taught in schools to future generations.

119. This is a principal fallacy of Chomsky's approach to language, discussed in chapter 5. Carter also says, "The notion of a universality of human experience is a confidence trick and the notion of a universality of female experience is a clever confidence trick" (*Sadeian*, 12), as Rosalind Morris demonstrated with Chuchad (see chapter 1).

fictions of romantic love, assists the process of false universalising." This may be called a "secret police" function: the genres themselves in their stable identity as the literature few admit they use urge the subordination of women in ordinary contexts of marriage and family through their collective action as providing standards of speech: it is sexy to say (using the imperative), "Suck my cock."[120] Neither the marriage nor the sex admits of flexible language, which is language available to change its references and uses through frequent use between partners and communities in unpredictable ways. Pornography is like other literature, Carter says: "It can never be art for art's sake. Honourably enough, it is always art with work to do."[121] Furthermore, "[P]ornographic writing retains this in common with all literature—that it turns the flesh into word." Literature and pornography are both words with work to do.[122]

The materiality of language identifies false universals only as figures or metaphors, which are also the stock-in-trade of any literature: readers know the universals are "false" in the sense that they are figurative in an aesthetic sense (and thus open to different readings) and provisional in a referential sense (and thus open to recursive revision). The materiality of these words emerges from this formulation by Carter:

> [S]exual relations between men and women always render explicit the nature of social relations in the society in which they take place and, if described explicitly, will form a critique of those relations, even if that is not and never has been the intention of the pornographer. So, whatever

---

120. Carter uses a term that feels similar to Dworkin's "secret police," but with a more complicated political purpose: "the pornographer has it in his power to become a terrorist of the imagination, a sexual guerilla whose purpose is to overturn our most basic notions of [sexual] relations, to reinstitute sexuality as a primary mode of being rather than a specialised area of vacation from being and to show that the everyday meetings in the marriage bed are parodies of their own pretensions, that the freest unions may contain the seeds of the worst exploitation. Sade became a terrorist of the imagination in this way" (*Sadeian*, 21–22). This reading invites women to read Sade more than Dworkin's reading does. Carter urges readers to read in a stance of self-examination as social figures; male supremacy is no less a degenerate ideology for her, but she gives grounds for formulating answers deriving from her adroit, practiced access to language.

121. Carter, *Sadeian*, 12, 13.

122. Catharine MacKinnon, *Only Words*, 32. MacKinnon says that pornographic words necessarily act: "To express eroticism is to engage in eroticism, meaning to perform a sex act. To say it is to do it, and to do it is to say it" (33). MacKinnon derives this thought from the more general speech act assumption that any use of language is a gesture. Carter and Kipnis include details of such uses of language that MacKinnon does not, namely, the caution that when the language is presented, there is a choice of how to use it: for example, whether as a mutually shared fantasy or as a come-on.

the surface falsity of pornography, it is impossible for it to fail to reveal sexual reality at an unconscious level, and this reality may be very unpleasant indeed, a world away from official reality. A male-dominated society produces a pornography of universal female acquiescence.[123]

The verbal action of pornography is its description, its writing of sexual relations into the experience of those with access to language. Carter observes that "access to pornography is usually denied to women at any level, often on the specious grounds that women do not find descriptions of the sexual act erotically stimulating."[124] Denied access to women was true in Sade's time but is not true now. Nevertheless, the denial took place through a social structure of writing and audience—a socialized genre action—rather than through signs saying "Keep out" or "No girls allowed." The almost-all-male audience for pornography now suggests that the genre action has changed little, although many more women are willing to announce that they are sex workers—actors, producers, and sellers of sex texts, sex toys, and sex acts—many more women are willing to say, "I masturbate." In any event, the salient fact of today's society is the access of women to texts, and critics such as those considered earlier provide understanding of those women who have better lives by being in the sex industry.

What action is performed by repeatedly telling the stories of cruelty and brutality that have been the stimulus for sexual arousal? Here is how Carter poses this issue:

> Violence, the convulsive form of the active, male principle, is a matter for men, whose sex gives them the right to inflict pain as a sign of mastery and the masters have the right to wound one another because that only makes us fear them more, that they can give and receive pain like the lords of creation. But to show, in art, erotic violence committed by men upon women cuts too near the bone, and will be condemned out of hand.[125]

This form of pornography "cuts too near the bone" because it really happens, because it teaches others to do it, as MacKinnon and Dworkin have claimed, and because it is unpleasant to read if one is not already so inclined to act. The perpetrators of sexual violence in Sade include women, for whom it may be retributive, but who, like O and Carol Cohn, recognize the ease with which they may adopt such feelings. Carter moves toward the position taken by many cited in this book: the structure of whole societies enable such writing as well as

---

123. Carter, *Sadeian*, 20.
124. Carter, *Sadeian*, 15.
125. Carter, *Sadeian*, 22.
126. Carter, *Sadeian*, 24.

such behavior. Carter takes the additional step of entertaining the thought that Sade's writing is an opportunity to decide anew what our society is:

> [Sade] describes sexual relations in the context of an unfree society as the expression of pure tyranny, usually by men upon women, sometimes by men upon men, sometimes by women upon men and other women; the one constant to all Sade's monstrous orgies is that the whip hand is always the hand with the real political power and the victim is a person who has little or no power at all . . . In this schema, male means tyrannous and female means martyrised, no matter what the official genders of the male and female beings are.[126]

The whip hand is usually that of small groups of powerful men as well as of the putatively benign "married head of household" identified on American internal revenue forms. This condition of society tolerates the monstrous and the brutal when it is comfortably remote. But Carter also implies that the condition is itself monstrous, as it suggests what it may mean for women to be free in this society: "A free woman in an unfree society will be a monster. Her freedom will be a condition of personal privilege that deprives those on which she exercises it of her own freedom. The most extreme kind of this deprivation is murder. These women murder."[127]

Twenty-five years after Carter's book came out, the film *Monster* (dir. Patty Jenkins, 2003) was made. Aileen Wuornos, having become a prostitute, was, in real life, identified as a monster, and the film gives a version of her life. She murdered several men, the first of whom was a john who was maliciously assaulting her. The others, except one, were also johns of varying degrees of offensiveness. Wuornos developed an intimate relationship with Selby, a young runaway. When Selby discovers what Aileen has been up to, she is angry, but not really appalled:

> *Selby: We can be as different as we wanna be, but you can't kill people!*
> *Aileen: SAYS WHO? I'm good with the Lord. I'm fine with him. And I know how you were raised, alright? And I know how people fuckin' think out there, and fuck, it's gotta be that way. They've gotta tell you that "Thou shall not kill" shit and all of that. But that's not the way the world works, Selby. Cuz I'm out there every fuckin' day living it. Who the fuck knows what God wants? People kill each other every day and for what? Hm? For politics, for religion, and THEY'RE HEROES! No, no . . . there's a lot of shit I can't do anymore, but killing's not one of them. And letting those fucking bastards go out and rape someone else isn't either!*

---

127. Carter, *Sadeian*, 27.

Aileen did deprive Selby of her own freedom, but only one of her murders, which was desperate and committed in the cause of honoring Selby's needs, would be taken as a deprivation of freedom. Her speech above, however, identifies how free she feels and acts. She is assuming the same freedom as those "heroes" who kill for political and religious causes. Killing for her is the answer to rape, which takes place against female victims, usually, without a response from society or from law enforcement. Rape is almost always unchecked, as Sade's "society" suggests, and is often used as an occasion for collective male stimulation. Just as Carter and Dworkin say that the source of that recursive perversion is religious and political, so does the monster, who seems to know what they know.

The monster has privileged access to language: she makes five uses of the word "fuck." She speaks like a wise guy or a goodfella. She has overtaken the discourse of male violence as well as the behavior. She understands to use God in a rhetorically powerful way: "Who the fuck knows what God wants." This woman, like the man, does the fucking. When you do the fucking, you also do the killing. In the words of Carter, "Women do not normally fuck in the active sense."[128] Carter views Sade as advocating egalitarian sex, which means active and passive for all parties, as desired. For *women* to use active *and* active-voice fucking in the world as it is means that women "will then be able to fuck their way into history and, in doing so, change it."[129] In this sentence "fuck" may also at the same time mean "speak and write."

Because obscene language is tolerated but generally censored in academic life, analyses such as Carter's and Dworkin's rarely make it into classrooms and curricula; if they do, there is a "So what?" discussion or perhaps a generic consignment of such writing to dismissible genres of polemic or rhetoric. But the way "fuck" is used in English cannot be separated from the recursive shrug at the association of violence with sex. Carter sees Sade as advocating a utopian vision of society (Who would read Sade with this thought?). Only an egalitarian society would move us away from sadism. But she sees also in Sade the same profound, ironic, even witty, doubt she sees in Kafka: "There *is* hope—but not for us."[130] But we might as well add the many literary figures already mentioned—Melville, Ibsen, Morrison, Atwood, and perhaps any writer from whose reading one feels an emancipation of language without an emancipation of society. Literature has *always* provided new language to its own and subsequent periods of history. It has *always* assumed that any person may read it or hear it with authority. But it has *almost always* been censored or reduced or cordoned off, segregated, patronized, rendered into fiction and amusement. Such actions are the gestures that

128. Carter, *Sadeian,* 27.
129. Carter, *Sadeian,* 27.
130. Carter, *Sadeian,* 26.

opposed the fundamental literary gestures of saying in a way that guides, leads, and urges people toward new action.

When literature became a part of university agendas, perhaps two centuries ago, universities collaborated with the political need to control the output and social consequence of new, powerful uses of language. Sometimes the language and literature themselves were censored. More often than not, however, universities sacralized and then academicized literature, and locked it in a tangled web of mindfuck and abstraction. In its familiar, reliable, upstanding, father-knows-best, acceptable ways, universities dematerialized language and literature systematically, regularly casting this valuable instrument of survival and success as an imaginary spiritual substance to such an extent that this substance assumed an absolute normality. In the work of a few readers, some of whom are cited in this book, the academic reduction has been resisted and the language has been released, just as the several writers cited in this chapter have succeeded in releasing obscene language to new, effective, uncensored uses.

Literature and any art, popular or not, has been the source of people's unlimited access to language. The historic pattern of limitation has been to sacralize a few so-called holy books and claim that language itself was exemplified by what was in those books: these were the only ones presented as material. Literacy itself was limited, so that those who might have direct access to these few books depended on the intermediate confidence games of interpretation by an elite group of men. The list of ways in which access has been limited does not need to be repeated.

What may better bear repetition is that some people in some societies in the last century have recognized the materiality of language and literature, that they have contributed some of their lives and fortunes to this understanding, that they have linked it to a politics that takes responsibility for all people, that they have contested the self-interested tyrannies of tradition, that they have taught others to live thoughtfully with uncertainty and change, and they have persuaded many that what all of us say matters.

BIBLIOGRAPHY

Aarsleff, Hans. *From Locke to Saussure: Essays on the Study of Language and Intellectual History.* Minneapolis: U of Minnesota P, 1982.

———. "The History of Linguistics and Professor Chomsky." *From Locke to Saussure: Essays on the Study of Language and Intellectual History.* Minneapolis: U of Minnesota P, 1982. 101–119.

———. "Introduction." Etienne Bonnot de Condillac, *Essay on the Origin of Human Knowledge.* Trans. and ed. Hans Aarsleff. Cambridge: Cambridge UP, 2001. xi–xxxviii.

———. "Introduction." Wilhelm von Humboldt, *On Language.* Trans. Peter Heath. Cambridge: Cambridge UP, 1988. vii–lxv.

Abrams, Meyer. Oral presentation. Modern Language Association. December 1974.

Adams, Marilyn McCord. *William Ockham.* 2 vols. South Bend, IN: U of Notre Dame P, 1987.

Ainsworth-Vaughn, Nancy. *Claiming Power in Doctor-Patient Talk.* New York: Oxford UP, 1998.

Allan, Keith, and Kate Burridge. *Forbidden Words: Taboo and the Censoring of Language.* New York: Cambridge UP, 2006.

Allison, Anne. *Nightwork: Sexuality, Pleasure, and Corporate Masculinity in a Tokyo Hostess Club.* Chicago: U of Chicago P, 1994.

Anonymous. *The* Manuale scholarium: *An Original Account of Life the Mediaeval University* (1481) trans. Robert Francis Seybolt. Cambridge MA: Harvard UP, 1921.

Archer, John, ed. *Male Violence.* New York: Routledge, 1994.

Aristophanes. *Lysistrata and Other Plays.* Trans. Alan H. Sommerstein. London: Penguin, 2002.

Armstrong, D. M. *Nominalism and Realism: Universals and Scientific Realism.* 2 vols. Cambridge: Cambridge UP, 1978.

Arnold, Matthew. "The Function of Criticism in the Present Time." *Critical Theory Since Plato.* 1864. Ed. Hazard Adams. New York: Harcourt Brace Jovanovich, 1971. 583–595.

Aronowitz, Stanley. *The Knowledge Factory: Dismantling the Corporate University and Creating True Higher Learning.* Boston: Beacon P, 2000.

Artz, Frederick B. *Renaissance Humanism, 1300–1550.* Kent, OH: Kent State UP, 1966.

Aston, Margaret. *Faith and Fire: Popular and Unpopular Religion, 1350–1600.* London: Hambledon P, 1993.

Atwood, Margaret. "Atwood on Pornography." *Chatelaine* 56 (September 1983): 61, 118, 126.

———. *The Handmaid's Tale.* Boston: Houghton Mifflin, 1986.

Augustine of Hippo. *Against the Academicians; The Teacher.* Trans. Peter King. Cambridge: Hackett, 1995.

———. *Confessions of St. Augustine,* Trans. Edward B. Pusey, D.D. New York: Modern Library, 1999.

Austin, J. L. *How to Do Things with Words.* 1955. Ed. J. O. Urmson. New York: Oxford UP, 1962.

———. *Philosophical Papers.* Oxford: Clarendon P, 1961.

Ayer, A. J. *Wittgenstein.* London: Weidenfeld and Nicolson, 1985.

Bainton, Roland H. *Hunted Heretic: The Life and Death of Michael Servetus (1511–1553).* 1953. Ed. Peter Hughes. Rev. ed. Providence, RI: Unitarian Universalist Historical Society; Blackstone Editions, 2005.

Bakhtin, M. M. *Speech Genres and Other Essays.* Ed. Caryl Emerson and Michael Holquist. Trans. Vern W. McGee. Austin: U of Texas P, 1986.

Barad, Karen. "A Feminist Approach to Teaching Quantum Physics." *Teaching the Majority: Breaking the Gender Barrier in Science, Mathematics, and Engineering.* Ed. Sue V. Rosser. Teachers College P, 1995. 43–75.

———. *Meeting the Universe Halfway.* Durham, NC: Duke UP, 2007.

———. "Posthumanist Performativity: Toward an Understanding of How Matter Comes to Matter." *Signs: Journal of Women in Culture and Society* 28.3 (2003): 801–831.

Barker, Drucilla K., and Edith Kuiper, eds. *Toward a Feminist Philosophy of Economics.* New York: Routledge, 2003.

Baron, Dennis. *The English Only Question: An Official Language for Americans?* New Haven, CT: Yale UP, 1990.

———. *Grammar and Gender.* New Haven, CT: Yale UP, 1986.

Bates, Elizabeth, Laura Benigni, Inge Bretherton, Luigia Camaioni, Virginia Volterra, Vicki Carlson, Karlana Carpen, and Marcia Rosser. *The Emergence of Symbols: Cognition and Communication in Infancy.* New York: Academic P, 1979.

Battersby, Christine. *Gender and Genius: Toward a Feminist Aesthetics.* Bloomington: Indiana UP, 1988.

Beatty, John. "Fitness." *Keywords in Evolutionary Biology.* Ed. Evelyn Fox Keller and Elisabeth A. Lloyd. Cambridge, MA: Harvard UP, 1992. 115–119.

Beck, Evelyn Torton. *Kafka and the Yiddish Theater.* Madison: University of Wisconsin P, 1974.

Benjamin, Jessica. *The Bonds of Love: Psychoanalysis, Feminism, and the Problem of Domination.* New York: Pantheon, 1988.

———. *Shadow of the Other: Intersubjectivity and Gender in Psychoanalysis.* New York: Routledge, 1998.

Berg, Jean de. *The Image.*1956. N.p.: Wet Angel, 2006.

Berlin, Isaiah. *The Age of Enlightenment.* New York: Mentor, 1956.

———. *Three Critics of the Enlightenment: Vico, Hamann, Herder.* Ed. Henry Hardy. Princeton, NJ: Princeton UP, 2000.

Bermann, Sandra, and Michael Wood, eds. *Nation, Language, and the Ethics of Translation.* Princeton, NJ: Princeton UP, 2005.

Bickerton, Derek. *Language and Species.* Chicago: U of Chicago P, 1990.

Bierwisch, Manfred. "Semantic Structure and Illocutionary Force." *Speech Act Theory and Pragmatics.* Ed. John R. Searle, Ferenc Kiefer, and Manfred Bierwisch. Boston: D. Reidel, 1980. 1–35.

Biller, Peter, and Anne Hudson, eds. *Heresy and Literacy, 1000–1530*. Cambridge: Cambridge UP, 1994.

Black, Laurel Johnson. *Between Talk and Teaching: Reconsidering the Writing Conference.* Logan: Utah State UP, 1998.

Blackwell, Antoinette Louisa Brown. *The Sexes Throughout Nature.* New York: Putnam, 1875.

Bleich, David. *The Double Perspective: Language, Literacy, and Social Relations.* New York: Oxford UP, 1988.

———. *Know and Tell: A Writing Pedagogy of Disclosure, Genre, and Membership.* Portsmouth, NH: Heinemann, 1998.

———. "New Considerations of the Infantile Acquisition of Language and Symbolic Thought." *The Psychoanalytic Review* 63.1 (Spring 1976): 49–71.

———. *Subjective Criticism.* Baltimore: Johns Hopkins UP, 1978.

———. *Utopia: The Psychology of a Cultural Fantasy.* Ann Arbor: UMI Research P, 1984.

Bleier, Ruth. *Science and Gender: A Critique of Biology and Its Theories on Women.* New York: Pergamon, 1984.

Bloom, Lois. *The Transition from Infancy to Language: Acquiring the Power of Expression.* Cambridge: Cambridge UP, 1993.

Bloom, Lois, Erin Tinker, and Ellin Kofsky Scholnick. *The Intentionality Model and Language Acquisition: Engagement, Effort, and the Essential Tension in Development.* Monographs of the Society for Research in Child Development, vol. 66, no. 4. Boston: Blackwell, 2001.

Boas, Franz. *The Mind of Primitive Man.* 1911. Rev. ed. New York: Macmillan, 1938.

Boas, Marie. *The Scientific Renaissance, 1450–1630.* New York: Harper, 1962.

Bordo, Susan, ed. *Feminist Interpretations of René Descartes.* State College: Pennsylvania State UP, 1992.

Botha, Rudolf P. *Challenging Chomsky: The Generative Garden Game.* Oxford: Blackwell, 1989.

Bourdieu, Pierre. *Masculine Domination.* 1998. Palo Alto, CA: Stanford UP, 2001.

———. *Unravelling the Evolution of Language.* Amsterdam: Elsevier, 2003.

Boyarin, Daniel. *Unheroic Conduct: The Rise of Heterosexuality and the Invention of the Jewish Man.* Berkeley: U of California P, 1997.

Brandt, Deborah. *Literacy in American Lives.* New York: Cambridge UP, 2001.

Bridgman, P. W. *The Logic of Modern Physics.* New York: Macmillan, 1927.

Briscoe, Ted. "Co-evolution of the Language Faculty and Language(s) with Decorrelated Encodings." *Language Origins: Perspectives on Evolution.* Ed. Maggie Tallerman. New York: Oxford UP, 2005. 310–333.

Brittan, Arthur. *Masculinity and Power.* New York: Blackwell, 1989.

Brockliss, Laurence. "Curricula." *A History of the University in Europe*, vol. 2: *Universities in Early Modern Europe: 1500–1800.* Ed. Hilde de Ridder-Symoens. Gen ed. Walter Rüegg. Cambridge: Cambridge UP, 1996. 563–620.

Brodkey, Linda. "The Troubles at Texas." *Writing Permitted in Designated Areas Only.* Minneapolis: U of Minnesota P, 1996. 181–192.

———. "Writing about Difference: The Syllabus for English 306." *Writing Permitted in Designated Areas Only.* Minneapolis: U of Minnesota P, 1996. 211–227.

Brody, Miriam. *Manly Writing: Gender, Rhetoric, and the Rise of Composition.* Carbondale: Southern Illinois UP, 1993.

Bronfenbrenner, Martha Ornstein. *The Rôle of Scientific Societies in the Seventeenth Century.* Chicago: U of Chicago P, 1928.

Brooke, Christopher. *Europe in the Central Middle Ages.* London: Longman, 1975.

Brooks, Cleanth. *The Well-Wrought Urn.* New York: Harcourt Brace Jovanovich, 1947.

Brown, Allison Leigh. *Subjects of Deceit: A Phenomenology of Lying.* Albany: SUNY P, 1998.

Brown, Michael E., and Sumit Ganguly, eds. *Fighting Words: Language Policy and Ethnic Relations in Asia.* Cambridge, MA: MIT P, 2003.

Brown, Peter. *The Body and Society: Men, Women, and Sexual Renunciation in Early Christianity.* New York: Columbia UP, 1988.

Brown, Roger. *Wilhelm von Humboldt's Conception of Linguistic Relativity.* The Hague: Mouton, 1967.

Bullough, Edward. "Psychical Distance as a Factor in Art and an Aesthetic Principle." *Critical Theory Since Plato.* 1912. Ed. Hazard Adams. New York: Harcourt Brace Jovanovich, 1971. 754–765.

Burling, Robbins. "The Slow Growth of Language in Children." *The Transition to Language.* Ed. Alison Wray. Oxford: Oxford UP, 2002. 297–310.

Butler, Judith. *Excitable Speech: A Politics of the Performative.* New York: Routledge, 1997.

Cantarella, Eva. *Bisexuality in the Ancient World.* 1988. 2nd ed. New Haven, CT: Yale UP, 2002.

Carre, Meyrick H. *Realists and Nominalists.* London: Oxford UP, 1946.

Carroll, James. *Constantine's Sword: The Church and the Jews, a History.* Boston: Houghton-Mifflin, 2001.

Carroll, Lewis. *Through the Looking Glass.* London: Penguin, Puffin, 1974.

Carter, Angela. *The Sadeian Woman And the Ideology of Pornography.* New York: Penguin, 1979.

Cassirer, Ernst. *The Philosophy of Symbolic Forms.* 1923. 4 vols. Trans. Ralph Manheim. Pref. and intro. Charles W. Hendel. New Haven, CT: Yale UP, 1953.

Catto, J. I. "Wyclif and Wycliffism at Oxford 1356–1430." eds. *The History of the University of Oxford,* vol. 2. Ed. J. I. Catto and Ralph Evans. Oxford: Clarendon P, 1992. 175–261.

Catto, J. I., ed. *The History of the University of Oxford,* vol. 1. Oxford: Clarendon P, 1984.

Cavell, Stanley. *The Claim of Reason: Wittgenstein, Skepticism, Morality, and Tragedy.* New York: Oxford UP, 1979.

———. *Philosophical Passages: Wittgenstein, Emerson, Austin, Derrida.* Cambridge, MA: Blackwell, 1995.

Cetina, Karin Knorr. *Epistemic Cultures: How the Sciences Make Knowledge.* Cambridge, MA: Harvard UP, 1999.

Charle, Christophe. "Patterns." *A History of the University in Europe,* vol. 3: *Universities in the Nineteenth and Early Twentieth Centuries (1800–1945).* Ed. Walter Rüegg. Cambridge: Cambridge UP, 2004. 33–80.

Chase, Stuart. "Foreword." *Language, Thought, and Reality: Selected Writings of Benjamin Lee Whorf.* 1957. Ed. John B. Carroll. Cambridge, MA: MIT P, 1997. v–x.

Chodorow, Nancy J. *Feminism and Psychoanalytic Theory.* New Haven, CT: Yale UP, 1989.

———. *The Reproduction of Mothering: Psychoanalysis and the Sociology of Gender.* Berkeley: U of California P, 1978.

Chomsky, Noam. *Aspects of the Theory of Syntax.* Cambridge, MA: MIT P, 1965.

———. *Cartesian Linguistics: A Chapter in the History of Rationalist Thought.* New York: Harper and Row, 1966.

————. Rev. of *Verbal Behavior*, by B. F. Skinner. *Language* 35 (1959): 26–58.

Christian, Barbara. "The Race for Theory." *Feminist Studies* 14.1 (1988): 67–79.

Christiansen, Morten H., Chris Collins, and Shimon Edelman, eds. *Language Universals.* New York: Oxford UP, 2009.

Christiansen, Morten H., and Simon Kirby, eds. *Language Evolution*. Oxford and New York: Oxford University Press, 2003.

Clanchy, M. T. *Abelard: A Medieval Life*. Oxford: Blackwell, 1997.

Clark, Eve V. *First Language Acquisition*. Cambridge and New York: Cambridge UP, 2003.

Clark, Stuart. *Thinking With Demons: The Idea of Witchcraft in Early Modern Europe.* Oxford: Clarendon P, 1997.

Clark, William. *Academic Charisma and the Origins of the Research University*. Chicago: U of Chicago P, 2006.

Cobban, Alan B. *English University Life in the Middle Ages*. Berkeley: U of California P, 1999.

————. *The Medieval English Universities*. Berkeley: U of California P, 1988.

Code, Lorraine. *What Can She Know? Feminist Theory and the Construction of Knowledge.* Ithaca, NY: Cornell UP, 1991.

Cohen, Ralph. "The Autobiography of a Critical Problem." Midwest Modern Language Association. Bloomington, IN. 4 November 1984.

Cohen, Roger. "No Time for Retribution." *New York Times* 23 April 2009. www.nytimes .com/2009/04/23/opinion/23iht-edcohen.html.

Cohn, Carol. "Sex and Death in the Rational World of Defense Intellectuals." *Gender and Scientific Authority*. Ed. Barbara Laslett, Sally Gregory Kohlstedt, Helen Longino, and Evelynn Hammonds. Chicago: University of Chicago P, 1996. 183–216.

————. "Wars, Wimps, and Women." *Gendering War Talk*. Ed. Miriam Cooke and Angela Woollacott. Princeton, NJ: Princeton UP, 1993. 227–246.

Cohn, Norman. *Europe's Inner Demons: The Demonization of Christians in Medieval Christendom*. 1973. Rev. ed. Chicago: U of Chicago P, 1993.

————. *Europe's Inner Demons: An Enquiry Inspired by the Great Witch-Hunt*. New York: Basic, 1975.

————. *The Pursuit of the Millennium*. 1957. New York: Harper, 1961.

Colapinto, John. "The Interpreter." *New Yorker* 16 April 2007: 118–137.

Cole, Michael, ed. *Cognitive Development: Its Cultural and Social Foundations*. Trans. Martin Lopez-Morillas and Lynn Solatoroff. Cambridge, MA: Harvard UP, 1976.

Coleman, Christopher B., trans. *The Treatise of Lorenzo Valla on the Donation of Constantine*. Toronto: U of Toronto P, 1993.

Colish, Marcia L. *Medieval Foundations of the Western Intellectual Tradition, 400–1400.* New Haven, CT: Yale UP, 1997.

————. *The Mirror of Language*. Lincoln: U of Nebraska P, 1968.

Colvin, Geoff. *Talent Is Overrated*. New York: Penguin, 2008.

Compayre, Gabriel. *Abelard and the Origin and Early History of Universities*. New York: Scribner's, 1893.

Condillac, Etienne Bonnot de. *Essay on the Origin of Human Knowledge*. Trans. and ed. Hans Aarsleff. Cambridge: Cambridge UP, 2001.

Cowan, Marianne. *Humanist without Portfolio*. Detroit: Wayne State UP, 1963.

Coyle, Daniel. *The Talent Code*. New York: Bantam, 2009.

Culler, Jonathan. *On Deconstruction: Theory and Criticism After Structuralism*. Ithaca, NY: Cornell UP, 1982.

——. *Structuralist Poetics: Structuralism, Linguistics, and the Study of Literature.* Ithaca, NY: Cornell UP, 1975.

Dante Alighieri. *De vulgari eloquentia.* Trans. Stephen Botterill. Cambridge: Cambridge UP, 1996.

Daston, Loraine, and Peter Galison. *Objectivity.* New York: Zone, 2007.

Dauber, Kenneth. "Beginning at the Beginning in Genesis." *Ordinary Language Criticism: Literary Thinking after Cavell and Wittgenstein.* Ed. Kenneth Dauber and Walter Jost. Evanston, IL: Northwestern UP, 2003. 329–345.

Dauber, Kenneth, and Walter Jost, eds. *Ordinary Language Criticism: Literary Thinking after Cavell and Wittgenstein.* Evanston, IL: Northwestern UP, 2003.

Davies, Paul C. W., and John Brown, eds. *Superstrings: A Theory of Everything?* Cambridge: Cambridge UP, 1988.

De Santillana, Georgio. *The Crime of Galileo.* 1955. Chicago: U of Chicago P, 1976.

Deacon, Terrence W. *The Symbolic Species: The Co-evolution of Language and the Brain.* New York: Norton, 1997.

DeJean, Joan. *The Reinvention of Obscenity: Sex, Lies, and Tabloids in Early Modern France.* Chicago: U of Chicago P, 2002.

Deleuze, Gilles, and Félix Guattari. *Anti-Oedipus: Capitalism and Schizophrenia.* 1972. Trans. Robert Hurley, Mark Seem, and Helen R. Lane. New York: Penguin, 2009.

——. *A Thousand Plateaus: Capitalism and Schizophrenia.* 1980. Trans. Brian Massumi. Minneapolis: U of Minnesota P, 1987.

Derrida, Jacques. "Freud and the Scene of Writing." *Writing and Difference* Trans. Alan Bass. Chicago: U of Chicago P, 1978. 196–231.

——. "The Law of Genre" (trans. Avital Ronell). *Critical Inquiry* 7.1 (Autumn 1980): 55–81.

——. "Limited, Inc a b c . . ." *Limited, Inc.* 1977. Evanston, IL: Northwestern UP, 1988. 29–110.

——. *Margins of Philosophy.* Trans. Alan Bass. Chicago: U of Chicago P, 1982.

——. *Monolingualism of the Other, or The Prosthesis of Origin.* 1996. Trans. Patrick Mensah. Stanford, CA: Stanford UP, 1998.

——. *Of Grammatology.* 1967. Trans. Gayatri Chakravorty Spivak. Baltimore: Johns Hopkins UP, 1974.

——. *On the Name.* 1993. Ed. Thomas Dutoit. Trans. David Wood, John P. Leavey, Jr., and Ian McLeod. Palo Alto, CA: Stanford UP, 1995.

——. "Signature Event Context." *Limited, Inc.* 1977. Trans. Samuel Weber. Evanston, IL: Northwestern UP, 1988. 1–24.

——. *Speech and Phenomena and Other Essays on Husserl's Theory of Signs.* Ed. David B. Allison and Newton Garver. Trans. David B. Allison. Chicago: Northwestern UP, 1973.

de Pizan, Christine. *The Book of the City of Ladies.* Trans., Introduction, Rosalind Brown-Grant. London: Penguin Books, 1999.

Deutscher, Guy. *Through the Language Glass: Why the World Looks Different in Other Languages.* New York: Metropolitan, 2010.

Di Simone, Marie Rosa. "Students." *A History of the University in Europe,* vol. 2: *Universities in Early Modern Europe: 1500–1800.* Ed. Hilde de Ridder-Symoens. Gen ed. Walter Rüegg. Cambridge: Cambridge UP, 1996. 285–325.

Dinnerstein, Dorothy. *The Mermaid and the Minotaur: Sexual Arrangements and Human Malaise.* New York: Harper, 1976.

DiPiero, Thomas. *Dangerous Truths and Criminal Passions: The Evolution of the French Novel, 1569–1791.* Stanford, CA: Stanford UP, 1992.

Donoghue, Frank. *The Last Professors: The Corporate University and the Fate of the Humanities.* New York: Fordham UP, 2008.

Dore, John. "Feeling, Form, and Intention in the Baby's Transition to Language." *The Transition from Prelinguistic to Linguistic Communication.* Ed. Roberta Michnick Golinkoff. Hillsdale, NJ: Erlbaum, 1983. 167–190.

Douglass, Frederick. *Narrative of the Life of Frederick Douglass, an American Slave.* New York: Dover, 1995.

Dreyfus, Hubert L. *What Computers Can't Do: A Critique of Artificial Reason.* New York: Harper and Row, 1972.

Du Bois, W. E. B. *The Souls of Black Folk.* 1903. New York: Bantam, 1989.

Dubrow, Heather. *Genre.* New York: Methuen, 1982.

———. "Thesis and Antithesis: Rewriting the Rules on Writing." *Chronicle of Higher Education* 49.15 (2002): B13.

Dunbar, Robin. *Grooming, Gossip, and the Evolution of Language.* Cambridge, MA: Harvard UP, 1996.

Dunbar, Robin, Chris Knight, and Camilla Power, eds. *The Evolution of Culture.* New Brunswick, NJ: Rutgers UP, 1999.

Dundes, Alan. *Holy Writ as Oral Lit.* Lanham, MD: Rowman and Littlefield, 1999.

Dworkin, Andrea. "Against the Male Flood: Censorship, Pornography, and Equality." 1985. *Feminism and Pornography,* ed. Drucilla Cornell. New York: Oxford UP, 2000. 19–38.

———. *Intercourse.* New York: Free P, 1987.

———. *Woman Hating.* New York: Penguin, 1974.

Dworkin, Andrea, and Catharine MacKinnon. *Pornography and Civil Rights: A New Day for Women's Equality.* Minneapolis, MN: Organizing Against Pornography, 1988.

Easlea, Brian. *Science and Sexual Oppression: Patriarchy's Confrontation with Woman and Nature.* London: Widenfield and Nicolson, 1981.

———. *Witch-Hunting, Magic, and the New Philosophy: An Introduction to the Debates of the Scientific Revolution, 1450–1750.* Sussex, NJ: Harvester, 1980.

Eisenstein, Elizabeth L. *The Printing Press as an Agent of Change: Communications and Cultural Transformations in Early-Modern Europe.* Cambridge: Cambridge UP, 1979.

Elyot, Thomas. "The Defence of Good Women." *Vives and the Renascence Education of Women.* Ed. Foster Watson. London: Edward Arnold, 1912. 211–239.

Emerson, Ralph Waldo. "Self-Reliance." 1841. *Ralph Waldo Emerson: Essays and Lectures.* New York, NY: Literary Classics of the United States, 1983, 257–282.

Ensler, Eve. *The Vagina Monologues.* New York: Villard, 1998.Erikson, Erik H. *Childhood and Society.* New York: Basic, 1949.

Everett, Daniel L. "Cultural Constraints on Grammar and Cognition in Piraha." *Current Anthropology* 46.4 (2005): 621–646.

———. *Language: The Cultural Tool.* New York: Pantheon, 2012.

Falk, Dean. "Brain Evolution in Females: An Answer to Mr. Lovejoy." *Women in Human Evolution.* Ed. Lori D. Hager. New York: Routledge, 1997. 114–136.

Fausto-Sterling, Anne. *Myths of Gender: Biological Theories about Women and Men.* New York: Basic, 1985.

Feingold, Mordechai. "The Humanities." *The History of the University of Oxford,* vol. 4. Ed. Nicholas Tyacke. Oxford: Clarendon P, 1997. 211–357.

Felman, Shoshana. *The Literary Speech Act: Don Juan with J. L. Austin, or Seduction in Two Languages.* 1980. Trans. Catherine Porter. Ithaca, NY: Cornell UP, 1983.

————. *The Scandal of the Speaking Body: Don Juan with J, L. Austin, or, Seduction in Two Languages.* Palo Alto, CA: Stanford UP, 2003.

Ferber, Marianne A., and Julie A. Nelson, eds. *Beyond Economic Man: Feminist Theory and Economics.* Chicago: U of Chicago P, 1993.

Ferguson, Frances. *Pornography, the Theory: What Utilitarianism Did to Action.* Chicago: U of Chicago P, 2004.

Fetterley, Judith. *The Resisting Reader: A Feminist Approach to American Fiction.* Bloomington: Indiana UP, 1978.

Fineman, Martha Albertson. *The Autonomy Myth: A Theory of Dependency.* New York: New P, 2004.

Fish, Stanley. "There's No Such Thing as Free Speech, and It's a Good Thing, Too." *There's No Such Thing as Free Speech, and It's a Good Thing, Too.* New York: Oxford UP, 1994. 102–119.

Fisher, John H. *The Emergence of Standard English.* Lexington: UP of Kentucky, 1996.

Fleck, Ludwik. *Genesis and Development of a Scientific Fact.* 1935. Chicago: U of Chicago P, 1979.

Folbre, Nancy. *The Invisible Heart: Economics and Family Values.* New York: New P, 2001.

————. "Socialism, Feminist and Scientific." *Beyond Economic Man: Feminist Theory and Economics.* Ed. Marianne A. Ferber and Julie A. Nelson. Chicago: U of Chicago P, 1993. 94–110.

Foucault, Michel. *The Archeology of Knowledge and The Discourse on Language* (1971), trans. Rupert Sawyer. New York: Pantheon, 1972.

Frazee, Charles. "The Origins of Clerical Celibacy in the Western Church." *Church History* 41 (1972): 149–167.

Freud, Sigmund. "The Antithetical Sense of Primal Words." *Collected Papers,* vol. 4. Trans. Joan Riviere. New York: Basic, 1959. 184–191.

————. *The Standard Edition of the Complete Psychological Works of Sigmund Freud.* Trans. James Strachey and Anna Freud. With Alix Strachey and Alan Tyson. 24 vols. London: Hogarth P, 1953–1974.

Frijhoff, Willem. "Patterns." *A History of the University in Europe,* vol. 2: *Universities in Early Modern Europe: 1500–1800.* Ed. Hilde de Ridder-Symoens. Gen ed. Walter Rüegg. Cambridge: Cambridge UP, 1996. 43–110.

Frye, Northrop. *Anatomy of Criticism: Four Essays.* 1957. Ed. Robert D. Denham. Toronto: U of Toronto P, 2006.

Gardner, Howard. *Frames of Mind: The Theory of Multiple Intelligences.* New York: Basic, 1983.

Gay, Peter. *Freud: A Life for Our Time.* New York: Norton, 1988.

Geertz, Clifford. *Local Knowledge: Further Essays in Interpretive Anthropology.* New York: Basic, 1983.

Gentner, Dedre, and Susan Goldin-Meadow, eds. *Language in Mind: Advances in the Study of Language and Thought.* Cambridge, MA: MIT P, 2003.

Georgescu-Roegen, Nicholas. *Analytical Economics.* Cambridge, MA: Harvard UP, 1966.

Gera, Deborah Levine. *Ancient Greek Ideas on Speech, Language, and Civilization,* New York: Oxford UP, 2003.

Gere, Anne Ruggles. *Intimate Practices: Literacy and Cultural Work in U.S. Women's Clubs, 1880–1920*. Urbana: U of Illinois P, 1997.

Ghosh, Kantik. *The Wycliffite Heresy: Authority and the Interpretation of Texts*. Cambridge: Cambridge UP, 2002.

Ginsparg, Paul, and Sheldon L. Glashow. "Desperately Seeking Superstrings." *Physics Today* May 1986: 7–9.

Glenn, David. "Nobel Prize in Economics Goes to 2 Scholars Who Developed Game Theory as Analytical Tool in Public Policy." *Chronicle of Higher Education* 10 October 2005. chronicle.com/article/Nobel-Prize-in-Economics-Goes/121295/.

Goldstein, Rebecca. *Betraying Spinoza: The Renegade Jew Who Gave Us Modernity*. New York: Schocken, 2006.

Goldstone, Lawrence, and Nancy Goldstone. *Out of the Flames: The Remarkable Story of a Fearless Scholar, a Fatal Heresy, and One of the Rarest Books in the World*. New York: Broadway, 2002.

Golinkoff, Roberta Michnick. "'I Beg Your Pardon?' The Preverbal Negotiation of Failed Messages." *Journal of Child Language* 13 (1986): 455–476.

Goodrich, Peter. "Distrust Quotations in Latin." *Critical Inquiry* 29.2 (Winter 2003): 193–215.

Gould, Stephen Jay. *The Mismeasure of Man*. New York: Norton, 1981.

Graff, Gerald. *Beyond the Culture Wars: How Teaching the Conflicts Can Revitalize American Education*. New York: Norton, 1993.

———. *Clueless in Academe*. New Haven, CT: Yale UP, 2004.

———. *Literature Against Itself: Literary Ideas in Modern Society*. Chicago: U of Chicago P, 1979.

———. *Teaching the Conflicts: Curricular Reform and the Culture Wars*. New York: Garland, 1994.

Graff, Harvey. *The Legacies of Literacy: Continuities and Contradictions in Western Culture and Society*. Bloomington: Indiana UP, 1987.

Grafton, Anthony, and Lisa Jardine. *From Humanism to the Humanities: Education and the Liberal Arts in Fifteenth- and Sixteenth-Century Europe*. Cambridge, MA: Harvard UP, 1986.

Grafton, Anthony. *Worlds Made by Words: Scholarship and Community in the Modern West*. Cambridge, MA: Harvard UP, 2009.

Green, Georgia M. *Pragmatics and Natural Language Understanding*. Hillsdale, NJ: Erlbaum, 1989.

Green, Donald, and Ian Shapiro. *Pathologies of Rational Choice Theory: A Critique of Applications in Political Science*. New Haven, CT: Yale UP, 1996.

Greenawalt, Kent. *Fighting Words: Individuals, Communities and Liberties of Speech*. Princeton, NJ: Princeton UP, 1995.

Grensted, L. W. *Psychology and God: A Study of the Implications of Recent Psychology for Religious Belief and Practice*. London: Longmans, 1930.

Grice, Paul. *Studies in the Way of Words*. Cambridge, MA: Harvard UP, 1989.

Gross, Michael, and Mary Beth Averill. "Evolution and Patriarchal Myths of Scarcity and Competition." *Discovering Reality: Feminist Perspectives on Epistemology, Metaphysics, Methodology, and Philosophy of Science*. Ed. Sandra Harding and Merrill B. Hintikka. Dordrecht: D. Reidel, 1983. 71–95.

Gross, Paul, and Norman Levitt. *Higher Superstition: The Academic Left and Its Quarrels with Science*. Baltimore: Johns Hopkins UP, 1994.

Grumet, Madeleine R. *Bitter Milk: Women and Teaching.* Amherst: U of Massachusetts P, 1988.

Grundmann, Herbert. *Religious Movements in the Middle Ages: The Historical Links Between Heresy, the Mendicant Orders, and the Women's Religious Movement in the Twelfth and Thirteenth Century, with the Historical Foundations of German Mysticism.* 1935. Trans. Steven Rowan. South Bend, IN: U of Notre Dame P, 1995.

Guillory, John. *Cultural Capital: The Problem of Literary Canon Formation.* Chicago: U of Chicago P, 1993.

Gumperz, J. J., and S. C. Levinson, eds. *Rethinking Linguistic Relativity.* Cambridge: Cambridge UP, 1996.

Hall, Kira, and Mary Bucholtz, eds. *Gender Articulated: Language and the Socially Constructed Self.* New York: Routledge, 1995.

Hamann, Johann Georg. *Schriften.* ed. F. Roth, G. J. Herder, and G. A. Wiener. 8 vols. Berlin: Bey G. Reimer, 1821–1843.

Hammerstein, Notker. "Epilogue: The Enlightenment." *A History of the University in Europe,* vol. 2: *Universities in Early Modern Europe: 1500–1800.* Ed. Hilde de Ridder-Symoens. Gen ed. Walter Rüegg. Cambridge: Cambridge UP, 1996. 621–640.

Hampshire, Stuart. *Spinoza and Spinozism.* 1951. New York: Oxford UP, 2005.

Handelman, Susan. *The Slayers of Moses: The Emergence of Rabbinic Interpretation in Modern Literary Theory.* Albany: SUNY P, 1982.

Hardin, Garrett. "The Tragedy of the Commons." *Science* 162 (1968): 1243–1248.

Harding, Sandra. *Is Science Multicultural? Postcolonialisms, Feminisms, Epistemologies.* Bloomington: Indiana UP, 1998.

———. "'Strong Objectivity' and Socially Situated Knowledge." *Whose Science, Whose Knowledge? Thinking from Women's Lives.* Ithaca, NY: Cornell UP, 1991. 138–163.

———. *Whose Science, Whose Knowledge? Thinking from Women's Lives.* Ithaca, NY: Cornell UP, 1991.

Harding, Sandra, and Merrill B. Hintikka, eds. *Discovering Reality: Feminist Perspectives on Epistemology, Metaphysics, Methodology, and Philosophy of Science.* Dordrecht: D. Reidel, 1983.

Harris, William V. *Ancient Literacy.* Cambridge, MA: Harvard UP, 1989.

Haskins, Charles Homer. *The Rise of Universities.* 1923. Ithaca, NY: Cornell UP, 1957.

Hauser, Marc D. *The Evolution of Communication.* Cambridge, MA: MIT P, 2000.

Hauser, Marc D., and W. Tecumseh Fitch. "What Are the Uniquely Human Components of the Language Faculty?" *Language Evolution.* Ed. Morten H. Christiansen and Simon Kirby. Oxford and New York: Oxford University Press, 2003. 158–181.

Heath, Shirley Brice. *Ways with Words: Language, Life, and Work in Communities and Classrooms.* Cambridge: Cambridge UP, 1983.

Heer, Friedrich. *The Medieval World: Europe 1100–1350.* 1961. Trans. Janet Sondheimer. London: Phoenix, 1998.

Heidegger, Martin. *On the Way to Language.* 1959. Trans. Peter D. Hertz. New York: Harper and Row, 1971.

Hennessy, Rosemary. *Materialist Feminism and the Politics of Discourse.* New York: Routledge, 1993.

Hess, Charlotte, and Elinor Ostrom, eds. *Understanding Knowledge as a Commons.* Cambridge, MA: MIT P, 2007.

Hester, Marianne. *Lewd Women and Wicked Witches: A Study of the Dynamics of Male Domination.* New York: Routledge, 1992.

Hingston, R. W. G. *Instinct and Intelligence*. New York: Macmillan, 1929.

Hirsh-Pasek, Kathy, and Roberta Michnick Golinkoff. *The Origins of Grammar: Evidence from Early Language Comprehension*. Cambridge, MA: MIT P, 1996.

Hoffman, Joel M. "Lost in Mistranslation." *Reform Judaism Online* Fall 2010. reformjudaismmag.org/Articles/index.cfm?id=1631.

Hubbard, Ruth. "Have Only Men Evolved?" *Discovering Reality: Feminist Perspectives on Epistemology, Metaphysics, Methodology, and Philosophy of Science*. Ed. Sandra Harding and Merrill B. Hintikka. Dordrecht: D. Reidel, 1983. 45–69.

———. *The Politics of Women's Biology*. New Brunswick, NJ: Rutgers UP, 1990.

Huber, V. A. *The English Universities*, vol. 1. 1839. Trans. Francis W. Newman. London: Pickering, 1843.

Hudson, Anne. *The Premature Reformation: Wycliffite Texts and Lollard History*. Oxford: Clarendon P, 1988.

Hughes, Geoffrey. *Swearing: A Social History of Foul Language, Oaths and Profanity in English*. New York: Penguin, 1991.

Humboldt, Wilhelm von. *On Language*. Trans. Peter Heath. Cambridge: Cambridge UP, 1988.

Humboldt, Wilhelm von, and Caroline von Humboldt. *Wilhelm und Caroline Humboldt in ihren Briefen*. Ed. Anna von Sydow. 7 vols. Berlin: E. S. Mittler, 1907–1919.

Hunt, Lynn, ed. *The Invention of Pornography: Obscenity and the Origins of Pornography, 1500–1800*. New York: Zone, 1996.

Hurford, James R., Michael Studdert-Kennedy, and Chris Knight, eds. *Approaches to the Evolution of Language: Social and Cognitive Bases*. Cambridge: Cambridge UP, 1998.

Ingarden, Roman. *The Literary Work of Art*. 1931. Trans. George G. Grabowicz. Evanston, IL: Northwestern UP, 1973.

Iwanicki, Christine. "The Materiality of Language." Ph.D. diss., Indiana University, 1995.

Jacob, Margaret C. "The Materialist World of Pornography." *The Invention of Pornography: Obscenity and the Origins of Pornography, 1500–1800*. Ed. Lynn Hunt. New York: Zone, 1996. 157–202.

Jacoby, Russell. *The Last Intellectuals: American Culture in the Age of Academe*. New York: Basic, 1987.

James, Henry. The Turn of the Screw *and* The Lesson of the Master. Amherst, NY: Prometheus Books, 1996.

Jardine, Alice, and Paul Smith, eds., *Men in Feminism*. New York: Routledge, 1987.

John of Salisbury. "How Bernard Drilled the Boys in Grammar at Chartres." *University Records and Life in the Middle Ages*. 1944. Ed. and trans. Lynn Thorndike. New York: Columbia UP, 1975. 7–10.

Johnson, Barbara. *The Critical Difference: Essays in the Contemporary Rhetoric of Reading*. Baltimore: Johns Hopkins UP, 1980.

———. *Persons and Things*. Cambridge, MA: Harvard UP, 2008.

Jolly, Alison. *Lucy's Legacy: Sex and Intelligence in Human Evolution*. Cambridge, MA: Harvard UP, 1999.

Jordan, June. "Nobody Mean More to Me than You and the Future Life of Willie Jordan." *On Call: Political Essays*. Boston: South End P, 1985. 123–139.

Jourdain, Charles M. *Histoire de l'Université de Paris au 17e et au 18e siècle*. Paris: Hachette, 1862–1866.

Joyce, James. *Finnegans Wake*. 1939. New York: Viking Press, 1964.

———. *Ulysses*. 1922. Philadelphia: Chelsea House, 2003.

Judovitz, Dalia. *Subjectivity and Representation in Descartes*. New York: Cambridge UP, 1988.

Juliard, Pierre. *Philosophies of Language in Eighteenth-Century France*. The Hague: Mouton, 1970.

Kafka, Franz. *Complete Short Stories*. Trans. Tania and James Stern. New York: Schocken, 1999.

———. *The Trial*. 1916. Trans. Willa and Edwin Muir, and E. M. Butler. New York: Modern Library, 1957.

Karmiloff-Smith, Annette. *Beyond Modularity: A Developmental Perspective on Cognitive Science*. Cambridge, MA: MIT P, 1992.

———. *A Functional Approach to Child Language: A Study of Determiners and Reference*. New York: Cambridge UP, 1979.

Keller, Evelyn Fox. *A Feeling for the Organism: The Life and Work of Barbara McClintock*. New York: W. H. Freeman, 1983.

———. *Reflections on Gender and Science*. New Haven, CT: Yale UP, 1985.

———. *Secrets of Life, Secrets of Death: Essays on Language, Gender, and Science*. New York: Routledge, 1992.

Keller, Evelyn Fox, and Elisabeth A. Lloyd, eds. *Keywords in Evolutionary Biology*. Cambridge, MA: Harvard UP, 1992.

Keller, Helen. *The Story of My Life*. Garden City, NY: Doubleday, 1954.

Kelly, Kristin. *Domestic Violence and the Politics of Privacy*. Ithaca, NY: Cornell UP, 2003.

Kendrick, Walter. *The Secret Museum: Pornography in Modern Culture*. New York: Viking, 1987.

Kenneally, Christine. *The First Word: The Search for the Origins of Language*. New York: Viking, 2007.

Kernan, Alvin, ed. *What's Happened to the Humanities?* Princeton, NJ: Princeton UP, 1997.

Kibre, Pearl. *The Nations in the Medieval Universities*. Cambridge, MA: Medieval Academy of America, 1948.

———. *Scholarly Privileges in the Middle Ages*. Cambridge, MA: Medieval Academy of America, 1962.

Kibre, Pearl, and Nancy G. Siraisi. "The Institutional Setting: The Universities." *Science in the Middle Ages*. Ed. David C. Lindberg. Chicago: U of Chicago P, 1978. 120–144.

Kieckhefer, Richard. *Magic in the Middle Ages*. New York: Cambridge UP, 1989.

Kimmel, Michael S.. *The Gendered Society*. New York: Oxford UP, 2000.

———. *Manhood in America: A Cultural History*. New York: Free P, 1996.

Kipnis, Laura. *Bound and Gagged: Pornography and the Politics of Fantasy in America*. Durham, NC: Duke UP, 1996.

Knight, Chris, Michael Studdert-Kennedy, and James R. Hurford. "Language: A Darwinian Adaptation?" *The Evolutionary Emergence of Language: Social Function and the Origins of Linguistic Form*. Ed. James R. Hurford, Michael Studdert-Kennedy, and Chris Knight. Cambridge: Cambridge UP, 2000. 1–15.

Kramer, Heinrich, and James Sprenger. *The Hammer of Witches: A Complete Translation of the* Malleus maleficarum. Ed. and trans. Christopher S. Mackay. New York: Cambridge UP, 2009.

Krauss, Lawrence M. "A Blip that Speaks of Our Place in the Universe." *New York Times* 9 July 2012. www.nytimes.com/2012/07/10/in-higgs-discovery-a-celebration-of-our-human-capacity.html.

————. *A Universe from Nothing: Why There Is Something Rather than Nothing*. New York: Free P, 2012.

Kripke, Saul A. *Naming and Necessity*. Cambridge, MA: Harvard UP, 1980.

————. *Wittgenstein on Rules and Private Language: An Elementary Exposition*. Cambridge, MA: Harvard UP, 1982.

Kristeva, Julia. *Desire in Language: A Semiotic Approach to Literature and Art*. Ed. Leon S. Roudiez. Trans. Thomas Gora, Alice Jardine, and Leon S. Roudiez. New York: Columbia UP, 1980.

————. *The Kristeva Reader*. Ed. Toril Moi. New York: Columbia UP, 1986.

————. *Language: The Unknown: An Initiation into Linguistics*. 1981. Trans. Anne M. Menke. New York: Columbia UP, 1989.

————. "The Materiality of Language." *Language: The Unknown: An Initiation into Linguistics*. 1981. Trans. Anne M. Menke. New York: Columbia UP, 1989. 18–42.

————. "Motherhood according to Giovanni Bellini." *Desire in Language: A Semiotic Approach to Literature and Art*. Ed. Leon S. Roudiez. Trans. Thomas Gora, Alice Jardine, and Leon S. Roudiez. New York: Columbia UP, 1980. 237–270.

————. *Revolution in Poetic Language*. 1974. Trans. Margaret Waller. New York: Columbia UP, 1984.

————. *Semeiotike: Recherches pour une sémanalyse*. Paris: Seuil, 1969.

————. "The System and the Speaking Subject." *The Kristeva Reader*. Ed. Toril Moi. New York: Columbia UP, 1986. 24–33.

Kristof, Nicholas D. "One Girl's Courage." *New York Times* 12 October 2011. www.nytimes.com/2011/10/13/opinion/one-girls-courage.html.

Kuhn, Thomas S. *The Structure of Scientific Revolutions*. Chicago: U of Chicago P, 1962.

La Marche, A. Lecoy de. *La chaire française au moyen âge: Spécialement au XIIIe siècle*. Paris: Renouard, 1886.

La Motte, Ellen N. *The Backwash of War*. 1916. St. Petersburg, FL: Hailer, 2007.

Lakoff, Robin. "The Growth of Little Gray Cells." *Washington Post* 23 November 1997: X06.

————. *Language and Woman's Place*. New York: Harper, 1975.

————. *Language and Woman's Place: Text and Commentaries*. Ed. Mary Bucholtz, New York: Oxford UP, 2004.

————. *The Language War*. Berkeley: U of California P, 2000.

————. Rev. of *Grammaire générale et raisonnée*, by C. Lancelot, A. Arnauld, and Herbert H. Brekle. *Language* 45.2 (June 1969): 343–364.

————. *Talking Power: The Politics of Language in Our Lives*. New York: Basic, 1990.

————. "The Way We Were; or, The Real Actual Truth About Generative Semantics." *Journal of Pragmatics* 13 (1989): 939–988.

Lakoff, Robin, and James C. Coyne. *Father Knows Best: The Use and Abuse of Power in Freud's Case of Dora*. New York: Teachers College P, 1993.

Lakoff, Robin, and Raquel L. Scherr. *Face Value: The Politics of Beauty*. New York: Routledge, 1984.

Lambert, Malcolm. *Medieval Heresy: Popular Movements from the Gregorian Reform to the Reformation*. Cambridge, MA: Blackwell, 1977.

Lane, Frederick S., III. *Obscene Profits: The Entrepreneurs of Pornography in the Cyber Age*. New York: Routledge, 2001.

Lange, Lynda. "Woman Is Not a Rational Animal: On Aristotle's Biology of Reproduction." *Discovering Reality: Feminist Perspectives on Epistemology, Metaphysics, Meth-*

odology, and Philosophy of Science. Ed. Sandra Harding and Merrill B. Hintikka. Dordrecht: D. Reidel, 1983. 1–16.

Langer, Susanne K. *Philosophy in a New Key.* New York: New American Library, 1941.

Larner, Christina. *Enemies of God: The Witch-Hunt in Scotland.* Baltimore: Johns Hopkins UP, 1981.

Lash, Joseph P. *Helen and Teacher: The Story of Helen Keller and Anne Sullivan Macy.* New York: Delacorte P, 1980.

Laslett, Barbara, Sally Gregory Kohlstedt, Helen Longino, and Evelynn Hammonds, eds. *Gender and Scientific Authority.* Chicago: U of Chicago P, 1996.

Laurie, S. S. *Lectures on the Rise and Early Constitution of Universities with a Survey of Mediæval Education, A.D. 200–1350.* London: Kegan Paul, Trench and Co., 1886.

Law, Vivien. *The History of Linguistics in Europe from Plato to 1600.* Cambridge: Cambridge UP, 2003.

Lawrence, D. H. *Lady Chatterley's Lover.* 1928. New York: Signet, 1959.

Le Boulluec, Alain. *La notion d'hérésie dans la littérature grecque, IIe–IIIe siècles,* vol. 1: *De Justin à Irénée.* Paris: Études augustiniennes, 1985.

Leader, Damien Riehl. *A History of the University of Cambridge,* vol. 1: *The University to 1546.* Cambridge: Cambridge UP, 1988.

Lee, Namhee, Lisa Mikesell, Anna Dina L. Joaquin, Andrea W. Mates, John H. Schumann. *The Interactional Instinct: The Evolution and Acquisition of Language.* New York: Oxford UP, 2009.

Lee, Penny. *The Whorf Theory Complex: A Critical Reconstruction.* Philadelphia: John Benjamins, 1996.

Lerner, Gerda. *The Creation of Patriarchy.* New York: Oxford, 1986.

Levack, Brian P. *The Witch-Hunt in Early Modern Europe.* New York: Longman, 1987.

Lévi-Strauss, Claude. "A Writing Lesson." *Tristes tropiques.* 1955. Trans. John Weightman and Doreen Weightman. New York: Atheneum, 1973. 294–304.

Lewin, Tamar. "Global Classrooms: In Oil-Rich Mideast, Shades of the Ivy League." *New York Times* 11 February 2008. www.nytimes.com/2008/02/11/education/11global.html.

———. "Global Classrooms: Universities Rush to Set Up Outposts Abroad." *New York Times* 10 February 2008. www.nytimes.com/2008/02/10/education/10global.html.

Lewis, Michael, and Louise Cherry. "Social Behavior and Language Acquisition." *Interaction, Conversation, and the Development of Language.* Ed. Michael Lewis and Leonard A. Rosenblum. New York: Wiley, 1977. 227–242.

Lieberman, Philip. *Eve Spoke: Human Language and Human Evolution.* New York: Norton, 1998.

———. *Human Language and Our Reptilian Brain: The Subcortical Bases of Speech, Syntax, and Thought.* Cambridge, MA: Harvard UP, 2000.

Lilla, Mark. *The Reckless Mind: Intellectuals in Politics.* New York: New York Review Books, 2001.

Lindley, David. *The End of Physics: The Myth of a Unified Theory.* New York: Basic, 1993.

Liptak, Adam. "No Argument, Thomas Keeps Five-Year Silence." *New York Times* 12 February 2011. www.nytimes.com/2011/02/13/us/13thomas.html.

Little, Daniel. *The Paradox of Wealth and Poverty: Mapping the Ethical Dilemmas of Global Development.* Boulder, CO: Westview P, 2003.

Locke, John L. *The Child's Path to Spoken Language.* Cambridge, MA: Harvard UP, 1993.

Long, Elizabeth. *Book Clubs: Women and the Uses of Reading in Everyday Life.* Chicago: U of Chicago P, 2003.

Lorenz, Konrad. *On Aggression.* 1963. Trans. Marjorie Kerr Wilson. New York: Harcourt, Brace and World, 1966.

———. *Das sogenannte Boese: Zur der Aggression.* 1963. Munich: Deutscher Taschenbuch Verlag, 1974.

Lucy, John A. *Language Diversity and Thought: A Reformulation of the Linguistic Relativity Hypothesis.* New York: Cambridge UP, 1992.

Lunsford, Andrea A., John J. Ruszkiewicz, and Keith Walter. *Everything's an Argument: With readings.* 4th ed. New York: Bedford St. Martins, 2007.

Lytle, Guy Fitch. "Patronage Patterns and Oxford Colleges, c. 1300–c. 1530." *The University in Society,* vol. 1: *Oxford and Cambridge from the 14th to the Early 19th Century.* Ed. Lawrence Stone. Princeton, NJ: Princeton UP, 1974. 111–149.

MacKinnon, Catharine A. *Only Words.* Cambridge, MA: Harvard UP, 1993.

MacKinnon, Catharine A., and Andrea Dworkin. *In Harm's Way: The Pornography Civil Rights Hearings.* Cambridge, MA: Harvard UP, 1997.

Macneilage, Peter, and Barbara L. Davis. "Evolution of Speech: The Relation Between Ontogeny and Phylogeny." *Approaches to the Evolution of Language: Social and Cognitive Bases.* Ed. James R. Hurford, Michael Studdert-Kennedy, and Chris Knight. Cambridge: Cambridge UP, 1998. 146–160.

MacWhinney, Brian, ed. *The Emergence of Language: Social Function and the Origins of Linguistic Form.* Mahwah, NJ: Erlbaum, 1999.

Malcolm, Norman. *Nothing Is Hidden: Wittgenstein's Criticism of His Early Thought.* Cambridge, MA: Blackwell, 1986.

———. *Wittgenstein: A Religious Point of View?* Ithaca, NY: Cornell UP, 1994.

Malthus, Thomas Robert. *First Essay on Populations.* New York: A. M. Kelley, 1965.

Marcuse, Herbert. *Eros and Civilization: A Philosophical Inquiry into Freud.* 1955. New York: Vintage, 1962.

Marrou, H. I. *A History of Education in Antiquity.* Trans. G. Lamb. London: Sneed and Ward, 1956.

Martin, Emily. "The Egg and the Sperm: How Science Has Constructed a Romance Based on Stereotypical Male-Female Roles." *Gender and Scientific Authority.* Ed. Barbara Laslett, Sally Gregory Kohlstedt, Helen Longino, and Evelynn Hammonds. Chicago: U of Chicago P, 1996. 323–339.

———. *The Woman in the Body: A Cultural Analysis of Reproduction.* Boston: Beacon P, 1987.

Mason, Mary Ann. "A Bad Reputation." *Chronicle of Higher Education* 6 February 2009. chronicle.com/article/A-Bad-Reputation/44843/.

Mason, Stephen Finney. *Main Currents of Scientific Thought.* New York: Abelard-Schuman, 1956.

Masters, William H., and Virginia E. Johnson. *Human Sexual Response.* New York: Bantam, 1966.

Mathiot, Madeleine, ed. *Ethnolinguistics: Boas, Sapir, and Whorf Revisited.* The Hague: Mouton, 1979.

Matsuda, Mari J., et al., eds. *Words That Wound.* Boulder, CO: Westview P, 1993.

McClelland, Charles E. *State, Society, and University in Germany, 1700–1914.* Cambridge: Cambridge UP, 1980.

McGinn, Marie. *Wittgenstein and the* Philosophical Investigations. New York: Routledge, 1997.

McSheffrey, Shannon. *Gender and Heresy: Women and Men in Lollard Communities.* Philadelphia: U of Pennsylvania P, 1995.

Mead, George Herbert. *Mind, Self, and Society from the Standpoint of a Social Behaviorist.* 1934. Ed. Charles W. Morris. Chicago: U of Chicago P, 1962

Melville, Herman. *Billy Budd, Sailor.* Chicago: U of Chicago P, 1962.

———. *Moby-Dick.* 1851. New York: Dover, 2003.

———. Bartleby *and* Benito Cereno. New York: Dover, 1990.

Mey, Jacob L. *Pragmatics: An Introduction.* Malden, MA: Blackwell, 1993.

Mill, John Stuart. *The Subjection of Women.* Cambridge, MA: MIT P, 1970.

———. *The Subjection of Women.* Ed. Susan Moller Okin. New York: Hackett, 1988.

Miller, Alice. *For Your Own Good: Hidden Cruelty in Child-Rearing and the Roots of Violence.* 1980. Trans. Hildegarde and Hunter Hannum. New York: Noonday P, 1983.

Miller, Arthur. *All My Sons: A Play in Three Acts.* New York: Reynal and Hitchcock, 1947.

Miller, Susan. *Textual Carnivals: The Politics of Composition.* Carbondale: Southern Illinois UP, 1993.

Millett, Kate. *Sexual Politics.* New York: Doubleday, 1970.

Miner, Valerie, and Helen E. Longino, eds. *Competition: A Feminist Taboo?* New York: Feminist P, 1987.

Mitchell, Juliet. *Psychoanalysis and Feminism: A Radical Reassessment of Freudian Psychoanalysis.* 1974. New York: Basic, 2000.

Moi, Toril. *Henrik Ibsen and the Birth of Modernism: Art, Theater, Philosophy.* New York: Oxford UP, 2006.

———. *Sexual/Textual Politics: Feminist Literary Theory.* New York: Routledge, 1985.

Monk, Ray. *Ludwig Wittgenstein: The Duty of Genius.* New York: Penguin, 1991.

Moore, A. W., ed. *Meaning and Reference.* New York: Oxford UP, 1993.

Moore, R. I. *The Formation of a Persecuting Society: Power and Deviance in Western Europe 950–1250.* Oxford: Blackwell, 1987.

———. "Literacy and the Making of Heresy c. 1000–c. 1150." *Heresy and Literacy, 1000–1530.* Ed. Peter Biller and Anne Hudson. Cambridge: Cambridge UP, 1994. 19–37.

Moran, John H., and Alexander Code, trans. *Two Essays On the Origin of Language: Jean-Jacques Rousseau and Johann Gottfried Herder.* 1966. Chicago: U of Chicago P, 1986.

Moraw, Peter. "Careers of Graduates." *A History of the University in Europe,* vol. 1: *Universities in the Middle Ages.* Ed. Hilde de Ridder-Symoens. Gen ed. Walter Rüegg. Cambridge: Cambridge UP, 1992. 244–279.

Morris, David. *The Culture of Pain.* Berkeley: U of California P, 1991.

Morris, Rosalind C. "Modernity's Media and the End of Mediumship? On the Aesthetic Economy of Transparency in Thailand." *Public Culture* 12.2 (2000): 457–475.

Morrison, Toni. "Friday on the Potomac." *Race-ing Justice, En-gendering Power: Essays on Anita Hill, Clarence Thomas, and the Construction of Social Reality.* Ed. Toni Morrison. New York: Pantheon, 1992. vii–xxx.

———. *Playing in the Dark: Whiteness and the Literary Imagination.* New York: Vintage, 1990.

———. "Unspeakable Things Unspoken: The Afro American Presence in American Literature." *Michigan Quarterly Review* 28.1 (Winter 1989): 1–34.

Moser, Paul K. *Philosophy after Objectivity: Making Sense in Perspective.* New York: Oxford UP, 1993.

Moulton, Ian Frederick. *Before Pornography: Erotic Writing in Early Modern England.* New York: Oxford UP, 2000.

Moulton, Janice. "A Paradigm of Philosophy: The Adversary Method."*Discovering Reality: Feminist Perspectives on Epistemology, Metaphysics, Methodology, and Philosophy of Science.* Ed. Sandra Harding and Merrill B. Hintikka. Dordrecht: D. Reidel, 1983. 149–164.

Müller, Rainer A. "Student Education, Student Life." *History,* ed. Ridder-Symoens, 2:326–354.

Muscio, Inga. *Cunt: A Declaration of Independence.* Emeryville, CA: Seal P, 2002.

Nadler, Steven. *Spinoza's Heresy: Immortality and the Jewish Mind.* New York: Oxford UP, 2001.

Nardi, Paolo. "Relations with Authority." *A History of the University in Europe,* vol. 1: *Universities in the Middle Ages.* Ed. Hilde de Ridder-Symoens. Gen ed. Walter Rüegg. Cambridge: Cambridge UP, 1992. 77–107.

Neiman, Susan. *Evil in Modern Thought: An Alternative History of Philosophy.* Princeton, NJ: Princeton UP, 2003.

Nelson, Cary. "Men, Feminism: The Materiality of Discourse." *Men in Feminism.* Ed. Alice Jardine and Paul Smith. New York: Routledge, 1987. 153–172.

Nelson, Julie A. *Economics for Humans.* Chicago: U of Chicago P, 2006.

———. *Feminism, Objectivity, and Economics.* New York: Routledge, 1996.

———. "The Study of Choice or the Study of Provisioning?" *Beyond Economic Man: Feminist Theory and Economics.* Ed. Marianne A. Ferber and Julie A. Nelson. Chicago: U of Chicago P, 1992. 23–36.

Nelson, Lynn Hankinson. *Who Knows: From Quine to a Feminist Empiricism.* Philadelphia: Temple UP, 1990.

Nelson, Mariah Burton. *The Stronger Women Get, the More Men Love Football: Sexism and the American Culture of Sports.* New York: Harcourt Brace, 1994.

Nesbitt, Richard. *Intelligence and How to Get It: Why Schools and Cultures Count.* New York: Norton, 2009.

Ng, Larry, ed. *Alternatives to Violence: A Stimulus to Dialogue.* New York: Time-Life, 1968.

Ninio, Anat, and Catherine E. Snow. *Pragmatic Development.* Boulder, CO: Westview P, 1996.

Noble, David F. "The Scientific Restoration." *A World without Women: The Christian Clerical Culture of Western Science.* New York: Oxford UP, 1993. 205–243.

———. *A World without Women: The Christian Clerical Culture of Western Science.* New York: Oxford UP, 1993.

Noble, Douglas D. *The Classroom Arsenal: Military Research. Information Technology, and Public Education.* New York: Falmer P, 1991.

Norris, Christopher. *Deconstruction: Theory and Practice.* London: Methuen, 1982.

Novick, Peter. *That Noble Dream: "The Objectivity Question" and the American Historical Profession.* Cambridge: Cambridge UP, 1988.

Ochs, Elinor, Emanuel A. Schegloff, Sandra A. Thompson, eds. *Interaction and Grammar.* New York: Cambridge UP, 1996.

Ochs, Elinor, and Bambi B. Schieffelin. *Acquiring Conversational Competence.* Boston: Routledge and Kegan Paul, 1983.

O'Flaherty, James C. *Johann Georg Hamann.* Boston: Twayne, 1979.

———. *Unity and Language: A Study in the Philosophy of Johann Georg Hamann.* Chapel Hill: University of North Carolina Studies in the Germanic Languages and Literatures, 1952.

Ofrat, Gideon. *The Jewish Derrida.* Trans. Peretz Kidron. Syracuse, NY: Syracuse UP, 2001.

Ohmann, Richard. "In, With." *Men in Feminism.* Ed. Alice Jardine and Paul Smith. New York: Routledge, 1987. 182–189.

———. *Selling Culture: Magazines, Markets, and Class at the Turn of the Century.* New York: Verso, 1996.

———. "Speech Acts and the Definition of Literature." *Philosophy and Rhetoric* 4 (1971): 1–19.

———. "Speech, Literature and the Space Between." *New Literary History* 5 (1974): 37–63.

———. "What's Happening to the University and the Professions? Can History Tell?" *Politics of Knowledge: The Commercialization of the University, the Professions, and Print Culture.* 2002. Middletown, CT: Wesleyan UP, 2003. 85–123.

Okin, Susan Moller. "John Stuart Mill's Feminism: The Subjection of Women and the Improvement of Mankind." *Mill's* The Subjection of Women. Ed. Maria H. Morales. Lanham, MD: Rowman and Littlefield, 2005. 24–51.

———. *Justice, Gender, and the Family.* New York: Basic, 1989.

Ong, Walter J., S.J. *Interfaces of the Word: Studies in the Evolution of Consciousness and Culture.* Ithaca, NY: Cornell UP, 1977.

———. *Fighting for Life: Contest, Sexuality, and Consciousness.* Ithaca, NY: Cornell UP, 1981.

———. *Orality and Literacy: The Technologizing of the Word.* New York: Methuen, 1982.

———. *Rhetoric, Romance, and Technology: Studies in the Interaction of Expression and Culture.* Ithaca, NY: Cornell UP, 1971.

Orwell, George. *Animal Farm.* New York: Harcourt, Brace, 1946.

———. *1984.* 1948. New York: New American Library, 1983.

Ostriker, Alicia Suskin. *The Nakedness of Our Fathers: Biblical Visions and Revisions.* New Brunswick, NJ: Rutgers UP, 1994.

Ostrom, Elinor. *Governing the Commons: the Evolution of Institutions for Collective Action.* New York: Cambridge UP, 1990.

Overbye, Dennis. "Giant Particle Collider Struggles." *New York Times* 3 August 2009. www.nytimes.com/2009/08/04/science/space/04collide.html.

———. "Physicists Find Elusive Particle Seen as Key to Universe." *New York Times* 5 July 2012. www.nytimes.com/2012/07/05/science/cern-physicists-may-have-discovered-higgs-boson-particle.html.

Ovid. *The Art of Love.* Trans. James Michie. New York: Modern Library, 2003.

Paetow, Louis John. *The Arts Course at Medieval Universities with Special Reference to Grammar and Rhetoric.* University of Illinois: The University Studies, vol. 3, no. 7. Urbana-Champaign, IL: University Press, 1910.

Pagels, Elaine. *Adam, Eve, and the Serpent.* New York: Vintage, 1988.

Parks, Winfield, and Richmond Croom Beatty, eds. *The English Drama: An Anthology, 900 to 1642.* New York: Norton, 1935.

Pawel, Ernst. *The Nightmare of Reason: A Life of Franz Kafka.* New York: Vintage, 1985.

Pedersen, Olaf. *The First Universities:* Studium generale *and the Origins of University Education in Europe.* Trans. Richard North. Cambridge: Cambridge UP, 1997.

Penn, Julia M. *Linguistic Relativity versus Innate Ideas: The Origins of the Sapir Whorf Hypothesis in German Thought.* The Hague: Mouton, 1972.

Percy, William Armstrong, III. *Pederasty and Pedagogy in Archaic Greece.* Urbana: U of Illinois P, 1996.

Perloff, Marjorie. *Wittgenstein's Ladder: Poetic Language and the Strangeness of the Ordinary*. Chicago: U of Chicago P, 1996.

Peters, Edward. *Heresy and Authority in Medieval Europe*. Philadelphia: U of Pennsylvania P, 1980.

———. *Inquisition*. New York: Free P, 1988.

Pharr, Suzanne. *Homophobia: A Weapon of Sexism*. Little Rock, AR: Women's Project, 1988.

Pinker, Steven. *The Blank Slate: The Modern Denial of Human Nature*. New York: Viking, 2002.

———. *The Language Instinct: How the Mind Creates Language*. New York: Morrow, 1994.

Pinker, Steven, and Paul Bloom. "Natural Language and Natural Selection." *Behavioral and Brain Sciences* 13 (1990): 707–784.

Pitkin, Hannah Fenichel. *Wittgenstein and Justice*. Berkeley: U of California P, 1972.

Plato. *Timaeus* (trans. Benjamin Jowett). *Plato: The Collected Dialogues*. Ed. Edith Hamilton and Huntington Cairns. New York: Pantheon, 1961. 1151–1211.

Popper, Karl R. *The Logic of Scientific Discovery*. 1935. New York: Harper, 1965.

Porter, Roy. "The Scientific Revolution and the Universities." *A History of the University in Europe*, vol. 2: *Universities in Early Modern Europe: 1500–1800*. Ed. Hilde de Ridder-Symoens. Gen ed. Walter Rüegg. Cambridge: Cambridge UP, 1996. 531–564.

Potter, Elizabeth. *Gender and Boyle's Law of Gases*. Bloomington: Indiana UP, 2001.

Pratt, Mary Louise. *Toward a Speech Act Theory of Literary Discourse*. Bloomington: Indiana UP, 1977.

Press, Eyal, and Jennifer Washburn. "The Kept University." *Atlantic Monthly* March 2000: 39–54.

Radway, Janice A. *Reading the Romance: Women, Patriarchy, and Popular Literature*. Chapel Hill: U of North Carolina P, 1984.

Randall, Lisa. *Warped Passages: Unraveling the Mysteries of the Universe's Hidden Dimensions*. New York: Harper Collins, 2005.

Rashdall, Hastings. *The Universities of Europe in the Middle Ages*, 3 vols. 1936. Ed. F. M. Powicke and A. B. Emden. New York: Oxford UP, 1997.

Ravitch, Diane. *The Language Police*. New York: Knopf, 2003.

Readings, Bill. *The University in Ruins*. Cambridge, MA: Harvard UP, 1996.

Réage, Pauline. *The Story of O*. 1954. Trans. Sabine d'Estrée. New York: Ballantine, 1965.

Reynolds, L. D., and N. G. Wilson. *Scribes and Scholars: A Guide to the Transmission of Greek and Latin Literature*. Oxford: Oxford UP, 1968.

Reynolds, Suzanne. *Medieval Reading: Grammar, Rhetoric, and the Classical Text*. New York: Cambridge UP, 1996.

Rich, Adrienne. "Compulsory Heterosexuality and Lesbian Existence." *Blood, Bread, and Poetry: Selected Prose, 1979–1985*. New York: Norton, 1986. 23–75.

Richlin, Amy, ed. *Pornography and Representation in Greece and Rome*. New York: Oxford UP, 1992.

Ridder-Symoens, Hilde de. "Management and Resources." *A History of the University in Europe*, vol. 2: *Universities in Early Modern Europe: 1500–1800*. Ed. Hilde de Ridder-Symoens. Gen ed. Walter Rüegg. Cambridge: Cambridge UP, 1996. 154–209.

———. "Mobility." *A History of the University in Europe*, vol. 1: *Universities in the Middle Ages*. Ed. Hilde de Ridder-Symoens. Gen ed. Walter Rüegg. Cambridge: Cambridge UP, 1992. 280–304.

Ridder-Symoens, Hilde de, ed. *A History of the University in Europe,* vol. 1: *Universities in the Middle Ages.* Gen ed. Walter Rüegg. Cambridge: Cambridge UP, 1992.

———. *A History of the University in Europe,* vol. 2: *Universities in Early Modern Europe: 1500–1800.* Gen ed. Walter Rüegg. Cambridge: Cambridge UP, 1996.

Rives, Standford. *Did Calvin Murder Servetus?* Charleston, SC: Booksurge, 2008.

Rorty, Richard. *Philosophy and the Mirror of Nature.* Princeton, NJ: Princeton UP, 1979.

Rosser, Sue V., ed. *Teaching the Majority: Breaking the Gender Barrier in Science, Mathematics, and Engineering.* New York: Teachers College P, 1995.

———. *Women, Science, and Society: The Crucial Union.* New York: Teachers College P, 2000.

Rothblatt, Sheldon. *The Modern University and Its Discontents.* New York: Cambridge UP, 1997.

Rowland, Ingrid, and Anthony Grafton. "The Witch Hunters' Crusade." *New York Review of Books* 49.14 (26 September 2002): 68–70.

Rubin, Joan Shelley. *Songs of Ourselves: The Uses of Poetry in America.* Cambridge, MA: Harvard UP, 2007.

Rubin, Miri. *Corpus Christi: The Eucharist in Late Medieval Culture.* Cambridge: Cambridge UP, 1991.

Rudy, Willis. *The Universities of Europe, 1100–1914: A History.* Cranbury, NJ: Associated UP, 1984.

Rüegg, Walter. "The Rise of Humanism." *A History of the University in Europe,* vol. 1: *Universities in the Middle Ages.* Ed. Hilde de Ridder-Symoens. Gen. ed. Walter Rüegg. Cambridge: Cambridge UP, 1992. 442–468.

———. "Themes." *A History of the University in Europe,* vol. 1: *Universities in the Middle Ages.* Ed. Hilde de Ridder-Symoens. Gen ed. Walter Rüegg. Cambridge: Cambridge UP, 1992. 3–34.

———. "Themes." *A History of the University in Europe,* vol. 2: *Universities in Early Modern Europe: 1500–1800.* Ed. Hilde de Ridder-Symoens. Gen ed. Walter Rüegg. Cambridge: Cambridge UP, 1996. 3–42.

———. "Themes." *A History of the University in Europe,* vol. 3: *Universities in the Nineteenth and Early Twentieth Centuries (1800–1945).* Ed. Walter Rüegg. Cambridge: Cambridge UP, 2004. 3–31.

———. "Theology and the Arts." *A History of the University in Europe,* vol. 3: *Universities in the Nineteenth and Early Twentieth Centuries (1800–1945).* Ed. Walter Rüegg. Cambridge: Cambridge UP, 2004. 393–458.

Rüegg, Walter, ed. *A History of the University in Europe,* vol. 3: *Universities in the Nineteenth and Early Twentieth Centuries (1800–1945).* Gen. ed. Walter Rüegg. Cambridge: Cambridge UP, 2004.

Rushdie, Salman. *The Satanic Verses.* New York: Picador, 1988.

Russell, Bertrand. *A History of Western Philosophy.* New York: Simon and Schuster, 1945.

———. *Introduction to Mathematical Philosophy.* London: Allen and Unwin, 1919.

Russell, Jeffrey. *Dissent and Order in the Middle Ages: The Search for Legitimate Authority.* New York: Twayne, 1992.

———. *A History of Witchcraft: Sorcerers, Heretics, and Pagans.* New York: Thames and Hudson, 1980.

Sainsbury, R. M. *Paradoxes.* 1987. Cambridge: Cambridge UP, 2006.

Salomon, Ludwig. *Geschichte des deutschen Zeitungswesen von den ersten Anfaengen bis zur Wiederaufrichtung des deutschen Reiches.* 3 vols. Oldenburg, Germany: n.p., 1900–1906.

Scheman, Naomi. *Engenderings: Constructions of Knowledge, Authority, and Privilege.* New York: Routledge, 1993.

————. "Epistemology Resuscitated: Objectivity as Trustworthiness." *Engendering Rationalities.* Ed. Nancy Tuana and Sandra Morgen. Albany: SUNY P, 2001. 23–52.

————. "Though This Be Method, Yet There Is Madness in It: Paranoia and Liberal Epistemology." *Engenderings: Constructions of Knowledge, Authority, and Privilege.* New York: Routledge, 1993. 75–105.

Schmidt-Biggemann, Wilhelm. "New Structures of Knowledge." *A History of the University in Europe,* vol. 2: *Universities in Early Modern Europe: 1500–1800.* Ed. Hilde de Ridder-Symoens. Gen ed. Walter Rüegg. Cambridge: Cambridge UP, 1996. 489–530.

Schwinges, Rainer Christoph. "Student Education, Student Life." *A History of the University in Europe,* vol. 1: *Universities in the Middle Ages.* Ed. Hilde de Ridder-Symoens. Gen ed. Walter Rüegg. Cambridge: Cambridge UP, 1992. 195–243.

Scott, Joan Wallach. *Gender and the Politics of History.* New York: Columbia UP, 1999.

Scribner, Bob. "Heterodoxy, Literacy, and Print in the Early German Reformation." *Heresy and Literacy, 1000–1530.* Ed. Peter Biller and Anne Hudson. Cambridge: Cambridge UP, 1994. 255–278.

Searle, John. *Intentionality: An Essay in the Philosophy of Mind.* New York: Cambridge UP, 1983.

————. *Speech Acts: An Essay in the Philosophy of Language.* Cambridge: Cambridge UP, 1969.

Senchuk, Dennis M. *Against Instinct: From Biology to Philosophical Psychology.* Philadelphia: Temple UP, 1991.

Sex and the City. Season 2, episode 2, "The Awful Truth." www.hbo.com/sex-and-the-city/episodes/index.html#/sex-and-the-city/episodes/2/14-the-awful-truth/index.html.

Siegel, Jerrold E. *Rhetoric and Philosophy in Renaissance Humanism: The Union of Eloquence and Wisdom, Petrarch to Valla.* Princeton, NJ: Princeton UP, 1968.

Silverman, David, and Brian Torode. *The Material Word: Some Theories of Language and Its Limits.* London: Routledge and Kegan Paul, 1980.

Shaw, Bernard. "Back to Methuselah: In the Beginning." *Complete Plays: With Prefaces,* vol. 2. New York: Dodd, Mead and Co., 1963. 6.

Simon, Joan. *Education and Society in Tudor England.* Cambridge and New York: Cambridge UP, 1966.

Skinner, B. F. *Verbal Behavior.* New York: Appleton-Century-Crofts, 1957.

Slobin, Dan Isaac, ed. *The Crosslinguistic Study of Language Acquisition.* Hillsdale, NJ: Erlbaum, 1985.

Smiley, Jane. *A Thousand Acres.* New York: Ballantine, 1991.

Smitherman, Geneva. *Black Language and Culture: Sounds of Soul.* New York: Harper and Row, 1975.

————. *Black Talk: Words and Phrases from the Hood to the Amen Corner.* Boston: Houghton Mifflin, 1994.

————. *Talkin' and Testifyin': The Language of Black America.* 1977. Boston: Houghton Mifflin, 1986.

————. *Talkin' That Talk: Language, Culture, and Education in African America.* New York: Routledge, 2000.

Spade, Paul Vincent, ed. *The Cambridge Companion to Ockham.* Cambridge: Cambridge UP, 1999.

Spanier, Bonnie B. *Im/Partial Science: Gender Ideology in Molecular Biology*. Blooming-ton: Indiana UP, 1995.

Spencer, Hamish C., and Judith C. Masters. "Sexual Selection: Contemporary Debates." *Keywords in Evolutionary Biology*. Ed. Evelyn Fox Keller and Elisabeth A. Lloyd. Cambridge, MA: Harvard UP, 1992. 294–301.

Spender, Dale. *Man-Made Language*. New York: Routledge, 1980.

Spivak, Gayatri Chakravorty. "Translator's Preface." Derrida, *Of Grammatology*. 1967. Baltimore: Johns Hopkins, UP, 1974. ix–lxxxix.

Sprat, Thomas. *The History of the Royal Society of London for the Improving of Natural Knowledge*. London: n.p., 1667.

Starhawk (pseud. of Miriam Simos). *Dreaming the Dark*. Boston: Beacon P, 1982.

Staten, Henry. *Wittgenstein and Derrida*. Lincoln: U of Nebraska P, 1984.

Stephens, Walter. *Demon Lovers: Witchcraft, Sex, and the Crisis of Belief.* Chicago: U of Chicago P, 2002.

Stern, Clara, and William Stern. *Die Kindersprache: Eine psychologische und sprachtheo-retische Untersuchung*. Leipzig: Johann Ambrosius Barth Verlag, 1928.

Stern, Karl. *The Flight from Woman*. New York: Farrar, Straus, and Giroux, 1965.

Sternglass, Marilyn. *Time to Know Them*. Mahwah, NJ: Erlbaum, 1997.

Stewart, Susan. *Crimes of Writing: Problems in the Containment of Representation* (New York: Oxford UP, 1991.

Stock, Brian. *The Implications of Literacy: Written Language and Models of Interpretation in the Eleventh and Twelfth Centuries*. Princeton, NJ: Princeton UP, 1983.

Strassman, Diana. "Not a Free Market: The Rhetoric of Disciplinary Authority in Eco-nomics." *Beyond Economic Man: Feminist Theory and Economics*. Ed. Marianne A. Ferber and Julie A. Nelson. Chicago: U of Chicago P, 1993. 54–68.

Strossen, Nadine. *Defending Pornography: Free Speech, Sex, and the Fight for Women's Rights*. New York: Scribner, 1995.

Stuckey, J. Elspeth. *The Violence of Literacy*. Portsmouth, NH: Heinemann Boynton-Cook, 1991.

Studdert-Kennedy, Michael. "Introduction [to Part II]: The Emergence of Phonetic Structure." *Approaches to the Evolution of Language: Social and Cognitive Bases*. Ed. James R. Hurford, Michael Studdert-Kennedy, and Chris Knight. Cambridge: Cam-bridge UP, 1998. 123–129.

Tallerman, Maggie, ed. *Language Origins: Perspectives on Evolution*. New York: Oxford UP, 2005.

J. L. Talmon. *The Myth of the Nation and Vision of the Revolution: Ideological Polarization in the Twentieth Century*. 1980. Piscataway, NJ: Transaction, 2005.

———. *Origins of Totalitarian Democracy*. London: Secker and Warburg, 1955.

———. *Political Messianism: The Romantic Phase*. London: Secker and Warburg, 1960.

Tannen, Deborah. *The Argument Culture: Moving From Debate to Dialogue*. New York: Random House, 1998.

———. *Conversational Styles: Analyzing Talk among Friends*. Norwood, NJ: Ablex, 1984.

———. "The Oral/Literate Continuum in Discourse." *Spoken and Written Language: Exploring Orality and Literacy*. Ed. Deborah Tannen. Norwood, NJ: Ablex, 1982. 1–16.

———. "Oral and Literate Strategies in Spoken and Written Discourse." *Literacy for Life: The Demand for Reading and Writing.* Ed. Richard W. Bailey and Robin Melanie Fosheim. New York: MLA, 1983. 79–96.

————. *You Just Don't Understand: Women and Men in Conversation.* New York: William Morrow, 1990.

Thurot, Charles. *De l'organisation de l'enseignement dans l'Université de Paris au moyen-âge.* Paris: Besançon, 1850.

Tice, Paul. "Foreword." *The* Malleus maleficarum *of Heinrich Kramer and James Sprenger.* Ed. and trans. Montague Summers. Escondido, CA: Book Tree, 2000. N.p.

Tiger, Lionel. *Men in Groups.* 1962. New York: Vintage, 1970.

Tilly, Charles. *The Politics of Collective Violence.* New York: Cambridge UP, 2003.

Todorov, Tzvetan. *Genres in Discourse.* 1978. Trans. Catherine Porter. Cambridge: Cambridge UP, 1990.

Tomasello, Michael. *Constructing a Language: A Usage-based Theory of Language Acquisition.* Cambridge, MA: Harvard UP, 2003.

————. *The Cultural Origins of Human Cognition.* Cambridge, MA: Harvard UP, 1999.

————. "Language Is Not an Instinct." *Cognitive Development* 10 (1995): 131–156.

————. "On the Different Origins of Symbols and Grammar." *Language Evolution.* Ed. Morten H. Christiansen and Simon Kirby. Oxford and New York: Oxford University Press, 2003. 94–95.

Trinkhaus, Charles Edward, Jr., trans. "Lorenzo Valla." *The Renaissance Philosophy of Man.* Ed. Ernest Cassirer, Paul Oskar Kristeller, and John Herman Randall, Jr. Chicago: U of Chicago P, 1948. 147–182.

Turkle, Sherry. *The Second Self: Computers and the Human Spirit.* New York: Simon and Schuster, 1984.

Turner, Howard R. *Science in Medieval Islam: An Illustrated Introduction.* Austin: U of Texas P, 1995.

Veblen, Thorstein. *The Higher Learning in America: A Memorandum on the Conduct of Universities by Business Men.* 1918. Stanford, CA: Academic Reprints, 1954.

Verger, Jacques. "Patterns." *A History of the University in Europe,* vol. 1: *Universities in the Middle Ages.* Ed. Hilde de Ridder-Symoens. Gen ed. Walter Rüegg. Cambridge: Cambridge UP, 1992. 35–74.

Villanueva, Victor. "Spic in English." *Bootstraps.* Urbana, IL: NCTE, 1994. 34–50.

Vives, J. L. "On the Learning of Women." *Vives and the Renascence Education of Women.* Ed. Foster Watson. London: Edward Arnold, 1912. 195–210.

Vygotsky, L. S. *Mind in Society.* 1930. Ed. Michael Cole, Vera John-Steiner, Sylvia Scribner, and Ellen Souberman. Cambridge, MA: Harvard UP, 1978.

Waquet, Françoise. *Latin, or, The Empire of the Sign.* 1998. Trans. John Howe. New York: Verso, 2001.

Watson, Foster, ed. and trans. *Vives, On Education: A Translation of* De tradendis disciplinis *of Juan Luis Vives.* Cambridge: Cambridge UP, 1913.

Weaver, Constance. *Reading Process and Practice: From Socio-Psycholinguistics to Whole Language.* Cambridge: Winthrop, 1980.

Weaver, Constance, Diane Stephens, and Janet Vance. *Understanding Whole Language: From Principles to Practice.* Portsmouth, NH: Heinemann, 1990.

Weinberg, Steven. *Dreams of a Final Theory: The Scientist's Search for the Ultimate Laws of Nature.* New York: Random House, 1992.

————. *The First Three Minutes: A Modern View of the Origin of the Universe.* 1977. Rev ed. New York: Basic, 1993.

————. "Why the Higgs Boson Matters." *New York Times* 14 July 2012. www.nytimes.com/2012/07/14/opinion/weinberg-why-the-higgs-boson-matters.html.

Welch, Kathleen E. *The Contemporary Reception of Classical Rhetoric: Appropriations of Ancient Discourse.* Hillsdale, NJ: Erlbaum, 1990.

West, Cornel. *Race Matters.* Boston: Beacon P, 1993.

White, Andrew Dickson. *Seven Great Statesmen in the Warfare of Humanity with Unreason.* New York: Century, 1910.

White, James Boyd. *Justice as Translation: An Essay in Cultural and Legal Criticism.* Chicago: U of Chicago P, 1990.

Whitehead, Alfred North. *Science and the Modern World.* 1925. New York: Free P, 1967.

Whorf, Benjamin Lee. *Language, Thought, and Reality: Selected Writings.* 1957. Ed. John B. Carroll. Cambridge, MA: MIT P, 1997.

———. "Science and Linguistics." *Language, Thought, and Reality: Selected Writings.* 1957. Ed. John B. Carroll. Cambridge, MA: MIT P, 1997. 207–219.

Williams, Linda. *Hard Core: Power, Pleasure, and the "Frenzy of the Visible."* Berkeley: U of California P, 1989.

Williams, Patricia J. *The Alchemy of Race and Rights: Diary of a Law Professor.* Cambridge, MA: Harvard UP, 1991.

Winders, James A. "Writing Like a Man (?): Descartes, Science, and Madness." *Feminist Interpretations of René Descartes.* Ed. Susan Bordo. State College: Pennsylvania State UP, 1992. 114–140.

Winnicott, D. W. "Transitional Objects and Transitional Phenomena." *Playing and Reality.* New York: Basic, 1971. 1–25.

Wittgenstein, Ludwig. *The Blue and Brown Books.* 1934. New York: Harper, 1965.

———. *Culture and Value.* 1929. Ed. G. H. von Wright and Hekki Nyman. Trans. Peter Winch. Oxford: Blackwell, 1980.

———. *Lectures and Conversations on Aesthetics, Psychology, and Religious Belief.* Ed. Cyril Barrett. Berkeley: U of California P, 1967.

———. *On Certainty.* Ed. G. E. M. Anscombe and G. H. von Wright. Trans. Denis Paul and G. E. M. Anscombe. New York: Harper, 1972.

———. *Philosophical Investigations.* 1953. Trans. G. E. M. Anscombe. New York: Macmillan, 1958.

———. *Tractatus Logico-Philosophicus.* 1922. Trans. C. K. Ogden. New York: Routledge, 1981.

Woodward, William Harrison. *Studies in Education during the Age of the Renaissance, 1400–1600.* 1906. New York: Columbia UP, 1967.

Woolf, Virginia. *Three Guineas.* 1938. New York: Harvest, 1966.

Wouk, Herman. *The Caine Mutiny.* Boston: Back Bay, 1951.

Zilsel, Edgar. "The Genesis of the Concept of the Physical Law." *The Philosophical Review* 51.3 (May 1942): 245–279.

INDEX

David Bleich is a faculty member in the English department of the University of Rochester. He is author of *Readings and Feelings: An Introduction to Subjective Criticism* (1975); *Subjective Criticism* (1978); *Utopia: The Psychology of a Cultural Fantasy* (1984); *The Double Perspective: Language, Literacy, and Social Relations* (1988); *Know and Tell: A Writing Pedagogy of Disclosure, Genre, and Membership* (1998). He is editor (with Sally Barr Reagan and Tom Fox) of *Writing With: New Directions in Collaborative Teaching, Learning, and Research* (1994), and (with Deborah H. Holdstein) *Personal Effects: The Social Character of Scholarly Writing* (2002).

CPSIA information can be obtained
at www.ICGtesting.com
Printed in the USA
LVHW112032080123
736729LV00001B/19